Organizations	Communities	Vulnerable Populations	Social Worker
		8.9	8.7, 8.8
All of Chapter 9			9.4
10.4, 10.11, 10.12	10.13	10.7, 10.8, 10.9	10.10
11.20, 11.21, 11.22	11.23, 11.24	11.19	
12.10, 12.11, 12.13	12.12, 12.13, 12.14		
13.24, 13.25, 13.26, 13.27, 13.28, 13.29, 13.30, 13.31, 13.32, 13.34, 13.35, 13.36, 13.37, 13.38, 13.39	13.33, 13.37, 13.40		
All of Section B			14.3
	15.20	All of Chapter 15	
16.1, 16.4, 16.5, 16.8, 16.9, 16.10			All of Chapter 16

Techniques and Guidelines for Social Work Practice

Techniques and Guidelines for Social Work Practice

EIGHTH EDITION

Bradford W. Sheafor
Colorado State University

Charles R. Horejsi
Professor Emeritus, University of Montana

PEARSON

Boston ■ New York ■ San Francisco ■
Mexico City ■ Montreal ■ Toronto ■ London ■ Madrid ■ Munich ■ Paris
Hong Kong ■ Singapore ■ Tokyo ■ Cape Town ■ Sydney

Series Editor: Patricia Quinlin
Series Editorial Assistant: Carly Czech
Marketing Manager: Laura Lee Manley
Production Supervisor: Beth Houston
Editorial Production Service and Electronic Composition: Elm Street Publishing Services
Composition Buyer: Linda Cox
Manufacturing Buyer: Debbie Rossi
Cover Administrator: Linda Knowles

For related titles and support materials, visit our online catalog at www.ablongman.com.

Between the time website information is gathered and then published, it is not unusual for some sites to have closed. Also, the transcription of URLs can result in typographical errors. The publisher would appreciate notification where these errors occur so that they may be corrected in subsequent editions.

ISBN-13: 978-0-205-57809-2   ISBN-10: 0-205-57809-8

Library of Congress Cataloging-in-Publication Data

Sheafor, Bradford W.
    Techniques and guidelines for social work practice / Bradford W. Sheafor, Charles R. Horejsi. — 8th ed.
        p.   cm.
    Includes bibliographical references and index.
    ISBN 978-0-205-57809-2
    1. Social service—United States.   I. Horejsi, Charles R. II. Title.

HV91.S48 2008
361.3'2—dc22

                                                                2007042668

Printed in the United States of America

10 9 8 7 6 5 4 3 2   11 10 09 08

To the next generation of social workers,
who have chosen to devote their time and talents to
the service of others and the struggle for social justice,

and

To our families,
Nadine, Laura, Brandon, Perry, Christopher,
Gloria, Angela, Martin, and Katherine,
for their love and support

Contents

Preface   xvii

CHAPTER 5
Guiding Principles for Social Workers   66

PART III   Techniques Common to All Social Work Practice   133

PART IV   Techniques and Guidelines for Phases of the Planned Change Process   195

CHAPTER 11
Data Collection and Assessment   239

CHAPTER 12
Planning and Contracting   322

CHAPTER 13
Intervention and Monitoring   363

CHAPTER 16
Techniques for Sustaining Social Work Practice   573

Preface

Many people are influenced, directly and indirectly, by the decisions and actions of social workers. Working in courts, clinics, hospitals, schools, businesses, private practice, and a myriad of social agencies, social workers deliver a wide variety of services directly to clients while they also work toward positive community and social changes. Improving the quality of life for an individual, a family, or the people of a community will ultimately have an impact on the general society and elevate the health, happiness, safety, and productivity of all its members.

This book is about what social workers actually do when helping their clients solve problems and/or enhance functioning. Although many books describe the general principles and theories used by social workers, *Techniques and Guidelines for Social Work Practice* focuses on a more concrete level. It describes many of the basic techniques and guidelines that social workers use in everyday practice.

Most social workers have been exposed to a wide variety of practice theories and conceptual frameworks reported in the literature and taught in social work education programs.* Although that knowledge base is essential, practice is much more than a set of ideas. In reality, practice is a set of actions and behaviors by the social worker. Clients are not directly affected by theory; rather, they are influenced by what the worker actually does—by the specific actions taken by the social worker. We do not intend to suggest that attention to the techniques can or should replace attention to theoretical frameworks. Rather, techniques and specific guidelines complete the package of knowledge and skills needed by the social worker.

■ PLAN AND STRUCTURE

Understanding the design of a book helps the reader make use of its contents. This book has five major parts.

Part I, "Social Work and the Social Worker," reviews the background knowledge and characteristics we believe a social worker must possess:

- A clear conception of the domain of social work and the competencies the social worker is expected to bring to the change process (Chapter 1)
- An understanding of the challenges a social worker faces in merging his or her personal life with professional roles and responsibilities (Chapter 2)

*A short synopsis of many of these basic frameworks is included in Chapter 6, "Practice Frameworks for Social Work."

- The native talents or artistic abilities necessary for perceptively creating and entering into the interpersonal relations that are at the heart of practice as well as a commitment to draw upon and apply the science of social work—that is, the profession's knowledge base and its ethical principles (Chapter 3)

Part II, "The Building Blocks of Social Work Practice," stresses the need for the social worker to become familiar with the central features of effective helping. To serve clients ranging from individuals to communities, a social worker must have these qualities:

- An understanding of the varied roles performed by social workers in delivering human services and the specific functions associated with these roles (Chapter 4)
- The ability to apply the fundamental practice principles of social work (Chapter 5)
- A basic knowledge of the various perspectives, theories, and models that have proven useful in practice (Chapter 6)
- Skill in selecting the best evidence available to inform the process of guiding clients through the planned change process and in helping them make sound decisions about how to improve their lives (Chapter 7)

From this point to the end of the book, we present specific techniques and guidelines. Each presentation follows the same format or structure. It begins with a technique or guideline ***Number*** and ***Name*** (e.g., 10.4: Making a Referral). In this example, 10.4 signifies the fourth technique or guideline in Chapter 10. This system of numbering is used to refer the reader to related information in other parts of the book. These numbers are also the keys to using the "Cross-Reference Guide," found inside the front cover, which is intended to help the reader easily locate techniques that may be useful when working with specific client groups.

Following each number and name is a one-sentence description of ***Purpose.*** This very brief statement is intended to help the reader quickly determine if the technique or guideline is relevant to his or her concern or interest.

Under the heading labeled ***Discussion***, anywhere from a few to many paragraphs describe the technique or guideline and its application. After the Discussion, we present a ***Selected Bibliography,*** which usually lists two or three books or articles that we consider particularly useful for obtaining additional information. We have made an effort to identify sources that are current and available in most university libraries.

In Part III of the book, "Techniques Common to All Social Work Practice," we have included techniques that strengthen the social worker's performance regardless of agency setting and independent of whether the client is an individual, family, group, organization, or community. Underlying our selection was the belief that the social worker must have these basic skills:

- The interpersonal competence to carry out effective communication and to engage in a set of basic helping activities (Chapter 8)
- The organizational ability to address the details of service delivery and to effectively manage his or her own workload (Chapter 9)

Part IV, "Techniques and Guidelines for Phases of the Planned Change Process," lists techniques and guidelines for both direct and indirect practice in chapters organized around the five phases of the planned change process. Although various authors use differing descriptions of this process, we have elected to use the following:

- Intake and engagement (Chapter 10)
- Data collection and assessment (Chapter 11)
- Planning and contracting (Chapter 12)
- Intervention and monitoring (Chapter 13)
- Evaluation and termination (Chapter 14)

We describe what should be accomplished in these phases in the introduction to each chapter. We then refine the general concepts to more clearly describe the direct practice applications (Section A) and the indirect practice applications (Section B) of those chapters. A worker can readily examine several suggested techniques or guidelines by identifying the phase of the change process, determining if the activity is a direct or indirect intervention, and then locating the appropriate chapter and section.

Part V, "Specialized Techniques and Guidelines for Social Work Practice," includes some items that cut across the five phases of the planned change process and thus did not fit into the classification system used in Part IV. To address these issues, we created chapters containing the items related to serving vulnerable client populations (Chapter 15) and the items related to maintaining one's position as a social worker (Chapter 16).

Although 151 different techniques and guidelines are described in Parts III through V of this book, many more exist. In fact, we have posted more than 40 on a website for this book: ***www.ablongman.com/sheafor8e.*** For the textbook, we have selected a sufficient range with the intent that one or more will be useful in most practice situations. If not, the ***Selected Bibliography*** at the end of each item will lead the worker to other approaches. Most of these techniques need not be applied rigidly. Rather, they should be approached with the idea of both *adopting* and *adapting* them for practice.

■ DEFINITION OF TERMS

Writing about social work practice inherently presents some language problems. One has to read only a few social work texts or articles to become at least a little confused with the terminology used to describe practice. Perhaps that is to be expected in a profession that focuses on complex and dynamic human and social interactions. This book cannot overcome these long-standing problems of terminology, yet the ideas presented here will be more readily understood if we make the meanings of three terms more explicit.

The reader should be alert to the term ***client.*** Common usage implies a narrow view of an individual who is the consumer of services. As used in this book, the term has a broader connotation. The client of the social worker may be an individual, a family or another form of household, or even a small group, committee, organization, neighborhood, community, or larger social system. Throughout the book, the term *client* is occasionally expanded to mention *clientele, clients, client groups,* or *client systems,* reminding the reader that the traditional narrow definition of *client* is not intended.

A ***technique*** is viewed as a circumscribed, goal-oriented behavior performed in a practice situation by the social worker. It is a planned action deliberately taken by the practitioner. The application of a simple technique (e.g., making the first telephone contact) may take only a few seconds, whereas more complex techniques (e.g., assessing a client's social functioning) may require an hour or more.

Guidelines, by comparison, are a set of directions intended to influence the social worker's behavior and decisions. Guidelines are essentially lists of do's and don'ts. They might be used when working with a specific type of client (e.g., a child or a client with mental illness) or when carrying out workload management tasks (e.g., recording or writing reports).

■ NEW TO THIS EDITION

Techniques and Guidelines for Social Work Practice has been carefully updated to provide students with easy access to the most current information on fundamental techniques required for social work practice from the generalist perspective. This text illustrates the multiple tools needed for both direct and indirect intervention activities. Touching upon everything from basic helping skills, to guidelines for preparing grant applications, the content of this text is so widely applicable it is a valuable aid for all professional social workers. New features of the eighth edition of *Techniques and Guidelines* include:

- Guidelines for the social worker serving persons affected by the "immigrant/refugee crisis" in the U.S.
- New information on the growing use of mediation in social work practice.
- Discussion of animal-assisted interventions—a new tool for practice.
- The social worker's role in assisting clients in parenting, as well as the new phenomenon of grandparents raising grandchildren.
- Due to the ever-increasing expectations from managed care and other funding sources, Chapter 14 has been revised to illustrate techniques for conducting empirical direct practice evaluation. (This includes current illustrations based on actual student applications of the most commonly used measurement and evaluation tools.)
- New descriptions of available practice approaches include narrative therapy and the psychoeducational model.
- The growing call for "evidence-based practice" is made more understandable for students through discussion of evidence-based assessment, evidence-based intervention (i.e., best practices), and evidence-based (or empirical) evaluation.

■ SUPPLEMENTS FOR INSTRUCTORS

For instructors using this book in their classes, two supportive resources are available. First, we have placed a document entitled "Ideas for Teaching from *Techniques and Guidelines for Social Work Practice*" on Allyn & Bacon's website (see ***www.ablongman. com/sheafor8e***). In that document, we describe ways we have used the materials in this book to help beginning-level students learn to serve clients using social work's knowledge, ethical prescriptions, and specific techniques and guidelines. Second, we have created an Instructor's Manual and Test Bank to assist instructors using this text. In addition to teaching suggestions, this supplement contains sample test questions (Chapters 1 through 7) and suggested exercises for applying these materials. This manual can be obtained from your campus Allyn & Bacon representative or by writing Allyn & Bacon (75 Arlington Street, Suite 300, Boston, MA 02116).

■ ACKNOWLEDGMENTS

We would like to recognize a number of people who have contributed to the techniques and guidelines presented in this book, including current and former students and professional colleagues who have graciously given their time and expertise to offer constructive criticisms on selected sections. A special thank-you is extended to each of the following individuals:

- Angeline Barretta-Herman, Ph.D. (staff meetings)
- Barbara Benjamin, M.S.W.; Bob Jackson, Ph.D.; Maxine Jacobson, Ph.D.; and Lowell Jenkins, M.S.W. (practice frameworks)
- Mary Birch, M.S.W. (small groups)
- Charlotte Booth, M.S.W. (hard-to-reach clients)
- Vicky Buchan, Ph.D. (understanding quantitative data)
- Timothy Conley, Ph.D.; Ted Lewis, B.S.W.; and Detective Mark Long (chemical dependency)
- Robert Deaton, Ed.D. (suicide)
- Jim Demuth, M.A.; Sr. Dot Feehan, M.A.; and Cindy Garthwait, M.S.W. (spirituality and religion)
- Jerry Finn, Ph.D. (using electronic technology)
- Kathleen Gallacher, M.A., and Kristin Dahl Horejsi, M.S. (child development)
- Cindy Garthwait, M.S.W. (working with the elderly)
- Ben Granger, Ph.D. (animal assisted interventions)
- Helen Holmquist-Johnson, M.S.W. (eating disorders)
- Cynthia J. Geissinger, M.S.W. (bisexual and transgender)
- Ken Hoole, M.S.W.; Suzanne Grubaugh, B.S.W.; and Deanna Morrow, Ph.D. (gay and lesbian issues)
- Mike Jakupcak, Ed.D. and George Camp, Ph.D. (mental retardation)
- Mike Johnson, M.A., and Sue Kenney, M.S.W. (poverty)
- Dan Morgan, M.S.W.; Cindy Bartling, M.S.W.; and Charlie Wellenstein, M.S.W. (children and adolescents)

- Kevin Oltjenbruns, Ph.D. (grief and loss)
- Peter Pecora, Ph.D. (evaluation)
- Maria Puig, Ph.D. (immigrants and refugees)
- Jeannette Sale, B.S.W.; Kelly Slattery-Robinson, B.S.W.; and Frank Clark, Ph.D. (battered women)
- David Schantz, Ph.D. (leadership)
- Mona Schatz, D.S.W. (social work roles and functions)
- Barbara W. Shank, Ph.D. (sexual misconduct)
- Michael Silverglat, M.D., and Mel Mason, M.S.W. (psychotropic medication and mental illness)
- John Spores, Ph.D.; Iris Heavy Runner, M.S.W.; Rodney Brod, Ph.D.; Victor A. Baez, Ph.D.; and Janet Finn, Ph.D. (cultural competence)
- Ryan Tolleson-Knee, M.S.W., and Shaen McElravy, M.S.W. (merging person and profession)
- Elizabeth Tracy, Ph.D., and James Whittaker, Ph.D. (social support assessment)
- Carmen Underwood, B.S.W. (family group conferencing)
- Deborah Valentine, Ph.D. (mentoring narrative therapy and mediation)
- Sue Wilkins, B.S.W. (involuntary and manipulative clients)

We would also like to acknowledge the following individuals, who reviewed this edition and offered suggestions for improving this publication: Sherry Edwards, University of North Carolina–Pembroke; Robyn Lugar, Indiana State University; and Katherine Palazzolo-Miller, Ferris State University. And for reviewing previous editions, we would like to continue to acknowledge Miriam Clubok, Ohio University; Michael Coconis, Grand Valley State University; Bob Jackson, University of Washington; and Anne Medill, Northern Arizona University. Thanks, as well, to those individuals who reviewed earlier editions: Mary Boes, University of Northern Iowa; Joan Dworkin, California State University–Sacramento; Patricia Ann Guillory, Southern University at New Orleans; Carolyn Knight, University of Maryland, Baltimore County; Larry Lister, University of Hawaii at Manoa; Martha Raske, University of Southern Indiana; Santos Torres, Jr., University of Pittsburg; and Kay van Buskirk, Mankato State University.

Techniques and Guidelines for Social Work Practice

PART 1

Social Work and the Social Worker

Social work is an indispensable profession in our increasingly complex and ever-changing society. But it is an often misunderstood profession, as well, in part because it cannot be easily described or explained. It is a profession characterized by diversity. Social workers engage in a broad range of activities within many types of settings and with many different people. Some work intensely with individuals and families, while others work with small groups, organizations, or whole communities. Some deal primarily with children, others with older persons. Some are counselors and psychotherapists, while others are supervisors, administrators, program planners, or fund-raisers. Some focus on family violence and others on how to provide housing or medical care to the poor. This variety is what makes social work so challenging and stimulating. But it is because of this diversity of both clients and activities that it is so difficult to answer the simple question: What is social work?

The task of concisely defining *social work* in a manner that encompasses all of the activities in which social workers engage has challenged the profession throughout its history. At a very fundamental level, ***social work*** is a profession devoted to helping people function as well as they can within their social environments and to changing their environments to make that possible. This theme of *person-in-environment* is clarified and illustrated throughout this book.

The authors' perspective of social work is made explicit in the following three-part definition of a social worker. A ***social worker***

1. has recognized professional preparation (i.e., education in the requisite knowledge, ethics, and competencies)
2. is sanctioned by society to provide specific services targeted primarily at helping vulnerable populations (e.g., children, the aged, the poor, minorities, women, families) engage in efforts to change themselves, the people around them, or social institutions
3. has the purpose of helping others meet social needs or eliminate difficulties so that they might make maximum use of their abilities to lead full and satisfying lives and contribute fully to society

In order to be a responsible professional, the social worker must understand and function within the profession's accepted areas of expertise. Chapter 1,

"The Domain of the Social Work Profession," elaborates on the authors' definition of social work and presents its central mission as helping people change so they fit and function more comfortably within their environments and also helping to modify those environments to be more supportive of the people. This help is provided through social programs that include making tangible social provisions available to people in need, offering intangible social services such as counseling or treatment, and engaging in organizational and community change activities.

The primary resource the social worker brings to the helping process is his or her own capacity to develop positive helping relationships and assist clients to take actions that will improve the quality of their lives. A social worker must have the ability to understand client issues, creatively select ways to address those issues (i.e., apply the appropriate techniques and guidelines), and assist clients in changing those factors that are negatively affecting their lives. To do this, the social worker must keep physically, intellectually, and emotionally "in shape" for this rigorous personal interaction with clients or client groups. At the same time, the social worker must avoid having one's personal life consumed by the events that arise in his or her work environment. Chapter 2, "Merging Person with Profession," identifies many of the factors a social worker should be prepared to address in keeping personally and professionally fit for practice.

Throughout its history, social work has been portrayed as both an art and a science. Chapter 3, "Merging the Person's Art with the Profession's Science," builds on the material introduced in Chapters 1 and 2 and provides a more detailed description of the personal characteristics (i.e., the art) that contribute to effective practice. The chapter also identifies the knowledge base (i.e., the science) required of beginning-level social workers. Chapter 3 introduces the consideration of the artistic features of the social worker by recognizing the central place that such factors as compassion, empathy, genuineness, creativity, hopefulness, energy, values, and professional style play in the helping process. However, the chapter also reflects the view that the professional social worker is obligated to bring the best scientific knowledge to the helping process.

Part I, then, addresses the most fundamental elements of social work practice—the blending of the person and the profession—in order to most effectively assist individuals, families or other households, small groups, organizations, and communities as they work to prevent or resolve the complex social problems that arise in their daily lives.

The Domain of the Social Work Profession

When a person sets out to help others, especially those most vulnerable to social problems, he or she assumes a serious responsibility. The responsible professional must practice within his or her ***professional domain*** (i.e., the profession's area of expertise, or its "professional turf") if clients are to receive the services that the profession is sanctioned to provide. Indeed, professional helpers can harm clients if the helpers' activities extend beyond their professional boundaries because these boundaries establish the content of the profession's formal education and identify the services its members are best prepared to deliver.

This book is concerned with the profession of social work and how social workers assist people in addressing a variety of different issues that confront them. Social work is, indeed, a curious name for a profession. In times that emphasize image over substance, it is clearly a title that lacks pizzazz. In fact, the use of the word *work* makes it sound dreary. It is a title that many social workers have wished they could change, possibly without understanding where it came from in the first place.

The title is attributed to Jeffrey Brackett (1860–1949). Brackett, initially an influential volunteer in the Baltimore Charity Organization Society, served for nearly 30 years on the Massachusetts Board of Charities and later became the first director of what is now the Simmons College School of Social Work. In the early 1900s, Brackett argued that the word *social* should be part of this developing profession's title because it depicts the focus on people's interactions with important forces that shape their lives, such as family members, friends, or a myriad of other factors, including their relevant cultural or ethnic group, school, job, neighborhood, community, and so on. He added the word *work* to differentiate professional practice from what he considered to be the often misguided and self-serving philanthropic activity of wealthy volunteers. He believed including work in the profession's title emphasized that its activities were to be orderly, responsible, and disciplined—not something to be engaged in by someone unprepared for these tasks.

Social work is an accurate title for a profession that applies helping techniques in a disciplined manner to address social problems. During the years since Brackett convinced early helping services providers to accept this title, the domain of social work has expanded and its approach has been reshaped by the increasing knowledge generated by the social and behavioral sciences. Yet the title continues to describe this profession's central focus today.

■ THE SOCIAL WORK DOMAIN

It is important for the social worker to examine periodically the *domain* of social work (i.e., to review its purpose, focus, scope, and sanction). This is especially important for the student or new social worker because educational programs divide the study of social work into units, or courses, and this can lead to a familiarity with the parts without necessarily understanding the whole. For the experienced practitioner, taking time to stand back from one's daily routine to view the profession as a whole may help the practitioner truly appreciate the depth and breadth of the profession's concerns and the varied and creative approaches used by its practitioners.

Conducting a periodic examination of the social work domain is also important to guard against ***professional drift:*** the neglect of the profession's traditional purpose and functions in favor of activities associated with another professional discipline. This happens most often in clinical settings when social workers align themselves too closely with models and theories used in medicine, psychology, and other disciplines, which tend to minimize social policy and social justice issues. These practitioners may come to view themselves as psychotherapists first and social workers second—or perhaps not as social workers at all. Professional drift is also seen among administrators and managers who were trained as social workers but identify primarily with their specific organizations rather than the social work profession. When professional drift occurs, it is a disservice to one's clients, employing agency, and community for it diminishes the commitment, perspective, and competencies unique to social work.

A precise and generally agreed upon understanding of the boundaries that mark the several helping professions does not exist. Different disciplines (e.g., social work, clinical psychology, school counseling, and marriage and family therapy) have claimed their domains without collaboration or mutual agreement about where one profession ends and another begins or where they appropriately overlap. This problem is further complicated by the fact that each state that chooses to license the practice of these professions is free to establish its own descriptions of professional boundaries. For this reason, a person who is licensed to practice social work in one state may not be eligible to be licensed in a neighboring state. It is important, therefore, to approach learning about social work's domain with a recognition that the boundaries between professions are sometimes blurred. However, being knowledgeable about social work's fundamental purpose, focus, scope, and sanction provides a reasonably clear picture of its domain.

Social Work's Purpose

An understanding of the social work profession begins with a deep appreciation of humans as social beings. People are, indeed, social creatures. They need other people. An individual's growth and development requires the guidance, nurturing, and protection provided by others. And that person's concept of self—and even his or her very survival, both physically and psychologically—is tied to the decisions and actions of other people. It is this interconnectedness and interdependence of people and the power of social relationships that underpins a profession devoted to helping people improve the quality and effectiveness of those interactions and relationships—in other words, to enhance their social functioning.

Improved Social Functioning. The concept of social functioning is a key to understanding the unique focus of social work and distinguishing social work from the other helping professions. Positive *social functioning* is a person's ability to accomplish those tasks and activities necessary to meet his or her basic needs and perform his or her major social roles, as required by a particular subculture of a community. *Basic needs* include such fundamental concerns as having food, shelter, and medical care, as well as being able to protect oneself from harm, finding social acceptance and social support, having meaning and purpose in life, and so on. Major social roles include, for example, those of being a family member, parent, spouse, student, patient, employee, neighbor, and citizen. A person's *social roles* change through life, and expectations associated with these roles differ somewhat depending on the person's gender, ethnicity, culture, religion, occupation, and community. (See Item 11.7 for more description of social role performance.) In sum, the concept of social functioning focuses on the match or fit between an individual's capacities and actions and the demands, expectations, resources, and opportunities within his or her social and economic environment.

Although the social work profession is concerned with the social functioning of all people, it has traditionally prioritized the needs of the most vulnerable members of society and those who experience social injustice, discrimination, and oppression. The most vulnerable in a society are often young children, the frail elderly, persons living in poverty, persons with severe physical or mental disabilities, persons who are gay or lesbian, persons of minority ethnic/racial backgrounds, or persons with a foreign country of origin.

To carry out their commitment to improving people's social functioning, social workers are involved in the activities of social care, social treatment, and social enhancement. *Social care* refers to those actions and efforts designed to provide people in need with access to the basics of life (e.g., food, shelter, protection from harm, etc.) and opportunities to meet their psychosocial needs (e.g., belonging, acceptance, and comfort in times of distress). In social care, the focus is on providing needed resources and/or on helping the client be as comfortable as possible in a difficult situation that either cannot be changed or cannot be modified in the immediate future. Examples of social care would be efforts to address the needs and concerns of young children who must live in foster care, adults living in a shelter for the homeless, adults who have a serious and persistent mental illness, and persons who are dying.

Social treatment involves actions designed to modify or correct an individual's or family's dysfunctional patterns of thought, feeling, and behavior. In social treatment, the focus is primarily on facilitating individual or family change through training, counseling, or various forms of therapy. In many cases (e.g., work with children in foster care), the social worker may provide both social care and social treatment to the same client.

A third form of intervention seeks to enhance, expand, or further develop the abilities and performance of persons who are already functioning well. *Social enhancement* services emphasize growth and development of clients in a particular area of functioning without a "problem" having necessarily been identified. Some examples of enhancement-oriented services are youth and senior citizen recreation programs, well-baby clinics, marriage enrichment sessions, and job training programs.

Improved Social Conditions.
Social work's second area of emphasis is on shaping and creating environments that will be supportive and empowering. Underpinning this goal is one of the most fundamental social work values: a strong belief in the importance of achieving and maintaining social justice. *Social justice* refers to fairness and moral rightness in how social institutions such as governments, corporations, and powerful groups recognize and support the basic human rights of all people. A closely related belief of social workers is that the society should strive for *economic justice* (sometimes called *distributive justice*), which refers to fairness in the apportioning and distribution of economic resources, opportunities, and burdens (e.g., taxes). In other words, the economic resources of a society should be distributed (and redistributed) through structures of taxation and other economic mechanisms so that all people have equal opportunities for economic advancement and can meet their basic needs.

Very often, political controversy has its origin in differing conceptions of what is truly fair and just and in differing beliefs on whether and how society should assume responsibility for addressing human needs and problems. Most social workers would argue that social and economic policies must recognize that all people have basic human rights—that is, claims on humanity at large, not because of individual achievement or by actions of government but simply by virtue of one's existence and one's inherent worth and dignity. Among those basic human rights are the following:

- The right to have the food, shelter, basic medical care, and essential social services necessary to maintain one's life
- The right to be protected from abuse and exploitation
- The right to work and earn a sufficient wage to secure basic resources and live with dignity
- The right to marry, to have a family, and to be with one's family
- The right to a basic education
- The right to own property
- The right to be protected from avoidable harm and injury in the workplace
- The right to worship as one chooses—or not at all, if one chooses
- The right to privacy
- The right to travel and associate with those one chooses
- The right to information about one's community and government
- The right to participate in and influence the decisions of one's government

Social workers would also agree that along with rights come responsibilities. Rights and responsibilities are two sides of the same coin; one cannot exist without the other. Situations of injustice develop when people are concerned only about their own rights and no longer possess a sense of responsibility for others and society in

general. To protect each right, there must be associated acts of respons
example, in relation to the first three rights identified above:

- If a human has the right to be alive, then others have the responsibility to make sure that he or she has food, shelter, and essential medical care.
- If people have the right to be protected from abuse and exploitation, then others have the responsibility to create social programs and take actions that will provide this protection when required.
- If a person has the right to work and earn a living, then others have the responsibility to make sure that employment opportunities exist and that those who work are paid a living wage.

Social workers sometimes perform the needed services to help achieve people's rights; at other times, they serve as a voice for those whose rights are ignored or abused by calling on others to recognize the basic rights of all people and to act responsibly, with fairness and justice. When working with individuals and families, these changes are often termed *environmental modifications*. An example would be efforts by a school social worker to prepare students for the return of a former classmate who was badly scarred in an automobile accident. Another example would be providing special training to a foster mother so she can respond thoughtfully and constructively to a young foster child who exhibits inappropriate sexual behavior.

When working with organizations and communities, the creation of an environment that is supportive, responsive, and empowering is also the goal of social workers. At this level, social workers seek changes in how community decision makers and state and national governments respond to human needs and social problems. This type of activity involves political action to encourage social change. Such efforts include those activities intended to develop and improve laws, social policies, social institutions, and social systems in ways that will promote social and economic justice, expand opportunities for people, and improve the everyday circumstances in which people live. Specific examples would be expanding the availability of safe and affordable housing, creating incentives for businesses to hire people with disabilities, amending laws so they better prevent discrimination, and empowering neighborhood and community organizations to become politically active in addressing the issues they face.

Efforts to modify environments are sometimes labeled programs of prevention. **Prevention** consists of those actions taken to eliminate social, economic, psychological, and other conditions known to cause or contribute to the formation of human problems. To be effective in prevention, social workers must be able to identify the specific factors and situations that contribute to the development of social problems and then select actions and activities that will reduce or eliminate their impact. Borrowing from the public health model, three levels of prevention can be identified:

Level 1: Primary prevention. Actions intended to deter the problem from developing
Level 2: Secondary prevention. Actions intended to detect a problem at its early stages and address it while it is still relatively easy to change

Level 3: Tertiary prevention. Actions intended to address an already serious problem in ways that keep it from growing even worse, causing additional damage, or spreading to others

Social Work's Focus

Social work is certainly not the only profession concerned with how individuals and families function, nor is it the only profession interested in social conditions and social problems. However, it is social work's simultaneous focus on and attention to both the person and the person's environment that makes social work unique among the various helping professions.

Elements or aspects of one's environment may be either supports or barriers to his or her effective social functioning. Because both the person and the environment are constantly changing, adaptations and adjustments must be ongoing. Social workers, therefore, must be especially vigilant regarding those aspects of a person's environment that are shaped by the social policies and programs that make up the social welfare system. It is this ***person-in-environment*** focus that sets social work apart from other helping professions.

The focus on person-in-environment requires that the social worker attend to several interrelated dimensions of the person: biological, intellectual, emotional, social, familial, spiritual, economic, communal, and so on. This concern for the ***whole person*** contributes to the breadth of concern by the social work profession— for example, the individual's capacity to meet basic physical needs (food, housing, health care, etc.), the person's levels of knowledge and skills needed to cope with life's demands and to earn a living, the person's thoughts about others and his or her own life, the individual's goals and aspirations, and the like. It is important to note the person-in-environment construct uses the word *person*, not *personality*. Personality is but one component of the whole person. A focus only on personality would be incongruous with the domain of social work and slant it toward psychology.

The term ***environment*** refers to one's surroundings—that multitude of physical and social structures, forces, and processes that affect humans and all other life forms. Of particular interest to social workers are those systems, structures, and other factors that most frequently and most directly affect a person's day-to-day social functioning (i.e., the person's *immediate environment*). One's immediate environment includes the person's family, close friends, neighborhood, workplace, and the services and programs he or she uses.

Based on their empirical analysis of social work practice tasks, Teare and Sheafor (1995) conclude that social workers devote a major part of their attention to clients' efforts to improve interactions with their immediate environment. Social workers focus to a lesser extent on the broader environment, possibly because the impact of problems in the more *distant environment* is less evident and more difficult to change. In order to grow, develop, and survive, humans need clean air, drinkable water, shelter, and good soil to produce food. And because biological well-being is a prerequisite to positive social functioning, social workers must also be concerned with problems such as prevention of disease and pollution. In addition, they seek to change damaging societal values, correct human rights violations, and address unjust political and economic structures that may affect their clients. Concern over factors in both the immediate and distant environments is central to fulfilling social work's mission.

Because social relationships are of central concern to their profession, social workers must understand the power of a social environment—both its potentially helpful and harmful purposes. As suggested earlier, humans are social creatures and have a strong need to be accepted by others. Humans are mimetic creatures, as well, which means they are drawn to imitate how others think and behave. The concept of *mimetic desire* refers to the drive people feel to have what others have. For example, we may have little or no interest in some object or activity until we see that others have it, and then we, too, will be interested in or want what they have. Observing what others in our social environment are doing can be a powerful force for change—either positively or negatively. Social workers understand that if a person's environment can be changed, that individual will be more likely to change what he or she thinks and how he or she behaves.

Social Work's Scope

A profession's **scope** can be thought of as the range of activities and involvements appropriate to its mission. One useful way of describing social work's scope involves classifying the intervention by the size of the client system. Practice at the **micro level** focuses on the individual and his or her most intimate interactions, such as exchanges between husband and wife, parent and child, close friends, and family members. The terms *interpersonal helping*, *direct practice*, and *clinical practice* are often used interchangeably with micro-level practice.

At the other extreme, **macro-level** practice may involve work with an organization, community, state, or even society as a whole. Obviously, macro-level practice also deals with interpersonal relations, but these are the interactions between people who represent organizations or who are members of a work group such as an agency committee or interagency task force. When engaged in macro-level practice, the social worker is frequently involved in activities such as administration, fundraising, testifying on proposed legislation, policy analysis, class advocacy, and social resource development.

Between the micro and macro levels is **mezzo-level** (midlevel) practice. Practice at this level is concerned with interpersonal relations that are somewhat less intimate than those associated with family life but more personally meaningful than those that occur among organizational and institutional representatives. Included would be relationships among individuals in a self-help or therapy group, among peers at school or work, and among neighbors.

Some practice approaches address more than one intervention level. For example, social treatment, as defined by Kemp, Whittaker, and Tracy (1997), includes the micro- and mezzo-levels, and the generalist perspective (Schatz, Jenkins, and Sheafor 1990) requires the social worker to be capable of practice at the micro, mezzo, and macro levels.

Social Work's Sanction

Sanction refers to the authorization, approval, or permission needed to perform certain professional tasks or activities. Sanction has the effect of defining the profession's domain. Four major sources provide sanction for social work activities. One source is government agencies—federal, state, and city—that authorize the actions of social workers through several means: legislation that creates social programs, the allocation of funds for social work activities, the licensing of organizations (e.g., licensed child-placing agencies) that employ social workers, and the licensing and regulation of individual social work practitioners.

A second source of sanction includes the many private human services organizations (both nonprofit and profit-making agencies) that sanction social work by recruiting and hiring social workers to provide services or by purchasing services from those who are in private practice or employed by other agencies. Indirectly, then, the community sanctions and pays social workers to provide specific services. In return for this sanction to practice, social workers are obliged to provide high-quality services and to take reasonable steps to make sure that all social work practitioners are competent and ethical.

Third, the profession, acting through the National Association of Social Workers (NASW), sets standards for appropriate and ethical practice. By requiring adherence to its *Code of Ethics*, offering certification (i.e., the Academy of Certified Social Workers and various specialty certifications [see http://www.socialworkers.org/credentials/default.asp]), and providing education to its membership through publications and conferences, the NASW serves as a vehicle for protecting the public trust.

Finally, the true test of public sanction for practice is the willingness of clients to seek out and use services offered by social workers. In order to win the trust of clients, social workers must demonstrate on a daily basis that they are capable of providing effective services and are committed to conducting their practice in a responsible and ethical manner.

■ AN OVERVIEW OF SOCIAL WORK PRACTICE

Figure 1.1 presents a model of the key factors that influence social work practice. It shows the client (or client system) and the social worker joining in a process of change while both are being influenced by the social agency (e.g., its policies and programs) and by the wider social environment.

The reason clients and social workers come together is to engage in a ***planned change process***. That process involves several phases of activity during which the client and social worker move from their decision to initiate a course of action, through the change activity, to an evaluation of its success and a decision to terminate the helping activity (see Chapter 7). Although the social worker is expected to guide this process, the client must ultimately make the decisions about whether to change his or her beliefs, thoughts, or behaviors or to make use of those resources identified by the worker.

FIGURE 1.1   An Integrative View of Social Work Practice

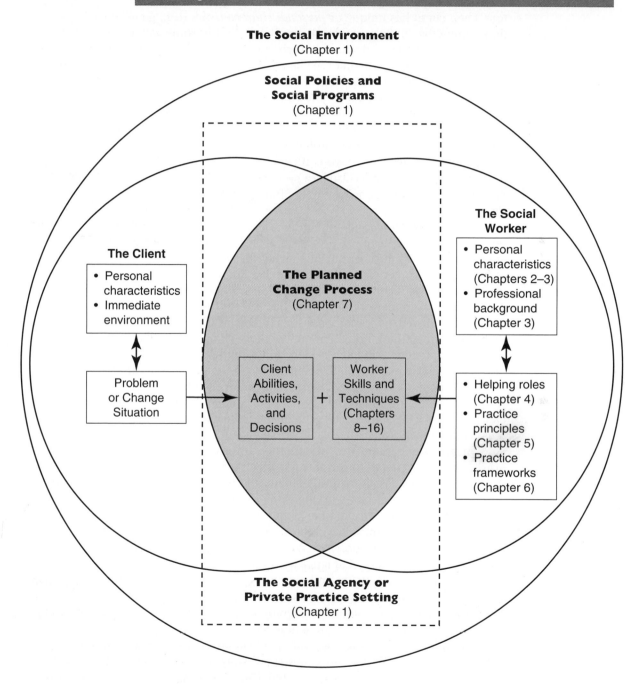

The Client side of Figure 1.1 indicates that the problem or situation the client seeks to change is the product of a combination of personal and environmental factors. Each client has unique or *personal characteristics* (e.g., goals, beliefs, perceptions, strengths, limitations) that have contributed in some way to the situation or problem being addressed and that might also be used to help bring about a desired change. Regardless of whether the client is an individual, family, or some larger system, every situation is unique to the client's special needs, wants, capacities, knowledge, beliefs, physical characteristics, and life experiences.

Clients do not exist in isolation. Their *immediate environment* might include friends, family, school personnel, employers, natural helpers, neighborhood or community groups, or even other professional helpers, to mention just a few. Because environmental influences have contributed to the problem or concern creating a need for change, they must also be a part of the solution; people in the client's immediate environment must be kept in the foreground as possible targets and resources for the change activity.

The Social Worker side of Figure 1.1 suggests that the worker brings unique personal characteristics and a professional background to the change process. These are experienced by the client through what the social worker actually does with the client (i.e., the worker's activities and application of skills and techniques). What the worker does is a function of the specific professional role he or she has assumed and the conceptual framework he or she has selected to guide practice. The worker's *personal characteristics* encompass such factors as life experience, talents, commitment to serving others, and the match of these characteristics with the demands of social work practice. (Chapter 2 offers an in-depth discussion of these characteristics.) The social worker's unique perspectives on the human condition, as well as his or her particular values, are inevitably introduced into the change process. The worker's view on life and human problems is shaped by his or her racial or cultural background, socioeconomic status, gender, age, sexual orientation, and the like. All of these characteristics affect the social worker–client relationship.

At the same time, the practitioner brings the special contribution of a *professional background* to social work, which differentiates the social worker from the client's friends, family, natural helpers, and the professionals representing other disciplines who may also be working with the client or who attempted to help in the past. What is this professional background? First and foremost, the social worker brings the belief system, values, ethical principles, and focus on social functioning that are common to the domain of social work. Through education and experience, the social worker develops a practice wisdom and an ability to use his or her personal characteristics, special talents, and unique style to help clients. In addition, the social worker brings a knowledge base, much of it derived from the social and behavioral sciences. Chapter 3 presents an overview of the necessary artistic abilities, knowledge base, and value positions relevant to practice.

As social workers carry out their responsibilities, they perform various *helping roles*. As Chapter 4 describes more fully, social workers must be prepared to perform a wide variety of roles and functions, ranging from linking clients to appropriate resources, to assessing case situations and providing direct services, to planning and conducting social action.

The profession has informally tested the applicability of its approach to providing human services, largely through trial and error. Some of these tried-and-true guidelines for practice have been reduced to *practice principles* that serve as the most fundamental directives to practice (see Chapter 5).

An important element of professional background is that portion of the social worker's knowledge base consisting of various *practice frameworks* that guide one's work (e.g., practice perspectives, theories, and models) and provide direction to the change process. The ways in which these frameworks might be selected and utilized are discussed in Chapter 6.

Finally, the social worker's *skills* and mastery of *techniques* are his or her most evident and tangible contribution to the change process. The skills or techniques selected by the social worker will depend, of course, on the nature of the client's problem or concern, the expectations of the practice setting, and the worker's own competence in using them.

Returning again to Figure 1.1, it is important to recognize that social work practice takes place within a ***social environment*** (sometimes called a *distant environment*) and, more specifically, usually within the context of a social agency. Typically, the agency has been shaped by local, state, and/or national social policies, and its programs are a reflection of society's values and beliefs. Commitment to the social welfare of its members varies among societies; within the United States, it even varies among regions, states, and communities. We know that having sound social programs supports quality living for all people—the more secure as well as the most vulnerable members of that society. Yet every social worker knows that our social policies and programs leave much to be desired. Moreover, U.S. society has demonstrated an ambivalent and transient commitment to people whose needs are not adequately met through their employment or help provided by family and friends. Therefore, social workers, who might be viewed as agents of the society, must frequently work with fewer than the desired tools for assisting their clients.

Through its legislative and other decision-making bodies, society creates ***social programs*** intended to help certain people. These programs take three forms:

- *Social provisions* involve giving tangible goods (e.g., money, food, clothing, and housing) to persons in need.
- *Social services* include intangible services (e.g., counseling, therapy, and learning experiences) intended to help people resolve and/or prevent problems.
- *Social action* programs are concerned with changing aspects of the social environment to make it more responsive to people's needs and wants.

The particular philosophy on which social programs are built has a significant bearing on how they operate, how effective they are, and how they affect both the client and the social worker. The dominant social welfare philosophy in the United States contends that social programs should be a safety net that is available only to people who can demonstrate "real need." In other words, social programs should exist only to help people solve already serious problems and be available only to those who are deemed eligible. A second philosophy, the social utilities conception, considers social programs to be first-line functions of society (similar to education and law enforcement). This approach places greater emphasis on prevention and avoids forcing the client to identify a problem or admit to some personal failure in order to benefit from human services.

The benefits and services associated with a particular social program are typically offered through a ***social agency***. Thus, for the most part, social work is an agency-based profession and most social workers are agency employees. A social agency might be a public welfare department, mental health center, school, hospital, neighborhood center, or any of a number of differing organizational structures. It may be a public agency supported by tax funds and governed by elected officials or a private agency operating under the auspices of a volunteer board and supported primarily by fees and voluntary donations. The basic functions of the agency are to administer social programs and to monitor the quality of the helping process. To perform these functions, the agency must secure money, staff, and other resources; determine which people are eligible for its services; and maintain an administrative structure that will meet targeted social needs in an efficient and effective manner. The most important ingredient of a social agency is its people. Receptionists, custodians, administrators, and service providers all must work together to deliver successful programs. Often, several helping professions are employed in the same agency. In such interdisciplinary programs, each profession brings its own perspective on helping—as well as the special competencies appropriate to the domain of that profession.

Increasingly, social workers are providing services through ***private practice***. In this setting, social workers and other professionals maintain an independent practice, as is typical in medicine and law, and contract directly with their clients to provide services.

CONCLUSION

Social work is one of several human services professions that have been sanctioned by society to help improve the quality of life for all people. Other such helping professions include clinical psychology, drug and alcohol counseling, marriage and family counseling, school psychology, medicine, rehabilitation counseling, nursing, and so on. The uniqueness of social work among these professions is its focus on the social functioning of people and helping people interact more effectively with their environments—both their immediate and distant environments. Social workers perform this role by assisting people to address issues in their social functioning and working to prevent social problems from emerging or, if they already exist, from getting worse.

Increasingly, conflict and competition arise among the various human services professions over issues of the domain (or turf) of each. These conflicts tend to center around competition for jobs, salary, status, and control, as well as disagreements over which profession is most qualified to perform certain tasks. To minimize the effect of these problems on clients, it is important for the members of these professions to engage in ***interprofessional collaboration*** as they provide their services.

However, each discipline must avoid letting its practice activities drift into the areas of expertise of the other professions.

Social workers have historically claimed they represent the profession best prepared to help people resolve problems in social functioning and to guide social change efforts to prevent problems from occurring or becoming worse. It is important that social workers maintain their focus on these central features of their domain.

SELECTED BIBLIOGRAPHY

Kemp, Susan P., James Whittaker, and Elizabeth Tracy. *Person-Environment Practice: The Social Ecology of Interpersonal Helping.* New York: Aldine de Gruyter, 1997.

Morales, Armando T., Bradford W. Sheafor, and Malcolm E. Scott. *Social Work: A Profession of Many Faces,* 11th ed. Boston: Allyn & Bacon, 2007.

National Association of Social Workers. *Code of Ethics.* Washington, DC: NASW, 1999.

Schatz, Mona S., Lowell E. Jenkins, and Bradford W. Sheafor. "Milford Redefined: A Model of Initial and Advanced Generalist Social Work." *Journal of Social Work Education* 26 (Fall 1990): 217–231.

2 Merging Person with Profession

$\mathbf{A}$ social worker's professional responsibilities and his or her personal life are intertwined. Most social workers cannot simply go to work, do their job, and then leave their thoughts and feelings about work at the office when returning home. They may try to keep professional concerns separate from their other roles and responsibilities but the nature of the work makes this difficult.

Social work professionals view the client, when an individual, as a *whole person* with various dimensions, including the physical, spiritual, emotional, psychological, social, and intellectual. They also view the client within a situational and ecological context. These same concepts apply to the social worker. The social worker responds to the challenges of practice with his or her whole being; therefore, the worker's beliefs, values, physical and emotional well-being, spirituality, family relationships, friendships, and all other facets of life and living will both influence and be influenced by the day-to-day experiences of social work practice.

A social worker has many roles, responsibilities, and interests besides those that are related to the job. For example, he or she is usually part of a family or household, often a spouse or partner, often a parent, part of friendship and social networks, and a resident in a particular neighborhood and community. Moreover, he or she may be a member of an ethnic group, affiliated with a religious denomination or faith community, a member of a special-interest group or political party, and a member of service and recreational groups. Given this multitude of social connections and roles, every social worker is challenged to resolve the inevitable tensions that arise between personal and professional obligations.

Although this book focuses primarily on the activities that occur during the hours that the social worker devotes to his or her job, this chapter examines how the realities of practice may impinge on the worker's private life. The observations presented here are intended to assist social workers to strike a healthy balance between their personal needs and responsibilities and the demands and responsibilities of practice.

■ SELECTING SOCIAL WORK AS A CAREER

Our lives are shaped by the choices we make. Because choosing social work as a career has some unique implications for self and family, those attracted to this profession must consider (and periodically reconsider) if social work should be their life's work. There must be a good fit between the person and his or her occupation. A mismatch can be destructive to one's health and emotional well-being. A person who feels trapped in the profession cannot bring the desired energy and commitment to the helping process, and consequently, clients will be poorly served.

Social Work as a Life Companion

An individual considering a social work career must be satisfied with his or her answers to the following questions:

- Is being a social worker a meaningful and worthwhile way for me to live my life?
- Is there a good fit between my personal beliefs, values, and needs and the values and demands of the social work profession?
- Is the practice of social work an appropriate and satisfying use of my unique gifts, abilities, and skills?
- What impact will being a social worker have on my physical and mental health, my intellectual development, my religious beliefs and practices, and my economic situation?
- What impact will my career in social work have on my family and friends?
- How will being a social worker affect the overall quality of my life?

Each person needs to identify his or her core values and decide what is really important in life. The work and rewards that accrue from being a social worker should be consistent with those beliefs and priorities.

The School-to-Job Transition

Many students do not fully realize that their program of social work education, including the practicum, takes place within a protected environment. Once they enter the world of full-time practice as a paid professional, they may experience reality shock. Many are surprised by the sheer difficulty of their jobs. For example, in describing her new job, a very capable recent graduate told one of the authors: "I simply had no idea that my clients would be so troubled, my job so difficult and frustrating, and my agency setting would be so overwhelmingly complex."

Those beginning their first social work job quickly discover that there is seldom enough time to do all that needs to be done. Many are upset and angered when they recognize that in far too many agencies, social work values and principles and a concern for clients have taken a backseat to the forces of political pressure, administrative convenience, budget limitations, the fear of lawsuits, and the day-by-day struggle to cope with an overwhelming caseload. Many are disillusioned by the discovery that some colleagues have lost their enthusiasm and are too fatigued and demoralized to be effective. Within such an environment, it can be a challenge to maintain one's professional ideals and standards.

Every new social worker is somewhat surprised and frustrated by the slowness of change, whether that change is by individual clients, organizations, or communities. They also discover that identifying what needs to change is relatively easy compared to achieving the change. Programs of social work education teach about the process of change and describe techniques for facilitating change but they cannot teach the personal qualities of patience, perseverance, tenacity, and tolerance that are so necessary to moving good ideas into reality.

Some new social work graduates who were high academic achievers face a special challenge when they move into an agency-based practice. Simply put, they are accustomed to doing grade A academic work and expect to do A-quality work on the job, but discover that there is only enough time and resources to do average work. Those unable to modify their expectations will experience much frustration.

Some agencies provide a superb work environment, but far too many offer an environment that is noisy, crowded, unattractive, and sometimes even dangerous. Dissatisfaction with an agency-based practice has led many experienced social workers to enter a private practice that offers a more pleasant place to work and more control over what they do and how they do it. Although this may be an understandable response to frustrations associated with bureaucratic settings, it has the effect of drawing social workers away from the profession's traditional commitment to the poor and oppressed. Throughout their careers, conscientious social workers must struggle to reconcile their desire for adequate income and a decent work environment with their concern for the poor and their commitment to social and economic justice.

Many new social workers become disenchanted when they discover that politics plays a significant role in the decisions and functioning of their practice settings. This issue needs to be put in perspective. Within every group and organization—whether a business, a social agency, a religious body, or a professional organization—people use power and authority to move the organization in directions they see as desirable. Thus, all organizations are inherently political. On the other hand, politics is certainly not the most important thing about an organization or a work setting. Social workers must guard against becoming so preoccupied with workplace politics that they lose sight of their agency's real purpose and the people it is to serve.

Earning a Living as a Social Worker

People do not choose the social work profession because of what social work jobs pay, but they cannot devote their time to the practice of social work unless they are paid and can earn a living as a social worker. The social worker and his or her dependents are directly affected by the worker's earning capacity. Social work has never been a high-paying profession and in contrast to some occupations, the earning power of social workers does not rise rapidly or continually as they gain skill and experience. Social workers earn a modest income and have limited opportunity to climb the economic ladder. However, the satisfaction of doing something truly worthwhile and making a difference in the lives of people is often viewed by social workers as an offsetting form of compensation.

Most entry-level jobs are ones involving the provision of services directly to clients. After a few years in direct services, many social workers apply for higher-paying jobs in supervision and administration as a way of increasing their income and prestige. This may be a wise job change for those attracted to management tasks such as budgeting, policy development, public relations, personnel selection, and staff training. It may be an unwise decision for those whose job satisfaction comes primarily from direct contact with clients.

Those entering social work should expect to change jobs from 5 to 10 times during their working years. Sometimes a job change is prompted by poor performance or an agency's staff reductions, but most often it is a matter of personal choice. Among the reasons that social workers change jobs are the following:

- Desire for higher salary, better benefits, or job security
- Desire to learn a new field of practice or test one's ability to perform certain tasks and activities
- Desire for more discretion and control over practice decisions and methods
- Desire to work in a setting that is more accepting of new ideas and new approaches to practice
- Desire to work with clients having a different set of problems, concerns, or situations
- Desire for a less stressful or a safer work environment
- Opportunity to receive better supervision and in-service training
- Desire to remove self from conflicts with a supervisor or agency administrator
- Need to adjust work to changes in personal or family life (e.g., marriage, divorce, birth of child, illness, etc.)

Those preparing to enter social work are advised to identify their personal and career goals and formulate a plan for reaching those goals. Examples of goals include obtaining a particular type of job, having the opportunity to design an innovative program, becoming an administrator of a certain type of agency, becoming skilled in work with certain client populations, conducting research on a particular topic, and so on. In these times of rapid change, it can be difficult to develop such a plan and even more difficult to follow it. However, career planning provides direction and a framework for making decisions about what special training and work experiences to pursue as preparation.

■ ESTABLISHING ONESELF AS A SOCIAL WORKER

It is not enough for the new social worker to carry his or her credentials into a job and assume that everything is in place for a satisfying and effective practice. The worker must first demonstrate to clients, colleagues, and other agencies in the community that he or she is competent and trustworthy. In addition, the worker will be challenged to reconcile his or her personal and professional standards with the everyday operations of human services systems.

Acquiring a Reputation

Every social worker acquires a reputation within his or her agency, within the local human services network, and among the clients he or she serves. That reputation, whether good or bad, has an impact on his or her effectiveness with clients, interagency and interprofessional communication and cooperation, and whether he or she is considered for promotion or offered other social work jobs. Social workers should regularly review how their statements, actions, and associations are shaping their reputations. Socrates observed that "the way to gain a good reputation is to endeavor to be what you desire to appear."

One need only sit in on a few support group meetings or spend an hour in an agency waiting room to realize that many clients talk freely about the social workers, doctors, teachers, and other professionals. They tell friends, neighbors, and other clients about how they have been treated and who does a good job and who to avoid. Clients are especially sensitive to whether social workers are willing to listen, available when needed, and fair in the decisions they make.

Within an agency, each social worker acquires a reputation as an employee. Over time, the other agency employees form an opinion about the worker's competence, whether he or she is dependable, and if he or she is a good team member. That reputation will affect the willingness of the other employees to offer their support, assistance, and cooperation.

Reputation is also a determining factor in whether a private practice or fee-for-service program will succeed. If they have a choice, clients will avoid agencies and professionals who have bad reputations. In addition, the professionals of a community who are in a position to refer clients to a particular social worker will do so only if that worker has a reputation for being competent and ethical.

A good reputation can take years to develop but can be quickly destroyed by others. For this reason, many cultures consider slander and the spreading of gossip that can ruin a person's reputation to be among the most reprehensible of moral transgressions.

Conflict over Agency Policy

One of the most painful situations social workers can experience is to find themselves employed by an organization that does not respect clients or value professional competence and ethical conduct. Such situations can arise when an organization's administration and policy board is more concerned about politics, cost cutting, or profit than providing needed and appropriate services.

All organizations develop a culture consisting of its values, expectations, and group norms. Employees are rewarded when they accept this culture and ostracized when they do not. Once established, an organization's culture tends to perpetuate itself while exerting a pervasive effect on employees and their job performance. A social worker employed by an organization with a destructive culture will need to work hard to change that culture or else look for another job.

Every social worker comes to his or her practice setting with a set of personal beliefs, values, standards, and expectations. It is inevitable that he or she will, from time to time, disagree with agency decisions and methods of operation. How is a worker to respond to such situations? In the final analysis, the social worker must follow his or her conscience. However, the worker's decision about what to do must be based on a thoughtful examination of the issue. One might begin this examination by seeking answers to the following questions:

- Why has my agency taken this position? What is the history behind this position? What are the arguments for and against this position? What data support this viewpoint? What political, economic, and social forces gave rise to this position? Was it prompted by political and administrative expediency or was it rooted in principles of social justice and efforts to allocate scarce resources in a fair and responsible manner? If it was driven by a lack of fiscal resources, what actions were taken to secure additional resources?
- Which of my beliefs, values, or standards is being threatened or violated? Are my concerns based on identifiable principles or possibly arising from bias or differences in personal, professional, and/or administrative style?
- Does the action or position in question recognize that every individual has worth and dignity, regardless of his or her strengths and limitations, successes and failings? Does it recognize that each person is unique and precious?
- Does the action or position recognize and respect the rights and responsibilities of each person? Does the position honor the principle that every mentally competent individual has a right to self-determination, as long as his or her actions do not harm others? Does the position recognize that every competent person is also responsible for his or her own actions and must accept the consequences for violating legitimate laws and rules?
- Does the action or position in question promote the common good? Does the position enhance and strengthen the functioning of individuals, families, and the community? Does it recognize the obligation of individuals, communities, and society to expand social and economic opportunities and, where necessary, to provide direct assistance to persons who are at risk of harm, deeply troubled, adversely affected by a physical or mental limitation, or socially or economically oppressed?

Once the social worker understands why the agency has taken the action or position in question and is also clear about why he or she disagrees, the worker must decide on a course of action. Each possible option needs to be examined in terms of its immediate and long-term consequences and in regard to what might be gained and lost. The following suggestions may prove useful:

- If the worker concludes that this is indeed a matter that demands a response, he or she might begin by seeking further advice and direction from trusted peers and/or the agency supervisor.
- If the worker is expected by his or her agency to take some action that would violate his or her professional or moral standards, the worker should voice these concerns, document them in a letter to the appropriate administrator,

and formally request to be excused from having to participate in the questionable activity.

■ In extreme cases and when there is no acceptable alternative, the worker will need to seek employment in a different agency.

When issues are complex, knowing what is right is never easy and doing what is right is always difficult.

Promoting Social Justice

Most individuals attracted to social work are idealistic. They want to make the world a better place. As discussed in Chapter 1, one of social work's fundamental purposes is to create a more just and humane society. Social workers believe that every individual has certain rights, such as those identified in the Declaration of Independence, the Bill of Rights, and the Universal Declaration of Human Rights issued by the United Nations. In short, they seek *social justice*, which Barker (2003, 404) describes as "an ideal condition in which all members of a society have the same basic rights, protection, opportunities, obligations and social benefits."

All considerations of social justice rest on a core belief: Every human being is intrinsically valuable. This worth is not something that must be earned or proved, nor is it a function of one's skin color, nationality, gender, social status, health, education, political affiliation, occupation, or other external characteristics or life circumstances. Simply by virtue of being human, every person has a right to be treated with fairness and respect, protected from abuse and exploitation, and granted opportunities to have a family, a basic education, meaningful work, and access to essential health care and social services. The Universal Declaration of Human Rights (United Nations, 1948, 1) observes that the "recognition of the inherent dignity and of the equal and inalienable rights of all members of the human family is the foundation of freedom, justice and peace in the world."

A multitude of interrelated economic, political, historical, and social forces give rise to and perpetuate injustice. The term *social injustice* refers to forms of exploitation, oppression, and discrimination that are embedded in societal beliefs and attitudes and reinforced by laws, policies, and social norms. Because the fundamental causes of social injustice tend to be woven into dominant belief systems and social and economic structures, an injustice and its effects may go unnoticed by all but those directly harmed. Social workers must be always open to the possibility that they or their agencies may unknowingly contribute to social injustice.

All too often, we do not feel personally responsible for the existence of social injustice. When an injustice is brought to our attention, we are likely to conclude that it is the fault of society and beyond our control. When we seriously examine a situation of injustice, we may end up feeling helpless and concluding that we are too small a force to make any difference. Social injustice is indeed a community or societal problem, but the responsibility to oppose injustice rests with the individual. Dr. Martin Luther King, Jr., reminded us that "whoever accepts evil without protesting against it, is really cooperating with it."

Achieving social justice is a complex undertaking, and even among people of goodwill and compassion, there will be different perspectives on what is truly fair and what specific actions will move us toward a more just and humane society. Social workers must work for social and economic justice and needed reforms in ways that recognize differences of opinion and maintain respect for those who may disagree with their own ideas about how best to achieve a just society.

In order to correct an injustice, people must become politically involved, speak out, and propose practical solutions. However, those who seek social reform must understand that they will pay a price for challenging powerful individuals and groups that stand to lose money, power, or position if the status quo is altered. Those who speak out may be ridiculed, lose their jobs, or, in extreme cases, subjected to physical threats and injury.

Political Involvement

Efforts to work for social and economic justice require participation in the political process. Basically, *politics* is the art of gaining, exercising, and retaining power. Some social workers are fascinated by politics; others find it distasteful. How and to what degree one involves himself or herself in political activity is a matter of choice, reflecting such factors as interest, available time, energy level, and personal style. Being an informed and conscientious voter is an essential first step, but more is required of social workers who wish to remain true to the "soul" of their profession.

A social worker's participation in the political process will usually involve one or more of the following activities:

- Evaluating how existing and proposed public policy affects people in need, the common good of society, and the profession
- Educating the public regarding the social dimensions and ramifications of law and public policy
- Entering into the debate on matters of public policy and advocating for desirable changes with or on behalf of persons affected by the policy
- Participating with other concerned parties in the formulation of public policy
- Working for the election of those who represent the worker's beliefs and values

As social workers become involved in the political process, they must make hard decisions about where they stand on complex issues. Most social workers tend to be on the liberal side of the conservative-to-liberal continuum. However, it is a mistake for social workers to assume that they must choose between being either a liberal or a conservative. Rather, they should be something of both. Everyone who is intellectually and spiritually alive is *liberal* in the sense of being open to the truth, regardless of its source; desirous of needed change; and accepting of governmental action if it will, in fact, improve the lives of people and promote the common good. Similarly, every thoughtful and responsible person is *conservative* in the sense of wanting to preserve those values, social arrangements, and approaches that have been fair and beneficial to people and because he or she knows that the newest idea is not necessarily the best one and that there is usually a negative side to government intervention. Thus, depending on the issue, a social worker might line up on either the liberal or conservative side of the debate. The merits and wisdom of a proposal, and not political ideology, should dictate one's stance on an issue.

The political health of a nation, state, or city depends on informed citizens debating the issues and ways of achieving justice and the common good. Such a debate requires not only mutual trust and goodwill among all involved but also a common language, respect for diversity, and agreement on a core of beliefs about people, society, and government. Debate, discussion, and decision making can be constructive only within a context of such fundamental agreement. Destructive to this process are those who replace dialogue with monologue, civility with coercion, and reason with slogans.

Political involvement can be tiring and frustrating. Some social workers begin to lose heart when confronted with setbacks. In order to continue working for desirable social and community change, year after year, social workers must strive to develop personal qualities of hopefulness, patience, perseverance, and tolerance. It is important to adhere to the following guidelines:

- Hold to your principles without being ideological.
- Be political without being partisan.
- Be respectful of those with whom you disagree.
- Be active and engaged without being used and manipulated.
- Focus on what brings people together, not what divides them, and focus on what people are for, rather than on what they are against.

Many social workers are in a position to observe the actual impact of social policies and programs on the lives of people. These direct observations are rarely available to the politicians who consider legislation and the administrators who develop policy and design programs. Thus, the social worker has both the opportunity and the obligation to document and communicate the effects of social legislation and administrative decisions, as well as to offer ideas on how policies and programs can be made more humane, effective, and efficient. Social workers with special abilities to speak and write can make valuable contributions to the education of decision makers and the citizenry.

■ THE INTERPLAY OF ONE'S PERSONAL AND PROFESSIONAL LIVES

Social workers receive many intangible gifts from their clients. For example, workers meet people who have overcome great obstacles and who care deeply about their families and communities. Getting to know such people can be an inspiring and life-changing experience. On the other hand, social work is often stressful and requires a heavy commitment of time and energy. Those factors also affect social workers and sometimes their families and friends.

Being Changed by Clients

In every type of practice, social workers will meet clients who are truly remarkable because of their courage, wisdom, compassion, and generosity. Some clients have survived and overcome great hardships and trauma. One of the great privileges of social work practice is the opportunity to meet these individuals and learn from them. Social workers open themselves to learning when they set aside their desire to learn *about* their clients and, instead, seek to learn *from* their clients. In a sense, the professional relationship is an exchange of gifts, and both the social worker and client stand to be changed by what they give and receive.

One cannot begin to really know a client without coming to understand how that individual thinks and feels about life. In many cases, the client's perspectives, beliefs, and values will be significantly different from those of the social worker. This may challenge the worker to rethink his or her own life experiences and values. Whenever one begins to understand things in a new way or look at the familiar from a different angle, one begins to change.

The social worker may also be changed by clients who are critical of his or her work. Clients may accuse workers of being uncaring and prejudiced or claim that their decisions are unfair. The worker must always remain open to the possibility that these clients are accurate in their assessments and, if that is the case, strive to modify the attitudes and behaviors that have offended clients.

The clients that cause the social worker great anguish are a particularly painful source of change. Not infrequently, the worker's skills and the available resources are insufficient to encourage or help clients to modify their behavior and social functioning. When this is the case, the worker must watch helplessly as clients make decisions that get them into trouble with the law, damage their health, or cause further disruptions in their lives. These humbling experiences teach the social worker that he or she is but one small influence in a client's life.

Personal Responses to Clients in Need

Many of the clients served by social workers live in poverty and experience constant stress because they cannot pay for even the basics such as food and shelter. By comparison, the social worker with only a modest income seems quite well off. This situation confronts the worker with hard questions of individual responsibility. Once a social worker has done all he or she can do as a professional and as an agency's representative, what, if anything, remains as a personal responsibility? Should a social worker use his or her own money to deal with a client's emergency?

Some would answer that meeting basic needs is a community and governmental responsibility and that the employees who work in human services agencies should not attempt to make up for system deficiencies. To even try would be an unfair and unreasonable drain on the employees' fiscal and emotional resources. It might also make it too easy for the community to avoid its responsibility to correct inadequacies in the system.

Others might answer that even when our social welfare systems fail to meet basic needs, the social worker still has a moral and ethical responsibility to respond personally. They might further argue that a social worker, because of his or her knowledge, has a unique obligation beyond that of the ordinary citizen.

Ultimately, one's answer is a matter of conscience and a judgment call concerning what action would be helpful to the client and reasonable and proper for the social worker. The social worker might consider the following questions in formulating his or her response:

- What situations, if any, require some extraordinary response? What if the situation involves a person who is especially vulnerable, such as a young child or a person who is sick or at risk of being injured?
- Is a personal response realistic for a social worker who encounters truly desperate situations on a daily basis? If a personal response is not reasonable, is some type of political or community action required?
- Is it appropriate for a social worker to make a personal contribution to a client (e.g., buy food, pay for a night's lodging, pay cab fare, etc.)? If yes, under what conditions and how is this to be done? If one decides to make a personal contribution, can it be done in a way that keeps the donor's identity confidential so as to maintain a proper boundary between worker and client and so the client is not placed in a position of feeling beholden to the worker?
- What personal, ethical, and legal pitfalls await the social worker who makes a donation directly to a client? What are the advantages and disadvantages of an agency having a policy on whether, when, and how a personal contribution is to occur? Is it appropriate for the workers of an agency to create and donate to a special, nonagency emergency fund?

The Social Worker's Family

It is difficult to keep work-related concerns from affecting one's personal life and family relationships. It is also difficult to keep one's personal and family problems from affecting professional performance. Nevertheless, social workers must strive to maintain a healthy separation.

Social workers, like everyone, experience personal and family problems. Sometimes the problems are serious and create stress, anxiety, or depression. When worry associated with personal concerns is added to the stress of practice, the social worker may become overwhelmed. During these times, the social worker needs the support of colleagues and friends and must be open to guidance provided by those able to see more objectively what is happening.

The social worker must protect his or her personal and family relationships from being adversely affected by work-related responsibilities. The daily transitions between one's family relationships and the often harsh realities and tension-filled relationships encountered at work can be difficult. The norms and expectations of these two environments are quite different.

Those who provide direct services to seriously troubled and highly dysfunctional clients will observe behaviors and situations that are extreme, depraved, and cruel. Long-term exposure to such behavior and circumstances can distort one's moral compass. In an adult correctional setting, for example, the daily exposure to intimidation, violence, and manipulation can dull one's sensitivity and gradually increase one's tolerance for abuse and inhumane treatment. Skewed views on what is usual and normal, if brought home to one's family or into one's friendships, can strain those relationships.

■ A FITNESS PROGRAM FOR THE SOCIAL WORKER

To be of maximum assistance to clients, a social worker must maintain a proper boundary in professional relationships. The worker's need for meaningful relationships and friendships must be met outside his or her relationships with clients. In addition, effective practice requires that the worker be intellectually alert and physically, emotionally, and spiritually healthy.

Friendships and Community

Good friends provide us with support and encouragement and help us to examine our assumptions, test reality, and maintain perspective. Good friends also provide constructive criticism when we behave inappropriately.

Because people tend to choose friends who are similar to themselves in age, interests, and socioeconomic status, many friendships develop in the workplace. While this is a natural occurrence, it has its disadvantages. For example, some social workers come to believe that no one except another social worker is capable of understanding their concerns and frustrations. Having friends only from one's work environment limits exposure to differing points of view and constricts the opportunity for personal growth. In some cases, it leads to an "us against them" type of thinking. The social worker should cultivate friendships with people from outside the work setting and from outside the profession in order to develop a broader community perspective and a more balanced and encompassing view of life.

All people need to feel that they belong and that they are participants in something greater than themselves. Unfortunately, a sense of community is increasingly missing in our society. So many people feel unconnected and lonely, in part because they are self-absorbed and more interested in receiving than in giving. A genuine sense of belonging and community cannot be artificially created, rushed, or forced into existence. Rather it grows slowly as individuals share what they have—time, energy, creativity, or money—with others in order to reach a shared goal. Long-term association, personal sacrifices, trust, mutual respect, and loyalty are the building blocks of community; there are no shortcuts.

Social workers often find a spirit of community and a sense of belonging through their participation in professional associations such as the National Association of Social Workers. Professional associations are important because they serve to advance the profession. However, social workers should not limit their involvements to professional or work-related groups and organizations. They are advised to also participate in neighborhood activities and local projects so they will meet a wide variety of people with differing perspectives.

Self-Worth and Self-Image

Social work is not an esteemed profession. To a large extent, this is because social work is inherently controversial. Social workers call attention to problems and deplorable social conditions that most in society prefer to ignore and deny. Because so many of the people served by social workers are devalued and disliked (e.g., the poor, parents who abuse their children, the mentally ill, individuals addicted to drugs, the homeless, etc.), social workers are also devalued. All too often, images of social work and social workers are linked to unpopular governmental welfare programs that many people perceive as a waste of taxpayer money.

Given the type of concerns they address, it is not surprising that social agencies and social workers become targets for criticism by politicians and others who do not want to be reminded of human need, injustice, and the inadequacy of existing programs and social structures. Not infrequently, social workers are blamed for systemic social and economic problems that are beyond the control of any one person, profession, or agency. Even when social workers understand that this criticism and denigration is unreasonable or misdirected, it is still painful. Social workers, like all people, want to be understood, valued, and respected.

In order to counteract feelings of being devalued and misunderstood, social workers must possess a sense of personal worth and confidence. This sense comes from belief in the importance of their work and the value of the services they provide. If the social worker doubts his or her own worth or the importance of the profession, he or she is likely to become discouraged and demoralized. No one should feel apologetic for being a social worker; the profession's mission and values are truly noble and reflect the very best of the human spirit.

Physical and Emotional Well-Being

When selecting a specific job, a social worker needs to consider his or her physical limitations, disabilities, and health problems, as well as anticipate the normal developmental changes that will occur over the years of work. There must be a suitable match between the worker's physical and emotional stamina and the demands of the job. Physical abilities change over time. As people grow older, their level of energy decreases and they experience some degree of loss in vision and hearing. Even such ordinary changes can affect the performance of specific social work tasks. Family and group therapy, for example, require excellent hearing. Also, one's age can make it either easier or more difficult to build relationships with clients who are in certain age categories.

For the most part, social work is a sedentary occupation. Physical inactivity can place the worker at risk of heart disease and other health problems. In order to counter this risk, it is important for workers to adhere to a program of regular exercise.

The expression of empathy and compassion by the social worker for the client is often necessary to support and encourage the client during the change process. However, those efforts to "be with" and to "feel with" the client are sometimes exhausting and even painful to the worker. The social worker must strive to strike a healthy balance between "feeling with client" and maintaining the emotional distance and personal boundaries appropriate to a professional relationship.

Social workers must be able to cope with and respond appropriately to the intense feelings and strong emotions (e.g., sadness, anger, fear) they often encounter and experience when working with clients who are in gut wrenching situations such as the father who has abused his child or the family that has lost a member to suicide. The frequent and long-term exposure to the distress of others can contribute to "compassion fatigue" and a numbing or hardening of the worker's own feelings.

Many clients are so overwhelmed by their problems that they develop *learned helplessness*—a pervasive feeling of hopelessness and a belief that no matter what they do, the pain will continue. Social workers who meet these clients on a daily basis or who work in inflexible organizations are vulnerable to developing this same sense of helplessness. The gallows humor observed in some agencies suggests that the workers are struggling to maintain perspective in the face of human conditions that defy acceptance, but have neither the time nor the resources needed to respond in a truly humane manner.

Social workers who have not satisfactorily resolved issues in their own family relationships or who carry emotional baggage related to traumatic life experiences are prone to distort and mishandle a professional relationship when their clients are struggling with issues similar to their own. In extreme cases, vulnerable workers have been so knocked off balance emotionally that they could no longer function as professionals. It is critically important that social workers be able to acknowledge their emotional weak spots and, if needed, obtain professional help. If that is not possible or successful, they should arrange for work assignments that help them avoid handling the types of cases and situations that might threaten their emotional well-being. (See Item 16.2 on worker self-awareness.)

In addition to the emotional demands placed on a social worker, other common sources of frustration on the job are heavy workloads, limitations on needed agency resources, and having to function within a complex and sometimes confusing set of laws, governmental regulations, and agency policies. All things considered, social work is a stressful occupation. Those entering this profession must be able to cope with this challenge. (See Item 16.3 for information on compassion fatigue and stress management.)

Intellectual Growth

Learning can and should continue throughout one's life. People can put themselves in touch with new ideas and clarify their thinking by engaging in reading and writing, listening to presentations by experts, and participating in thoughtful discussions with family, friends, and colleagues. It is helpful to occasionally place oneself in situations that will generate pressure to study and think. Examples include teaching a class, making a presentation, or writing an article (see Items 16.11 and 16.12). Ideally, every new social worker will find a mentor within his or her field of practice who will provide encouragement and direction as the worker seeks to learn a new job or develop his or her knowledge and skills (see Item 16.10).

In order to learn, people must allow themselves to feel unsure about what they "know" and open themselves to new and sometimes disturbing ideas. Learning begins with a question and an inner dissatisfaction with one's level of skill or understanding. It continues as the individual searches for answers, either alone or with others. Learning requires a willingness to give up familiar ideas and experience the uncertainty of moving in new directions.

It is hard to imagine a type of work that can evoke as many truly significant and challenging questions as does the practice of social work. The situations social workers encounter each day touch the very heart of questions about social justice; human rights and responsibilities; ethical behavior; the causes of individual, family, and organizational problems; and the nature of personal and social change. However, those who seek to become a social worker must recognize that social work is not an academic discipline nor a pure science wherein the search for knowledge is driven by the excitement of ideas and the joy of discovery. Those who want most of all to acquire a theoretical understanding of behavior and social problems and to build new knowledge are usually not content in the role of a social work practitioner. Social workers spend most of their time trying to patch together practical solutions to very serious but quite ordinary human problems, dilemmas, and crises.

It is important to strike a balance between personal and professional learning. Too much attention to professional interests can narrow one's vision. On the other hand, if attention is devoted mostly to topics of purely personal interest, one's professional knowledge will soon be outdated.

Religion and Spirituality

Given that a social worker's clients typically come from diverse backgrounds in terms of culture, religion, and spirituality, a worker must be accepting of how different individuals and groups have constructed or arrived at different answers to the really "big questions" in life. Throughout human history, people have sought answers to enduring questions such as these: Does my life have some ultimate purpose and meaning? How should I live my life? How am I to decide what is right and wrong? Am I being foolish and naïve when I strive to do what is right and fair to others? Why is there so much evil and suffering in the world? Why is there so much good and love in the world? How do I relate to God? Is there a God? What is God? These are not questions that the scientific method can answer. Rather, they are matters of religious faith, spirituality, and choice. The major religions of the world offer answers and perspectives that have been meaningful to millions of people over thousands of years, but, ultimately, each individual must choose his or her own spiritual path.

Although the concepts and experiences of religion and spirituality are intertwined, it is helpful to make a somewhat arbitrary distinction. A ***religion*** is a set of beliefs, stories, traditions, and practices that nurture and support particular approaches to spiritual growth. A religion provides a language and a conceptual framework for describing and understanding the spiritual life. Religions are passed from one generation to another by various forms of leadership and institutional structures. The elements of a religion typically include public prayer and worship by the community of believers, various rituals that mark transitions in the life cycle or the spiritual journey, a prescribed moral code, and a reverence for certain sacred writings and sacred places.

As compared to a religion, which is public and institutional in nature, ***spirituality*** is more a quality of the inner self or soul—that deepest recess of our being, where we are conscious of who we really are, what is right and wrong, and what gives us meaning and purpose. Both religion and spirituality involve a sense of the sacred and the recognition that some creative power, life force, or divine being transcends the visible and material world.

Although most of the world's people do not think of their spirituality as being separate from their religion, this distinction is helpful because some individuals appear to possess a deep and active spiritual life but engage in few public and observable religious practices. On the other hand, some participate in many religious activities without seeming to possess much in the way of a deep inner faith or spirituality. Still others attempt to develop a spirituality that is separate from all religion, often because they have been somehow hurt by formal religion.

To a considerable extent, a person's spirituality is his or her unique way of interpreting and assigning meaning to life and living. Our spirituality becomes visible to others in how we respond to other people, what we do with our money, how we react to success and setbacks, and the value and meaning we place on very ordinary aspects and events of living.

As people struggle to make sense of their experiences, especially those that bring great joy or cause great distress, they often gain new insights and their beliefs slowly change. Thus, spirituality is dynamic and an ongoing journey. The deeply religious and spiritual people who describe their spiritual struggles and growth emphasize the importance of occasional solitude for reflecting on life experiences, striving to achieve self-knowledge and self-discipline, providing service to others, developing a sense of humility, and having patience with themselves and compassion for others. They also identify common barriers to spiritual growth such as a desire for control, power, prestige, and possessions, and the fear of change.

One's spirituality must be durable in the sense that it provides meaning and direction throughout the life cycle, during both good times and bad, and especially as the person faces hardship, suffering, and death. As Moore (1992) suggests, the development and nurturing of such spirituality is difficult without the assistance of a group or community that provides guidance, encouragement, and challenge.

> Religions around the world demonstrate that spiritual life requires constant attention. . . . For good reason we go to church, temple, or mosque regularly and at appointed times: it's easy for consciousness to become lodged in the material world

and forget the spiritual. Sacred technology [e.g., prayer, meditation, solitude, ritual, study, fasting, etc.] is largely aimed at helping us remain conscious of spiritual ideals and values. (p. 204)

As people grow spiritually, they see more clearly that they are capable of great love and generosity as well as hate and selfishness. An important task in one's spiritual journey is to recognize and come to terms with one's own potential to be cruel, dishonest, and destructive as well as one's capacity for self-deception.

Social workers appreciate the complexity of human behavior and the uncertainties and fragility of life. Every day, social workers meet people who have been hurt by acts of ignorance, injustice, discrimination, and violence. In order to cope with the pain and harshness encountered on a daily basis, the social worker must strive to develop a hopeful spirituality—one that views all people, including those that hurt others, as having inherent worth and dignity and as being capable of positive change. In order to maintain a healthy and positive perspective, the social worker must seek opportunities to observe and to celebrate the basic goodness of people. (See Item 15.18 for more information on spirituality and religion.)

Artistic Expression

Another piece of the social worker's fitness program should be to develop and/or maintain his or her own capacities for artistic expression. There is evidence that creative people are effective social workers (see Chapter 3); it is not uncommon to meet social workers who are talented in various forms of artistic expression such as music, painting, acting, creative writing, sewing, photography, dance, woodworking, and so on.

It is important for social workers to cultivate and share their artistic talents. Such activities can be a diversion from the stress of practice and a gift that enhances the quality of life of other people.

■ HAVING FUN IN SOCIAL WORK

Human beings need to play and have fun. Adults often satisfy this need by introducing various forms of humor (e.g., jokes, kidding, playful pranks, and silly antics) into their work environment. How is a social worker to reconcile his or her need for fun with the serious business of social work? In many ways, the practice of social work is a rather grim and emotionally heavy endeavor. Clients are often in truly desperate and tragic situations, and the helping resources at a social worker's disposal are woefully inadequate. Although human distress is not a laughing matter, humor can be a counterbalance to the frustrations and despair experienced in practice.

Despite the risks associated with inappropriate expressions of humor, without an active sense of humor, social work practice can be unbearable and social workers can be very boring. Social workers must take their work seriously yet acknowledge and appreciate those things that are genuinely funny about themselves, their jobs, and the situations they encounter. They must allow themselves to laugh at the absurdities of life and temporarily to slip out from under societal demands for conformity and the many restrictions they place on themselves.

The use of humor with clients is always somewhat risky, but given proper precautions, it has a place in helping relationships. Often, it is the clients who teach the workers the importance of finding the humor in the clients' situations. It is always wrong to laugh *at* clients, but it may be appropriate and even helpful to laugh *with* them as they describe the humorous aspects of their experiences. Humor is an essential coping mechanism that should be affirmed and supported. Many individuals who live with harsh realities come to deeply appreciate the importance of humor as a way of achieving self-detachment from painful situations.

Humor is an antidote to adversity, stress, and frustration. Social workers, who work with clients facing some of the most difficult issues people can experience, need to cultivate an appropriate use of humor in working with their clients and with their colleagues.

CONCLUSION

Social work practice involves the blending or merging of a unique human being with a set of professional responsibilities. The social worker, like the client and all other people, has many dimensions, including the physical, emotional, intellectual, spiritual, and social. The social worker responds to his or her professional role and responsibilities as a whole person, and all these dimensions affect and are affected by the moment-by-moment activities of practice.

The social worker may be closely identified with his or her professional role but is not in that role 24 hours a day. He or she has a life, relationships, and responsibilities apart from those of a social worker. Each worker must achieve a proper and healthy balance between his or her personal and professional lives.

SELECTED BIBLIOGRAPHY

Barker, Robert. *The Social Work Dictionary*, 5th ed. Washington, DC: NASW Press, 2003.

Gibelman, Margaret. *What Social Workers Do*, 2nd ed. Washington, DC: NASW Press, 2005.

Moore, Thomas. *Care of the Soul*. New York: Harper-Collins, 1992.

Reichert, Elisabeth. *Social Work and Human Rights*. New York: Columbia University Press, 2003.

United Nations General Assembly. *Universal Declaration of Human Rights*. New York: United Nations, December 1948.

3 Merging the Person's Art with the Profession's Science

The social worker must combine his or her personal qualities, creative abilities, and social concern with the profession's knowledge in order to help clients enhance their social functioning or prevent social problems from developing. Each person has unique personal qualities that represent the artistic component of social work practice. Professional education cannot teach these artistic features, although it can help the learner identify such strengths and develop the ability to focus and apply them in work with clients. Professional education can also assist the learner in developing a beginning understanding of the knowledge (or science) that is necessary for effective practice. This merging and blending of one's art and the profession's science is initiated in social work education programs, but it is a lifelong activity, as social work knowledge is constantly expanding and the worker is being continually changed by life experiences.

■ THE SOCIAL WORKER AS ARTIST

Art is defined as "skill arising from the exercise of intuitive faculties" (*American Heritage Dictionary of the English Language* 2000, s.v. "art"). One need not look far to observe successful helpers who rely entirely on their artistic or intuitive abilities. Natural helpers, volunteers, and untrained human services providers demonstrate daily that even without formal education, they can be helpful in many situations. Similarly, it is not uncommon to see well-educated and knowledgeable people fail in their efforts to serve clients because they lack intuitive skills required for their practice.

What factors comprise the art of social work? There are numerous components: the compassion and courage to confront human suffering; the capacity to build a meaningful and productive helping relationship; the creativity to overcome barriers to change; the ability to infuse the change process with hopefulness and energy; the exercise of sound judgment; the appropriate personal values; and the formation of an effective professional style.

Compassion and Courage

A prerequisite to effective social work practice is the social worker's **compassion**. The word compassion means to suffer with others; it refers to a willingness to join with and enter into the pain of those who are distressed or troubled. Although most people see themselves as compassionate, it is important to recognize that a high level of compassion is not typical of most people. In fact, it is natural to want to avoid involvement in the pain of others. A social worker who lacks compassion is likely to distance himself or herself from client concerns.

Social work also demands personal ***courage***, not in the sense of being bold or daring but rather in being able to confront on a daily basis human suffering and turmoil and, not infrequently, negative and destructive human behaviors. Day after day, case by case, the social worker must be able to respond constructively to people who are directly affected by disease, disability, violence, neglect, sexual abuse, addiction, criminal exploitation, poverty, bizarre and chaotic family life, separation from a loved one, loneliness, abandonment, and other types of human suffering. Moreover, the social worker must be able to respond constructively to people who have directly or indirectly inflicted suffering on others. They must be able to deal with sometimes appalling human problems without becoming distracted or immobilized by their emotional reactions.

Over time, an individual can develop this fortitude or courage, but it is not something that can be learned from books or in a classroom. If it can be learned at all, it is learned from being with those who model an inner strength and a capacity to accept human suffering as part of the human condition. Those who have this courage are able to value and treat with dignity even those who have hurt others.

Professional Relationship

A bond of trust must exist before people are willing to risk that difficult human experience—change. Thus, the most fundamental tool of the trade is the use of a ***professional relationship*** to help people become open to the possibility of change and actively engage in the change process. A positive relationship is a precondition for effective work with individuals, families, or groups of clients, but it is also important in work with the people who make up organizations and communities.

How important is this relationship to the helping process? Lambert (1992) has carefully reviewed the research on factors that contribute to successful helping and concluded there are four:

1. *Client factors* (e.g., quality of the client's participation in treatment, satisfaction with what the worker is doing, the client's personal strengths and resources)
2. *Relationship factors*
3. *Placebo, hope, and expectancy factors* (e.g., the client's sense of hope and positive expectations from the helping process)
4. *Model/technique factors* (e.g., the specific practice approach used by the worker)

Lambert's research indicates that of these four, client factors account for 40 percent of successful outcomes, relationship factors for 30 percent, expectancy factors for

15 percent, and helping approach factors the remaining 15 percent. In other research, Hubble, Duncan, and Miller (1999) did not find significant differences in the success rates among the more than 200 intervention models now available to therapists. They conclude that the elements of a particular model are less important than the worker's confidence that following a certain approach will help achieve the desired change and thus encourage the client's trust in the process. Of the variables the worker can affect, relationship is the most important.

What are the essential qualities of successful helping? Within many Native American tribes there is a saying: "If you want to understand another person, you must first walk a mile in his [or her] moccasins." In other words, one must get inside that person's thoughts, beliefs, and life experiences. But before that is possible, one must first set aside his or her own values, attitudes, and judgments. This ability to take on another's perspective is known as having ***empathy***.

Although no one can ever fully appreciate the viewpoint of another person, the social worker needs to get as close as possible to that level of understanding. Empathy is needed, for example, to understand the fear and anger of a battered wife and her possible love and concern for the man who hurt her; to be sensitive to the anger and guilt of an abusive parent; to appreciate the difficulty of a teenager risking criticism by peers for speaking up in a group; or even to hear out the frustrations of an overworked staff member. A capacity for empathy is critical to all social workers, from caseworker to administrator.

Empathy requires an investment of energy; it is difficult to live vicariously—even temporarily—in another person's world. Moreover, it is easier to have empathy for some people than for others. For these reasons, a social worker cannot maintain the same level of empathy for all clients or for the same client at all times. Fatigue and stress, for example, can diminish one's capacity for empathy.

Warmth is a quality of relationship that communicates respect, acceptance, and interest in the well-being of others. However, warmth is much more than just saying "I care," although at times, that is important. Warmth is transmitted in many forms of communication, from a reassuring smile to an offer of concrete and tangible assistance. Warmth is a highly individual quality that is expressed differently by each person, but inherent in all expressions of warmth is acceptance and a nonjudgmental attitude.

Linked to warmth and empathy is the quality of ***genuineness***. Trite as it may sound, the social worker must behave like a "real" person and must truly like people and care about their well-being. The social worker may know the correct words to say or the proper action to recommend, but the client will assign them little value if the worker appears phony.

Creativity

Creative thinking is characterized by the integration of diverse facts and information leading to the formation of original ideas. Creativity is important in social work because each client's situation is unique and constantly changing. So-called textbook answers to human problems cannot accommodate this uniqueness.

A social worker with ***imagination*** can identify a variety of ways to approach and solve a problem, whereas the unimaginative one sees only one or two options—or perhaps none at all. For example, an agency board attempting to improve the accessibility of people with physical disabilities to public facilities might think only of encouraging local merchants or the city parking control office to create more "handicapped parking" spaces. On the other hand, the imaginative social worker might help the board identify additional ways to address the problem. Perhaps more effective enforcement of parking restrictions is a better solution. Another option might be to deputize people with disabilities to ticket an auto illegally parked in a restricted parking space. The imaginative social worker might also encourage the board to examine the possibility of increased public information programs, or expanded public transportation, or any of a dozen other strategies.

Another area in which the social worker must be imaginative is in interpreting and implementing agency policies. Policies are created to serve the typical client, yet people are characterized by infinite variety. Although the social worker cannot ethically (or legally) ignore or subvert agency policy, he or she must find ways to adapt or bend a policy to meet unique client needs. The social worker who is bound by a literal interpretation of "The Manual" is simply not able to make the system work for many clients.

Flexibility is also a dimension of creativity. Helping others change requires an ability to continually modify and adapt prior plans and decisions. The social worker making a foster home placement, for example, must have the flexibility to adapt his or her thinking to the often diverse perspectives of biological parents, foster parents, the child, the court, the agency, and even the neighborhood. To align oneself rigidly with any of the affected parties limits the social worker's ability to help resolve problems and conflicts. At times, one needs to be supportive; at other times, it is necessary to challenge the client; and at still other times, the social worker must be hard nosed, be directive, or exercise legitimate legal or professional authority. The effective social worker must be able to shift from one approach to another and correctly decide when a shift is appropriate.

In addition, the creative social worker must possess the trait of ***persistence***—the capacity to continue on a course of action, despite difficulties and setbacks. Self-discipline and goal directness are needed to translate creative ideas into action. The term *flexible persistence* emphasizes the need for both flexibility and persistence in the problem-solving process.

Hopefulness and Energy

The willingness and motivation of a client to work for change, when the prospect of change is anxiety producing or painful, is often a reflection of the social worker's ability to communicate the perspective that together the worker and client can improve the client's situation. Two characteristics of the social worker that are central to increasing client motivation are hopefulness and energy.

Hopefulness refers to a firm belief and a trust in the basic goodness of people, in their capacity to change in positive ways, and in their willingness to work cooperatively with others for the common good. Clients have typically been unsuccessful when attempting other avenues to address their issues or they would not be seeking professional help. Consequently, they often approach professional services with a carryover of skepticism and despair. Given the serious and intractable nature of many of the situations encountered in practice, the social worker, too, is vulnerable to feelings of discouragement. The worker's hopefulness makes it possible for him or her to approach each practice situation with a genuine sense that this helping effort can make a difference.

Energy may be defined as the capacity to move things along, get results, and bounce back from mistakes and failures. The social worker's energy is needed to activate the client or client group and counteract the client's hesitation. The worker should be careful, however, to avoid communicating a false sense of optimism. To simply reflect one's willingness to commit time and effort to the change process can encourage clients to also invest themselves in that activity.

Judgment

The responsibilities that are inherent in any professional activity, the complex nature of the helping process, and the uniqueness of every client's situation requires social workers to make difficult and important *judgments*. That which we term human judgment is the ability to discern relationships, make distinctions, choose between alternatives, and arrive at a decision on how to proceed. Judgment is at the very core of such professional activities as assessing client situations, formulating intervention plans, choosing techniques or procedures to utilize, and deciding when to terminate services. A particularly critical judgment is that of deciding when the services needed by the client are beyond the capacities of the social worker.

Needless to say, some of us are better than others when it comes to forming judgments and making decisions. Some of us make poor judgments because it is easier to *feel* than to *think*; given that, we may be inclined to make decisions on the basis of emotion rather than careful and logical thinking. Ultimately, professional judgment depends on clear and critical thinking by the social worker.

The qualifier *mature* is often used to describe the type of judgments expected of a social worker. Sometimes, we assume that chronologically mature people are better at making sound judgments. Certainly, life experience presents opportunities to gain insight, and if one learns from those experiences, then age and wisdom are surely associated. Similarly, providing human services over many years affords opportunities to test and refine one's ability to make wise practice decisions. However, the repetition of an experience by itself does not assure that the social worker will gain insight. To grow in practice wisdom, the social worker must be analytical, reflective, and open to learning from successes as well as failures.

Personal Values

The reasons one might enter social work are varied, but the motive is almost always a concern for others and a desire to make the world a better place. However, it is important to remember that when a person becomes an instrument for change, there is in that person's mind some notion about what constitutes a desirable and good life for people. In other words, social workers, like all people, possess personal values. A ***value*** is a consistent preference that affects one's decisions and actions and is based on that person's deepest beliefs and commitments. Values are our fundamental beliefs about how things should be and what is right and worthwhile.

The dilemma arises when there is a difference of opinion over what is "right." The social worker's view of the "right" outcome or the best course of action may be different from the client's, and both may differ from those who fund and sanction the agency that employs the social worker. Is it "right," for example, to encourage a single mother to find employment if having a job necessitates placing her children in day care? Is it "right" to refer a woman to an abortion clinic? Is it "right" to withhold further financial assistance from a client who has violated an agency rule by not reporting income from a part-time job? Is it "right" to force homeless people to reside in shelters against their will? Whose "right" is right? Whose values are to be followed?

Given that one person's values and conscience cannot serve as absolute guides for all others to follow, is it appropriate to expect the client to conform to what the social worker or his or her agency considers desirable or the right thing to do? Logic would answer no, but many clients feel pressured to go along with what they think the agency or social worker expects. If a social worker accepts the principle of maximizing clients' self-determination, he or she must allow clients to make the decisions and to move toward outcomes they believe are most desirable. And apart from those values codified in law and universally recognized moral principles, the social worker should hold his or her personal beliefs and values in abeyance in favor of client self-determination.

This is not to suggest that the social worker is always to remain neutral with regard to client behaviors or decisions that are socially irresponsible, self-destructive, or harmful to others. A social worker is of little help to a client if he or she sidesteps or avoids discussing moral and ethical issues directly related to a client's concerns. Laws, basic moral principles, and even the rules of civility do matter. They are an essential part of our social fabric, and they are an important aspect of the client's social functioning. However, when such issues are discussed, it must be done in ways that are nonjudgmental and respectful of the client.

Prerequisite to developing a ***nonjudgmental attitude*** is a knowledge of one's own belief system. As new value conflicts arise, it is important for the social worker to consider what he or she believes about the situation and why. It is useful to discuss values and various moral dilemmas with family, friends, and colleagues to obtain alternate views that might contribute to refinements in one's thinking.

The social worker's personal values should be compatible with the values of the social work profession. If these two value systems are in conflict, one of two things is likely to happen: (1) the worker will go through the motions of being a professional social worker but because his or her heart is not in it, the lack of genuineness will be apparent to both clients and colleagues; or (2) the worker will reject the profession's values and principles as a guiding force and respond to clients entirely on the basis of personal beliefs and values. In both instances, the client and the employing agency will lose the benefit of the social work perspective.

What values characterize professional social work? The *NASW Code of Ethics* (NASW 1999) is predicated on six core values that drive this profession:

1. *Service.* The primary purpose of social work is to help clients deal with issues of social functioning. The obligation to serve clients takes precedence over the workers' self-interests.
2. *Social justice.* As social workers engage in efforts to change unjust societal conditions, they are particularly sensitive to the most vulnerable members of the population (i.e., those individuals and groups who have experienced poverty, discrimination, and other forms of injustice). In doing this, social workers are committed to promoting public understanding of the effects of such oppression and encouraging an appreciation of the richness to be gained from human diversity.
3. *Dignity and worth of the person (and the society).* Social workers are committed to considering each client a person of value, and therefore treating the client with respect—even when his or her behavior may have been harmful to self or others. At the same time, social workers are committed to improving societal conditions and resolving conflicts between clients and the broader society.
4. *Importance of human relationships.* Social workers understand that relationships are central to human development as well as to a successful helping process, whether serving individuals, families, groups, organizations, or communities. Further, clients are hesitant to risk change unless they are true partners in the helping process, feel supported by a meaningful relationship with the social worker, and maintain as much control as possible over the decisions about how to achieve change.
5. *Integrity.* A helping relationship cannot be sustained unless clients can trust social workers to be honest and to respect the clients' rights to privacy. Moreover, workers are obligated to assure that any human services agency with which they are affiliated treats clients and client information in an appropriate and professional manner.
6. *Competence.* Social workers are committed to bringing the best knowledge and skill possible to the helping process. They are obligated to practice within their areas of expertise (i.e., the social work domain), to search for the best knowledge and skills related to the practice situation (i.e., evidence-based practice), and to contribute to the profession's knowledge base.

None of these values is unique to social work, but the effect of the combined set of values differentiates social work from other professions.

Professional Style

In the final analysis, it is the social worker himself or herself who is the instrument of change and, as such, each social worker has an unique style of practice. According to

Siporin (1993, 257), "The social worker's personality, craftsmanship, and artistry in the application of knowledge and skill are articulated through professional and personal styles." One's style can open up and facilitate the helping process or close it down.

Style is expressed in how social workers relate to clients—their energy, creativity, wisdom, and judgment, as well as their passion and commitment to particular social issues. In addition, their uniqueness is expressed in their clothing, hairstyle, posture, speech, and in a hundred other choices and behaviors that send out messages about who they are and what they believe about themselves and others.

One's professional style must be appropriate to the situation, the clients served, and the agency setting. For example, a social worker dressed in a three-piece suit will surely have difficulty establishing rapport with a group of street people yet may be highly effective in persuading a city council to create needed services for people living on the street. Similarly, a worker might dress casually when working with children and families but should dress more formally when making a court appearance in their behalf.

"Know thyself" is an important admonition for the social worker, but putting that advice to practice is never easy. It is helpful for the social worker to step back periodically and examine how others perceive his or her style. Clues from clients, family, friends, colleagues, and supervisors are helpful in making these assessments.

A social worker's practice style emerges as he or she balances individuality with the behaviors required for practice. Inherent in professional socialization is pressure to conform. The need to balance expectations of profession, agency, and clients with one's individuality is an issue for every social worker. The social worker must ask: How far am I willing to compromise my individuality and personal preferences in order to serve my clients and meet agency expectations? So long as clients are properly served and not alienated or harmed, one has considerable latitude. In fact, the profession is enriched by the varied styles of its members.

■ THE SOCIAL WORKER AS SCIENTIST

Social workers must use both heart and head when interacting with clients and providing services. With artistic abilities as a foundation, the social worker builds professional capacity by drawing from the available knowledge about his or her clients and the most effective methods of helping. One form of knowledge, *practice wisdom*, is derived from the worker's personal observations and the collective experiences for several generations of social workers who informally share their understanding with colleagues. It is expected that professionals will also use tested knowledge (i.e., science). *Science* is defined as "the objective identification, description, experimental investigation of theoretical explanations and phenomena" (*American Heritage Dictionary of the English Language* 2000, s.v. "science"). Like other professions, social work strives to increase the amount of scientific knowledge available to its practitioners.

The *scientific method* is the most accepted approach in Western societies for studying phenomena and building knowledge. In its most rigorous applications, the scientific method involves carefully defining and isolating the problem under study, precisely defining all concepts and terminology used, formulating hypotheses to be tested, following appropriate sampling procedures and an established protocol for gathering data, using control and experimental groups for comparison, using valid and reliable tools of measurement, and, finally, submitting the research findings to scrutiny by professional peers so they can replicate the study and either confirm or repudiate the findings. Although the use of the scientific method is not the only source of knowledge, it is one that helps to minimize errors of judgment caused by bias and subjectivity.

The application of the scientific method is difficult within social work because many of the problems that concern social workers cannot be easily quantified, client confidentiality prohibits some studies, and identical client situations seldom exist for rigorous comparison and testing. Also, for ethical reasons, social workers and agencies cannot assign vulnerable, at-risk clients (e.g., an abused child) to a no-treatment or control group. Single-subject designs may be used or the relative effectiveness of two or more interventions may be studied, but seldom can the effectiveness of an intervention be directly compared to doing nothing at all.

For ethical reasons, social work may never be a completely scientific discipline, nor should it. Practice wisdom, values, and beliefs will inevitably shape the social worker's practice. Nevertheless, the worker must strive to be scientific in his or her thinking. Social work is not a science to the same degree as, for example, physics, botany, or chemistry. However, social work can be said to be scientific in the following ways:

- It gathers, organizes, and analyzes data that describe the social functioning of people.
- It uses its observations, experiences, and formal studies to create new techniques, formulate new practice guidelines, and develop new programs and policies.
- It uses data as the basis for formulating propositions and conceptual frameworks that guide social work interventions.
- It objectively examines its interventions and their impact on the social functioning of people.
- It exchanges and critically evaluates the ideas, studies, and practices described by others in the profession.

To the extent that social work is scientific, it should be viewed as an applied science, rather than a pure science. And like many other professionals, the social worker is more a technologist than a scientist. For example, as a technologist, the physician draws upon and applies the findings derived from the biological sciences; likewise, the mechanical engineer applies knowledge derived from the science of physics. The social worker, too, is a technologist who draws upon and applies the knowledge derived from the social and behavioral sciences. Whereas the primary goal of the scientist is to understand, the primary goal of the technologist is to bring about certain types of change.

To assist clients with problems of social functioning, social workers need knowledge of the social phenomena (e.g., individual, family, group, organization, or community) with which they will be working. Because social workers are also concerned with the social environment of people, they must be knowledgeable about the social conditions in communities, agencies, and the human services delivery system. Finally, because they are representing one of several helping professions, social workers need to have knowledge of the social work profession and possess the requisite knowledge to be effective in social work practice.

Knowledge of Social Phenomena

Given their focus on the social functioning of people as an outcome of person-in-environment interaction, social workers are especially concerned with interactions between and among people and interactions between people and the systems that deliver social programs. Thus, they must understand social phenomena and the various levels of person-in-environment interaction. As described in Chapter 1, social work requires an exceptionally broad knowledge base.

In addition to understanding the interrelatedness of the various system levels and the kind of situations being addressed in the social worker's practice, the worker must understand the individual person, for which a knowledge of physical and psychological development (including both normal and abnormal functioning) is essential. The social worker must also understand families and other households. The family has long been a dominant point of intervention for social workers, and knowledge of family dynamics is critically important. With the increase of nontraditional family structures, understanding alternate living and intimacy patterns has become especially important. Further, a considerable amount of practice takes place with small groups, including support groups, therapeutic groups, and committees. Thus, the social worker needs to understand small-group behaviors and processes.

Most social work practice takes place under the auspices of a formal organization, such as a social agency, school, hospital, or correctional facility. The social worker must understand how clients and other members of the community view these organizations and how people are affected by the behavior of organizations. To work effectively within an agency or program, a social worker must understand organizational development, structure, methods of operation, and communication patterns. Indeed, the social worker is required to possess substantial knowledge regarding the people and organizations with which he or she works.

The social worker must also understand cultural and religious differences and personal and social issues related to ethnic identity, cross-cultural interaction, and the impact of racism and discrimination. Since people are influenced by the neighborhoods and communities in which they live, the social worker must be familiar with, for example, theories of decision making, intergroup conflict, and community change. In addition, he or she needs to understand prevailing community beliefs and attitudes related to ethnicity, race relations, gender roles, aging, sexual orientation, and disabling conditions.

Knowledge of Social Conditions and Social Problems

Social workers must not only understand the problems commonly brought to the attention of social agencies, but also must recognize how human problems cluster together and overlap. In discussing the problems of adolescent crime, school-age childrearing, school dropout, poverty, unemployment, drug abuse, family violence, and so on, Schorr (1989) states the following:

> Each can be studied separately, but in the real world they interact, reinforce one another, and often cluster together in the same individuals. Increasingly, the individuals also cluster [together in families] and the damage that begins in childhood and becomes so visible in adolescence reverberates throughout a neighborhood as part of an intergenerational cycle of social devastation. (p. 15)

The interrelatedness of human problems is an inescapable fact.

As background for dealing with social problems, the social worker should be familiar with factors that contribute to the overall quality of life on this planet. Some of these are clean air and water, a safe and sufficient supply of food and energy, opportunities for employment, worldwide political and economic conditions that support personal freedom and social justice, the wise use of technology to improve human welfare, success in controlling communicable illnesses and promoting wellness, and a world free of racial hatred and war. In short, the well-informed social worker possesses a world view.

Social work practice and related social programs and services are particularly influenced by conditions at the national or regional level. When practicing in the United States, for example, the social worker must understand the beliefs, values, and organization of U.S. society and its governmental, political, and economic systems.

Although some social conditions and problems are national and international in scope, others are a function of regional and state characteristics. For instance, regional drought conditions or low prices for farm products directly affect people in the agricultural states of the Midwest or Rocky Mountains differently than people in urban centers.

Finally, some social conditions affect local communities but not whole states or regional areas. The well-publicized crime rate in Washington, DC, and the high incidence of juvenile gang activity in Los Angeles have dramatically affected those cities, whereas towns a few miles away are relatively free of those problems. Rural areas may also experience locality-relevant social and economic problems caused by, for example, a decline in available timber in Montana and Oregon or the closing of a small town's single industry in Alabama.

When social conditions are perceived as either harmful to people or a threat to the community or the society, social policies may be formulated and social programs created to help those in need or to address the threatening problem. Essentially, a *social policy* is a set of principles, usually expressed in law and governmental regulation, that guides the assignment of specific benefits and opportunities or the regulation of behavior. We have policy clusters related to areas such as health care, mental illness, crime, child welfare, education, disabilities, old age, poverty, unemployment, and so forth. Social workers must be familiar with the policies that most strongly influence the programs through which they work and understand how these policies affect the clients served by those programs.

Social programs consist of three major elements: organizational structure, benefits or services, and providers. Social programs must be delivered through some form of *organization* or *agency*. No matter what service or benefit is provided, there must be an organizational and administrative structure that determines who is eligible, how it will be provided, who will provide it, and what costs are acceptable. Thus, social workers must be knowledgeable about the fiscal, administrative, and organizational aspects of service delivery.

The *benefits and services* provided by a social program can take the form of social provisions, social services, and/or social action. The social worker must understand the programs offered by his or her own agency and be familiar with those provided by the agencies to which clients might be referred.

Finally, social programs require *providers*, people who are in direct contact with the client, or the consumers of the services and benefits. Providers may be volunteers, but most often they are paid professionals. Social work is only one of the professions that deliver services and benefits. Teachers, psychologists, physicians, nurses, occupational therapists, and others provide a wide array of human services. Each has its own focus but there are areas of overlap. Understanding the competencies of each profession, as well as the dynamics of teamwork and interprofessional cooperation, is important to developing the social worker's knowledge base.

Knowledge of the Social Work Profession

The social worker must understand the functions that a profession performs in society and the benefits, as well as the responsibilities, that accrue from this status. When society grants professions the authority to provide the specific services that fall within their domain, in essence, a monopoly is given to that profession to determine the qualifications of its members (e.g., educational and experiential prerequisites for membership). In return, the profession is charged with monitoring and policing its members to protect the public against abuses of that monopoly.

Social workers have been ambivalent about professionalizing their discipline. They have devoted considerable effort to identifying their knowledge base, creating professional organizations, staking out their domain, specifying criteria for identifying qualified social workers, and taking other steps to become a valued profession. At the same time, they have been uncomfortable about the inherent elitism that characterizes any profession and have struggled with the conflict between assuring quality services to clients and keeping access to the profession open to as many people as possible.

The balance between maintaining openness and having clear standards for recognition as a professional social worker changes through time. At this time in history, the entry point is through completion of a baccalaureate or master's degree from a social work education program that is accredited by the Council on Social

Work Education. To move to more advanced or more specialized levels of recognition, one must gain experience, and through demonstration of appropriate levels of knowledge and competence, he or she can receive professional certification through the National Association of Social Workers. Additionally, all states now have some form of licensing or certification for at least some social work practice activities.

Closely linked with professional recognition is the social worker's compliance with the profession's ***ethical principles***. Workers must be both competent and ethical in their practice if the profession is to maintain the public trust. Thus, it is essential that the social worker possess a thorough understanding of the ethical principles that guide practice. Ethics are concerned with what is morally right or, in a profession, what is the correct course of professional action. Perhaps no single document is more important to the practice of a social worker than the *NASW Code of Ethics* (1999). When a social worker joins the NASW, he or she pledges to practice within the profession's ethical code. The NASW uses the *Code* as a standard for determining if charges of unethical practice have a basis. If accusations are made that an individual worker has violated the *Code*, the local NASW chapter and NASW's National Committee on Inquiry may review the complaint and possibly apply negative sanctions to that social worker.

Knowledge of Social Work Practice

In a profession such as social work, it is not possible to separate theory from practice or concept from action. In fact, practice is the process of using knowledge and applying theory in order to bring about specific change. A practice uninformed by theory tends to become repetitive and sterile, whereas theory uninformed by the realities of practice tends to be merely interesting and often irrelevant.

The many theories, models, and perspectives discussed in the social work literature can all be considered conceptual frameworks. A ***conceptual framework*** is composed of a coherent set of concepts, beliefs, values, propositions, assumptions, hypotheses, and principles. Such a framework can be thought of as an outline of ideas that help one to understand people, how people function, and how people change. These frameworks are important because they have utility. Consider the following:

- They provide a structure for analyzing complex and often highly emotional human problems and situations.
- They organize information, beliefs, and assumptions into a meaningful whole.
- They provide a rationale for action and decision making.
- They promote a systematic, orderly, and predictable approach to work with people.
- They facilitate communication among professionals.

Social workers use a variety of theories, models, and perspectives. Although these terms have somewhat different meanings, they are often lumped together and simply termed *theory*. However, it is helpful to make some distinctions when

FIGURE 3.1 | Types of Conceptual Frameworks

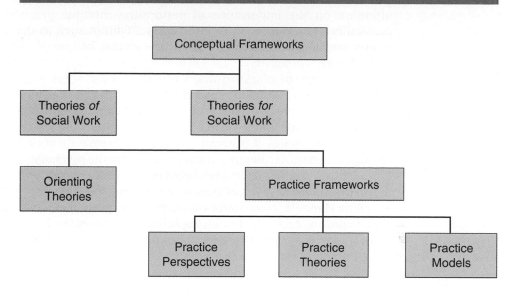

describing these conceptual frameworks (see Figure 3.1). Howe (1987, 166) explains that there are theories *of* social work and theories *for* social work. The ***theories of social work*** focus on the profession and explain its purpose, domain, and character within a society. They describe what the profession is all about and why it functions as it does. By contrast, the ***theories for social work*** focus on clients and helping activities. They explain human behavior, the social environment, how change occurs, and how change can be facilitated by the social worker in order to benefit clients.

In their work, social workers make use of orienting theories and practice frameworks. Mailick (1990) indicates that ***orienting theories*** describe and explain behavior and how and why certain problems develop. They provide important background knowledge and are usually borrowed from other disciplines such as biology, psychology, sociology, economics, cultural anthropology, and the like. Examples include the various theories related to human development, personality, family systems, socialization, organizational functioning, and political power, as well as theories related to specific types of problems such as poverty, family violence, mental illness, teen pregnancy, crime, and racial discrimination. Orienting theories, by themselves, provide little guidance on how to bring about change. For such guidance one must look to ***practice frameworks***. There are three types: practice perspectives, practice theories, and practice models.

A ***practice perspective*** is a particular way of viewing and thinking about practice. It is a conceptual lens through which one views social functioning and it offers very broad guidance on what may be important considerations in a practice situation. Like a camera lens, a perspective serves to focus on or magnify a particular feature. Two perspectives, the general systems perspective and the ecosystems perspective, are commonly used in assessing relationships between people and their environment. The generalist perspective focuses a worker's attention on the importance of performing multiple practice roles and the possibility of various levels of intervention. Others, such as the feminist and the ethnic-sensitive perspectives, remind the worker of special challenges faced by certain groups in society.

A second type of framework, a ***practice theory***, offers both an explanation of certain behaviors or situations and guidance on how they can be changed. A practice theory serves as a road map for bringing about a certain type of change. Most practice theories are rooted in one or more orienting theories. An example is psychosocial therapy, which is based primarily on psychodynamic theory and ego psychology. Another is behavioral therapy, which derived from the psychology of learning.

A distinction is made here between a *practice theory* and a *practice model*. A ***practice model*** is a set of concepts and principles used to guide intervention activities. However, in contrast to a practice theory, a model is not tied to a particular explanation of behavior. For example, crisis intervention is viewed as a practice model rather than a practice theory because it does not rest on a single explanation of crisis situations. For the same reason, task-centered practice is termed a model. Most often, a model develops out of experience and experimentation rather than as a derivation from a theory of human behavior.

The term *model* is also used when referring to a conceptual framework that is borrowed from one field and applied in another. For example, when someone refers to an approach to change based on the medical model, he or she is describing practice activity that mirrors that used in medicine—one that places emphasis on the practitioner as an expert and an authority figure, the careful gathering and categorization of data (study), the application of a classification system to properly label the problem (diagnosis), and an intervention (treatment) dictated by the diagnosis. Similarly, social workers may refer to the legal model as a way of describing an approach to social action and client advocacy—one that involves competition and conflict among adversaries. Other innovations in practice are spread from agency to agency by borrowing the essence of a successful program. Thus, we hear such terms as the *self-help model,* the *grass-roots model,* the *12-step model,* the *case-management model,* and so on.

It is rare for a social worker to use a single orienting theory or a single practice framework. Rather, most social workers utilize a variety of orienting theories and a set of compatible and complementary perspectives, theories, and models. Such a combination can be termed one's *theoretical frame of reference* or *theoretical orientation* to practice.

This book presumes that social workers use many of the same techniques and guidelines, regardless of practice perspective, theory, or model. A ***technique*** is a set of actions directed at accomplishing a particular outcome. Although a worker's frame of reference might lead him or her to select particular techniques, they are, for the most part, independent of specific theories. ***Guidelines***, on the other hand, are typically a mix of prescriptions (do this) and proscriptions (avoid this). (More precise definitions of these two terms appear in the Preface.)

CONCLUSION

In order to perform effectively, the social worker uses a combination of art and science. It is recognized that a worker brings certain intangibles to the practice situation that affect both the process and the outcome—the art encompassed in building relationships, creative thinking, compassion and courage, hopefulness and energy, using sound judgment, and committing to appropriate values. At the same time, the social worker must combine his or her artistic abilities with the profession's knowledge and scientific base. Without art, the knowledge base is of little value. But without the knowledge, the art is of limited effectiveness.

The social worker merges his or her art and the profession's science into a practice framework. Chapter 6 provides descriptions of over two dozen selected practice perspectives, theories, and models that commonly are included in practice frameworks. The intent is not to provide a comprehensive description of any of these frameworks nor is it to provide a complete listing of all those available to the social worker. Rather, the chapter is intended to supply enough information to suggest how practice frameworks differ and what might be required for constructing one's own theoretical orientation to practice.

SELECTED BIBLIOGRAPHY

American Heritage Dictionary of the English Language, 4th ed. Boston: Houghton Mifflin, 2000.

Howe, David. *An Introduction to Social Work Theory.* Hants, England: Wildwood House, 1987.

Hubble, Mark A., Barry L. Duncan, and Scott D. Miller. *The Heart and Soul of Change: What Works in Therapy.* Washington, DC: American Psychological Association, 1999.

Lambert, Michael J. "Implications of Outcome Research for Psychotherapy Integration." In *Handbook of Psychotherapy Integration,* edited by John C. Norcross and Marvin R. Goldstein. New York: Basic Books, 1992.

Mailick, Mildred. "Social Work Practice with Adolescents: Theoretical Saturation." In *Serious Play: Creativity and Innovation in Social Work,* edited by Harold Weissman. Silver Spring, MD: NASW, 1990.

National Association of Social Workers. *NASW Code of Ethics.* Washington, DC: NASW, 1999.

Schorr, Lisbeth. *Within Our Reach: Breaking the Cycle of Disadvantage.* New York: Doubleday, 1989.

Siporin, Max. "The Social Worker's Style." *Clinical Social Work Journal* 21 (Fall 1993): 257–270.

PART 2

The Building Blocks of Social Work Practice

Once the social worker is personally prepared to engage in practice, several other factors will shape the nature of that practice: (1) the roles and functions performed in an agency and with a specific client, (2) the basic principles that should guide each social worker's approach to practice activities, (3) the conceptual frameworks that direct the manner in which clients are served, and (4) the social worker's competence in selecting the best available evidence about the client and the situation, and then leading clients through the change process to make decisions that will result in desired outcomes. An understanding of these four building blocks is prerequisite to the selection and application of the techniques and guidelines described in the remainder of this book.

In Chapter 4, "The Roles and Functions Performed by Social Workers," attention is directed to 10 primary roles typically performed by social workers. One can readily discern that social work differs from other helping professions simply by examining these roles. Although other disciplines perform some of these roles and the associated functions, the collection of roles (e.g., broker, advocate, case manager, social change agent) reflects social work's breadth and its emphasis on helping people interact more effectively with their environments.

Chapter 5, "Guiding Principles for Social Workers," describes 24 fundamental principles that should guide the social worker's practice. These principles provide the "bottom line" for consistently offering appropriate and effective service to clients. To many social workers, the phrases used to communicate these principles have becomes clichés: "Begin where the client is," "Help the client help himself (or herself)," "Guide the process, not the client." The casual use of these phrases too often masks the wisdom of these principles.

A social worker selects and uses specific techniques that have been individualized to the needs and situation of the client or client group being served and to the resources that are applied to help resolve the client's problem or concern. In helping the client formulate a plan, the worker draws on various conceptual frameworks that provide an overall strategy for the change process. Chapter 6, "Practice Frameworks for Social Work," identifies criteria one should consider in selecting practice frameworks. It also highlights the central features of 24 perspectives, theories, and models that are commonly used in social work practice. Although no one social worker is expected to master all of these conceptual frameworks, each should be familiar with these possible approaches to practice in order to help clients connect with social workers who are competent to use the most appropriate framework for a given practice situation.

Two key elements in successful practice are the social worker's ability to (1) guide clients through the phases of the change process and (2) assist clients in making decisions that will result in enhancement of their social functioning or the improvement of a social condition. In Chapter 7, "Using Evidence to Guide the Change Process," the five phases of the change process are introduced (to be expanded in the introductions to Chapters 10 through 14), and the importance of critical thinking and good decision making during the change process are reviewed.

By examining these building blocks for social work practice, the foundation is established for the rest of the book. It is within this context that the social worker should select and apply the techniques and guidelines described in Chapters 8 through 16.

4 The Roles and Functions Performed by Social Workers

Every occupation (e.g., engineer, teacher, farmer, etc.) is expected to perform a set of **occupational roles**. For example, when functioning as a physician, an individual is expected to conduct tests to diagnose a patient's condition, prescribe treatment, and monitor the results. Similarly, when functioning as a social worker, an individual is expected to think and behave in a manner consistent with the expectations of a social worker. Although there is individuality in how a person performs an occupational role, there are also boundaries that govern what should and should not be done.

Associated with the roles are a number of **job functions** that can best be described as the tasks or activities one performs within a specific role. This chapter describes 10 roles and nearly 40 distinct functions expected of social workers. In the course of a day, most social workers engage in several practice roles. Someone in specialized practice will assume a more limited number of these roles and functions, whereas the generalist worker will engage in a broader array of activities in conducting his or her practice.

■ DEFINING PROFESSIONAL ROLES

The roles and job functions expected of the members of a given profession are defined by social norms and historical traditions, by the legal codes and administrative regulations that sanction the activity, and by agency policy and procedure. In any practice role, the performance of several distinct functions may be required. Similarly, a specific job function may be applied in the performance of more than one role. For example, a social worker might engage in an assessment of a client's situation in the role of a broker of human services, a counselor or clinician, and a case manager. In the following pages, however, each function is described only once.

1. The Social Worker as Broker

Purpose.   To link clients to appropriate human services and other resources.

Description.   Social work's particular emphasis among the helping professions is to assist people in relating to their social environment. That places the social worker in the position of being the professional person most likely to facilitate linkage

53

between client and community resources (i.e., to bring together a person needing a service and a provider of that service). To carry out the **broker role**, the social worker identifies clients' needs, assesses their motivation and capacity to use various resources, and helps them gain access to the most appropriate resources.

As a broker of human services, the social worker must be knowledgeable about the various services and programs available, maintain an up-to-date assessment of each one's strengths and limitations, and understand the procedures for accessing those resources. These resources may include social provisions (e.g., money, food, clothing, and housing) and/or social services (e.g., counseling, therapy, group interaction experiences, and rehabilitative services).

Functions

Client Situation Assessment.   The first step in brokering is to thoroughly understand and accurately assess the needs and abilities of the client or clients. An effective broker should be skilled at assessing such factors as the client's vulnerability, culture, verbal ability, emotional stability, intelligence, and commitment to change.

Resource Assessment.   The social worker must assess the various resources available to meet client needs. For his or her own agency, as well as for other community agencies, the social worker must be familiar with what is offered, the quality of staff, the general eligibility requirements, and the costs of those services. Additionally, the social worker must know the best way to help clients gain access to those resources.

Referral.   The process of connecting the client to a resource requires that the social worker make a judgment regarding the motivation and ability of the client to follow through and the likelihood that the resource will accept the client for service. Depending on these judgments, the social worker will be more or less active in the referral process. A proper referral also entails a follow-up activity wherein the worker checks to assure the client-resource connection is working to meet the client's needs. If there has been a breakdown, further action may be warranted.

Service System Linkage.   Brokering requires that the social worker facilitate continuing interaction between various segments of the service delivery system. To strengthen the linkage among agencies, programs, and professionals, the social worker may engage in networking to strengthen communication channels, negotiate resource sharing, and/or participate in interagency planning, information exchange, and coordination activities.

Information Giving.   Brokering often requires the transmittal of information to clients, community groups, and legislators or other community decision makers. As a repository of knowledge about the service delivery system, the social worker helps others by sharing this knowledge. Also, the social worker may make the general public aware of gaps between client needs and available services.

2. The Social Worker as Advocate

Purpose.   To assist clients in upholding their rights to receive resources and services or to actively support causes intended to change programs and policies that have a negative effect on individual clients or client groups.

Description.   Advocacy is fundamental to social work's mission and is clearly embodied in the *Code of Ethics* (NASW 1999). For example, Section 3.07 of the *Code* calls for social workers to *advocate* "within and outside their agencies for adequate resources to meet clients' needs" and to assure that the resource allocation procedures are open and fair for all clients. At the macro level, Section 6.04 indicates that social workers are expected to "*advocate* for changes in policy and legislation to improve social conditions in order to meet human needs and promote social justice."

Mickelson (1995) defines social work **advocacy** as "the act of directly representing, defending, intervening, supporting, or recommending a course of action on behalf of one or more individuals, groups, or communities with the goal of securing or retaining social justice" (p. 95). Social workers must balance their methods of advocacy with the principles of maximizing client self-determination and client participation in the change process. To the extent possible, advocacy should take the form of assisting clients to be their own advocates.

Advocacy within one's own agency or with the community service system is a necessary function performed by social workers. What is right, however, is not always popular. The social worker should be prepared for negative and even hostile responses to advocacy activities.

Functions

Client or Case Advocacy.   A common goal in this type of advocacy is to assure that the services or resources to which an individual client is entitled are, in fact, received. Such advocacy efforts may be directed toward one's own agency or to others in the human services network. Critical steps include gathering information and determining if the client is entitled to the desired service. If so, negotiation, mediation, and, if necessary, more strident and confrontational tactics are used to secure the service. The client is helped to make use of available appeal procedures and, in some instances, to take action against the agency or service provider.

Class Advocacy.   The social worker must often serve as an advocate for groups of clients or a segment of the population that have a common problem or concern. Typically, class advocacy entails action intended to remove obstacles or barriers that restrict a class or category of people from realizing their civil rights or receiving entitlements or benefits due them. It usually requires efforts aimed at changing agency regulations, social policies, or laws. Consequently, class advocacy requires activity within the political and legislative arena and building coalitions with organizations that are concerned about the same issue.

3. The Social Worker as Teacher

Purpose.   To prepare clients or the general public with knowledge and skills necessary to prevent problems or enhance social functioning.

Description.   Much of social work practice involves teaching clients or client groups to deal with troublesome life situations or to anticipate and prevent crises. Some of the knowledge the social worker has gained through education and experience is shared with the client. This is empowering to clients. In the *Social Work Dictionary*, Barker (2003, s.v. "educator role") defines this ***teaching role*** as "the responsibility to teach clients necessary adaptive skills . . . by providing relevant information in a way that is understandable to the client, offering advice and suggestions, identifying alternatives and their probable consequences, modeling behaviors, teaching problem-solving techniques, and clarifying perceptions."

A fundamental purpose of social work practice is to help clients change dysfunctional behavior and learn effective patterns of social interaction. This may require teaching clients to adhere to the various rules or laws and norms of society, modify their immediate environment, develop social skills, learn role functioning, and gain insights into their own behavior. The teaching may occur informally during one-on-one interviews or in more structured educational activities such as presentations and workshops.

The teaching role also has a macro-level application. Social workers should be prepared to engage in activities that educate the public about the availability and quality of needed human services and the adequacy of social policies and programs for meeting client needs.

Functions

Teach Social and Daily Living Skills.   Teaching skills in conflict resolution, money management, use of public transportation, adjusting to new living arrangements, personal care and hygiene, and effective communication are examples of activities regularly engaged in by some social workers.

Facilitate Behavior Change.   The social worker may use intervention approaches such as role modeling, values clarification, and behavior modification in teaching clients more effective interpersonal behaviors. When dealing with larger social systems, the social worker may, for example, educate a board of directors about an emerging social issue or teach a client advocacy group how to redesign a change strategy that is failing.

Primary Prevention.   Throughout its history, the social work profession has been mostly concerned with addressing and modifying serious human problems and conditions. In recent years, social workers have given greater attention to primary prevention (i.e., preventing the development of problems). Many such prevention efforts place the social worker in the role of a teacher or even a public educator.

Examples include such activities as providing premarital counseling, teaching parenting skills, offering information on family planning, and informing the public of ways to address a social problem or issue (see Item 12.14).

4. The Social Worker as Counselor/Clinician

Purpose.   To help clients improve their social functioning by helping them better understand their feelings, modify their behaviors, and learn to cope with problematic situations.

Description.   Perhaps the most visible and frequently performed role in social work is that of **counselor** or **clinician**. This role, according to the *Social Work Dictionary* (Barker 2003, s.v. "clinical social work"), involves the "professional application of social work theory and methods to the treatment and prevention of psychosocial dysfunction, disability, or impairment, including emotional and mental disorders."

In order to perform this role, the social worker needs a knowledge of human behavior and an understanding of how the social environment impacts on people, an ability to assess client needs and functioning and to make judgments about what interventions can help clients deal with these stresses, skill in applying intervention techniques, and the ability to guide clients through the change process.

Functions
Psychosocial Assessment and Diagnosis.   The client's situation must be thoroughly understood and his or her motivation, capacities, and opportunities for change assessed. This involves selecting conceptual frameworks to organize the information in ways that promote an understanding of both the client and the social environment. The labeling and categorizing inherent in diagnosis is necessary in some settings for purposes of interprofessional communication, research, program planning, and obtaining payment for services provided. The *Diagnostic and Statistical Manual of Mental Disorders*, or *DSM* (APA 2000; see Item 11.18), is a commonly used tool for clinical diagnosis.

Ongoing Stabilizing Care.   The counselor/clinician role does not always involve efforts to change the client or social situation. Sometimes it consists of providing support or care on an extended basis. For example, counseling people who are severely disabled or terminally ill—or working with their families—may involve efforts to increase their choices and help them to more comfortably deal with difficult but unchangeable situations or conditions.

Social Treatment.   This function involves such activities as helping clients understand the relationships among relevant persons and social groups, supporting client efforts to modify social relationships, engaging clients in the problem-solving or interpersonal change efforts, and mediating differences or conflicts between individuals and/or between individuals and social institutions. Whittaker and Tracy (1989, 9) define *social treatment* as "interpersonal helping that utilizes direct and indirect strategies to aid individuals, families and small groups in improving social functioning and coping with social problems." Direct strategies might include face-to-face meetings with the client, whereas indirect strategies often involve helping the client negotiate the human services system by using such tools as advocacy, referral, and the provision of concrete services.

Practice Evaluation.   At the direct-service level, practice evaluation takes two forms. First, the social worker examines his or her own performance to assess the effectiveness of the interventions utilized. In this way, the social worker can be accountable to clients, the employing agency, the general public, and the profession. Second, the social worker collects client data to detect emerging social problems that might need to be addressed by new or revised services and public policies (see Chapter 14, Section A).

5. The Social Worker as Case Manager

Purpose.   To achieve continuity of service to individuals and families through the process of connecting clients to appropriate services and coordinating the utilization of those services.

Description.   The social worker's role as case manager is of critical importance for clients who must utilize services provided by several agencies. This role has become increasingly prominent in social work as more and more highly vulnerable people are residing in their own homes and communities, rather than in institutional settings. Among these groups are the frail elderly, dependent children from dysfunctional families, persons with physical disabilities, and persons experiencing chronic mental illness.

As a *case manager*, the job of the social worker involves a wide range of activities. The work typically begins with identifying the type of help needed and moves on to exploring ways to overcome barriers to successful living, advocating for clients as they attempt to connect with potential helpers, and, on occasion, providing some of the services directly to the client. Finally, the worker monitors the success of the services plan and helps solve problems that may emerge.

Effective case management requires a social worker to be goal oriented, proactive, and assertive. A case manager must be able to get things done.

Functions.   Case managers have several core functions.
Client Identification and Orientation.   This involves directly identifying and selecting those individuals for whom service outcomes, quality of life, or the cost of care and service could be positively affected by case management.

Client Assessment.   This function refers to gathering information and formulating an assessment of the client's needs, life situation, and resources. It may also involve reaching out to potential clients who have not requested services.

Service/Treatment Planning.   In concert with the clients and other relevant actors, the social worker identifies the various services that can be accessed to meet client needs. Bertsche and Horejsi (1980, 96) describe these tasks as the work necessary to "assemble and guide group discussions and decision-making sessions among relevant professionals and program representatives, the client and his or her family, and significant others to formulate goals and design an integrated intervention plan."

Linkage and Service Coordination.   As in the broker role, the case manager must connect clients with the appropriate resources. The case manager role differs, however, in that the social worker remains an active participant in the delivery of services to the individual or family. The case manager places emphasis on coordinating the clients' use of resources by becoming a channel and a focal point for interagency communication.

Follow-Up and Monitoring Service Delivery.   The case manager makes regular and frequent follow-up contacts with both the client and the service provider to ensure that the needed services are actually received and properly utilized by the client. If not, action is taken to correct the situation or modify the service plan. Typically, it is the case manager that completes the necessary paperwork to document client progress, service delivery, and adherence to the plan.

Client Support.   During the time the services are being provided by the various resources, the case manager assists the client and his or her family as they confront the inevitable problems in obtaining the desired services. This activity includes resolving personality conflicts, counseling, providing information, giving emotional support, and, when appropriate, advocating on behalf of clients to assure that they receive the services to which they are entitled.

6. The Social Worker as Workload Manager

Purpose.   To manage one's workload to most efficiently provide client services and be responsible to the employing organization.

Description.   Social workers must simultaneously provide the services needed by clients and adhere to the ***workload management*** requirements of the employing social agency. In other words, they must balance their obligations to both clients and agency. Although the emphasis on accountability to funding sources has increased in recent years, social workers have always needed to maximize the services provided within an environment of scarcity.

Functions

Work Planning.   Social workers must be able to assess their workloads, set priorities according to importance and urgency, and make plans that will accomplish work in the most efficient and effective way possible. They must be effective in managing heavy workloads.

Time Management.   If the social worker is to give each client proper attention, priorities for the use of one's time must be set and the working hours carefully allocated. Time management requires that the worker learn to use the agency's computer systems and other technological resources (see Item 9.6).

Quality Assurance Monitoring.   The social worker should regularly evaluate the effectiveness of his or her own service provision and also be involved in the assessment of services provided by colleagues. These activities might include reviewing agency records, conducting job performance evaluations, and holding performance review conferences with colleagues or volunteers.

Information Processing.   Social workers must collect data to document need and justify service provision, complete reports, maintain case records, and substantiate various expenditures. Further, information about agency regulations and procedures must be understood by all, which requires that workers be skilled at preparing and interpreting memoranda, participating in staff meetings (see Item 13.26), and engaging in other activities that facilitate communication.

7. The Social Worker as Staff Developer

Purpose.   To facilitate the professional development of agency staff through training, supervision, consultation, and personnel management.

Description.   Social workers often serve in middle-management positions. In that capacity, they devote a part of their energies to maintaining and improving staff performance. That might involve working with secretaries, receptionists, volunteers, and others, but most often the *staff developer role* centers on maximizing the effectiveness of professional helpers.

Staff development requires many of the skills used in the teacher role. In this case, however, the knowledge is transmitted to peers rather than clients or the general public. Staff development is predicated on an accurate assessment of the training needs, with the training taking the form of individualized instruction such as job coaching, supervision and consultation, and/or conducting or participating in training sessions and workshops.

Functions

Employee Orientation and Training.   Orientation to the agency and training for specific job assignments are necessary for all new employees and volunteers. Among the tasks required to perform this function are specifying job expectations, orienting workers to the organizational policies and procedures, and teaching helping skills and techniques.

Personnel Management.   Personnel management activities may range from the selection of new employees to the termination of someone's employment. Many of these middle-management activities affect the professional development of other workers. For example, the selection of case assignments not only involves judgments about workers' capacities but also provides opportunities for workers to have new and challenging professional experiences.

Supervision.   This function involves overseeing and directing the activities of other staff members to enhance the quality of services they provide and making sure that agency rules and regulations are followed. It includes such tasks as making and monitoring work assignments, developing performance standards, and negotiating staffing changes to better address the needs of clients (see Item 16.9).

Consultation.   As compared to supervision, which is a part of the agency's administrative hierarchy, consultation is given on a peer level—from one professional to another. The consultee is free to use or not use the advice offered by the consultant. Typically, consultation focuses on how best to handle a particularly challenging practice situation.

8. The Social Worker as Administrator

Purpose.   To plan, develop, and implement policies, services, and programs in a human services organization.

Description.   In an *administrative role*, the social worker assumes responsibility for implementing the agency's policies and managing its programs. When performing this role, the social worker might be a public or private agency's chief administrative officer or executive director. Or he or she might be in a middle-management position, in which the administrative responsibility spans only the social workers in an agency (e.g., the social work unit) or perhaps one program area (e.g., the child welfare division). The tasks one would be expected to perform might include giving leadership to program planning, implementing programs that have been adopted, and evaluating the effectiveness of the programs. At the same time, social worker administrators often continue to carry a small caseload or otherwise engage in the primary work of the agency in order to have firsthand knowledge of the day-to-day issues in operation of the agency.

In the role of administrator, the social worker is responsible for implementing policies, programs, and laws made by others. Agency boards or elected officials typically define agency purposes, establish administrative guidelines, and allocate the funds required to operate the agency. Normally, either the governing board of a volunteer agency or, in a public agency, an elected official or officials appoints the chief administrative officer (or executive director) to administer the organization. Depending on the size and complexity of the organization, the social worker occupying an administrative position in the agency may perform all or some of the following functions.

Functions

Management.   The management function calls for the administrator to maintain operational oversight of a program, service unit, and/or the entire organization. It includes such responsibilities as facilitating the work of the agency board, recruiting and selecting staff, directing and coordinating staff activities, developing and setting priorities, analyzing the organizational structure, promoting professional standards within the organization, adjudicating employee conflicts, and obtaining the necessary resources to operate the organization. In addition, management involves budgeting, documenting the use of resources, and arranging for the acquisition and maintenance of buildings and equipment.

Internal and External Coordination.   A primary task of the administrator is to coordinate the work of the agency. Internally, this involves developing plans for implementing the agency's programs in an efficient and effective manner. Often, this requires negotiating among several units or programs and working with staff to assure that new programs are understood and integrated into the agency's functioning. The administrator also serves as the primary representative of the agency to external constituencies. These external tasks include serving as a buffer to protect staff from external pressures, negotiating disputes with consumers, and interpreting programs to the community in order to maintain viability. Thus, the administrator is engaged in external work not only with the governing board but is also a key figure in the agency's public relations and communication with consumers, other social agencies, and the general public.

Policy and Program Development.   The effective administrator is proactive. Although considerable time and energy must be devoted to maintaining established programs, an administrator should regularly assess the need for new or different services by conducting a needs assessment, being knowledgeable about social trends, generating alternative policy goals for the governing body to consider, and translating new program or policy goals into services.

Program Evaluation.   Finally, the administrator is responsible for quality control. When overseeing the functioning of an agency, the social worker must monitor and evaluate the agency's programs and collect data that will help document the adequacy of the services and/or suggest actions that might be taken to improve them. Program evaluation, then, is concerned with both program development and program compliance (see Items 14.9 and 14.11).

9. The Social Worker as Social Change Agent

Purpose.   To participate in the identification of community problems and/or areas where the quality of life can be enhanced, and to mobilize interest groups to advocate for change or new resources.

Description.   Social work's dual focus on both the person and environment requires that the social worker facilitate needed change in neighborhoods, communities, or larger social systems. The role of *social change agent* has been a part of social work since its beginnings. Its inclusion in the social worker's repertoire of practice roles distinguishes social work from the many other helping professions.

When working directly with clients, social workers are in an excellent position to recognize conditions that are contributing to people's distress and the need for human services. The social worker must take responsibility for assuring that resources are available to meet those needs and/or for stimulating action to create resources or change conditions that contribute to social problems. Social change typically does not occur rapidly or easily, and the authority to make the political decisions to achieve change is rarely held by social workers. Rather, change requires skill in stimulating action by influential groups and decision-making bodies that have the power to address the problems.

Functions

Social Problem or Policy Analysis.   A first requirement for social change is to understand the nature of the problem. Trends must be analyzed, data collected and synthesized, and findings reported in ways that are understandable to decision makers. Without this background work, change efforts have little chance of success. The tasks involved in such analysis include identifying criteria for the analysis, ascertaining the impact of the policy on clients and social problems, and analyzing community values and beliefs that affect the issue (see Item 11.24).

Mobilization of Community Concern.   Translating one's understanding of problems into social change efforts requires mobilizing and energizing concerned individuals, groups, and organizations. This might involve encouraging clients, special-interest groups, human services organizations, and/or other citizen groups to address and speak out on the problem. Mobilization for action might involve assembling interested parties and presenting an analysis of the situation, helping expand their understanding of the issues and identify goals they could achieve, aiding in the selection of change strategies, identifying the decision makers who can effect the desired change, and planning and/or carrying out the activities necessary to induce change.

Social Resource Development.   The social change agent might also work toward the development of needed programs and services. *Resource development* involves creating new resources where they do not exist, extending or improving existing resources, planning and allocating available resources in order to avoid unnecessary duplication of human services, and increasing the effectiveness and efficiency of services offered by a unit, an agency, or a group of agencies. This may involve lobbying and providing expert testimony to legislative committees or more informal communication with decision makers (see Item 13.41).

10. The Social Worker as Professional

Purpose.   To engage in competent and ethical social work practice and contribute to the development of the social work profession.

Description.   Basically, a *professional* is a person whose actions are thoughtful, purposeful, competent, responsible, and ethical. It is incumbent on the social worker to practice in a manner that reflects the highest professional standards. The social worker must constantly seek to develop his or her knowledge and skills, to examine and increase the quality of his or her practice, and to perform in a highly ethical manner.

As one who benefits from professional status, the social worker should actively engage in the enhancement and strengthening of the profession. Active participation in professional associations at the local, state, and national levels is an essential component of the professional role.

Functions

Self-Assessment.   The autonomy required for professional decision making carries with it the responsibility for ongoing self-assessment. In their national task analysis of social work practice, Teare and Sheafor (1995) found social workers serving virtually every type of client, working in virtually every type of human services organization (including private practice), and performing virtually every social work role while also devoting a substantial amount of effort to self-assessment and their own professional development based on that assessment.

Personal/Professional Development.   The corollary to self-assessment is further developing one's abilities and addressing any performance problems that have been identified. Teare and Sheafor (1995) also found that most social workers regularly read articles in professional and scientific journals, newspapers, and magazines related to their job responsibilities; seek critique of their practice from colleagues; and periodically attend workshops, seminars, and other programs intended to improve their job knowledge and skills for practice.

Enhancement of the Social Work Profession.   Social workers should contribute to the growth and development of the profession and the expansion of its knowledge base. Maintaining membership in the National Association of Social Workers and contributing time and energy to the efforts of NASW to strengthen the quality of professional practice and support legislative initiatives are obligations of each social worker. In addition, social workers should contribute knowledge gained from their practice or research to colleagues through presentations at conferences and by contributing to the professional literature (see Items 16.11 and 16.12).

CONCLUSION

The range of practice roles performed by the social worker is large and varied. The effective social worker must master at least the basic job functions associated with most of these roles. The specialist practitioner might develop more in-depth competence in fewer roles, but the generalist social worker, in particular, must continually seek to expand his or her competence in each.

SELECTED BIBLIOGRAPHY

American Psychiatric Association. *Diagnostic and Statistical Manual of Mental Disorders, DSM-IV-TR*, 4th ed., revised. Washington, DC: APA, 2000.

Barker, Robert L. *The Social Work Dictionary*, 5th ed. Washington, DC: NASW Press, 2003.

Bertsche, Anne Vandeberg, and Charles R. Horejsi. "Coordination of Client Services." *Social Work* 25 (March 1980): 94–98.

Mickelson, James. "Advocacy." In *Encyclopedia of Social Work*, Vol. 1, 19th ed., edited by Richard L. Edwards, 95–100. Washington, DC: NASW Press, 1995.

National Association of Social Workers. *NASW Code of Ethics*. Washington, DC: NASW, 1999.

Teare, Robert J., and Bradford W. Sheafor. *Practice-Sensitive Social Work Education: An Empirical Analysis of Social Work Practice and Practitioners*. Alexandria, VA: CSWE, 1995.

Whittaker, James, and Elizabeth Tracy. *Social Treatment*, 2nd ed. New York: Aldine deGruter, 1989.

Guiding Principles for Social Workers

5

Within each profession there exists a number of fundamental principles that guide practice decisions and actions. These principles apply in all practice situations, regardless of client characteristics, practice setting, or roles assumed by the professional. In addition, they are independent of any specific theories, models, and techniques selected in a specific practice situation. *Principles* are basic rules or guides to one's practice behavior, but they are not to be applied without careful analysis.

Social work's practice principles are grounded in the profession's philosophy, values, ethical prescriptions, and practice wisdom. Most are not supported by empirical verification nor are they compiled in a single document. Social work's practice principles are largely unwritten and typically are passed on informally from seasoned workers to those who are entering the profession. They are often expressed as clichés such as "start where the client is" or "accept the client as he or she is." Many of the principles seem so obvious to the experienced worker that they often are not consciously taught in professional education programs or during supervision. However, they are central to effective social work practice and should be fully understood.

This chapter presents a synopsis of 24 fundamental principles that should guide social work practice. The first 6 focus on the social worker. The remainder are concerned with the social worker in interaction with a client or client group—whether it be an individual, family, small group, organization, neighborhood, community, or even larger social structure.

■ PRINCIPLES THAT FOCUS ON THE SOCIAL WORKER

1. The Social Worker Should Practice Social Work

This fundamental principle seems so obvious that it appears trite. We expect the teacher to teach, the physician to practice medicine, and the social worker to practice within the boundaries of the social work profession. Yet it is not uncommon to find professionals extending their activities into the domain of another profession. This principle admonishes the social worker to do what he or she is sanctioned and trained to do.

Social work is sanctioned to focus on social functioning and help improve the interaction between people and their environment—that is the social work domain. The requisite educational preparation equips the social worker with the knowledge, values, and skills to work at the interface of person and environment, and that, more than anything else, is the unique contribution of social work among the helping professions.

Due to areas of overlap, the "turf" problems among the disciplines are difficult enough when each practices within professional boundaries. Such problems are magnified when a member of one discipline strays into another discipline's area of operation. Ethical practice requires that the social worker function within his or her professional expertise. Although individual social workers may have special talents that exceed the profession's domain, the social worker who drifts from the profession's area of focus deprives clients of a critically important perspective on human problems and associated change activities.

2. The Social Worker Should Engage in Conscious Use of Self

The social worker's primary practice tool is the self (i.e., his or her capacity to communicate and interact with others in ways that facilitate change). The skilled worker is purposeful in making use of his or her unique style of relating to others and building positive helping relationships with clients.

In professional relationships, workers reveal—verbally or nonverbally, directly or indirectly—their values, lifestyles, morals, attitudes, biases, and prejudices. Workers must be consciously aware of how their own beliefs, perceptions, and behaviors may have an impact on their professional relationships, as these personal attributes will surely affect the ability to be helpful to clients. Part of the "art" that the social worker brings to the helping process (see Chapter 3) is his or her enthusiasm for helping people improve the quality of their lives. This personal commitment to serving others facilitates communicating energy and hope to the client.

The social worker must also be comfortable with his or her unique personality and be at peace with whatever problems he or she has experienced in life. For most people, acquiring such self-knowledge and self-acceptance is a lifelong journey that requires a willingness to take risks, for taking a close look at who we are can indeed be disquieting. (See Item 16.2 for more information on developing self-awareness.) But the worker must discover and build on his or her special strengths and minimize the impact of deficiencies, identify the types of clients and situations that respond positively to his or her practice style, and develop a pattern of regular, objective, and nondefensive examination of how one's professional self is functioning.

3. The Social Worker Should Maintain Professional Objectivity

By the time most clients come into contact with a professional helper, they have attempted to resolve their troublesome situation themselves—by either struggling alone or seeking assistance from family, friends, or other helpers. Often, these efforts are thwarted by high levels of emotion and the conflicting advice they receive. This may only add to the person's frustration and preclude clear understanding and response to the situation.

The professional adds a new dimension to the helping process by operating with a degree of personal distance and neutrality. Maintaining this neutrality without appearing unconcerned or uncaring is a delicate balancing act. The worker who becomes too involved and too identified with the client's concerns can lose perspective and objectivity. At the other extreme, the worker who is emotionally detached fails to energize clients or, even worse, discourages clients from investing the energy necessary to achieve change. The social worker can best maintain this balance through a controlled emotional involvement.

Further, this professional objectivity is important to the social worker's own mental health. A degree of emotional detachment is needed, allowing the worker to set aside the troubles of clients and society and separate the professional and personal aspects of one's life. Professional objectivity is perhaps the best antidote to worker burnout.

4. The Social Worker Should Respect Human Diversity

The practice of social work involves activity with and in behalf of people from virtually all walks of life, most racial and ethnic backgrounds, a variety of cultures and religions, a range of physical and intellectual abilities, both genders, as well as various sexual orientations and ages. This diversity is expressed in the beliefs and behaviors of individuals, families, communities, and even societies.

The worker must understand and respect such differences and human uniqueness and recognize that what may appear to be unusual behavior from one perspective may be quite appropriate given a different set of values and life experiences. To the social worker, diversity brings richness to the quality of life and failure to accept and appreciate difference creates barriers to helping.

Respect for diversity requires sensitivity to the fact that various population groups have had differing experiences in U.S. society. In addition, individuals within a particular group or class may have had quite different experiences from other persons in that group. The social worker, then, must also appreciate the variations within any group and avoid making assumptions about any one person's cultural identity, beliefs, or values on the basis of that person's external characteristics or membership in a particular population or demographic group. Practitioners who respect diversity are careful to guard against jumping to conclusions or making decisions based on overgeneralizations and stereotypes.

5. The Social Worker Should Challenge Social Injustices

Central to social work is the recognition that many human problems are caused by discrimination, oppression, or more subtle social factors that limit people's opportunities or create difficulties for them. The lack of health insurance by one in every six American families, the failure of employers to accommodate the needs of persons with disabilities, and the tradition of higher pay for men over women doing comparable work are just a few well-known examples of social injustices. If not addressed, these social injustices will continue to burden the individuals affected and the society as a whole. Eliminating these injustices will improve the quality of life for all and, for the most vulnerable members of society, will prevent many social problems from occurring in the first place.

Challenging social injustices is a long-term proposition. The social worker cannot expect social issues that developed over time to dramatically be resolved with only short-term effort. However, unless social workers, clients, and other concerned citizens effectively identify, document, analyze, strategize, and carry out social change efforts, social injustices will surely continue.

6. The Social Worker Should Seek to Enhance Professional Competence

Social work is a contemporary discipline. Its focus is on the here-and-now concerns of ever-changing people living in a dynamic environment. Helping people interact more effectively with their environments requires that the social worker be in tune with the world as it is experienced by others. One cannot be empathic and creative in working with a wide range of clients while holding a narrow and uninformed view of life. The social worker must continuously seek growth and development—both personally and professionally.

The person who becomes immersed in social work to the exclusion of other activities and experiences actually limits the ability to be helpful by restricting his or her knowledge and awareness of broader issues that affect human functioning. To appreciate the infinite variety of the human condition, one must understand life from various orientations. Gathering ideas from history, literature, science, the arts, and travel and interacting with a wide range of people are vital to the continuing development of the social worker.

However, the social worker must also be current with the latest professional information. The rapid growth and change in the knowledge relevant to social work requires constant updating. New concepts, theories, and intervention techniques regularly appear in the literature and are presented at workshops and conferences. It is incumbent on the social worker to regularly participate in such activities in order to continue to grow as a competent social worker.

■ PRINCIPLES THAT GUIDE PRACTICE ACTIVITIES

In addition to the principles related to the social worker as an individual and a professional person, a number of other principles are concerned with the social worker's intervention with individual clients and client groups.

7. The Social Worker Should Do No Harm

Social work practice is about the facilitation of desired change. However, there is always an element of risk in any effort to bring about change, no matter how well intended or desirable the goal. Because planned change is a very human process, the responsible professional must anticipate that mistakes will be made. The social worker must anticipate such possibilities and have a plan for dealing with the things that can go wrong in an intervention. In the effort to do good and enhance the social functioning of people, the social worker must strive to at least minimize any harm.

A social worker's change goals and intervention activities should not damage appropriate and healthy levels of client social functioning. Professional actions and the programs social workers implement should in no way discourage or undermine responsible client behaviors nor erect barriers to appropriate social functioning. Furthermore, social workers engaged in efforts to change an unjust condition or unfair social policies must avoid creating other injustice to people affected by the change.

8. The Social Worker Should Engage in Evidence-Based Practice

At the very core of society's trust in professions is the expectation that the professional will bring to the change effort the latest and most professional knowledge; even so, consciously using the best available evidence regarding the client condition and successful interventions in one's practice requires considerable discipline. With the pressure of heavy caseloads and busy schedules, there is a tendency to fall into a pattern of reacting to client situations without carefully considering what is known about people who experience similar conditions, what research has shown on the effectiveness of different intervention approaches related to this condition, and so on. Unless one's work is knowledge driven, it will fail to meet the expectation for professional practice.

A social worker cannot possibly stay abreast of all the knowledge that relates to the many dimensions of social work practice. However, the worker is obligated to be familiar with the most current knowledge that directly relates to his or her practice activities and to be able to retrieve needed knowledge from the social work literature, from the vast resources on the web, and from colleagues.

It is also important that social workers are careful consumers of the knowledge available through electronic technology, presented in the social work literature, and discussed at social work conferences. After all, it is the clients that are most at risk if practice assessments and intervention decisions are based on faulty information. Each social worker should be prepared to engage in critical review of social work's theoretical knowledge and "best practices" research before adopting that as a basis for his or her practice activities.

9. The Social Worker Should Engage in Value-Guided and Ethical Practice

It is critical that the social worker make a conscious effort to identify and address relevant value and ethical issues as a part of social work practice. Value choices and value conflicts are at the center of many practice situations. The social worker must recognize that one's values are powerful forces in human behavior and that helping clients clarify and understand value issues in their lives can be a critical step in bringing about change. However, in many cases, if clients are to change themselves or their situations, they must take some action to adjust or adapt their values to be more congruent with those of others in their lives—or learn to help others adjust or adapt their values to be more congruent with those of the client. When working directly with clients, then, the social worker must be sensitive to the value issues that inevitably arise.

Organizations and communities also operate from values about who should be served, who should pay for the services, and how the services should be delivered. When engaged in practice activities that relate to the agencies that employ them, the social conditions that exist in the community, or the social programs that are created at the city, county, state, or federal level, the social worker should attempt to understand the values that have affected that situation. Societal problems are often a result of value differences, and an important step in finding solutions to those problems is to address the value issues.

Social workers must also be sensitive to their own values and beliefs and be prepared to suspend or set aside their own preferences and perspectives to avoid inappropriately imposing their beliefs on their clients. Social work practice, however, is not value free. At times, the social worker must take actions to protect the health and safety of others or achieve a broader social benefit than the interests of a single client. Making those practice decisions ethically requires careful consideration. (See Item 8.8 for guidelines on sorting out ethical dilemmas.)

10. The Social Worker Should Be Concerned with the Whole Person

Most professions focus on a single dimension of the person. Physicians are primarily interested in physical well-being, teachers focus on intellectual development, and psychologists are concerned with emotional and cognitive processes. Social work, however, is unique among the professions because of its concern for the whole person—biological, psychological, social, and spiritual. For the social worker, practice activities rarely relate to a single dimension of human life and living.

Concern for the whole person requires attention to the client's past, present, and future. It requires the social worker to look beyond the client's immediate or presenting problem and be alert to the possible existence of other issues, ranging from a lack of food and shelter to a lack of meaning and purpose in life. The social worker must focus attention on both the client's problems and strengths. He or she must attend to the client's presenting problem or concern and to possible underlying causative factors (i.e., the symptoms as well as their causes). In keeping with the person-in-environment construct, the social worker must be concerned with the well-being of the client and also the many other people who may be affected by the client's behavior and by the worker's intervention. Finally, the social worker must be concerned with both the short-term and long-term implications of the change process for both the client and others.

11. The Social Worker Should Serve the Most Vulnerable Members of Society

From its inception, the profession of social work has concerned itself with those people most likely to experience difficulties in social functioning. Persons who are poor, mentally or physically disabled, from a minority race or culture, and who otherwise may be devalued often face special challenges of discrimination, ostracism, and neglect by the dominant society. Needless to say, not every person who is part of a vulnerable population actually experiences problems and requires the assistance of a social worker. But as a group, these individuals are at risk and frequently encountered by workers when delivering various social programs.

Not infrequently, ill-conceived social policies and laws treat devalued groups unfairly and place them at a social and economic disadvantage. Social workers have often been champions of efforts to remedy these conditions, even though advocacy for (and with) these groups may be politically unpopular. Such advocacy, if successful, forces members of the dominant society to face the existence of social and economic injustice and the need for change in the social order. In fact, those who have power and privilege often benefit from the status quo and typically resist change. They may therefore dislike what social workers are trying to do and seek to discredit the profession. To be a social worker, one must be willing to accept the criticism that follows from service to devalued groups and engage in the advocacy needed to accomplish social change.

12. The Social Worker Should Treat the Client with Dignity

Philosophically, the social worker must accept the proposition that each person or group deserves to be treated with dignity, respect, and understanding. The phrase "Accept the client as he or she is" reminds and encourages the social worker to approach clients as people with dignity who deserve respect, regardless of behavior, appearances, and circumstances. Acceptance occurs when the worker views the client as he or she is, with all of the endearing and maddening characteristics that every human possesses. That means recognizing that clients sometimes make wise decisions and at other times make irrational choices that damage themselves and others. Nevertheless, the social worker is obligated to treat the client as a person who is valued and deserves to maintain his or her dignity throughout the helping experience.

Communicating acceptance and respect requires that the social worker avoid making moral judgments concerning clients. The worker's nonjudgmental attitude helps clients overcome the common fear of being criticized by others and frees up the helping relationship for positive, rather than defensive, action. Treating the client with dignity also helps guard against the inappropriate intrusion of the social worker's biases into the client's life. Weick, Rapp, Sullivan, and Kisthardt (1989, 353) observe that the importance of acceptance and the nonjudgmental attitude in practice rests on the belief that people have "an inner wisdom about what they need and that ultimately, people make choices based on their own best sense of what will meet that need [and that] it is impossible for even the best trained professional to judge how another person should best live his or her life."

The need to treat each and every client with respect and acceptance does not imply approval of all behavior by a client. One can accept and care for the client with dignity without approving of, for example, illegal, harmful, or socially destructive behavior. The key to adhering to this principle is to remember that the purpose of social work is to help people make changes, and it has been amply demonstrated that acceptance of and respect for the person are prerequisite for change and that condemnation and judgmentalism erect barriers to such change.

13. The Social Worker Should Individualize the Client

To individualize the client—whether an individual, family, group, or community—is to be cognizant of and sensitive to the uniqueness of the client and the uniqueness of his or her situation, concerns, history, and possibilities. The social worker must adapt his or her approach to this uniqueness and to the client's capacities, limitations, and readiness to participate in a particular intervention or change effort. What works well with one client may not work at all with another.

Closely related to the principle of individualization is the precept "Start where the client is." In other words, the social worker must strive to identify and tune in to the client's current thoughts, feelings, and perceptions. The worker should always begin the professional relationship, an intervention, and each contact with the client by focusing first on the concerns, issues, and circumstances that are most relevant to and most pressing for the client. The client's highest priority or greatest concern may, of course, change from day to day or week to week. A skillful social worker will be alert to such shifts and adapt his or her approach accordingly.

14. The Social Worker Should Consider Clients Experts on Their Own Lives

Who knows more about a client than the client himself or herself? Too often, social workers and other helping professionals become enamored with their theoretical knowledge of human functioning and forget to consult with their clients to learn the actual circumstances of their lives. There are many things social workers will never know about their clients—and, in fact, many things that are not the business of the workers to know. Where possible, clients should be viewed as the primary experts on their lives.

What, then, is the social worker's role in assessing a client's situation? The expertise a social worker brings is to help the client recall factors that have affected his or her life, to provide alternative interpretations of the meanings of those factors, to provide possible explanations by connecting multiple factors, to link this information to knowledge that aids in understanding, and to help the client decide how to act on the basis of this knowledge. The client will be empowered to realize that the worker recognizes him or her as the expert on his or her own life.

15. The Social Worker Should Lend Vision to the Client

A central feature of professional helping is to bring vision: new ideas, new perspectives, and more effective change strategies to a problem situation. If an individual or group is to invest in the difficult process of changing, they must be convinced that the outcome will be worth the effort. One element of vision that the social worker must introduce and nurture is a sense of hopefulness; the social worker should offer a vision that change is possible and that there are new and better ways to deal with the situation. The client will become more hopeful and more open to change if the worker can display a genuine belief and faith in the client's potential for change, in his or her power to overcome obstacles, and in the capacity to build working alliances with others who can become resources to the client.

While offering new perspectives, encouragement and support, and techniques for change, the social worker must also be realistic and honest about limits and possibilities. Clients are not helped by raising false hopes or by projecting unrealistic outcomes for the helping process. A tempered infusion of energy and vision allows the client or client group to make real progress toward achievable outcomes.

16. The Social Worker Should Build on Client Strengths

All too often, social workers and other human services professionals become preoccupied with client problems and invest considerable effort in identifying all that is wrong with a situation and in describing the specific limitations or deficiencies of a client or client group. Such an essentially negative way of thinking about clients and their situations is reinforced by the diagnostic labels now required for statistical purposes within many human service agencies or by insurance companies that pay for social work services.

For the social worker, it is the clients' abilities and potentials that are most important in helping to bring about change. Since a change in social functioning is largely under the control of the client, it is important to help clients recognize and utilize their strengths. The emphasis on maximizing and building on clients' strengths helps change the tone of the helping relationship from one of gloom over problems to one of optimism.

17. The Social Worker Should Maximize Client Participation

"Help your clients to help themselves" is a principle based on the belief that if meaningful and lasting change is to occur for an individual, group, community, or other client system, the people who will need to change must be active participants in the change process. It is the responsibility of the social worker in guiding the process to be sure that, as far as possible, all relevant persons participate in identifying the problem, formulating a plan of action, and implementing that plan.

In order to maximize client participation, the social worker should "Do *with* the client and not *to* or *for* the client." For example, it does little good for the social worker to construct a sophisticated diagnosis of a client's situation if that client does not understand or accept those conclusions. Meaningful change will occur only when those who must change clearly understand the need for change and are willing and able to take action.

Similarly, an intervention plan is most likely to be followed when it is developed with active client participation. As compared to an attorney, who single-handedly presents a case for the client, or a physician, who injects the patient with a chemical that can cure an illness with minimal patient involvement, a social worker must assume a very different posture. The social worker must view himself or herself as primarily a collaborator, facilitator, and catalyst. Although situations do arise in which a social worker must act in behalf of clients, the social worker should always seek to maximize client involvement.

18. The Social Worker Should Maximize Client Self-Determination

The instruction to "Guide the process—not the client" captures another important principle. This principle maintains that those who must ultimately live with the outcomes of decisions should have the freedom to make those decisions. The job of the social worker is to help clients explore alternatives and the implications of various options but not to prescribe their final choices.

The principle of self-determination must be qualified in its application. It assumes that the client is capable and legally competent to make decisions in relation to self and others. Sometimes that is not a valid assumption. Some clients may not understand the consequences of an action or may lack the mental capacity to make sound judgments and might therefore make choices that are clearly harmful to themselves or others. At times, the social worker must take on a decision-making role for these clients (e.g., children, the person who is mentally ill, etc.). This may involve persuading them to take a particular action, using the authority or power that the social worker's position might command, securing a court order declaring mental incompetence, or, in the most extreme situations, calling for police assistance in order to prevent a tragedy.

The social worker should reluctantly assume the responsibility for making decisions in behalf of clients and then only after careful review of the situation, after consultation with others, and always with the intent of returning that responsibility to the client as soon as possible. In the final analysis, the social worker should attempt to maximize the client's ability to determine his or her own destiny.

19. The Social Worker Should Help the Client Learn Self-Directed Problem-Solving Skills

Most social workers are familiar with the idea of helping people help themselves. Perhaps this should be extended to "helping people help themselves now and also in the future."

Many of us have had the experience of being pleased with our loss of weight only to discover a few months later that we had slipped back into old eating patterns and regained the lost pounds. Similarly, the changes in social functioning made by a client with the assistance of a professional helper can come unraveled unless the client is prepared to sustain that change over time. Ideally, a social work intervention helps prepare clients to cope successfully with future difficulties and to engage in self-directed problem solving when faced with another problem.

Hopefully, what the client learns during his or her interaction with the social worker can be applied to additional concerns in day-to-day living—in the present and in the future. The admonition "Don't do for clients what they can do for themselves" relates to this principle of helping clients learn the skills needed to be independent and self-reliant.

An important aspect of preparing clients for the future is to teach them how to identify and make use of resources that might be found in their immediate environment. Such resources may include family members, relatives, friends, service clubs, and church, mosque, or synagogue groups.

20. The Social Worker Should Maximize Client Empowerment

Because social workers are committed to serving society's most vulnerable citizens, they regularly work with people who have been victims of various forms of discrimination and oppression. One especially helpful contribution social workers can make to their clients' social functioning is to help them gain increased power over their lives. While some of the principles described here have the effect of giving clients more control over some dimensions of their lives (e.g., maximizing participation, maximizing self-determination, or helping to develop problem-solving skills), a principle that should guide all of a social worker's practice activity is the goal of empowerment.

The goal of helping people, both individually and collectively, to gain the power needed to change their life circumstances and to gain control over how they live their lives has been part of social work's philosophy from its founding. The term *empowerment* reflects efforts to help people gain control over their life circumstances, to obtain needed information and resources, and to develop skills needed to make the decisions and take the actions necessary to attain a higher level of self-reliance and modify one's social and political environment. In order to empower others, social workers place a special emphasis on the activities of encouraging, teaching, and facilitation, as well as collaboration and shared decision making within the professional relationship.

21. The Social Worker Should Protect Client Confidentiality

Individuals and families seeking help from a social worker often discuss very private aspects of their lives. In groups, clients may reveal secrets and self-perceptions that could be embarrassing or damaging if made public. The community worker, too, encounters instances when information about individuals, agencies, and organizations must be protected. All social workers must therefore be capable of handling private and sensitive information in a confidential manner.

There are two basic forms of confidentiality: absolute and relative. *Absolute confidentiality* refers to a situation when information imparted by the client can never go beyond the social worker. That degree of confidentiality is rare in social work practice. It is only under the protection of some professional licensing statutes that a client can claim a legal right to privileged communication. Most social work practice involves *relative confidentiality*, meaning that the most the social worker can promise is to treat information responsibly, as prescribed in the profession's *Code of Ethics;* adhere to existing laws; and to follow agency policy concerning the handling of client information.

The degree of confidentiality that can be provided will, of course, depend on the type of information communicated, the nature of the agency where the practice occurs, the state and federal laws and regulations that govern its operation, and the existence of other legal requirements such as the mandated reporting of child abuse. In correctional programs (e.g., prison, parole, probation), the client can expect little confidentiality. On the other hand, a client who receives social services within a hospital setting will have a much higher level of protection. But even here, a client's records might be reviewed by nonhospital personnel such as insurance companies, Medicaid or Medicare authorities, worker's compensation officials, hospital accreditation teams, and others who have authority to review patient records for purposes of quality control (see Item 10.5). The clients should be advised early in the helping process of the limits of confidentiality the social worker can guarantee.

The social worker must be prudent regarding what information is placed in agency files, and care must be taken in preparing clerical staff to respect the confidential nature of any materials they may type, file, or inadvertently overhear. To protect confidential information, social workers must carefully plan the location of interviews and cautiously select the information to be discussed during professional consultations and in case conferences. Further, clearly separating one's personal life and work life is important in protecting against breaches of confidentiality that might occur when discussing work experiences with family and friends.

22. The Social Worker Should Adhere to the Philosophy of Normalization

Many social work clients have significant mental and physical disabilities. Because of these limitations, they often experience discrimination and social isolation. The philosophy of normalization is a powerful force in efforts to integrate persons with disabilities into the life of the community and ensure that their lives resemble that of the so-called normal person as much as possible. This philosophy originated in the field of mental retardation but has spread to programs serving other groups such as the elderly, the physically disabled, and the seriously mentally ill.

Normalization connotes helping people, especially those experiencing disabling conditions, to live their lives within an environment and in a manner considered typical and culturally normative for persons without disabilities. This approach has the effect of minimizing social stigma and increasing social acceptance of persons who are in some way different from most others. For example, a person with mental retardation should, to the greatest extent possible, live in a typical or ordinary home, attend a conventional school, and perform work that is useful and valued. His or her recreation, religious participation, clothing, transportation, and daily routines should be as conventional and mainstream as possible. Moreover, the individual should receive medical and social services in ways and in settings that closely resemble how others in society would receive them.

23. The Social Worker Should Continuously Evaluate the Progress of the Change Process

The practice of social work is far from an exact science. It involves working with ever-changing people and ever-changing situations. The objectives of helping activities, therefore, must be clearly delineated and regularly reviewed to be certain that they remain relevant to the client's needs. It is not enough to set the course of an intervention strategy and assume that the desired outcome will be achieved. Rather, a continuous monitoring and evaluation of the change process by both the social worker and the client is necessary. To achieve this, both the worker and the client or client group must regularly collect and record data that are indicators of change and these data must be reviewed and carefully analyzed. If the desired change is not occurring, the worker is obligated to try another approach or redesign the intervention plan.

24. The Social Worker Should Be Accountable to Clients, Agency, Community, and the Social Work Profession

One factor that complicates practice is that the social worker must answer to a number of parties. Practitioners in some disciplines might feel that they are accountable only to the client, but the social worker—working at the interface of person and environment—faces multiple sources of accountability.

Social workers are obligated to give their best service to all clients at all times and therefore must be accountable to those individuals, families, and groups they directly serve. In addition, since most social workers are employed by a social agency or as part of a private practice group, they must be accountable to their employing organizations by carrying out their work as effectively and efficiently as possible. Furthermore, the existence of a professional monopoly demands that the members of a profession also be accountable to the community. For many social workers, this accountability is formalized through licensing. For others, the accountability is less structured but nevertheless expected.

The social work profession, as reflected in the *NASW Code of Ethics* (NASW 1999), expects accountability to clients, colleagues, employers, the profession, and society. At times, practice situations place the individual worker in a position that makes it impossible for him or her to be fully and equally accountable to all audiences. In those situations, the social worker should attempt to maximize the accountability to each—but accountability to one's clients should be given priority.

CONCLUSION

The new social worker is often inundated with information that reveals, in bits and pieces, the knowledge and values that guide social work practice. Some of this information is formally taught in professional education programs, whereas other information, such as the principles described in this chapter, is typically transmitted in a more subtle and informal manner.

Practice principles reflect that combination of values and knowledge that should underlay all practice activities. If all else fails, the worker cannot go too far wrong if he or she is operating within these principles. They might be viewed as a fail-safe mechanism in social work practice. With these principles firmly in mind, the social worker is prepared to engage the client in a change process and to identify and select appropriate techniques for addressing the problems or enhancement needs of the client.

SELECTED BIBLIOGRAPHY

National Association of Social Workers. *Code of Ethics.* Washington, DC: NASW, 1999.

Weick, Ann, Charles Rapp, W. Patrick Sullivan, and Walter Kisthardt. "A Strengths Perspective for Social Work Practice." *Social Work* 35 (July 1989): 350–354.

6 Practice Frameworks for Social Work

It is said that "There is nothing so practical as a good theory." Some social workers may question that notion when faced with the rather daunting task of trying to understand and sort through the multitude of conceptual frameworks and theoretical orientations described in social work textbooks and professional journals and at conferences and workshops. For example, dozens of the frameworks used in both direct and indirect practice are described in the *Encyclopedia of Social Work* (1995) and books by Brandell (1997), Dorfman (1994, 1998), Payne (2005), Turner (1996), Greene (1999), Allen-Meares and Garvin (2000), Lehmann and Coady (2000), Roberts and Greene (2002), and Walsh (2006). Nevertheless, conceptual frameworks are important and their proper application does improve social work practice.

At the end of Chapter 3, under the heading "Knowledge of Social Work Practice," the topic of practice frameworks was introduced and three types of practice frameworks—perspective, theory, and model—were described. The reader may want to review those pages before proceeding. Basically, a ***practice framework*** consists of a set of beliefs and assumptions about how and when people and systems change and what a social worker can do to facilitate desired and needed change. Some practice frameworks focus mostly on individual change, whereas others focus on families, small groups, organizations, or communities. This chapter suggests criteria for selection, explains how different frameworks may be more or less useful depending on the phase of the helping process, and provides brief descriptions of commonly used practice perspectives, theories, and models. In each description, an effort has been made to identify the primary reasons social workers use the framework. Key concepts are noted, and suggested readings about each framework are provided.[*]

■ REQUIREMENTS OF A PRACTICE FRAMEWORK

A framework for social work practice should meet the following criteria:

- It should be consistent with the purpose, values, and ethics of the profession.
- It should be capable of being communicated to others (i.e., its concepts, principles, and assumptions should be clearly described and defined).

[*]If a reference mentioned or cited does not appear under the relevant list of Suggested Readings, the full citation will be found in the Selected Bibliography at the end of the chapter.

- It should make sense to laypersons (i.e., most clients and volunteers should be able to understand the framework's connection to their concerns and life experiences).
- It should help the worker analyze and understand complex and often chaotic situations.
- It should provide guidance and direction during the various phases of the change process.
- It should rest on an empirical foundation (i.e., be based on facts and careful and systematic observations).

Because of the wide variety of practice settings, types of clients, and situations addressed by social workers, it is not possible to identify a single social work practice framework that is superior to all others. However, a framework is most likely to yield the desired outcomes for the client if it encourages the social worker to do the following:

- Focus on those factors, issues, and conditions that can, in fact, be changed and over which the client or the social worker has influence and control.
- Address both personal and environmental factors in the client situation (e.g., view children in the context of their family and families in the context of their neighborhoods and communities).
- Build a collaborative relationship with the client based on mutual trust and on the worker's respect, empathy, caring, and compassion for the client.
- Permit and encourage the client to make decisions on the intervention goals and the methods to be used to reach those goals.
- Recognize and build on client strengths and avoid focusing only on limitations, deviance, and psychopathology.
- Be proactive and reach out to the client with offers of services that he or she wants and considers relevant.
- Offer services and use approaches that are congruent with the client's values, culture, and religion.
- Offer services for which the costs to the client in time and money are reasonable given the probable benefits or outcome.
- Achieve some immediate success so as to demonstrate the usefulness of intervention and maintain client motivation.
- Encourage the client's use of those mutual support and self-help groups available in his or her community.
- Facilitate the client's acquisition of knowledge and skills that will decrease his or her need for professional assistance and formal resources in the future.

■ GUIDELINES FOR SELECTING A PRACTICE FRAMEWORK

The choice of a particular practice framework can either enlarge or narrow the social worker's vision and options. Students and new workers especially must guard against becoming locked into a single practice framework and then assuming that it has universal applicability. During their formal education, social workers often become committed to a single theory or modality and remain invested in that approach throughout their careers. Such a narrow "Have theory—will travel" mentality is both shortsighted and a disservice to clients. An additional caution is important: Within the human services, the term *theory* is loosely used. For example, some people apply the term to ideas that have no empirical basis or are so vague that they cannot be tested. For others, the ideas called a "theory" are little more than a description of someone's personal style.

Professionals must also avoid falling into the habit of using practice frameworks in an uncritical manner. The concepts, beliefs, and assumptions that are the elements of particular frameworks must be continually reexamined and tested against changing times and new research findings. The usefulness and the appropriateness of a practice framework does change over time.

The utility of a given framework depends on the nature of the problems or issues receiving the worker's attention, the characteristics of the clients or consumers, the phase in the helping process, and the setting or organizational context of practice. For example, a framework that is helpful in guiding work with voluntary clients may be of little value in work with involuntary, court-ordered clients. A framework that is useful with teenagers may not be useful with elderly persons, and one that is useful with persons of one ethnic group may prove ineffective when used with clients of another group.

When selecting a framework, one must grapple with the question: With what types of clients, with what kinds of problems, in what practice settings, and under what circumstances will a particular conceptual framework provide relevant and useful guidance? In addition, the worker must always ask: Does the framework allow me to address the uniqueness of this particular client or client group? Social workers must beware of frameworks that are either so narrow or so abstract that they no longer describe life's realities as experienced by the clients.

In working with a specific client or client group, social workers may use several practice frameworks together or sequentially. They may shift from one to another as they move through the phases of the helping process (see Chapter 7). For example, the general systems perspective and the ecosystems perspective are most helpful in the beginning phases (e.g., problem definition and assessment), but neither are prescriptive when it comes to the later phases of planning, implementing, or evaluating an intervention. On the other hand, a framework such as behavior modification provides detailed guidance on implementing behavior change, but its use presumes that changing a specific behavior will be the focus of the intervention. Questions that a social worker might consider when selecting a practice framework include the following:

1. What client system does the framework address? Does the framework focus on the individual? Couple? Family unit? Peer group? Organization? Community?
2. What type of client change is expected? For example, changes in values or attitudes? Changes in behavior? Expanded knowledge? Access to new resources? Acquisition of new skills?
3. Does the framework offer an explanation of how and why change occurs?

4. When applying the framework, what is the role of the social worker? For example, is the worker an advisor? Teacher? Counselor? Broker of services? Case manager? Administrator? Planner? Researcher? Advocate?

5. What are the implicit or explicit assumptions concerning the relationship between the professional and the client? For example, consider the differing assumptions of some theories:
   - *Clients as objects.* Professionals are the experts and know what should be done; the clients are expected and encouraged to do what the professionals decide is "best" for them.
   - *Clients as recipients.* Professionals possess and control the services needed by the clients; the clients are expected to utilize the services given to them in a cooperative and appreciative manner.
   - *Clients as resources.* Professionals presume that the clients are in the best position to know what they need and what will and will not work. They actively solicit the clients' ideas on the problems they face and on possible solutions. The clients' thoughts and decisions are respected.

6. What power balance exists in the client-worker relationship? For example, is the worker to be viewed by the client as a friend? Expert? Authority figure? Advisor? Consultant? Companion? Colleague?

7. What is the primary medium of communication? Does the framework rely on verbal exchanges? Expression through art or games? Writing and reading? Precise and planned communication or unplanned and freewheeling exchanges?

8. Does the framework specify when its use is appropriate and effective, as well as when its use would be inappropiate or possibly harmful? Are data used to support these beliefs?

9. Does the framework acknowledge the importance of the client's cultural or ethnic background and religious values and beliefs? Can it be adapted to clients of various backgrounds?

10. Does the framework describe the setting or organizational context required for effective application? Agency-based practice? Private practice? Will the client be seen in an office? In the client's home?

11. Is the framework applicable when the client is involuntary or court ordered? When the client is not cooperative?

12. Does the framework offer an explanation of how it is similar to and different from other commonly used frameworks?

13. Does the framework require the application of a unique set of techniques or are the suggested techniques the same as those used with other frameworks?

14. Does the framework exclude certain clients or situations, either explicitly or implicitly? For example, what about the individual who does not read? The individual who cannot meet at the professional's office or during regular office hours? The individual who cannot pay a fee? The individual whose primary concerns are a lack of food, shelter, health care, protection from harm, and so on? The individual with significant physical, sensory, or intellectual limitations?

15. Does the framework emphasize keeping the client within his or her family and social networks? Or does it emphasize removal of the client from the influence of family, peers, or others in the client's near environment?

The social worker's selection of a practice framework is never a completely objective process. A worker brings subjective factors to the selection process, such as the feeling that a particular approach fits best with his or her practice style or that it works better than other approaches. However, subjective factors alone are not sufficient. By passing the various practice approaches through a screen of questions such as those just described, a greater degree of rationality can be applied to the worker's selection of a practice framework.

■ SELECTED PRACTICE FRAMEWORKS

Typically, a social worker draws upon several practice frameworks that offer guidance and direction in work with the types of clients served. This repertoire or set of perspectives, theories, and models can be termed a *practice frame of reference*. When first developing one's frame of reference, the worker may adopt only a limited number of frameworks. Gradually, the number can be expanded to fit the needs of one's agency and one's interests and abilities.

To aid in the selection process, a sampling of commonly used frameworks is described next. Each brief description highlights a few key concepts and assumptions that set the framework apart from others. Taken as a whole, these descriptions heighten one's awareness of how different professionals may view the problems of social functioning and how and why they might approach the change process in different ways. These descriptions begin with six perspectives: generalist, general systems, ecosystems, strengths, ethnic-sensitive, and feminist. A sampling of practice theories and models is also provided, beginning with those that are more individually oriented and progressively moving to families, small groups, organizations, and concluding with the identification of a few frameworks used in work with communities. The reader is reminded that no one approach is always best. Most social workers draw ideas and techniques from several theoretical frameworks and are therefore somewhat eclectic.

Selected Practice Perspectives

One element of a social worker's practice framework is his or her practice perspective(s). As identified in Chapter 3, a *practice perspective* directs the worker to focus most attention on certain factors when approaching a practice situation. One or more of the following (or other) perspectives might be selected as part of the worker's frame of reference.

THE GENERALIST PERSPECTIVE

Purpose.   To ensure that the social worker will approach every client and situation in a manner open to the use of various models, theories, and techniques and will consider several levels of intervention, from micro to macro.

Application.   This way of thinking about practice is most relevant and most needed during the beginning phases of the helping process, when the problem is initially defined and assessed and when decisions are being made concerning what needs to be changed and what approaches might be used. This perspective directs the worker to identify several possible points and levels of intervention and then select the one or ones that are most appropriate and feasible.

Description.   Social work practice has been described as inherently generalist. According to the *American Heritage Dictionary*, a ***generalist*** is "a person with broad general knowledge and skills in several disciplines, fields, or areas." Thus, the terms *generalist practice* and *generalist social worker* refer to a social work practitioner who has a broad range of knowledge and skills, who draws on several perspectives, theories, and models, and who can move with minimal difficulty from one field of practice to another. The opposite of generalist practice is one characterized by specialization, either by type of client served, by method used, by level of intervention, or by role assumed by the social worker.

The social worker utilizing the generalist perspective is willing and able to identify and focus on a variety of factors that may contribute to problems in social functioning. These include conflicts among values and beliefs; broken relationships; distortions of thinking; lack of knowledge and information; destructive individual and family patterns; alienation and loneliness; oppression, injustice, and racism; poverty and the lack of basic resources; misuse of power by those in authority; misguided or unworkable programs and policies; and so on.

The generalist social worker is prepared to engage and work with a variety of client systems—for example, an individual; a whole family; a group formed for a purpose such as therapy or social support; a committee or task group; a formal organization, such as an agency or a network of agencies; and legislators and policymakers. In addition, the generalist is prepared to assume a variety of social work roles—for example, advocate, case manager, counselor or therapist, group facilitator, broker of service, fund-raiser, program planner, policy analyst, and researcher. The generalist expects to mold and fit his or her approach to the client's unique situation and concerns and to characteristics of the local community, rather than expect the client to conform to the professional's or agency's preferred way of responding.

Based on their study of the generalist conception of practice, Schatz, Jenkins, and Sheafor (1990, 223) identify four elements that most clearly characterize the generalist perspective:

1. *A multidimensional orientation that emphasizes an interrelatedness of human problems, life situations, and social conditions.* At the heart of this perspective is the view that both the type and level of intervention should not be decided until after carefully considering the different ways in which the client's concern or problem might be defined and approached. This perspective is compatible with both the general systems and ecosystems perspectives, as they too assist the social worker in assessing a situation by focusing on system interactions without predisposing that worker toward a specific intervention strategy.

2. *An approach to assessment and intervention that draws ideas from many differ-ent practice frameworks and considers all possible actions that might be relevant and helpful to the client.* The generalist perspective requires that the social worker be *eclectic* (i.e., draw ideas and techniques from many sources). It requires that the worker be versatile enough to at least initiate practice activities in a variety of situations. That is not to say that the generalist is expected to be an expert in the application of all theories and models. Rather, the generalist is knowledgeable enough to know when he or she can responsibly serve the client and when it is necessary to refer elsewhere for more specialized interventions.

3. *Selection of intervention strategies and worker roles are made primarily on the basis of the client's problem, goals, situation, and the size of the systems that are targeted for change.* The generalist perspective calls for the social worker to adapt his or her practice activities to the unique client situation. Sometimes that may require working directly with the client, with key persons in the client's immediate environment, and at other times working to change agency and community factors that affect the clients or the services.

4. *A knowledge, value, and skill base that is transferable between and among diverse contexts, locations, and problems.* The more specialized frameworks may, implicitly or explicitly, prescribe or limit the settings where a worker is prepared to practice or the type of client, problem, or concern the worker is prepared to address. However, the generalist perspective can be applied in any human services organization or geographic context and used with a wide variety of clients and concerns. That transferability has job mobility value to the worker, but is a trade-off for the more in-depth knowledge and skills that are required in specialized settings.

The flexibility offered by this perspective is particularly useful when the social worker's job description demands the performance of multiple roles (see Chapter 4). However, it is recognized that many agencies have missions, job descriptions, and policies that limit the scope of practice activities or point practitioners in certain directions (e.g., toward individual change, group services, community development) that will make use of the generalist perspective especially difficult or inappropriate.

Generalist is, perhaps, the most universally held perspective among social workers. The accreditation standards of the Council on Social Work Education (CSWE) require that all baccalaureate programs prepare graduates for generalist practice. Also, master's-level social work education programs are required to build their more specialized programs on a generalist base and several schools offer advanced generalist practice as the primary practice approach for which their gradu-ates are prepared.

SUGGESTED READINGS

Johnson, Louise, and Stephen Yanca. *Social Work Practice: A Generalist Approach*, 8th ed. Boston: Allyn and Bacon, 2004.
Kirst-Ashman, Karen. *Understanding Generalist Practice*, 4th ed. Belmont, CA: Brooks/Cole, 2006.
Poulin, John. *Strength-Based Generalist Practice*, 2nd ed. Belmont, CA: Brooks/Cole, 2005.

THE GENERAL SYSTEMS PERSPECTIVE

Purpose.   To assist the social worker in maintaining a focus on the dynamic interplay of the many biological and social systems that affect client behavior and functioning.

Application.   This way of thinking about clients and their situations is most useful in the beginning stages of the helping process, especially during assessment. Given that every part of a system affects and is affected by every other part, this perspective reminds the worker that there are usually several points at which an intervention can be applied in order to facilitate change. Systems theory offers social work some useful terminology and a number of metaphors for describing client systems (e.g., individuals, families, groups, organizations) within a dynamic context.

Description.   With conceptual roots in biology and computer science, general systems theory seeks to describe the common principles by which all biological and social systems function internally and interact with other systems. These principles are then used to predict the behavior of a system and formulate strategies for bringing about a desired change.

A *system* can be defined as an aggregation of interrelated and interconnected elements and activities that form an identifiable, organized, and functioning whole. Organization is the essence of "systemness." A system has a hierarchic, multilevel structure and displays a particular pattern of behavior. A system consists of numerous parts. If, for example, a family is the primary system of attention—the *focal system*—it is possible to identify several *subsystems*: the spouse subsystem (husband-wife relationship), the parental subsystem (parent-child relationship), and the sibling subsystem (child-child relationships). Each system is also part of a larger *suprasystem*. The suprasystem for a social agency, for example, would be the community social welfare system.

A *symbiotic relationship* is assumed to exist among the parts of a system. Each component is, to some degree, affected by all other parts of the system. A change in one part will have an impact on all other parts. Because of this, a social worker's assessment must anticipate how a given intervention will affect others in the client's immediate environment. For example, social workers usually want to work with both the husband and wife when focusing on a marriage problem, recognizing that a change by one will affect the other.

All systems have boundaries. The outer skin of a person's body, for example, is the physical boundary of that individual. The boundary of a social system (e.g., family, organization, community) is less distinct. The *boundary* of a social system distinguishes between those who belong and those who do not. That determination often requires a judgment call related to the situation being addressed. For instance, regarding a family's plans to purchase an automobile, an emancipated 30-year-old child would probably not be considered part of the system. However, if funeral plans for a grandparent were being made, that same adult-aged child might be an essential component of the family system. All biological and social systems are *open systems*, which means that the boundary is permeable and allows the exchange of matter, energy, and information across the boundary. However, systems vary in degree of openness. Some have such a "thick" boundary that the system is highly resistant to outside influences. On the other extreme, some have boundaries that are so "thin" and permeable that the system is so easily influenced by outside forces that it is unstable and easily destroyed.

Systems are constantly changing and are often more chaotic and unpredictable than it seems. However, systems tend to function in ways that preserve a dynamic equilibrium, or a *steady state*, but these times of relative stability are temporary at best. Although systems naturally seek a certain amount of growth and development, they resist radical change, attempting to maintain a safe degree of sameness. When significant change does occur, the system tends to move rather quickly to a more stable level of functioning, thereby establishing a new steady state. A pattern of ongoing change, then, tends to involve movement from one plateau to another rather than change at a constant pace. It is useful for the social worker to recognize every system's inherent resistance to rapid or extensive change.

The concept of *entropy* refers to the tendency of systems to become disorganized, to disintegrate, or to run down and die. Without a minimum level of organization, a system loses its identity and ability to interact meaningfully with other systems. *Negative entropy* (or negentropy) refers to the forces that preserve the system's organization, promote its development, and keep it alive. All systems need matter (resources), energy, and/or information to counteract entropy and maintain organization. Social work practice often involves helping systems achieve a favorable steady state by preserving or increasing their negentropy.

System functioning includes four interrelated activities: (1) *input* (taking in needed energy, information, etc.); (2) *conversion operations* (activities that process the input and convert it into forms that can be used by the system to sustain functioning); (3) *output* (interactions with other systems); and (4) *feedback* (processes by which the system monitors its own functioning and makes needed adjustments in order to maintain a steady state).

We are reminded by systems theory that cause-and-effect relationships are complex and not nearly as predictable as we may think. The principle of *equifinality* (same end) tells us that a single effect or outcome may result from several different causes, and the principle of *multifinality* (many ends) helps us understand that a single action (one cause) may produce many different effects or outcomes.

Finally, the concept of *interface* refers to the meeting or overlapping of two or more systems. One can visualize, for example, the interface of a family and a school or the interface of a patient and his or her family with a hospital. The social worker works at the interface of these systems (i.e., does "boundary work") in order to improve the interactions between the client system and other relevant systems in that client's environment.

SUGGESTED READINGS

Chetkow-Yanow, Benjamin. *Social Work Practice: A Systems Approach*, 2nd ed. New York: Haworth, 1997.

Norlin, Julia, Wayne Chess, Orren Dale, and Rebecca Smith. *Human Behavior and the Social Environment: A Systems Model*, 4th ed. Boston: Allyn & Bacon, 2003.

THE ECOSYSTEMS PERSPECTIVE

Purpose.   To help the social worker maintain a focus on the interplay between the person and his or her environment.

Application.   This conceptual lens adds to our understanding of the various ways a client system may adapt to an ever-changing environment in order to cope, survive, and compete for needed resources. It is most useful during the phases of assessment and planning because it conceptually places the client system within a situational and environmental context. For example, it reminds the social worker that families must function within and adapt to a certain neighborhood, community, and cultural environment and that the social agencies and social programs designed to serve families must operate and compete for resources within a particular economic and political context.

Description.   The ecosystems perspective takes selected concepts and terminology from the science of ecology, a branch of biology, and uses them as metaphors for describing social processes. Social workers have been drawn to these concepts in a search for better ways of describing the interdependencies and exchanges among and between people and social systems. The use of ecological metaphors reminds us that the behavior of an individual always occurs within a particular environment and that the actions of every individual and every group affect every other person and group in society. The use of these concepts also serves to remind social workers that the process of planned change is both facilitated and limited by a myriad of factors and the larger economic, political, and cultural contexts in which the change occurs.

When borrowing concepts from this biological science, it is important to understand that ecology is focused on the adaptations and functioning of a *species* (i.e., a type or category of organism) within the ecosystem and not on the adjustments or functioning of an individual who is a member of that species. By contrast, social work is very focused on the individual.

Ecology is the study of the relationship between organisms and their biological and physical environments. Smith (1986, 344) defines an ***ecosystem***, the unit of study in ecology, as "a partially or completely self-contained mass of organisms . . . [that engages in] interactions and material cycling that link the organisms in a community with one another and their environment."

An individual can adapt to and will function better in some environments (i.e., settings or contexts) than in others. In other words, we all have niches where we seem to "fit best." The ecological concept of *niche* refers to that combination of conditions and circumstances (e.g., temperature, soil, chemistry) needed by a particular species. Most plant and animal species have a rather narrow niche, but humans are quite adaptable and have widened the human niche through the use of technology. Unfortunately, modifying that environment has caused long-term damage to the water, air, and land and has also damaged the fabric of communities and cultures.

The population density of a neighborhood or community has a rather profound impact on the people who live there. The term *carrying capacity* is defined as the maximum number of individuals of a species that can live in an ecosystem. If the population of a species exceeds the ecosystem's carrying capacity for that species, the forces of disease, starvation, and predation will usually decrease that population. A rapid growth or decline in a species' population can upset the delicate balance necessary to an ecosystem's health and survival.

Ecosystems are never static, and each species in an ecosystem is slowly but constantly adapting to an ever-changing environment. If the environment changes rapidly or if the species cannot adapt quickly enough, the species may be overpowered or replaced by a more adaptable species. One form of adaptation is *specialization*. A species that is specialized in terms of what it requires to survive is at an advantage because its specialization has the effect of reducing competition. However, a highly specialized species is more vulnerable in a rapidly changing environment. As a general rule, specialization will increase a species' survivability in a stable environment but decrease its survivability in a rapidly changing environment.

Smith (1986, 12) explains that *competition* is a major force in shaping ecological communities. Since resources (e.g., food, water, space) are usually limited, the various species that make up an ecosystem must compete in order to survive. When the resources needed by a particular species are scarce, the individual members of that species must, in addition, compete with each other.

The interactions between the many different species in an ecosystem can take several forms. In one type of interaction, termed *predation*, one species (the predator) feeds on or utilizes another (the prey). *Symbiosis* refers to a close and frequent interaction between two species, wherein one or both benefit from this interaction. There are three major types of symbiosis: In *mutualism*, both species benefit from the interaction (e.g., bees and flowers); in *commensalism*, one species benefits while the other is neither helped nor harmed; and in *parasitism*, the parasite benefits while its host is harmed.

Despite the difficulty of borrowing biological concepts to build a conceptual framework for social work practice, the ecosystems perspective has provided some new ways of thinking about and describing the functioning of the individual, the family, and the organization and the interactions between various groups in a society. People must cope with and adapt to changes in themselves, in other people, and in wider society. When people cannot make effective adaptations, they experience distress and are disadvantaged in their ability to compete. Competition can be a positive force in that it may lead to a higher level of functioning, but it can also be destructive in that it may lead to social and economic injustice and the oppression of some groups. Cooperation, mutualism, and respect for diverse groups in society are needed to counter the potentially negative effects of raw competition.

The ecosystems perspective helps us recognize that we cannot understand the functioning of an individual without examining his or her environmental context. This perspective also reminds us that people shape their environments and are also shaped by them. Both success in social functioning and problems in social functioning arise from people-environment transactions, not solely from within the individual or from environmental forces. From an ecosystems perspective, social work interventions seek to enhance the growth, development, and adaptive capacities of people; to remove environmental obstacles to effective functioning; and to expand the availabilty of scarce resources. Social work aims to maintain or restore an adaptive balance between people and their environments by helping them adapt, by changing the environment, or both.

SUGGESTED READINGS

Germain, Carel, and Alex Gitterman. *The Life Model of Social Work Practice*, 2nd ed. New York: Columbia University Press, 1996.

Kemp, Susan, James Whittaker, and Elizabeth Tracy. *Person-Environment Practice*. New York: Aldine de Gruyter, 1997.

Meyer, Carol, and Mark Mattaini. "The Ecosystems Perspective: Implications for Practice." In *The Foundations of Social Work Practice*, 3rd ed., edited by Mark Mattaini, Christine Lowery, and Carol Meyer, 3–19. Washington, DC: NASW, 2002.

THE STRENGTHS PERSPECTIVE

Purpose.   To ensure that the social worker is attentive to client strengths during assessment and intervention.

Application.   This perspective is necessary in work with all clients and during all phases of the helping process. It is an important counterbalance to the preoccupation with client problems, pathology, and deficits that is so pervasive in the service delivery system and inherent in many of the practice theories and models used by social workers.

Description.   Basically, the ***strengths perspective*** is a way of thinking about clients and their situations. It is an orientation or a philosophical stance that anticipates the existence of positive and constructive elements, even in the most tragic of situations and even when the client's behavior is seriously dysfunctional. It encourages the social worker to always look for client strengths, examine them, and make use of them during the helping process. It must be noted that most of the practice theories and models used by helping professionals are quite different in that they emphasize uncovering and examining the client's problems, limitations, and pathology. In those approaches, the client's strengths are often overlooked or dismissed as irrelevant to the change process.

A *client strength* can be defined as any attribute, experience, or skill that contributes to positive social functioning. Strengths take many forms, such as the capacity to learn from life experience, fortitude, a special talent, a commitment to help others, and personal integrity. This perspective presumes that all clients have strengths and that it is the social worker's task to uncover those strengths and build upon them. Recognizing strengths usually has the effect of increasing client motivation, elevating the client's sense of hope and self-confidence, and uncovering new possibilities and untapped resources.

Positive elements exist within every environment, no matter how harsh it might be. For example, every social network, neighborhood, and community contains individuals and groups who care and who will contribute their time and resources to helping others. Such helping resources can be mobilized if an individual is creative and persistent.

It is presumed that a client generally knows what will and will not be effective and helpful in addressing his or her concerns. A client is considered to be an expert on his or her life situation and circumstances. Thus, a social worker utilizing this perspective takes seriously the client's suggestions or ideas on how best to proceed. The helping relationship is collaborative in nature, and the professional's role is mostly that of a consultant to the client and a facilitator.

While it is true that traumatic life experiences are injurious and that an illness or disability can impose some limitations on a person, these events and situations may also become sources of positive challenge and opportunity for the individual. No one can know for certain the upper limits of a person's capacity to grow, change, and overcome life's difficulties (see Item 11.4).

SUGGESTED READINGS

Glicken, Morley. *Using the Strengths Perspective in Social Work Practice*. Boston: Allyn and Bacon, 2004.

Rapp, Charles, and Richard Guscha. *The Strengths Model*, 2nd ed. New York: Oxford University Press, 2007.

Saleebey, Dennis. *The Strengths Perspective in Social Work Practice*, 4th ed. Boston: Allyn and Bacon, 2006.

THE ETHNIC-SENSITIVE PERSPECTIVE

Purpose.   To ensure that the social worker is attentive to ethnic, cultural, and religious diversity among clients and that the problems and effects of discrimination and minority status are addressed in practice.

Application.   This perspective is needed whenever the worker is involved with a client who is a member of an ethnic or minority group or who has a cultural background different than that of the worker and especially when there is reason to believe that oppression and discrimination are related to the client's presenting problem or concern. It is relevant during all phases of the helping process.

Description.   This conceptual lens draws attention to the fact that a client's social class, culture, ethnicity, and religious beliefs have a significant impact on his or her help-seeking behavior and on whether a particular approach by a professional or even a specific type of service will be perceived by the client as needed, relevant, and useful. These same factors will have a bearing on whether the client defines a situation as a problem in need of attention, on how the client expects to be treated by service providers, and which of the suggestions made by the professionals are helpful versus offensive.

Every person must simultaneously negotiate and reconcile two sets of beliefs, values, and expectations. One set consists of the rather impersonal influences exerted on us by economic, political, legal, media, and educational systems. The second set of influences are the more intimate ones in our lives, such as those we experience within our family, friendships, and neighborhood. Conflict, alienation, and self doubt can result if there is a significant incongruence between these two sets of beliefs, values, and expectations. That incongruence is most likely to occur among ethnic minorities and recent immigrants.

Given the increasingly diverse nature of U.S. society, it is important for every social worker to become a culturally competent practitioner—namely, one who has the ability to work with a client in ways that are congruent with his or her cultural, ethnic, and religious beliefs, values, traditions, and expectations. In order to develop this ability, the social worker must, first and foremost, be cognizant of how his or her own beliefs, values, and expectations have been shaped by his or her particular culture, education, religious orientation, and social class and how these influences have given rise to a set of assumptions about the way things are or should be. In addition, the social worker must be truly open to learning about the client's culture, ethnicity, and religion and be able to integrate this knowledge into his or her professional roles and responsibilities, manner of building a relationship, assessment process, and interventions. (See Items 8.9, 15.18, and 15.19).

SUGGESTED READINGS

Appleby, George, Edgar Colon, and Julia Hamilton. *Diversity, Oppression, and Social Function.* Boston: Allyn and Bacon, 2007.

Diller, Jerry. *Cultural Diversity: A Primer for the Human Services,* 3rd ed. Belmont, CA: Brooks/Cole, 2007.

Lum, Doman. *Culturally Competent Practice: A Framework for Understanding Diverse Groups and Justice Issues,* 3rd ed. Belmont, CA: Brooks/Cole, 2007.

Paniagua, Freddy. *Assessing and Treating Culturally Diverse Clients,* 3rd ed. Thousand Oaks, CA: Sage, 2005.

THE FEMINIST PERSPECTIVE

Purpose.   To insure that the negative effects of bias, prejudice, and stereotypes concerning gender and sex roles are addressed in social work practice.

Application.   This perspective is helpful and probably needed whenever the client is female and always when there is reason to believe that sexism and sex role stereotyping are related to the concerns brought to the social worker's attention. It is applicable throughout the helping process but is especially important during the phases of problem definition and assessment.

Description.   The feminist perspective heightens the practitioner's awareness of how societal beliefs and attitudes related to sex, gender, and sex roles may affect the way a client's problem is defined by a client and by a professional or agency, the relationship formed between helper and client, and the type of assistance or service actually provided. It has added relevance when one recognizes that most of the social policies and social programs that impact women are formulated and designed by male-dominated institutions, governmental organizations, and corporations. There is a cultural and political dimension to all personal problems; this is especially true for women who have minority status in terms of political and economic power.

The terms *sex* and *gender* are often used interchangeably but they have somewhat different meanings. The concept of **sex** refers to the classification of people as either male or female based on anatomy and a particular assemblage of the X and Y chromosomes. By contrast, the concept of **gender** refers to socially constructed differences as reflected in the meanings, beliefs, and attitudes that people commonly associate with ideas of "femininity" and "masculinity." Sex is biological whereas gender is cultural. In many societies, femininity is associated with the qualities of compassion, cooperation, loyalty, intuition, caring, sharing, openness, and the attention to human relationships. Masculinity, on the other hand, is associated with the characteristics of rationality, competition, authority, leadership, courage, decisiveness, fortitude, honor, and attention to things and objects. Needless to say, many of the perceived differences between the sexes have their origin in historical forces and cultural and societal dynamics, rather than in biological characteristics.

This practice perspective challenges two assumptions, or ways of interpreting reality, that give rise to the oppression and exploitation of women: patriarchy and sexism. *Patriarchy* refers to a hierarchical system of societal organization in which men control family, political, and economic structures. It rests on the belief that the male is inherently more important, superior to the female, and naturally suited for leadership and decision making. *Sexism* refers to subordinating one sex (usually female) to the other resulting in an unfair ordering of roles and responsibilities and an unfair distribution of social and economic benefits and opportunities.

Central to practice utilizing the feminist perspective is the idea that the professional helping process cannot be limited to clinical or direct service activities; it must also emphasize political action and advocacy. Other principles important to this perspective are the following:

- The helping process emphasizes empowerment and building on client strengths. It has a strong educational component, including teaching the client about sexism, sex-role stereotyping, gender discrimination, and historical factors that have shaped attitudes toward women and how women view themselves.
- Client concerns and personal problems are assessed within a sociopolitical context. Special attention is given to the impact of power relationships.
- The helping relationship is egalitarian; the professional seeks to be a partner or colleague to the client, not an expert or authority. The professional is willing to share relevant personal experiences and the client is expected to be an active participant in the helping process.
- There is an emphasis on creating and utilizing women's social networks and support groups.

The feminist perspective is especially important in work with women, but it has many characteristics—such as its emphasis on empowerment, social justice, and political action—that should be a part of social work practice in all settings and also in work with male clients.

SUGGESTED READINGS

Bricker-Jenkins, Mary. "Feminist Issues and Practices in Social Work." In *Social Workers' Desk Reference*, edited by Albert Roberts and Gilbert Greene, 131–136. New York: Oxford Press, 2002.

Kopala, Mary, and Merle Keitel, eds. *Handbook of Counseling Women*. Thousand Oaks, CA: Sage, 2003.

Saulnier, Christine. *Feminist Theories and Social Work*. Binghamton, NY: Haworth, 1996.

Selected Practice Theories and Models

A practice perspective does not stand alone; it is used in conjunction with various practice theories and models. For example, a social worker operating from the generalist perspective may elect to use behavioral techniques, small group theories, and/or theories of organizational change, depending on the roles being performed and the demands of the practice situation. More specialized practitioners may draw on a smaller number of theories or models, but apply them with more depth of knowledge and skill.

In addition to the reference books mentioned in the opening paragraph of this chapter and those listed in the "Suggested Readings" sections, there exist a number of general reference books that provide one-chapter overviews of the common theoretical frameworks used in therapeutic work with individuals, families, and small groups. These include, for example, Corsini and Wedding (2005), Prochaska and Norcross (2007), Gilliland and James (2003), Forte (2007), and Sommere-Flanagan (2004).

PRACTICE BASED ON PSYCHODYNAMIC THEORY

Purpose.   To improve the social functioning of individuals by helping them understand and work through their conflicting thoughts and feelings.

Application.   Prerequisite to the use of this approach is a client who is motivated, verbal, and willing and able to participate actively in a series of regularly scheduled sessions. This approach is seldom useful if the client has limited intellectual ability, is chemically dependent, or is overburdened by problems related to adverse social or economic conditions (e.g., poverty, inadequate housing, etc.).

Description.   This practice framework frocuses mostly on the client's inner life, his or her deeply personal thoughts, feelings, and conflicts. Psychodynamic explanations of behavior presume that many problems and dysfunctions originate in negative childhood experiences that disrupt or distort the normal processes of personality development. This approach recognizes the power of intense emotions (e.g., fear, anger, envy, revenge, sexual attraction) and the inner turmoil or psychological conflicts that can arise when trying to control them in a socially acceptable manner. Various types of largely unconscious **defense mechanisms** (e.g., repression, projection, rationalization) operate to minimize or mask the anxiety associated with these intrapsychic conflicts (see Item 11.6). It is believed that many of the choices we make in life are driven by unconscious motivations and that our behaviors and decisions often serve some underlying and hidden purpose. Various *object relations* (people relations) concepts are used to explain how current patterns of thought, feeling, and behavior reflect, at an unconscious level, one's childhood relations with others. Social workers who use this practice framework believe that the client often acts and feels toward the worker as he or she did toward an important figure from childhood, especially a parent or sibling. In some instances, the client can be engaged in an analysis of this phenomena called *transference* and thereby helped to understand how and why he or she feels and behaves as such.

The term **ego** refers to those aspects of psychological functioning that are involved in coping and decision making. In a sense, the ego mediates between primitive drives (e.g., flight or fight) and the demands of social norms. The ego is understood to be the problem-solving aspect of intrapersonal dynamics. Thus, a term such as *ego supportive treatment* refers to an intervention intended to maintain or enhance a client's problem-solving and adjustment activities as he or she struggles with some difficulty in life.

Change results from the client's cathartic expression of inner conflicts and emotion; from gaining insight (understanding) into how life experiences gave rise to troublesome thoughts and behaviors; and from working through one's inner turmoil. The change process requires a lengthy and in-depth therapeutic relationship wherein the client feels safe to explore and express very private thoughts and feelings.

Social workers have adapted various therapeutic methods rooted in psychodynamics to the realities of an agency-based practice and to the social work profession's emphasis on viewing the client within an environmental context. As a general rule, however, a practice that is based on psychodynamic concepts will give relatively more attention to client's psychology (inner thoughts and feelings) than to social and situational factors. Recent contributions to this literature incorporate concepts drawn from the cognitive-behavioral approach and various theories of family treatment.

SUGGESTED READINGS

Brandell, Jerrold. *Psychodynamic Social Work*. New York: Columbia University, 2004.
Goldstein, Eda. *Object Relations Theory and Self Psychology in Social Work Practice.* New York: Free Press, 2001.
Leiper, Rob, and Michael Maltby. *The Psychodynamic Approach to Therapeutic Change.* Thousand Oaks, CA: Sage, 2004.

PRACTICE BASED ON BEHAVIORAL THEORY

Purpose.   To improve the functioning of individuals, couples, families, or organizations by helping them learn new behaviors.

Application.   In order to use this approach successfully, it must be possible to operationally define a behavior(s) that needs either to increase or decrease in frequency, duration, or intensity. Also, either the client or the professional must be able to control the consequences that will follow the behavior targeted for change. This approach can be used with a nonvoluntary client if the professional has the ability to monitor the client's behavior closely and the authority to allocate reinforcement (rewards) to the client. It has less applicability when the client's concerns or problems are related primarily to decision making, value conflicts, and distorted thinking.

Description.   A central assumption in behavioral theory is that human behavior, and even certain types of emotional reactions, result from a learning process. Both functional (healthy) behaviors and dysfunctional behaviors (psychopathology) are learned in essentially the same ways. People will usually repeat those actions that are rewarded and abandon those that are not rewarded or that are punished. In other words, how a person behaves is shaped and patterned by the consequences he or she experiences.

In this approach, the process of planned change involves modifying the client's immediate environment (i.e., reactions by others to him or her) so that it elicits and rewards (reinforces) the desired behaviors and no longer reinforces the undesirable or dysfunctional behaviors. This approach, more than any other, emphasizes the need for precise and detailed data collection in order to determine what factors encourage or suppress specific behaviors as well as the need for careful measurement during the intervention in order to determine if it is working. The decisions that guide the change process are made on the basis of data and observations, not assumptions about what might or should work.

The behavioral approach has been attractive to professionals working in residential treatment and correctional settings, where it is possible to observe the behavior of clients and exercise control over the rewards they receive. In many applications, the client is taught how to modify his or her own behavior through the self-administration of reinforcers. (See Item 13.4 for more explanation.)

<u>**SUGGESTED READINGS**</u>

Bronson, Denise. "A Behavioral Approach to Social Work Treatment." In *Social Workers' Desk Reference*, edited by Albert Roberts and Gilbert Greene, 137–143. New York: Oxford Press, 2002.

Sundel, Martin, and Sandra Sundel. *Behavior Change in the Human Services*, 5th ed. Thousand Oaks, CA: Sage, 2005.

Thyer, Bruce, and John Wodarski. *Handbook of Empirical Social Work Practice*. New York: Wiley, 1998.

PRACTICE BASED ON COGNITIVE-BEHAVIORAL THEORY

Purpose.   To improve social functioning by assisting the client to learn more realistic and positive ways of perceiving, thinking about, and interpreting his or her life experiences.

Application.   This approach requires that the client have the requisite intellectual capacity and be willing to invest the time needed to monitor and analyze his or her ways of thinking and to practice techniques designed to change long-standing habits of thought. Cognitive-behavioral theory is especially useful in work on problems of depression, low self-esteem, and self-defeating thoughts. It can be used with children (age 10 and older), adolescents who are developing their patterns of thinking, and, of course, adults.

Description.   This framework integrates selected concepts from learning theory and applied behavioral analysis with ones drawn from the study of cognitive processes (i.e., how people think and process information). It focuses on the interplay among cognitions (thoughts), emotions, and behavior.

How and what people think strongly influences their emotional reactions (feelings) and their behaviors. In a sense, we humans live at the mercy of our beliefs and assumptions. These patterns of thought, termed *schemas*, typically develop during childhood as the individual interacts with his or her environment and forms a set of enduring convictions about self, others, and what one can and should expect in life.

Problem behaviors and personal distress are often rooted in faulty, irrational, and rigid thinking and in unfounded and unrealistic beliefs about the way things ought to be. For example, if people operate on the belief that one must always keep others from getting upset, they face a lifetime of distress because this is an unrealistic expectation. During a course of cognitive-behavioral therapy, the client is helped to identify, monitor, examine, and modify those patterns of thought and the faulty assumptions that give rise to problems. The client is usually taught specific skills and procedures to recognize the content and impact of their cognitions, evaluate the validity of their perceptions and assumptions, and view events and situations with greater objectivity. A variety of techniques are used: cognitive restructuring, logical analysis, role modeling, behavioral rehearsal, paradoxical instruction, desensitization, covert extinction, cognitive flooding, and so on.

Within this general framework there are subdivisions, such as rational emotive therapy and cognitive therapy. Practitioners and theoreticians tend to differ on whether to emphasize the cognitive side or the behavioral side of the cognitive-behavioral construct and the degree to which they work to modify fundamental cognitive process such as perception, memory, information processing, judgment, and decision making (see Items 8.5, 13.8, and 13.11).

SUGGESTED READINGS

Corcoran, Jacqueline. *Cognitive Behavioral Methods: A Workbook for Social Workers.* Boston: Allyn and Bacon, 2006.

Ronen, Tammie, and Arthur Freeman, eds. *Cognitive Behavior Therapy in Clinical Social Work Practice.* New York: Springer, 2006.

Ledley, Deborah, Brian Marx, and Richard Heimberg. *Making Cognitive-Behavioral Therapy Work.* New York: Gilford, 2005.

PRACTICE BASED ON PERSON-CENTERED THEORY

Purpose. To improve individual social functioning by increasing the client's self-understanding and self-acceptance through a nondirective helping process that emphasizes empathetic and reflective listening.

Application. This approach usually requires that the client be voluntary, highly motivated, articulate, thoughtful, and not overburdened by problems caused by external or environmental factors.

Description. With roots in humanistic and existential philosophic traditions, this approach emphasizes the uniqueness of every person and the power of the meanings assigned to personal experience. It is built on a positive and optimistic view—people are fundamentally good, prosocial, striving for self-actualization, and in search of life's meaning.

Change occurs when self-imposed psychological barriers are identified and examined, thereby freeing the client's innate potential for positive personal growth. The social worker strives to demonstrate openness, empathy, warmth, and genuineness and makes frequent use of paraphrase, reflection, and other techniques of active listening (see Item 8.4). The practitioner must be nonjudgmental, refrain from giving advice, and avoid diagnosing and labeling. The focus is on the here and now, rather than on past experience.

SUGGESTED READINGS

Mearns, Dave, and Brian Thorne. *Person-Centered Counseling in Action*, 2nd ed. Thousand Oaks, CA: Sage, 1999.
———. *Person-Centered Therapy Today: New Frontiers in Theory and Practice*. Thousand Oaks, CA: Sage, 2000.
Purton, Cambell. *Person-Centered Therapy*. New York: Palgrave, 2004.

PRACTICE BASED ON EXCHANGE THEORY

Purpose. To improve the social functioning of individuals, groups, and organizations by recognizing people's tendency to act in their own self-interest and their desire to secure benefits and avoid costs.

Application. Being aware of the power of self-interest in a client's choices and behaviors will increase the accuracy of an assessment and thus the effectiveness of any intervention. Client self-interest should be identified and incorporated, to the extent possible, in the formulation of intervention plans.

Description. The basic ideas of *exchange theory* are drawn from the fields of behavioral psychology and economics. (See the previous section on behavioral theory.) This approach rests on the observation that self-interest is a key factor in human motivation and that people's desire to achieve benefits and avoid costs can, to a considerable extent, explain and predict the behaviors and decisions of individuals, families, groups, and organizations. Exchange theory suggests that clients will do what they perceive to be in their self-interest and that which moves them closer to securing whatever they define as valuable, desirable, and beneficial. Moreover, clients will avoid actions that will cause them to lose what they value or desire.

Clients' values and belief systems are key predictors of what they will define to be a benefit, advantage, or reward and what they will judge to be a cost, disadvantage, or punishment. Different individuals and groups will have different ideas about what is desirable. For example, some people may focus on money, possessions, power, social status, and privilege as being important, whereas others may believe that personal freedom and autonomy, honor, social approval, friendship, a sense of belonging, and the feeling of a "job well done" have the greatest value. For still others, adhering to a moral code, performing religious practices, and holding to traditions may be more important than anything else. Similarly, costs will be defined differently by different individuals, groups, and organizations. Examples of costs are the loss of money or time, the loss of status or respect, negative attention, dishonor, humiliation, or knowing one has done wrong. Understanding how clients' define *costs* and *benefits* is central to understanding their motivation, predicting how they will behave in certain situations, and anticipating the effectiveness of particular interventions.

Among the core principles of exchange theory are the following:

- When a client (i.e., individual, family, group, or organization) is asked to choose from among various alternatives, the client will make the choice and engage in the behaviors that will secure the greatest benefits and incur the least costs, as the client defines benefits and costs.
- When a client concludes that all possible alternatives will result in about the same level of reward or benefit, the client will usually select the alternative that has the fewest perceived costs (i.e., disadvantages) and risks.
- When a client believes that all possible alternatives will have immediate outcomes that are about equal, he or she will usually select a course of action that may result in some long-term benefit.
- When a client believes that all possible alternatives will have long-term outcomes that are about equal, he or she will usually select a course of action that might provide an immediate benefit.
- When a client's values have been shaped by a Western industrialized society, the client will usually choose a course of action that promises the greatest financial gain for the least financial cost.

In the context of micro-level social work practice, exchange theory suggests that a client will make use of a certain service (e.g., counseling, support group, treatment group) only if and only as long as he or she believes the benefits of doing so (e.g., feeling better, avoiding negative consequences) outweigh the costs. In this situation, costs might include fees, time, loss of privacy, and stress.

Exchange theory also helps predict intergroup and interorganizational behavior. As a general rule, people's desire to obtain rewards and avoid costs will determine whether they cooperate and collaborate with others, whether they engage in competition and conflict, and whether they attempt to overpower others through coercion. For example, one organization will collaborate with another if it perceives that doing so is in its own self-interest. On the other hand, one organization will compete with another organization if it believes it can gain more through competition than through cooperation. If, for example, social agencies are expected to cooperate and work together, there must be clear advantages for them to do so. If there is no incentive to cooperate, the agencies will compete for limited resources, such as funding, press coverage, status, staff, and the like.

Closely related to exchange theory is the conceptual framework known as *rational choice theory*. This theory is drawn from the study of economics and rests on the assumption that people are rational and will, when given a choice, select those alternatives or behaviors that maximize their benefits and minimize their costs. Thus, by creating a system of rewards and penalties, it is possible to guide people toward desired social goals and away from behaviors that are deemed undesirable. In recent decades, this theory has been the rational for many social policy changes in the areas of health care and welfare assistance.

SUGGESTED READINGS

Blau, Peter. *Exchange and Power in Social Life*. New York: Wiley and Sons, 1964.

Nye, F. I., ed. *The Relationships: Rewards and Costs*. Beverly Hills, CA: Sage, 1982.

Robbins, Susan, Pranab Chatterjee, and Edward Canda. *Contemporary Human Behavior Theory*. Boston: Allyn & Bacon, 1998.

THE INTERACTIONAL MODEL

Purpose.   To improve social functioning by mediating the interactions between people.

Application.   This model developed out of practice experience with social work clients in a variety of social agencies. It presumes that many clients will be involuntary. The model can be used to guide work with individuals, families, groups, and communities.

Description.   This model of social work practice consists of four major elements: (1) people (i.e., clients); (2) the interactions among and between people; (3) the social systems and people with whom the client interacts; and (4) the element of time or the phases in the helping process. In addition to providing concepts for understanding interactions, this model describes numerous specific skills or techniques that might be applied in the four phases of helping. These phases are the preliminary or preparatory phase, the beginning contracting phase, the middle or work phase, and the ending or transition phase. Each phase has unique dynamics and requires the application of a special set of skills. (See Item 8.4.)

Neither the client's relationships with others nor the client's problem can be understood apart from their social and environmental contexts. And, of course, the social worker is part of that ever-changing context. The model calls on the worker to be very active, responsive, and human—a "third force" who functions as a mediator among people and between people and systems.

This process-oriented approach focuses on the client's here-and-now experiences. It presumes that both the client and those with whom the client interacts are striving toward deeper involvement and connectedness in interpersonal relationships, even though there is often conflict and ambivalence about these relationships.

SUGGESTED READINGS

Shulman, Lawrence. *The Skills of Helping Individuals, Families, Groups, and Communities*, 5th ed. Belmont, CA: Brooks/Cole, 2006.

———. *Interactional Supervision*. Washington, DC: NASW, 1993.

———. *Interactional Social Work Practice: Toward an Empirical Theory*. Itasca, IL: F. E. Peacock, 1991.

THE STRUCTURAL MODEL

Purpose.   To ensure that a social work intervention gives adequate and appropriate attention to the client's social environment and to social change.

Application.   This model is intended for use in all social work interventions involving direct practice with individuals, couples, and families.

Description.   Given the social work profession's focus on the person-in-environment and the inherent difficulty of giving equal attention to both dimensions, social workers have tended to choose either a clinical orientation or a social change orientation. The structural approach addresses this tension by asking practitioners to consider, first, changing the client's environment. Whereas most other orientations to direct practice focus mostly on helping individuals adjust to their situations, the structural approach aims to modify the environment first so it better meets the needs of the individual.

This approach rests on the belief that most of the client situations encountered in social work practice are a manifestation of inadequate social arrangements and insufficient resources, rather than individual pathologies or personal deficiencies. Moreover, social change (i.e., improving social conditions and societal structures) is the responsibility of all social work practitioners, including direct-service workers, and not just the obligation of certain specialists, such as those working in the areas of community organization, social policy development, and social planning.

The model identifies four social work roles (conferee, broker, mediator, and advocate) and assumes the worker will move from role to role, depending on the needs of the client. It is built on several fundamental principles: Be accountable and responsible to the client; take actions that identify and engage others who have concerns or problems similar to those of the client; maximize the supports that exist in the client's environment; proceed on the basis of "least contest" (e.g., take on the role of broker before mediator and mediator before advocate); and teach behaviors and skills that will help the client take control of his or her life.

SUGGESTED READINGS

Goldberg, Gale, and Ruth Middleman. *The Structural Approach to Direct Practice in Social Work.* New York: Columbia University Press, 1989.
Mullaly, Robert. *Structural Social Work: Ideology, Theory and Practice,* 2nd ed. New York: Oxford University Press, 1997.

THE CRISIS INTERVENTION MODEL

Purpose.   To address the needs and concerns of a client in an acute, psychological crisis.

Application.   The crisis intervention model is applicable whenever the functioning of an individual or family has been suddenly and dramatically affected by some personal loss or tragedy. It is to be used during a four-to six-week period following the event that precipitated the crisis.

Description.   This model describes basic principles of helping someone who is in a state of *crisis*, or a time-limited period of psychological disequilibrium that can arise when a person experiences a highly stressful or disrupting experience. During this period, the person is unable to function because his or her customary ways of coping and adapting prove ineffective. If he or she does not reestablish a pattern of adequate functioning, there is the danger that serious and long-term problems may develop. *Crisis intervention* is an effort to cushion the immediate impact of the disruptive event by providing "emotional first aid," helping the individual clarify his or her situation, mobilize inner strengths, and reach out to needed family and social resources.

When using this approach, the professional is quite directive. Key elements of the model include (1) quick access to the client and rapid response by the helper; (2) use of time limits (e.g., five sessions over four-week period); (3) focused attention on the crisis configuration (i.e., on the nature of the precipitating event and its subjective meaning to client); (4) emphasis on helping the client make decisions and take action; and (5) contact with the client's social network. Those using the model may draw on a variety of theories, techniques, and intervention procedures. (For more information on crisis intervention, see Item 15.6.)

SUGGESTED READINGS

James, Richard. *Crisis Intervention Strategies,* 6th ed. Belmont, CA: Brooks/Cole, 2008.
Kanel, Kristi. *A Guide to Crisis Intervention,* 3rd ed. Belmont, CA: Brooks/Cole, 2007.
Roberts, Albert. *Crisis Intervention Handbook,* 3rd ed. New York: Oxford University, 2005.

THE TASK-CENTERED MODEL

Purpose.   To improve the social functioning of a client through the use of an intervention structure that emphasizes action steps by the client.

Application.   This approach can be used with individuals, couples, families, and small groups and can be adapted to work with the nonvoluntary client. Because of its emphasis on taking action and the completion of agreed upon tasks, it is especially useful with clients who are attempting to manage problems caused by insufficient resources such as a job, housing, day care, transportation, and so on.

Description.   After discussing their problem or situation, some clients know what they need to do but are unable to move ahead and take the actions necessary to significantly change their situation. The emphasis of this model is on helping the client take those actions. Specific actions are called *tasks*.

The tasks to be worked on can take many forms: making a decision within a certain time frame, securing a needed resource, learning a skill, expressing concerns to an employer, and so forth. Large tasks are broken down into several smaller ones so the client will experience success and sustain motivation. Priority setting is used to limit the number of tasks to only two or three per week. Such structuring and the time limits help the client stay focused and mobilize inner resources. The model is largely empirical, stressing the monitoring and measurement of task completion.

This model's emphasis on action and the completion of tasks should not be interpreted as a lack of concern about clients' inner thoughts and feelings. However, this approach rests on the belief that people are more likely to change as a result of taking action than as a result of simply discussing their thoughts and feelings. Task-centered practitioners draw on a variety of theories and techniques to help clients accomplish agreed upon tasks (see Items 12.1, 12.2, and 14.4).

SUGGESTED READINGS

Epstein, Laura, and Lester Brown. *Brief Treatment and a New Look at the Task Centered Approach*, 4th ed. Boston: Allyn & Bacon, 2002.

Reid, William. *The Task Planner*. New York: Columbia University Press, 2000.

———. *Task Strategies: An Empirical Approach to Clinical Social Work*. New York: Columbia University Press, 1992.

THE PSYCHOEDUCATION MODEL

Purpose.   To improve the functioning of individuals and families by educating them about the psychosocial problems they are experiencing.

Application.   This type of intervention is applicable whenever a client or client's family could benefit from an understanding of the illness, problem, or troublesome situation that is impacting on their lives. Although the psychoeducation model was first developed within the field of psychiatric treatment, it is now used in a wide variety of practice settings.

Description.   When faced with a specific problem or condition, such as a mental illness, both the client and members of the client's family need information; they need to understand what is happening in their lives and what they can do about it.

When people have accurate information they are better able to mobilize personal resources, make informed decisions, and use available services.

Psychoeducation can be defined as a specialized type of education or training designed to help people learn about some specific condition or situation. As such, it is seldom a stand-alone intervention but is used to complement or supplement another treatment or therapy. For example, consider the case of John, a man recently diagnosed as having schizophrenia. Both John and his family need information about this disorder, its etiology, progression, prognosis, and the treatment options so they can make use of available services and better cope with the bewildering symptoms associated with this illness. Another example of psychoeducation occurs in alcoholism treatment programs when the family of an alcoholic is invited to attend educational sessions that explain the nature of addiction, the effects of alcohol on mind and body, the 12-step program, signs of relapse, the phenomena of co-dependency, and the like.

A wide variety of problems or situations might become the focus of psychoeducation sessions; for example: living with bipolar disorder, going through a divorce, parenting a teenager, dealing with the death of a loved one, managing a child with attention deficit disorder, and so on. Psychoeducation lowers anxiety, corrects possible misunderstandings, and teaches relevant problem-solving skills and coping strategies. A social worker using psychoeducation must be clear on the goals for the educational session(s), what a client expects and needs to learn, and how the material can be presented so the client can most easily grasp and make use of key ideas. (See the section titled, "The Social Worker as Teacher" in Chapter 4, and Item 13.34).

SUGGESTED READINGS

Brown, Nina. *Psychoeducational Groups: Process and Practice*, 2nd ed. New York: Brunner-Routledge, 2003.

DeLucia-Waak, Janice. *Leading Psychoeducational Groups for Children and Adolescents*. Thousand Oaks, CA: Sage, 2006.

Pollio, David, Carol North, and Douglas Foster. "Content and Curriculum in Psychoeducation Groups for Persons with Severe Mental Illness." *Psychiatric Services*, June 1998: 816–822.

PRACTICE BASED ON THE ADDICTION MODEL

Purpose.   To improve the social functioning of individuals with an addiction by helping them overcome compulsive behavioral patterns.

Application.   Given the nature of addiction, this model presumes that most clients are nonvoluntary. Since a direct confrontation of the client's defenses is a first step in treatment, the structure and control provided by an institutional or hospital setting are often necessary during the beginning stages of the intervention.

Description.   The addiction model recognizes that many people are unable to discontinue patterns that cause them much misery. These patterns often take the form of alcohol, drug, and tobacco abuse; eating disorders; child molestation; dangerous risk taking; and compulsive sexual activities, spending, gambling, or physical exercise. Even the compulsive pursuit of money or power can be viewed as an addiction. It is believed that during the beginning phases of an addiction, the individual uses the substance or activity mostly as a means of coping with distress caused by emotional pain or some unmet need. When it works to help the person feel better, usage is further reinforced and, subsequently, it is used again and again. Over time, the substance or activity consumes more and more of the individual's attention and resources and displaces other aspects of living. As the addiction spins out of control, the individual develops a system of denial, rationalizations, and behaviors that ensure access to the substance or activity.

Successful treatment requires the breakdown of the denial and helping the client learn more functional means of meeting his or her needs and coping with life's problems. The process of treatment and recovery from an addiction typically moves through six stages:

1. The person lets go of denial and defensiveness and recognizes that he or she has an addiction problem.
2. The person develops a sense of hope based on an awareness that other people with similar problems have made a successful recovery.
3. The person comes to understand how the addiction developed and why it has gotten worse over time.
4. The person acquires the resolve, strength, and social support necessary to change the patterns of thought, behavior, and lifestyle that reinforce the addiction.
5. The person takes action, one step at a time and over an extended period of time, to abandon old patterns and practice healthy patterns.
6. The person continues to monitor and manage his or her life so as to stay free of the addictive substance or activity.

Both one-on-one counseling and small-group experiences (e.g., 12-step programs) help the person move through these stages and achieve sobriety and a healthy life-style. Even after the individual is able to function without the addictive substance or activity, he or she must constantly work to avoid being drawn back into the addiction. (For further information on chemical dependency, see Item 15.12.)

SUGGESTED READINGS

Barsky, Allan. *Alcohol, Other Drugs, and Addictions.* Belmont, CA: Brooks/Cole, 2006.
Doweiko, Harold. *Concepts of Chemical Dependency,* 6th ed. Belmont, CA: Brooks/Cole, 2006.
McNeece, C. Aaron, and Diana DiNitto. *Chemical Dependency,* 3rd ed. Boston: Allyn and Bacon, 2005.

THE SELF-HELP MODEL

Purpose. To improve social functioning through a group experience and discussions with others who have or have had similar concerns or problems.

Application. In order for this approach to be effective, the client must be willing and able to attend a series of group meetings, listen to others, and share personal information and concerns. However, some self-help groups include nonvoluntary and even court-ordered participants.

Description.   Alcoholics Anonymous, Parents Without Partners, and Overeaters Anonymous are but a few of the many self-help groups that can be found in most communities. Most self-help groups are designed around five basis assumptions and beliefs:

1. People have a need to tell their story and to be heard by others. They are especially receptive to suggestions from those who have similar concerns and life experiences.
2. All people have strengths that can be mobilized. People are helped as they help others. We all have much to learn from and to teach others.
3. People are attracted to and feel most comfortable in small groups that are informal, noncompetitive, nonbureaucratic, nonintellectual, and nonelitist.
4. People want and can use simple rules and principles that provide practical guidance on how to cope with day-to-day problems (e.g., live one day at a time, walk your talk, etc.).
5. Helping and caring for others is a natural human activity and not a commodity to be bought and sold.

Self-help groups usually depend on leaders indigenous to the group. Some rotate the leadership role from one member to another. A few look to leadership by professionals or members who have received special training on how to conduct and facilitate meetings.

SUGGESTED READINGS

Gitterman, Alex, and Lawrence Shulman. *Mutual Aid Groups, Vulnerable and Resilient Populations, and the Life Cycle*, 3rd ed. New York: Columbia University Press, 2005.
Kurtz, Linda. *Self-Help and Support Groups.* Thousand Oaks, CA: Sage, 1997.
Powell, Thomas. *Understanding the Self-Help Organization.* Newbury Park, CA: Sage, 1994.

THE SOLUTION-FOCUSED MODEL

Purpose.   To improve social functioning and facilitate client change by assisting the client to identify and expand upon actions that he or she views as relevant and effective solutions to his or her presenting problem.

Application.   This approach is used with individuals, couples, and families. It is appropriate when the client and worker are limited in the number of times they can meet together. The model can be adapted for use with the nonvoluntary client.

Description.   A variety of influences, some of them economic, are forcing social workers and agencies to place great emphasis on efficiency and to limit the number of times they meet with a client. This has given birth to new models of brief and time-limited counseling and therapy. Solution-focused therapy is one of the better-developed approaches. It is built on several assumptions and principles:

- Rapid change and rapid resolution of problems are possible. Because of the ripple effect, small positive changes will, over time, have a positive impact on all other parts of the client system.
- Clients do not resist changes that make sense and provide relief from distress. Problems do not serve a hidden purpose; clients are not invested in maintaining their problems for some unconscious motive.
- It is not necessary to understand the cause of a problem in order to resolve it.
- There are many possible ways of viewing a situation and many right ways of dealing with a troublesome concern.
- Clients are the true experts on their situations and in the best position to know what will and will not solve their problems.
- Clients (individuals and families) have within them the ideas, strengths, and resources to begin resolving their problems; these must be identified, mobilized, and supported by the social worker.

Rather than trying to analyze and understand the client's problem, the social worker using this model tries to help the client identify what he or she wants to change and what he or she is already doing to bring about that change. Emphasis is placed on helping the client envision ways to continue doing whatever is already working, even if only to a small degree. The social worker uses various questioning techniques to help the client recognize that he or she already has some control over the problem and to discover workable ideas on how best to solve it (see Item 11.5).

Because this approach accepts the client's definition of the problem, of what needs to change, and of how to change it, it is inherently more culturally sensitive than approaches that place the social worker in the position of identifying, diagnosing, and treating the client's problem.

SUGGESTED READINGS

Christensen, Dana, and Jeffrey Todahl. *Solution-Based Casework*. Hawthorne, NY: Aldine de Gruyter, 1999.

Dejong, Peter, and Insoo Kim Berg. *Interviewing for Solutions*, 2nd ed. Pacific Grove, CA: Brooks/Cole, 2003.

O'Connell, Bill. *Solution-Focused Therapy*, 2nd ed. Thousand Oaks, CA: Sage, 2005.

THE NARRATIVE THERAPY MODEL

Purpose.   To help clients choose to view their lives in ways that are positive and constructive rather than as negative and dominated by problems and shortcomings.

Application.   In recent years, narrative therapy has become increasingly attractive to many social workers providing therapeutic services. The concepts and techniques of narrative therapy are used in work with individuals, families, and small groups.

Description.   At the heart of this approach is the observation that individuals and families construct stories about who they are, about their lives, and about why things are the way they are. These narratives or interpretations help people make sense of their life experiences. In a certain sense, people construct their own "reality." They are the "makers of meaning" and, in turn, react to the meanings, beliefs, and stories they have constructed.

Kelly (2002, p. 121) explains that these stories or narratives or interpretations of one's life ". . . incorporate the dominant social and cultural stories of gender, ethnicity, and power, as well as personal stories co-constructed in interactions with others (families, friends, and professional helpers). These stories constitute the knowledge people hold about themselves and their worlds." The words we choose to describe our life and situation strongly influence whether we value and respect ourselves and other people. When stories are negative and distorted they often produce skewed attitudes, problems, and dysfunctional patterns.

The construction of one's story is strongly influenced by societal and community beliefs and values and also by themes and plots drawn from movies and pop culture. For example, and unfortunately, many people derive their ideas about and evaluations of their own marriage, parenting, children, work, and the way life should be from the images and stories they see on television.

A professional using the narrative therapy model places great emphasis on careful listening and on striving to understand the client's perceptions about his or her life and situation. Clients are helped to examine and unravel the assumptions, experiences, and interpretations on which their personal stories have been constructed and to then construct alternative interpretations and new, more positive stories that explain and shape their lives. (A reading of Items 11.5, 11.8, and 13.8 provides some insight into how a social worker might help clients examine their stories.)

A key technique in narrative therapy is termed "externalizing the problem." This is an effort to separate the person from the problem. A problem is talked about as an "opponent" and "oppressor." The client and therapist work together to "combat" the problem. A problem, not the person with a problem, is the target of change. According to Walsh (2006, p. 256), the goals of the process are to:

- Awaken the client from a problematic pattern of living.
- Liberate the client from externally imposed constraints and conditions.
- Help the client create or author stories of personal dignity and competence.
- Recruit supportive others to serve as audiences to the client's new life story.

In some respects, this model is similar to the strengths perspective and the solution-focused model. However, narrative therapy is different from other models in that it draws heavily on presumptions that are common to postmodern philosophy and to related ideas of constructivism and social construction. This set of beliefs questions the existence of objective reality and also doubts the usefulness of the scientific method. Thus, in contrast to most of the other practive frameworks used in social work, the narrative model does not incorporate concepts of data collection, assessment, a specification of desired outcomes, treatment plans, or evaluation. Neither does it strive to be methodical.

SUGGESTED READINGS

Brown, Catrina, and Tod Agusta-Scott. *Narrative Therapy*. Thousand Oaks, CA: Sage, 2006.

Goldenberg, Herbert and Irene Goldenberg. *Family Therapy*, 7th ed. Belmont, CA: Brooks Cole, 2008.

Kelly, Patricia. "Narrative Therapy." In *Social Workers Desk Reference*, edited by Albert Roberts and Gilbert Greene. New York: Oxford University, 2002.

Walsh, Joseph. *Theories for Direct Social Work Practice*. Belmont, CA: Brooks/Cole, 2006.

PRACTICE BASED ON THE FAMILY THERAPIES

Purpose.   To improve the social functioning of families by working with the family as a system and changing the interactions among family members.

Application.   Prerequisite to the use of the various family therapies are family members who have at least a minimum level of concern for each other and want to preserve or strengthen their families. At least some of the members should be voluntary clients, although it is expected that others will have been coerced into participation by more powerful family members.

Description.   Within this broad framework, there are numerous theories and models that have much in common: The family system is the unit of attention, all or most family members are engaged in the change process, focus is on the interaction of members within the family system, emphasis is on current behavior (here and now), and active techniques are employed (e.g., family sculpture, role-play, homework, etc.). The differences between the approaches are mostly a matter of emphasizing certain concepts and procedures over others. The practitioner of family therapy must be eclectic. In order to illustrate how work with families might differ from one practitioner to another, a few of the key assumptions associated with commonly used approaches are presented.

The *communications approach* presumes that family problems are caused mostly by faulty communication. Change occurs when family members learn to really listen to each other and express themselves openly and honestly. The practitioner models forthright communication and uses various experiential exercises to help family members express themselves.

As suggested by its name, the *structural approach* focuses primarily on a family's structures. Special attention is given to the delineation and interaction of the spousal, parental, and sibling subsystems and their interaction. Unhealthy alliances and splits among these subsystems and either overly rigid or overly flexible boundaries are major sources of family dysfunction. Change occurs when the roles and responsibilities of the family's members and the subsystems are clarified and agreed to by all.

The *family systems approach* focuses on the struggle of family members to simultaneously be a part of a family group and be individuals apart from the family.

Problems arise when an individual either suppresses the self and is overly involved (enmeshed) with his or her family or, at the other extreme, rejects his or her family connection. This approach also recognizes the tendency of a family to repeat patterns established in prior generations (i.e., the intergenerational transmission of dysfunction) and is sensitive to issues related to the family life cycle.

The **strategic family therapy** approach gives primary attention to family rules (the often unstated family beliefs about how family members should think and behave) and to the distribution and use of power. The word *strategic* connotes an active and directive role by the therapist in strategically selecting interventions that move the family toward a pattern of behavior deemed desirable by the therapist.

A model termed the **social learning approach** draws its concepts and techniques from behavior therapy and behavior modification. It presumes that family conflicts and problems arise because the members have not learned basic skills such as communication and conflict resolution, and/or that appropriate behavior is not reinforced within the family system. Thus, the practitioner places much emphasis on teaching. *Functional family therapy* resembles the social learning approach but also examines the social context of family problems and the function served by problem behaviors. Problem behaviors are viewed as unsuccessful efforts by family members to cope with issues of dependence versus independence, freedom versus control, and intimacy versus distance.

The **narrative approach** to working with families focuses on the personal and family stories and anecdotes that family members use as frames of reference when they explain and interpret their own lives, situations, and problems. People also use the stories embedded in a community and culture (e.g., fables, novels, biographies, movies, etc.) to make sense of their own life experiences. Special questioning techniques are used to help family members reexamine the way they think about themselves and to help them construct alternative stories and interpretations that lead to new patterns of interaction. (See section on Narrative Therapy in this chapter.)

As is true of psychotherapy in general, most approaches to family therapy developed out of work with middle-class and upper-class families. They may not work as well with families that are economically poor or members of a minority group. Social workers are challenged to select approaches that can be adapted to agency-based practice and their profession's emphasis on social functioning and the person-in-environmental construct. To help them make that selection, Kilpatrick and Holland (2006) offer a practical **integrative model** that ties the use of various approaches or types of family interventions to four levels of family need and functioning. Consequently, the recommended approach for a family that is struggling with meeting basic needs (food, safety, equality, etc.) is different from the approaches recommended for the family having problems around issues of unclear boundaries or a lack of intimacy in family relationships. (For additional information on work with families, see Items 11.2, 11.9, 12.8, and 13.13.)

SUGGESTED READINGS

Becvar, Dorothy, and Raphael Becvar. *Family Therapy*, 6th ed. Boston: Allyn & Bacon, 2006.

Collins, Donald, Catheleen Jordan, and Heather Coleman. *An Introduction to Family Social Work*, 2nd ed. Belmont, CA: Brooks/Cole, 2007.

Janszen, Curtis, and Catheleen Jordan. *Family Treatment*. 4th ed. Belmont, CA: Brooks/Cole, 2006.

Nichols, Michael, and Richard Schwartz. *Essentials of Family Therapy*, 3rd ed. Boston: Allyn and Bacon, 2007.

PRACTICE BASED ON SMALL-GROUP THEORIES

Purpose.   To improve the social functioning of individuals or couples through participation in a small-group experience under the guidance of a professional.

Application.   The client must be willing to participate in discussions and small-group activities and behave in ways that do not disrupt the group or harm other members. Group experiences can be designed for a number of purposes (e.g., training, therapy, mutual support, social action, etc.). A skillful group leader will be able to engage clients who are nonvoluntary participants.

Description.   Work with groups occurs in a variety of settings for a multitude of purposes. Although there are some differences in approach, these differences are usually a matter of emphasis, rather than in terms of fundamental concepts and skills. The differences are related to the purpose of the group (e.g., a task group versus a treatment group); the role assumed by the professional (e.g., group leader, therapist, teacher, mediator, or facilitator); and whether attention is focused mostly on the behavior of the individuals that make up the group or mostly on the functioning of the group as a social system. Numerous small-group-related orienting theories provide social workers with background knowledge on such dimensions as group leadership, goals, structure and norms, group cohesion, conflict, stages of group development, and intragroup communication. For purposes of illustration, it is useful to identify some of the ways in which work with groups may differ and a few of the frameworks that influence practice.

Task groups are common to practice when providing indirect services. These goal-oriented groups tend to be quite structured and formal. Examples include agency boards, committees, staff meetings, and community planning groups. Such groups are characterized by the use of a written agenda, *Robert's Rules of Order*, and clear assignments of leadership roles and member responsibilities.

The *interactional model*, or mediating model, places the social worker in the role of a mediator between members of the group and between the group and its environment, including the agency that has sanctioned the group's formation. This approach places a high value on client self-determination.

The *group treatment approach* views the group as a therapeutic environment and a behavior-changing influence on its members. The focus is mostly on the members as individuals and on the problems they are having outside the group. However, a client's behavior within the group may be used as a way of assessing and illustrating his or her attitudes and behavioral patterns. In these groups, the social worker assumes the role of a therapist, expert, and group leader. In some groups, such as those used in the treatment of sex offenders and persons addicted to alcohol or drugs, there is heavy use of confrontation and members are required to complete assigned home-work and strictly adhere to established rules. In such groups, self-determination is not a priority.

In many agency settings, groups are used to promote normal growth and develop-ment and the learning of ordinary skills for living rather than for the purpose of coping with serious problems or correcting dysfunctional behavior. Many of the groups that are part of the YMCA/YWCA programs, summer camps, after-school programs, and senior citizen programs are of this type. These groups make use of the ***developmental approach***. The worker typically assumes the role of leader, planner, and arranger of group activities and makes heavy use of programming (see Item 13.23).

When groups are used for the purpose of ***teaching and training***, they are goal oriented and the worker assumes the roles of leader and teacher. Depending on the topic being addressed (e.g., parent training, learning communications skills, learning job skills, learning about a medical condition, etc.) and the number of times the group will meet, there may or may not be an emphasis on member interaction, build-ing trust, and developing a sense of belonging to the group.

A number of theoretical influences from outside the social work profession have had an impact on how social workers approach their practice with groups and, of course, also with individuals and families. These include *Gestalt therapy, transac-tional analysis, encounter groups, psychodrama, behavior modification,* and *positive peer culture.* (For additional information on group work, see Items 11.10, 11.22, 12.9, 13.22, and 13.27.)

SUGGESTED READINGS

Fatout, Marian, and Steven Rose. *Task Groups in Social Services.* Thousand Oaks, CA: Sage, 1995.

Garvin, Charles, Maeda Galinsky, and Lorraine Gutierrez. *Handbook of Social Work with Groups.* New York: Guilford, 2004.

Greif, Geoffrey, and Paul Ephross, eds. *Group Work with Populations at Risk,* 2nd ed. New York: Oxford University Press, 2004.

Toseland, Ronald, and Robert Rivas. *An Introduction to Group Work Practice,* 5th ed. Boston: Allyn & Bacon, 2005.

MODELS FOR CHANGING ORGANIZATIONS

Purpose.   To change the functioning of a human services agency in order to increase its ability to address the needs and concerns of its clients and staff.

Application.   Various models of organizational development and change can be used with both private and public agencies. An organizational change effort may be the result of a carefully articulated process to analyze agency functioning and establish a plan for incrementally making needed changes (i.e., *strategic planning*), or it may stem from concerns by staff members and/or clients that some problem in agency functioning must be repaired. In either case, the change effort will typically involve the agency's top administrative staff, the agency's board of directors in the case of a private agency, and in the case of a public agency, certain elected officials and legislative committees.

Description.   The complexity of organizational change becomes evident when one recognizes that organizations are made up of numerous individuals, each with a unique personality and each with numerous roles and tasks to perform; a set of formal and informal structures, procedures, and norms; and a set of power and authority relationships. Moreover, an organization is a legal entity whose purpose and functioning is tied to a charter and bylaws or to certain legislation, in the case of a public or governmental organization. Every organization is shaped by its financial resources and all must function within an ever-changing social, political, and economic environment.

Every social worker employed by an organization, regardless of position, must give some attention to how well it is functioning. A social agency, for example, must operate in an effective and efficient manner if it is to provide appropriate services and continue to receive the funding it needs to achieve its goals. As one moves from line worker to supervisor or middle manager, or to agency administrator, the responsibility to engage in organizational maintenance and change activities increases. The activities at any level, however, may include informing upper-level administrators of staff concerns and client needs, proposing specific changes in agency policies and procedures, arranging input from consultants, participating on committees to study specific aspects of the organization's performance, conducting program evaluations, and so on.

The selection of a method or an approach to planned organizational change will depend on the organization's culture regarding its nature and functioning. Descriptions of an organization's culture are usually drawn from three conceptual models. The ***rational model*** assumes that those who are part of the organization are in agreement about its goals and committed to those goals. Thus, an organization is primarily a way of structuring the work that needs to occur in order to reach a goal. Given that view, proposed changes (e.g., restructuring, personal assignments, adoption of new technologies, reallocation of resources, etc.) will be accepted if it becomes apparent that they would improve the organization's capacity to achieve its goals. Change, therefore, results from such activities as self-study, obtaining the advice of consultants, examining the complaints or suggestions made by clients or consumers, in-service training on new technologies, and so forth.

The ***natural-system model*** views an organization as a system made up of a multitude of individuals, roles, subsystems, and formal and informal processes striving to function and survive in a wider social environment. It recognizes that the personnel of an organization can be easily distracted from the organization's official mission by such things as job stress, unclear work assignments, and disagreements over duties and responsibilities. This model views an organization as needing to balance its goal achievement with maintenance functions. Change efforts emphasize the clarification of goals and objectives, improving communication, recognizing and addressing the social and emotional needs of personnel, morale building, and the like.

The ***power-politics model*** assumes that an organization is essentially a political arena in which various individuals, departments, and other units compete for power, resources, and personal advantage. Consequently, the achievement of the organization's official or stated goals may take a backseat to other agendas. To change such an organization, one needs access to persons in positions of influence over the organization and must be able to persuade those within the organization that a specific change is in their self-interest. External forces such as media exposure, investigations by citizen groups, legislative oversight, and lawsuits might be necessary for modifying organizations.

There are five fundamental approaches a social worker might adopt for generating change in a human services organization. The ***policy approach*** achieves change by developing and adopting new policies that will guide the organization and its operation. Those working for change direct their efforts toward the groups and individuals who are authorized to make policy and allocate resources at either the local, state, or national level. They provide these decision makers with data and new insights concerning a specific condition, problem, need, or issue, and advocate for a specific policy change.

The ***program approach*** seeks to change the organization by designing and introducing new or additional programs and services to better express and implement existing policy. Change efforts are directed primarily at people in administrative and managerial positions (i.e., those who have authority to modify specific programs and alter the procedures and technology used to carry out the work of the organization).

The ***project approach*** introduces change at the interface between line staff and the clients or consumers of the organization's services. Small-scale projects are used to try out or demonstrate new ways of working with agency clients. Policies and programs remain the same but staff skills and performance are enhanced. Change efforts often take the form of in-service training and increasing sensitivity to clients' needs and behavior.

An approach known as ***client-centered management*** focuses attention on the relationship between managerial behaviors and client outcomes. It is predicated on the belief that an excessive emphasis on powerful decision makers, funding bodies, interagency communication, and personnel issues has diverted the attention of administrators from their primary purpose—assuring that the social agency provides high-quality services that truly respond to client needs. This approach strives to secure client input into agency decision making and planning (see Item 14.10).

The ***teamwork model*** is primarily concerned with the manner in which workers interact to implement agency programs. It is based on two premises. First, it recognizes that the typical bureaucratic organization places excessive control in the hands of administrators, which, in turn, reduces innovation and consensus among workers about how best to provide services. Second, it recognizes that given the explosion of knowledge and technology, specialization is increasingly required in almost every occupation. But with specialization comes the need for better coordination. The providers of human services must be especially able to coordinate practice activities since services to clients are often provided simultaneously by several disciplines and several different agencies. Unfortunately, the typical department structure used in many agencies may erect barriers to coordination because the lines of communication and decision making are organized by profession, role, and job title, rather than by the need for an integrated approach to service delivery.

The teamwork approach has proven especially useful as a means of retaining the specialized knowledge and competencies of the several helping professions, and at the same time coordinating their practice activities. To make multidisciplinary teams viable working units, they are given the authority to plan and implement programs and to make decisions about the personnel and resources necessary to carry out their assignments. In this process, the teams become powerful forces for innovation and policy and program change.

SUGGESTED READINGS

Gibelman, Margaret. *Navigating Human Service Organizations*, Chicago: Lyceum, 2003.

Netting, Ellen F., and Mary K. O'Connor. *Organization Practice: A Social Worker's Guide to Understanding Human Services*. Boston: Allyn and Bacon, 2003.

Poertner, John, and Charles A. Rapp. *Textbook of Social Administration: The Consumer-Centered Approach*, New York: Haworth Press, 2007.

MODELS FOR CHANGING COMMUNITIES

Purpose.   To improve the functioning of a community and increase its capacity to address the social needs and concerns of its members.

Application.   Whenever community change is being considered, it is important to recognize that the word *community* can be defined in several ways. For example, a community might be defined as the people who live in a particular geographical area (e.g., neighborhood, town, or city) or the word community might be applied to the people who share a common interest, focus, or concern (e.g., people who are working to protect the environment or those who share a particular religious orientation.) The selection of a particular approach to community change must be based on an assessment of the problem or concern targeted for change and, to a large extent, on political factors. If the social worker has the authority, responsibility, and/or support of others to work toward a specific community change, his or her efforts will most likely succeed. Yet even under the best circumstances, community change is a slow and difficult process.

Description.   Social work embraces three models of community practice, and each rests on a different set of assumptions concerning how community is defined, the change process to be followed, and the role of the professional. The three models are locality development, social planning, and social action.

The ***locality development model*** (or community development) presupposes that the community consists of people who share a sense of belonging to their local area and can reach a consensus on the nature of community problems and what should be done about them. It emphasizes broad citizen participation, sharing of ideas, democratic decision making, cooperative problem solving, and self-help. In the process of working on problems, people learn the practical and leadership skills needed to tackle other concerns of the community. In performing most community-level social work practice (including activities connected to federated fund-raising, coalitions of human services organizations, ad hoc task forces, and neighborhood organizations), the professional performs such functions as enabling, facilitating, coordinating, and teaching.

The model known as *social planning* focuses on specific social problems (i.e., crime, inadequate housing, lack of health care, etc.) and the response of the human services delivery system to these problems. It recognizes the complex legal, economic, and political factors that must be addressed in solving a major community problem. Although involvement by ordinary citizens is welcome, the key to community problem solving and change is involvement by influential persons, government officials, and organizations that have authority, power, and influence. This approach also recognizes the vertical dimension in community dynamics and therefore the need to involve influential persons and organizations from outside the immediate locality such as state and federal government agencies, as well as major national corporations that do business in the community. The social worker using this approach gives much attention to fact gathering, data analysis, policy analysis, sharing technical information, and program planning.

The third model, *social action*, is usually associated with efforts to correct a social injustice or achieve a needed change for a devalued or disadvantaged group (e.g., those living in poverty, those who suffer discrimination, etc.). It views a community as consisting of diverse groups and special interests that are competing for power and limited resources. Thus, in order to bring about a change in human services programs, there must be a shift in the decisions of those who exercise power and influence—or new decision makers must be given authority to take action. Since it is assumed that those in control will not easily relinquish their power, change requires confrontation with those who have power. The functions of the professional within this model include those of organizing, advocating, and negotiating.

SUGGESTED READINGS

Eichler, Mike. *Consensus Organizing: Building Communities of Mutual Self Interest*. Thousand Oaks, CA: Sage, 2007.

Hardcastle, David, Stanley Wenocur, and Patricia Powers. *Community Practice: Theories and Skills for Social Workers*, 2nd ed. New York: Oxford University Press, 2004.

Kirst-Ashman, Karen, and Grafton Hull. *Generalist Practice with Organizations and Communities*, 3rd ed. Belmont, CA: Brooks/Cole, 2006.

Weil, Marie. *The Handbook of Community Practice*. Thousand Oaks, CA: Sage, 2005.

CONCLUSION

As suggested by this survey of conceptual frameworks, the intervention approaches used by social workers have similarities but may differ in what they emphasize. Some differ in terms of basic assumptions about how and why change occurs (see Chapter 7 for additional ideas about the nature of change) and others differ in the characteristics of the clients they are intended to serve. A lifelong activity of the social worker is to carefully select a configuration of perspectives, theories, and models that matches his or her practice style and best meets the needs of his or her clients.

The reader is reminded that no one approach is always superior to others and that a social worker needs to have a basic understanding of several. One's practice framework might include multiple perspectives and an ever-growing repertoire of practice theories and models. Since all frameworks are concerned with helping people change, the worker must always be cognizant of the whole person—humans are thinking, feeling, and behaving biological beings whose survival, growth, and development depend on constant interaction with others and their environment.

SELECTED BIBLIOGRAPHY

Allen-Meares, Paula, and Charles Garvin. *Handbook of Social Work Direct Practice*. Thousand Oaks, CA: Sage, 2000.

Brandell, Jerrold, ed. *Theory and Practice in Clinical Social Work*. New York: Free Press, 1997.

Corsini, Raymond, and Danny Wedding. *Current Psychotherapies*, 7th ed. Belmont, CA: Brooks/Cole, 2005.

Dorfman, Rachelle, ed. *Paradigms of Clinical Social Work*, vol. 1. New York: Brunner/Mazel, 1994.

———, ed. *Paradigms of Clinical Social Work*, vol. 2. New York: Brunner/Mazel, 1998.

Encyclopedia of Social Work, 19th ed., edited by Richard L. Edwards. Washington, DC: NASW, 1995.

Forte, James. *Human Behavior and the Social Environment*. Belmont, CA: Brooks/Cole, 2007.

Gilliland, Burl, and Richard James. *Theories and Strategies in Counseling and Psychotherapy*, 5th ed. Boston: Allyn & Bacon, 2003.

Greene, Roberta. *Human Behavior Theory and Social Work Practice*, 2nd ed. New York: Aldine de Gruyter, 1999.

Kilpatrick, Allie, and Thomas Holland. *Working with Families: An Integrative Model by Level of Functioning*, 4th ed. Boston: Allyn & Bacon, 2006.

Lehmann, Peter, and Nick Coady. *Theoretical Perspectives for Direct Social Work Practice*. New York: Springer, 2000.

Payne, Malcolm. *Modern Social Work Theory*, 3rd ed. Chicago: Lyceum Books, 2005.

Prochaska, James, and John Norcross. *Systems of Psychotherapy*, 6th ed. Belmont, CA: Brooks/Cole, 2007.

Roberts, Albert, and Gilbert Greene, eds. *Social Workers' Desk Reference*. New York: Oxford Press, 2002.

Rothman, Jack. "Approaches to Community Intervention." In *Strategies of Community Intervention*, 6th ed., edited by Jack Rothman, John Erlich, and John Tropman, 27–64. Itasca, IL: F. E. Peacock, 2001.

Schatz, Mona S., Lowell E. Jenkins, and Bradford W. Sheafor. "Milford Redefined: A Model of Initial and Advanced Generalist Social Work." *Journal of Social Work Education* 26 (Fall 1990): 217–231.

Smith, Robert. *Elements of Ecology*. New York: Harper & Row, 1986.

Sommers-Flanagan, John, and Rita Sommer-Flanagan. *Counseling and Psychotherapy Theories in Context and Practice*. Hoboken, NJ: John Wiley and Sons, 2004.

Turner, Francis. "Psychosocial Therapy." In *Paradigms of Clinical Social Work*, edited by Rashelle Dorfman. New York: Brunner/Mazel, 1988.

———, ed. *Social Work Treatment: Interlocking Theoretical Approaches*, 4th ed. New York: Free Press, 1996.

Walsh, Joseph. *Theories of Direct Practice*. Belmont, CA: Brooks/Cole, 2006.

7 Using Evidence to Guide the Change Process

The admonition that the social worker should "Guide the process, not the client" is fundamental to effective professional practice, yet perhaps oversimplifies the complexity of guiding the change process. One must first fully understand the client situation, help the client identify the change needed, engage the client in efforts to bring about that change, and, finally, evaluate the success of the change effort. To perform these tasks, the social worker must carefully consider available knowledge and intervention strategies, engage in critical thinking about the application of the knowledge to the practice situation, and guide the client through the often difficult process of changing.

■ EVIDENCE-BASED PRACTICE

Increasingly, social work and other helping professions are emphasizing ***evidence-based practice***, a term suggesting that the practitioner is to draw upon the strongest documented information to guide his or her practice-related judgments and decisions. This approach or way of thinking about practice seeks to identify and utilize those treatments or interventions that are indeed effective and also to identify and end the use of those that are ineffective or cause harm. Such an orientation enhances and expands the scientific basis of practice and is consistent with the NASW Code of Ethics (1999), which states: "Social workers should base practice on recognized knowledge, including empirically based knowledge, relevant to social work and social work ethics" (Section 4.01c, p. 22). This approach calls on social workers to critically examine and evaluate their own practice, keep current on the professional literature, and remain open to the implications of new research, especially research findings on the effectiveness of various interventions.

In times past, many social workers assumed that their good intentions, compassion, common sense, and adherence to core social work values were sufficient to bring about desired changes. We now recognize that something more is required. Research tells us that some approaches and interventions are more effective than others; some approaches are ineffective; and some are even harmful. Clients deserve social workers who will think critically about their practice-related beliefs and assumptions and will search for and apply procedures and interventions that have been evaluated and found effective.

Given their heavy caseloads and the demands placed on their time, social workers can easily find rationalizations and excuses for not spending time searching professional journals, textbooks, and the Internet for information that can guide their practice. But all too often, those excuses provide only a short respite from the time crunch and, in the long run, often create added time pressures because the most effective assessments and interventions were not applied to the client's situation and, as a result, the client's concerns or problems continue to occupy the worker's time.

Because many client situations are unique and highly complex, not all social work practice can or should be based only on professional literature. Indeed, many decisions and actions must be based primarily on professional values, ethics, legal statutes, agency policy, and court orders. Moreover, practice-related decisions must always consider such factors as the client's personal preferences and values and special circumstances. But, to the extent possible, social workers must strive to base their practice on a body of evidence. When the professional literature does not offer the guidance sought, the best available evidence will be a consensus reached by experienced professionals. The demands of evidence-based practice can be made less burdensome if the worker is selective in deciding when to examine the evidentiary support for certain procedures, interventions, or approaches. For most social workers, evidence-based practice will take the form of evidence-based assessment, evidence-based intervention, and/or evidence-based evaluation.

In an *evidence-based assessment* the social worker seeks out and makes use of theory and research data that will expand his or her understanding of the practice situation. Two sets of data are utilized; one focuses on the client's specific condition or problem while the other focuses on the client group or population being served.

As part of one's educational preparation for social work practice, the courses that fall under the heading of "human behavior and the social environment" provide general knowledge about the behavior and functioning of individuals, families, groups, and communities. Although this information is typically extensive, it usually does not provide enough depth to adequately inform or guide interventions related to a client's particular condition or problem. Thus, the worker must search the literature for more specific information to better understand, for example, the implications for a family if a child is diagnosed with Down syndrome, or if an older parent is exhibiting signs of dementia, or perhaps if a couple is experiencing sexual dysfunction.

Another aspect of evidence-based assessment seeks to learn more about the client group or client population being served. For example, if the worker's client is an adolescent, what does the worker need to know about adolescence as a stage in human development? When working with a client who is a member of a minority or a devalued group, the worker may want a better understanding of what it is like to experience discrimination. Or the worker may need to find information about the religion that plays a big part in a specific client's life and decisions.

Fortunately, much information on various human problems, illness, disabling conditions, social problems, and various population groups is now available online, and various search engines (see Item 9.4) provide links and easy access to relevant websites. Additional sources are, of course, social work journals, textbooks, and documents published by organizations that focus on particular conditions, social problems, and issues.

Evidence-based practice also involves drawing on the most substantial information available about how to help the client change the situation, i.e., *evidence-based intervention*. Chapter 6 contains short descriptions of a number of commonly used intervention approaches; a social worker might select one or more of these approaches, depending on the specific client situation. But how does one decide which approach is most appropriate? To answer that question, the professions are beginning to engage in "best practices" research, in which the available evidence is carefully scrutinized in relation to success rates when different approaches are applied to specific client conditions or specific client populations. Best practices research typically begins with a key word search around the intervention being assessed and usually involves identifying a large number of articles. These articles are then screened to a smaller number by maintaining in the pool for study only those that empirically evaluate the effectiveness of the intervention. The articles or research reports making the final cut are then subjected to a rigorous protocol by which a panel of experts rates each study on the quality of evidence for answering such questions as:

- How would you rate the alignment of the intervention to commonly held ideas regarding this intervention approach?
- How would you rate the replicability of the intervention approach?
- How would you rate the adequacy of the outcome measures used?
- How broadly was the intervention tested statistically across important populations that might be served?
- How adequate were the controls placed on the manner in which the intervention approach was applied to the clients in the study?

Through this filtering process relatively few studies typically meet the rigor of providing sufficient evidence of the effectiveness of the intervention approach relative to the client conditions analyzed. Where these studies agree, best practices are identified. The Campbell Collaboration is a good source for current best practices conclusions relative to social work (http://www.campbellcollaboration.org/SWCG/titles.asp).

The growing need for empirical evidence related to the outcomes of social work interventions has generated an interest in *evidence-based evaluation*. In part this is a response to those who demand that social workers provide evidence to support their recommendations and requests. For example, a managed care organization may refuse to pay for client services unless the social worker offers evidence that a particular intervention is both appropriate and effective. Increasingly, social workers must clearly describe the changes or outcomes that they anticipate from the application of a specific intervention. Moreover social workers must be able to empirically measure these changes, a topic addressed in Chapter 14.

■ CRITICAL THINKING WHEN MAKING PRACTICE DECISIONS

The social worker's skills in critical thinking are also essential for successful practice outcomes. *Critical thinking* involves consciously thinking about how we arrive at our decisions and conclusions. The skills of critical thinking include the following:

- Clarifying and defining key terms and concepts and using them in a consistent manner
- Determining the credibility of an information source
- Differentiating relevant from irrelevant information
- Distinguishing between verifiable and unverifiable claims and statements
- Checking the accuracy of a statement or claim
- Recognizing proper and improper use of statistics
- Separating thoughts and logic from emotions and feelings
- Identifying biased, ambiguous, irrelevant, and deceptive arguments
- Recognizing logical fallacies and inconsistencies in an argument or line of reasoning
- Reaching conclusions about the overall strength of an argument or conclusion

Critical thinking is especially important in social work because all people develop systems of beliefs or bundles of ideas that they draw upon to interpret new experiences. While such frames of reference or conceptual maps are necessary to human thought and reasoning, they are also a potential source of errors, bias, and distortion. A critical thinker, however, recognizes that all ideas (e.g., concepts, theories, definitions) are essentially inventions constructed to describe and explain our understandings and judgments at a particular point in time. Critical thinking requires recognition that these inventions may not represent "truth" about the topic, are invariably incomplete, and are likely to shift as we have new experiences or acquire more information.

Critical thinking requires an ability to distinguish between a fact, an assumption, an opinion, and a value. A *fact* is a statement of what is or of what happened that can be independently verified by empirical means. A fact is more or less solid, depending on how easily it can be confirmed. An *assumption* is an idea that is taken for granted or presumed for the sake of making an argument but is recognized as possibly untrue or inaccurate. An *opinion* puts forward one particular interpretation or viewpoint when it is understood that other credible interpretations are also possible. A useful opinion has some factual basis, is rooted in extensive experience, and is derived from careful judgment. A *value* is a strongly held belief concerning what is truly worthwhile, right or wrong, and the way things are supposed to be.

In our efforts to think clearly, it is also useful to distinguish between information, knowledge, and wisdom. The term *information* refers to a more or less random collection of concepts, facts, and opinions. *Knowledge* refers to an orderly and coherent arrangement of relevant and trustworthy information related to a specific topic. The term *wisdom* refers to a higher level of knowledge that has a truly lasting quality. Typically, wisdom is a distillation of key ideas and principles drawn from a broad base of knowledge, a careful and in-depth examination, and many years of practical experience. These distinctions help us realize that a person can possess much information but lack real knowledge. Also, a person can be very knowledgeable on a topic but lack wisdom.

The critical thinker is aware of his or her capacity for self-deception. All too often, we believe what we want to believe and what is convenient and comfortable for us to believe. We tend to ignore facts and ideas that do not fit with our expectations. We often hold tightly to whatever we believe even in the face of evidence to the contrary. Another aspect of our capacity for self-deception is our tendency to find what we are looking for. When we want support for our ideas, positions, and personal agenda, we usually find it. Moreover, we tend to look harder for evidence that supports our views than for evidence that refutes it.

An important dynamic giving rise to uncritical thinking is our desire to be right and to have others believe we are right. That is why we so often become defensive when our beliefs are questioned. The more fragile our self-esteem, the more likely we are to be threatened by new ideas; the more likely we are also to uncritically accept ideas proposed by others.

To think critically about a claim or assertion one should consider the following:

Purpose
- Who is making this claim? How reliable and trustworthy are these individuals or sources?
- Why do those making the claim or assertion want me to believe it?
- What motives or circumstances might cause them to make erroneous claims?
- Do they have something to gain from my acceptance of this claim or assertion?
- Am I attracted to this argument or claim because I want to believe it or perhaps because it meets some emotional need?

Evidence
- Are the terms used to present the claim clearly defined and explained?
- Is the claim or assertion rooted in facts? Opinion? Values? Ideology?
- Does the claim or assertion recognize the complexity of the matter being considered, or is it based on an oversimplification or superficial understanding of the topic?
- Are the facts and figures used to support the argument correct and complete? Have relevant facts been omitted or distorted?

Interpretation
- Could the facts and figures be interpreted in other ways or assigned different meanings?
- Have irrelevant and extraneous facts been added to the argument in order to create confusion or divert the focus from the central question?
- Has the claim or assertion been framed or stated in a way that allows it to be subjected to independent verification, objective observation, and scientific study?

- Has the claim been subjected to careful studies? Were the studies as free as possible from bias? Have the studies been replicated? Has the claim been tested in experimental studies?

Critical thinking and a search of the literature for best practices are especially important when an unconventional intervention (such as rebirthing or conscious energy breathing, aroma therapy, crystal therapy) has been requested or suggested for use in a particular case situation. A social worker must first decide if this is a valid approach and make an informed judgment about its effectiveness and the risk of this approach for the client—and the social worker. A social worker is more vulnerable to a malpractice suit if he or she is unable to demonstrate that an intervention or treatment is the one most effective and appropriate to the client's problem or situation (see Item 16.6). Reamer (2005) suggests that a social worker should follow the *procedural standard of care* guidelines to help consider the ethical and legal implications of selecting such intervention approaches. He notes that this includes "eight key elements: 1) consulting colleagues; 2) obtaining proper informed consent; 3) obtaining proper supervision; 4) reviewing relevant ethical standards; 5) reviewing relevant regulations, laws, and policies; 6) reviewing relevant literature; 7) obtaining legal consultation when necessary; and 8) documenting and evaluating decision-making steps" (p. 194).

■ GUIDING THE PLANNED CHANGE PROCESS

Change is inevitable. Humans and all of the social systems created by humans are constantly adjusting and adapting within their ever-changing environments. Many of the changes experienced by individuals and families are set in motion by the natural consequences of biological maturation and aging, and also by personal choices such as selecting a certain occupation, taking a specific job, choosing a particular person as a spouse or partner, raising children, or getting a divorce. Still other changes are imposed on people by illness, accidents, natural disasters, and even world events such as wars and shifts in the economy. These events and experiences change the way people think, feel, and behave, and they may constrict or expand their choices and opportunities.

Although many of the changes experienced by individuals, families, groups, and organizations are unplanned, unintended, and unwelcome, others are deliberately chosen and achieved through individual and group effort. These can be termed *planned changes*. Within social work, professional efforts to help clients bring about a planned change are called *interventions*. Interventions are designed to alter some specified condition, pattern of behavior, or set of circumstances in an effort to improve a client's social functioning or well-being.

An intervention or a planned change is accurately described as a *process*: a planned series or sequence of actions directed toward the achievement of a specific end. However, the use of the word process should not be interpreted to mean that the change effort, once begun and underway, will naturally unfold and proceed on a predictable path toward its goal. Quite the opposite is usually true. Given the complexity of change, change efforts can easily come apart, and movement toward a goal can easily be derailed.

In some ways, a planned change is similar to a scientific experiment: Based on knowledge and a working hypothesis, the social worker takes certain steps and then monitors the effects to determine what, if any, change has occurred. However, an intervention will usually have both expected and unexpected outcomes.

Change—even if wanted and planned—is often difficult to achieve and requires time and effort. Consequently, some degree of reluctance and conflict, accompanied by emotion, can be expected during periods of change. The social worker who is helping others make a change must be ready to address these conflicts and be comfortable with the client's expressions of fear, frustration, and anxiety.

Resistance to change is also a characteristic of humans and their social systems. People tend toward preserving the status quo. They resist change, particularly if it is rapid or especially upsetting to familiar patterns. The social worker must anticipate and be prepared to deal with resistance, even in a case where the client has demonstrated a strong desire to change.

Closely related to resistance is *ambivalence*, which is a condition of both wanting and not wanting a particular change. For example, an abused wife may want to leave her abusing husband in order to escape the abuse but at the same time not want to risk the loss of the financial security she has while married. Such a client is pulled in opposite directions and may become immobilized and unable to make decisions or take action to change the situation.

Helping clients sort through their perceptions of the *risks and rewards* associated with change is another important social work activity. If the potential rewards far outweigh the risks, most clients will attempt the change. On the other hand, if the change involves high risk or promises few or uncertain rewards, many clients will be reluctant to work toward change.

Success in making change is largely a function of the client's motivation to change, capacity for change, and opportunity to change. *Motivation*, which can be viewed as a state of readiness to take action, represents the balance of the pull of hope and the push of discomfort. Clients will work and struggle toward a desired change if they believe this change is truly possible (i.e., the pull of hope) and if they are dissatisfied or distressed with their current situation (i.e., the push of discomfort). A client can be highly motivated toward one action while having little or no motivation toward another. Moreover, a person's level of motivation varies over time and from one social context to another. Thus, a meaningful and useful description of a client's motivation must be tied to some specified goal or action rather than being viewed as a personal trait or characteristic.

One's *capacity* for change can be thought of as the various abilities and resources that clients or other people in the clients' environment bring to the change process. These capacities include time, energy, knowledge, experience, self-discipline, optimism, self-confidence, communication skills, problem-solving skills, money, political power, and so on. Different types of change require different capacities. For example, the capacities needed by someone to perform successfully as a participant in a therapy group may be significantly different from those needed to communicate effectively with his or her teenaged son and different still from those needed to adjust to the limitations of a chronic illness.

Change further requires *opportunities*—that is, various conditions and circumstances within the client's immediate environment that invite and support positive change. For example, consider the situation of a young man on probation who wants to find a job and stay out of trouble. His environment consists of his family, peer group, neighborhood, law-enforcement agencies, and so on, that will influence his ability to bring about the desired change. His opportunity for change may also be affected by community attitudes, the availability of jobs, discrimination, and other social forces.

When a social worker becomes involved in the change process as a facilitator of planned change, he or she adds *professional resources and knowledge* to the client's motivation, capacities, and opportunities. The role of the social worker in helping people to make changes can be conceptualized as taking action and applying knowledge and skills designed to increase motivation, expand capacity, and create or uncover opportunities for change.

■ THE CONTEXT OF PLANNED CHANGE

Whether the social worker's client is an individual, a family, a group, an organization, or a community, the client's concern or problem always exists within a wider context. A multitude of social, economic, cultural, legal, and political factors are known to affect client functioning. However, many of these factors are beyond the influence of both the client and worker. Reality demands that the client and social worker narrow their focus and zero in on those aspects of the situation that can be influenced and changed.

For the purpose of further explaining the process of planned change, the term *client situation* is used here to describe that segment of the client's total existence, experience, and circumstances that are the focus of the planned change effort. *Decision making* is the activity of consciously choosing among available options. The social worker must be able to make difficult decisions—and help clients make difficult decisions—and do so with an awareness of the evidence being used to inform those decisions.

The *observed situation* (or objective situation) is the client's situation as observed by people in the client's environment and perhaps described by professionals using commonly understood terminology, categories, and classifications. By contrast, the *perceived situation* (or the subjective situation) is the situation as it is felt by and uniquely interpreted and subjectively constructed by the client. It consists of the client's hopes and fears, desires and aspirations, and it usually reflects the client's history and life experiences. The situation as perceived by the client may be significantly different from the client's observed situation as understood and interpreted by the social worker and others in the client's environment.

The importance of the client's perceived situation to the change process is recognized in the social work axiom, "Start where the client is." It is necessary for the worker to understand the client's concern and situation from the client's subjective point of view. It is this element of subjectiveness that makes it so difficult to predict how clients will respond to a given intervention.

An awareness of the contextual and situational aspects of social functioning and planned change yields several fundamental guidelines for social work practice:

- The social worker must give primary attention to the client's problem or concern as it is defined, perceived, and experienced by the client.
- The worker must focus primarily on those aspects of the situation and the client's environment that most immediately and directly affect the client.
- The intervention must address those aspects of the situation over which the client and/or the worker have some control and influence.
- The social worker must recognize the multitude of forces pushing and pulling on the client but understand that the actual impact of those forces is at least partially dependent on the client's subjective interpretation.
- The worker must be prepared to intervene at one or more levels (e.g., individual, family, organization, community, etc.), depending on the nature of the client's concern, the client's interpretation of the situation, what the client wants to do about it, and what the client can reasonably expect to be able to do about it.
- The worker must be prepared to use a variety of techniques, approaches, and services since whatever is done must make sense to the client, given his or her perceptions and interpretations of reality.

Within all client situations, there are factors and forces pushing and pulling the client toward healthy, positive, and constructive functioning. These are often called *strengths* (see Items 11.4 and 11.13). At a fundamental level, most social work approaches to planned change are efforts to encourage, guide, and build on the positive forces already at work in the client's life and, at the same time, to remove or overcome barriers that block change.

■ IDENTIFYING THE ACTORS IN PLANNED CHANGE

Efforts by a social worker or agency program to facilitate change typically involves numerous individuals, groups, and organizations. In complex situations, and especially in mezzo- and macro-level practice, dozens or even hundreds may be involved. To be effective, the social worker must be clear about the purpose and goal of each intervention and clear as to what is expected of each of the many actors in the change process. Drawing from a conceptualization proposed by Pincus and Minahan (1973, 63), we suggest the following terminology to help make needed distinctions among the various actors:

- ***Change agent system***. The social worker and the worker's agency
- ***Client system***. The person, group, or organization who has requested the social worker's or agency's services and expects to benefit from what the worker

does. (It is the client system that enters into an agreement or contract with the change agent system.)

- *Target system*. The person, group, or organization that needs to change and is targeted for change in order for the client to benefit from the intervention. (In many situations of direct practice, the client system and the target system are one and the same.)
- *Action system*. All of the people, groups, and organizations that the change agent system (e.g., the social worker) works with or through in order to influence the target system and help the client system to achieve the desired outcome.

An episode of practice typically begins with the client system and the change agent system coming together and contracting to address a particular client concern. They identify the person(s), group(s), or organization(s) that need to change and then reach out to and involve others to help facilitate the change. For example, a single mother (the client system) may approach and contract with a human services agency to receive counseling from an agency social worker (the change agent) on how to help her 10-year-old son who is withdrawn and socially isolated because he is ridiculed by schoolmates. If both the mother and child need to change, both would be target systems. If the social worker draws the child's teacher, the school principal, and the school psychologist into the helping process, these become part of the action system. If the intervention also attempts to change the behavior of the other children at school, they are also part of the target system.

■ PHASES OF THE PLANNED CHANGE PROCESS

An intervention or planned change activity typically moves through several sequential phases, with each phase building on previous ones. The uniqueness of each phase is that the social worker is focusing on a specific action, information, decision, or outcome. If the social worker is to guide the change process, he or she must become an expert regarding the tasks that must be accomplished at each phase.

Descriptions of these phases have been a part of the social work literature throughout the history of the profession. In her classic book, *Social Diagnosis* (1917), Mary Richmond described several steps necessary in helping people. Forty years later, Helen Perlman (1957) echoed the same theme when describing helping as a problem-solving process that involved three major phases: (1) beginning with **study** that would ascertain and clarify the facts of the problem, followed by (2) **diagnosis**, where the facts would be analyzed, and concluding with (3) **treatment** that involves making choices and taking actions to resolve the problem. In subsequent years, various authors divided these phases into more discrete units, described them in more detail, and demonstrated their application in a range of helping approaches and in work with client systems of various sizes. The **phases of planned change** presented here are typical of such descriptions:

- Identify, define, and describe the client's concern, troublesome situation, or problem.
- Collect additional data needed to better understand the client's concern or situation and its context.
- Assess and analyze the concern and situation and decide what needs to change, what can be changed, and how it might be changed.
- Identify and agree upon the goals and objectives (outcomes) to be achieved by the process of planned change.
- Formulate a relevant and realistic plan for reaching the goals and objectives.
- Take action based on the plan (i.e., implement the plan carry out the intervention).
- Monitor progress of the intervention and determine if it is achieving the desired outcomes and, if not, modify the plan and try again.
- Once goals and objectives have been reached, terminate the intervention and evaluate the change process to inform future practice activities.

The logical progression of these phases makes the process appear to be a linear, step-by-step of activities. In reality, change rarely proceeds in an orderly fashion; rather, it is more of a spiral, with frequent returns to prior phases for clarification or a reworking of various tasks and activities (see Figure 7.1). During each phase, the

FIGURE 7.1 | **Phases of the Planned Change Process**

Intake and Engagement	Data Collection and Assessment	Planning and Contracting	Intervention and Monitoring	Final Evaluation and Termination
Begin the relationship; identify and define the client's concern or problem; determine eligibility for service.	Gather information and "study" the problem or situation; decide what needs to change, what can be changed, and how it can be changed.	Formulate objectives; evaluate possible strategies; agree on an intervention plan; determine who will do what and by when.	Carry out the plan; monitor progress; revise the plan if it is not achieving the desired results.	Evaluate overall progress; bring the relationship to an end; give feedback to the agency about how services and programs might be improved.

worker also anticipates future phases, tasks, and activities and lays the groundwork for their completion.

At any given time, it is helpful to be clear about where the client is in the process of planned change, because the worker draws on somewhat different techniques to accomplish the tasks of each phase. What is helpful in one phase might be ineffective or even counterproductive in another. For example, it would be an error for a worker to discuss with an abusive mother her possible participation in an anger-management group (i.e., planning and contracting) when she has not yet concluded that there is something inappropriate and harmful about how she disciplines her child (i.e., data collection and assessment).

CONCLUSION

The belief that change is possible and that planned change can resolve problems or create better lives for people is embedded in Western culture and especially in U.S. society. Faith in the ability to change human interactions and social conditions is at the very heart of social work practice and is a prerequisite characteristic of effective social workers.

When engaged in guiding a planned change process, the social worker makes several important contributions. The social worker understands the whole process necessary for change and guides the client(s) through several phases, being sure that the key decisions or actions to be accomplished at each phase are indeed completed. The social worker also contributes critical insights that the client would not normally be expected to possess. This includes seeking out and engaging in evidence-based assessment—in terms of drawing on the best evidence found in the literature regarding people with the client's characteristics, evidence regarding the issues to be addressed in the practice situation, and the relationship between the two factors. In addition, the social work will have researched the "best practices" to use in that client situation (evidence-based intervention) and should be competent in using that approach or skilled in referring the client to someone who is. Finally, throughout the process the social worker must engage in critical thinking that can lead to sound decision making to improve the chances of a successful practice outcome.

The five phases of the planned change process are an important part of the structure of this book. Because the phases reflect certain activities that should be accomplished as the practice episode unfolds, it is possible to identify various practice techniques and guidelines that are most likely to be helpful in each phase. In Chapters 10 through 14 more than 100 techniques and guidelines are presented. A description of the work to be done in each phase is provided in each chapter's introduction and the various items are divided into those most likely to be used in providing services directly to clients, and those that support the indirect practice activities in which social workers are typically engaged.

SELECTED BIBLIOGRAPHY

Briggs, Harold E., and Tina L. Rzepnicki, eds. *Using Evidence in Social Work Practice*. Chicago: Lyceum, 2004.

Cournoyer, Barry R. *The Evidence-Based Social Work Skills Book*. Boston, Allyn and Bacon, 2004.

Perlman, Helen. *Social Casework: A Problem Solving Process*. Chicago: University of Chicago Press, 1957.

Pincus, Allen, and Anne Minahan. *Social Work Practice: Model and Method*. Itasca, IL: F.E. Peacock, 1973.

National Association of Social Workers. "Code of Ethics." Washington, DC: NASW, 1999. (http:\\www.naswdc.org/pubs/code/default.asp)

Reamer, Frederic G. "Nontraditional and Unorthodox Interventions in Social Work: Ethical and Legal Implications." *Families in Society: The Journal of Contemporary Social Services* 87, no. 2 (2006): 191–197.

Richmond, Mary. *Social Diagnosis*. New York: Russell Sage Foundation, 1917.

Thyer, Bruce, and John S. Wodarski, eds. *Handbook of Empirical Social Work Practice*, 2 Vols. Hoboken, NJ: John Wiley & Sons, 1998.

PART 3

Techniques Common to All Social Work Practice

The two chapters in Part III focus on techniques and guidelines basic to social work practice, regardless of agency setting or type of client served. In every practice setting, the social worker must be a skillful communicator, be able to develop relationships, know how to manage a workload, cope with job-related pressures, and continue to learn and grow as a professional person.

Chapter 8, "Basic Communication and Helping Skills," presents information on effective communication and relationship building. The chapter lays a foundation for understanding and applying the more specialized practice techniques and guidelines discussed in Parts IV and V. Although many of the examples used to illustrate these skills are drawn from direct service, most can and are applied in administrative, community organization, and social planning activities. It is assumed that those using this book have been exposed to the ideas in this chapter; however, the authors' experiences suggest that readers will appreciate this concise review.

Chapter 9, "Basic Skills for Agency Practice," is especially important to the social worker who is going into a social agency for the first time. Few new workers are adequately prepared to cope with the time pressures and paperwork they encounter. This chapter provides practical guidance on such things as time management, how to write reports, how to maintain records, and how to use information technology. The worker's ability to master these tasks often determines whether he or she can make it in social work.

8 Basic Communication and Helping Skills

INTRODUCTION

This chapter presents what might be called "the basics" of social work communication and relationship building. The focus is on generic communication and helping skills—those used with all clients, whether the client is an individual, a family, a small group, an organization, or a community.

The purpose of a social worker's interaction with a client will determine what type of relationship he or she attempts to create and, of course, the types of messages he or she will communicate to the client. A social worker providing direct services to individuals and families will strive to develop a professional relationship characterized by qualities known to positively affect the outcome of the helping process. More specifically, he or she will strive to display and communicate acceptance, empathy, personal warmth, and genuineness. Such communication will tend to be fairly informal. By contrast, the indirect-services worker—who is, for example, interacting with members of a committee, representatives of an organization, or legislators—will form relationships that are more formal and place an emphasis on communication characterized by precision, clarity, and goal directness.

Essentially, ***communication*** is a process in which one individual conveys information—either intentionally or unintentionally—to another. It exists or occurs when one person attaches meaning to the verbal or nonverbal behavior of another. Communication is a form of behavior, but not all behavior is communication; it depends on whether a person perceives a message in the words or behavior of another. Communication is primarily a receiver phenomenon; regardless of what one says in words or intends to communicate, it is the person on the receiving end that assigns meaning to those words and body movements.

It is important to recognize the complexity and limitations inherent in our efforts to communicate. Because each individual is a unique personality and has had a unique set of life experiences, he or she has developed various perceptual filters and patterns of thought that affect how messages are sent and received. Thus, one individual may notice things that others overlook, and messages that are important to one person may seem inconsequential to another.

Communication involves the use of words. We need to remember, however, that a word is but a symbol; thus, it may have somewhat different meanings to different people, depending on their belief system, life experiences, capacity of abstract thinking, and familiarity with the language being used. The words of a language have literal, or *denotative,* meanings (i.e., dictionary definitions), but they may also have implied, or *connotative,* meanings. It is important to recognize that the meaning of a word, phrase, or nonverbal gesture may change according to who is using it and the context of when and where it is being used.

Communication depends on the functioning of the senses (e.g., vision, hearing, etc.) and the cognitive activities of the brain, which include ***attention*** (focusing on certain stimuli while disregarding others); ***perception*** (using pattern recognition and sensory memory to interpret stimuli picked up by our senses); ***memory*** (retaining information over time); ***language*** (interpreting, expressing, and remembering verbal and written words and symbols); ***conceptualization*** (organizing information and ideas into categories); ***reasoning*** (drawing conclusions from information); and ***decision making*** (making choices based on an anticipation of future events). These cognitive processes are interrelated and overlapping. If the physical senses are impaired or if the brain has been damaged, the ability to communicate will be limited to some degree. Common causes of brain damage are strokes, trauma, chemical intoxication, tumors, and dementia-type illnesses.

One of the most important factors affecting people's communication is their ***self-concept,*** or how they define and view themselves in relation to others (see Item 11.8). One's self-concept is like a screen or a lens through which he or she sees, hears, and interprets all experiences and messages from others. An individual with a poor or a negative self-concept is often guarded and defensive. Moreover, being insecure and lacking confidence may make it difficult for an individual to express his or her true thoughts and feelings, to voice ideas that are different from those of other people, and to listen attentively to others. The defensive individual may find it difficult to accept important direction, instruction, or constructive criticism.

The capacity to send and receive messages accurately can also be limited or distorted by one's emotional state and expectations. In general, we tend to hear what we want to hear, hear what we have learned to expect, and hear what serves our self-interests at the moment. We often distort messages in order to avoid discomfort and to meet our emotional needs. In addition, individuals with certain personality disorders characteristically distort messages in a self-serving fashion.

Situational and social-interactional factors also have a powerful influence on how words and gestures are interpreted. How, when, and where a message is sent are usually as important as the literal meaning of the words used.

The lack of clear communication is a common cause of problems within families, organizations, and other social systems. In general, communication problems develop in these situations:

- We speak for others rather than let them speak for themselves.
- We do not take the time or make the effort to really listen.
- We allow prejudices, stereotypes, and presumptions to color how we interpret what others are saying.
- We keep things to ourselves because we fear others will disapprove of what we believe and feel.

- We make no attempt to communicate because we assume others already know, or should know, how we feel and what we think.
- We discourage or suppress communication by ordering, threatening, preaching, patronizing, judging, blaming, or humoring.
- We allow negative feelings about ourselves to keep us silent, fearing that we have nothing worthwhile to say and that no one will want to hear what we think or feel.

In addition to all these issues, it is important to recognize that a person's ethnicity, gender, religion, and socioeconomic class can also have a significant impact, not only on his or her communication but also on help-seeking activity, problem definition, and expectations of a professional relationship.

8.1   CREATING AN EFFECTIVE HELPING RELATIONSHIP

Purpose: To develop a helping relationship with a client.

Discussion: A positive relationship between the social worker and client is essential but not sufficient for client change. The application of appropriate change-producing techniques and procedures is also necessary. Without a positive relationship, change is not likely to occur. With a positive relationship, the various intervention techniques are more likely to have their intended effect.

Some type of relationship will develop whenever a social worker and client interact. This relationship may be either positive or negative, depending on the client's interpretation of the worker's words and actions. Thus, the social worker cannot *make* a positive relationship happen. At most, a social worker can strive to be the type of person and type of professional that most clients find to be helpful.

The nature of a professional relationship will be shaped by various factors, such as the reason the social worker and client are meeting, the agency's program and procedures, the purpose of the intervention or change effort, and the practice framework selected by the social worker. It is important to recognize that even an effective helping relationship is not free of interpersonal tension. Because change is difficult, a change-producing relationship is often challenging and somewhat stressful for both the client and the social worker.

At the very heart of effective helping relationships is human caring. A social worker must genuinely care about his or her clients. Clients expect a social worker to be knowledgeable, but they will not pay much attention to what the worker knows until they are convinced that he or she really cares. Trust is always basic to a professional relationship. When clients trust a social worker they have faith and confidence in the worker's integrity, ability, and character. Trust develops when the client experiences the social worker as truthful, dependable, and competent.

Research within the fields of counseling and psychotherapy has identified four characteristics of a therapeutic relationship. These qualities or *core conditions* of a change-producing relationship are empathy, unconditional positive regard, personal warmth, and genuineness.

The quality of ***empathy*** is the social worker's ability to understand the client's inner experiences, as if the worker were that client. Empathy is often described as the ability to "step into the client's shoes" and to think and feel as the client is thinking and feeling. Empathy is conveyed primarily by giving the client undivided attention and by responding sensitively to his or her nonverbal communication. A worker will often use the techniques of active listening (e.g., paraphrasing, reflection) to display empathy for his or her client (see Item 8.4).

The quality of ***unconditional positive regard*** exists when the social worker believes that the client is a person of inherent worth and treats him or her with respect, regardless of what the client may have done in the past, of how he or she might behave during an interview, and how he or she appears. The word *unconditional* is meant to convey the idea that clients are to be treated with fairness and respect simply because they are human beings, not because they have somehow earned the right to such treatment.

The display of unconditional positive regard is closely related to the admonition to maintain a *nonjudgmental attitude* in work with clients. We have a judgmental attitude when we make harsh and negative moral judgments and express them in ways that disparage clients, whether verbally or nonverbally. Whenever a person perceives that he or she is being judged or criticized, he or she will tend to become defensive and withdraw from the relationship.

Thus, in order to be helpful and to facilitate positive change by the client, the social worker must be willing and able to suspend making moral judgments within the professional relationship. Needless to say, this can be a difficult task. A social worker is most likely to become judgmental when the client has violated the worker's own deeply held values or moral principles (e.g., by committing a murder, abusing a child, raping someone, or exploiting a helpless elderly person).

To say that the social worker should strive to be nonjudgmental is not to suggest that he or she cannot make judgments concerning the client's attitude, behavior, or functioning. Neither does it mean that the social worker must condone harmful and inappropriate behavior. The client's negative or destructive behavior must be discussed when it is related to his or her presenting concerns and/or is the reason he or she is involved with the worker's agency. However, the unacceptable behavior must be discussed and assessed in a factual and objective manner, not in a manner that will denigrate or deprecate the client and possibly cause him or her to withdraw from using the services he or she needs to change the behavior.

The relationship characteristic of ***personal warmth*** exists when the social worker responds to clients in ways that make them feel safe and accepted. Without the quality of warmth, the worker's words will sound hollow and insincere and will have no therapeutic impact. Warmth is mostly nonverbal communication and is expressed in a smile, a soft and soothing voice, a relaxed but interested posture, appropriate eye contact, and gestures that convey acceptance and openness.

Genuineness means being one's self, being real, and "speaking from the heart." Social workers who are genuine are nondefensive and spontaneous, and what they say matches what they do. They lack pretentiousness and any hint of phoniness. What they reveal about their own thoughts and feelings is true and real. They are honest with others, but that does not mean that they strive to be totally honest, for they are sensitive to the needs and feelings of other people. When they have a negative feeling toward a client's behavior, they exercise self-discipline so it does not damage the professional relationship or harm the client.

Those who are new to social work sometimes worry that they cannot simultaneously take on a professional role and be genuine in their relationships with clients. Being professional has nothing to do with "playing the role" or trying to imitate some particular image of a professional person. A true professional is knowledgeable, self-disciplined, responsible, ethical, and, most of all, effective. There is no conflict between possessing those qualities and being genuine.

In addition to the worker's demonstration of empathy, positive regard, personal warmth, and genuineness, certain other conditions have been identified as important to an effective helping relationship: ***concreteness*** (being able to communicate one's thoughts and ideas clearly and specifically), ***competence*** (proficiency in carrying out professional tasks and activities), and ***objectivity*** (being unbiased and able to appreciate differing points of view).

Relationship building can often be enhanced through the use of ***structuring***, a term that refers to various arrangements (e.g., worker-client matching) and symbols (e.g., worker dress and office environment). The use of structuring is based on the observation that a client is most likely to be influenced by someone he or she respects and to whom he or she is attracted. People are usually attracted to and feel most comfortable with those who have beliefs, backgrounds, and a lifestyle similar to their own. It follows, therefore, that a social worker who wants to increase his or her attractiveness to a client and decrease a client's uncomfortableness should look for similarities and mention them to the client. For example, the worker might point out that he or she and the client both have children of about the same age or that both grew up on a farm.

Whether certain differences between the client and the worker have a significant impact on the helping relationship is mostly a function of the client's expectations and perceptions. Davis and Proctor (1989) suggest that a client who is different from the social worker in terms of race, gender, or socioeconomic status is likely to have three major concerns:

1. Is the helper a person of goodwill? That is, does this person have my best interests at heart? Does he or she dislike . . . people like me? The client's answer to this question determines the extent to which the client will initially trust the helper.
2. Does the worker have professional expertise or mastery of skills that can resolve my problems? . . . The answer to this question will also affect the client's trust in the worker. . . .
3. Does the worker have sufficient understanding of my social reality or my world view? That is, is this person sufficiently familiar with people like me? Will this person understand my life experiences? The answer to this question will determine the extent to which the worker is seen as credible, and the extent to which advice and suggestions can be accepted as valid and meaningful. (p. ix)

How the client answers such questions will determine if and how he or she uses the services of the social worker.

The social worker's waiting room and office also can have a significant impact on clients, either positive or negative. For example, if a client must talk with the social worker in a space that lacks privacy and comfort, respect for the worker is greatly diminished. It is important to make offices and meeting rooms as comfortable as possible for clients.

Expertness—or at least the appearance of expertness—can have a positive impact on the initial phases of the helping process. Such things as certificates and diplomas on the wall, a large office, proper use of language, and professional dress can increase the client's respect for the helper and result in the client being more open to influence. While the social worker must be alert to the importance of such factors, he or she should remember that clients, like all people, make deliberate decisions about whose influence they accept and whose they reject.

SELECTED BIBLIOGRAPHY

Brammer, Lawrence, and Ginger MacDonald. *The Helping Relationship*, 8th ed. Boston: Allyn & Bacon, 2003.

Davis, Larry, and Enola Proctor. *Race, Gender and Class: Guidelines for Practice with Individuals, Families and Groups.* Englewood Cliffs, NJ: Prentice Hall, 1989.

8.2   VERBAL COMMUNICATION SKILLS

Purpose: To improve verbal communication with other professionals and agencies.

Discussion: Social workers make frequent use of two broad categories of communication skills: (1) those intended to facilitate interpersonal helping and (2) those intended to facilitate the exchanges of information within an agency, between agencies, and among professionals. The communication skills used in direct-practice activities (e.g., face-to-face work with individual clients, families, therapeutic groups) are described in Item 8.4. The other category, basic communication skills, is used frequently when the social worker is communication with another social worker, another professional (e.g., physician, lawyer, judge, etc.), an agency supervisor or administrator, or members of a committee or other task group. A description of those skills is presented here.

Among the attitudes that provide a foundation for good communication are the following:

- A willingness to understand that every human being is unique; consequently, each person experiences and perceives events and interpersonal exchanges in a unique manner. Thus, you should anticipate some degree of misunderstanding and take steps to minimize the problems of miscommunication.
- A willingness and desire to organize your thoughts and present your message in a way that will make it easy for others to follow and understand
- A willingness to listen carefully to other people and to lower your defenses so you can hear and understand what others are saying

- A willingness to take responsibility for your statements and behaviors
- A willingness to take the time needed to communicate effectively

Communication involves both a message sender and a message receiver. The sender has a responsibility to convey his or her message in a way that is easily received and not likely to be misunderstood. The receiver has a responsibility to make sure that he or she has accurately received the sender's intended message and has not, in some way, distorted or misunderstood that message.

When in the position of listening to or *receiving a message,* remember these rules:

- Stop talking. You cannot listen when you are talking.
- Put the message sender at ease. Do what you can to lessen his or her anxiety and remove distractions (e.g., close the door).
- Be patient with the message sender. Do not interrupt.
- Ask questions if it will help you understand or help the sender to clarify his or her message.
- Do not show disapproval of what the sender is saying. Do not criticize or enter into an argument, for that will erect a barrier to further communication.

When *sending a message,* follow these rules:

- Use clear, simple language. Speak distinctly and not too fast.
- Pay attention to your body language; make sure it is congruent with your message. Maintain appropriate eye contact and utilize gestures.
- Do not overwhelm or overload the receiver with information. Break up a lengthy or complex message into several parts so it can be more easily followed and understood.
- Ask for comments, questions, or feedback so you will know whether you are being understood.

The skill of *planning a message* refers to the worker thinking about an upcoming episode of communication and planning the message around the answers to questions or concerns, such as the following:

- How much time is available for this exchange?
- When and where am I most likely to have the full attention of the person who is to receive my message?
- What are the essential points of my message?
- What aspects of my message are most likely to be misunderstood or confusing?
- How can I organize or frame my message so it will be easily understood and accepted by the receiver?
- Do I have the credibility, position, and status to deliver this message or should it be sent by someone else?

It is the middle portion of a message that is most likely to be distorted by the receiver. Thus, the most important points should be placed at the beginning and the end of your message.

The skill of *identifying self* is an important first step in meaningful communication. It requires a concise description of who you are and how your role and responsibilities relate to the intended message or exchange of information. For example:

> You may remember me from a previous meeting, but let me begin by introducing myself. My name is Mary Jones. I am a social worker with the Evergreen Family Services Center. A client of mine has asked me to speak with you to find out if . . .

The skill of *explaining the purpose of the communication* refers to the sender's statements that explain the reason behind the message. This helps the receiver place the message in a proper context. For example, a child welfare worker speaking to a prosecuting attorney might say:

> As you know, my agency has Jimmy Johnson in one of our foster homes. I need to talk with you and get a clear idea about when you plan to have Jimmy testify in court. This information is important to us because we have to inform his school of a planned absence and also work out his transportation to the courthouse.

Sometimes, it is important to respond to a receiver's nonverbal communication when it suggests confusion or disagreement with the message. The skill of *following up on nonverbal communication* refers to such efforts. For example:

> John, I noticed that you looked a bit puzzled when I was explaining the new agency procedure. If you have any questions, please feel free to ask me at this time.

Similar follow-up efforts are important when the receiver's nonverbal communication suggests that he or she disagrees with the message. For example:

> When I was explaining the proposed policy change, I could not help but notice that several of you were looking rather distressed. It is important for me to know how you feel about the proposal. I really want to know what you are thinking. Bob, Anna, and Judy—please react to the proposed policy change.

Sending a message of complaint or criticism is especially challenging because it can so easily put the receiver on the defensive and block further communication. The communication technique called the *I-statement* refers to a way of structuring and wording a message so as to minimize that possibility. To understand the I-message, it is important to recognize that during times of conflict, confrontation, and hurt feelings we often use

"You-statements"; for example: "You need to study more," "You make me angry," and "You are being selfish and rude." Such messages cause the person on the receiving end to feel put down and wanting to strike back.

In an I-statement the focal point is the sender. It allows the person bothered by the behavior of another to say, in effect: "This is my concern, this is how your behavior bothers me or affects me, and this is how I am feeling." Implicitly it says: "I will trust you to decide what change is needed." It gets a point across without sounding accusatory. An I-statement consists of three parts: (1) a brief, clear description of a *specific behavior*, (2) the *resulting feeling* experienced because of that specific behavior, and (3) a description of the *tangible impact* this behavior has had. For example, a social worker using an I-statement might say to a client:

> ***Worker:***   When you did not show up for our scheduled appointment (specific behavior), I felt upset and put down (feeling) because I don't like having to wait around and because I could have spent that time with another client (tangible impact).

The skill of **checking for message reception** refers to various questions and probes intended to verify that your message was completely and accurately received by the other party. For example:

> I am aware that what I have described as needed modifications in the agenda for our meeting might be confusing. I want to make sure you understand. Would you please repeat to me what you heard me say?

When on the receiving end of a message, it is desirable to use the skill of **checking one's own receipt of a message.** This refers to various probes and questions intended to verify that you have, in fact, received the message and did not misunderstand what was intended by the sender. For example:

> Before we end this conversation, I want to make sure I understand completely what you have said. Let me take a minute and repeat what I heard you say. If it sounds as if I have misunderstood, please correct me.

It is surprisingly difficult to ask questions so that they can be answered in a clear and concise manner. All too often, we attach unnecessary words and extraneous topics to our questions, and this can confuse the point of our query. In order to receive a clear answer, your question must be focused and precise. This calls for the skill termed **asking a focused question.** Consider first this example of a confusing question directed to an agency administrator:

> I am confused about these new agency policies, especially the ones about foster care and, in some ways, about a lot of the policies. This manual is organized in an unusual way. What is really expected of us? I mean, what are

we supposed to do with new cases and how do we handle the court-ordered evaluations?

It would be difficult for the administrator to give a clear answer to this communication because many different questions are being asked at the same time and all of them are rather vague. The question would be much more focused like this:

I have a question about policy number 86 on page ninety-nine of our agency manual. In order to secure a psychological evaluation on a foster child, do I need my supervisor's written approval?

The skill of ***answering a question*** refers to the ability to use statements that respond directly to the question asked and that answer the question in a complete manner. This seems simple; however, people often fail to really listen to the question. In the following example, a supervisor makes this error but then makes a correct response:

Worker: I need some direction on where to send this report. Do I send it to the County Attorney or directly to Judge Smith?

Supervisor: Just remember that Judge Smith is a real stickler for details. Also, he wants the report as concise as possible.

Worker: Well, yes, I know that but what I want to know is where to send the report.

Supervisor: Oh, I'm sorry. I didn't answer your question. Send it directly to Judge Smith.

When responding to a question, do not make assumptions or engage in mind reading about what the person meant to ask or should have asked. Listen carefully to the question and answer it without adding extraneous details.

Many communication problems arise because people use words or phrases in different ways. The skill of ***checking for word meaning*** refers to inquiries intended to make sure that all parties in an exchange agree on the meaning of key words. Consider the following example:

Chair of Planning Group: I think we need to shift about 20 percent of our budget into child abuse prevention programs.

Committee Member (checking for meaning of words):   Well, I may or may not agree, depending on what you mean by prevention. What level of prevention are you talking about? Primary or secondary?

SELECTED BIBLIOGRAPHY

Allen, Gina, and Duncan Lanford. *Effective Interviewing in Social Work and Social Care*. New York: Palgrave, 2006.

Burley-Allen, Madelyn. *Listening: The Forgotten Skill*. New York: John Wiley and Sons, 1995.

8.3   NONVERBAL COMMUNICATION SKILLS

Purpose: To understand and use nonverbal messages.

Discussion: Research suggests that about 65 percent of the communication that occurs during a face-to-face exchange is nonverbal, meaning that the messages are conveyed by means of facial expressions, eye movements, gestures, and voice qualities such as tone, pitch, and resonance. Much of our nonverbal communication is beyond our awareness. Consequently, we sometimes say one thing with our words and, without knowing it, say something else with our actions and expressions.

The social worker must be careful to avoid sending unintended messages to the client by way of nonverbal expressions. And through paying attention to the client's nonverbal cues, the social worker can determine how his or her messages are being received. Observing nonverbal behavior may also tell the worker if what the client is saying in words truly reflects his or her thoughts and feelings.

Eye contact is a powerful means of communication. Our eyes reveal much about our emotional state and our sensitivity to and understanding of the immediate situation. In most Western cultures (e.g., North America, Europe), making eye contact indicates openness and a willingness to engage in communication, whereas avoiding eye contact is viewed as being anxious and closed to communication and sometimes even as an indicator of dishonesty. In other cultures, such as those of many Native Americans and people from Asia and the Middle East, making direct eye contact is considered intimidating, disrespectful, and/or sexually aggressive. Moreover, in these and other cultures, private conversations between unmarried men and women may be perceived as inappropriate.

Gestures of greeting are important to relationship building. In North America and Europe, a firm handshake is the expected gesture of greeting among both males and females. However, the social worker must be alert to cultural differences. For example, for people from Asia and the Middle East, a firm handshake may suggest aggression. Bowing is the appropriate gesture among the people of Japan, Thailand, and India; the lowest-ranking person bows first, and the depth of the bow reflects the status of the person to whom the bow is offered. An embrace or hug is a common greeting for males in Russia, the Middle East, and Latin America.

Personal space is another important nonverbal element in interpersonal communication. In general, being close to someone communicates trust and involvement, but being too close is threatening. People from North America typically prefer to be about an arm's length from one another, whereas those from Asian cultures usually prefer a greater distance. People from the Middle East and Latin America are used to being toe-to-toe during their conversations. Each client will have his or her own *comfort zone* in terms of how close he or she will want to be to the social worker. The worker can avoid invading a client's personal space by reading his or her body language and adjusting accordingly.

Body positioning conveys various attitudes and intentions. It is best to face the client at a 90-degree angle, since this suggests both safety and openness. Facing the client directly may communicate aggressiveness. A desk separating the client and worker inhibits closeness and openness and also suggests the worker is in a superior position. Leaning slightly toward the client communicates interest and acceptance.

Facial expressions—such as smiling, frowning, nodding and shaking the head, lip quivering, and blushing—register and convey our thoughts and emotions. The face is the most expressive part of our body and makes us most vividly present to others. Quite often, facial expressions reveal that the person is saying one thing but thinking another. And it is often facial expressions that reveal a worker's disapproval of a client, even when the worker is trying hard to be nonjudgmental.

Touch is a powerful means of communication. For example, by touching another's hand, arm, or shoulder or by offering a gentle hug, we can convey a message of reassurance, sympathy, or understanding. A social worker must be cautious about touching a client, however, especially if the client is of the opposite sex or from an unfamiliar cultural or ethnic background. Also, an innocent and well-meaning touch can be misinterpreted as a sexual advance or as intimidation by someone who has been physically or sexually abused or who has any of certain mental disorders.

Arm and hand movements frequently communicate strong emotions. Crossed legs, arms folded across the chest, and body rigidity usually suggest defensiveness, whereas arms and hands at the body's side or in an outreached position suggest openness to others. Clenched fists indicate anger or anxiety. Fidgety movements, toe and finger tapping, leg bouncing, and similar movements suggest impatience, nervousness, or preoccupation.

Tone of voice reveals feelings. A loud, forceful tone suggests aggressiveness, control, and strength. A meek, scarcely audible tone suggests withdrawal, fear, and weakness. A monotonous or flat voice suggests a lack of interest.

Dress and appearance are important forms of nonverbal communication. Our choice of clothing and accessories (e.g., jewelry) and our hairstyle sends a message about who we are or who we want to be and reveals information about our membership in a social class, group, or subculture. A social worker must give careful thought to his or her appearance and avoid making choices that might distract clients or make them feel uncomfortable or out of place. Dress that would be appropriate in an agency serving children may be inappropriate in a hospital or court setting. Likewise, dress that is acceptable to adolescent clients may be offensive to elderly clients. Clothing that is highly unusual, flashy, or sexually suggestive always should be avoided.

Some agencies have dress codes. The new worker should consult his or her supervisor for guidance on selecting appropriate dress. In sum, a well-groomed appearance connotes a seriousness about one's professional role and responsibilities.

SELECTED BIBLIOGRAPHY

Kavanagh, James. *Worldwide Gestures.* Blaine, WA: Waterford Press, 2000.

Knapp, Mark, and Judith Hall. *Nonverbal Communication in Human Interaction*, 6th ed. Belmont, CA: Wadsworth, 2006.

Remland, Martin. *Nonverbal Communication in Everyday Life.* Boston: Houghton-Mifflin, 2004.

8.4   HELPING SKILLS

Purpose: To use verbal messages that can assist and encourage a client during the intervention process.

Discussion: As used here, the term ***helping skill*** refers to a message that the practitioner conveys to the client because the worker believes it will have a beneficial effect on the client's thinking, feelings, or behavior. The moment-to-moment decisions concerning what message to send should be guided by the purpose of the interview and based on what the social worker knows about the client and his or her situation. Moreover, a specific skill or message will be more or less useful depending on the phase of the change process (i.e., intake, assessment, planning, intervention, and termination). The appropriateness of a message also depends on whether it is offered during the beginning, middle, or ending phase of an interview or meeting. Needless to say, all communication has a significant nonverbal component—including the use of eye contact, gestures, and other movements—to help convey the message; information on nonverbal communication appears in Item 8.3.

On the following pages, brief descriptions of commonly used helping skills are offered. In several instances, terminology is borrowed from Shulman (1981, 2006). The examples that illustrate how a particular skill might be used are drawn from one-on-one interviews, but these same skills can be adapted for use in work with families and therapeutic groups. Many of the more specialized techniques presented in the remainder of this book can be viewed as elaborations and special applications of the basic skills described here.

Getting Ready

In a sense, the social worker's helping actions begin *before* the first face-to-face meeting with the client. Prior to the meeting, the worker should imagine what the client might be thinking and feeling as he or she enters the agency or office expecting to discuss personal matters with a stranger. By trying to anticipate how the client might feel, the worker begins to develop empathy for the client and mentally prepares to address the client's initial feelings (e.g., anger, fear, confusion, etc.) and to identify ways to ease the client into the helping relationship. Shulman (2006) has termed this the *tuning-in phase* of the helping process. (See Items 10.1, 10.2, and 13.1 for more information on how to prepare for an interview.)

Getting Started

During the intake and engagement phase of the change process and also at the beginning of each session with a client, the social worker must give special attention to clarifying the purpose of the meeting and the worker's role. The helping skill of ***explaining purpose*** refers to a simple, nonjargonized statement by the worker about the general purpose of the meeting. It serves to define expectations and reduce client confusion and anxiety. For example:

> *Worker:*   I am pleased that you were able to meet with me today. As you know, your wife first came to this agency about three weeks ago. She expressed concern about your marriage. I would like to hear your thoughts and find out if you also believe there are problems in the marriage.

When the first contact is initiated by the client, the worker should encourage the client to begin by describing the reason for requesting the interview. If the client has a hard time explaining his or her purpose, the worker might ask some general questions about the circumstances that led up to the request for an interview and what the client hopes will come from the meeting.

When the social worker initiates the first contact, he or she should begin by explaining the purpose. The explanation should be clear and to the point, as in this example:

> *Good Explanation:*   I need to talk with you about your son Max. He has missed 14 out of the last 20 school days. This is a serious problem.
>
> *Poor Explanation:*   Hi there. I know your son Max. I was in the neighborhood so I decided to stop by to chat. How are things going?

The skill of ***encouraging the client's feedback on the purpose of the communication*** (Shulman 1981) refers to statements that encourage the client to respond to the worker's explanation. This gives the client an opportunity to ask questions or perhaps voice disagreement. Consider these two examples:

> *Worker:*   What are your reactions to what I have said about the purpose of this meeting? Do you see things differently?

or

> *Worker:*   It's quite possible you and I have different thoughts about why we are talking today. I want to know if you were expecting something else.

The skill of ***describing the worker's role and method*** refers to statements intended to give the client a beginning idea of how the worker might be able to help and the approaches or methods to be used. For example:

> *Worker:*   As you get ready to leave this hospital, it is important to anticipate the problems you may face when you get home and to figure out how to deal with them. Basically, that is why I want to meet with you two or three times before you leave. I will ask for your ideas and I will share my ideas, as well. Between the two of us, I hope we can come up with a plan that will minimize the difficulties you will have when you return home.

Each session with a client has three time phases: (1) getting started, (2) the central work of the session, and (3) drawing the session to a close. At the beginning of each session, the social worker should provide an opportunity for what Shulman (1981, 12) terms ***sessional contracting***. Even when there has been a prior agreement on how the session's time will be used, it is important to check once again for consensus. Quite possibly, some change in the client's situation has altered the client's sense of priorities. The skill of ***reaching for between-session data*** (Shulman 1981) is used to initiate sessional contracting. This form of "checking in" involves asking the client to bring the worker up to date and to identify the key topics to be discussed, even if they are different from what was planned during the previous meeting. This can be viewed as an attempt to adhere to the principle of *starting where the client is*. For example:

> **Worker:**   You will recall that during last week's session we agreed to spend today's session talking about your reluctance to visit your children in foster care. Do you still think that is how we should spend our time today, or do you now have a more pressing concern?

Asking Questions

A social worker uses various types of questions to obtain needed information and assist the client in expressing his or her thoughts and feelings. A question such as "What are the names of your children?" is termed a ***closed-ended question***; it limits how the client can respond. By contrast, a question such as "Tell me about your children" is called an ***open-ended question*** because it gives the client an opportunity to say whatever he or she thinks is important. However, open-ended questions can vary in the amount of freedom they allow. These three questions are all open ended, but some are more open than others:

"Tell me about your job."

"What do you like and what do you dislike about your job?"

"What tasks and responsibilities are part of your job?"

During counseling sessions, the worker will use mostly open-ended questions. Closed-ended questions are appropriate when the worker needs specific information or when the client is so confused or overwhelmed that structure is needed to maintain focus and direction.

The skill of ***narrowing the focus*** (or *funneling*) refers to a series of questions intended to assist the client in describing his or her concerns or situation with more specificity. For example:

> **Client:**   Things are really a mess at home.
> **Worker:**   I'm not sure what you mean by "a mess." What happened?
> **Client:**   We were eating when Dad came home from work. He was drunk and ended up hitting Mom.

> ***Worker:***   What did you do when all this was happening?
> ***Client:***   First I ran out of the room. Then I came back and yelled at my dad to stop it or I would call the cops.
> ***Worker:***   What were you thinking and feeling at the time you threatened to call the police?

A worker should never ask questions out of mere curiosity or to fill a silence. Other common errors in questioning include the overuse of closed-ended questions, stacking questions, asking leading questions, and asking too many "why" questions. *Stacking questions* refers to the undesirable practice of asking several questions all at once. Consider this example:

> ***Worker:***   So, you are interested in adoption. How long have you been thinking about adoption? Have you known others who have adopted? Are you thinking about an infant? Have you thought much about an older child or one who has a disability?

Stacked questions are confusing to clients. It is best to ask questions one at a time.

Leading questions are those that push or pull the client toward a certain response—for example, "Didn't you think that was wrong?" or "I assume that you explained to your boss why you missed work?" or "Isn't it true that you were hoping for a fight?" Leading questions are intimidating and insulting to clients. A leading question may prompt the client to lie rather than openly disagree with the worker.

Another common error is to ask "*why*" questions—for example, "Why do you get so angry when Maria spills food?" Essentially, "why" questions ask the client to justify his or her behavior, and this tends to produce defensiveness. Moreover, most people do not know or cannot articulate the "whys" of their behavior, so, when asked, they simply guess or give socially acceptable answers. Instead of asking why, use questions that focus on the what, where, when, and how of the client's behavior and situation.

Active Listening

In active listening, the worker attends to both the client's verbal and nonverbal messages. The worker also reflects back to the client what has been heard so that the client will know that his or her message has been accurately understood. The skills of active listening are those of using encouragers, clarification, paraphrase, reflection, summarization, and exploring silences.

An ***encourager*** (also called a *prompt*) refers to a single word, short phrase, or nonverbal gesture that encourages the client to continue talking. Examples of verbal encouragers are "Uh-huh," "Tell me more," "Please go on," and the repetition of a key word just uttered by the client. Nonverbal encouragers include nods of the head and hand gestures that signal an invitation to say more.

Clarification refers to asking a question designed to encourage a client to become more explicit or to verify the worker's understanding of what the client has said. Such questions might begin with "Are you saying that . . . " or "Do you mean that . . . " and end with a rephrasing of the client's words. For example:

> *Client:* My life is a disaster. I thought I could get things squared away, but it doesn't look like that will be possible.
>
> *Worker:* I am not sure I am following you. Are you saying that things are changing more slowly than you expected or that your situation is now worse than before?

Another example follows:

> *Worker:* I am not sure what you mean when you say that you and your wife had a fight. Did this involve hitting?

When a worker becomes confused by what a client is saying, it is best to acknowledge the confusion and seek clarification. Here are a couple of examples:

> *Worker:* You have been talking very fast. I cannot keep up and I am getting confused. Please start over, one point at a time. Also, try to slow down so I will not miss anything that you have to say.

or

> *Worker:* I am sorry, but I didn't follow that. Please tell me once more.

A skilled social worker focuses on both the client's words and on the affect associated with those words. To do this, he or she will make frequent use of the paraphrase and reflection. The skill known as ***paraphrasing*** is a rephrasing of the literal meaning of the client's statement, whereas the skill termed ***reflection of feeling*** is an expression of the feeling or emotional component of the message. Examples of paraphrase and reflection are as follow:

> *Client:* That guy down at the employment office is a real jerk. How does he get away with treating people like that? I feel three inches tall when I go down there.
>
> *Worker:* I hear you saying that when you go to that office you are treated badly. (paraphrase)

or

> *Worker:* It sounds like you feel shamed and humiliated at the employment office. (reflection of feeling)

The skill of ***summarization*** refers to pulling together the content and affective components of several messages. For example, a worker might use summarization to draw together the key elements of what was discussed during the previous few minutes. Here is an example of summarization:

> *Worker:*   From what you have been saying, I am hearing a number of things. You are desperate for a job and feel a mix of anger and depression because you haven't found one. You have been going to the employment office but that adds to your feelings of frustration and humiliation. On top of that, you have begun to feel deep regret for having dropped out of high school. Is that an accurate summary of what you have been saying?

Active listening also requires careful attention to times when the client is silent. Silence is a behavior that has meaning, and sometimes it is important to discover that meaning. The skill of *exploring the client's silence* refers to efforts to gently probe the silence. For example:

> *Client:*   (thoughtful silence)
> *Worker:*   You appear to be puzzling over something. Can you tell me what you are thinking about?

> *or*

> *Client:*   (thoughtful silence)
> *Worker:*   Discussing your mother's illness seems difficult for you. Am I asking you to talk about something that is too painful to discuss?

An error commonly made by beginning social workers is to respond to silence with a change of topics. This happens because the worker becomes uncomfortable when the client is quiet. A brief silence is best responded to with polite quietness. If the silence is a long one, the worker should attempt to explore the silence.

Displaying Empathy, Genuineness, and Warmth

Item 8.1 of this chapter described the importance of the social worker's capacity for empathy, genuineness, and personal warmth in a helping relationship. A number of skills or techniques are used to display these qualities to the client. The skill of *displaying understanding* refers to verbal and nonverbal communication intended to demonstrate that the social worker comprehends and can identify with the client's thoughts and feelings. For example:

> *Client:*   Having to place Susan in foster care is one of the most difficult decisions I have ever made.
> *Worker:*   It must be hard to make a decision that is going to be very upsetting to Susan. It seems like this decision is tearing you apart inside.

It is especially important to acknowledge and display an understanding of a client's negative feelings such as anger and resentment. For example:

> *Client:*   I am sick of this place. I don't need to be in a treatment program. I feel like punching the next person who asks me about my drinking.
>
> *Worker:*   Well, I am part of this treatment program and you know that I will ask about your drinking. I guess that means you want to hit me. I am not sure how to respond to your threat. What are you expecting me to do?

The skill of ***putting the client's feelings into words*** refers to the articulation of what the client is feeling but has stopped just short of expressing in words. For example:

> *Worker:*   How did the visit with your mother go?
>
> *Client:*   OK, I guess, but I don't know if I can take this much longer.
>
> *Worker:*   Watching your mother die is putting you under a lot of stress. It sounds like you hope death will come soon, but I am wondering if such a thought makes you feel guilty. Is that the way you are feeling?

This helping skill gives the client a supportive invitation to express what he or she is feeling but is reluctant to say aloud. Here is another example:

> *Worker:*   Do you have any other questions about adoption or our agency's adoption program?
>
> *Client:*   No, I don't think so. You explained it pretty well. I guess it's just a lot different from what I expected.
>
> *Worker:*   You look disappointed. Can you tell me how you are feeling about what I have told you?

It is important to recognize that encouraging a client to express feelings is appropriate only when those feelings are directly related to the overall goals of the professional relationship and intervention.

The helping skill of ***self-disclosure*** refers to a worker's statements that reveal some of his or her own thoughts, feelings, or life experiences. When properly used, self-disclosure has the effect of making it easier for the client to talk about a sensitive topic and to feel more at ease with the worker. Consider these three examples of worker self-disclosure:

> *Worker:*   I can understand how frustrated you feel about your teenaged son. I went through a similar experience with my son, Bob. There were times when it seemed like Bob was from another planet. His self-centeredness and concern about what I felt were superficial fads just drove me nuts! Now, 15 years later, he is married, has two kids, and has a very responsible

job. I once heard grandchildren described as "God's reward for not killing your children." I'd have to agree with that!

Worker: I feel disappointed and angry. You and I invested a lot of time and energy in finding you a job—a job you wanted and needed desperately. Now, after just one week, you are talking about quitting the job.

Worker: I am sorry about how I reacted on the phone. I guess you noticed that I become sad when we talk about your mother's death. That touches me deeply. I had a real hard time adjusting after my mother died of cancer two years ago.

As a general rule, the use of self-disclosure should be avoided in the early stages of relationship building and used sparingly at other times. The information revealed by the worker should always have a clear connection to the client's concern. It is inappropriate for the worker to talk about personal experiences that are unrelated to the purpose of the interview.

Another complicated issue for social workers is deciding how to go about *answering personal questions.* Clients might ask workers a whole range of personal questions, such as these: Do you have children? Did you ever go through a divorce? What is your religion? Have you ever used drugs? Have you ever been fired from a job? Whether and how the worker answers questions like these will depend on his or her best guess as to why the client wants to know. The workers' answers will, most likely, affect the professional relationship.

There are many reasons clients might ask social workers personal questions. For example, the client may want to know if the worker is capable of understanding the client's situation. The client also may be checking out whether the worker is going to be judgmental. Not infrequently, the client asks personal questions simply because he or she is curious. And in some cases, the client is trying to manipulate the worker (see Item 10.9).

Typically, we feel most comfortable with people whom we perceive are similar to us in terms of values, beliefs, and life experiences. This holds true for the client-worker relationship, as well. Thus, when asked a personal question, the worker may want to offer a simple, straightforward answer, if doing so will establish some common ground for mutual understanding. On the other hand, the worker should avoid answering the client's personal question if the answer will underscore their differences in values, beliefs, and so on. Also, the worker should sidestep any question that seems to be a client's attempt to manipulate the worker or to divert the discussion away from the purpose of the meeting.

Sustaining Client Motivation

In order for people to make a change, they must feel hopeful about the possibility of change as well as feel some discomfort or dissatisfaction with their current behavior or situation. Several skills can be used to increase or sustain a client's motivation for change.

Displaying a belief in the potential of work (Shulman 1981) refers to statements intended to convey the worker's belief that professional intervention can be helpful. It is an offer of realistic hope to the client. For example:

> **Worker:**   The problems you have described are serious. I can understand why you feel overwhelmed. But I think you can successfully deal with these problems if we work together and start chipping away at the problems, one at a time. It won't be easy, but I believe we can make some progress over the next few weeks.

The skill of *recognizing client strengths* refers to expressions of confidence in the client's ability to accomplish some specific tasks or to cope with a difficult situation (see also Item 11.4). Here are two examples:

> **Worker:**   I know it is going to be difficult and painful for you to visit your kids in their foster home, but your visits are important to them, and I think you can handle it because you have been through this experience once before.

or

> **Worker:**   You faced this problem in the past, and somehow you weathered the storm. I know you just want to run away from the whole thing, but you are an intelligent person and I really believe that you can figure out a solution.

The skill of *pointing out negative consequences* refers to statements that remind the client that change is needed in order to avoid undesirable consequences. For example:

> **Worker:**   When you talk about wanting to drop out of the sex offender treatment program, I feel that I must warn you of the consequences. If you do not work on your problems and demonstrate a capacity to control your attraction to children, the judge may revoke your probation and you will go to prison.

or

> **Worker:**   When we first met, you were frantic because you owed so much money on your credit cards. Over the past months, you have made some real progress on controlling your spending. Now, you are talking about a very expensive vacation. I am concerned that you might slip back into your old habits.

In some situations, it is necessary to use the skill of *persuasion* to encourage a reluctant or fearful client to take an important step. The worker can do several things to increase the chance that the client will follow through:

- Present and explain the suggested course of action using words, descriptions, and examples that the client will easily understand.

- Present and explain the suggested course of action after first identifying and acknowledging the other options or positions that may appeal to the client. This demonstrates to the client that you understand the dilemma and hesitation he or she may feel.
- Explain how the suggested course of action is compatible with the client's values and usual ways of doing things. Also point out how not taking this action will be inconsistent with his or her stated goals, values, and belief system.
- Identify and describe the advantages of following the suggested action while also pointing out the negative consequences of not doing so.
- Describe how this course of action was helpful or useful to persons in circumstances similar to those of the client.
- Offer an approach or plan that will allow the client to move ahead in small steps or phases so he or she can gradually try out or experiment with the suggested course of action.
- Enlist the assistance of persons whom the client trusts and respects and ask them to encourage the client toward the suggested course of action.

Maintaining Progress toward Change

Effective helping involves much more than understanding the client's problem or situation. The client needs to be helped and encouraged to make decisions and take action. Realistic, gentle, and supportive demands for change are necessary. Change usually involves having to reexamine one's assumptions and reevaluate past behavior; this can be painful and embarrassing. Change also involves trying out new behaviors and completing unfamiliar tasks; this can be frightening because it requires risk taking. It is important to recognize that a degree of fear, ambivalence, and resistance is a normal part of change. In fact, a lack of ambivalence and resistance may indicate that what looks like an effort to change is, in reality, only an illusion. Shulman (1981) explains that

> the worker must make a consistent ***demand for work.*** The demand may be expressed in many ways, but it is generally experienced by the client as the worker saying "I mean business." It is a critical skill because it conveys to the client the worker's belief in the client's strength and the worker's willingness to deal with even the toughest problems and feelings faced by the client. It is precisely this additional pull that clients need at that moment to mobilize their strength and to take their next steps. . . .
>
> The demand for work needs to be linked closely to the empathic skills. . . . A worker who is demanding, but not empathic, will be seen by the client as rejecting. On the other hand, the worker who is empathic, but makes no demands, will appear to the client as easy to put off. It is a critical synthesis of these two behaviors that will lead to effective work. (p. 20)

Several skills are helpful in maintaining momentum in the change process. One of these, ***partialization,*** refers to breaking down a seemingly insolvable problem into smaller, more manageable components. Clients often feel overwhelmed or helpless when faced with large, complex problems. When a problem is broken down into several smaller concerns, it seems less frightening, and the client is better able to focus his or her attention and energy. For example:

> ***Client:***   I cannot believe what is happening. Jimmy cut his head and I took him to the hospital. That crazy doctor notified child protective services and accused me of abusing Jimmy. Then my oldest son got into a fight with the landlord, and now the landlord has asked me to find another apartment. I cannot afford a lawyer, my child support check is late, and, on top of everything else, our car won't start. Things are so screwed up I cannot even think straight. All of a sudden the whole world has fallen in on me.
>
> ***Worker:***   I think we better talk about your concerns one at a time. Otherwise, we will get confused and feel even more frustrated. Let's first focus on the child abuse report. We will return to the other problems later. First, tell me more about Jimmy's injury and the abuse report. For now, let's talk only about that problem, OK?

The skill of ***staying on track*** involves worker statements intended to keep the client's attention focused on a specific concern or objective. This is especially important if the client tends to ramble or wants to avoid work on a relevant concern. For example:

> ***Worker:***   Because your boss has threatened to fire you, I think we better focus on that problem.
>
> ***Client:***   Yeah. I guess so. I really wish I could get a transfer. But the company has such old-fashioned policies on things like that. I'm surprised they make any money at all. With the economy the way it is, you would think they would change the whole operation. They are not prepared for global markets. I recently read an article on new styles of management and . . .
>
> ***Worker:***   I think we better come back to the conflict between you and your supervisor. You have lost other jobs because of conflict. I know you need this job, so I think we better figure out a way of dealing with the problem between you and your supervisor.

The skill of ***building a communication link*** refers to efforts by the worker to establish a connection between the client and those with whom he or she needs to communicate. For example:

> ***Worker:***   This is the third time you have told me that you haven't been able to tell your doctor about your concerns. What do you think about me giving her a call and explaining that I know you have something to talk to her about? I think that might cause her to spend more time with you when she visits you in the hospital tomorrow. Is that OK with you?

Sometimes, a client will outwardly agree to take a certain course of action but inwardly have no real commitment to that plan. It is also fairly common for a client to decide on an action without being fully aware of the difficulties he or she will encounter. The skill of ***checking for acquiescence*** is used to flush out a client's resistance to or ambivalence regarding a certain decision or action. For example:

> ***Worker:*** I certainly agree that you should talk to your math teacher about your failing grade. That needs to be done and I am pleased to hear that you intend to do it. But I also know that you often feel intimidated by that teacher. How might this be a difficult step for you?

Because genuine personal change is often an emotional struggle, the helping process and the content of the client-worker communications are usually emotionally charged. If, over a period of several sessions, there is little or no affectively charged discussion and no significant change in the client's behavior or situation, it is likely that the client is not really engaged in the change process. This needs to be discussed with the client. The skill of ***challenging the client's avoidance of change*** is a type of confrontation aimed at pointing out the client's resistance. The next example illustrates the use of this challenge during a marriage counseling session:

> ***Worker:*** Something concerns me. When you two came to this agency a few weeks ago, you requested help with your marriage. We have met three times. However, both of you have spent most of our time talking about your jobs, your kids, and your wish for a new house. You have said that there have been times when you were close to a divorce. You seem to be avoiding any discussion of your marriage relationship. Unless we focus on your relationship, we are not going to make any progress.

(See Item 13.10 for additional information on challenge and confrontation.)

A client's movement toward change may be blocked because he or she does not want to grapple with painful feelings. The skill of ***identifying emotional blocks*** refers to messages aimed at increasing the client's awareness of how these feelings are getting in the way of progress. For example:

> ***Client:*** I know I said I wanted to visit my kids more often, but I have been too busy at work to get away for a visit.
> ***Worker:*** You are a hard worker and your job demands much of your time, but I suspect the anger and guilt you feel about your divorce is also causing you to avoid visiting your kids. Perhaps we need to discuss those feelings and how they keep you from doing what you want to do.

Another example follows:

> ***Worker:*** I have noticed something, and I think we need to talk about it. We started meeting together because you wanted help in learning how to handle your children. Yet each time I ask about Gloria, you become tense and start talking about the other children. What is it about your relationship with Gloria that makes you so uncomfortable?

In some cases, the change process is blocked when a client has unusual difficulty talking about an important but embarrassing topic such as sexual behavior, spending habits, or irresponsible behavior. The skill of *supporting the clients in taboo areas* (Shulman 1981) refers to communication intended to assist the client in discussing sensitive topics. For example:

> *Client:*   I always feel nervous when I get to the topic of sex. It's hard for me to talk about it because of the way I was raised.
>
> *Worker:*   You are not alone. Many of us were raised the same way. But I want you to try. You and your husband need to discuss your sexual relationship. That area in your marriage is causing you some real problems. It's difficult to discuss, but let's keep at it.

Some clients have had difficulties with authority figures (e.g., parents, employers, police, etc.) and view the social worker as one more authority wanting to control them. It is important to invite the client to talk about this concern. The skill of *addressing the authority issue* refers to worker communication that invites the client to express concerns or complaints about the worker or the helping process. Consider this illustration:

> *Client:*   I think things are a lot better now at home. I don't think we need to set up another meeting.
>
> *Worker:*   I hope things are better, but I think something else is going on here. I have the impression that you think my job is like that of a parole officer and that I am trying to catch you doing something wrong. How about that? Are you scared of me and the trouble I might cause you?

(See Item 10.7 for more information on authority and the helping process.)

Bringing Things to a Close

Not infrequently, clients will wait until the last few minutes of a session before bringing up an important issue. There are several possible motives behind this *doorknob communication*, such as fear of the topic, wanting to inform the worker of a concern but not wanting to discuss it, and so on. The skills of *setting time limits* and *giving a 10-minute warning* are ways of encouraging the client to bring up difficult topics and to stay focused on high-priority topics. Here are a couple of examples:

> *Worker:*   Before we begin, I want to remind you that we can talk until 4:00 P.M. I say that because I want to make sure that we use our time to discuss issues that are of greatest importance to you.

or

> *Worker:*   I just noticed that we have to end this session in 10 minutes. Have we gotten to all the topics you wanted to discuss or is there something else that you wanted to talk about today?

The skill of ***looking ahead to the end*** is designed to remind the client of a planned ending for the intervention so the best possible use can be made of the remaining sessions. For example:

> *Worker:*   When we began meeting a month ago, we agreed to meet for eight times. We have three sessions left. Let's discuss what remains to be done so we use those three sessions to focus on high-priority concerns.

The client–social worker relationship may end because their work together is finished, because the social worker must transfer the client to another worker, because insurance benefits have elapsed, or for other reasons. If the relationship has been a meaningful one, the ending can be difficult. Because so many clients have experienced losses during their lives, the ending may be painful because it reactivates feelings attached to prior losses. These feelings must be addressed directly by the worker. Shulman (1981) explains that

> because of the general reluctance to face endings, both on the part of the worker and the client, endings often are handled too quickly, without an opportunity for the client and worker to deal with the complex feelings involved. . . . Since the client needs time to deal with the ending, encompass it, and not experience it as a sharp rejection by the worker, it is important for the worker to point out the ending well in advance in order to allow the process to become established. . . . It is only when workers can come to grips with their own feelings that they can begin to help the client in this important phase. (pp. 26–27)

The worker can help the client deal with the separation by voicing feelings about termination. Doing so is termed ***sharing ending feelings*** (Shulman 1981). For example:

> *Worker:*   I have been thinking about our relationship. Since you came to this hospital in September, we have gotten to know each other very well. I am glad you are finally able to go home, but I want you to know that I will miss our discussions and your positive attitude.

The review of what the client and worker have done to address the client's concerns is an important element in termination. This skill is referred to as ***reviewing progress.*** Here is an example:

> *Worker:*   Altogether, we have been meeting for about four months. A lot has happened since you were reported for child abuse. You have made some positive changes in how you deal with your son, Michael. What have you learned from this whole experience?

It is important to encourage the client to express his or her feelings about termination. These feelings may be positive or negative or a mix of both. The skill of ***reaching*** *for ending feelings* (Shulman 1981) refers to worker communication that helps the client articulate his or her feelings. For example:

> *Worker:*   I know you are pleased about getting off probation. You are no longer required to see me. But I also sense that you have mixed feelings about our meetings coming to an end. I wonder if it will be difficult for you to say good-bye. How about that?

(See Item 14.7 for more information on termination.)

SELECTED BIBLIOGRAPHY

Farber, Barry A. *Self-Disclosure in Psychotheraphy*. New York: Guilford Press, 2006.

Hill, Clara. *Helping Skills*, 2nd ed. Washington, DC: American Psychological Association 2004.

Murphy, Bianca, and Carolyn Dillon. *Interviewing in Action*, 3rd ed. Belmont, CA: Brooks/Cole, 2007.

Shulman, Lawrence. *The Skills of Helping: Individuals, Families, Groups, and Communities*, 5th ed. Belmont, CA: Brooks/Cole, 2006.

———. *Identifying, Measuring and Teaching Helping Skills*. Alexandria, VA: CSWE, 1981.

8.5   UNDERSTANDING EMOTIONS AND FEELINGS

Purpose: To assist the client in understanding and expressing his or her feelings.

Discussion: A social worker's capacity to understand and communicate with others depends on his or her ability to accurately read and tune in to human emotions and feelings. Many of the clients served by social workers are confused, frightened, or overwhelmed by their emotions, and many have not learned to express their feelings in a healthy manner. A social worker must be able to discuss the nature of emotions in ways that clients can understand and in ways that help clients learn how to gain greater control over troublesome feelings and emotions.

Emotions are complex, physical, biochemical, and psychological responses to conscious and unconscious interpretations of an event or experience. Neuroscience is just beginning to understand how emotions arise within us and how normal emotions can go awry, as when, for example, fear grows into a phobia or sadness turns into a disabling depression.

The word *emotion* means "to move." Our emotions move or motivate us to take action. They are a type of innate and primitive survival wisdom that is programmed into our very being. Emotions warn us of danger and push us away from or pull us toward activities that are likely to protect us from harm or assist us in meeting our basic needs. For example, the emotion of fear moves us to withdraw from a dangerous situation, whereas anger moves us to attack those who threaten harm. The emotion of anticipation moves us to persist in efforts to reach a goal, whereas the emotion of sadness attracts the attention and caring of other people. The emotion of remorse or guilt moves us to correct misbehavior, to rebuild damaged relationships, and make amends for harm we have caused.

Emotion is a type of communication that signals our state of mind and intentions to others. The facial representations of emotions such as sadness, fear, anger, disgust, joy, and so on, are recognizable around the world, regardless of culture.

Each emotion can vary in intensity. For example, joy can range from serenity to ecstasy, fear can range from apprehension to terror, and anger from annoyance to rage. While all emotions involve some level of physiological change, the bodily reactions that accompany the primitive fight-flight emotions such as fear, anger, panic, and terror are the most intense of all. Strong emotional reactions can overpower one's ability to think, concentrate, and learn. The power of emotion is most apparent in children and adolescents. As an individual matures, he or she grows in the ability to use reason to maintain self-control.

Although the words *emotion* and *feeling* are often used interchangeably, it is useful to define an *emotion* as a particular physiological and psychological response and a ***feeling*** as one's subjective awareness of that response. As explained earlier, emotions motivate us to take action when our physical or psychological survival or our well-being is perceived by us to be threatened or when the satisfaction of our needs is perceived to be blocked. It is important to understand that our emotions are a response to our subjective interpretation of what is happening, and this may or may not be an accurate interpretation.

The usual sequence between perception and thought and emotional and behavioral responses is as follows:

1. An event or situation occurs.
2. We notice, interpret, and think about the event.
3. Depending on our interpretations and thoughts, we experience a certain emotion.
4. The emotion moves us to engage in a certain behavior.

Some emotional reactions are immediate and do not involve thinking or cognition at a conscious level. For example, no real thought or analysis is necessary to interpret the danger of an attacking dog, to elicit the emotion of fear, and to move us to escape. Also, because of past conditioning (learning), we may interpret certain experiences in a habitual and almost automatic (unconscious) manner that involves little or no conscious thought. For example, the conditioning or learning associated with prior painful life experiences may cause us to misread a situation or event and thereby elicit emotions and behaviors that are seen as inappropriate by others. An example would be a woman who feels fearful around all men because during childhood she was sexually abused by one man.

We respond emotionally not only to our interpretations of events and situations but also to our own feelings and behavior. For example, as we experience an emotion, we often think about whether it is right or wrong to be feeling as we do, and these thoughts may, in turn, elicit still other emotions. We frequently pass judgment on our own behavior, and these judgments may give rise to still other emotions and behaviors or perhaps prompt us to reinterpret the situation in a different light. Thus, our thoughts, emotions, and behaviors are dynamic and interactive.

Because of the interplay between thought and emotion, we can, to a degree, alter and control our emotions and feelings by striving to change the usual ways we think about and interpret events and experiences. Several steps are involved in this learning process:

1. *Noticing our feelings.* People who are aware of their feelings are, by definition, in touch with their bodies, since all emotions have physiological correlates. Certain bodily sensations inform us that an emotional response is occurring. However, many of us tend to ignore or deny these sensations. Consequently, we may need help in learning to recognize the bodily reactions associated with emotion. One approach is to stop periodically throughout the day and reflect on our body's reactions and ask, for example, "What part of my body is experiencing emotion?" "Does some part of my body feel tense or strange?" "Is my body trying to get my attention?" "Why?" "What thoughts and interpretations are giving rise to these emotions?" Our bodily reactions during difficult interpersonal encounters or during times of stress are important windows to our underlying assumptions about self and others and our habitual ways of interpreting experiences.

2. *Naming our feelings.* Assigning a name to emotions and feelings helps us to accept them as real and provides a beginning sense of control. But attaching a label to something as subjective and nebulous as feelings is more difficult than it sounds. Many people lack a vocabulary for feelings. A list of feeling words may be of assistance in this naming process (see Item 13.17). If we reflect on an emotion, locate it in our body, and give it a name, it becomes more familiar and is less upsetting.

3. *Owning our feelings.* Before we can really examine an emotion or feeling, we need to claim it as ours. Taking ownership of a feeling can be difficult if we are in the habit of denying and ignoring our feelings. Owning and accepting a feeling can be made easier if its name is spoken aloud, possibly to another person (e.g., "I am afraid" or "I am feeling sad"). Many people are surprised to discover that this simple verbalization helps them cope with troublesome feelings.

4. *Examining our habits of thought.* Our ways of interpreting and thinking about events and situations are often habitual. To a large degree, those patterns are learned during childhood and carried into adulthood. Thus, in order to understand and modify troublesome thoughts and feelings, it may be necessary to reevaluate what we were taught during our childhood—a time when we uncritically form beliefs about ourselves and others. We must then decide if what we came to believe years ago as a child is still valid.

5. *Looking under and behind our emotions.* It is useful to think of our emotions as windows through which we can view the underlying and often unconscious interpretations of events and situations. For example, when feeling anxious or fearful, we might ask ourselves, "Why does this situation seem frightening or threatening?" "Is it really so or am I interpreting it this way out of habit or because of a prior painful experience?" "Are there alternative ways of interpreting this experience?" By looking at things from a different angle or coming up with other interpretations, we can often gain some control over the direction and intensity of our emotions and feelings.

6. *Choosing a course of action.*   Even when we cannot significantly change our emotional reaction to a particular situation or event, it is still possible to make choices about how to behave. We begin to gain control over our behavior by asking ourselves, "When I feel this way, what choices do I have?" "Is my instinctive response (e.g., running if I am afraid, attacking if I am angry) an appropriate one under the circumstances?" "What destructive responses must I avoid?" "What responses would hurt me or others?" "Which response would be most positive for me and others?"

SELECTED BIBLIOGRAPHY

Greenberger, Dennis, and Christine Padesky. *Mind over Mood.* New York: Guilford, 1995.

Lewis, Michael, and Jeanette Haviland, eds. *Handbook of Emotions*, 2nd ed. New York: Guilford, 2000.

Plutchik, Robert. *Emotions in the Practice of Psychotherapy.* Washington, DC: American Psychological Association, 2000.

8.6	RESPONDING TO DEFENSIVE COMMUNICATION

Purpose: To reduce the client's defensiveness.

Discussion: A social worker, especially one who is working with nonvoluntary clients, will encounter individuals who are defensive and guarded in their communication, often because they are angry or fearful or somehow feel threatened. The client may use a number of defensive maneuvers to keep the social worker at a distance and to avoid or minimize interaction and meaningful communication. Consider these examples:

- *Denial:* "I do not have a drinking problem!"
- *Blaming:* "I wouldn't have hit her if she didn't make me so mad."
- *Labeling:* "She can't help it; she's retarded."
- *Avoidance:* "I got busy and forgot about our appointment."
- *Helplessness:* "It's no use trying; nothing will change."
- *Using crisis or distraction:* "Johnny got into another fight; I have to talk about that now."
- *Being fragile:* "If I hear one more complaint, I will go absolutely crazy."

Some individuals use their physical environment (e.g., drawn shades, vicious dogs, terrible smells) and even their style of dress as means of intimidation and keeping people at a distance. Still others use cursing, aggression, and threats.

Often, the client is defensive before he or she even meets the social worker, but sometimes, the worker's behavior or style can add to the problem. Behaviors that increase client defensiveness include appearing rushed, being brusque or insensitive to a client's feelings, making judgmental statements, using jargon or quoting agency rules and policy without explanation, failing to identify yourself and your role clearly, calling an adult by his or her first name without permission, being authoritarian, and creating long waits and delays.

By following these guidelines, the social worker can reduce a client's defensiveness:

1. Remember that defensiveness is fundamentally an attempt to protect oneself from real or imagined danger. Within a context of social service delivery, the dangers or threats perceived by clients are those of embarrassment, humiliation, loss of control over one's life, loss of privacy, or failure to receive a desired social provision. Thus, do not respond to the defensive behavior as such but rather focus on what might be the client's underlying fear. Determine what is causing your client to feel threatened and try to remove that cause. Acknowledge those aspects of the situation that may cause your client to feel awkward, threatened, or humiliated (e.g., "I know it can be embarrassing to have to ask for financial assistance"). Use a generous amount of active listening (see Item 8.4), and make it as easy as possible for your client to verbalize feelings; do not pressure him or her to do so, however.

2. Expand your tolerance of your client's defensive behavior by understanding that it may have served a purpose in the past. If the client's defensiveness is a long-term pattern rather than situational behavior, hypothesize how it may have protected the client from pain associated with some fundamental disruption (e.g., rejection by a parent, breakup of one's family, or separation from loved ones) or a frightening event (e.g., major personal problem, family violence, or a life-threatening illness). Patterns of defensiveness often develop in response to such fear and pain. Your gut reactions to the client will often provide clues as to the function served by the defensiveness. For example, if you feel a strong desire to walk away from the client, the client's defensiveness may serve as protection against interference by outsiders. If the client's sad and helpless behavior makes you feel sorry and want to rescue the client, this defensive pattern may help the client avoid a frightening responsibility.

3. If your client exhibits a nondefensive behavior, respond in a way that will reinforce or reward this behavior. Also use the technique of ***mirroring***, which can be described as speaking at the client's pace and in a manner that matches his or her nonverbal behavior. In other words, follow a nondefensive conversational exchange with a vocal tone and cadence, posture, and nonverbal behavior that mirrors or imitates the client's verbal and nonverbal behavior. On the other hand, if your client assumes a defensive posture or tone of voice, respond with exactly the opposite (e.g., an open, nondefensive posture and a soft comforting tone of voice). If your client's conversation speeds up as a result of anxiety or anger, respond with a slow and nurturing manner; this usually has a calming effect on the client.

4. To the extent possible, use words and phrases that match your client's dominant mode of receiving information. The three basic modes are visual, auditory, and touch. A client reveals his or her dominant mode in the frequent use of certain predicates in phrases such as "I see what you mean" (visual), "I hear what you are saying" (auditory), or "That goal is beyond my reach" (touch). If you can identify your client's dominant mode, try to match your phrases to his or her mode—for example, "Do you have a clear picture of what I am suggesting?" (visual), "Does this plan sound OK to you?" (auditory), or "I think the plan you have suggested is one we can both get hold of" (touch).

5. Whenever possible, give your client opportunities to make choices and remain in control of what is happening in his or her life. Use words such as *we, us, together,* and *it will be your decision;* these imply cooperation, respect, and choice.

6. Consider using the technique of ***joining the resistance*** by aligning yourself with the client's feelings—for example, "After such a long wait, you deserve to be angry. I would be angry also." Such an alignment with the client's hurt feelings reduces resistance by removing the client's need to keep defenses up and it gives the client permission to vent feelings.

7. Do not label or categorize your client (e.g., "All Medicaid recipients have to fill out this form"). People become defensive when they experience a loss of individuality. Also, do not embarrass or back your client into a corner, either physically or psycho-logically. Arrange your office and your own seating position so your client does not feel confined. Allow your client to save face in embarrassing situations.

8. A defensive or resistant individual may attempt a number of maneuvers to block a worker's engagement efforts. In situations where it is critically important to engage the resistant client (e.g., in cases of child abuse), you will need to be assertive and deal directly with the issue. For example, if your client is silent, you might say something like, "I can see you do not want to talk to me about how your child was injured, but I am going to stay here until we have discussed it." If your client appears overly agree-able to what you have said, you could say, "I certainly hope you will take the actions you have promised, but how will I know that you have followed through on those plans?" Some defensive clients attempt to divert attention away from the real issue. When that happens, you might say, "I can sense you do not want to focus on the child abuse report, but that is why I am here and we have to get back to that topic." If your client attempts to avoid the central issue by talking about secondary concerns, you may need to take control by saying something like, "You have mentioned at least five other problems and I can understand that they are of concern to you, but we have to come back to the question of how Joey got those bruises—that must be the primary focus of this interview." In some cases, clients defend themselves by trying to make the worker feel guilty. When that happens, you may need to say, "I know you are upset and I don't like to see people cry, but your child has been seriously injured and it is my job to find out what happened. Take a few minutes to compose yourself and then we must get to the bottom of this. If you cannot talk to me I will ask someone from the prosecu-tor's office to speak with you." If your client verbally or physically threatens you, you will need to say something like, "I have no intention of harming you. I will not argue with you and I cannot continue the interview under these conditions. If you are too angry to talk now, I will come back this afternoon with a police officer. Do you prefer to talk now or later?" (see Items 10.7, 10.8, 10.9, and 10.10).

9. If your client uses obscene or abusive language, remain calm and do not respond in ways that might reinforce the unacceptable behavior. Respond immediately with verbal and nonverbal attention and reinforcement to any part of the client's communication that is appropriate and constructive.

10. If the client persists in verbal attacks, consider using the technique termed *fogging.* This name comes from the notion that rocks thrown into a fog bank have no effect. If the person under verbal attack can mentally and emotionally behave like the fog, the verbal "rocks" have no impact and, hopefully, the attacker will soon abandon his or her efforts to cause discomfort. This technique works because the person under attack offers no resistance and avoids responding with either anger or defensiveness and because it calmly acknowledges that the angry person may have a point and is possibly accurate in his or her criticism and judgments. For example:

> *Angry Client:*   All you ever do is talk!
> *Worker:*   You're right. I do talk a lot.
> *Angry Client:*   If you would pay attention to what I have been saying, you wouldn't have to ask these dumb questions!
> *Worker:*   That may be true. I could be more attentive to what you say.
> *Angry Client:*   You are just like all the other lazy government employees and state social workers! You are always telling people what to do and butting into things that are none of your damn business.
> *Worker:*   I am a state employee. It does make sense that state employees would do their job in similar ways.

SELECTED BIBLIOGRAPHY

Cormier, Sherry, and Paula Nurius. *Interviewing and Change Strategies for Helpers*, 5th ed. Belmont, CA: Brooks/Cole, 2003.

Kottler, Jeffrey. *Nuts and Bolts of Helping*. Boston: Allyn & Bacon, 2000.

Rooney, Ronald. *Strategies for Work with Involuntary Clients*. New York: Columbia University Press, 1992.

8.7   ELEMENTS OF PROFESSIONAL BEHAVIOR

Purpose: To clarify the nature of professional behavior.

Discussion: It has been said that "A *professional* is someone who knows what to do and can be counted on to do what needs to be done, even when he or she does not feel like doing it." There is much wisdom in that description. It suggests that a professional knows what should be done, can be trusted to do it, and does not let matters of personal convenience or personal feelings interfere with his or her performance.

It is important for social workers to continually examine their performance and make sure their behavior is of a professional nature. Consider the following comparison of professional and nonprofessional behavior:

Professional Behavior	*Nonprofessional Behavior*
1. Views social work as a calling and a lifetime commitment to certain values and actions	1. Views social work simply as a job that can be easily abandoned if something better comes along
2. Bases practice on a body of knowledge and research findings that have been learned through formal education and training	2. Bases practice on personal opinions or on agency rules and regulations
3. Makes decisions primarily on the basis of facts, analysis, and critical thinking	3. Makes decisions primary on the basis of personal feelings and traditions
4. Develops relationships with clients that are purposeful and goal directed; does not expect to meet own emotional needs within these relationships	4. Develops relationships with clients that are perfunctory or resemble friendships; expects to meet own emotional needs within these relationships
5. Considers client's well-being and needs to be of primary concern	5. Considers own well-being and needs to be of primary concern
6. Adheres to the principles of good practice, regardless of other pressures	6. Allows political and fiscal pressures to dictate decisions and actions
7. Uses the profession's *Code of Ethics* to examine and address ethical concerns	7. Uses only personal moral judgments and opinions to address ethical concerns
8. Upgrades knowledge and skills continually so that services to clients can be improved	8. Learns only what is required to keep the job
9. Takes responsibility for creating new knowledge and sharing it with peers	9. Does not see self as responsible for the development of new knowledge
10. Assumes personal responsibility for examining the quality of services provided and for working to make agency, program, or policy changes that will improve services to the client	10. Is concerned only about doing the job as assigned or described by others; does not see self as responsible for agency, policy, or program changes
11. Exercises self-discipline; keeps own emotions under control	11. Lacks self-discipline; expresses emotions in a thoughtless and hurtful manner
12. Expects and invites review of own performance by peers	12. Avoids peer review of own performance
13. Keeps accurate and complete records of practice decisions and actions	13. Avoids recordkeeping

SELECTED BIBLIOGRAPHY

Lauffer, Armand. *Working in Social Work.* Newbury Park, CA: Sage, 1987.

Morales, Armando, Bradford W. Sheafor, and Malcolm E. Scott. *Social Work: A Profession of Many Faces,* 11th ed. Boston: Allyn & Bacon, 2005.

8.8 MAKING ETHICAL DECISIONS

Purpose: To clarify ethical issues and make practice choices that are consistent with social work's ethical principles and professional values.

Discussion: Each day, social workers make decisions concerning complex ethical issues. Sometimes the task is to help clients sort out their own ethical concerns, and at other times it involves the social worker determining if an action he or she is about to take is appropriate from an ethical perspective. Occasionally all possible practice options will cause harm or distress to someone, creating an ethical dilemma for the social worker.

Essentially, an ***ethical dilemma*** is a situation in which the worker has two or more ethical obligations but cannot follow or adhere to one without violating another. For example, ethical dilemmas faced by social workers increasingly involve decisions on how best to allocate scarce resources in times of budget cutbacks and staff short-ages or to limit services when an insurance company will not pay for the cost of services required by a client. In some cases, the decision to provide services to one client may result in limiting or withholding the services needed by others.

A first step toward resolving ethical dilemmas is to answer several questions that supply important background information and clarify the matter:

- Who is your primary client (i.e., usually the person, group, or organization that requested the social worker's services and expects to benefit from them)?
- What aspects of the agency's activity or worker's roles and duties give rise to the dilemma (e.g., legal mandates, job requirements, agency policy, questions of efficient use of resources, possible harm caused by an intervention, etc.)?
- Who can or should resolve this dilemma? Is it rightfully a decision to be made by the client? Other family members? The worker? The agency administrator?
- For each decision possible, what are the short-term and long-term conse-quences for the client, family, worker, agency, community, and so on?
- Who stands to gain and who (if anyone) stands to lose from each possible choice or action? Are those who stand to gain or lose of equal or of unequal power (e.g., child vs. adult)? Do those who are most vulnerable or those with little power require special consideration?
- When harm to someone cannot be avoided, what decision will cause the least harm with fewest long-term consequences? Who of those that might be harmed are least able to recover from the harm?
- Will a particular resolution to this dilemma set an undesirable precedent for future decision making concerning other clients?

Once those questions have been answered, the worker must answer three additional questions:

- What ethical principles and obligations apply in this situation?
- Which, if any, ethical principles are in conflict in this situation and therefore create an ethical dilemma?
- In this situation, are certain ethical obligations more important than others?

To answer these questions, the social worker must be very familiar with the National Association of Social Worker's **Code of Ethics** (1999), which lists and describes ethical standards and principles and provides general guidelines for professional conduct. The *Code* is also the NASW's basis for evaluating and responding to any charges of unethical conduct made against a social worker. A copy of the *Code* should be on the desk of every social worker.* The *NASW Code of Ethics*, therefore, is an important benchmark that may be used to survey a practice situation to determine if a specific alternative or action is ethically responsible. It serves as an ethical screen or filter through which the acceptable practice alternatives should pass.

The Code of Ethics Worksheet (see Figure 8.1) is offered here as a tool for comparing the ethical dimensions of practice alternatives. To use the worksheet, the worker should first list each practice option (e.g., each possible action or decision). For example, Option A might be "I will prevent my client from making a serious mistake by pressuring him to follow my advice and not quit this job until other employment is secured," and Option B might be "I will respect my client's decision to quit his job even if that choice will make his problems even worse." There could be other options (e.g., Options C, D, E, etc.).

Second, the worker should make notes of issues and concerns that might arise for each option directly on the Code of Ethics Worksheet. This worksheet is built on the NASW *Code*'s six areas of ethical consideration—that is, the social worker's ethical responsibilities (1) to clients, (2) to colleagues, (3) to practice settings, (4) as professionals, (5) to the social work profession, and (6) to the broader society. The Canadian *Code of Ethics* is organized differently but could readily be placed in a similar format. The 10 areas addressed in the Canadian *Code* are (1) primary professional obligation, (2) integrity and objectivity, (3) competence, (4) limits on professional relationships, (5) confidential information, (6) outside interests, (7) limits on private practice, (8) responsibilities to the workplace, (9) responsibilities to the profession, and (10) responsibilities for social change.

*The latest version of the *NASW Code of Ethics* can be obtained from the National Association of Social Workers. It can be downloaded from NASW's website at www.naswdc.org/code.htm. Also, NASW maintains a "hotline" a few hours each week (800–638–8799) where members can recieve consultation regarding ethical issues in social work practice. Information regarding the Canadian Association of Social Workers' *Code of Ethics* can be obtained from CASW's website at www.casw-acts.ca and search the practice section.

FIGURE 8.1

Code of Ethics Worksheet

What options, actions, or decisions are being considered as a practice intervention?

List and briefly describe the practice option(s) being considered.

Option A: *Pressure client to not quit job*

Option B: *Allow client to make a poor decision and quit job*

Does the option potentially place you in violation of any of the following ethical areas identified in the *NASW Code of Ethics*? If so, make a brief note regarding the potential violation.

1. **Standards related to the social worker's ethical responsibilities to clients.**
   This section of the *Code of Ethics* is concerned with such factors and principles as: the worker's primary responsibility is to the client; respect for client self-determination; securing client's informed consent; worker's competence to provide needed services; worker's cultural competence; avoiding conflict of interest; respecting clients' right to privacy and confidentiality; the prohibition of sexual involvement, sexual harassment, inappropriate physical contact, and abusive or derogatory language; special considerations when clients lack decision-making capacity; avoiding the interruption of services; careful termination of services.

   Potential issues and problems to consider:

   Option A: *Compromises client self determination? (Section 1.02)*

   Option B: *Is client able to make own decisions? (Section 1.14)*

2. **The social worker's ethical responsibilities to colleagues.**
   Section 2 of the *Code of Ethics* is concerned with social workers' responsibility to treat colleagues with respect; concern for maintaining confidentiality among professionals; appropriate collaboration and teamwork; proper handling of disputes and disagreements; appropriate consultation relationships; proper referral of clients to colleagues; the prohibition of sexual harassment and sexual involvement with one's supervisees or students; and the requirement for responsible action in relation to a colleague who is impaired, incompetent, or is unethical in his or her practice.

   Potential issues and problems to consider:

   Option A: *Not applicable*

   Option B: *Not applicable*

3. **The social worker's ethical responsibilities in practice settings.**
   This section of the *Code of Ethics* relates to services performed in relation to social workers and other professionals, and only indirectly relates to clients. The items addressed include competence in providing supervision, consultation, education,

(continued)

and training; evaluating the performance of other workers; maintaining proper client records and billing properly; carefully evaluating client needs before accepting transfers; assuring an appropriate working environment and providing ongoing education and training in human services agencies; demonstrating commitment to agency employees; and acting responsibly in labor disputes.

Potential issues and problems to consider:

Option A: *Not applicable*

Option B: *Not applicable*

4. **The social worker's ethical responsibilities as a professional.**
This section of the *Code of Ethics* includes items related to the social worker accepting employment and job assignments when he or she may not be competent to perform that work; practicing, condoning, or participating in any form of discrimination; engaging in private conduct that compromises the ability to fulfill professional responsibilities; engaging in dishonesty, fraud, and deception; addressing one's own problems if impaired; clarification of public statements regarding whether acting as a professional or a private citizen; making uninvited solicitations for business; and properly acknowledging any contributions to one's written or other work made by others.

Potential issues and problems to consider:

Option A: *Not applicable*

Option B: *Not applicable*

5. **The social worker's ethical responsibilities to the social work profession.**
Section 5 of the *Code of Ethics* concerns issues related to the social worker promoting high standards for social work and contributing time and energy to its growth and development, as well as items related to social workers monitoring and evaluating social policies, programs, and their own practice interventions.

Potential issues and problems to consider:

Option A: *Not applicable*

Option B: *Not applicable*

6. **The social worker's ethical responsibilities to the broader society.**
In this section of the *Code of Ethics*, social workers are charged with promoting the general welfare of the society and the realization of social justice; participating in public debate to shape social policies and institutions; providing services in public emergencies; and actively engaging in social and political action.

Potential issues and problems to consider:

Option A: *Not applicable*

Option B: *Not applicable*

Third, once potential issues are identified, the worker should examine the specific language in each section of the *Code of Ethics* for clarification and eliminate any specific issues that no longer seem relevant after this closer scrutiny. Finally, for each practice option, the worker should prepare a summary of the *Code of Ethics* items that would be compromised if that option were selected.

If the worker determines that the client possesses adequate decision-making ability as expressed in Section 1.14 of the *NASW Code of Ethics,* the appropriate ethical decision would be to allow the client to be self determining (Section 1.02) even if the result would be a poor decision for the client and his family.

A limitation of the *NASW Code of Ethics* as a tool for resolving ethical issues is that all standards in the *Code* are given equal weight. Thus, it is useful for the worker to apply a second tool when making ethical decisions: the Ethical Issue Priority Checklist (see Figure 8.2). This checklist is derived from a ranking of ethical priorities developed by Dolgoff, Loewenberg, and Harrington (2005). Although all seven principles are

---

FIGURE 8.2   **Ethical Issue Priority Checklist**

What options, actions, or decisions are being considered by the social worker?

Option A: ___*Pressure client to not quit job*___

Option B: ___*Allow client to make a poor decision and not quit job*___

Answer the following questions for each of the options you have identified with "Yes," "No," or "Cannot Determine." (*Note:* Avoid making too many assumptions about possible but unlikely long-range implications of the action.)

1. Does this option/action threaten or risk someone's life, physical well-being, or chances of survival?

    | Option A | Yes | (No) | Cannot Determine |
    | Option B | Yes | (No) | Cannot Determine |

2. Does this option treat someone in a fundamentally unjust, unfair, or unequal manner and/or violate basic human rights?

    | Option A | Yes | (No) | Cannot Determine |
    | Option B | Yes | (No) | Cannot Determine |

3. Does this option significantly and unreasonably limit someone's self-determination or autonomy?

    | Option A | (Yes) | No | Cannot Determine |
    | Option B | Yes | (No) | Cannot Determine |

4. Does this option cause someone significant personal distress or economic hardship?

    | Option A | Yes | (No) | Cannot Determine |
    | Option B | (Yes) | No | Cannot Determine |

(continued)

5. Does this option decrease the quality of life for those of a neighborhood, community, or society as a whole?

Option A	Yes	(No)	Cannot Determine
Option B	Yes	(No)	Cannot Determine

6. Does this option cause someone to lose his or her right to privacy and confidentiality?

Option A	Yes	(No)	Cannot Determine
Option B	Yes	(No)	Cannot Determine

7. Does this option involve distorting or withholding the truth from an individual or a community?

Option A	Yes	(No)	Cannot Determine
Option B	Yes	(No)	Cannot Determine

The checklist would indicate that limiting the clients' self-determination should have priority over the economic hardship that might follow when the client quits his job.

---

important, it lists the principles in order, with Principle 1 (i.e., the protection of life) viewed as most important and Principle 7 (i.e., telling the truth) considered least important among the seven. An individual social worker might identify additional principles or order the priorities differently, yet the ranking by Dolgoff et al. provides a useful starting point.

The process followed in using the Ethical Issue Priority Checklist begins with identifying the various practice options in a manner identical to completing the Ethics Worksheet. In this case, however, the worker then responds to questions 1 through 7 on the checklist by circling an answer "Yes," "No," or "Cannot determine" for each option. If a circled yes answer appears higher among the priorities (i.e., higher on the page) for one option as opposed to others, the worker should seriously question the appropriateness of using that practice option.

When the two checklists are completed and analyzed, the worker should be prepared to make a decision regarding which option to exercise—at least as far as the ethical issues are concerned. If the action selected violates a provision of the *Code of Ethics*, it is suggested that the worker write out the rationale for that decision and include such a statement in the client's file, as this documentation may be useful if the worker is subsequently charged with a *Code* violation as a result of this decision.

SELECTED BIBLIOGRAPHY

Dolgoff, Ralph, Frank M. Loewenberg, and Donna Harrington. *Ethical Decisions for Social Work Practice*, 7th ed. Belmont, CA: Brooks/Cole, 2005.

National Association of Social Workers. *Code of Ethics.* Washington, DC: NASW, 1999.

Reamer, Frederic G. *Ethical Standards in Social Work: A Critical Review of the NASW Code of Ethics.* Washington, DC: NASW Press, 2006.

Robison, Wade, and Linda Reeser. *Ethical Decision Making in Social Work.* Boston: Allyn & Bacon, 2000.

Strom-Gottfried, Kim. *Straight Talk About Professional Ethics.* Chicago: Lyceum, 2007.

8.9   APPLYING CULTURAL COMPETENCE TO HELPING

Purpose: To become sensitive to the significance of cultural factors in the helping process.

Discussion: The United States has been and continues to be a nation of many diverse cultures. Social workers interact with many individuals who have cultural, ethnic, religious, and socioeconomic backgrounds that are significantly different from their own. Thus, it is critical for social workers to understand that culture affects many aspects of clients' lives, including how families raise their children, how men and women perceive gender roles, what beliefs and values drive people's behavior, use of language, forms of religious expression, and so on. Intervention strategies that are relevant to and compatible with the client's culture are far more likely to succeed than those that ignore this important factor in human functioning.

What is a culture? A **culture** can be defined as a set of interrelated behaviors, beliefs, values, attitudes, and practices that is transmitted or communicated from generation to generation. In this definition, the phrase regarding transmittal from one generation to the next is critical to the identification of a culture. In fact, *transmittal* is what distinguishes a culture from a segment of a population that shares beliefs, attitudes, and values because they have been shaped by a particular life experience or event—for example, the camaraderie that exists among combat veterans, members of a particular profession, or persons who have a particular disease or disability.

It is important to recognize that the word *culture* is often used in a rather loose and imprecise manner, as, for example, in the phrases *teen culture, drug culture,* and *agency culture.* These are not true cultures, as just defined, because the social phenomena that characterize them are not passed on to and imitated by the next generation. The communication and transmittal of a whole set of beliefs, behavioral patterns, and values from generation to generation requires the influence of multiple societal institutions and social forces (e.g., families, schools, laws, language, etc.).

A culture strongly influences how people meet their basic needs, cope with the ordinary problems of life, make sense out of their experiences, and negotiate power relationships, both within and outside their own group. One's culture is, to a large degree, the source of what one expects of self and others, as well as his or her ideas about the way things are or should be. Our minds and our culture do not create reality but they do create or construct what we believe to be reality. A culture is like a lens or screen through which people view life. That lens typically becomes so internalized and such a central part of his or her way of interpreting experiences that he or she may not even recognize its existence and its power in shaping his or her thoughts, behaviors, and judgments about self and others.

Because social work involves making judgments about clients when determining how practice will be performed, sensitivity to each client's cultural background becomes a fundamental skill. In addition, the social worker must be aware of his or her own culture and how it affects the manner in which he or she perceives clients and provides services.

Closely related to the idea of culture is the concept of ethnicity. An *ethnic group* is a segment of a larger population that identifies itself and is regarded by others as being a distinct group who share a common language, religion, ancestry, physical appearance, or some combination of such characteristics. Ethnicity is mostly related to people's perception of social boundaries and how perceived differences among people are defined, explained, proclaimed, or denied. If people believe that they belong to a distinct group and are somehow different from other people, that belief will have a significant effect on their behavior and on their relationships with others—including how they interact with their social workers.

A particular ethnic group may or may not also be a minority group. A *minority group* is one whose members have significantly less power, resources, and control over their own lives when compared to those who are members of the dominant group in society. Typically, the members of a minority group have some physical or cultural characteristics that distinguish them from members of the dominant group, and they frequently experience prejudice and discrimination.

Whereas culture and ethnicity have to do with people's values, beliefs, and behaviors, the term **race** refers to the categorization of people on the basis of certain observable physical characteristics, such as skin color, hair texture, eye shape, and body structure. **Racism** exists when people judge others on the basis of such physical features and view them as somehow inferior. Racist beliefs and attitudes give rise to discrimination and oppression. Those who encounter racism and other forms of discrimination—including discrimination based on gender, class, ethnicity, disability, sexual orientation, and age—are more likely to experience social and economic inequality and are vulnerable to various psychosocial problems. American society— and many others around the world—falls short of Martin Luther King, Jr.'s, dream of a society in which people "would not be judged by the color of their skin, but by the content of their character."

An additional related concept is that of *social and economic class*. Within every society and cultural or racial group, there are subgroups whose life situations and conditions are closely tied to factors of income, level of education, and type of occupation. One's income and access to financial resources (e.g., credit, business contacts, job information) have a far-reaching effect on his or her social functioning, self-image, and attitudes. For example, people who have few financial resources often feel very vulnerable and are afraid to say or do anything that might put their jobs or incomes at risk. People who have wealth, however, come to understand and use its power—often at the expense of those with lower socioeconomic status.

Belief systems such as racism, classism, ageism, and sexism usually arise from personal and societal prejudice and often lead to discrimination against particular groups. It is important to distinguish between prejudice and discrimination. **Prejudice** refers to beliefs that negatively prejudge others on the basis of their group identity. Although prejudice may lead to acts that are damaging to others, or **discrimination,** it is fundamentally a belief about others that has little effect until it is acted upon. Thus, prejudice might not always lead to discrimination, and discrimination can exist apart from prejudice. For example, one can discriminate out of ignorance or carry out insensitive and discriminatory organizational policies without being prejudiced.

Acts of discrimination may be as blatant as deliberately causing physical injury to a member of a particular group or refusing to hire a person because of his or her race; these are acts of *personal discrimination. Institutional discrimination*, on the other hand, can be more difficult to detect because it is built into the fabric of society through laws, longstanding patterns of assigning wages to particular jobs, and other systematic patterns that have the effect of placing specific groups at a social and economic disadvantage. For example, the "glass ceiling" for women in management positions and the substantially higher poverty rates for African American and Hispanic families in the United States are indication of institutionalized discrimination.

Most people, whatever their background, possess some level of prejudice against groups other than their own—and sometimes even toward their own ethnic, cultural, or gender group. Social workers must be alert to the existence of prejudice (including their own) and constantly assess, modify, and suspend their prejudices so that these beliefs and attitudes do not lead to discrimination. Social workers must also be alert to the existence of institutional discrimination and be prepared to address and combat it, lest it affect their clients negatively.

Guidelines for Culturally Sensitive Social Work Practice

People tend to be ***ethnocentric***—that is, they assume that their way of life is a superior or appropriate standard for judging others. It is difficult to completely rid oneself of the prejudices acquired during his or her upbringing, but social workers must constantly guard against falling into the ethnocentric trap when assessing and working with clients. The professional helper should watch for these signals that his or her thinking is racist or otherwise prejudiced:

- Stereotyped explanations are given for the behavior of people of a specific ethnic, age, gender, or other minority group.
- The same practice strategies and techniques are used for all clients who are members of a particular group.
- The factors of culture, race, and ethnicity are minimized or ignored or, at the other extreme, used to explain nearly all behavior.

One of the social worker's first goals in practice should be to understand and appreciate each client's cultural background while recognizing that we seldom acquire more than a superficial knowledge of another culture, especially when language differences are involved. Even so, the social worker can achieve at least a beginning understanding of a culture by reading about it, interacting with people from that culture, attending various cultural and religious events, and so on. The worker must remember that every attempt to describe a group of people—whether the people be White middle class, blind, African American, or Republican or Democrat—requires the use of generalizations and thus he or she runs the risk of labeling and stereotyping people. Among the members of every cultural or ethnic group, there are always significant individual differences.

The practice principle "The social worker should consider clients experts on their own lives" (see Chapter 5) should guide the social worker's approach to learning about a client's culture. The need for cultural sensitivity is not limited to work with individuals. It also applies to agencies and communities. Social workers should be alert to the fact that their agencies' policies and programs might, in some way, discriminate against certain ethnic groups or other groups of people. Being open to this possibility, conducting ongoing self-studies, including minority group members on governing or advisory boards, and soliciting reviews by persons from outside the agency who are members of various population groups can be of critical importance in developing and maintaining appropriate cultural sensitivity as an organization.

Social workers should also recognize that most social agencies and their programs were created by members of the dominant group in society and that the social workers employed by these programs may be viewed with suspicion by clients who are members of minority population groups. Furthermore, cultural difference between the worker and client can have other effects on practice. Whittaker and Tracy (1989, 158), for example, explain that a major obstacle in working with a member of an ethnic minority is the "differing expectations as to what constitutes 'help,' making it extremely difficult to select appropriate and effective intervention methods." They warn that some of the most popular and commonly used techniques may not be effective when working cross-culturally. To illustrate:

- Self-disclosure may be particularly difficult between dominant-culture workers and discriminated minority groups, since it presumes a degree of trust which may not exist initially.
- Short-term, task-oriented styles of social work may be ineffectual with clients who feel that extended periods of time "just talking" is an appropriate way to enter a relationship. . . .
- Reflection, reaching for feeling, or asking for insights may appear inappropriate or intrusive.
- Some ethnic groups, for example Asian-Pacific Americans, may view help-seeking as a shame-inducing process and will be extremely reticent to disclose personal problems. . . .
- Many ethnic minority groups (e.g., Puerto Rican, Hispanic) expect a more active helping relationship with the worker offering advice and tangible assistance.
- Techniques that rely on intrapersonal solutions versus social resolutions may be less appealing.
- Cognitive behavioral or rational emotive techniques . . . [e.g., challenging irrational beliefs, etc.] may run counter to important cultural values and beliefs. (pp. 158–159)

Closely related to demonstrating ethnic sensitivity is the need to adapt practice to the client's religious beliefs and spirituality. In fact, one's ethnicity, culture, and religion are usually interwoven. The social worker should be aware that the lives and decisions of a large portion of the clients they serve are influenced by particular religious and moral beliefs. Practice that neglects the client's religion may miss opportunities to be helpful to the client (see Item 15.18). Loewenberg (1988) observes that

> avoiding one segment of a person's life, such as religion, will handicap the interaction, even if it is a professional relationship between a social worker and client. One may wonder whether a social worker can really have a meaningful or helpful relationship with clients who have a strong religious commitment when such a social worker avoids the religious aspects of their lives. (p. 86)

In work with all clients, but especially with clients of a different cultural or ethnic background, the social worker is advised to individualize the client. The social worker must be alert to human diversity and never assume that a client's physical features or ethnic identity will predict the client's values, beliefs, or behavior patterns.

The social worker also should keep in mind these guidelines:

1. Appreciate the subjectiveness involved in how people see themselves and others. Remember that human differences are whatever people define them to be and their relevance is whatever people believe them to be.

2. Self-awareness is of critical importance. Constantly examine your attitudes and behavior and be alert to the possibility that you are making judgments based on racism, prejudice, and stereotypes, or perhaps behaving in a discriminatory manner. Frequently ask yourself, "What is my attitude toward people of different cultural backgrounds?" "How do I feel about people who have a different skin color or speak a different language?" "How do I feel about people who have religious beliefs different from my own?"

3. Early in the relationship with a client, you should acknowledge the existence of obvious differences of ethnicity or race as a way of giving the client permission to talk about these matters and express possible concerns about not being accepted or understood. Encourage the client to identify perceived differences and to explain how these differences might be addressed in the professional relationship and service delivery.

4. Show a special interest in your client's name, place of birth, and home community, for these topics are good icebreakers and lead naturally to a discussion of the client's cultural background and ethnic identity.

5. A client who might experience difficulty with the English language should be asked if an interpreter is needed. If you will be working with many people who speak another language as their first or primary language, strive to learn as much of that language as possible. Make an effort to speak the client's language, even if you can master no more than a few words and phrases. Doing so will be viewed as a basic courtesy and as showing respect for the client's native language and culture.

6. Overlooking client strengths, misreading nonverbal communication, and misunderstanding family dynamics are among the most common errors made in cross-cultural helping. Behaviors motivated by religion and spirituality, family obligation, and sex roles are often misunderstood. Because of the difficulty in reading nonverbal cues cross-culturally, the worker should move slowly when reaching for feelings and putting the client's feelings into words. Overlooking strengths results when the worker does not fully appreciate the situation—especially the contextual and systemic aspects—with which the client must cope.

7. Be alert to the fact that in many ethnic groups, certain family members are the key decision makers and other family members will not make important decisions without consulting them. For example, in many Hispanic families, the husband and father typically has considerable authority, and his wife and even his adult children may feel obligated to obtain his approval before taking a course of action. Also, within the extended families common to the American Indian tribal cultures, certain individuals perform the role of advisor and other family members will delay making a decision until they have obtained his or her advice on the matter. Thus, it is always a good idea to ask the client if he or she wants to invite others to the interview or somehow involve them in decision making. Not infrequently, clients will simply bring these respected individuals to important meetings.

8. Be alert to the subtleties and limitations inherent in the use of language. Recognize the influence of language on how one thinks or is able to think about certain matters. Whenever we use a word, we call up in our minds a concept or "picture" of what that word means. A given word may call forth somewhat different thoughts and ideas, depending on one's culture. Clearly, it is in our use of language that we encounter differences in how people think and interpret experiences.

9. Because members of many ethnic minority groups have experienced discrimination, it is to be expected that they will be somewhat distrustful of professionals and agencies that represent and reflect the dominant groups in society. They will enter a helping relationship with caution as they size up the social worker. For example, they may evaluate the worker's trustworthiness by asking, directly or indirectly, about his or her life experiences, family, children, and opinions. The worker needs to respond to these probes with honest, nonevasive answers. Because visiting people in their own home is usually seen as an indication of caring and respect, the home visit may help the worker build trust.

10. Ask your clients to explain their beliefs and culture, and ask for their advice in how you might adapt your helping methods to their values, traditions, and customs. Do not be afraid to say that you do not understand. If you genuinely care for the clients and demonstrate concern for their situation, most will explain what you need to understand about their way of life. It often helps to use a bit of self-effacing humor (i.e., laughing at your own ignorance) when asking questions about things you do not understand. This display of humility makes you less threatening.

11. When you need to better understand certain cultural or ethnic factors, seek appropriate consultation. Contact leaders in the ethnic community and express your desire to learn about their values, beliefs, and way of life. They will usually offer their assistance if they perceive your interest to be genuine. Also attend celebrations, ceremonies, and other cultural and religious events sponsored by the group.

12. Be alert to the fact that societal or systemic problems (poverty, unemployment, poor housing, lack of access to health care, etc.) bring ethnic minorities to agencies more often than do psychological problems. Thus, the provision of concrete services and the practitioner roles of broker and advocate are of special importance.

SELECTED BIBLIOGRAPHY

Diller, Jerry. *Cultural Diversity*. 3rd ed. Belmont, CA: Brooks/Cole, 2007.

Fong, Rowena, and Sharlene Furuto, eds. *Culturally Competent Practice: Skills, Interventions, and Evaluations*. Boston: Allyn & Bacon, 2001.

Loewenberg, Frank. *Religion and Social Work Practice in Contemporary American Society*. New York: Columbia University Press, 1988.

Lum, Doman. *Culturally Competent Practice*, 3rd ed. Belmont, CA: Brooks/Cole, 2007.

Whittaker, James, and Elizabeth Tracy. *Social Treatment*, 2nd ed. New York: Aldine de Gruyter, 1989.

Rothman, Juliet. *Cultural Competence in Process and Practice: Building Bridges*. Boston: Allyn & Bacon, 2008.

Basic Skills
for Agency Practice

INTRODUCTION

Most social workers are employed by some type of human services agency. Within these organizational contexts, social workers typically struggle with two interrelated sets of tasks: managing their time and managing the required paperwork. This chapter offers guidance on how social workers might increase their efficiency by incorporating into their daily routines the skills of time management, effective phone use, and information technology. Also included are guidelines on report and letter writing and preparing client records.

Paperwork and recordkeeping consume much of a social worker's time. Most workers dislike these tasks, but they are an essential component of service provision. Professional records must be complete, concise, legible, and accurate. Ideally, an agency's recordkeeping system will create documentation useful for the following purposes: (1) provide an accurate account of services provided; (2) provide data that can be used to identify needed changes in policy, service delivery, and staff deployment; (3) provide data for retrospective and prospective research; (4) provide data that reveal the judgments behind key decisions and are therefore useful in staff development and professional education; (5) provide documentation of adherence to relevant legal and policy requirements; and (6) provide information that is understandable to and will withstand scrutiny by external reviewers (e.g., accreditation bodies, ombudsmen, lawyers, insurance companies, quality control personnel, etc.).

In our litigious society, social workers are sometimes named in lawsuits alleging professional negligence or misconduct. Accurate and complete recordkeeping is of critical importance in defending oneself against such an allegation. In the absence of proper documentation, there may be no evidence that a social worker's decision or action was appropriate, responsible, and justified by the situation and circumstances.

The new social worker learns quickly that there is not enough time to do all that needs to be done. Faced with that reality, the worker must make the best possible use of limited time and focus on matters of highest priority. The worker must strive to be efficient, but measures taken in the name of efficiency must not compromise an effective helping process or shortchange client services.

9.1   REPORT WRITING

Purpose: To prepare a clear and useful professional report.

Discussion: A social worker must write many reports. Reports that are inaccurate, incomplete, or unclear create misunderstanding and sometimes costly errors. A number of guidelines can improve the quality of reports.

1. Before you begin to write, carefully consider the report's audience (i.e., who will be reading this report?). Determine what information or content the readers need and expect. Also, consider whether the report may be passed on to still other readers such as another agency or possibly to newspapers or agency clients. Keep these potential readers in mind as you write and imagine how they will interpret or perhaps misinterpret your words.

Select an appropriate format and writing style. As a general rule, a formal writing style and format that yields a tightly organized report is required for court reports and interagency or external communication. A less formal approach is usually acceptable for internal communications (i.e., within an agency or organization). Formal reports require close attention to agency protocol and prescribed format, use of proper names and titles, and accurate use of terminology. By contrast, the use of first names, abbreviations, and jargon may be acceptable for internal or intraagency communication. Copies of sample agency reports—ones judged by others in the agency to be good models—can be used as guides to your report writing.

2. Before writing the first draft, organize the content to be presented into a logical structure that outlines the main topics, the various subtopics, and the key points under each. If you present your ideas in an orderly manner and use various headings to set sections apart, the reader will be better able to follow your reasoning and understand your message.

Two or three drafts or revisions of a formal report may be needed before the final version is produced. Ask peers to review your draft. If they are not sure of what you are trying to say, you can be certain that the intended reader will not understand either. Also read the draft aloud; if it does not sound right, revise it. Be committed to your ideas, not your words.

Always use the spelling check, grammar check, and the thesaurus that are features of a computer's word-processing program. A thesaurus, which lists synonyms and antonyms for a word, will help you add variety and freshness to word selection.

3. Use words, sentences, and writing style that are simple, clear, and direct. Select your words carefully, using only those your reader will understand. Use the dictionary whenever in doubt about the exact meaning of a word. Use the number of words necessary, but no more. Wordiness lessens the force of expression and may distract the reader from the point you want to make.

4. Keep your sentences short, usually 15 to 20 words or less. Most often, the straightforward subject-verb-object sentence is the best arrangement because it can be read quickly and is seldom misunderstood. Consider these two sentences:

- After much discussion, not all of which was productive, a foster home placement—the agreed upon arrangement—was made for the child.
- The child was placed in a foster home.

The second sentence is easier to read and understand; it is short and it follows the subject-verb-object structure.

5. Use the active voice whenever possible. The passive voice adds unnecessary words, weakens the statement, and makes the meaning less clear. For example, "Don hit John" has a clearer, stronger impact than "John was hit by Don."

6. Give special attention to paragraph construction. Each paragraph should focus on a single idea. The outline for a good paragraph is as follows:

- In the first sentence, state the central point of the paragraph.
- If necessary for purposes of clarification, restate the central point in other words.
- Present the evidence, examples, background information, and the logic supporting the central point and your conclusions or observations.
- Finally, draw the paragraph to a close, summarizing the key point in a single sentence.

By reading only the first and last sentence of a paragraph, the reader should be able to pick up the core idea of what you are trying to communicate. In general, a page of double-spaced typewritten copy should contain two or three paragraphs. If there is only one paragraph per page, it is likely that too many ideas have been crammed into a single paragraph.

7. Do not use weak and evasive language such as "There may be a tendency toward," "It would appear that," "It seems as though," and "There is some reason for believing." Such phrases give the reader the impression that the writer is either unsure of what to say or unwilling to take responsibility for what is being said. Also avoid so-called weasel words such as *feel* and *seems*. Instead of saying "I feel placement is necessary," be direct and state "I believe placement is necessary" or simply "I recommend placement for this child." Wishy-washy language and weasel words cause the report reader to question the worker's professional competence and confidence.

8. Avoid hackneyed expressions such as "It certainly merits study," "The matter is receiving our closest attention," "We will explore every avenue," and "Naturally, the child's interest is our concern." Such trite phrases suggest that the writer is insincere or responding as a mere formality.

9. Avoid using slang or phrases that might offend the reader. For example, consider the following series of words: *determined, obstinate, stubborn, pig-headed*. Each has about the same meaning, but each will strike the reader differently. Also, avoid redundant phrases such as *first beginnings, the present time, join together, and exact same*.

SELECTED BIBLIOGRAPHY

Alfred, Gerald, Charles Brusaw, and Walter Oliu. *Handbook of Technical Writing,* 7th ed. New York: St. Martin's Press, 2003.

Beebe, Linda, ed. *Professional Writing for the Human Services.* Washington, DC: NASW, 1993.

9.2   LETTER WRITING

Purpose: To communicate ideas and information clearly and concisely in letters.

Discussion: Most of the principles that should guide report writing (see Item 9.1) also apply to letter writing. In addition, the guidelines presented in this section will improve the effectiveness of written correspondence. Some of these are relevant to writing e-mail messages, as well. Consider the following suggestions:

1. Before you send even the shortest letter, think carefully about its purpose and the recipient's need for and use of the information or content written into the letter. Remember that your image as a professional is shaped by the appearance, quality, and tone of your written work. Proper grammar and correct spelling is essential in all professional writing. Incomplete sentences, while now common to email messages, are not appropriate in letters and reports.

As a general rule, all letters to other agencies and professionals should be prepared on letterhead stationery. Ordinarily, letters to clients should also be typed. In some instances, a personalized letter or note to a client can be appropriately handwritten.

A copy of all letters sent should be retained in the agency file or case record because they document a professional action and the service provided. Use certified or registered mail when necessary to document that a specific letter was delivered.

2. Be cautious about including in a letter any information that would violate a client's right to confidentiality if read by persons other than the intended recipient. Also, be alert to the fact that an agency's name on an envelope may reveal the client's involvement with the agency.

3. A formal letter will have at least the following parts: letterhead, date, inside address, reference line or subject line, salutation, body, complimentary close, typed signature, and written signature. When appropriate, there should also be an enclosure notation (*enc.*) and a copy notation (*cc* or *pc*) that names others receiving copies of the letter.

4. Always use proper titles, such as *Mr., Mrs., Miss, Dr., Rev.*, and so on. The use of *Ms.* is appropriate when a woman's marital status is unknown. First names should be used only when addressing children or persons with whom you have a close relationship.

5. A letter in which you are registering a complaint or arguing your point of view should be written with directness and clarity. Make your point emphatically but without being abrasive. If you have written this type of letter while angry or

frustrated, wait a day before putting it in the mail. Reread it and consider what you have said and how it is likely to be perceived by the recipient. This wait and reconsideration may prevent you from saying something you will later regret.

SELECTED BIBLIOGRAPHY

Berger, Arthur. *Improving Writing Skills: Memos, Letters, Reports, and Proposals.* Newbury Park, CA: Sage, 1993.
Davis, Kenneth. *Business Writing and Communication.* New York: McGraw Hill, 2005.

9.3 EFFECTIVE TELEPHONE COMMUNICATION

Purpose: To communicate clearly when using the telephone.

Discussion: The telephone is a frequently used tool in social work practice. However, it is not always the most effective method of communication.

The telephone should be used when a quick response is needed and the matter under discussion is relatively uncomplicated. It is important to remember that a phone call does not establish a permanent record of the transaction. A letter or memo may be preferred when time is not critical, when a record must be established, or when the message involves many details. Following these guidelines will help improve telephone use:

1. Before placing a phone call, consider its purpose and jot down the major points you wish to address during the phone conversation. Plan to take notes and if it is important to document the phone call and its content these notes can be placed in the agency file or case record. Begin all phone communications by identifying yourself and your organization. Before saying "good-bye" it may be appropriate to summarize the information you intended to convey and the information you received.

2. The task of communicating on the telephone must be accomplished entirely by voice. The person to whom you are speaking does not have the advantage of observing your gestures or other body language. Take time to enunciate clearly. Give your undivided attention to the person with whom you are speaking; do not attempt to "multitask" while on the phone.

3. The widespread use of cell phones is a boon and a bane to social work practice. For sure, the cell phone contributes to efficiency and better time management. On the other hand, cell phone use, especially in public places, can jeopardize client confidentiality and it is often an irritant to the people nearby. It is truly difficult for a social worker to give undivided attention to a client while also driving a car or walking down a busy street. Common courtesy requires that cell phones be turned off during client interviews and agency meetings.

4. If the person on the other end is talking at length, interject a brief comment at intervals: "Yes, I see" or "I understand." This lets the other person know that you are listening. If your caller gets sidetracked, steer him or her back to the main point of the call.

5. If you must leave a message for a person you did not reach by phone, keep the message short (e.g., your name, phone number, and reason for calling) and assume there is a good chance that the message will get garbled or lost. Repeat the phone number two times, and speak slowly while doing so. Suggest a specific time for the person to return your call. You will save time by calling back yourself rather than waiting for your call to be returned.

6. Master the skills of using your agency's phone system such as transferring calls, using voice mail, and so on. When transferring calls to other lines, let callers know what you are doing: Tell them the name and title of the person to whom they will be speaking and why you are transferring their call. When you must leave the phone, explain why: "Please hold on for a few seconds while I get that file." Unless you are sure you will be away for only a few moments, tell your caller that you will call back. If you have left the phone, alert your caller to your return before resuming the conversation: "Hello" or "Thanks for waiting" or "I have that file now."

7. Realize that the voice mail systems used in many agencies can be confusing to callers. The caller may be upset after having to listen to a recorded voice, select from a menu of options, and perform numerous dialing maneuvers. Instruct your clients and other frequent callers how to use the system.

SELECTED BIBLIOGRAPHY

Tarbell, Shirley. *Office Basics Made Simple.* New York: Learning Express, 1997.

9.4   USING INFORMATION TECHNOLOGY

Purpose: To use various forms of information technology to increase practice effectiveness, workload efficiency, and administrative accountability.

Discussion: In recent years, computer use has become an essential part of social work practice, agency operation, and administration. At a minimum, social workers should be skilled at word processing, the use of a spreadsheet program, accessing online information, and communicating by way of the internet. A desktop computer equipped with a basic software package and a modem connected to a standard telephone line is sufficient for performing these activities—although a high-speed Internet connection is much more desirable.

Here are the applications and information technologies that are used in most social work settings:

1. *Online resources.* The forms of information technology used most often by social workers are likely the various online resources. ***Electronic mail*** or ***e-mail***, is an excellent communication tool for transmitting information, scheduling meetings, obtaining consultation, and providing support for both professionals and clients. At the most advanced level, email can be used even for client counseling and advice giving. For the professional using email to improve efficiency, messages can easily be sent and stored, meetings can be efficiently announced and scheduled, clients can be contacted, and reports can be transmitted and received. Participating in email-based professional discussion groups can also add to social workers' practice knowledge and stimulation, even for workers who live in remote areas. Clients, too, can use email and electronic discussion groups to connect with people experiencing similar social issues as a form of self-help or mutual-aid group experience.

Another widely used online resource is the ***World Wide Web (WWW)***, which links Internet information through webpages. Once basic web access fees have been paid, an unlimited amount of information is available to the user at no cost. Many government agencies, human services organizations, universities, and individuals create and maintain webpages. These pages often provide built-in links to related pages, making it relatively easy for a social worker to access many sources of information on a specific topic, even when in a location far from a well-stocked library. Many articles and some books are available on the web and can be downloaded free or at a nominal cost. With the growing emphasis on evidence-based social work practice, it is essential to be able to search for evidence of best practices for specific services or the latest information on specific client conditions.

Web-based online advocacy represents a growing use of this technology. Groups who are concerned about local, state, national, and even international matters of social policy are able to rapidly exchange social and political information and reach large numbers of people to encourage them to take action regarding these issues. Figure 9.1 provides a listing of particularly useful web resources for social workers.

2. *Word processing.* Another almost universal use of computer technology by social workers is word processing. Much of the necessary correspondence; preparation of case summaries; completion of agency information sheets; writing memoranda, agendas, reports, and journal articles (see Item 16.11); and other routine agency paperwork now bypasses clerical staff and is done entirely by social workers. A specialized form of word-processing software, created for what is known as ***desktop publishing***, is used in many agencies to prepare newsletters, bulletins, flyers, and public relations information (see Item 13.36). Finally, ***presentation software*** packages assist in creating text and graphics for making presentations at professional meetings (see Item 16.12) and for interpreting agency services to other agencies, civic clubs, United Way allocation committees, potential clients, and so on.

3. *Spreadsheets.* When the information to be recorded is numerical, ***spreadsheet software*** is extremely useful. Spreadsheets are used in maintaining data about services provided and clients seen, in accounting and bookkeeping tasks, and in collecting program evaluation and research data. The primary advantage of using a spreadsheet is being able to use formulas so that data summaries can be quickly compiled. In addition, columns can be easily and accurately summed, basic statistical formulas can be readily applied to data, and graphs and charts can be professionally developed. One particularly useful application of spreadsheet software is in making projections; namely, "what if" questions can be tested by changing one value and then observing how doing so will modify other values. This application is useful, for example, in

FIGURE 9.1	Useful Web Resources for Social Workers

Professional Organizations

Association of Social Work Boards (information on licensing requirements in all states and schedule of licensing examinations) http://aswb.org

Canadian Association of Social Workers (CASW programs, *Code of Ethics*) www.casw-acts.ca

Council on Social Work Education (CSWE programs, lists of accredited BSW and MSW programs, publications) www.cswe.org

International Federation of Social Workers (IFSW position papers, *Code of Ethics*) www.ifsw.org

National Association of Social Workers (NASW activities, *Code of Ethics,* and publications) www.naswdc.org

Search Engines for Social Work–Related Topics

Federal Legislation (texts of recent bills and status of pending legislation) www.thomas.loc.gov

Information for Practice (news and new scholoarship from around the world) http://www.nyu.edu/socialwork/ip

Google Scholar (search of scholarly literature including books, articles, and theses) http://scholar.google.com

Government Printing Office Access (links to policy databases including federal budget, economic indicators, *Federal Register,* legislative reports, presidential papers, judicial decisions) www.gpoaccess.gov/index.html

Healthfinder (guide to health-related information) www.healthfinder.gov

Library of Congress (search for all books with U.S. copyrights) http://catalog.loc.gov

Social Work Access Network (links to relevant information sources, social work chat room, message board, etc.) http://cosw.sc.edu/swan

Statistical Information (centralized data source for most government agencies) www.fedstats.gov

Welfare Information Network (clearinghouse for information, policy analysis, and technical assistance related to welfare, workforce development, and other human and community services) www.financeprojectinfo.org

---

estimating the need for financial resources when preparing a grant application, in identifying the potential savings from purchasing a more efficient photocopy machine, or in increasing the fees charged for services.

4. *Database programs.* As the electronic equivalents of filing cabinets and file folders, ***database programs*** provide an efficient way of maintaining and accessing important information. Regarding a specific client, social workers might include in a database such items as demographic characteristics, a social history, intake information, treatment plans, and progress notes. These data can be readily retrieved to track the progress of the client or merged with data from other clients to prepare a report. Database programs also can be used to schedule appointments, manage "to do" lists, and otherwise reduce paperwork.

5. *Research-related software.* Social workers are obligated to assess their practice effectiveness. That might be done by tracking the progress of individual clients (see Items 14.3 through 14.6) or by engaging in program evaluation (see Item 14.9). In addition, social workers are expected to add to the knowledge base of the social work profession as they become interested in answering questions and testing hypotheses that arise in their practice. Software is available to facilitate such research by selecting a sample size, constructing data-entry forms, calculating the margin of error for a given return rate, suggesting and performing statistical tests, analyzing qualitative data, and presenting the results in graphic format.

6. *Distance learning.* Social work practice constantly changes, which means social workers at all levels must learn new theories and techniques on an ongoing basis. Whenever a worker moves from one practice setting or field to another (e.g., from mental health to corrections), a period of intensive study is usually required. In addition, some state licensing boards require licensed social workers to update their credentials periodically by participating in workshops, classes, and other instructional activities. These educational needs often can be met through participation in distance learning programs. Some are offered in an online format, which will allow the worker to participate in courses from his or her home or office.

As social work practice makes increasing use of information technology, practitioners at all levels must participate in shaping the technology to fit the practice, rather than permitting the technology to shape and drive practice. Social workers also should understand both the benefits and the dangers associated with this technology. For instance, they should be aware of inherent ethical issues, such as the risk of transmitting confidential information electronically, as well as the potential to further distance disenfranchised populations from mainstream society by expecting that people have ready access to this technology. (This is sometimes referred to as the *digital divide.*)

In the end, however, social workers must recognize that electronic technology only provides tools to assist practice. It is the workers themselves who must decide how to use this technology in an appropriate and responsible manner.

SELECTED BIBLIOGRAPHY

Finn, Jerry, and Gary Holden. *Human Services Online: A New Arena for Service Delivery.* Binghamton, NY: Haworth Press, 2001.

Vernon, Robert, and Darlene Lynch. *Social Work and the Web.* Belmont, CA: Wadsworth, 2000.

Yaffe, Joanne, and Doug Gotthoffer. *Socialwork on the Net.* Boston: Allyn & Bacon, 2001.

9.5 PREPARING CLIENT RECORDS

Purpose: To maintain accurate and useable client records.

Discussion: What and how much information should be included in the client's record? How should this information be arranged and organized? Every social worker and agency must come up with workable answers to those questions. What is recorded and the format used will depend on factors such as the agency's mission, the type of service provided, relevant state and federal laws and regulations, and who will have access to the records.

A client record describes the client and his or her problem or situation and the social work intervention. It shows the rationale underlying the intervention, documents the client's involvement in decision making and actions taken, documents compliance with key agency policies, and provides a coherent picture of the specific services provided. All client records contain identifying data such as names, addresses, and phone numbers. A "good record," according to Kagle (2002, 30), will be accurate, unbiased, objective, up-to-date, well written, and well organized. Given that a court can subpoena client records for use as evidence in lawsuits and because a social worker may be asked to read aloud from this record in open court, a worker must be very thoughtful about what information is placed in a record and how it is stated (see Item 16.7). Kagle (2002, 30) also notes that certain types of information should not be placed in a client record, such as information not relevant to the services provided, unsubstantiated hypotheses, unfounded judgments, and rumors about the client. Maintaining client confidentiality is an overriding concern in all recordkeeping and documentation (see Item 10.5).

Depending on agency policy, a client record may be handwritten, dictated, or typed directly into a computer document. Increasingly, agencies use software programs that aid in the preparation and the management of client records and make the retrieval of information faster and easier (see Item 9.4).

The use of *progress notes* or *case notes* is a common method of recording in direct service agencies. This approach describes the worker's contacts with the client, chronologically arranged. After each contact with the client or with persons collateral to client service, the worker writes a few sentences or paragraphs (progress notes), which succinctly captures the essence of what happened during the session and, typically, states what the worker plans to do in future sessions with the client.

In order to prepare progress notes for easier reading and retrieval, the notes are often placed within an organizing structure. The DAP (Data, Assessment, Plan), PIG (Problem, Intervention, Goal), and SOAP formats are three such structures. The acronym SOAP refers to the following key elements or headings:

S   *Subjective information* describes how the client feels about or perceives his or her situation. It is derived from client self-report. By definition, subjective information does not lend itself to independent or external validation.

O   *Objective information* is that which has been obtained by way of direct observation by professionals, clinical examinations, systematic data collection, and the like. This category of information can be independently verified.

A   *Assessment* refers to the professional's conceptualization or conclusions derived from reviewing the subjective and objective information.

P   The *Plan* spells out how the professional intends to address or resolve the client's concern or problem.

FIGURE 9.2   **Sample SOAP Entry**

Subjective: Mrs. Brown states she worries about children's diet. The children complain of being hungry and to her embarrassment they have asked neighbors for food. Since Mrs. B grew up on welfare, she has vowed "never to go on the dole." She says she is in a "panic" about the thought of losing her children.

Objective: Her job earns $325 take-home pay per week. Rent is $700 per month. It is hard to follow Mrs. Brown in conversation; she jumps from topic to topic. Agency records indicate that she was herself neglected as a child and placed in foster care for two years.

Assessment: Family does not have enough money for food. Mrs. Brown is probably eligible for food stamps. Much of her disorganization is due to her anxiety about losing her children to foster care, which is, in turn, related to her own experience in foster care. She fears that accepting welfare will label her as a "bad parent."

Plan: (Problem #2) Need to support Mrs. Brown's application for food stamps and show her that application is a way to be a "good mother" under these very trying circumstances. Need to assure her that agency has no plans to place her children. Begin effort to help Mrs. B find higher-paying job. Complete food stamp application by 5/25.

Figure 9.2 is an illustrative SOAP entry related to problems faced by a client, Mrs. Brown.

The shorter DAP and PIG formats collapse both the "subjective" and the "objective" information into a single category.

At monthly or quarterly intervals, the information contained in progress notes or case notes may be consolidated into a *narrative summary* and also may be used to update or modify a client's service contract or treatment plan (see Item 12.6).

Many agencies utilize various *forms and outlines* to collect and arrange client information. Such instruments are created by the agency's professional staff and administrators familiar with the work of the agency and the type of concerns it addresses. The headings written into the forms and outlines remind the social worker of the types of data to be recorded and also facilitate the retrieval of information. Examples of headings that appear on such forms are: client's presenting concern or problem, client's family and social supports, client's health, client's employment and occupation, client's cultural background, activities and changes since last contact with client, and so on.

A consideration in all approaches to preparing client records is developing a mode of documentation that can monitor and measure client progress in order to determine if a given intervention is working. The starting point for all such measurement is clarity regarding the intervention goals and objectives (see Items 12.1 and 12.5). Chapter 14 describes scales and techniques used to measure client change. The documentation of client change is critically important when a client is using a public or private insurance to pay for the service. Several books offer guidance on the preparation of a client record that will meet requirements imposed by managed care. Such books list hundreds of prewritten progress notes that are keyed to various client problems and to the DSM categories (see Item 11.18 and Item 16.8).

SELECTED BIBLIOGRAPHY

Jongsma, Arthur. *The Adult Psychotherapy Progress Notes Planner*. Hoboken, NJ: Wiley, 2003.

Jongsma, Arthur, L. Mark Peterson, William McInnis, and David Berghuis. *The Child Psychotherapy Progress Notes Planner*. Hoboken, NJ: Wiley, 2003.

Kagle, Jill. "Record-Keeping." In *Social Worker's Desk Reference*, edited by Albert Roberts and Gilbert Green, 28–33. New York: Oxford Press, 2002.

Wiger, Donald. *The Psychotherapy Documentation Primer*, 2nd ed. Hoboken, NJ: Wiley, 2005.

Wiger, Donald. *Clinical Documentation*, 3rd ed. Hoboken, NJ: Wiley, 2005.

9.6 MANAGING TIME AND WORKLOAD

Purpose: To make the best possible use of limited time.

Discussion: Nearly every social worker is faced with having too much work and too little time. Thus, the worker must strive to control his or her workload and use time management skills to increase efficiency on the job. Consider these guidelines:

1. Understand your agency's mission and your job description. Unless you are clear about what needs to be done, you cannot figure out ways to do it effectively and efficiently. If your assignments and responsibilities are not clear, discuss them with your supervisor or administrative superiors. Find out what tasks and assignments are of highest priority.

2. Plan your work. At the end of each day, as well as at the end of each week, write down what you must work on or accomplish the next day and the next week. Start each day with a "to do" checklist. Estimate how much time is needed for each item on the list and plan to allocate the time needed. Anticipate deadlines and begin work on those tasks that must be completed within a certain time frame. It is usually best to tackle lengthy tasks before those that can be completed in a short time. Work on the most difficult tasks when your energy level is highest (e.g., first thing in the morning). Reserve some time at the end of each day for clearing your desk and taking care of last-minute activities.

3. Adopt a system for setting priorities. One such system is the ABC priority system. On your list of work tasks, write *A*'s next to those that are most important and have highest priority. Write *C*'s next to tasks that are of least importance and *B*'s next to tasks in the middle range. Next, prioritize the *A* tasks in order of importance, labeling them *A–1, A–2, A–3*, and so on. The *B* tasks can be labeled in the same way: *B–1, B–2*, and so on. At the beginning of the working day, start at once on task *A–1* and stay with it until it is completed. Then move to *A–2* and on down the list.

A less complex approach is to classify all tasks into three categories: (1) tasks that must be completed today, (2) tasks that should be started today, and (3) tasks that can wait a few days. Realize that priorities may change over the course of a day or week. Thus, it is necessary to continually review and revise your "to do" list.

4. Plan for the unexpected. Allow time in your schedule for emergencies. Remember Murphy's Laws: "Nothing is as simple as it seems," "Everything will take longer than you think," and "If anything can go wrong, it will."

5. Reduce interruptions to a minimum. When you are interrupted, maintain control of the situation by giving the interruption full attention, avoiding irritation, and, where appropriate, setting a time limit on the interruption. Drop-in clients are often less of a problem than staff who interrupt other workers. Being able to say no to the question, Do you have a minute? is an important time-management skill. Closing your office door or standing up to converse with someone who just stopped by can help limit unnecessary interruptions.

6. Make decisions in a timely manner. Some workers are too afraid of making mistakes; as a result, they delay making decisions. Some avoid making decisions because they cannot arrive at a perfect solution. There are few, if any, perfect solutions in the real world of social work practice. One must strive for excellence, but striving for perfection will result only in frustration. If you make a mistake, learn from it; do not waste time brooding over it. A "good" mistake is one from which you learn and do not repeat. A "bad" mistake is one you will repeat again.

7. Keep your agency's policy and procedures manual up to date. As changes occur, insert the new information and discard the old. Much time can be lost searching for misplaced information or following an outdated procedure.

8. Develop a *tickler file* to keep track of deadlines for submitting monthly reports and other tasks that must be completed according to a schedule. A tickler file can take several forms: notations on a calendar, a desktop file, a computerized calendar, or electronic date book. Also, develop a workable system for the storage and rapid retrieval of frequently used information such as the names, addresses, phone numbers, and email addresses of professionals and agencies that you regularly contact. That system might be a Rolodex or a personal digital assistant.

9. Minimize the time spent in agency meetings. Unnecessary and poorly planned meetings can waste much valuable time. Do not schedule a meeting if an alternative is possible, such as a telephone conference call or email exchanges. If you must have a meeting, make sure all those attending know its purpose and are given an agenda in advance so they can come properly prepared. Start on time and end on time. Stick to the agenda and stay on task. Consider attending the meeting for only the amount of time necessary to make your contribution. (See Items 13.25 and 13.27 for additional guidelines on meetings.)

10. When possible, structure your day by using scheduled appointments for interviews, collateral contacts (contacts with other service providers), and the like. Reduce travel time by scheduling all meetings in a given locality for the same day.

11. Organize your desk and eliminate clutter in your workspace. Keep those things you are working on in front of you, but clear your desk of other materials. This will help keep your attention on the task at hand. Focus on one thing at a time until you either complete the task or reach a preset time limit for that activity. Avoid jumping from task to task.

12. An important rule in managing paperwork and paper flow is to handle each paper only once. If you pick up a letter or report, take the action required or discard it if no action is necessary. Do not set it aside; do not let papers pile up on your desk.

13. If a lack of some specific skill is slowing you down or causing time-consuming mistakes, obtain the additional training you need. Ask experienced colleagues to help you devise more efficient approaches to your work. Secure their suggestions on how to reduce time spent writing agency records and routine reports (see Item 9.1). Become proficient in the use of office machines and communications systems (e.g., email, fax, word processor, etc.).

14. To the extent feasible, control your workload. If a social worker does not exercise such control, he or she will be spread too thin and effectiveness will diminish. When asked by others to take on additional work that will require more time than you have, consider the following:

- Decide if the proposed assignment or request for your time is reasonable, given your job description and current workload. Ask yourself: Is this a matter of high priority? Am I responsible for this matter or is someone else? If I say yes, will I soon regret it and feel angry and put upon? Am I tempted to say yes mainly because I want to avoid a conflict or the appearance of selfishness?
- When unsure if the request is reasonable, obtain more information before saying yes or no. If still in doubt, ask for time to think about the request and set a deadline for making the decision (e.g., "I'll let you know in a half hour").
- If you must refuse, say no firmly and calmly. Give a straightforward explanation of why you must say no, but do so without offering excuses and rationalizations. If you have a good reason for refusing, there is no need to apologize.

It must be noted that the above discussion of refusing additional assignments presumes a situation in which there is opportunity to negotiate. In many practice settings that situation does not exist. An agency supervisor or administrator has the authority to make work assignments, even when he or she knows you are already overloaded.

In some work situations you can reduce an excessive workload by assigning certain tasks to other agency staff such as a secretary, case aide, or paraprofessional. When assigning work do not ask others to take on tasks that are beyond their ability or job description.

SELECTED BIBLIOGRAPHY

Davidson, Jeff. *Complete Idiot's Guide to Managing Your Time*, 3rd ed. New York: Alpha Books, 2002.

Morgenstern, Julie. *Time Management from the Inside Out*, 2nd ed. New York: Henry Holt and Co., 2004.

Zeigler, Kenneth. *Getting Organized at Work*. New York: McGraw Hill, 2005.

PART 4

Techniques and Guidelines for Phases of the Planned Change Process

Many social work supervisors have heard practicum students and new social workers say something like "I understand the basic theory of working with people, but what should I do when I see Mrs. Jones and her daughter this afternoon?" Obviously, these novice workers have discovered that there is a difference between *knowing* and *doing* in social work practice. They sense a need for direction and guidance that is more specific than that provided by various practice perspectives, theories, and models.

Part IV of this book addresses this need. As was explained in the Preface, the authors chose to prepare a book focusing mostly on techniques and guidelines. This decision reflects their belief that many texts do an excellent job of presenting the theoretical frameworks of practice, yet few provide the concrete guidance so often requested by students and new workers.

Many social workers engage in some combination of both direct and indirect practice. The term ***direct practice*** refers to those activities that involve frequent face-to-face interaction with an individual or family who has requested a service or is experiencing some difficulty. Direct social work practice might include, for example, individual and family counseling, case assessment, case management, referral work, group treatment, guiding a support group, advocating for the services needed by a specific individual, and so on. By contrast, the term ***indirect practice*** is used to describe practice activities that do not involve extensive contact with the clients or consumers of services but which indirectly benefit those who need various types of services or forms of assistance. Examples are agency administration, staff supervision, program planning, program evaluation, fund-raising, public education, work with community groups and coalitions of agencies that are concerned about a particular social problem or condition, advocacy on behalf of a large group of persons in need, and efforts to enact legislation and change public policy that would enhance peoples' lives.

The five chapters of Part IV correspond to the five phases of the planned change process, as described in Chapter 7. The reader will notice that each of these chapters has a Section A and a Section B. Techniques and guidelines related to direct social work practice are provided in Section A, whereas techniques and guidelines used in indirect practice are provided in Section B.

Chapter 10, "Intake and Engagement," is concerned with start-up activities, or the beginning phase of work with clients. Also included is information on new beginnings that are part of joining an agency and starting work in a new community.

Chapter 11, "Data Collection and Assessment," provides a sampling of techniques and guidelines for gathering information about the client situation and assigning meaning to that information. Some form of data gathering and assessment will be required, whether the social worker's client is an individual, a family, a neighborhood, or a community.

Chapter 12, "Planning and Contracting," presents techniques and guidelines for helping the client and worker arrive at a set of agreed upon goals and objectives for their work together. The failure to secure such an agreement and to formulate a clear plan for the change effort or intervention is one of the most common errors made by human services professionals, whether working with a family, agency committee, or other client system.

Chapter 13, "Intervention and Monitoring," provides a sampling of direct practice and indirect practice techniques and guidelines for encouraging and facilitating the process of change and for bringing about specific types of change. The selections included in this chapter alert the student and new worker to the wide variety of techniques available to the practitioner and the wide range of situations in which they might prove useful.

Finally, Chapter 14, "Evaluation and Termination," anticipates the practical problems associated with finding a valid and feasible means of measuring whether the change effort has been effective. Determining how to evaluate one's practice is a difficult task for most social workers. This chapter also includes information on the termination of a professional relationship.

10 Intake and Engagement

INTRODUCTION

This chapter presents guidelines and techniques for use during the beginning, or start-up phase, of the change process. Although the activities differ somewhat when providing direct services (Section A) as opposed to indirect services (Section B), the intent is essentially the same. During this phase, a client, whether an individual or even an organization, is typically ambivalent about entering a helping relationship and beginning the change process. Making a favorable first impression on the client and setting a positive tone for working with the client can decrease the client's ambivalence and have a positive influence on all that follows.

During this initial period, the social worker typically undertakes three sets of activities: preparation, initial engagement, and intake. First, he or she *prepares* for the first contact by reviewing whatever information is available on the client (e.g., agency records), selecting a meeting time and place that will be convenient and comfortable for the client, determining who should be involved in the initial meeting, and remaining sensitive to other factors that might affect the client's perspective on and investment in the helping process.

Second, the worker will begin the process of *engagement* by establishing rapport and helping clients articulate and clarify the nature of their concerns or requests. Usually, individuals or families have already unsuccessfully attempted to deal with their issues through friends or other professional helpers when they come to a social worker. If the client is an agency or community, they too have often unsuccessfully attempted to deal with the matter of concern. In these situations, people are likely to approach the social worker and the change process with some degree of skepticism and ambivalence. It is important, therefore, to quickly help the client become truly invested in this process by starting to build trust and actively engaging the client in working toward meaningful change.

Third, the worker must determine if he or she can appropriately address the client's need or request. In short, some form or *intake* or screening decision must be made. In most communities, the human services delivery system is complex and those in search of service may begin with an agency or worker who will not be able to address the client's concern. Or at the indirect-service level, the initial group created to address an agency or community issue may not, on more thorough examination of the matter, be the best structure or set of actors to proceed with the change process. The decision to be made by the social worker, then, is whether it is appropriate to continue the contact or relationship or to make a referral to another organization or professional that is better suited to address the situation.

SECTION A

TECHNIQUES AND GUIDELINES FOR DIRECT PRACTICE

Many clients are anxious and ambivalent during the start-up phase of a helping relationship. They may wonder, for example: Will I be treated with respect? Will this social worker be able to help? Will he or she really care about me or just treat me as another case? Will this worker listen to what I have to say? Is there a good chance that my concern or situation can be resolved in a reasonable amount of time at a reasonable cost to me?

Preparatory Activities.   When providing direct services, it is not always possible to plan for the initial meeting, as sometimes a social worker first meets a client under crisis conditions when there is not an opportunity to adequately prepare. However, since the first contact is critical in setting the tone for a helping relationship, the worker should carefully plan for that meeting whenever possible.

One useful preintake activity is to reflect on the fact that the typical client has already unsuccessfully sought assistance and may be skeptical, discouraged, or distrustful of entering still another professional relationship. If the client is *involuntary* (court ordered or pressured to see the worker by someone else), he or she may be angry or resentful. To prepare for issues that might arise at a first meeting, it is useful, especially for the inexperienced social worker, to review guidelines for working with clients who are involuntary, hard to reach, manipulative, or dangerous.

It is also important to consider a number of factors when planning the first meeting, such as carefully establishing the time and place for that critical contact. Some clients cannot conveniently leave work to see a social worker during usual business hours, and thus weekend or evening appointments may be necessary. These meetings might be conducted in the worker's office, the client's home, or some other location such as a hospital, jail, group home, neighborhood center, or other convenient location for both the client and worker. When the meeting is held, it is the social worker's responsibility to attend to such concerns as comfort, privacy, freedom from distractions, and accommodations for special needs (e.g., space for a wheelchair, arrangements for an interpreter, etc.). The worker, too, should be concerned with personal preparation for the contact such as wearing appropriate clothing, being on time, and being prepared to guide the session.

The social worker also should be sensitive to factors of agency environment or milieu that might affect the helping relationship. For instance, Is the receptionist courteous and helpful when the client telephones or stops by the agency to initiate contact? Is there a comfortable reception or waiting area for clients? Is child care available if needed? Is the worker's office or a group meeting room appropriately furnished to create a favorable environment for interacting with clients? Agency atmosphere sets the stage for what is to follow.

Engagement Activities.   A critical factor in successful helping is involving the client in the change process. The following activities can help clients take the risk to invest themselves in a helping relationship:

- Greet and speak with the client in a way that is nonthreatening and puts him or her at ease.
- Demonstrate genuine interest in the client and concern for his or her request, problem, or situation.
- Explain any legal or ethical obligations the social worker may have regarding the confidentiality of information divulged by the client.
- Help the client articulate and clarify his or her request or concerns.
- Learn about the client's expectations of the agency and worker.
- Identify any fears or misunderstandings the client may have about the social worker, the agency, or its services.
- Explain pertinent eligibility requirements that may affect service provision.
- Address the client's possible ambivalence about receiving services.

During this phase of helping, the worker should be particularly sensitive to the client's fear of the unknown and people's inherent *resistance to change.* Even a small change can create discomfort or fear for clients, especially if they hold rigid beliefs, are inflexible in their thought processes and behaviors, or are fearful about risking change in their relationships with others. The social worker's role is to help clients examine new ways of thinking and behaving that may result in improved functioning and to help them determine if various options are sufficiently benefical and feasible to risk an effort at change. The social worker should also recognize that when clients are anxious or unsure of what is happening, they are likely to become somewhat defensive and hold tightly to their usual patterns of thought and behavior. However, these patterns must be examined and even challenged if clients are to make the changes necessary to deal with their problems or improve their level of functioning. This is only possible within a supportive and nonthreatening helping relationship.

Intake Activities.   One decision the social worker must make during the intake and engagement phase is concerned with the continuation of service. The worker must rapidly determine if there is a fit between agency eligibility criteria requirements and the client's need or request. If so, the next decision is whether the worker should provide continuing services (i.e., guide the remainder of the process) or transfer the matter to another worker in the agency. That decision will depend on the division of labor in the agency and the competence of the worker to address the client's specific issues. If it is determined that the worker should continue to provide services to the client, some actions that should be taken include the following:

- Assess the urgency of the client's needs or presenting problem and attend to the emergency, if one exists.
- Explain the responsibilities that both the client and worker will assume during the helping process.
- Explain to the client that he or she will need to provide information (in some cases, very personal information) needed to assess the problem or situation.
- Secure the client's signed release of confidential information (if one is needed).
- Reach tentative agreement on the minimum and, if possible, maximum number of meetings that probably will be necessary.
- Explain procedures to be followed or fees to be paid in order to receive services. If approval to provide services must be given by a managed care company (see Item 16.8), begin the process of acquiring approval and learning of any associated restrictions on practice activities.
- Reach agreement on the time, place, and frequency of future meetings.

If the client's request or needs do not match this agency's programs, a referral to an appropriate source of help must be made. Social workers are the professionals who are typically expected to be well versed in the human services resources available to clients. However, making successful referrals is a complex and challenging task (see Item 10.4).

10.1   MAKING THE FIRST TELEPHONE CONTACT

Purpose: To engage the person contacting the agency by phone.

Discussion: The first contact between the worker and client is often by telephone. Most clients feel nervous; many are confused and uncertain about what to expect. Others have a distorted idea about what the agency can or will do for them. Thus, the worker must use the time on the telephone to lessen the client's fears, secure at least a general understanding of what the client expects from the agency, and, if appropriate, arrange for the first face-to-face interview. Several guidelines should be kept in mind:

1. Remember that during a telephone conversation, you cannot read the client's nonverbal behavior. You will not always know if the caller is becoming confused or fearful in response to what you are saying. Keep your messages clear and simple.

2. If speaking with a voluntary client, briefly explore the client's presenting concern or request so you can evaluate the appropriateness of this referral to your agency. However, avoid gathering detailed intake information by phone; that is best done during a face-to-face interview. Also, avoid overwhelming the client with extraneous information about your agency and its services and procedures. Explanations of complex or detailed concerns also should be saved for a face-to-face meeting.

3. If speaking to an involuntary client, it is usually best to confine the phone conversation to arranging the first face-to-face interview unless explanations and encouragement are needed to get the client to attend such a meeting. The involuntary client often has negative feelings about having to meet with a social worker. Such feelings are much easier to read and effectively addressed during a face-to-face interview (see Item 10.7).

4. When arranging the first office visit, make sure the client knows your name and the location of your office. Some clients may need guidance on how to use public transportation to reach the agency. In some cases, a follow-up letter should be sent to the client, repeating the time and place of the appointment.

5. Be aware of the client's relationships and roles (e.g., child, spouse, parent, etc.), and assess how family or household members will be impacted by the caller's decision to seek professional assistance. When taking a call from one member of a family or household, ask if others in the home know about the caller's request for assistance. If the call is being kept secret from others, ask why secrecy is important. Determine if making the call places the caller in physical danger.

6. The first telephone contact can be an opportune time to ask the caller if others in his or her family or household also should perhaps attend the first face-to-face meeting. Except in situations in which secrecy is necessary to protect the caller, encourage the caller to consider involving significant others (e.g., spouse, child) in at least the assessment phase of the helping process. Perhaps explain, for example, that the assessment of a problem will be more accurate and the intervention more effective if everyone directly affected by it can share his or her perception of what is happening and voice his or her ideas on what actions or services might prove helpful. If the caller is open to involving significant others and they are willing to participate, hold out for such a meeting. If the caller does not want others involved, then respect his or her wishes and set up a meeting with the caller alone. Later in the helping process, you might again try to involve the client's significant others, if their participation will make the helping process more effective.

SELECTED BIBLIOGRAPHY

Martin, David, and Allan Moore, eds. *First Steps in the Art of Intervention.* Belmont, CA: Brooks/Cole, 1995.
Ragg, D. Mark. *Building Effective Helping Skills.* Boston: Allyn & Bacon, 2001.

10.2   CONDUCTING THE FIRST FACE-TO-FACE MEETING

Purpose: To conduct the initial interview in a manner that lays the foundation for a good working relationship.

Discussion: It is quite common for the social worker to feel a bit nervous when meeting a client for the first time. It can be safely assumed that the client has similar feelings. It is during this first meeting that the worker and client size up each other and form initial impressions. These first impressions can have a powerful effect on what follows. Several guidelines can help the social worker get the interaction off to a good start:

1. Before meeting a client for the first time, try to anticipate what he or she might be thinking and feeling about this meeting. Prepare yourself to respond in an understanding manner to the client's possible feelings of fear, confusion, ambivalence, and anger. Realize that the client may perceive you as an unwanted intrusion, an unwelcome stranger, and an authority figure.

2. Create a physical arrangement conducive to good communication. For a two-person meeting, the chairs should face each other. The chairs for a family interview should be arranged in a circle. Make sure the room temperature is comfortable. Be aware that your body language, how you are dressed, your posture, facial expressions, and gestures all send messages to the client.

3. If the client requested the meeting, begin with some introductory remarks and possibly some small talk, but soon move on to the concerns that brought the client to the agency. If you initiated the interview, begin by explaining who you are, who you represent, and why you need to speak to the person.

4. Explain the rules of confidentiality that apply and inform the client if what he or she says cannot be held in complete confidence. For example, you might say, "Before we begin, I want to make certain you understand that I will be preparing a report for the court that is based on our meetings. So, what you tell me may end up in my report to the judge. Do you understand that?"

5. If you have only limited time to spend with a client, explain that at the beginning of the interview so the topics of highest priority to the client will be sure to receive attention. Begin with whatever topic the client considers important and wants to talk about (i.e., begin where the client is). Realize, however, that many clients will first test the worker's trustworthiness and competence before deciding whether to reveal their real concerns or whole stories.

6. Do not rush the client. Convey the message, "I will give you the time necessary to develop your thoughts and decide what you want to say." Do not jump to conclusions about the nature or cause of the client's presenting concern or problem. Do not display surprise or disbelief in response to what the client tells you.

7. Adapt your language and vocabulary to the client's capacity to understand. If you do not understand what the client is saying, ask for clarification. Use mostly open-ended questions, unless you need specific data. Do not ask a question that you believe the client will be unwilling to answer. This may force the client to lie and that may obstruct the further development of a working relationship.

8. When you do not know the answer to a service-related question asked by the client, explain this in a nonapologetic manner and offer to find the answer. Be careful not to make promises that you may not be able to keep.

9. Some notetaking during the intake phase is usually necessary and appropriate. Writing down pertinent client information can demonstrate a desire to understand and remember important details. Notetaking can be distracting, however. If the client is bothered by notetaking, show him or her your notes and explain why they are needed. If the client still objects, cease taking notes. If you are completing an agency form, give the client a copy to follow along as you talk.

10. Plan the next meeting with the client, if one is necessary. Be sure the client has your business card and that it lists your name and phone number. Also be sure that you have his or her full name, address, and phone number.

The social worker will encounter a number of *clients who have significant physical or sensory disabilities.* The place and usual patterns of first meetings may need to be altered in order to accommodate their special needs. A few guidelines should be kept in mind:

1. When interviewing a person who is lying in a hospital bed or using a wheelchair, sit or position yourself at eye level with the client. Do not stand over him or her. Not only might this place the client in a psychologically inferior position, but it may also force the client to strain his or her neck or body in order to look at you.

2. If the client moves about in a wheelchair or by using crutches or a walker, respect his or her wish to remain in control and move independently. Do not offer assistance unless it is clearly needed, and respect the client's right to decline your offer. Be patient if it takes him or her longer to complete tasks and movements. Avoid fixation on the client's medical equipment or prosthesis.

3. When you meet with a person who is blind and in an unfamiliar physical environment, you may need to provide information he or she needs to move about. When walking with a person who is blind and using a cane, simply stay at his or her side and let the person maneuver. Never grab or move the individual, for this is both insulting and frightening. If the client wants your assistance, he or she will ask or reach out; respond by offering your elbow to hold and then walk about a half-step ahead. It is appropriate to alert the person to an unusual obstacle or danger he or she might not detect and to mention things like overhead obstructions, sharp turns, and stairs. If the person is using a guide dog, do not touch, feed, or speak to the dog. Guide dogs are trained to walk down the center of a sidewalk or hallway.

4. Individuals with a hearing loss may confuse words that sound similar, and they may have difficulty accurately interpreting the human voice when there is background noise and/or several people are talking at once. A form of hearing loss that is caused by long-term exposure to loud sounds is fairly common among older people. Because it involves diminished capacity to hear high-frequency sounds, individuals with this type of hearing loss may understand a male voice more easily than a female voice. Many hearing aids amplify all sounds, so even persons wearing hearing aids may have trouble hearing in a noisey enviornment.

If your client is struggling to hear, ask what you can do to minimize the client's difficulty. You may need to slow down your pace slightly, speak as clearly as possible, and check often to see if the client is able to follow the conversation. Do not mistake nodding and smiling as a sign of comprehension, for that may be the client's response to being embarrassed.

If your client uses speech reading (lip reading), be sure to position yourself so he or she can see your face. In addition, do not speak while looking away or down at papers, and do not position yourself in front of a window or bright light. A heavily mustached mouth may impede speech reading, as well. Do not exaggerate your words, since this will make speech reading more difficult.

A person who is totally deaf is usually prepared to communicate in writing, by sign language, or through adaptive technology. If the individual will be using sign language, find out what system he or she uses and arrange for the services of an interpreter. Some who are deaf use hearing dogs that are trained to detect certain sounds such as traffic and alarms. These dogs usually wear an orange collar and leash.

5. Most governmental offices, hospitals, and other essential services are equipped with devices that can be used by persons who have difficulty communicating because of blindness, hearing loss, or speech impairments. A social worker likely to encounter clients with these limitations should become familiar with amplifiers, signaling devices, puff-blow devices, electronic artificial larynx devices, telebraille, TDD (telecommunications device for the deaf), TTY (teletypewriter), and other assistive technology.

SELECTED BIBLIOGRAPHY

Allen, Gina, and Duncan Lanford. *Effective Interviewing in Social Work and Social Care*. New York: Palgrave, 2006.

Lukas, Susan. *Where to Start and What to Ask: An Assessment Handbook*. New York: Norton, 1993.

Murphy, Bianca, and Carolyn Dillon. *Interviewing in Action*, 3rd ed. Belmont, CA: Brooks/Cole, 2007.

10.3   CLARIFYING THE CLIENT'S PROBLEM, CONCERN, OR REQUEST

Purpose: To define and clarify the nature of the client's presenting concern.

Discussion: An important activity performed by the social worker during the phase known as intake and engagement is to obtain from the client a description of the problem, concern, or need that brought him or her into contact with the social worker or agency. Careful interviewing by the social worker is necessary in order to obtain a description that is clear, accurate, and useful. The ways in which clients describe their concerns tend to differ somewhat, depending on whether the client is voluntary or is being pressured by others to seek help. Nonvoluntary clients will often minimize the seriousness of their problem, describe it in only a vague and general manner, and withhold significant but unflattering information. Many who are voluntarily seeking a service tend to overstate the seriousness of their problem and the urgency of their request.

Here are examples of the types of questions or statements a social worker can use to encourage adult clients to clearly describe their problems or concerns:

- Did someone suggest that you come here and talk to me (or come to this agency)? Who was that? Why did he or she think it was important for you to come here?
- Describe the most recent example of the problem or situation that is adversely affecting your life.
- Describe a fairly typical example of having this problem. Describe the time when this problem was the most serious it has ever been.
- If today's meeting with me accomplishes what you hope it will, what will be different in your life? How will your situation change?
- What have you attempted to do about this problem? How well did that work?
- What have others tried to do about your problem? How well did that work?
- Do you know of other people who have had a similar problem or concern? What did they do about it? What seemed to work for them?
- Who else have you talked to about this concern? What did they have to say about it? What suggestions or assistance did they offer?
- How have you managed to cope with this problem up to now? What have you done to keep it from getting even worse or more serious?
- If you could do it, what is the one thing that you would do to make things better for yourself and the other people who are affected by this problem?
- If someone close to you—such as your spouse, child, or parent—were to describe and explain your problem or concern, what would they say about it?
- If someone videotaped your problem and then I watched that tape, what would I especially notice, hear, or see? What would stand out on the video?
- On a scale of 1 to 10—with 1 meaning "of little concern" and 10 meaning "of great concern"—how would you rate the seriousness of your problem today? How would you have rated it two weeks ago? What has changed in the last two weeks? On this scale of 1 to 10, how would your spouse (or child, parent, probation officer, etc.) rate this problem?
- Is there a time of day or a particular day of the week when this problem is the most troublesome to you? When?
- In what places or in what types of situations is this problem most evident or most serious? Less evident and least serious?
- Think of times when you have experienced this problem. Now, tell me what is usually going on just *before* the problem occurs or turns worse? What usually happens *after* you have experienced an episode of this problem?
- If your best friend came to you with this same problem or request and asked for your advice, what would you tell him or her?
- If, all of a sudden, this problem or concern disappeared, what would you do differently? How would each day or each week of your life be different?

What would you do instead of devoting time and energy to cope with this problem?

■ What is your theory about your problem or concern? Why has it developed or appeared at this point in your life? How do you explain it? Do you think your problem could have somehow been prevented?

Every effort to bring about change begins with an assessment of the current situation and a consideration of how things could be different. But unless action follows the assessment, nothing will change. Every change begins with someone in the situation doing something different from what they have been doing.

SELECTED BIBLIOGRAPHY

Hill, Clara. *Helping Skills,* 2nd ed. Washington, DC: American Psychological Association, 2004.
Kottler, Jeffrey. *Nuts and Bolts of Helping.* Boston: Allyn & Bacon, 2000.

10.4   MAKING A REFERRAL

Purpose: To link a client with an agency, program, or professional person that will provide the services he or she needs.

Discussion: An important social work activity is to link the client with the community resources, services, and opportunities that he or she needs, wants, and can use. Many people view referral as a relatively simple task. However, studies indicate that many attempted referrals end in failure. This high rate of failure, possibly 50 percent, indicates that referral is actually very complex. By following these guidelines, the worker can increase the rate of success in the referral process:

1. A *referral* is an action (i.e., a type of intervention) that is intended to help a client better address some specific problem, concern, or request. Thus, the social worker is not in a position to make an appropriate referral until he or she has clearly identified and explored the client's concern. Some data gathering and preliminary assessment is prerequisite to making a successful referral. That assessment must determine what the client wants and expects in the way of service and what type of service he or she is ready to utilize. Any attempt to refer a client for help with a concern that he or she does not consider a priority will likely end in failure.

2. Referral is appropriate when your agency cannot provide the service needed and wanted by a client. Referral to another professional is appropriate when you do not have the knowledge or skills needed to work with a particular client or when you have reason to believe your own values, attitudes, religious beliefs, or language will be a barrier to developing an effective helping relationship. Attempting to rid yourself of responsibility for dealing with a difficult client is never an acceptable reason for referral. "Passing the buck" or "dumping" a frustrating difficult client on another agency or professional is unprofessional and unethical.

3. Be realistic about what other agencies and professionals have to offer your client. Before deciding that referral is necessary, make sure you have considered all possible sources of assistance available within your own agency. Because any attempted referral carries a risk of failure and may add to the client's frustration, the social worker should first use the resources of an agency to which the client is already linked. Also be sure to consider the client's friends, relatives, neighbors, natural helpers, and other informal resources as a possible source of assistance.

4. Make sure you know of all the agencies already involved with the client before considering a referral. Some client concerns and issues may be best handled through interagency case coordination and improved case management, rather than by expanding the number of agencies and professionals involved. Professionals and other agencies already working with a client should be consulted prior to referring a client to yet another agency. The client's permission will usually be needed before this discussion can take place. Whenever necessary, obtain releases of information signed by the client prior to engaging in the referral process.

5. When the client is in need of a service for which there is a fee, you must address the issues of cost and the client's ability to pay. Some clients will need guidance and assistance in order to obtain information from insurance companies, managed care organizations, or public programs and then determine whether they have a way of paying for a service. In this era of managed care, you must consider the questions of whether the client's private insurance or public medical program (e.g., Medicaid) will cover certain medical procedures or specific types of services and whether a particular professional is on the list of providers acceptable to the managed care company. Helping a client secure the proper preauthorization from the managed care company may be an important step in making a referral to a health care provider.

6. Agency decisions concerning eligibility for services, benefits, and entitlement are usually tied to questions about whether the applicant fits into a legally defined category and meets established criteria. Thus, referral work requires skill in gathering information and documents related to, for example, citizenship, marriage, parent-child relationships, prior employment, income, household composition, medical conditions, and so forth. It is important to know how to verify information and obtain key documents such as citizenship papers, birth certificates, marriage certificates, divorce decrees, death certificates, tribal enrollment numbers, and military service papers.

7. All agencies and private practitioners have their own procedures, policies, and eligibility criteria. Do not expect them to suspend their ordinary procedures as a favor to you or your client. Be careful not to tell a client that he or she is eligible for a particular service, unless you have the authority to make such eligibility decisions. Do not attempt to speak for another professional or agency.

8. In order to make an effective referral, you must know about existing community resources. A social worker must invest the time and energy necessary to learn about resources and keep up with the constant change that occurs within the community resource system. Just knowing that a resource exists is seldom sufficient. It is important for the worker to know someone on the agency staff who can be used as a contact point. Use agency visits as well as NASW and other professional meetings as an opportunity to meet people working in the agencies to which you will be referring clients. Most communities have a clearinghouse and/or computerized database designed to help the user identify existing health and social service agencies, programs, and providers. Know how to access these listings.

9. When considering the referral of a client to a particular resource, give special attention to the practical problems that may be a barrier to its utilization (e.g., client's lack of transportation or phone, inability to read, lack of child care during appointments, fearfulness associated with travel in a high-crime area, inability to take time away from job, etc.).

10. Help the client tell his or her story about the agencies and resources he or she has used or rejected in the past. Also determine how the client approached and interacted with these resources; this will provide clues as to what needs to be done to facilitate the referral. A prior negative experience with an agency can contribute to referral failure. Anticipate possible barriers, and take action to lay the groundwork for success.

11. View the referral as the first step in a new helping process. It sets the stage for what will follow. If done well, the referral process itself will be an empowering and therapeutic experience for the client. Because the referral involves the use of problem-solving skills such as problem definition, gathering information, and decision making, your involvement with the client during the referral process gives him or her an opportunity to learn these skills and to learn how to secure still other needed resources.

12. If possible, give the client several options from which to choose the agency or professional he or she wishes to utilize. If the client asks for advice on which one to select, you have an obligation to give your honest assessment.

13. Ordinarily, when telling a client about services available through another professional or agency, you should explain both the advantages and limitations of those services. However, with clients who are confused, fearful, or highly dysfunctional, it is best not to focus on the limitations. Doing so may create an added barrier to the client's use of a needed service.

14. When helping a client select a provider of a professional service such as counseling or psychotherapy, ask yourself this question: Would I refer my own mother or my own child to this professional? Refer clients only to those professionals whom you know to be competent and ethical.

15. Whenever possible, clients should make their own arrangements for the services they want. In some cases, however, the frightened, immature, or overwhelmed client will need help in setting up an appointment, securing transportation, arranging child care, and the like. As a general rule, the client should be expected to assume as much responsibility as possible, without, of course, placing the success of the referral in jeopardy. If a referral is critically important to a client, you should do whatever is needed to establish the linkage. Sometimes you will need to accompany clients if they are confused or fearful about going to an agency. Family members, friends, or volunteers may also be able to provide this support.

16. Going to a new or unfamiliar agency will be stressful and frustrating for many clients. They may encounter a rude or harried receptionist, an overwhelmed intake worker, complex application forms, confusing eligibility requirements, and long waiting lists. Some clients will need a great deal of emotional support during the referral process, and some will need to be coached in some detail on how to approach an agency and apply for services. Without this extra help, some clients may abandon efforts to get the services they need.

17. In some cases, the referral of a client to another agency or professional means that the client must end a satisfying, familiar relationship and face the task of building new relationships with unfamiliar persons. Although the client may see the logic of the referral and the need to use another resource, he or she may be fearful, ambivalent, or even resentful about having to do so. Explore and address those feelings so they do not block the referral.

18. Whether an attempted referral is successful often depends on whether others in the client's immediate environment support the plan. Thus, it is often a good idea to ask the client if family members or friends might be opposed to the referral being discussed. It is also important to ask the client if he or she wants others to participate in deciding or planning the referral. Whenever appropriate and desired by the client, the client's family and significant others should be involved in making these decisions. Doing so will, of course, increase the number of persons who have opinions about the referral and may slow down the process. However, in the long run, involving those persons who exert a strong influence on the client will increase the chances that the referral will be successful. In addition, involving other persons will reduce the chances that they will later sabotage the client's utilization of the service or program to which he or she was referred.

19. Do all that you can to make sure your client successfully connects with the resource (professional, agency, or program) to which you are referring him or her. These ***connecting techniques*** have proven effective:

- Write out for the client the name, address, and phone number of the resource, and, if necessary, provide him or her with detailed instructions on how to get there (e.g., draw a map or plot the bus route to take).
- Provide the client with the name of the person he or she is to contact.
- Compose a brief letter addressed to the resource that the client will deliver to the resource. This statement should briefly describe the client's concern or request, and the client should be involved in composing this message.
- Contact the resource by phone when the client is with you. After speaking to the resource and briefly explaining the intended referral, hand the phone to the client so he or she will experience some conversation with the resource.

It is important to remember that all too often, the client's initial contact at the agency will be with someone who does not listen carefully and instead launches into a explanation of the service, program, eligibility, and so on. Some instruction, support, and modeling for the client may be necessary to prepare him or her to ask the right questions and to be assertive during the phone conversation or meeting.

Applying these connecting techniques creates several advantages:

- The client has support during the introductory contact.
- The social worker can assist with drawing out needed information and clarification from both sides, serving to repeat and reinforce instructions given, as well as express immediate appreciation to the accepting agency.
- The client and social worker share the experience. This can be especially valuable if the contact turns out to be disappointing.

20. Even after the client has had the first interview with a referral resource, take steps to encourage or cement this beginning connection. Doing so will increase the chance that the client will continue using this resource. For example:

- Ask the client to call you after he or she has had the first contact and summarize what happened. Find out what he or she is thinking and feeling about making use of this resource.
- With the client's agreement, contact him or her after the first scheduled meeting with the resource to see if things went as expected.
- Plan a series of interviews with the client while he or she is using the new resource in order to provide encouragement and detect any possible problems the client may be encountering with the new resource.

By following these steps, you will help uncover any misunderstandings or problems the client may be having with the resource. If detected early, these issues can be resolved before they result in the client withdrawing from the resource.

21. Evaluate your referral work. It is important to do a follow-up evaluation on referrals to assess whether the client actually received what he or she wanted from the agency, if the client is making progress, and if additional information is available to help guide the referral experience with other clients in the future.

SELECTED BIBLIOGRAPHY

Abramson, Julie. "Six Steps to Effective Referrals." In *Agency-Based Social Work,* edited by Harold Weissman, Irwin Epstein, and Andrea Savage, 65–71. Philadelphia: Temple University Press, 1983.

Crimando, William, and T. F. Riggar. *Community Resources: A Guide for Human Service Workers,* 2nd ed. Long Grove, IL: Waveland Press, 2005.

Levinson, Risha, ed. *New Routes to Human Services: Information and Referral.* New York: Springer, 2002.

Reamer, Frederic. *Pocket Guide to Essential Human Services.* Washington DC: NASW, 2005.

10.5   OBTAINING, PROTECTING, AND RELEASING CLIENT INFORMATION

Purpose: To protect client confidentiality in the use, exchange, and storage of client information.

Discussion: During the engagement and intake phase, the social worker will begin to gather client information and construct some form of client record. Once obtained, this information must be handled and stored in ways that will protect the client's privacy. During intake, the social worker also may decide that it is important to obtain client information contained in records maintained by another agency or professional. For example, the social worker may feel that it would be helpful to review a child's school record or medical report or to read a child welfare agency's record that describes how a child adjusted in a prior foster care placement.

In recent years, the laws and regulations concerning the creation, storage, and exchange of client information have grown more complex. Moreover, different federal and state laws apply in different settings (e.g., hospitals, schools, adoption agencies, substance abuse programs, child protection agencies, correctional programs, etc.). Thus, it is critically important for the social worker to understand the laws and procedures that apply in his or her practice setting.

The newer laws provide consumers of health and social services with greater privacy and make providers of these services more accountable for the records they keep. In addition, they generally give clients and patients greater access to their records and more control over who may view them. For example, the Health Insurance Portability and Accountability Act (HIPAA)[*] is a federal law that applies to providers of health and mental health services, including clinical social workers and social workers employed in medical settings, if they or their organization engages in the electronic exchange of information with health insurance providers, health clearinghouses, or other health or mental health care providers. Among the many general HIPAA rules and regulations, the following are critical for social workers:

- At the beginning of the professional relationship, the client or patient must be notified of his or her privacy rights and informed of how the provider of services intends to use and disclose his or her health information.
- The client or patient has a right to see, copy, and supplement (i.e., correct) his or her records. However, the provider may deny a patient access to records in certain circumstances, such as when there is reason to believe that disclosure will cause harm to the patient or to some other person or will result in the disclosure of other protected information.
- The provider of services is required to have in place certain technical and administrative procedures designed to safeguard client information, especially information that is stored in a computer or transferred electronically.
- Providers are barred from disclosing health information to a client's employer.

---

*The purpose of HIPAA is broader than addressed here. That is, the legislation is intended "to improve portability and continuity of health insurance coverage in the group and individual markets, to combat waste, fraud and abuse in health insurance and health care delivery, to promote the use of medical savings accounts, to improve access to long-term care services coverage, to simplify the administration of health insurance, and for other purposes" (Preamble to Public Law No. 104–191, 110 Stat.1936). For human services providers, the requirement for *accountability* relative to clients' private information is what makes being familiar with this legislation especially important.

- Under ordinary circumstances, the provider can release a client's health information only with the client's permission. However, a provider may share client information with others on a need-to-know basis if his or her purpose is to secure a professional consultation; to arrange care, treatment, and other services for the client or patient; to secure payment; and/or to conduct an audit, quality of care assessment, or the like.
- Providers of mental health services can refuse to disclose psychotherapy notes to the client's health insurance company without first obtaining the client's authorization.
- Health insurance companies and health plans may not condition enrollment or the delivery of benefits on obtaining the client's authorization to release information.
- A hospital patient has a right to opt out of having his or her name and health status made available to interested and concerned persons.
- When records and notes are to be discarded, they must be shredded. They cannot be placed whole in a waste container.

In all practice settings, social workers must follow the ordinary procedures intended to safeguard client information. For example:

- All client information and files should be stored in locked files. Only those professionals or agency employees with a legitimate need to know should have access to such materials.
- Computer screens, appointment books, and files containing client information must be kept away from and out of the sight of all other clients, persons in waiting rooms, janitors, and other agency personnel.
- Professionals should discuss matters related to clients only when behind closed doors. Phone conversations with clients or about clients should be made only in areas where they cannot be overheard by others.
- When a client's file is being used, it should be placed face down on the desk so as not to reveal the client's name or any other client information.
- The possibility of violating a client's privacy must by evaluated before sending him or her a letter (e.g., an appointment reminder), since even the return address on an envelope and letterhead stationary will reveal an association or connection with a certain type of professional or organization.

Fundamentally, the client record maintained by a social agency or private practice group belongs to *the client,* which means he or she has the right to decide whether and to whom this information will be released. (Parents and legal guardians control the release of information concerning minor-age children.) If a social worker wants information contained in a client record that is maintained by another agency or professional, the worker must first secure the client's written permission to proceed. Similarly, the worker must never release client information to someone outside his or her own agency without first obtaining the client's written permission to do so. There are, however, some exceptions to this general principle. For example, a client's records may be released to a judge in response to a subpoena or court order, and in most states, a protective services investigator (e.g., someone investigating child or elder abuse or neglect) may by law access client records without the client's permission.

The permission granted by the client is often called a ***consent for release of confidential information.*** Most agencies have developed a standard form for this purpose, and in most situations, a signed consent form will automatically expire six months after it is signed. Legally and ethically, the client's permission must constitute ***informed consent.*** In other words, before signing a release, the client should do the following:

- Know what information is being requested, by whom, and for what purpose.
- Have an opportunity to read the material being requested, or if necessary, have it read and explained in words he or she can understand.
- Have an opportunity to correct any errors in the record before it is released.
- Be informed of the possible negative consequences if the information is released and the possible consequences if the information is not released.
- Understand that a signed consent form can be revoked at a later date.

The rules surrounding the release of client information can make it difficult for professionals and agencies to share information needed for an accurate diagnosis or assessment and can create an added barrier to effective case management and the coordination of services provided to the client by several different agencies. Laws giving clients access to their records have had a profound effect on what is written into the record. Professionals may be reluctant to include information that could be upsetting or damaging to the client or family if they were to read the record. A school social worker, for example, may be reluctant to record the content of a discussion with a student about the parent-child relationship if the worker knows that the parent can review the school record.

When a social worker is documenting service to a client (i.e., writing an entry into the client record), the worker should always assume that the client—or the client's parent or guardian, if the client is a minor or legally incompetent—has a right to read this record. Moreover, the social worker should assume that the client may copy the record, question what is written, and ask that the record be changed to correct any errors.

Deciding what is and is not part of an official agency record is more difficult than it might seem. For example, is a report prepared by a private psychologist part of the agency record just because it has been placed in the client's file? Or what about a report the social worker obtained from a school? The social worker must clearly understand agency policy and procedure concerning such questions before responding to a written request to release a client record.

In the absence of legal guidance to the contrary, the social worker should presume that records and reports prepared by and obtained from a third party (e.g., a doctor, another agency) are not a part of his or her own agency's record. In other words, an agency record consists only of those materials that were prepared by or written by the agency's personnel. Thus, the worker should not release letters or reports that were prepared by persons outside his or her agency, even if they are contained in the client's file.

Within the context of this discussion concerning the protection and release of client information, it is important that the reader understand a related concept. Some professional licensing laws provide for what is termed *privileged communication.* The extent of the privilege is governed by state statutes. It usually applies to doctor-patient, attorney-client, husband-wife, and priest-penitent relationships. Some laws might also extend the privilege to the social worker–client relationship. This privilege belongs to the client, not to the professional; it can be claimed by the client when he or she learns that information covered by the privilege has been subpoenaed and could be disclosed in a trial. The client might then ask the judge to recognize the privilege and prevent the disclosure, and the judge might then make the decision on the basis of whether there is a compelling need to reveal the information.

SELECTED BIBLIOGRAPHY

Dickson, Donald. *Confidentiality and Privacy in Social Work.* New York: Free Press, 1998.

National Association of Social Workers. "HIPAA Highlights for Social Workers." 2004. Available online: www.naswdc.org/hipaa/default.asp.

Roberts, Albert, and Gilbert Greene, eds. *Social Worker's Desk Reference.* New York: Oxford University Press, 2002.

Saltzman, Andrea, and David Furman. *Law in Social Work Practice,* 2nd ed. Chicago: Nelson-Hall, 1999.

10.6   CONDUCTING AN IN-HOME INTERVIEW

Purpose: To engage and deliver services to the client who cannot or will not meet in an office setting and/or to secure a more accurate assessment by observing the client in his or her natural environment.

Discussion: The terms **in-home interview** and *home visit* refer to a meeting between the social worker and client in the client's home. In the early days of social work, home visiting was the *modus operandi* of the worker. In later years, the home visit was abandoned by many because it did not seem professional and did not fit the popular office-based models of therapy. Of course, the home visit has always been used by social workers in child protection and public health agencies and by those providing services to the elderly. The home visit is a component in all outreach activities and of critical importance in work with the hard-to-reach client (see Item 10.8).

Despite its usefulness and necessity in many cases, the in-home interview is a source of anxiety for many social workers. Following these guidelines can help the worker make proper use of this valuable diagnostic and treatment tool:

1. Understand the rationale for meeting with clients in their natural environment. Meeting in an agency building or in a professional's office is often necessary and appropriate, but such a setting can be awkward for many clients. Most people are most comfortable and relaxed when in familiar surroundings. Thus, for many clients, participating in an in-home interview, on their own "turf," will decrease their discomfort and defensiveness. In a familiar setting, clients often are thus more open and revealing and more real and authentic. The home visit or in-home interview is especially valuable in helping the worker obtain an accurate picture of the client's family and neighborhood contexts and an appreciation of how various forces within the client's environment either support or undermine his or her social functioning.

2. Appreciate the depth of understanding that can be gained from an in-home interview. Ebeling and Hill (1983) explain that a person's home is his or her sacred space and a reflection of the individual's personality and lifestyle:

> Within the walls of a home, people experience the intimate moments of their lives. They sleep, wake up, bathe, eat, drink, make love, raise children. They fight, scream, and rejoice; they cry, laugh, and sing. They may experience the warmth of positive object relationships, the anguish of negative ones, or isolation and loneliness. . . .
>
> Their outer space reflects their inner space. The way the homes are decorated and furnished can reveal either the chosen lifestyle of the occupants or their economic position. It can also indicate depression, despair, and disorganization. (p. 64)

3. Do not confuse the in-home interview with a purely social or friendly visit. This technique, like all others, is to be used in a purposeful manner. When it is the social worker who requests an in-home interview, the client should be given a clear explanation as to how and why it will make the service more effective.

4. An in-home interview should be scheduled at a mutually convenient time. Unannounced visits should be avoided but may be unavoidable when it is necessary to speak with a client who does not have a phone or is unable to read a letter. If you must stop by a client's home unannounced, explain immediately your previous efforts to reach him or her and use the conversation to set up a scheduled visit. (Often, the client will immediately invite you in.)

5. When you enter the home of a client, extend the same respect and courtesy you expect when someone enters your home. Ask where you are to be seated. Accept an appropriate offer of food or drink. Convey a genuine interest in family pictures and household furnishings that are an expression of the client's identity, interests, and culture. Ebeling and Hill (1983, 66) remind us that it is essential that the social worker never show shock or disapproval upon entering the client's home—his or her sacred space: "No matter what the condition of the building, . . . regardless of the number of dogs, the darkness of the halls, or the odors of the stairways; no matter how barren or cluttered or 'hospital' clean; even no matter what signs of impulsivity, violence, or sexual acting out are encountered."

6. Obtaining sufficient privacy is often a problem during a home visit. Children may run in and out, neighbors may stop by, the telephone may ring, and the TV may be blaring. This will be distracting to you but possibly not to your client. On the positive side, such distractions provide an accurate picture of the family's environment. Significant distractions are best dealt with directly by expressing a need for privacy and for attention to the interview's purpose. When friends or neighbors are in the home, the client should be asked if it is permissible to discuss private matters in their presence. Some clients may invite their informal helpers and supportive friends to sit in on the interview, and this choice should be respected.

7. If the client lives in a dangerous neighborhood, it is important to schedule the home visit for a time of day when the risks are minimal. Also ask the client for suggestions on how best to minimize the risks. If the client or others in the household are possibly dangerous and/or if you are concerned about being falsely accused of inappropriate behavior, you should bring along a colleague for added protection and to serve as an observer or witness (see Item 10.10).

SELECTED BIBLIOGRAPHY

Ebeling, Nancy, and Deborah Hill, eds. *Child Abuse and Neglect.* Boston: John Wright, PSG, 1983.
Newton, Nancy, and Kadi Sprengle. *Psychosocial Interventions in the Home.* New York: Springer, 2000.
Wasik, Barbara, and Donna Bryant. *Home Visiting: Procedures for Helping Families,* 2nd ed. Newbury, CA: Sage, 2000.

10.7   ENGAGING THE INVOLUNTARY CLIENT

Purpose: To begin building a working relationship with a client who was forced into contact with a social worker and agency.

Discussion: The term ***involuntary client*** refers to an individual who is required or mandated to seek and make use of professional help. The external pressure bringing the person into contact with the worker may be a legal authority such as a judge, probation officer, or child protection agency; a powerful family member; or an employer. Such a client is often resentful, angry, and sometimes belligerent. Needless to say, social workers would much rather work with a client who asks who am I? Rather than the client who asks who are you? What are you doing here? And when are you going to get out of my life? It is a challenge to engage the involuntary client in the helping process, but it can be done.

In most cases involving an involuntary client, the social worker will possess some degree of official authority. For example, social workers employed in child protection, probation, and parole are granted authority by law to impose a certain course of action on a client. Many social workers are uncomfortable with such authority and avoid using it; others overuse or misuse legitimate authority. Workers must use their authority in a purposeful and thoughtful manner. A worker's compassionate and fair exercise of legitimate authority can be a therapeutic experience for clients who associate authority with abuse and exploitation.

Filip, McDaniel, and Schene (1992) remind child protective service (CPS) workers of the therapeutic use of authority with the following guidelines:

- Use your authority in a warm, personal, supportive manner and show an understanding of the parents' feelings about the problem.
- A family may feel less fearful of your authority if you demonstrate a nonthreatening and noncoercive attitude.
- Help your client to see that you represent a reasonable authority so that (s)he can learn that other authority figures can also be reasonable. . . .

■ Clarify your protective service role and function. Do not retreat from your responsibility; make the family aware of the expectations for change and the consequences of no change in their behavior. Make them aware that you will develop a plan for your work together and that there are consequences should the changes in their behavior not occur and their child be considered at-risk.

■ Make the family aware of your knowledge that CPS intervention can be traumatic and you will do your best to minimize that trauma. Remember the experience may be traumatic for both children and parents. . . .

■ Avoid insensitivity to parental feelings since insensitivity may create anger, hostility, and resistance and will make it difficult for you to establish a helping relationship. (p. 45)

Consider these guidelines when working with an involuntary client:

1. Prepare yourself for the session by anticipating how the client may respond and recalling how it feels when you are forced to do something you do not want to do.

2. When you first meet with your client, reveal the factual information you have about why he or she is involved with your agency. Invite the client to explain his or her side of the story. Explain that you will check the record and speak to the people he or she has mentioned in order to verify facts and resolve any apparent misunderstandings. Seek clarification from the referring source if there is a significant discrepancy between what the client has been told about why he or she must seek professional help and what you have been told by the referring person.

3. Provide a clear and honest explanation of both your role and responsibility and what you or your agency expect of the client. Also, explain the rules of confidentiality that apply. For example, if you are expected to prepare a report to the court, the client has a right to know that what he or she tells you may end up in this report and be discussed by the judge and attorneys in open court.

4. Inform the client of any adverse consequences that may occur if he or she does not cooperate. However, respect the client's right to choose the consequences rather than your services. Remind the client who decides not to cooperate that he or she is, in effect, giving up the control he or she has to influence the outcome.

5. Assume that the client has negative feelings about being forced into contact with a social worker. Be prepared to encounter hostility, anger, shame and embarrassment, and a number of defensive reactions (see Item 8.6). Foremost, be sure to address the client's negativism. Do not ignore or avoid these feelings; acknowledge them and deal with them directly.

6. Make it clear to the client that you do not want him or her to lie, using an explanation something like this:

I am aware that you are unhappy and perhaps angry about having to talk to me. I can understand that. I can also understand that there may be times during our sessions when you will be tempted to lie to me. More than anything else, I do not want you to lie. If you lie, you may then feel guilty or begin to worry about me catching you in a lie. That would not be good for you, and it would be a waste of my time. Rather than lie, I want you simply to tell me that you do not want to answer my question. Is that something you can agree to?

Do not ask questions that could be construed as an attempt to trap the client or catch him or her in a lie.

7. Discuss the client's previous experience with professionals or the social services system, along with any preconceived notions he or she has about social workers, counselors, or other professional helpers. Be aware of the client's cultural background or experience with discrimination and how this might add to his or her feeling of being overpowered by or alienated from social institutions.

8. Within the limits and legal constraints placed on the client, give him or her as much choice as possible. Allowing the client to make some choices and have some degree of control over even minor details will usually lower his or her resistance—for example: "We have to meet each Wednesday for the next six weeks. We can meet either at 2:00 P.M. or 4:00 P.M. What is your choice?"

9. If other efforts to engage the client and establish a beginning level of cooperation have not worked, consider using the "Let's make a deal" tactic. In this approach, the worker agrees to do something that will lessen the client's discomfort or help the client get something he or she wants (something legal and legitimate) in exchange for the client's cooperation or the client's completion of certain specified tasks. An example of this approach would be a worker who says something like the following:

> Well John, it is clear to me that you do not want to come here for counseling. But you and I both know that your probation officer, Mr. Roberts, is insisting that you get help with what he is calling "your anger problem." If you don't do what your PO wants, then he may make your life even more difficult. How about us making a deal? If you see me for five one hour sessions, answer my questions, and talk honestly about the relationships you have with your wife and children, I will, in return, write a letter to Mr. Roberts and say that you have made a good faith effort to use counseling to examine what others are calling your anger problem.

10. Always remember that there is no such thing as an unmotivated client. All clients are motivated—all have wants, needs, and preferences. When a social worker labels a client "unmotivated," he or she is simply acknowledging that what the client wants is different from what the worker wants for the client. Successfully engaging the involuntary client requires that the worker tap into the client's own needs and wants and establish intervention goals that are at least partially consistent with the client's own wishes and inclinations. Some workers call this "moving with the motive." Work hard to identify something that both you and the client agree is a goal or a desirable course of action. Once there is an agreed upon goal, you can more easily engage the client in problem solving. For example, you might say, "Well, we both want you to get off probation so you won't have to see me each week. What ideas do you have on how we can work together to reach that goal?"

11. With most clients, some degree of self-disclosure by the worker has the effect of breaking down client defensiveness. However, when working with a prison inmate population, sociopathic individuals, or persons who are skilled manipulators, you should avoid sharing personal information (see Item 10.9). The use of self-disclosure with these individuals will usually have unwanted consequences, as many have an uncanny ability to spot and exploit a helper's personal weakness. For similar reasons, you must never break or even bend agency rules as a favor to the client; even a minor concession quickly leads to further requests or a "blackmail" situation (e.g., "Look, if you won't do . . . for me, I'll let your supervisor know that you violated program rules when you allowed me to . . .").

SELECTED BIBLIOGRAPHY

Filip, Judee, Nancy McDaniel, and Patricia Schene, eds. *Helping in Child Protective Services.* Englewood, CO: American Humane Association, 1992.
Ivanoff, Andre, Betty Blythe, and Tony Tripodi. *Involuntary Clients in Social Work Practice.* New York: Aldine de Gruyter, 1994.
Trotter, Chris. *Working with Involuntary Clients,* 2nd ed. Thousand Oaks, CA: Sage, 2006.

10.8   ENGAGING THE HARD-TO-REACH CLIENT

Purpose: To build a working relationship with a client who is distrustful and reluctant to become involved in the helping process.

Discussion: The term **_hard to reach_** is used here to describe a client with whom it is especially difficult to build a relationship. Most of these clients are socially isolated, fearful, and distrustful. Many have a mental illness and/or are extremely uncomfortable in interpersonal relations. The term hard to reach should not be confused with the term *involuntary client;* some hard-to-reach clients are, in fact, voluntary, and many involuntary clients are actually quite easy to engage. In working with a client who is hard to reach, the greatest challenge will be to break through his or her distrust. Several guidelines should be followed:

1. Be prepared to tolerate a great deal of testing behavior, and be patient when progress is slow. Many hard-to-reach clients have been so beaten down by life that they feel hopeless about ever making a change in their situation. Many have been hurt and abused by others, and as a result, they are fearful and distrustful. In order to engage them in the helping process, you must demonstrate that you will not hurt them and that you can be trusted.

2. Be tactful with hard-to-reach clients. Their feelings are easily hurt, and many are supersensitive to any hint of rejection. Do nothing that could be construed as criticism. If you accidentally say or do something that is hurtful to the client, discuss it immediately and repair the damaged relationship; if you do not, the client may withdraw from the relationship, once again convinced that no one can be trusted.

3. Remember that first impressions are extremely important to these clients. They are quick to form judgments, and more often than not, they interpret situations in the most negative ways possible. To be effective, you must be a warm, giving, and dependable person. Use a liberal dose of self-disclosure to help the client see you as a real and genuine person. In many ways, you must become like a good parent figure to the client—loving but firm and fair. That firmness and concern may express itself in the gentle setting of limits on what is and is not acceptable behavior in a professional relationship.

4. In the early stages of relationship building, you will probably need to do things *for* the client before reaching the point where you do things *with* the client. Strive to demonstrate your good will and usefulness to the client in a concrete way. Home visits, sending birthday cards, sharing food, and other tangible expressions of concern are usually necessary. By doing things for the client and by "feeding" the client's dependency needs, you provide assurance that you are "safe." By becoming useful to the client, you gain some psychological leverage. Do not worry about creating overdependency. That problem can be addressed later. The first objective is simply to build a human bond or connection.

5. Encourage frequent contact with the hard-to-reach client. As a general rule, the more often people interact, the more important they become to each other. Use phone calls and brief letters to supplement face-to face contact and to demonstrate your ongoing concern and interest in the client.

6. While demonstrating your awareness that change can be difficult, gradually introduce the idea that if the client wants to change his or her situation, then he or she will have to do some things differently. Remind the client that if he or she keeps doing the same thing, he or she will keep getting the same result. Thus, it will be necessary for the client to try out some new ways of addressing concerns and problems.

7. If the client announces that he or she does not want to talk about certain topics, explain that his or her decision is acceptable and that you will not ask the client to talk about those topics. But then follow up with an effort to engage the client in a discussion of why some topics might be hard for people to discuss and why people often want to withhold and protect certain information. These reasons might include feelings of shame and embarrassment, not knowing what words to use, not knowing how the social worker will react, not knowing if the worker would understand, fear that the worker might be judgmental, fear of a lack of confidentiality, fear that the information will be used to exploit the client, and so on. Very often, this general discussion of common fears and concerns will reveal to the client that the worker understands and can be trusted, and the client will then decide to talk about previously protected topics.

8. In order to engage and begin building a relationship with hard-to-reach clients, you must be willing to utilize some unconventional methods, ones not common to programs that provide counseling and psychotherapy, methods that are often inconvenient and unattractive to professionals. Among those methods are the following: (a) reaching out to clients when they are in a crisis or emergency and most likely to accept an offer of assistance, (b) responding to the clients within 24 hours of their request for help, (c) meeting clients in their home rather than in an office setting, and (d) demonstrating a willingness and ability to respond in whatever ways the clients perceive as useful in dealing with their current problem. Unconventional methods of assistance might include helping clients clean the kitchen floor, finding a way to fix the plumbing, securing emergency child care, meeting basic needs for food and shelter, coordinating services, and so on.

SELECTED BIBLIOGRAPHY

Harris, George. *Overcoming Resistance: Success in Counseling Men*. Laurel, MD: American Correctional Association, 1995.

Harris, George, and David Watkins. *Counseling the Involuntary and Resistant Client*. Laurel, MD: American Correctional Association, 1987.

Kinney, Jill, David Haapala, and Charlotte Booth. *Keeping Families Together: The Homebuilders Model*. New York: Aldine de Gruyter, 1991.

10.9 RESPONDING TO THE MANIPULATIVE CLIENT

Purpose: To respond appropriately to the client who frequently manipulates other people.

Discussion: Most people, at least occasionally, attempt to manipulate others as a way of getting what they want. However, some individuals rely on manipulation and "conning" as a primary means of coping with life. These individuals can be difficult clients because they are skilled in using other people. Social workers who are unable to detect a manipulation may quickly find themselves in legal, ethical, and moral difficulties.

Some of the most practiced manipulators are labeled as *sociopaths* or *psychopaths* or as having an *antisocial personality disorder*. Many have a history of criminal activity. A hallmark of psychopaths is their lack of a conscience; they do not experience genuine remorse or guilt. They also lack empathy. Additional common characteristics include a glib and superficial manner of relating, egocentric and grandiose thinking, shallow emotions, impulsiveness and poor self-control, a strong need for excitement and risk taking, and antisocial behavior. For them, truth is whatever fits their purpose at the moment. Many grew up in environments where manipulation was the key to their physical and psychological survival; thus, it is useful to view manipulation as the continuation of behavioral patterns that proved effective in the past.

Here are a few guidelines for dealing with a manipulative client:

1. The manipulative client, like all clients, is deserving of respect. With this client, however, you need to be much more cautious and deliberate. You must be explicit in outlining your role, what you can and cannot do as a professional person, and your expectations of the client. You must demonstrate firmness. Yochelson and Samenow (1985) remind us that the habitual manipulator is always behaving in ways that help him or her gain control of others:

He tries to determine what others want to hear and feeds it to them. He finds and uses opportunities for digression and diversion. He discloses as it suits his purposes.

He slants his version of events to make himself a victim and blames others for his plight in life. He tries whatever he thinks will impress the [professional helper], enlist his sympathy and compassion, or convince him of a particular point of view. Failing this, he uses a variety of tactics to put [the helper] on the defensive. These may be couched in highly intellectual terms as the criminal argues the meaning of a word, disputes a philosophic issue, and generalizes a point to absurdity. However, there are also open power plays as he intimidates, threatens, ridicules and erupts with angry reactions.

The agent of change [a helper] has no hope of being successful if he allows a criminal to set the conditions of a meeting. . . . The [helper] must stand firm. . . . [A professional] who is indecisive or lacks confidence does not instill confidence or respect in a criminal. Nor can [a professional] who is permissive later establish himself as a firm authority. Many criminals have had experience with permissive change agents and have exploited them. A person who is shy, timid, or reserved may do well in many endeavors, but he will fail to effect change in criminals. (p. 541)

2. Suspect manipulation whenever your client takes an inordinate interest in your personal life or your feelings about your job. Be especially cautious when your client says such things as "You are the only person who really understands me," "No one else has ever been as helpful as you," "You are the most caring person I have ever met," "If you could just do this one thing for me (often something illegal or unethical), I can get my life straightened out," "I have a wonderful opportunity to pull my life together—I just need a small loan," and "I need to tell you something but you must promise not to tell this to anyone else." Also be alert to the possibility of manipulation if your client makes frequent use of the word *but* as a way of avoiding responsibility or downplaying the seriousness of a behavior (e.g., "Well yes, I did steal some money but only 30 dollars" or "I hit him with a baseball bat but not very hard").

3. If you suspect that you are being drawn into manipulation, immediately consult with another professional. If you are part of a team, raise your concerns with team members. You may discover that the client is saying very different things to other team members. An elevated level of communication and coordination is necessary to keep team members from being drawn into a manipulation where one is played against another.

4. Inform your client that, above all else, you do not want him or her to lie. Say, for example, "I want to be very clear on one point. If I ask you a question that you do not want to answer, tell me so. Do not lie to me. If you lie, it will only confuse our relationship; it will not help you and it will not help me."

Unfortunately, there is no completely reliable way of detecting a lie, especially when the person who is lying has little or no conscience and is practiced in the art of lying. Nevertheless, making a few observations may help you detect when someone is lying:

- Engage the person in several minutes of friendly small talk before addressing a topic about which he or she may lie and before asking pointed questions aimed at detecting a deception. An obvious change in voice, facial expressions, or other body language suggests a deception.

- Most people feel at least a bit uncomfortable when they lie. Consequently, when lying, their voices often become higher in pitch and they are more likely to stumble over words.
- When lying, people tend to use fewer descriptive phrases and fewer hand motions than when not engaged in deception. Also, when lying, they are more prone to frequent blinking and fidgeting.
- Even a clever, confident, and experienced liar cannot completely control his or her facial expressions. Thus, the individual may exhibit a momentary look of panic upon wondering if he or she has been detected.
- The experienced liar has prepared and practiced responses to commonly asked questions, but his or her response often sounds emotionally flat. A really unusual or unexpected question may catch such a person off guard and uncover a deception.
- When asked a question, someone telling the truth will respond quickly because he or she has only one thing to say—the truth. By contrast, someone who wants to deceive will hesitate before answering because he or she must first weigh the pros and cons of the various answers he or she could give.
- A person who is lying tends to decrease the level of intimacy. Thus, he or she will look away, avoid touching, and move back slightly from the person to whom he or she is lying. The person who is lying will also use words that are less intimate. For example, he or she will avoid pronouns (*I, me, my, we*) and instead use more distant, objective words (*them, that, it*).
- People who are telling the truth will not hesitate to give detailed and specific answers to questions. Those who are lying will usually answer with generalities because they fear being tripped up by details and specifics. Some who are very skilled at lying, however, will attempt to bolster their credibility by overwhelming the questioner with details, which they assume the questioner will not take the time to verify. But once these skillful liars are told that their answers can and will be checked for accuracy, they usually back away from specifics.
- Individuals who are right handed typically move their eyes up and to the left when trying to accurately remember an image or set of details. When trying to fabricate a visual image or put together a deceptive story, their eyes usually move up and to the right. The right and left movements are reversed for a left-handed person.

5. Be fair but unwavering in your expectations of clients who are manipulative. Hold them accountable for their behavior, and do not rescue them from the natural consequences of their choices. Before deciding to change their behavior, they usually need first to experience the punishing consequences of their actions.

SELECTED BIBLIOGRAPHY

Allen, Bud, and Diana Bosta. *Games Criminals Play*. Sacramento: Rae John, 1981.
Lieberman, David. *Never Be Lied to Again*. New York: St. Martin's Press, 1998.
Yochelson, Samuel, and Stanton Samenow. *The Criminal Personality*, vol. 2. Northvale, NJ: Jason Aronson, 1985.

10.10   INCREASING PERSONAL SAFETY IN DANGEROUS SITUATIONS

Purpose: To respond to a potentially violent client or a dangerous situation in a manner that reduces the risk of being harmed.

Discussion: At times the practice of social work places the worker in danger. In the 2006 NASW Workforce Study of licensed social workers, 44 percent of the workers reported that they experienced some safety issues in their jobs. However, 70 percent of these workers indicated that their employers adequately addressed the safety issues—leaving 13.2 percent of social workers facing safety risks in their jobs. In particular, workers in criminal justice, child welfare, and the addiction field were considerably more likely to experience dangerous situations than workers in other areas of practice. It is not surprising that workers dealing with clients experiencing high levels of distress will at times face problems of workplace safety. Also, a social worker may encounter various biohazardous materials in health care facilities and possibly during visits to clients' homes, especially if the client's home has been involved in the use or manufacture of illegal drugs. To minimize the risk of being injured, the social worker should adhere to the following guidelines:

1. Never enter a potentially dangerous situation without first consulting with others about your plans. Consider the situation to be high risk whenever you are to meet with individuals who have a history of violence and whenever you are to meet an unfamiliar client in a nonpublic or isolated place. An inadvertent encounter with illegal activity such as drug dealing is also dangerous. If you must enter a dangerous environment or situation, do not hesitate to call for police protection.

2. A history of violent behavior is the best predictor of future violence. Statistically speaking, an individual with one or more the following characteristics and life experiences is more likely to commit violent acts:
- Has a history of committing violent acts
- Is violent when under the influence of alcohol or drugs
- Is or was the target of family violence during childhood
- Is or was the target of violence in his or her community
- Has been publicly humiliated
- Is part of a violent peer group
- Is experiencing a high level of stress
- Is a male teen or a young adult
- Has experienced a traumatic brain injury

3. The office or meeting room where the social worker will encounter a dangerous client should be set up so the worker has quick and easy assess to the door or another escape route. Also, the room should be clear of items that easily could be grabbed and used as weapons (e.g., letter openers, staplers, paper weights, etc.).

4. An agency's recordkeeping system should use some method of flagging the case record of a dangerous client so the social worker who is to meet the client for the first time can take appropriate precautions. In addition, the agency should have a preestablished emergency communication code so all staff will recognize a disguised request for assistance. For example, in a telephone message such as, "Hello, Bob. This is Jim. Would you please send a copy of our red resource book to my office?" the phrase *red resource book* might be code for "Send the police to my office."

5. When making a home visit that could develop into a dangerous situation, keep your office informed of your itinerary and check in by phone according to a pre-arranged schedule. Before entering a home or building, take a few seconds to look around and think about your safety. Are you alone? Where are the escape routes? Do you hear a violent argument in process? Do the people inside sound out of control?

6. Never move through a doorway as a response to an invitation to "come in" unless you can see the person who is speaking and he or she has seen you. (Being mistaken for someone else can be dangerous.) When entering a room containing a hostile person, move in slowly. Remain on the periphery until you can assess the situation, and then move in slowly. Do not move into the person's space. Intrusive movements may trigger violent behavior.

7. Be alert to anything about the situation that feels or looks unusual or out of place. We all possess an unconscious danger detector. Thus, trust your gut feelings. If you feel afraid, assume that you are in danger, even if you cannot pinpoint why you are feeling this way.

8. Most people who are very angry will vent for 2 or 3 minutes and then begin to calm down. However, some individuals are further stimulated and aggravated by what they are saying and thinking. If an angry individual is not calming down after a few minutes, assume that the situation has become more dangerous.

9. Do not touch an angry person; do nothing that could be interpreted as threatening. If possible, sit rather than stand, because sitting is a less aggressive stance. Also encourage the client to sit, as it usually has a calming effect. However, avoid sitting in a overstuffed chair or sofa because it can be difficult to rapidly get up and out of a well-cushioned chair. Also avoid sitting on a cushioned chair or sofa, because it might contain a needle left over after a drug injection. Rather, pick a hard, movable chair that can be used for protection if you are attacked.

10. Be alert to signs of imminent attack, such as flaring nostrils, rapid breathing, dilated pupils, pulsing veins, grinding teeth, pointing fingers, clenching fists, choppy movements and speech, crouching upper body, and bobbing or dipping movements of the body. Do not turn your back to an angry or distraught person or let that person walk behind you. If the danger level of the situation escalates, leave.

11. When in the home of a potentially violent person, be alert to the facts that guns are usually kept in the bedroom and that the kitchen contains numerous potential weapons. If the person has threatened you and then moves quickly to one of these rooms, leave immediately.

12. An attack on others is often a reaction to being afraid; thus, do what you can to lessen the person's need to be afraid of you. Remain composed and speak in a gentle and soothing manner. Do not argue, accuse, or give advice. Demonstrate empathy for the person's feelings of frustration and anger. Use active listening skills (see Item 8.4) to secure an accurate understanding of his or her feelings. If an inappropriate statement on your part causes the client to become angry, admit your error and apologize.

13. Aggressiveness and attacks often arise out of a feeling of being trapped or controlled by others. Thus, for an office interview, position your furniture and yourself so the client has easy access to the door. To the extent possible, increase the client's sense of being in control by offering options and choices and using language such as "Of course, it is up to you to decide what is best" and "Think about what we have discussed and decide which course of action you want to follow."

14. Select clothing and shoes that permit running and rapid movement. Do not wear long earrings that can be easily grabbed. Maintain a neat, well-groomed appearance and an attitude of confidence that projects the impression that you take your job seriously and are able to handle any situation. An angry person is more likely to attack someone who appears weak, afraid, and insecure.

15. Do not attempt to disarm a person who has a weapon. Leave that to the police! If your client has a weapon, calmly explain that you intend no harm and then slowly back away or otherwise extricate yourself from the situation.

16. The social worker's family (e.g., spouse, children) may become the target of a client's anger and violence. Thus, family members should be prepared for that possibility.

17. If you work in a dangerous neighborhood, secure guidance from experienced peers, local merchants, and the police on how to protect yourself. If you are likely to encounter dangerous clients, ask your agency for in-service training on nonviolent self-defense. You must be able to protect yourself from harm without inflicting physical injury on your clients. If you secure training in self-defense be sure to select an instructor who has had personal experience with violent persons. Remember, even excellent training does not adequately prepare you for the real thing. Never overestimate your ability to handle a situation or underestimate the paralyzing effect of fear.

18. If you work in a hospital or another health care setting, be alert to biological hazards and receive instruction on how to protect yourself and vulnerable patients against exposure and possible infection. That includes knowing how to handle items stained with body fluids, such as bandages, tissues, clothing, and bedsheets. In some instances, the social worker will need to wear a protective mask and gloves when interviewing a hospitalized client.

19. Social workers and other human services personnel who make home visits should be alert to the possibility of inadvertently encountering a clandestine laboratory where illegal drugs are being manufactured. For example, methamphetamine, or "meth," can be cooked using easily obtained chemicals, ordinary kitchen equipment, everyday jars and rubber tubing, and a propane burner. Needless to say, someone who is manufacturing drugs may take drastic action to prevent the lab from being reported to law enforcement. In some cases, clandestine laboratories are booby-trapped with explosives. Such laboratories are also extremely dangerous because the chemicals used in making drugs are both corrosive and flammable.

SELECTED BIBLIOGRAPHY

Cambell, Jacquelyn. *Assessing Dangerousness.* New York: Springer, 2006.

Jones, David, ed. *Working with Dangerous People.* San Francisco: Radcliff Medical Press, 2004.

National Association of Social Workers. *Assuring the Sufficiency of a Frontline Workforce: A National Study of Licensed Social Workers, Executive Summary.* Washington, DC: NASW, Center for Workforce Studies, 2006, p. 23.

Newhill, Christina. *Client Violence in Social Work Practice.* New York: Guilford, 2004.

Weinger, Susan. *Security Risk: Preventing Client Violence against Social Workers.* Washington, DC: NASW, 2001.

SECTION B

TECHNIQUES AND GUIDELINES FOR INDIRECT PRACTICE

At the indirect service level, the planned change process usually involves the social worker in activities aimed at making existing programs work better or creating new programs to meet client needs or to prevent problems from developing. For example, the social worker might give formal or behind-the-scenes leadership to a change effort, or he or she may actively advocate with agency administrators, legislators, or others to effect change. Usually, indirect service work is done with a committee or some other group that comes together to provide services more effectively and efficiently or to develop strategies to accomplish the needed change in a policy, program, or budget.

As in most change efforts, it is important for the participants to be invested in the process, committing their time, talent, and (sometimes) resources. Participants need to be involved early in the process and have opportunities to influence its direction as the change effort develops. In the intake and engagement phase of the change process, the worker must first do the background work that prepares him or her for this activity. Next, the other interested people must be helped to engage in the process, and third, a decision must be made to continue or discontinue the effort.

Preparatory Activities.   Social workers attempting to facilitate organizational or community change must know their "turf," or territory. Even new social workers must be able to assess the agency where they are employed (see Item 10.11) and the dynamics of their community (see Item 10.13). Establishing that foundation is prerequisite to any effort to facilitate change in an agency or community.

Typically, the work of the social worker involves bringing together groups of people from within an agency or from a community to address new problems or ones that have not been successfully resolved in the past. Gaining knowledge of past efforts, barriers that existed, and the people or organizations that were involved is a necessary part of one's homework. When providing indirect services, it is rare that the worker faces an emergency or crisis situation that does not allow time for gathering this background information. Such preparation is expected.

When leading a group for the purpose of addressing an issue, the worker should carefully select, invite, and recruit participants; identify a meeting time that accommodates as many potential participants as possible; select a convenient meeting place and arrange the meeting room to facilitate interaction; and have a prepared agenda that includes ample opportunity for participants to discuss the issue at hand (see Item 13.27).

Engagement Activities.   A social worker rarely will have the power or authority to individually resolve problematic issues in an agency or community. Rather, the worker must secure support and resources from others in order to solve problems. It is important, then, that the first meeting of a group or committee is structured to involve the participants in identifying concerns and issues from their own perspectives and encouraging the expression of differing viewpoints. Also, participants should leave the meeting having some responsibility for an action to be reported at the next meeting as a means of maintaining their involvement.

Intake Activities.   The first meeting of a group or committee must, among other things, reach a decision regarding the desirability of this group continuing to address the matter, deferring to another group that may already be addressing this topic, joining a parallel effort to deal with the matter, or dissolving. The social worker's role, as convenor of the group, is to help the group decide which of these options should be followed.

For the social worker involved in administration, the intake phase takes on a second meaning. It also may involve selecting and training personnel, the most essential resource for human resource delivery, to work in a human services agency. This activity includes selecting volunteers (see Item 10.12) to perform needed services that are appropriate for unpaid personnel.

10.11   LEARNING ABOUT YOUR AGENCY

Purpose: To become knowledgeable about an agency's purpose, structure, and procedures.

Discussion: Most social workers are employed by either a private or a public agency. ***Public agencies*** (whether at the city, county, state, or federal level) are established by legislation adopted by elected officials and are funded by tax dollars. By contrast, most ***private agencies*** (also called *voluntary agencies*) are nonprofit corporations funded primarily by voluntary contributions and possibly by fees, grants, or contracts. It should be noted that some of the organizations providing mental health and substance abuse treatment may be ***for-profit corporations*** designed to yield income for investors and stockholders. Some private agencies enter into the purchase of service contracts with public agencies and are paid to deliver specified services; thus, such private agencies are funded, in part, by tax dollars. The term ***membership agency*** refers to a private agency that derives a significant portion of its funds from membership fees (e.g., a YMCA or YWCA). The term ***sectarian agency***

describes a private agency that is under the auspices of a specific religious body (e.g., Jewish Community Services, Catholic Social Services, etc.).

In order to deliver social services and programs effectively, the social worker must understand the agency's mission, structure, funding, policies, and procedures. The following activities will help the worker learn about his or her agency:

1. Ask your supervisor and experienced agency staff for guidance on how best to become familiar with the agency's purpose, policies, and operation. Study the agency's organization chart and determine how you and your department or unit fit into the agency structure.

2. If your agency is a *public agency,* read the law(s) that established the agency and those describing the specific programs that the agency is to administer (e.g., state child protection laws) and examine relevant state and federal administrative rules and regulations. If your agency is a *private agency,* read the bylaws that describe the agency's purpose and the functions of the board of directors and its officers and committees and how board meetings are to be conducted. The bylaws will also describe the responsibilities assigned to the executive director, who is typically responsible for carrying out the work of the organization.

3. Examine your agency's manual of policies and procedures. Pay special attention to any ethical guidelines that prescribe employee behavior. For example, many agencies will have guidelines for such potential issues as the following:
- Use of time at work for personal matters
- Use of agency property (e.g., telephones, fax, automobiles, copy machines, computer, office space) for personal use
- Receipt of gifts from clients, other employees, or persons who are in a position to receive referrals of fee-paying clients from agency employees
- Use of the agency's name or the worker's affiliation with the agency in outside activities
- Provision of agency services to friends and family
- Situations wherein personal or financial interests might conflict, or appear to conflict, with official duties
- Publication and dissemination of research reports or other information prepared or developed during agency employment
- Sale of materials prepared on agency time or with agency resources
- Matters related to the confidentiality of client information

4. Read documents that describe your agency's history, mission, and philosophy. Find out how the agency has changed during the past 5 to 10 years and what community or political forces are having a significant impact on the agency. Seek information about the agency's goals and objectives for the current year and its goals and plans for the next 3 to 5 years.

5. Examine the agency's personnel policies, the tools or forms that will be used in the evaluation of your job performance. Read the union contract, if one exists.

6. If your agency must conform to standards issued by a national accrediting organization (e.g., Child Welfare League of America, Council on Accreditation of

Rehabilitation Facilities, etc.), review those portions of the accreditation standards that apply most directly to your areas of service.

7. Examine your agency's budget. Pay special attention to the sources of income, because the agency must be responsive to these sources if it is to continue to attract needed funding. Also review any purchase of service agreements, interagency agreements, or protocol statements that tie the services and operation of your agency to other agencies or funding sources. If you are working on a project funded by a grant or a contract, read the relevant documents so you know what the funding source is expecting of the project.

8. Examine annual reports and statistical data compiled by your agency, and determine which of its programs and services are most used and least used by clients and consumers. Also, examine data that describe the people served by your agency in terms of age, gender, socioeconomic status, race, ethnicity, religion, and so on.

9. Determine what procedures are used to evaluate agency performance and the quality of services provided. Also determine how the agency's clients and consumers are involved in the evaluation and planning of services and programs.

10. Identify the agencies and organizations with which your agency frequently interacts. Determine what community or state planning agencies have an impact on your agency and how the services and programs provided by your agency are to be coordinated with other agencies in the community.

11. Determine what specific roles, tasks, and activities are assigned to the agency's social work staff and those assigned to persons of other disciplines and professions. Also find out what practice frameworks guide service delivery (see Chapter 6).

12. Talk to community leaders and professionals outside your agency to ascertain how your agency and its programs are perceived by others. Determine the public image attached to your agency and how it acquired that reputation.

SELECTED BIBLIOGRAPHY

Gibelman, Margaret. *Navigating Human Service Organizations.* Chicago: Lyceum, 2003.
Netting, F. Ellen, and Mary Katherine O'Connor. *Organizational Practice: A Social Worker's Guide to Understanding Human Services.* Boston: Allyn & Bacon, 2003.

10.12   RECRUITING, SELECTING, AND TRAINING STAFF AND VOLUNTEERS

Purpose: To secure and prepare competent paid and volunteer staff members to conduct agency programs.

Discussion: Although some tangible resources (e.g., social provisions, equipment, and supplies) are important to the operation of human services agencies, the heart and soul of helping rests with the people who deliver those services. Perhaps no indirect service task is more important to clients than getting the right personnel in place to provide needed services.

Securing a group of competent and committed volunteers is essential to the operation of most social agencies. Boraas (2003) reports that 27.6 percent of the U.S. population volunteer to serve in their communities each year. However, if this level of volunteer effort is to continue, it is essential to make sure that there is a good match between the volunteer and the service needed, that the work is carefully planned and rewarding, and that volunteers are properly rewarded for their contributions. Many human services agencies have a staff member (often a social worker) assigned to the tasks of recruiting, screening, selecting, orienting, training, and evaluating volunteers. Even before this process begins, it is vital to sort out the service tasks that are appropriately performed by volunteers from those that require professional expertise.

Being able to secure and prepare professional staff for an agency is expected of persons in agency management roles. Although the agency managers may have the final decision regarding who will be chosen, an important prior step is to screen applicants and recommend the strongest candidates. Virtually every social worker, whether or not in management, will at some time be part of a search committee. And once a new employee has been selected, the agency social workers may also have a role in helping the hiree develop or sharpen his or her competencies to better fit the needs of the agency.

Developing a Cadre of Volunteers

The first step in conducting any successful search for volunteers is to determine as precisely as possible the competencies that are needed. For a *volunteer* (i.e., a person who provides services without compensation), this requires clear specification of who the clientele will be, what services he or she will be expected to provide, and how much time will be required to perform the duties. Nothing is more frustrating for a volunteer than being recruited to an agency and then not having his or her time and talents used efficiently.

A second step in securing volunteers is to advertise the agency's need for such help. In general, widely circulated announcements in local newspapers and on the agency website are the minimum effort at advertising. These formal announcements should describe the major tasks to be performed, the time demands, and the expectations for skills the volunteer would bring to the work. It is important for the ads to target specific organizations or groups of people and to attempt to generate applications from those most likely to be interested in the position. When seeking volunteers, for example, civic groups, religious organizations, and word-of-mouth recruiting by other volunteers are often the best sources.

Once the applications have been received, the screening process will begin. The initial screening of volunteers is usually restricted to reviewing information provided on an application form. In general, this information is intended to determine, at a minimum, if anything in the person's background might indicate that clients could be placed at risk by working with this volunteer and if the person brings any unique strengths to the helping process.

Following the paper screening, the face-to-face interviewing process will begin. When interviewing persons for volunteer positions, the goal should be to assess each person's motivation, commitment, and capacity for addressing the identified client needs. Questions such as these should be asked:

- Why are you interested in being a volunteer in this agency?
- What type of activity is of greatest interest to you? Are there tasks or activities you might be asked to perform that are of little or no interest to you?
- Are you hoping to have direct contact with clients? If yes, with what type of clients? What types of interaction do you want to have with clients?
- What do you expect to gain personally from this experience?
- Have you been a volunteer for other agencies? If so, what was satisfying about that experience? Not satisfying?
- For how long do you expect to serve as a volunteer? How much time can you contribute each week or month?
- What special skills and experience would you bring to the agency? Do you have any limitations that would affect your work at the agency?
- What type of training and supervision do you expect from the agency?
- What is your view of the importance of the confidentiality of client information?

The final selection of volunteers usually rests with a volunteer coordinator or other staff member assigned to that function. Once capable volunteers have been identified, the coordinator will be responsible for matching each volunteer's talents with the agency's needs and initiating the volunteer into the agency. Each volunteer should be given a thorough orientation to the agency and will usually need training to perform the specific tasks to which he or she has been assigned. This training might be conducted on an individual basis, or it might be conducted in a group session for new volunteers. The important point is that the orientation and training should be specific to the tasks to be performed.

Formalizing an ongoing support system for new volunteers is also important. A staff member should have the clear responsibility for assisting new volunteers in clarifying the tasks to be performed, determining when and where clients will be seen, and identifying the best means of carrying out the work.

Securing a Competent Professional Staff

For *professional staff* (i.e., persons with specific professional preparation who are to be employed and compensated for their work), a successful job search will carefully match the abilities of each applicant with the requirements of a given job. Therefore, being clear about the requirements of the job is prerequisite to a good search. A beginning point for the specification of competencies usually is found in a job description. Most agencies will have such descriptions, but it is helpful to review the list of tasks and then identify the competencies (i.e., knowledge and skills) required to perform each task.

The position should be advertised widely to attract a diverse and qualified pool of applicants. The advertisement should appear in local newspapers and identify the minimum requirements (e.g., experience in working with older adults, a bachelor's or master's in social work degree, grant-writing skill), the closing date for applications, a description of how to apply, and the expected starting date for the position. If a position requires a professional social worker, advertising in the newsletter of the NASW chapter or sending flyers to other human services agencies may further stimulate applications from qualified persons.

Typically, the staff-screening process has two phases: a credential review based on information submitted by the applicant and a personal interview with a small number of applicants who appear from their credentials to be the most prepared to assume the responsibilities of the position. The goal of the credential review is to obtain sufficient information for the committee to rate the applicants on the characteristics established in the job description. In most cases, the candidate will have been asked not only to submit a professional resumé but also to provide a narrative statement regarding his or her interest in and preparation for the position. With this information, the committee will review the applications completed, compare their independent assessments of the candidates and discuss differences in perception, eliminate unacceptable candidates from consideration, and create a priority list of applicants to invite for interviews.

When interviewing a person for a staff position, the process usually involves members of the organization beyond the committee membership. This interview process should be viewed as providing opportunities to surface the best candidate(s) for recommendation to the manager or other hiring authority, to provide a chance for the applicant to learn about the agency and job and judge if he or she is a good fit, to allow the candidate to ask questions about the job and agency, and to provide an opportunity to convince the applicant to accept the position if it should be offered. The search committee will often prepare a list of questions to be asked of all candidates and/or develop a short case example to be discussed so that comparisons among finalists can be made. Questions such as these might be asked:

- What about the population group served by this agency makes you interested in our position?
- What special skills do you bring to working with these clients?
- Why are you considering leaving your current position, and what about this job seems more attractive to you?
- From a career development perspective, how would taking this job fit into your future plans?
- What can we tell you about this agency (or community) that would assist you in considering this position?
- What support, training, or professional development opportunities would you see as valuable in getting started on this job?

All agency personnel engaged in conducting interviews should be warned against asking inappropriate personal questions about a candidate's marital status, plans for having children, child care arrangements, sexual orientation, and so on. It should be assumed that professionals make appropriate provisions for their personal lives and are responsible for making sure that personal matters do not negatively affect their professional performance.

Before a staff search is turned over to the person with final hiring responsibility, the committee must collect feedback from persons who were involved in the interview process (a form might be developed to get consistent feedback on key factors), contact the finalists' references to gain a more detailed and candid appraisal of each candidate, analyze all the information gathered, and rank the candidates or designate those who would be acceptable or unacceptable in the committee's judgment. The committee should compile the documentation under-pinning its recommendations, and the agency should maintain that information for three years in case an unsuccessful applicant should challenge the fairness of the process. The final decision maker will then have the responsibility to offer the job, negotiate the conditions, and plan for the entry of the new employee into the agency.

All new staff members will require orientation to the agency. Some of the orien-tation should relate to the basics of how the agency functions, whom to ask when needing various types of information, where to find supplies, procedures to maintain confidentiality, and so on. Also, new staff members usually require some training to adapt their general skills to the unique needs of the agency. This might involve in-service training or the investment of agency funds for participation in professional workshops or conferences. Bringing new personnel into an agency should not be considered complete until he or she is given appropriate training. And when client services are being provided, there must be careful monitoring to be sure that expecta-tions for the worker's performance are being achieved.

For the new employee, the person who provides administrative supervision (see Item 16.9) is critical to the success of the hire, as this person, at least at first, will closely monitor the staff member's work. The monitoring function offers both the clients and the agency a level of protection by closely observing the service activities being performed and, if necessary, using administrative authority to protect clients from errors or incompetence until the new person becomes more experienced. It is also useful for another person in the agency to support the new worker as a *mentor* (i.e., a trusted counselor or guide) to help the worker develop into a competent staff member (see Item 6.10). While a supervisor must be responsible for monitoring the new employee's work and protecting agency interests, a mentor should focus on the new worker's professional development.

SELECTED BIBLIOGRAPHY

Boraas, Stephanie. "Volunteerism in the United States." *Monthly Labor Review* 126 (August 2003): 3–11.

Young, Richard D. *Volunteerism: Benefits, Incidence, Organizational Models and Participation in the Public Sector.* Columbia, SC: University of South Carolina Institute for Public Services Policy Research, 2004. Available online: www.iopa.sc.edu/publication/Volunteerism%20FINAL.doc.

10.13   LEARNING ABOUT YOUR COMMUNITY

Purpose: To conduct an informal assessment of a community in order to understand the context in which an agency's services are delivered.

Discussion: A *community* is a group of people who feel a bond with each other because they share an identity, common interests, a sense of belonging, and usually a common locality. Thus, one can think of a community as a group of people who share a common interest (e.g., the social work community, the African American community, etc.) or as a geographic community such as a neighborhood, town, or city. Geographic communities are expected to perform one or more of the following functions:

- *Provision and distribution of goods and services.* Water, electricity, gas, food, housing, garbage disposal, medical care, education, transportation, recreation, social services, information, and the like are provided.
- *Location of business activity and employment.* Commerce and jobs exist from which people earn the money needed to purchase goods and services.
- *Public safety.* Protection from criminal behavior and hazards such as fires, floods, and toxic chemicals is provided.
- *Socialization.* Opportunities are available to communicate and interact with others and to develop a sense of identity and belonging beyond that provided by the family system.
- *Mutual support.* Tangible assistance and social supports beyond those provided by one's family are available.
- *Social control.* Rules and norms necessary to guide and control large numbers of people (e.g., laws, police, courts, traffic control, pollution control, etc.) are established and enforced.
- *Political organization and participation.* Governance and decision making related to local matters and public services are in place (e.g., streets, sewer, education, public welfare, public health, economic development, zoning of housing and businesses, etc.).

For the social worker who is new to a geographic area, conducting an informal study of the community where he or she is employed is an important part of moving into a new job. Such an assessment has three purposes:

1. *To understand the context of one's practice.* The social worker must become knowledgeable about the community's history, as well as its economic and political structures and the prevailing values, norms, and myths that affect decision making and intergroup behavior.

2. *To evaluate the existing human services system.* The social worker needs to know what services are available and to understand community attitudes toward people who have psychosocial problems and utilize the human services. Communities differ in their willingness to respond to human needs and in regard to how well local professionals and agencies work together.

3. *To acquire understanding of the community decision-making structure.* At some point, the social worker's desire for more adequate human services should lead to efforts to bring about changes in the community's response to a particular problem or need. To succeed in those efforts, he or she must understand the power structure operating in the community, the beliefs and values of the leaders and key actors who decide what programs and services will be provided and funded, and the formal and informal processes used to reach those decisions.

The social worker's study and assessment of his or her community is an ongoing activity that must be continually updated as new information surfaces. However, it is essential that this process be initiated when beginning work in a new community. This might be done in collaboration with several other professionals who are also new to the community.

Information that describes a community and its functioning can be gleaned from documents such as census data, economic forecasts, public health reports, prior studies of a community problem, reports related to community planning projects, directories of health and human services agencies, and the like. Helpful documents may be available from the local library, Chamber of Commerce, United Way, and government offices. Supplemental data might be obtained by reading historical accounts of how the community grew and developed and how it responded to recent problems, by interviewing long-time residents, and by closely following current issues and controversies reported in the local news. It is important to record the names of the organizations and individuals who are important decision makers, especially those associated with human services concerns.

Although the social worker's area of practice will determine the nature and depth of information sought in relation to particular aspects of the community and its service systems, certain general information is essential. The following points will help the social worker develop a profile of the community in which he or she is working:

1. *Demographics*
   - Total population
   - Age distribution (e.g., number of preschoolers, number in grade school and high school, number of people over age 65, etc.)
   - Minority and ethnic groups; languages spoken by various groups

2. *Geography and environmental influences on community*
   - Effect of climate, mountains, valleys, rivers, lakes, and so forth on local transportation patterns, economic development, and population distribution
   - Effect of transportation routes and other corridors and barriers on neighborhood patterns, social interaction, agency location, and service delivery

3. *Beliefs and attitudes*
   - Dominant values, religious beliefs, and attitudes of the population and its various subgroups

- Types of human services agencies and programs that are valued and respected and that attract community support, favorable publicity, and funding

4. *Local politics*
   - Form of local government
   - Relative power and influence of political parties and various interest groups
   - Current political debates, issues, and controversies at local level

5. *Local economy and businesses*
   - Types of jobs and work available in area (i.e., wages; part time or full time; seasonal or year-round; hours and times of work)
   - Reasons new businesses move to area; move away from area
   - Percentage of labor force unemployed

6. *Income distribution*
   - Median income for women; for men; for minority groups
   - Number of persons/families below official poverty line
   - Number of persons/families/children receiving various types of public assistance (e.g., cash grants, Medicaid, food stamps, etc.)

7. *Housing*
   - Most common types of housing (e.g., single-family dwellings, apartments, public housing)
   - Cost and availability of housing
   - Percentage of units overcrowded or substandard

8. *Educational facilities and programs*
   - Locations and types of schools (i.e., public, private, neighborhood, magnet, etc.)
   - School programs for children with special needs
   - Schools sensitive to problems and strengths of persons from minority and ethnic groups; schools with bilingual programs
   - Dropout rate for all students; for members of various socioeconomic and minority groups

9. *Health and welfare systems*
   - Names and locations of providers of health care (e.g., emergency services, acute care, home health programs, long-term care, public and private hospitals, public health programs, private clinics, etc.)
   - Names and locations of agencies providing social and human services (e.g., housing, substance abuse treatment, child welfare, protection from child abuse and domestic abuse, financial assistance, etc.)
   - Service providers sensitive to special needs or concerns of minority and ethnic groups; bilingual staff members; clients treated with respect
   - Self-help groups and informal helping networks exist in the community

10. *Sources of information and public opinion*
    - Influential TV and radio stations and newspapers to which the people look for information and perspectives on current events

- Key leaders and spokespersons for various segments of the community, including racial or ethnic and religious groups

11. *Summary assessment of community issues*
    - Assessment of major social problems within the community (e.g., inadequate housing, inadequate public transportation, lack of jobs, youth gangs, poverty, teen pregnancy, domestic abuse, etc.)
    - Major gaps among existing social, health care, and educational services
    - Efforts underway to address these issues; leaders in these efforts

SELECTED BIBLIOGRAPHY

Hardina, Donna. *Analytical Skills for Community Organization Practice.* New York: Columbia University Press, 2002.

Weil, Marie, ed. *Handbook of Community Practice.* Thousand Oaks, CA: Sage, 2005.

11 Data Collection and Assessment

INTRODUCTION

The social worker's focus during the second phase of the planned change process is on collecting sufficient information from the client and others in the client's environment to comprehend the client's concern or problem and situation, understand his or her goals and motivation, and assess his or her capacity and opportunity to make needed changes. In this phase, the worker brings an expertise not usually possessed by the general public, including skill in determining what data are needed, where they can be obtained, and how they should be interpreted.

Data collection is the activity of securing the information needed to understand the practice situation as a prerequisite to formulating a plan of action. It is important to gather factual information from the client, from other involved people, and, in some cases, from other sources such as medical records, school reports, probation records, and so on. Also, the worker should identify the subjective perceptions, assumptions, and beliefs regarding the situation held by the client, family members, teachers, employers, and perhaps even a referring agency (e.g., a court, school, spouse, etc.). Depending on the situation, the worker may need skills ranging from interviewing to data compilation in order to obtain the needed impressions or facts to assess the problem or case situation.

When does data collection end? To some degree, new data are always being collected. Certainly, it is essential that a social worker obtain sufficient information to have a clear picture of what is occurring in the client's life before arriving at an assessment. However, it is equally important to avoid delaying or stalling the change process by collecting too much data or irrelevant data.

Assessment is the thinking process by which a worker reasons from the information gathered to arrive at tentative conclusions. During assessment, the available information is organized and studied to make sense of the client's situation and lay a foundation for a plan of action. When the assessment is complete, the social worker should be able to describe the problem accurately and identify what needs to be changed to improve the client's situation.

The best assessments are *multidimensional*—that is, they are drawn from numerous sources that reflect varying perceptions and points of view. If the perceptions and conclusions of the worker, client, and other people involved in the situation are in conflict, it may be necessary to return to data collection and bring more information to bear on the analysis that will eventually inform the intervention plan.

239

Social workers must guard against unconsciously making the client's situation fit a particular theory or a preconceived diagnostic category. One protection against the worker's own biases having undue influence on the assessment is to have the client actively involved in sorting through the information when arriving at an assessment. Further, when a conclusion is reached, the worker should view that as tentative and be open to revising that assessment as additional information is obtained during other phases of the change process.

SECTION A

TECHNIQUES AND GUIDELINES FOR DIRECT PRACTICE

In direct practice with individuals, families, and small groups, a social worker's emphasis should be on gathering and interpreting information that allows the worker, client, and others to understand the situation from the *person-in-environment* framework (i.e., the needs, wants, and abilities of the person as well as the demands and constraints of his or her external world). Ultimately, it is finding a suitable match between the person and his or her environment that becomes the focus of the intervention (see Chapter 13).

Data-Collection Activities.   A social work assessment should give some attention to all dimensions of the person and to all relevant factors that impinge on that person's social functioning. Here are some aspects of the client's functioning about which the worker might seek information:

- *Volitional:* the personal choices and decisions, both large and small, that shape one's life; the impact of these decisions and choices on oneself and others
- *Intellectual:* the ideas, knowledge, and beliefs used to understand oneself, others, and the world; the ability to interpret and give conceptual order to one's experiences; the cognitive processes needed to understand, form judgments, and make decisions
- *Spiritual and religious:* one's deepest core beliefs concerning the meaning and purpose of life; one's relationship with his or her Creator; the meaning assigned to pain and suffering; one's religious identity, traditions, and practices
- *Moral and ethical:* one's standards of right and wrong; the criteria one uses to make moral decisions; one's conscience
- *Emotional:* one's feelings and moods, such as joy, love, sadness, anger, fear, shame; the inclination to be drawn toward or move away from certain situations and persons
- *Physical:* one's level of energy; capacity for movement; health and nutritional status (e.g., illness, disabilities, pain, care and treatment needed)
- *Sexuality:* one's sexual identity and orientation; libido; place of sexual attraction in relationships; the capacity for reproduction; the meaning assigned to being male or female; one's sex-role expectations

- *Familial:* relationships with one's parents, siblings, spouse, partner, children, and relatives; one's sense of loyalty to and responsibility for family members; one's family history and traditions; one's ethnic identity
- *Social:* interactions with friends and peers; one's social support network; one's interests and leisure time/recreational activities
- *Community:* one's sense of belonging to a group beyond family and friends; one's sense of loyalty to and responsibility for others in the neighborhood and local area; one's place or status in the community; one's use of various formal and informal resources to meet personal and family needs
- *Work/occupation:* the nature of one's work; one's source of income; relationships with others in one's work organization or occupation; the place and meaning of work in one's life
- *Economic:* one's material resources; one's capacity to secure the money needed to purchase goods and services; consumer decisions
- *Legal:* one's rights, responsibilities, protections, and entitlements

There are several different modes of data collection. Since each mode has limitations, the social worker should use more than one whenever possible to increase the accuracy of the inferences that result from these data. Data-collection modes a social worker might use include the following:

- Direct verbal questioning, such as the face-to-face interview or a group interview (see Chapter 8)
- Direct written questioning, including the use of problem checklists and questionnaires (see Item 11.12)
- Indirect or projective verbal questioning, such as the story completion or the use of vignettes (see Item 11.12)
- Indirect or projective written questioning, such as sentence completion
- Observation of the client in the client's natural environment, such as home visits (see Item 10.6), visits to a classroom, and so forth
- Observations of the client in a simulated situation that is analogous to real life, including such techniques as role-playing a job interview
- Client self-monitoring and self-observations by means of written recording tools, such as a personal log, journaling, or recording information about one's actions, feelings, or beliefs
- The use of existing documents, such as agency records, newspapers, school records, and physician reports

Assessment Activities. An assessment tool combines data collection with a format that facilitates interpretation. Often, this format provides a way to compare the client's responses to those of a larger collective to whom the instrument has been administered (i.e., a standardized assessment tool; see Item 14.2). Literally hundreds of such instruments are available to the social worker. Sometimes, it is useful for the worker to develop an assessment tool that is tailored to fit the manner of communication and experiences of an individual client or family (see Item 14.1). Techniques for organizing data to maintain an ongoing assessment of practice achievements are reported in Chapter 14.

Particular attention needs to be given to assessing client strengths. Too often, both the client and worker become preoccupied with the presenting problem and all that is going wrong. This can generate a sense of pessimism and yield an incomplete or distorted intervention plan. Including an analysis of client strengths builds hopefulness and uncovers possibilities for dealing with a problem.

Value preferences also affect assessments. The client and the social worker will hold beliefs about the way things ought to be, and these views affect the way a problem is defined and the outcomes sought. To the extent possible, these values and beliefs should be made explicit and discussed during the assessment process.

Finally, during assessment (but hopefully earlier), there must be clarity as to who is the client and who will become the target system. In other words, who is asking for and expects to benefit from the social worker's services (the *client system*) and who is expected to change (the *target system*). They are not always the same. For example, when a mother requests counseling for a rebellious daughter who is forced to attend the counseling sessions, who is the client? We would probably conclude that the mother is the client and the daughter is the target of intervention.

It is in direct social work practice that social workers encounter the concept of diagnosis, which is related to the processes of data gathering and assessment yet essentially different. In *diagnosis,* the client's problem, condition, or situation is classified and assigned to a particular category within a given taxonomy, such as the Person-in-Environment (PIE) system or the *Diagnostic and Statistical Manual of Mental Disorders* (*DSM*) (see Items 11.16 and 11.18). The act of diagnosis applies a standardized terminology to the client's condition or situation in order to facilitate communication among professionals and to aid in the gathering of data needed for research and program administration. Labeling and categorization may or may not make a useful contribution to the worker's intervention planning, however. In many instances, clients assigned to the same *DSM* diagnostic label may require somewhat different forms of treatment and intervention because of individual contextual or environmental factors.

11.1   THE SOCIAL ASSESSMENT REPORT

Purpose: To convey to other professionals relevant social information about a particular individual or family.

Discussion: A *social assessment report* (often called a *social history*) is a type of professional report frequently prepared by social workers in direct practice. This report focuses on and describes the social aspects of the client's functioning and his or her situation. The word *social* refers to the interactions between and among people and between people and the significant systems of their social environment (e.g., family, school, job, hospital, etc.). Social workers are particularly concerned about the match (or lack thereof) between client needs and the resources (formal and informal) available to meet those needs.

Past behavior is the best predictor of future behavior; this fact is the rationale for compiling a social history. If a social worker can gather accurate descriptions of how a client previously reacted to new situations, handled stress, and coped with problems and can also identify patterns in those prior responses, the worker can then make an informed prediction about how the client will respond to various situations in the future. A social history or assessment is especially useful to professionals responsible for making decisions concerning the type of program or service that would be most appropriate for a particular client and to those responsible for facilitating a client's adjustment to a new environment (e.g., treatment program, foster home, nursing home).

A social assessment report presents the reader with two types of information: (1) the social data, consisting of facts and observations, and (2) the worker's interpretation of those data along with implications of the data for those who will work with the client. The information presented in the report should lay a foundation for doing something with the client about his or her problem or situation.

The organization, format, and content of a report will vary from agency to agency and reflect the agency's purpose and program. Also, the content will vary depending on the audience for which it is prepared: doctors, judges, psychologists, school personnel, interdisciplinary teams, and so on. A good report is characterized by these qualities:

1. *Shortness.* The report should say no more than needs to be said to those who will use the report. Everyone is busy. Do not ask others to read more than is necessary.

2. *Clarity and simplicity.* Select the least complicated words and phrases. Avoid jargon and psychiatric labels. Rather than using labels, describe and give examples of the behavior you are discussing.

3. *Usefulness.* Keep the report's purpose in mind while you are preparing it. Ask yourself who will read the report and what they need to know.

4. *Organization.* Use logical headings to break the information into easy-to-find topical categories. Here are some of the headings commonly used in social assessment reports:

- Identifying Information (name, date of birth, address, etc.)
- Reason for Report
- Reason for Social Work or Agency Involvement
- Statement of Client's Problem or Concern
- Client's Family Background (family of origin)
- Current Family Composition and/or Household Membership
- Relationships to Significant Others
- Ethnicity, Religion, and Spirituality
- Physical Functioning, Health Concerns, Nutrition, Home Safety, Illness, Disabilities, Medications
- Educational Background, School Performance, Intellectual Functioning
- Psychological and Emotional Functioning
- Strengths, Ways of Coping, and Problem-Solving Capacities
- Employment, Income, Work Experience, and Skills
- Housing, Neighborhood, and Transportation
- Current and Recent Use of Community and Professional Services
- Social Worker's Impressions and Assessment
- Intervention and Service Plan

The sample social assessment report presented in Figure 11.1 illustrates the use of various topical headings.

FIGURE 11.1   **Sample Social Assessment Report**

Greystone Family Service Agency

Identifying Information

Client Name: _____Shirley McCarthy_____   Case Record #: _____3456_____

D.O.B: _____July 4, 1988_____ Age: _____20_____   Date of Referral: _____Oct. 8, 2008_____

Soc. Security #: _____505–67–8910_____   Social Worker: _____Jane Green, BSW_____

Address: _____2109 B Street_____   Report Prepared: _____Oct. 13, 2008_____

_____Greystone, MT 09876_____

Phone: _____555–0123_____

Reason for Report

This report was prepared for use during consultation with Dr. Jones, the agency's psychiatric consultant, and for purposes of peer supervision. (The client is aware that a report is being prepared for this purpose.)

Reason for Social Work Involvement

Shirley was referred to this agency by Dr. Smith, an emergency room physician at City Hospital. Shirley was treated there for having taken an unknown quantity of aspirin in an apparent suicide attempt. She is reacting with anxiety and depression to her unwanted pregnancy. The father is a former boyfriend with whom she has broken off. She does not want him nor her parents to learn that she is pregnant.

She does not want an abortion and does not want to care for a child. She has thought about adoption but knows little about what would be involved. She agreed to come to this agency in order to figure out how she might deal with her dilemma.

Source of Data

This report is based on two one-hour interviews with the client (Oct. 9 and 11) and a phone conversation with Dr. Smith.

Family Background and Situation

Shirley is the youngest of three children. Her brother, John, age 30, is a chemical engineer in Austin, Texas. Her sister, Martha, age 27, is a pharmacist in Seattle. Shirley does not feel close to either sibling and neither knows of her pregnancy.

Her parents have been married for 33 years. They live in Spokane, Washington. Her father, Thomas, is an engineer for a farm equipment company. Her mother, Mary, is a registered nurse.

Shirley describes her parents as hard-working, honest people who have a strong sense of right and wrong and a commitment to family. The family is middle class and of Irish

(Continued)

heritage. The McCarthy's are life-long Catholics. The three children attended Catholic grade and high schools. Shirley says that if her parents knew of the pregnancy "it would just kill them." Her wish to keep her parents from learning of the pregnancy seems motivated by a desire to protect them from distress.

Physical Functioning and Health

Shirley is 5'7" tall and weighs 115 pounds. She is about three months pregnant. Dr. Smith reports that she is underweight but otherwise healthy. He has concern about her willingness to obtain proper prenatal care; he had referred Shirley to Dr. Johnson (an OB/GYN physician), but she did not keep that appointment.

Shirley says that she is in good health, eats well, exercises minimally, and reports no medical problems. She is not taking any medication.

Intellectual Functioning

Shirley completed two years at the University of Washington and then transferred to the University of Montana where she is currently a junior in computer science. She has an overall GPA of A–. Despite her good grades, Shirley describes herself as a "mediocre student."

She is attracted to subjects where there is a clear right and wrong answer. She does not like courses such as philosophy, which seems "wishy-washy" to her. Although she values the logical and precise thinking that is part of computer science, she explains that she tends to make personal decisions impulsively and "jumps into things without considering the consequences."

Emotional Functioning

Shirley describes herself as "moody." Even before the pregnancy, she had bouts of depression when she would sit alone in her room for hours at a time. She never sought treatment for the depression. In describing herself, Shirley uses the words *childish* and *immature;* she has always felt younger than others her age.

She often feels anger and sadness, but tries to keep her feelings from showing. In this sense, she is like her father, who always keeps things to himself until he finally "blows up."

In spite of her accomplishments, Shirley seems to have poor self-esteem and focuses more on her limitations than her strengths.

Interpersonal and Social Relationships

Shirley has no "close friends." She says it is difficult for her to interact with others and she wishes she had better social skills. She has held various part-time jobs during high school and college, but socialized only minimally with co-workers. In college, Shirley had trouble getting along with her roommates in the dorm, so she moved to an apartment so that she could be alone.

When she drinks alcohol, she feels more outgoing and friendly. However, this fact scares her because several uncles are alcoholic. For the past year, she worked hard at not drinking at all. She was not drinking when she took the aspirin.

Her former boyfriend, Bob (father of her baby), was the first person she ever dated for more than a few months. The relationship ended one month ago. Bob is also a student.

Religion and Spirituality

Shirley was raised as a Catholic and retains many of the beliefs and values she learned as a child. She describes herself as a spiritual person and one who prays quite often. She has clear ideas of right and wrong but also feels she is in a stage of life when she is trying to

(Continued)

FIGURE 11.1	Continued

decide what she really believes and is in the process of constructing a system of values, morals, and ethical principles.

Strengths and Problem-Solving Capacity

Although Shirley tends to minimize her strengths, she exhibits intelligence, an ability to work hard, a desire to make friends, a loyalty to her family while also wanting to make her own decisions, and a moderate motivation to deal with her situation constructively. She displays a good vocabulary and expresses herself in a clear manner.

She tends to avoid making hard decisions and lets things pile up until she is forced by circumstances to follow the only option still open to her. She usually knows what she "should do" but does not act; she attributes this to a fear of making mistakes. When faced with interpersonal conflict, she is inclined to withdraw.

Economics/Housing/Transportation

Shirley's parents are assisting her with the costs of her education. She also works about 30 hours per week at the Baylor Department Store, earning minimum wage. With this money, she pays rent and keeps her eight-year-old car running.

Aside from her college student health insurance, she has no medical coverage. She does not know if that policy covers pregnancy. Shirley lives alone in a two-room apartment which she says is located in a "rough area" of town. She is afraid to be out alone after dark.

Use of Community Resources

This is the first time Shirley has had contact with a social agency. During our sessions, she asked many questions about the agency and expressed some confusion about why she had been referred here by Dr. Smith. She acknowledged that feelings of embarrassment and shame make it difficult for her to talk to about her concerns.

Impressions and Assessment

This 20-year-old is experiencing inner conflict and depression because of an unwanted pregnancy. This gave rise to a suicide attempt. In keeping with her tendency to avoid conflict, she has not told others of the pregnancy, yet the father (Bob) will need to be involved if she chooses the legal procedure of relinquishment, and her parents' involvement may be needed for financial support. Prenatal care is needed, but it too has been avoided. Abortion is not an acceptable solution to Shirley, and she is ambivalent about adoption and how to manage her life while pregnant.

Goals for Work with Client

In order to help Shirley make the necessary decisions to deal with this pregnancy, I hope to engage her in pregnancy options counseling. Issues to be addressed include making a further assessment of her depression and suicide attempt, obtaining and paying for medical care, and deciding on whether to inform Bob and her own parents. She will need emotional support, some structure, and a gentle demand for work so she can overcome her avoidance, make decisions, and take necessary action.

Note: The names in this report are fictitious.

5. *Confidentiality and client access.* Respect the client's privacy. Assume that the client may want to read the report and has a right to do so. Do not include information that you would not want the client or family (or their lawyer) to read.

6. *Objectivity.* Select words that express your observations in an accurate and nonjudgmental manner. Beware of value-laden words and connotative meanings such as, for example, "welfare mother," "chauvinist," "The client admits she doesn't attend church," and "He claims to have completed high school." Label your opinions and personal judgments as such and support your conclusions with data. Do not present an opinion as if it were a fact. The best way to do this is to place your conclusions, opinions, and hypotheses under a separate topical heading called "Worker's Impressions and Assessment."

When it is necessary to include information or draw conclusions that might offend the client/family, do so, if possible, by using the client's own words. Note these examples:

Inappropriate: It is apparent that Jane is a hostile and uncaring individual who is too self-centered and immature to cope with the demands of her elderly father.

Acceptable: While I was talking with Jane, her father requested a glass of water. She responded in a loud voice and said, "Go to hell, you old fool. I hope you dry up and blow away."

7. *Relevance.* The information included in the report should have a clear connection to the client's presenting concern and/or the reason the social worker and agency are involved with the client.

8. *Focus on client strengths.* Avoid preoccupation with pathology and family disorganization, personal weakness, and limitation. To the extent possible, emphasize whatever strengths exist. Focus on what the client/family can do, not on what they cannot do. Successful intervention is built on client strength; the social assessment report must identify these strengths (see Item 11.4).

SELECTED BIBLIOGRAPHY

Kagle, Jill. *Social Work Records,* 2nd ed. Belmont, CA: Wadsworth, 1991.
Zuckerman, Edward. *The Clinician's Thesaurus: The Guide for Wording Psychological Reports,* 6th ed. New York: Guilford, 2005.

11.2   GENOGRAMS AND ECOMAPPING

Purpose: To graphically depict family and interactional data as an aid in the social assessment process.

Discussion: A *genogram* is a diagram similar to a family tree. It can describe family relationships for two or three generations. (Attempting to depict more than three generations becomes very complex.) An *ecomap* drawing places an individual or a family within a social Context.

FIGURE 11.2   Symbols for Ecomaps and Genograms

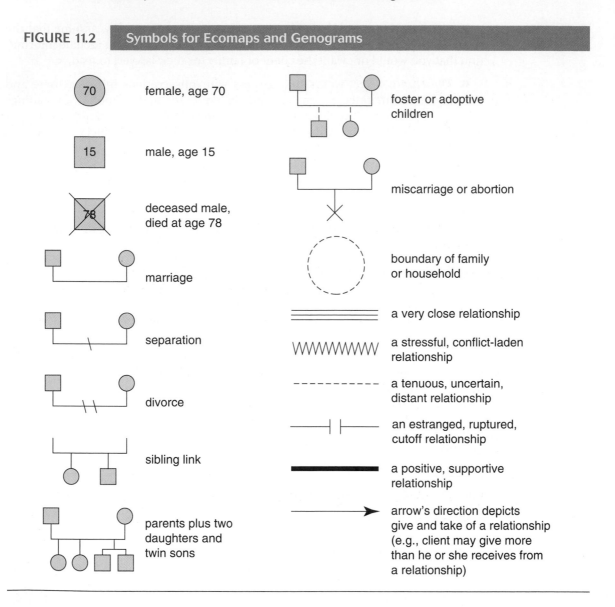

In addition to their value in assessment, genograms and ecomaps can shorten the case record. Descriptions that might require two or three pages of narrative can often be reduced to a single page of genogram and ecomap diagrams. For example, a typical record or social history will include information such as the following:

- Age, sex, marital status, and household composition
- Family structure and relationships (e.g., biological children, stepchildren, parents, etc.)

- Job situation, employment, and responsibilities
- Social activities and interests (hobbies, recreational activities, etc.)
- Formal associations (church membership, participation in union, membership in service club, etc.)
- Sources of support and stress in social interactions (between people and between people and community systems)
- Utilization of community resources (Medicaid, economic assistance, public health, mental health, schools, Social Security, doctors, etc.)
- Informal resources and natural helpers (extended family, relatives, friends, neighbors, self-help groups)

All of these data can be "drawn" into a one-page ecomap.

Although the user of these diagrams can create his or her own symbols and abbreviations, certain symbols are commonly used, as shown in Figure 11.2. Words and notations—such as "m" for "married," "div" for "divorced," and "d" for "died"—may also be used in the family diagram and ecomap.

Figure 11.3 is a diagram of a reconstituted family, which appears within the dotted circle (boundary). It indicates that a man (age 45), his wife (age 33), and three children (ages 3, 1, and 10) live in the household. The 10-year-old is from his mother's former marriage; the boy's biological father died in 2004. The 45-year-old husband was divorced from his former wife (age 42) in 2003. Also, we see that he has two daughters (ages 20 and 18) by this former wife and is now a grandfather, since his 20-year-old daughter has a 1-year-old daughter. The former wife is now married to a man who is age 44.

An ecomap places the family or client within their social context by using circles to represent organizations or factors impacting their lives. Various symbols or short phrases are used to describe the nature of these interactions. Figure 11.4 is an ecomap of Dick and Barb and their two children, John and June.

FIGURE 11.3   Genogram of a Reconstituted Family

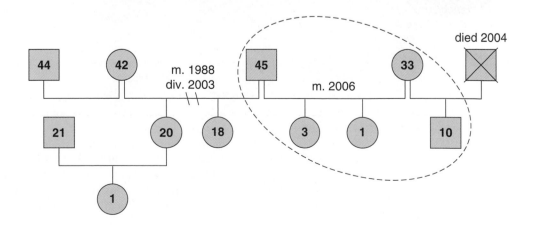

FIGURE 11.4   Ecomap

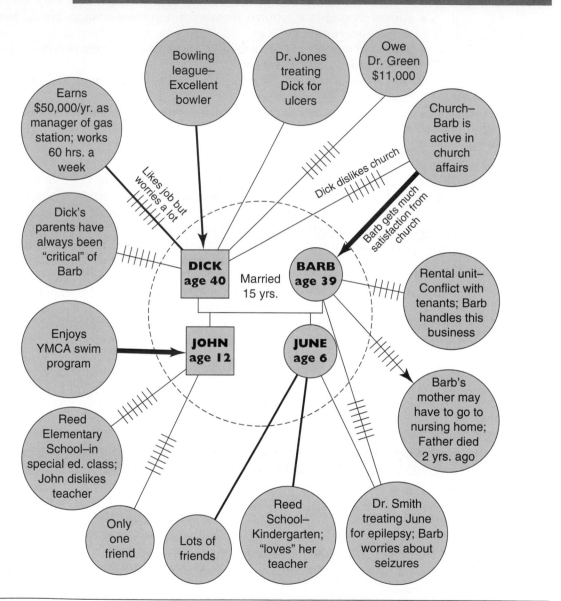

Usually, an ecomap is developed jointly by the social worker and client and helps both to view the family from a system's or ecological perspective. Ecomapping can be used by the worker to build a relationship and demonstrate a desire to learn about the client and his or her situation. It has been used in adoption and foster-care home studies and in marriage and family counseling. Many clients report that doing an ecomap helps them see their situation more clearly.

When examining an ecomap, consider a number of basic questions: Does the family have an income adequate to cover basic needs such as food, shelter, transportation, and health care? Are family members employed? Do they enjoy their jobs? Does the family live in a neighborhood that is safe? Does the family interact with relatives, friends, and neighbors? Does the family participate in social, cultural, religious, and community activities? Are the family's values, beliefs, or lifestyle in conflict with those dominant in the neighborhood? Do the children have access to needed educational resources? Do they enjoy their school experience? Are some of the family members experiencing high levels of stress? Answers to such questions yield important information for assessment and intervention.

SELECTED BIBLIOGRAPHY

Kaslow, Florence. *Projective Genogramming*. Sarasota, FL: Professional Resource Press, 1995.

McGoldrick, Monica. "Using Genograms to Map Family Patterns." In *Social Workers' Desk Reference*, edited by Albert Roberts and Gilbert Greene, 233–245. New York: Oxford University Press, 2002.

McGoldrick, Monica, Randy Gerson, and Sylvia Shellenberger. *Genograms,* 2nd ed. New York: W. W. Norton, 1999.

11.3   SOCIAL SUPPORT ASSESSMENT

Purpose: To identify people to whom a client might turn for certain types of social support.

Discussion: The term *social support* refers to various types of assistance and helping, offered by others, and perceived by the person as desirable and beneficial. Social support can take several forms, such as the following:

> *Tangible or concrete assistance* (e.g., a ride to a doctor appointment, a small cash loan, help with grocery shopping, unpaid child care)
>
> *Guidance and teaching* (e.g., providing sought-after information, helping a friend make a difficult decision, teaching a needed skill)
>
> *Emotional caring and support* (e.g., listening respectfully or providing reassurance and empathy)

Social support is usually provided by a family member or relative, friend, or neighbor, but in some situations, it is provided by a paid professional or agency volunteer.

In order to help clients make appropriate and effective use of social supports, it is necessary to engage clients in the identification and evaluation of their potential social supports. Questions such as the following can assist in this assessment process:

- What people are important to you? As you answer that question think of the people who are in your household or family, your friends and neighbors, the people at work or school, and the people who are members of the organizations or religious groups to which you belong.
- Of those you have listed, which ones do you consider to be especially supportive and helpful and a positive influence on your life? And of these, which ones do you see, talk to, write to, or email on a regular basis?
- Are there individuals to whom you often turn to for advice or help in making decisions?
- Are there individuals in your life that you would feel comfortable asking for a ride to work, a ride to the grocery store, or for a small loan?
- Who among those in your network of relatives and friends knows you and understands you better than anyone else?
- Do you have individuals in your life that you really trust and could turn to for help or advice concerning a personal problem or dilemma?
- Who is the one person within your network of family and friends that you can always count on for help, no matter what the problem and no matter what might be involved?

Once a client has identified the individuals or groups that are potential social supports, the social worker engages the client in a discussion of whether and how the client might reach out to and utilize these sources of support. Whether the supports are likely resources will depend on the nature of the client's problem or needs and the client's willingness to use these supports. Questions such as those presented below may help determine if the client is willing and able to utilize the potential social supports within his or her social network:

- Of those that you have identified as helpful and positive influences in your life, which ones have you actually asked for some sort of help or assistance? When was that? Were you satisfied with how they responded to you?
- Are there reasons why you might feel reluctant to ask others for assistance, even though you believe that they would probably be glad to help?
- Are there ways that you could "repay" these people for the help they could provide to you?

In some situations, a client may experience support just knowing that there are people or agencies that they could call upon, even if they never do actually reach out to and utilize these potential resources.

Social support resources are a part of one's *social network,* which can be defined as all those individuals and groups with which one interacts on a regular basis. The size or extent of a person's social network is not necessarily correlated with the amount or the quality of support available to him or her. By definition, social support is a positive and helpful influence. However, other exchanges with persons and groups that constitute one's social network may have a harmful impact on one's functioning and sense of self.

SELECTED BIBLIOGRAPHY

Kemp, Susan, James Whittaker, and Elizabeth Tracy. *Person-Environment Practice*. New York: Aldine de Gruyter, 1997.

Sarason, Barbara, and Steve Duok, eds. *Personal Relationships: Implications for Clinical and Community Psychology*. New York: Wiley, 2001.

Tracy, Elizabeth. "Identifying Social Support Resources of At-Risk Families." *Social Work* 35, no. 3 (May 1990): 252–258.

11.4   IDENTIFYING CLIENT STRENGTHS

Purpose: To identify individual and family strengths.

Discussion: A social worker's assessment of a client's functioning and his or her situation should always strive to identify client strengths. A ***client strength*** can be defined as an important, positive, and prosocial action or activity that the client is doing, can do, or wants to do. The assessment should focus mostly on positive and functional patterns, not only on negative and dysfunctional ones. This is not to suggest a Pollyannaish approach that ignores or overlooks real problems, but it does ask the worker to search for strengths even in the most dysfunctional and chaotic of cases. The reason for this emphasis is simple: To be successful, *an intervention must be built on and around client strengths*. If the worker focuses only on problems and only on what is going wrong in the client's life, the client will soon feel even more frustrated and discouraged and the worker will feel pessimistic about being able to be of help.

For many in the helping professions, focusing on client strengths requires a paradigm shift—a new way of thought and analysis. Several forces encourage and reinforce a focus on client problems and limitations rather than on strengths. Consider the following:

- *Agency policy and funding.* Most human services agencies are created for the purpose of addressing or correcting some personal or family problem, pathology, deficiency, or dysfunction. Thus, agency staff may assume that their primary "duty" is to identify and focus on problems.
- *Diagnostic labels.* Commonly used terminology and reference books (e.g., *DSM*) focus attention on pathology and on all that is wrong and troublesome in a person's life. Frequent use of this terminology creates a rather negative mindset that looks for and finds only problems and pathology.
- *Lack of skill.* Identifying personal and family problems can be described as a beginning level or elementary skill. Most people can do it with little or no

training. On the other hand, identifying strengths is an advanced or high-level skill.

■ *Personality and temperament.* Many people tend to be negative in their outlook. They see the glass as "half empty" rather than "half full." They just naturally focus on what is missing and on what is wrong. Some sociobiologists believe that the human tendency to notice quickly what is wrong and out of place has a survival or protective value for animals and the human species. Consequently, evolution has "wired" our senses and perceptual processes so we will quickly notice things that are different or wrong, because doing so helps us to detect and avoid dangers in our environment.

As suggested earlier, a strength is something positive and important that an individual or a family can do and will do. The social worker can identify strengths by carefully observing individual and family behavior. Here are some examples of *individual strengths:*

■ Assuming responsibility for one's actions
■ Taking reasonable risks in order to make needed changes
■ Demonstrating loyalty and a sense of duty to family, relatives, and friends
■ Showing affection, compassion, and concern for others; demonstrating a willingness to forgive others
■ Assisting and encouraging others; protecting others from harm
■ Seeking employment, holding a job, being a responsible employee, meeting one's financial obligations
■ Exercising self-control and making thoughtful decisions and plans; choosing not to engage in problem or self-defeating behavior (e.g., an angry youth wanted to beat up another teen but chose to walk away)
■ Being trustworthy, fair, and honest in dealing with others
■ Experiencing true and appropriate sorrow and guilt; making amends or restitution for having harmed others
■ Seeking to understand others and their situations and accepting differences among people
■ Willingness to keep trying despite hardship and setback
■ Participating in social, community, or religious organizations and working to improve one's neighborhood and community
■ Expressing one's point of view and standing up for one's own rights and the rights of others
■ Making constructive use of special abilities and aptitudes (e.g., mechanical, artistic, interpersonal, athletic, etc.)

Important *family strengths* include the following:

■ Members trust, respect, and enjoy each other.
■ Members listen to and respect each other's opinions, even when they disagree. Their communication is clear, positive, and productive.

- The family has clear and reasonable rules that govern behavior and interaction.
- Each member's ideas, preferences, and needs are considered before making a decision that would affect the family.
- The family has traditions, rituals, and stories that provide a sense of history, belonging, and identity.
- Family members share what they have and make personal sacrifices in order to help each other; members stick together and support each other in times of adversity.
- Conflicts are acknowledged and resolved.

(Additional client strengths are described in Item 11.13.)

Strengths can be identified by asking the client questions such as the following: Can you tell me about times when you successfully handled problems similar to those you now face? Where did you find the courage and energy to deal with those problems? How have you managed to cope up to this point? What kept you going? Despite your current problems, what parts of your life are going fairly well? What do other people like about you? What strengths or advantages do others see in your approach to life? What would you not change about yourself, your situation, and your life?

Building on client strengths may require looking at a client's problems from a different angle. For example, consider the man who has been labeled uncooperative and unmotivated. If one views this so-called uncooperative behavior from another perspective, one uncovers a strength: He is asserting his rights to disagree and resist doing what does not make sense. In other words, he is being logical and assertive. When problems are reframed in ways that reveal strengths, one usually also discovers more effective ways of helping. (See Item 13.11 for other examples of redefining a problem as a strength.)

Another way of orienting your approach to one that recognizes and builds on client strengths is to operate on the assumption that within all people, there are innate tendencies toward psychological health and prosocial behavior. Just as there are natural healing processes that are constantly repairing the human body, there appears to be natural forces that, over time, tend to heal and repair psychological damage, ruptured relationships, and the many other hurts that are part of human life and living. If such a belief is a reasonable one, it lends hope to the worker's helping efforts. It informs the social worker of the importance of supporting those natural forces and creating conditions and environments that allow the client's natural healing processes to work.

Drawing on suggestions made by Cowger and Snively (2002), these guidelines will help the worker maintain a focus on strengths:

1. Believe the client. Assume that he or she is honest and trustworthy, unless it is proven otherwise. Assume that all people are capable of making positive changes in how they cope with the challenges of life and in how they interact with others.

2. Display an interest in strengths. Listen for and call to the client's attention all indicators of the client's competence, skill, resourcefulness, and motivation to make his or her situation better.

3. Assume that the client is an expert on his or her behavior, life, and situation, and knows best what will and will not work in a change effort or treatment plan. Give primary attention to the client's own perceptions and understanding of his or her situation.

4. View the assessment and the service planning processes as joint worker-client activity. Both the client and the professional share responsibility for determining what concern or issue needs to be addressed and how this can be done.

5. Assess but do not diagnose. Avoid the use of diagnostic labeling, for it draws attention away from client strengths and places the focus on pathology and deficits.

6. Avoid discussions of blame and what the client or others should or should not have done previously. Attempts to assign blame lead nowhere and use time and energy better spent on problem solving. Rather, focus on what can be done now. Also, avoid pointless discussions of cause and effect. Typically, problems of social functioning arise from many complex and interrelated factors. Trying to figure out the exact cause of a problem is usually nonproductive. Time is better spent on here-and-now problem solving.

7. Assume that within the client's family, social network, and community there is an oasis of potential resources, both formal and informal, that can be drawn into the helping process. Every family, every neighborhood, and every community contains people who are willing and capable of being helpful and supportive of others.

8. Formulate an intervention plan that is specific and individualized to the client and his or her situation. Because every individual and every family is unique and unlike every other one, all treatment plans or service plans should be unique.

SELECTED BIBLIOGRAPHY

Cowger, Charles, and Carol Snively. "*Assessing Client Strengths*" In *Social Workers Desk Reference*, edited by Albert Roberts and Gilbert Greene. New York: Oxford University, 2002.
Glicken, Morley. *Using the Strengths Perspective in Social Work Practice.* Boston: Allyn & Bacon, 2004.
Saleebey, Dennis, ed. *The Strengths Perspective in Social Work Practice,* 4th ed. Boston: Allyn & Bacon, 2006.

11.5   EXPANDING A CLIENT'S VISION OF CHANGES THAT ARE POSSIBLE

Purpose: To stimulate a client's thinking about goals and possibilities.

Discussion: Most approaches to assessment ask the client to provide a detailed description of his or her problem or concern. While doing so is necessary for some purposes, such as making a clinical diagnosis, such descriptions are not necessarily helpful to the process of bringing about needed change. In fact, giving undo attention to the problems and all that is wrong in a client's situation can make him or her feel defeated and conclude that the problem is even worse than he or she had assumed.

An alternative approach, one based on the principles of *solution-focused therapy* (see Chapter 6), is to help the client provide detailed descriptions of those times and situations when the problem does not have such a strong negative effect on his or her functioning and also to encourage the client to imagine how he or she would think, feel, and behave if the problem would suddenly disappear. This approach helps the client put his or her difficulty in perspective, recognize his or her strengths, and begin to visualize specific steps and options that could effectively address the problem. The techniques of *exploring exceptions, scaling questions*, and using the *miracle question* facilitate these purposes.

The technique of **exploring exceptions** refers to a type of questioning intended to help the client realize that there are times or situations when the problem is less frequent or less intense. Once these exceptions have been identified, the social worker can encourage the client to consider why they occur and to figure out what might be done to prolong these desirable times and situations. Even when the client feels the problem exists "all the time" and "everywhere," it is usually possible to find exceptions. Here are some examples of questioning intended to uncover and explore exceptions:

> "This is obviously a very serious problem. How have you managed to keep it from getting even worse?"

> "You have said that you are in trouble with your parents most of the time. Tell me about a time in the last couple of weeks when you and your parents were getting along better than usual. What did you do to make that happen?"

> "You are failing all of your school courses except one. What have you done in order to pass this one course?"

> "Have things been even a little better since you called me to arrange this appointment [the answer is usually yes]? What did you do to make things better?"

> "Are those times when things are going a bit better for you usually in the morning? Afternoon? Evening? Who is with you at these times? What are they saying and doing to make things go more smoothly?"

> "During the next week and before we meet again, please notice the times when things are going better and write a note about what is happening each time the problem is less troublesome."

The technique of **scaling questions** is designed to help the client realize that the seriousness and the impact of a problem varies over time and also that bringing about desirable change is a matter of taking many small steps, rather than making some large and sudden shift in functioning. The technique consists of asking the core scaling question and several follow-up questions, as in this example:

> **Social Worker:**   On a scale of 1 to 10—with 1 being the worst your problem has ever been and 10 meaning that the problem had been solved and is no longer of concern to you—how would you rate your situation today?
>
> **Client:**   Oh, probably about a 4 today, but it was about a 2 last week.

> ***Social Worker:*** Great! I am glad to hear that things are going better. Given your answer, I have two questions for you: First, how did you manage to improve your situation from a 2 to a 4 during this last week? And second, what do you think you can do in the next week to move the rating from a 4 to about a 4.5 or a 5?

Here is an application of the scaling question intended to assess the client's motivation:

> ***Social Worker:*** We have talked about some of the things you might be able to do in order to address your concern. On a scale of 1 to 10—with 1 meaning that you are not willing to do anything to solve the problem and 10 meaning that you are willing to try just about anything to find a solution—how hard are you willing to work on this problem?
>
> ***Client:*** Probably about a 9.
>
> ***Social Worker:*** Wow! You feel strongly about wanting to deal with this problem. Tell me, why do you feel so strongly motivated about this matter?

Another solution-focused technique, the ***miracle question,*** encourages the client to visualize and describe what his or her life would be like without the problem. Doing so helps the client think about the future, rather than the past, and encourages him or her to identify a range of options and more clearly identify the changes he or she needs to make. The miracle question is asked deliberately and rather dramatically. De Shazer (1988, 5) suggests wording something like this:

> "Now, I want to ask you a rather strange question. Suppose that while you are sleeping tonight, a miracle happens: The problem that brought you here for professional help has been solved! However, because you were sleeping, you do not know that this miracle has occurred. So, after you wake up tomorrow morning, how will you know? What will be different? What will tell you that something miraculous has happened and that the problem that brought you into counseling has disappeared?"

The social worker then asks various follow-up questions to help the client further describe the hoped-for changes. The following examples are from work with a married woman:

> "What might your husband [child, friend] notice about you that would give him the idea that things are going better for you?"
>
> "When he notices that positive change in you, what might he do differently in response?"
>
> "When he behaves differently toward you, what will you do in response to him?"
>
> "When you are doing better, how will your time at home and time at work be different than they are now?"

DeJong and Miller (1995) offer the following suggestions on follow-up questioning:

> When a client responds to the miracle question with "I'd have a sense of peace," the worker might ask, "What might your husband notice as being different about you and tell him that you are beginning to 'have a sense of peace'?" With this question, the worker is attempting to help the client develop more concrete goals. . . . Or, to give another example, when a client responds to the miracle question with, "I'd cry less," the worker would ask, "What would be there instead of the crying?" recognizing that well-formed goals are the presence of something rather than the absence. (p. 731)

As clients begin to visualize and think seriously about their everyday lives without their given problems, they typically come up with practical ideas about what they can do to better cope with their problems and make things better.

SELECTED BIBLIOGRAPHY

DeJong, Peter, and Insoo Kim Berg. *Interviewing for Solutions,* 2nd ed. Belmont, CA: Brooks/Cole, 2002.

DeJong, Peter, and Scott Miller. "How to Interview for Client Strengths." *Social Work* 40 (November 1995): 729–736.

de Shazer, Steven. *Clues: Investigating Solutions in Brief Therapy.* New York: W. W. Norton, 1988.

Miller, Scott, and Insoo Kim Berg. *The Miracle Method: A Radically New Approach to Problem Drinking.* New York: W. W. Norton, 1995.

11.6 COPING STRATEGIES AND EGO DEFENSES

Purpose: To identify a client's usual methods of coping and defenses in order to anticipate how the client will respond to difficult situations.

Discussion: Some professionals use the terms *coping strategy* and *ego defense mechanism* interchangeably, but it is useful to make a distinction based on the degree to which the response is under conscious and voluntary control and whether self-deception and reality distortion are involved. Thus, we shall define a **coping strategy** as a fairly deliberate and conscious effort to solve a problem or handle personal distress. By contrast, an **ego defense mechanism** is a habitual or unconscious problem-avoiding maneuver.

Coping strategies have two functions: to solve a problem (task-focused coping) and to reduce the emotional discomfort caused by stressors (emotion-focused coping). Often, an individual must first deal with emotional reactions before moving on to problem solving, but emotion-focused and task-focused coping frequently occur simultaneously.

Individuals vary widely in the type of emotion-focused strategies they use to cope with painful feelings and stressful situations. For example, given a situation that causes much anxiety, some individuals might elect to go off by themselves, others might visit friends, some pray and meditate, and still others might engage in a brisk physical workout. Other coping strategies—some functional, some not so functional—include ignoring the problem, sleeping more, eating more, and becoming absorbed in work. Since an individual tends to use certain coping strategies habitually, the social worker can form a fairly accurate picture of which ones a client typically uses by asking how he or she has responded to or dealt with other stressful situations.

Regardless of culture, people react to shocking events and intense distress by using ***emotion-focused coping strategies*** such as the following:

- *Crying.* Crying is a common and normal means of alleviating tension and responding to loss. It is a necessary part of successful grief work.
- *Talking it out.* People who have undergone traumatic experiences often need to repeatedly describe and talk about the experience. As a result of this natural desensitization process, they eventually learn to accept and tolerate the painful thoughts and feelings associated with the traumatic experience.
- *Laughing it off.* Joking and viewing painful experiences with a sense of humor serves to release tension and place the matter in perspective. In healthy grieving, for example, there is often a good mix of crying and laughter among those adjusting to the death of a loved one.
- *Seeking support.* It is natural for both children and adults to seek support, attention, and affection from others as a means of regaining emotional equilibrium.
- *Dreaming and nightmares.* These do not fit the authors' definition of a coping strategy (i.e., conscious and voluntary) but they are a common reaction to traumatic experience. These dreams and nightmares are often repetitive. And, like the desensitization process involved in talking it out, the recurring dream encourages the individual to consciously grapple with the experience.

When working with a client who has moved beyond these emotion-focused responses or who has not experienced a traumatic event, the social worker should help him or her make use of ***task-focused strategies.*** These strategies consist of deliberate and rational actions that will likely bring about changes in one's functioning, one's environment, or both. The strategies listed below are of a rather general nature, but they illustrate what the social worker should be looking for in data collection and assessment. A client with good task-oriented coping strategies will have the motivation, the capacity, and the opportunity to do these things:

- Express thoughts and feelings in a clear, positive, and, when necessary, assertive manner.
- Ask questions and gather new information, even when the new information may challenge current beliefs.
- Identify one's personal needs and learn socially acceptable means of meeting those needs.
- Model one's own behavior after persons who behave in an effective and responsible manner.
- Recognize that one does have choices and can exert influence on one's own behavior, feelings, and life events.

- "Cut one's losses" and withdraw from relationships or situations that are unhealthy or stressful and unchangeable.
- Examine the religious and spiritual dimension of life and draw on one's beliefs for insight, strength, and direction.
- Identify early signs or indicators of a developing problem so action can be taken before the problem becomes serious.
- Take positive and appropriate steps to solve problems even when such actions are a source of fear and anxiety.
- Release pent-up emotion in ways that do not verbally or physically harm self or others.
- Take care of one's body and maintain one's health.
- Delay immediate gratification in order to stick with a plan that will attain a more distant but desired goal.
- Use mental images of future actions or events to mentally rehearse how to handle anticipated difficulties.
- Ignore unjustified criticism by others and remove one's self from situations that lead to self-defeating or harmful outcomes.
- Seek out and use additional skills training and needed professional services.

If the assessment reveals that a client lacks necessary coping strategies, the intervention plan should focus on helping the client learn specific *coping skills.* Of course, the skills needed will depend on the client's problem, situation, and goals. For example, an abusing parent may need to learn parenting skills, an individual in need of a job will need to focus on job finding skills, a married couple in conflict may need communication skills, and a youth leaving the foster-care system will need to acquire independent living skills.

A ***defense mechanism*** is usually defined as a largely unconscious mental process that serves to protect the individual against overwhelming anxiety, psychological threat, and emotional pain. The defense mechanisms frequently mentioned in the professional literature include denial, projection, rationalization, repression, reaction formation, displacement intellectualization, fantasizing, and acting out. Everyone uses defense mechanisms to some degree in coping with the ordinary anxieties and stresses of living. However, the excessive or rigid use of defense mechanisms is problematic because it poses a barrier to realistic problem solving. The individual may have an impaired ability to perceive reality and to get along with others. A high level of defensiveness and distortion of reality is characteristic of a disturbed personality.

An individual who uses the ego defense of ***denial*** screens out certain realities by refusing to acknowledge them. Denial is often used in combination with ***rationalization,*** which involves the justification of inappropriate behavior by manufacturing logical or socially acceptable reasons for the behavior. An example is the abusing parent who justifies physical abuse on the basis that "the only thing he understands is pain." Although clearly a distortion of the truth, a rationalization is not the same as a lie because the defensive pattern is so habitual that the person is not consciously and deliberately trying to fabricate a falsehood. Denial and rationalization are predominant defenses used by people who are chemically dependent. Behaviors that suggest rationalization by a client include: (a) groping for reasons to justify an action or belief, (b) inability to recognize inconsistencies in his or her own "story," and (c) unwillingness to consider alternative explanations and becoming angry when one's "reasons" are questioned.

In **projection,** others are seen as being responsible for one's own shortcomings or unacceptable behavior. For example, the child molester may believe that he was seduced by the young child and sees himself as the victim rather than the offender.

Repression refers to a mental process in which extremely threatening and painful thoughts or experiences are excluded from consciousness. For example, a child may repress experiences of sexual abuse and not remember them until years later.

Emotional insulation is a maneuver aimed at withholding an emotional investment in a desired but unlikely outcome. This defense creates a shield that protects the individual from loss or a recurrence of pain and disappointment. For example, a child who is moved frequently from foster home to foster home may use emotional insulation as a defense against the pain of separation and loss; unfortunately, such a child often carries this pattern into adulthood and is then unable to develop emotional attachments to a marriage partner or to his or her own children. This defense is closely related to the concept of *learned helplessness*—after a long period of frustration, many people simply give up and quit trying to escape their misery. These are the "broken" individuals who become passive recipients of whatever life brings them. Emotional insulation is commonly used by persons who have grown up in extreme deprivation.

Intellectualization involves the use of mental abstractions as a way of distancing and sparating oneself from emotional pain. The intensity of one's pain or hurt is softened by looking at one's situation through the lens of theoretical analysis. For example, the individual who was turned down for a sought-after job may cope with feelings of disappointment by explaining his or her disappointment within a context of free-trade economics and changing global markets.

Regression represents a retreat from one's present level of maturity to one that has fewer demands and stressors. For example, when a new child is born to a family, the 5-year-old may begin behaving like an infant (e.g., wetting pants, sucking thumb, etc.) as a way of getting more attention and coping with fears of being overlooked by his or her parents. Regression is common among physically ill persons who are experiencing much fear or pain.

When using **reaction formation,** a person adopts behaviors that are the opposite of inner thoughts, desires, or impulses that he or she finds abhorrent and unacceptable. An example is an individual who comes to realize that he is sexually attracted to children and, in response, works tirelessly to create programs designed to prevent child sexual abuse.

Displacement refers to transferring troublesome emotions (often hostility) and acting-out behaviors (e.g., violence) from the person(s) who arouses the emotion to another less threatening and less powerful person or thing. The classic example is the man who kicks his dog because he is angry with his boss.

The person using **fantasy** as a defense spends much time daydreaming and dwells on imaginary situations, either as a way of meeting emotional needs or as shields against anxiety and feelings of inadequacy. Problems develop when the person finds his or her reality so painful that he or she prefers an imaginary world. An inability to distinguish between fantasy and reality is a symptom of serious mental illness.

Acting out is an attempt to cope with frustration or inner turmoil by taking action, often impulsively, or by striking out physically. For example, a frustrated adolescent boy who is unable to verbally express his feelings may seek a release from tension by attacking the person he views as the source of his problems. Another example would be the battered wife who is feeling the tensions build and knows she will soon be beaten by her abusive husband, so she proceeds to provoke him so she can "get it over with." Combat soldiers who can no longer tolerate the stress and fear of waiting for an attack have been known to leave the safety of their foxhole and blindly charge the enemy.

Several guidelines can be offered to assist the social worker in assessing and responding to a client's defense mechanisms:

1. When using defense mechanism terminology, certain precautions are necessary. The patterns we call defenses are only hypothetical constructs inferred from the way people behave. At best, they are a shorthand language for describing behavior. Simply labeling a client's behavior as projection or rationalization, for example, in no way explains or changes the behavior. You must look behind the surface behavior and identify and address the unmet needs and pain that cause the client to rely on the defense mechanism.

2. Because defenses are mostly learned and habitual, an individual tends to utilize those defenses he or she has used in the past. For example, if, in the past, an individual frequently used denial and rationalization, you can expect him or her to use those same defenses when again faced with anxiety or conflict.

3. People hold tightly to their defensive patterns. The more anxiety they experience, the more rigidly they use the defense. People do not easily give up these habits of thought and behavior. It is usually only within a relationship characterized by empathy, warmth, and genuineness that a person can feel safe enough to let down his or her defenses and examine the underlying pain.

SELECTED BIBLIOGRAPHY

Blackman, Jerome. *101 Defenses: How the Mind Shields Itself.* New York: Routledge, 2003.
Conte, Hope, and Robert Plutchik. *Ego Defenses: Theory and Measurement.* New York: Wiley and Sons, 1995.

11.7 ASSESSING A CLIENT'S ROLE PERFORMANCE

Purpose: To clarify and describe the nature of a client's difficulty in performing role-related behaviors.

Discussion: A great many social agencies and programs seek to enhance or improve people's performance of social roles such as parent, spouse, employee, student, and citizen. Concepts and terminology borrowed from role theory can help a social worker assess and describe a client's role-related behavior and functioning. These concepts are useful because they bridge psychological and social perspectives on human behavior.

The concept of ***social role*** derives from the observation that within a society's structure, certain behaviors are expected of particular persons simply because they occupy a particular status or position within that society. For example, once a person becomes a parent (a social role), he or she is expected to provide his or her young children with food, shelter, protection, guidance, and so on. Within a school setting, the teacher (a social role) is expected to teach, and the student (another social role) is expected to adhere to school rules and learn that which the teacher judges to be important. The term *role*, borrowed from the world of theater, implies that a script, an actor, and an audience are components of our social functioning. If we use this analogy from theater, the script corresponds to role expectations, and the audience corresponds to society and its various institutions.

The term ***role expectation*** suggests that for a given role, there is a cluster of behaviors that are deemed appropriate and acceptable by a reference group or by society as a whole. In other words, the reference group expects the individual to behave in a certain way and will either approve or disapprove of the person, depending on whether he or she conforms to those norms or expectations. Role expectations define the limits or the range of acceptable and tolerated behavior.

The term ***role conception*** refers to an individual's personal beliefs and assumptions about how he or she is supposed to behave in a particular role. What the individual expects of himself or herself may or may not conform to the role expectations defined by others and the wider society.

An individual's actual behavior while performing a role is termed his or her ***role performance*** (or *role enactment*). In some instances, an individual's role performance may be consistent with his or her role conception but not conform to others' role expectations. For example, a father may live up to his own beliefs about parenthood, but his parental behavior may be labeled as neglectful by the wider community or its court system. In order to successfully perform a given role, an individual must possess certain knowledge, skills, physical and mental abilities, and other personal attributes. These prerequisites to acceptable role performance are often termed ***role demands*** (or *role requirements*).

A number of terms are used to describe problems in role performance. ***Interrole conflict*** refers to an incompatibility or clash between two or more roles. For example, a woman may experience a conflict between her role as parent to a young child and her role as a corporate executive who is expected to make frequent out-of-town business trips. ***Intrarole conflict*** exists when a person is caught up in a situation where two or more sets of expectations are assigned to a single role. For example, a high school boy may not be able to reconcile the role of student as defined by his teacher with how the role is defined by his peers. ***Role incapacity*** exists when, for some reason, an individual cannot adequately perform a role; possible reasons include physical or mental illness, lack of needed knowledge or skills, drug addiction, mental retardation, and so on. ***Role rejection*** occurs when an individual refuses to perform a role; an extreme example is when a parent abandons his or her child.

A problem of ***role ambiguity*** (or *role confusion*) exists when there are few clear expectations associated with a role—a condition most likely to occur in times of rapid social change. Consequently, the individual is unsure of what is expected and is unable to evaluate his or her own performance. ***Self-role incongruence*** exists when there is little overlap between the requirements of a role and the individual's personality. For example, an individual may occupy the role of a professional but not feel comfortable in that role. Another example is when an individual finds that his or her values, ethics, or lifestyle is at odds with the expectations of a role. The problem of ***role overload*** exists when a person occupies more roles than he or she can perform adequately. In reality, most individuals are unable or do not choose to conform to the expectations of all their social roles. Thus, most people live with some degree of ***role strain,*** a situation that necessitates making compromises and trade-offs, setting priorities, and using various defense mechanisms and coping strategies to reconcile their role conceptions with their limited time and energy.

A number of questions can help the social worker analyze problems of role performance and make decisions concerning the type of intervention needed. The questions that follow are based, in part, on ones proposed by Mager and Pipe (1997) for the analysis of job-related performance problems:

1. *What is the nature and degree of the discrepancy between actual performance and role expectation?*
  - How does the client's behavior differ from that considered appropriate or normal for persons in this particular role?
  - What observations, events, or experiences have caused you and/or the client to conclude that a discrepancy exists?
  - Why are you and/or the client dissatisfied or concerned about the client's role performance? Why is this role important? What will happen if there is no change in the client's role performance?

2. *Is the discrepancy caused by a lack of knowledge or skill?*
  - Does the client possess the knowledge or skill needed to perform this role?
  - Could the client adequately perform this role if he or she really had to or really wanted to? Could he or she do it if life depended on it?

3. *If the discrepancy is caused by a lack of knowledge and skill, how best can the problem be addressed?*
  - Was there a time when the client could perform this role? If so, what experience or condition has caused the client to lose the capacity or motivation to perform this role?
  - What can be done to help the client regain a capacity that has deteriorated?
  - Is the client now able to learn the behaviors needed to perform the role?
  - What teaching methods or techniques will help the client learn the behaviors needed to perform this role?

4. *If the discrepancy is caused by a rejection or a lack of interest in the role, how can the problem be addressed?*
  - Does this role really matter to the client? Is it important to the client?
  - What roles or activities does the client consider more important?

■ Does the client see any benefits in performing this role?
■ Is the client rewarded or reinforced for the performance of this role? If not, how can rewards be increased?
■ Is the client punished by others or the social environment for attempting to perform this role? How can the client be helped to avoid this punishment?

SELECTED BIBLIOGRAPHY

Davis, Liane. "Role Theory." In *Social Work Treatment,* 4th ed., edited by Francis Turner, 581–600. New York: Free Press, 1996.

Mager, Robert, and Peter Pipe. *Analyzing Performance Problems,* 3rd ed. Atlanta: Center for Effective Performance, 1997.

11.8   ASSESSING A CLIENT'S SELF-CONCEPT

Purpose: To understand a client's perceptions and thoughts about herself or himself as a person.

Discussion: The term *self* refers to that private and inner world of assumptions, perceptions, and thoughts about the "I" or the "me." Basically one's sense of self answers the questions: Who am I? and What am I really like, regardless of what others may think of me? The term ***self-concept*** refers to a set of beliefs that a person has about his or her nature, characteristics, and typical behavior. These beliefs may or may not be shared with others. Our self-concept or our sense of self is of critical importance to our social functioning because how we respond to others and to life events is strongly influenced by how we think and feel about ourselves.

Nurius and Berlin (1995, 517–518) remind us that each of us has not one, but rather "multiple concepts about who she or he is, sometimes is, was, should be or could be." They also state that the concept of self that is activated is, to some degree, responsive to the situation and the circumstances or tasks most salient at that time.

Several other terms and concepts are used to explain and describe various aspects of the private, inner world of the self. ***Self-identity*** is how we define and describe ourselves to ourselves and differentiate ourselves from other people. It is important to recognize that what we think about ourselves (our private thoughts) may be different from the image we present to other people. Thus, we have a private self and a public self. Others may view us quite differently than we view ourselves. ***Self-efficacy*** has to do with our feelings of being competent and effective and in control of our life. The term ***self-worth*** (or *self-esteem*) refers to our evaluation of our own value or adequacy as human beings. Self-worth is a very subjective evaluation, not an objective one. The term ***self-acceptance*** can be thought of as the degree to which we are satisfied and at peace with our qualities and attributes, assets and limitations. The term ***ideal-self*** (or *self-expectation*) refers to our inner thoughts about who we could be, should be, or want to be. ***Body image*** refers to our perceptions and evaluations of our own body and physical appearance.

To a large degree, one's sense of self is formed during early childhood but experiences during adolescence also exert a strong influence. However, experiences throughout one's lifetime can lead one to reevaluate and modify the answer to the questions: Who am I? and How did I come to be the person I am? Deeply personal thoughts and core beliefs have much to do with the meanings we assign to our lives and life experiences; thus, a person's sense of self—one's inner self—is an element of spirituality.

Whether a particular aspect of a client's self-concept or life experiences needs to be discussed during the assessment process depends on the client's presenting concern or problem and the reasons the client and professional are meeting. Some clients are reluctant to share personal information, whereas many others are eager to tell their stories and will easily describe very personal life experiences. To draw out this type of information, the social worker can ask questions that are organized around five fairly common human experiences: love, loss, fear, having been hurt, and having hurt others. Many clients will respond non-defensively to questions like these:

1. *Who and what do you love?* Who do you really care for? What is most important to you? For whom do you make personal sacrifices? For what purposes do you donate your time and money? Are you able to love others as you want to?

2. *Who and what have you lost?* Have you lost parents, children, and close friends to death or separation? Have loved ones become disabled or seriously ill? Have you lost your hopes and dreams because of divorce, abandonment, or relocation? Have you lost some physical abilities as a result of illness or injury (e.g., mobility, vision, hearing, etc.)? Have you lost your sense of emotional security and personal safety as a result of abuse, exploitation, violence, or war? Have you lost purpose and meaning in life? Have you lost contact with your homeland or native language? Have you lost touch with meaningful religious and cultural activity? Have you lost a home or important possessions to a flood, fire, or natural disaster?

3. *Who and what do you fear?* Do you live with a fear of hunger, violence, illness, pain, disability, or death? Do you fear that no one cares for you? Do you fear that you are incapable of loving others? Do you fear the loss of respect and status? Do you fear the loss of important relationships, a job, money, or a home?

4. *How have you been hurt in life?* How and when were you hurt by others (physically, emotionally, financially, etc.)? How do you explain these painful life experiences? Who is responsible? Have these past hurts given rise to fears of being hurt again or a desire for revenge? How have these experiences affected the way you think and feel about yourself and others?

5. *Whom have you hurt?* How and when have you hurt others, deliberately or inadvertently? Why did it happen? How do you explain these experiences? How has your hurting of others shaped the way you think and feel about yourself? What have you done to correct or make amends for the pain and injury you caused?

Next are some other lines of questioning that might be used, in one form or another, to explore a client's sense of self:

1. *Family membership.* Who is your family (tribe or clan)? For whom do you feel responsible and obligated to care for, help, or look after? With whom do you live? Where do other family members live? How often do you talk with these family members? To which members of your family do you feel especially close? Are you comfortable with your membership in this family?

2. *Identity.* How do you define yourself in terms of the groupings and labels commonly used to describe people? (For example: Gender? Sexual orientation? Occupation? Nationality? Ethnicity? Religion? Socioeconomic class? Language? Political orientation?)

3. *Body image.* What do you notice most about your body? What do others see when they look at your body? Are you satisfied with your body? To what extent do you worry about illness and a loss of physical capacity? What specifically do you worry about?

4. *Self-acceptance.* To what degree are you comfortable with your answer to the question: Who am I? Do you enjoy times when you are alone? When by yourself, are you comfortable with your thoughts and feelings? Are you usually at ease or usually tense when you are with people you know? If you could change yourself, what, if anything, would you change?

5. *Self-worth.* What criteria do you use when you judge the worth or value of another person? How do you measure up on those same criteria? Do you like yourself? What are your major strengths, talents, and abilities? In what ways are you a unique person?

6. *Ideal-self.* To what degree are you doing or accomplishing what you expect of yourself? Are your hopes and dreams within reach? How do you define personal success? In what areas are you successful? In what areas are you falling short of your expectations? What do you want to accomplish or achieve in your lifetime? What contributions do you want to make to others, your family, or your community? How do you want to be remembered after you die?

7. *Self-efficacy.* Do you feel that you are in control of your life? Which has more influence in your life: the decisions that you make or the decisions that other people make? Do you usually respond to change with anticipation and enthusiasm or with fear? Are you hopeful about your future? Is what you expect to happen mostly good or mostly bad?

8. *Spirituality.* Do you have spiritual or religious beliefs or particular moral standards that I should know about in order to better understand your concerns and situation? Do you have a set of beliefs that help you find meaning and purpose in your life? How do you explain or make sense out of the pain and suffering that you and others experience in life?

9. *Past self and future self.* Do you see yourself as about the same or somewhat different from who you were one year ago? Five years ago? Ten years ago? Do you have regrets or guilt feelings about the past? Do these feelings have a significant impact on your life? Do you expect that you and your life situation will be different in five years? Will this be a desirable or an undesirable change?

10. *Sense of place.* In what kind of a physical environment are you most comfortable? To what degree are you satisfied with your home? Your neighborhood? Your community? Is there some place you really want to live? Where? Why?

SELECTED BIBLIOGRAPHY

Bracken, Bruce, ed. *Handbook of Self-Concept.* Hoboken, NJ: John Wiley and Sons, 1996.

Nurius, Paula, and Sharon Berlin. "Cognition and Social Cognitive Theory." In *Encyclopedia of Social Work*, 19th ed., vol. 1, edited by Richard Edwards, 513–524. Washington, DC: NASW Press, 1995.

Raskin, Nathaniel, and Carl Rogers. "Person-Centered Therapy." In *Current Psychotherapies*, 7th ed., edited by Raymond Corsini and Danny Wedding, 130–165. Belmont, CA: Brooks / Cole, 2005.

11.9   ASSESSING FAMILY FUNCTIONING

Purpose: To identify the nature and structure of interactions among those who make up a family system.

Discussion: Given the dramatic societal changes of recent decades, it is increasingly difficult to define the term family. The U.S. Census Bureau defines a *family* as "two or more persons related by birth, marriage or adoption who reside in the same household," and it defines a *household* as "all the persons, related or not, occupying a housing unit."

For purposes of planning human services and maintaining a family-centered approach in the delivery of these services, the authors prefer a definition based on family functions. Thus, a ***family*** will be defined as a group of persons related by biological ties, a legal relationship, and/or expectations of long-term loyalty and commitment, often comprising at least two generations and usually inhabiting one household. Moreover, in order to be defined as a family, some of the adults of this group must have the intention and the capacity to carry out all or most of the activities or functions common to a family:

- *Provide for the rearing and socialization of children* (e.g., prepare children for adulthood; teach children what they need to know in order to function within a particular culture and society; teach and model basic values, morals, and social skills such as honesty, responsibility, cooperation, compassion, trust, sharing, communication, and self-acceptance).
- *Provide its members with intimacy and a sense of belonging* (e.g., acceptance and love).

- *Provide an emotionally secure environment for sexual expression among consenting adults.*
- *Provide its members with a place of privacy and respite* (e.g., respite from other and more formal and more public social roles such as those related to community, work, and school responsibilities).
- *Provide its members with a legal and social identity* (e.g., an identity and location for the purposes of legal transactions, especially those related to parental rights and responsibilities).
- *Serve as an economic unit* (e.g., make decisions concerning the purchase of goods and services, budget and plan for future, and manage and care for possessions and property).
- *Protect, assist, and care for those family members who are vulnerable or cannot care for themselves* (e.g., young children, the frail elderly, the sick or disabled).
- *Serve as an advocate for family members in need of community resources* (e.g., parent identifies her child as being ill or disabled and seeks out medical care, parent makes sure his child gets a proper education, etc.).

In addition to nuclear and extended family structures, other variations in family form are increasingly common. These include *single-parent families* (i.e., one biological parent or adoptive parent or foster parent plus children), *blended families* or stepparent families (i.e., two married adults plus each one's children from a prior marriage and possibly children born to them as a couple), and *functional families* (i.e., two or more unmarried and unrelated adults plus their children). We are also seeing a growing number of families headed by what some call *second-time-around parents*, referring to grandparents who have assumed primary responsibility for rearing their grandchildren. In part, this is due to the growing number of biological parents who have been incarcerated or whose functioning is seriously impaired by addiction to drugs and alcohol.

The family is indeed a complex system and it is challenging task to identify and assess its interactional patterns. The social worker should keep in mind these questions as he or she gathers information about a family's functioning:

1. *How is family membership defined?* One can view membership in a number of ways. For example, who are members of the *biological family* (e.g., bio-parents, biological offspring)? Who are members of the *legal family*, as defined by marriage, divorce, and adoption laws and by court orders affecting child custody? What is the composition of the *functional family* (i.e., who is part of household and who assumes responsibility for child care and other tasks of daily living)? Who belongs to the *perceived family* (i.e., those who the members consider as belonging to the family regardless of biological and legal ties)? And finally, who belongs to the *family of long-term commitments*, as defined by an expectation of lifelong loyalty, duty, and "being there for me" regardless of changes in household composition or legal definitions?

2. *What facts and realities describe the family?* What are the names and ages of the members? How is the family's functioning affected by the various developmental stages of its members, such as the presence of young children, teens, and the elderly? How does the family's functioning relate to the family life cycle? Does the family have a particular religious, ethnic, or cultural identity? What is the source of income? Are family members employed? Where? What are their occupations? How do the demands of these jobs affect family roles and functioning? What personal and social circumstances surrounded the marriage or the formation of the family and the birth of the children? Is there a history of divorce, abandonment, or violence? Is the family's functioning affected by a member's physical or mental illness, disability, or addiction?

A social worker's efforts to assist or encourage a client to describe his or her family and relationships to family members will be more productive if the client brings family photographs or albums to the interview. Browsing through snapshots and photos will make it easier for the client to describe family members, explain family interactions, and remember important family events.

3. ***Is family functioning supported by the community?*** In what neighborhood and community does this family live? How is the family affected by living there? Is it a safe place to be? Is decent and affordable housing available? Are jobs available? Are basic public utilities and services available (e.g., police protection, sanitation services, transportation, library)? Do the local schools provide the educational programs needed by the children?

4. ***How well are family functions performed?*** How does the family function as an economic unit (i.e., secure income, pay bills, etc.)? Does it successfully manage tasks of daily living (e.g., cooking, cleaning, laundry, etc.)? Does the home serve as a place of rest, recuperation, and privacy for its members? Does the family provide its members with a sense of identity and belonging? Does it provide nurturing, love, companionship, and intimacy? Do the children receive the encouragement and guidance needed to prepare for success in school and work roles? Does the family provide appropriate socialization experiences for its children so they learn the interpersonal and social skills they will need in adulthood? Is the family able to adhere to customs, traditions, and religious beliefs it considers important?

5. ***What boundaries, subsystems, rules, and roles govern family interaction?*** As suggested above, various societal customs, mores, and laws establish and define a family and the social boundaries that separate one family system from another and the family from other social systems in its wider social environment. (See Chapter 6 for more information on system concepts.)

As the members of a family live together, their interactions become habitual and organized. In short, a social system is created. Once the patterns are well established, there is a tendency for the family members and the family as a whole to preserve the status quo and repeat that which is familiar and habitual, even when a particular pattern is the source of a problem. Moreover, when adults form a new family they tend to repeat the behavioral patterns they learned in their own family of origin. Thus, both family strengths and family problems can be transmitted from one generation to another.

The nature of a family's boundary will determine whether that particular family is open or closed to external influences from the community and society and how that family will interact with, for example, its neighbors and the school system. The family's boundary must be sufficiently open so the family can take in new information and make necessary adaptations to its ever-changing environment. However, if a family lacks boundary and is indiscriminately and completely open to outside influences, the family may destroy its internal organization (i.e., its "systemness") and lose for its members a sense of identity, unity, and belonging. Such a family soon becomes little more than a group of people who happen to live under the same roof. On the other extreme, if a family's boundary is rigidly closed to outside influences, the family may become isolated, estranged from other families, and separated from its community. An example would be parents that prohibit their children from having any exposure to, or contact with, such influences as TV, newspapers, schools, and the people living in the neighborhood. Such a family may preserve a sense of belonging and unity but may be unable to make healthy and needed adaptations to its dynamic social and cultural environment.

Within a family system consisting of both adults and children, there will typically be four subsystems: the *spouse subsystem* (i.e., two adults, usually involved in a sexual relationship); the *parental subsystem* (i.e., those family members—usually adults—responsible for childrearing); one or more *parent-child subsystems* (i.e., a special closeness between a particular parent and child); and the *sibling subsystem*. In a healthy family, the boundaries that define and separate these subsystems are clear and are in keeping with societal norms. By contrast, for example, in an incest family, the child has been drawn into the spouse subsystem. In a similar vein, the child with an alcoholic parent will sometimes enter the parental subsystem, reverse roles, and end up looking after and taking care of the adult parent.

When subsystem boundaries are unclear, members may become intrusive or overly involved in the lives of other family members. Such relationships are termed *enmeshed, fused,* or *merged.* On the opposite extreme is when there is little or no communication or interaction among family members as, for example, when the parents know nothing about their adolescent son's friends or his day-to-day activities. Such families are said to have a *disengaged* pattern of interaction.

The social worker should give special attention to the role structure within a family and the expectations assigned to those roles. Role expectations guide many of the common tasks of living, such as who drives the car, who pays the bills, and who cares for the children. It is important to determine why certain tasks are assigned to certain family members. The role structure may be strongly influenced by the family's culture and religion.

During childhood, individuals often learn certain roles or patterns of interaction within their family of origin that are resistant to change and thus remain with them in later life. Pet expressions for such roles include "black sheep," "mama's boy," "peacemaker," "family worrier," "disciplinarian," "lone wolf," "message carrier," and "family banker." Family therapy literature often makes reference to the family roles of "scapegoat," "identified patient," "infantalized child," "parentified child," "hero," "mascot," "lost child," and "rescuer."

Family rules are the explicit and implicit principles that maintain the family's organization, or "systemness" by governing and guiding member behavior. These rules may be evident in something so simple as the seating arrangement during family meals or in who is responsible for putting gas in the car. An explicit family regulations might be: "You must always clean the bath tub when finished." Although most family rules are practical, innocuous, and sometimes even silly (e.g., "Don't take a trip in the car without first changing your underwear.") others can be destructive and dysfunctional. Rules that suppress emotion, cover up irresponsible behavior, promote dishonesty, or generate feelings of shame are especially harmful. Examples include: "When Dad is drinking, never mention his brother Ed" or "Pretend you don't see Mom and Dad fighting" or "Only an evil person would ever feel anger toward a parent." The children of parents who are alcoholic often grow up with the rules of "don't talk" (about the drinking or other real issues), "don't feel" (suppress all feelings), and "don't trust" (always be on guard and keep people at a distance). The social worker must identify family rules and, more importantly, observe whether they can be openly discussed and what happens when rules are broken.

The boundaries, rules, and roles at work within a family can only be inferred after careful observation. Some family members may be able to articulate family rules, but most of these patterns are so ingrained that they seem natural and normal and are never questioned.

6. ***How well does each member fit within the family system?*** Although there is value in viewing the family from a systems perspective, it is important to remember that this system is made up of separate human beings, each of whom has a unique genetic makeup, biology, personality, and life experience. Thus, the worker needs to be cognizant that each member has his or her own thoughts and feeling; hopes, expectations, and obligations; talents; sense of identity; spirituality; coping strategies and ego defenses; special emotional needs; and physical or mental limitations. It is useful to consider whether there is a good match or a possible mismatch between each family member and the norms and values of his or her family system.

7. ***What are the moral and ethical dimensions of the family's functioning?*** This dimension of family dynamics refers to issues such as obligation, loyalty, fairness, sacrifice, accountability, and entitlement that relate rather directly to a person's moral standards, religious beliefs, notions of good and evil, and spirituality. Many of the conflicts among family members revolve around moral and ethical issues.

8. ***What aspects of life are considered beyond human control?*** In order to understand a client's behavior and decisions, it may be necessary to understand his or her sense of the sacred—that which is in the sphere of the mysterious, the awesome, the uncontrollable, and the supremely important. These views and beliefs are in contrast to views concerning aspects of life that one can control or at least attempt to control. An individual's or family's sense of the sacred is closely related to their religious beliefs, spirituality, concepts of God, and the meanings assigned to life, death, and human suffering.

9. ***How does the family make decisions?*** All families develop patterns or styles of decision making. In some families, all members can express opinions and participate in decision making. On the other extreme are families in which one member makes all major decisions. Some practitioners learn about a family's way of making decisions by meeting with the whole family and asking them to perform a task (e.g., plan a vacation or family outing) and then observing how they reach a decision.

10. *What is the mood of the family?* Much like an individual, a family is often characterized by a prevailing mood. Is the family warm and caring? Optimistic? Pessimistic? Excitable? Outgoing? Depressed? Fun loving? Angry? Controlled? Spontaneous?

11. *How do family members handle differentness?* Everyone is unique and everyone must learn to live with others. A common source of interpersonal difficulty is the inability to accept others as being different from one's self and/or the inability to accept one's self as being different from others. Thus, when assessing a family, consider how each member deals with differentness. There are four basic ways of handling differences:

- *Eliminating others.* Attempting to deal with differentness by beating down or suppressing the individuality of others (e.g., finding fault with others, blaming, attacking, etc.)
- *Eliminating self.* Handling differentness by suppressing one's individuality (e.g., always agreeing, submitting to others, accommodating, hiding one's true feelings, etc.)
- *Avoiding issues.* Attempting to handle differentness by denying or avoiding issues that would reveal differences (e.g., keeping family communication on "safe" topics, etc.)
- *Open and honest communication.* Dealing with differentness by acknowledging the existence of differences, discussing them in a respectful manner, and working to resolve whatever conflicts exist

Like all social systems, families tend to resist change. Family members will engage in various maneuvers to maintain the status quo or hold onto their usual and habitual ways of interacting and functioning. In some extreme cases and when other adaptations have not worked, a family may attempt to preserve itself from a threat—whether real or perceived—by scapegoating or sacrificing a family member for the good of the whole family. A request by parents to have their disruptive teenager placed in foster care could be viewed as such a maneuver. A related adaptive phenomena, often termed *re-peopling*, refers to the family system's efforts to enhance its functioning or regain stability by either adding or excluding a member. The decision by a couple having marriage problems to have a child could be viewed as a re-peopling maneuver.

12. *How clearly do family members communicate their own expectations and needs?* In order for family members to respond appropriately to each other's needs, there must be communication concerning those needs. Sometimes we are unwilling or unable to communicate our wants and needs but still feel angry and disappointed when others do not respond in the desired way. Problems arise when family members expect others to be skilled at mind reading.

13. *What communication patterns exist within the family?* A pattern of verbal and nonverbal communication develops whenever two or more people interact on a regular basis; certain unwritten rules begin to guide interaction. The pattern reveals how each member regards himself or herself in relation to the others. There are many forms of workable communication patterns. What is functional for one family may not work for another. As with so many aspects of family functioning, culture and ethnicity have a strong impact on family communication and on what works for the family. To decipher this pattern, the worker needs to observe the following: Who speaks to whom? Who speaks first? Who responds? Who listens to whom? Who speaks most? Who speaks least? Who speaks last? Who sits next to whom? Are messages directed to one person but meant for someone else? Are the messages clear? Do the words say one thing but mean another? Are the family's communications character-ized by respect, openness, and honesty or by evasiveness, denial, double messages, blaming, threats, hurtful jokes, interruptions, or defiance?

14. *Do family members allow other members to get close emotionally?* Everyone has a need for intimacy, but at the same time most of us have some fear of closeness. Sometimes people avoid getting close to others because they fear that if they reveal their vulnerabilities, others will take advantage of their weakness. Some people hide behind a facade because they fear others will not care for the real them. Even within a family, members may keep others at a distance. Within a well-functioning family, members are able to reveal many of their inner thoughts and feelings but also maintain a comfortable level of privacy.

15. *To what tasks and activities do the adults and older children devote their time?* For example, how many hours each week are devoted to paid employment? Travel to and from work? Child care? House cleaning and laundry? Cooking? Shopping? Medical and health care? Education and training? Study and homework? Clubs and organizations? Religious activities? Recreation and leisure? Reading? TV? What portion of each day and week is spent at home and with other family members?

16. *What are the interpersonal payoffs of troublesome behavior?* To understand a troubled family, the social worker must see beyond the problem behavior and develop working hypotheses about why members repeatedly engage in interactions that create so much distress and misery. Two interrelated themes of family interac-tion explain many problem and nonproblem behaviors: the desire by a member for closeness versus his or her desire for distance and the member's desire for belonging versus his or her desire for independence. People want intimacy but not to be oppressed by the closeness. Also, people want to be part of a family but not to be consumed or controlled by family loyalty. When observing the family's struggle with a problem, the worker should constantly ask: How does this behavior bring the family members closer emotionally or create a feeling of belonging? How does this behavior promote a sense of separateness and independence?

17. *Who supports and who opposes change?* Whenever a change is being consid-ered, some degree of resistance can be expected. However, family members will differ in the degree to which they will oppose change. In order to assess support and opposition, the social worker might ask the family members to speculate on the effects of a hypo-thetical change. For example, the worker might ask: "How would a move to another city affect your family? How would each family member try to adjust to this change?"

SELECTED BIBLIOGRAPHY

Collins, Donald, Cathleen Jordan, and Heather Coleman. *An Introduction to Family Social Work,* 2nd ed. Belmont, CA: Brooks/Cole, 2007.

Manuchin, Salvador, Michael Nichols, and Wai Yung Lee. *Assessing Families and Couples.* Boston: Allyn & Bacon, 2007.

Thomlison, Barbara. *Family Assessment Handbook,* 2nd ed. Belmont, CA: Brooks/Cole, 2007.

Walsh, Froma, ed. *Normal Family Processes,* 3rd ed. New York: Guilford, 2003.

11.10   ASSESSING SMALL-GROUP FUNCTIONING

Purpose: To observe the functioning of a small group and assess its effectiveness.

Discussion: A social worker will typically work with and within many different types of groups, including, for example, committees, interagency planning groups, educational and training groups, therapeutic groups, and self-help groups. In general, a *well-functioning group* is one in which the members are clear about the group's purpose and are all working together to achieve that purpose. A well-functioning group energizes its members, brings out their creativity, and, of course, achieves its purpose. A *dysfunctional group,* on the other hand, seldom achieves its purpose, and participating in such a group is frustrating to its members and viewed as a waste of their time.

When working with or within a group, the social worker should constantly observe and assess the group's functioning in order to decide what he or she can do to increase its effectiveness and efficiency. To do this, the worker should be attentive to both content and process. Basically, *content* refers to the group's observable decisions and activities (i.e., what the group talks about and does), whereas *process* describes the how and why behind what the group says and does or perhaps avoids.

It is group content, for example, that is described by the formal minutes of a committee meeting. Content is, of course, shaped by the group's stated purpose, formal structure, and official agenda. By contrast, group process is a less visible dimension of a group's functioning. Process is characterized by such matters as how members interact, who influences whom, how decisions are made, the degree to which members feel allegiance to the group, and how members are affected by their participation in the group. Group process is shaped by such matters as the motivations and values of each member, the existence of hidden agendas, the formation of subgroups and cliques, the occurrence of power struggles, the level of morale, the use of communication patterns and leadership styles, and the degree of cooperation and competition among members.

When a social worker participates in a group, he or she must keep three questions in mind:

1. Why are we here? What is the *purpose* of this group?
2. What are we to do? Given the group's purpose, what *activities* must it perform?
3. Given the group's purpose and activities, how must it be *organized* or *structured*?

The following sections identify several aspects of group functioning and questions to consider when assessing a group's functioning and deciding what actions might improve its functioning.

Purpose

Agreement and clarity on the group's purpose is fundamental to effective group functioning. Unless all members are working toward the same general outcome or goal, the group is likely to drift off in many directions or get bogged down in conflict. However, it not uncommon for different people, both inside and outside the group, to hold differing ideas about what the group is to accomplish. There is, for example the group's purpose as defined by the sponsoring or host agency, the purpose as defined by the group's designated leader, the purpose as generally agreed to by all who participate in the group, and the purpose that is personally perceived or experienced by each of the group's members. To assess a group's clarity of purpose, the answers to the following questions should be informative: What is the group's stated or official purpose? Who decided or selected the group's purpose? Are all group members in agreement on the purpose? If the members disagree over what the group is to achieve, what is the source of their disagreement?

If a group lacks clarity and agreement on its purpose, the social worker should try, in a nonthreatening way, to bring this to the group's attention and encourage members to discuss this matter. Conflict among members may, however, begin to surface as they voice their differing expectations of the group.

Organizational and Community Contexts

Each group exists and functions within a context of organizational and/or community forces that push and pull it in various directions. These external forces are often the source of hidden agendas and conflict within a group, especially disagreements over the group's purpose and composition. For example, individuals outside the group may pressure the group's leader or members to move the group in a certain direction or to make a particular decision.

Answers to the following questions will reveal how a group is being influenced by external forces: What organization sponsors, hosts, or funds the group or wanted to see it formed? What does this organization expect of or require of the group? In what ways is the group's functioning impacted by external events and contexts (e.g., political pressures, agency policy and program requirements, funding concerns, community controversy, etc.)?

In situations where external forces are having an adverse effect on the performance of individual members and on the ability of the group as a whole to achieve its purpose, it is usually best to openly acknowledge and discuss these concerns and outside influences.

Membership and Participation

In order for the group to achieve its purpose, it must be made up of persons who have the motivation, skills, and power to achieve that purpose. In other words, there must be a logical and workable match between the group's purpose and membership. Moreover, a group will be effective only when its members are active participants in the work that it does.

To assess these aspects of group functioning, seek answers to the following questions: Given its purpose, is the group about the right size? Does the group consist of individuals who are necessary to achieving its purpose? Is the group membership either too homogenous or too diverse to carry out its activities and achieve its purpose? Has the membership or level of participation changed significantly since the group was first formed? What factors draw the members to this group, and what factors keep members from participating? What members are most active? Least active? Do some members dominate the group? Are some members ignored or isolated? Are quiet or hesitant members encouraged by others to participate? Do members feel free to express disagreement, address conflicts, and take risks? Do members listen to each other, respect each other, and support each other? Is open and honest communication expected or perhaps discouraged and punished? Do members ignore real conflict, suppress disagreement, and punish those who express strong feelings or divergent opinions?

In situations where a group's effectiveness is hampered by a mismatch between its purpose and the ability or the authority of its members to make the decisions and perform the activities necessary to achieve that purpose, the social worker should look for ways of modifying the group's size and composition. If level of attendance or participation is a problem, this should be brought to the group's attention and discussed in an attempt to find a workable solution. A social worker in such a group should strive to model those behaviors and ways of communicating that are important to effective group functioning.

Individuals within the Group

The functioning of a group ultimately depends on the behaviors, attitudes, and skills of the individuals who comprise it. Having a few highly motivated and skilled individuals can be pivotal to a group's effectiveness. On the other hand, having a few negative, unmotivated, or disruptive members can severely limit the group's capacity for achieving its purpose.

Answers to the following questions can reveal how well each member is contributing to group effort or perhaps distracting the group from its goals: What values, attitudes, and belief systems (e.g., cultural, ethnic, religious, political) does each member bring to the group? What specific strengths, motivations, expectations, needs, and problems does each member bring to the group? Does each member attend the group's meetings because he or she wants to or because attendance is required?

If the group's members do not have the skills or abilities needed to achieve its purpose, then membership may need to be expanded. If an individual within the group is clearly a disruptive force that keeps the group from performing essential activities, the group as a whole needs to address this concern. If the disruptive member cannot modify his or her behavior, he or she may need to be excluded from the group.

Structure, Norms, and Rules

Over time, a group develops both formal and informal structures, as well as a set of norms or rules that shape how it functions and how its members behave. Different structures may be considered and will be more or less effective, depending on the group's size, purpose, and history. The norms and rules that develop are typically a mix of stated or *explicit* guidelines and unstated or *implicit* guidelines.

Seeking answers to several questions can help to assess the appropriateness of the group's structure, norms, and rules: Do the group's structure, norms, and rules encourage all members to participate and keep them focused on the group's purpose and essential tasks and activities? Are members expected to behave in certain ways when attending the meeting (e.g., dress code, seating arrangement, etc.)? Are the frequency and length of meetings appropriate to the group's purpose and methods? Is the discussion of certain topics or the expression of certain viewpoints either encouraged or prohibited? Does a formal or informal structure or hierarchy of authority determine who speaks most, who listens to or sides with whom, and who makes decisions?

If a group is not achieving its goals because it lacks a workable structure and/or effective procedures, the social worker may want to encourage group members to develop a set of agreed upon rules, procedures, and expectations. Or if a group has a structure that no longer works because it is either too rigid or too informal, the social worker should encourage its members to reexamine the existing structure in light of the group's purpose and perhaps adopt a more workable structure and approach to performing its essential tasks and activities.

Leadership

Having effective leaders is essential to the process of moving and guiding a group toward its goals. If the designated group leader lacks the skills of leadership, the group will flounder and the conflicts that are inevitable in any group will likely smolder and eventually undermine its functioning. The answers to several questions can help assess the leadership dimension within the group: How and by whom was the leader selected? Does the designated or official leader of the group have credibility among group members and command their respect? Does the leader provide the vision and direction needed to help the group achieve its goals? Does the leader display or model the behavior and level of commitment that he or she expects from the group's members? Does the leader take actions to clarify and test out ideas, build consensus, promote needed compromises, and resolve conflicts between factions within the group? Is there someone within the group who is a natural leader or an unofficial leader to whom other members look for leadership? Do some members undercut, undermine, or sabotage the group's leader?

When the work of a group is being impeded by the lack of effective leadership, a change of leaders is usually necessary. In some cases, this may occur as the result of an open and critical evaluation of the group's functioning. Problems related to inadequate leadership sometimes can be prevented or at least minimized by holding regularly scheduled elections of a leader. In groups that have a more informal structure, an agreed-upon rotation of the leadership role may help prevent the ongoing negative impact that can be caused by poor leadership.

Decision Making

A truly effective group can make good and timely decisions after considering the perspectives and preferences of all its members. Decision making can be examined by seeking answers to the following questions: Do all members contribute their ideas to the decision-making process? Does the leader encourage everyone to participate in making decisions? Does a subgroup or clique within the membership push its own agenda in the decision-making process? Does the group use a formal procedure to arrive at its decisions (e.g., *Robert's Rules of Order*)? If so, do all members understand this procedure (see item 13.30)? Do members rush into making decisions, or are they deliberate and thoughtful?

Power and Influence

Leadership and decision making are interrelated in terms of the use of power and influence within the group. The misuse or abuse of power is a problem in many groups. In order to assess the place of power and influence in the functioning of a group, the following questions should be explored: Does the leader have the authority to insist that the group take certain actions or make certain decisions? Do other group members have that authority? Which members exert the greatest influence on the group? If some members are especially influential, what is the source of that influence? Which members have little or no influence?

Physical Environment and Resources

Levels of attendance and meaningful participation, and thus the ability of the group to achieve its goals, are related in part to whether members remain focused and comfortable during their meetings. In addition, the group's overall effectiveness often depends on having access to the resources it needs to perform essential group tasks. Examples of such resources might include a written agenda, minutes of previous meetings, fact sheets, copies of reports under discussion, training materials, and money for supplies, photocopying, administrative assistance, and refreshments. This dimension of a group's functioning can be assessed by considering several questions: Is the meeting space physically comfortable for everyone and arranged in a way that will facilitate participation and maintain a focus on the work of the group? Do all members have access to supplies and other resources needed for an efficient and focused meeting?

SELECTED BIBLIOGRAPHY

Corey, Marianne, and Gerald Corey. *Group Process and Practice,* 7th ed. Belmont, CA: Brooks/Cole, 2006.

Northhouse, Peter. *Leadership: Theory and Practice,* 4th ed. Thousand Oaks, CA: Sage, 2006.

Toseland, Ronald, and Robert Rivas. *An Introduction to Group Work Practice,* 5th ed. Boston: Allyn & Bacon, 2005.

| **11.11** | **THE ABC MODEL AND THE BEHAVIOR MATRIX** |

Purpose: To achieve greater precision in the observation and analysis of client behavior.

Discussion: Social workers often look to behavioral analysis and behavior modification for techniques of helping clients learn new behaviors or eliminate problem behaviors. The influence of behavior-oriented approaches has done much to help practitioners be more precise in data gathering and assessment. Two tools commonly used in behavioral analysis, the ABC model and the behavior matrix, are particularly useful.

The ABCs of Behavior

In the ***ABC model,*** the letter *A* stands for *antecedent*, *B* for *behavior*, and *C* for *consequences*. For example, when assessing a problem behavior, such as a child's temper tantrum, the worker first clearly identifies and operationally defines the behavior under study. In this example, the tantrum is the *B* (i.e., target behavior).

Next, the worker looks for the *A*, or the antecedent, which comprises the various situational factors or cues that set up the behavior. In the tantrum example, it might be a particular action by the parent that sets the stage for the child's tantrum; perhaps the parent begins to work in the kitchen or turns on the TV news.

Finally, the worker looks for the immediate consequences of the behavior, which is the *C* in the model. This may identify factors that reinforce or reward the behavior. For example, once the tantrum starts, the parent may try to comfort the child and, in the process, reinforce the tantrum behavior. By using the ABC model, the worker may be able to identify those factors that can be changed in order to reduce or eliminate a problem behavior.

Behavior Matrix

A second tool, actually an observational aid, is a three-cell matrix known as the ***Behavior Matrix*** (see Figure 11.5). After observing the interactions of an individual client, family, or small group, the worker records his or her observations in the appropriate cell. What emerges will be a picture of what positive behaviors should be

| **FIGURE 11.5** | Behavior Matrix |

	Behavior Exists	**Behavior Does Not Exist**
Positive or Appropriate	1	2
Negative or Inappropriate Behavior	3	

TABLE 11.1 **Behavioral Observations and Intervention Techniques**

Observation	Possible Behavioral Interventions
Desired behaviors do not occur at all	Instruction, modeling, prompting, shaping
Desired behaviors occur but infrequently	Additional reinforcement, shaping, behavioral rehearsal
Behaviors occur but not at appropriate times	Behavioral contracting, prompting, and other reminders
Desired behavior occurs so frequently as to be inappropriate	Reduce frequency of reinforcement, differential reinforcement, remove from reinforcing environment
Behaviors that occur are dangerous to self or to others	Remove from reinforcing environment, reinforce incompatible behavior

reinforced, what negative behaviors should be extinguished, and what new behaviors will need to be learned by the client.

As an example, assume that the worker is attempting to help a man who is developmentally disabled learn to interact more appropriately when greeting other adults. While observing and using the matrix, the worker sees that when introduced to another person, the client giggles, reaches for a handshake, and fails to look directly at the person he is greeting. The worker would record his or her observations as follows:

1. The giggle is an existing inappropriate behavior—enter comment in cell 3.
2. The handshake is an existing appropriate behavior—enter comment in cell 1.
3. Eye contact when shaking hands is a nonexisting appropriate behavior—enter comment in cell 2.

Having made such observations, the next step is to develop an appropriate intervention strategy. Table 11.1 matches recommended behavioral techniques to findings derived from the matrix. (See Items 13.4, 13.5, and 13.6 for information on behavior techniques.)

SELECTED BIBLIOGRAPHY

Miller, L. Keith. *Principles of Everyday Behavior Analysis,* 3rd ed. Pacific Grove, CA: Brooks / Cole, 1997.

Sundel, Sandra, and Martin Sundel. *Behavior Change in the Human Services,* 5th ed. Thousand Oaks, CA: Sage, 2005.

Thyer, Bruce, and John Wodarski. *Handbook of Empirical Social Work Practice.* New York: Wiley, 1998.

11.12   USING QUESTIONNAIRES, CHECKLISTS, AND VIGNETTES

Purpose: To create data-gathering tools for use with clients in a particular practice setting.

Discussion: Various types of data gathering tools (e.g., questionnaires, checklists), when specifically designed for certain types of clients and client situations, are useful when these clients have difficulty verbalizing their concerns, either because they feel confused or embarrassed or because they do not have the words to express their thoughts. Such tools are also useful when a practitioner needs to collect the same basic information from all of his or her clients and do so in a more efficient manner.

A *problem checklist* is a data-collection tool designed to help the client identify and state his or her concerns. It is basically a list of problems and concerns commonly reported by a particular group of clients served by a particular agency. It is compiled by a worker familiar with how people with these concerns think and feel. If a client is having difficulty articulating concerns, he or she is presented with the list and asked to identify those statements that come close to describing his or her concerns.

Consider the case of a 15-year-old who has just given birth to a baby in a hospital and will be dismissed in one day. In such a case, the hospital social worker would like to meet with the young mother, do a quick assessment, and perhaps refer the mother to relevant community resources. Many such clients may be reluctant to verbalize their worries, and the worker's task is further complicated because there is so little time to build a relationship. Figure 11.6 is a checklist that could be used with this client. In addition to helping the youth identify and express her concerns, it focuses the communication so that she and the worker can make the best possible use of very limited time together.

Frequently, clients are unaware of the services that can be offered by the social worker. If a worker and a client examine a problem checklist together, the client begins to understand how the worker or agency might be of assistance. In this sense, the checklist serves as an educational tool. A checklist can also help to structure interviews with clients who are easily distracted. In addition, the completion of the checklist might be assigned as "homework" between the first and second meeting (see Item 13.14).

Figure 11.7 is a *questionnaire* developed by a social worker who provides counseling to married couples in conflict. Its purpose is to help the clients quickly identify those aspects of the relationship that are troublesome. Because the questionnaire is simple and brief, clients can complete it in only a few minutes and they do not find it burdensome. By substituting another set of questions, the basic format illustrated in this example can be adapted for use with other groups of clients in other practice settings.

In some practice situations, the worker needs a type of information that cannot be elicited by specific questions such as those written into questionnaires. For example, social workers often need to gather information about a client's values and attitudes but recognize that direct questioning is not likely to yield complete or accurate information. Consider a child welfare worker faced with the task of deciding whether an individual should be licensed as a foster parent. Among other things, the worker needs to gather information about the person's beliefs and attitudes related to child care. The

FIGURE 11.6   **Sample Problem Checklist**

Concerns of Young Mothers: A Checklist

The birth of a baby is a time of happiness and joy. But along with the good feelings are concerns about the changes in lifestyle and responsibility that lie ahead. A new mother often feels uncertain and a bit scared about the responsibility of caring for a baby. If we know about your concerns, we may be able to help you find ways to address them.

Directions: Below is a list of worries and concerns that have been expressed by other new mothers who have had babies in this hospital. Please read through this list and place a check (✓) by all statements that are similar to the concerns you now have. Your responses will be held in strict confidence.

1. _____ Have worries about paying hospital and doctor bills.
2. _____ Have worries about my baby's health and physical condition.
3. _____ Have worries about my own health and physical condition.
4. _____ Uncertain about how to feed and care for an infant.
5. _____ Uncertain where to turn when I have questions about child care.
6. _____ Afraid I may become pregnant before I am ready to have another child.
7. _____ Worried about not having enough money to care for my baby.
8. _____ Concerned about whether I can finish school.
9. _____ Worried about getting or keeping a job when I have a baby to care for.
10. _____ Concerned when I feel resentment or anger toward my baby.
11. _____ Worried about the effects of drugs or alcohol on me and my baby.
12. _____ Worried that my friends will not accept me and my baby.
13. _____ Worried about my relationship with my baby's father.
14. _____ Concerned that I do not feel love toward my baby.
15. _____ Feeling sad and depressed about my situation.
16. _____ Worried that I will be a burden to my own parents.
17. _____ Worried about living alone with my baby.
18. _____ Concerned that my own parents and family will not accept me and my baby.
19. _____ Afraid I am going to lose my independence and freedom.
20. _____ Please describe or list any other concerns not covered by the checklist:

_____

Now, look over all of those items you have checked and draw a circle around the one or two that seem most important. Please feel free to discuss these concerns with a hospital social worker.

FIGURE 11.7 | Sample Questionnaire

Questionnaire on the Husband-Wife Relationship

Explanation: Below are questions about how satisfied you are with what goes on between you and your spouse. Your answers will help us understand and clarify your concerns. To the right of each statement, place a check (✓) to indicate if you are mostly satisfied, or mostly dissatisfied, or perhaps unsure and confused about this aspect of your marriage relationship. If a statement does not apply to your situation, write NA next to the statement.

	Mostly Satisfied	Mostly Dissatisfied	Unsure or Confused
The way we make decisions	_____	_____	_____
The way we divide up responsibility for child care	_____	_____	_____
The way we handle and budget money	_____	_____	_____
The way we divide up housework	_____	_____	_____
The way we talk to the children	_____	_____	_____
The amount of money we earn	_____	_____	_____
The way we resolve conflict	_____	_____	_____
The way we discipline our children	_____	_____	_____
The way we get along with in-laws	_____	_____	_____
The way we use our free time	_____	_____	_____
The way we talk to each other	_____	_____	_____
The way we care for our home	_____	_____	_____
The amount of time we have together	_____	_____	_____
The way we help and encourage each other	_____	_____	_____
The amount of privacy we have	_____	_____	_____
The way alcohol or drugs affect our relationship	_____	_____	_____
The way we handle birth control	_____	_____	_____
The sexual part of our relationship	_____	_____	_____
The way we plan for our future	_____	_____	_____
The way we get along with the neighbors	_____	_____	_____
The way we deal with moral or religious concerns	_____	_____	_____
The way we handle anger and frustration	_____	_____	_____

Please list here any other concerns you may have about your relationship:

_____

_____

What do you consider to be the major strengths in your marriage?

_____

_____

What do you consider to be the one or two major problems in your marriage?

_____

_____

worker could ask direct questions such as: Do you believe in spanking a child who misbehaves? and How would you respond if a 10-year-old frequently wets the bed? Such direct questions are likely to elicit answers that the individual thinks the worker wants to hear and may not reveal much about the person's underlying attitudes that are so central to parenting.

An alternative approach is for the worker to write a set of vignettes and use them as springboards for discussion and exploration. Basically, a *vignette* is a brief story to which the client is asked to respond. Thus, this techniques is an indirect or a projective method of gathering information that draws feelings and beliefs from the client. Figure 11.8 presents two examples that were written for use in the foster home-study process. Needless to say, the worker using this tool must create vignettes that will elicit the type of information needed to better understand the client.

In general, social workers underutilize data-gathering tools such as those described above. However, these tools are useful in many situations and not difficult to devise and develop. Here are some guidelines that will help:

1. As you reflect on the possible design of a paper-and-pencil, data-gathering tool, be clear about its intended purpose, the reasons for using written questions rather than verbal questioning, the type of information sought, and the type of client and client situation for whom it is being prepared. Rather than attempting to develop one all-purpose data-gathering tool, it is better to design several, each with a specific purpose in mind.

FIGURE 11.8   **Sample Vignettes**

The Peterson Family: A Situation to Discuss

The Petersons have been foster parents to 15-year-old Sharon for about six years. Religion is very important to Mr. and Mrs. Peterson. They attend church services and participate in several church-related activities on a regular basis. Until about two months ago, Sharon also attended the Petersons' church even though she had been raised in another religious denomination. Sharon now refuses to attend church and tells her foster parents that religion is a bunch of superstition and foolishness. The Petersons are worried and upset by Sharon's attitude because religion is so central to their life and family.

1. What could have caused this situation?
2. How should the Petersons respond to Sharon?

The Allen Family: A Situation to Discuss

Mr. and Mrs. Allen have three children. In order to celebrate Mrs. Allen's birthday, the whole family goes to a restaurant. During the meal, 6-year-old Jimmy throws a tantrum—he cries and throws food at his parents. Others in the restaurant stare at the Allens and obviously disapprove of what they are seeing.

1. What is your evaluation of Jimmy's behavior?
2. How should the parents respond to Jimmy?

2. Paper-and-pencil tools (e.g., questionnaires, checklists) should focus on issues that the client will recognize as being similar to or relevant to his or her own concerns. They should be relatively short so they are easy to understand and so they do not tax the client's capacity. A short and focused questionnaire is more likely to be accurately completed than a long one. In general, the higher the client's level of education and motivation, the more likely he or she is to deal successfully with a paper-and-pencil, data-gathering tool. Remember, many people lack the basic skills of reading and writing.

3. The writing of questions or items to be included in a data-gathering tool requires knowledge of possible and probable responses by clients. For example, if a written question asks the client to select his or her answer from a provided list of possible answers, the questionnaire designer must know beforehand the answers most likely to be given by clients. When it is difficult to anticipate the range of probable client answers, it will be necessary to use an open-ended question to which the client writes out his or her answer in a space provided on the paper. However, a client's written answer is often difficult to read and understand. Consequently, a data-gathering tool that contains many open-ended questions will have few advantages over verbal questioning during a face-to-face interview.

4. Each question or item should focus on a single idea and should in no way lead or point the client toward a particular answer. The wording of the question should be clear, concise, and free of jargon, bias, and offensive language. When possible, the wording of each question in a series of questions should follow a similar format and structure because this helps the client move more easily from question to question and minimizes the chances that he or she will misinterpret a question.

5. A sequence of questions should follow a logical and unfolding order and should usually begin with the general questions and end with the more specific ones. The questions that will be easiest for the client to answer should appear at the beginning of a series, whereas the most personal or probing questions should usually appear toward the end. To the extent possible, a question should flow from the previous one and lead to the ones that follow.

6. A pretest should be used to determine if clients understand all the items and questions that appear in the data-collection tool, whether clients can complete the questionnaire in a reasonable amount of time, and whether the data obtained are indeed useful to practitioners.

SELECTED BIBLIOGRAPHY

Corcoran, Jacqueline. *Evidence-Based Social Work Practice with Families.* New York: Springer, 2000.

Horejsi, Charles. *Assessment and Case Planning in Child Protection and Foster Care Services.* Englewood, CO: American Humane Association, 1996.

Jordan, Cathleen, and Cynthia Franklin. *Clinical Assessment for Social Workers,* 2nd ed. Chicago: Lyceum Books, 2003.

| 11.13 | ASSESSING A CLIENT'S SOCIAL FUNCTIONING |

Purpose: To examine and assess the various dimensions of a person's social functioning.

Discussion: As explained in Chapter 1, the social work profession seeks to enhance social functioning and to prevent and correct problems of social functioning. The concept of *social functioning*, when applied to an individual, can be thought of as the person's motivation, capacity, and opportunity to meet his or her basic needs and perform his or her major social roles such as those of parent, spouse, partner, family member, employee, citizen, and so on.

At a fundamental level, assessing a client's social functioning involves the client and social worker examining various facets of the client's need-meeting activity and role performance and then drawing conclusions about his or her current level of functioning. Depending on the client's presenting concerns or problem, some areas are examined in more depth than others.

The statements in the following sections should serve to remind the social worker of the various dimensions of an individual's social functioning. Each statement describes a prosocial behavior or situation. If a client's current behavior or situation departs significantly from the description given, he or she is likely facing some special challenges or experiencing problems in social functioning. Because all of the statements are written in positive language, they can be viewed collectively as a list of possible client strengths. This list can also provide a starting point for the social worker who is writing goals and objectives to be included in a service agreement or treatment plan (see Items 12.5 and 12.6).

Adults

Fundamentals of Independent Living

- The client manages basic self-care tasks such as bathing, toileting, eating, and food preparation.
- The client is sufficiently mobile, has the range of body movement, and possesses the energy necessary to safely care for self.
- The client recognizes and responds to dangerous situations (e.g., criminal activity, gas leak, malfunctioning electric circuit, etc.) and knows how to call police and fire department, request emergency medical assistance, and alert neighbors of danger.
- The client can grasp and mentally process new information, make decisions, and take action needed to complete the ordinary tasks and activities of day-to-day living.
- The client speaks, reads, and writes the language(s) needed in his or her community for such activities as shopping, work, school, obtaining medical care, and calling for help.
- The client has the time and energy needed to perform his or her key social roles and fulfill his or her responsibilities.
- The client takes personal responsibility for his or her own behaviors, decisions, and choices.

- The client initiates interactions with others and influences them to cooperate or assist in meeting his or her own legitimate needs.
- The client has positive self-image and self-confidence and expresses feelings of self-worth. He or she does not overlook or underestimate abilities and strengths and does not deny or ignore real limitations.

Citizenship and Legal Concerns

- The client has a basic understanding of right and wrong, as well as legal and illegal activity, and strives to live in accord with existing laws and basic moral principles that recognize the rights and needs of others and the common good.
- The client understands his or her basic rights and responsibilities as a citizen and the functions of police, lawyers, and the court system.
- The client has a basic knowledge of laws related to ordinary concerns such as marriage, parent-child relationships, contracts, insurance, leases, loans, taxes, driving an automobile, use of alcohol and drugs, firearms, and so on.
- The client expresses his or her views on public policy and legislation through such activities as voting and participation in political and advocacy organizations.
- The client avoids situations, associations, and activities that could draw him or her into dangerous or illegal conduct.

Use of Community Resources

- The client is aware of and knows how to access common resources such as those providing medical care, mental health services, legal counsel, consumer counseling, recreation, employment services, library services, and so on.
- The client knows of some agencies and organizations that provide services pertinent to his or her special concerns and life circumstances and knows how to access those resources, if needed.
- The client knows how to use Yellow Pages, directories of community services, and information and referral agencies in order to identify and contact needed resources.
- The client knows how to use telephone, letters, and other means of communication necessary to obtain needed services and resources.
- The client has access to transportation, child care, and other types of support or assistance that are prerequisites to the use of most community resources.

Family Life

- The client has a relationship with a spouse or partner that is mutually satisfying and meets his or her need for intimacy and companionship.
- The client experiences mutual and nonexploitative sexual activity that is satisfying to self and partner.
- The client behaves toward his or her children in a manner that is accepting, supportive, and encouraging. He or she recognizes and is able to meet a child's need for nurturing, guidance, protection, and limits.
- The client has an income sufficient to meet the needs of his or her family.

- The client has family members who care for each other, help each other, and are a source of support and encouragement for each other.
- The client is willing to make sacrifices for his or her family and put the needs of the children before his or her own needs and wants.
- The client has children who consider the provided guidance, limits, and discipline to be fair and reasonable.
- The client experiences adults in his or her family who encourage each other and their children to participate in community, school, job, recreation, religious, civic, or other activities and to build healthy relationships with people outside the family.

Friendships and Social Supports

- The client maintains satisfying and lasting relationships with family, friends, neighbors, and co-workers.
- The client has access to and is willing to utilize a social support network that can provide encouragement, information, and some forms of tangible assistance.
- The client selects companions who provide acceptance and encouragement and who have qualities of warmth and genuineness. He or she avoids those individuals who are discouraging, manipulative, or exploiting.
- The client can build and maintain new friendships that are age appropriate, positive, and satisfying.

Spirituality and Religious Activity

- The client possesses values, beliefs, and perspectives that provide meaning, purpose, and direction in life.
- The client possesses and uses a framework of moral principles for making responsible and ethical decisions.
- The client is part of a group or faith community that provides a sense of hope, encouragement, and guidance, especially in times of difficulty.
- The client is able to attend religious services of his or her choice.

Interaction with Community

- The client lives in a community and neighborhood that meets basic standards of public health and safety.
- The client is not limited by forces of discrimination or oppression within community or society in his or her efforts to work and care for self and family.
- The client participates in social, recreational, and political activities of the neighborhood and community.
- The client participates in activities intended to benefit and improve his or her community and the lives of its people.
- The client feels accepted in and has a sense of belonging to a positive and prosocial neighborhood and community.
- The client takes initiative to help neighbors and is willing to be helped by others in the neighborhood.

Personal Appearance and Hygiene

- The client maintains the level of personal hygiene needed to prevent illness and infections.
- The client is able to obtain those items and services needed to maintain appropriate appearance (e.g., hair care, deodorant, shampoo, washing machine, dry cleaning, etc.).
- The client selects clothing, accessories, and body decorations that are appropriate to the occasion or situation and that enhance personal appearance and social acceptance.

Education and Training

- The client is free of any cognitive or sensory difficulties that impede or seriously limit learning or is able to effectively compensate for these limitations.
- The client explores new areas of knowledge that stretch and challenge self in order to discover new interests and abilities.
- The client is aware of and has access to types of education and training needed to maintain and develop needed job skills.
- The client is interested in and stimulated by the education and training needed to prepare for and maintain a job.
- The client assesses his or her own learning needs, seeks out instruction, and then learns what is needed in order to perform social roles and fulfill responsibilities at work, home, and school.
- The client has realistic understanding of his or her capacity to learn and to complete programs of education and training.

Employment and Job Performance

- The client knows about various types of jobs, how to apply, and how to act during job interviews and can determine if a particular job matches his or her skills and financial needs.
- The client has a satisfying job that provides an adequate level of income and is appropriate to his or her level of skill and experience. Working conditions and environment are safe. If the client is a parent, he or she has access to suitable and affordable day care.
- The client is a responsible employee, is able to perform assigned work, is on time for work, dresses appropriately, gets along with most others at work, and understands employment-related policies and procedures.
- The client prepares for and works toward those job changes and promotions that expand opportunity, increase job satisfaction, and provide needed income and benefits.

Money Management and Consumer Awareness

- The client monitors spending and financial transactions by using some type of budgeting and bookkeeping effort.

- The client plans and budgets for unanticipated emergencies, for seasonal expenses, and so on.
- The client understands the difference between necessities and wants and has sufficient self-discipline to avoid unwise expenditures and debt.
- The client understands basic money concepts such as interest, debt, charge accounts, loans, and late payment penalties, and understands that the purpose of commercial advertising is to encourage spending.
- The client understands payroll deductions such as taxes, FICA, and insurance.
- The client understands basic eligibility requirements for assistance (e.g., unemployment insurance, SSI), reporting rules, and time limitations.

Recreational and Leisure Activity

- The client participates in enjoyable recreation or leisure activities that provide a respite from the demands of other responsibilities.
- The client is aware of various forms of recreation and leisure and is willing to explore some of them in order to expand opportunity for physical exercise, new learning, and new friendships.
- The client selects recreation and leisure activities that are safe and wholesome and does not expose self to social influences that could prove harmful (e.g., excessive drinking).

Housing and Housekeeping

- The client has housing that provides adequate space and privacy and offers basic protection from fire, cold weather, excessive heat, break-in, and so forth.
- The client has safe drinking water and a safe method of food storage.
- The client keeps the living area and food preparation area clean and sanitary.
- The client has access to and knows how to safely use the various tools, soaps, and household chemicals needed to keep the living area and kitchen area free of disease-causing microbes, roaches, and rodents.

Nutrition and Health Care

- The client plans, shops for, and prepares a variety of nutritious meals within his or her food budget.
- The client engages in health-building behaviors (e.g., adequate sleep, proper diet, exercise) and avoids misuse of medicines, harmful foods, street drugs, and alcohol.
- The client has access to and capacity to pay for appropriate treatment of illness or injury.
- The client avoids high risk or daredevil activities that could result in injury.

Coping with Ordinary Problems of Living

- The client completes assigned tasks and carries out responsibilities in various areas of life (e.g., home, job, school) even when they are a source of frustration. He or she is able to stick with and follow through in order to complete important tasks.

- The client recovers at a reasonable rate from anxiety or depression brought on by an upsetting event or life disruption such as a death in the family, loss of job, and so on. He or she resumes responsibilities without serious or unusual interruption.
- The client carefully and purposely rebuilds alternate intimate relationships following a loss such as a divorce, separation, or death of significant other. Over-all feelings of self-worth and self-confidence are not permanently damaged by loss and disruption.
- The client is comfortable with his or her own identity, self-concept, ethnicity, gender, sexual orientation, economic situation, and life circumstances.
- The client is able to set priorities and reasonable limits on demands by others for his or her time and energy.
- The client uses knowledge of past experiences to decide how best to cope with current difficulties and to anticipate challenges.

Coping with Mental Health Problems or Addiction

- The client recognizes the nature of his or her problems and their present and future consequences. He or she does not deny the existence of significant problems.
- The client makes full and appropriate use of effective therapies, medications, and support groups.
- The client who has prior problems with addiction has the addiction controlled and monitored in order to prevent relapse.
- The client interacts with a wide variety of people. (Current relationships and activities are not limited to ones with people having similar problems.)

Adjustments to Physical Disability

- The client makes full and appropriate use of rehabilitation programs, medications, and assistive technology (e.g., communication devices, artificial limbs, wheelchair, etc.) to minimize the impact of the disability.
- The client's expressions of frustration and concerns over his or her disability are reasonable and do not offend or drive away family members, friends, relatives, and other helpers.
- The client is able to discuss the disability and the need for assistance without embarrassment or apology. The client lets others know what he or she can and cannot do.
- The client recognizes disability-related risks and vulnerabilities and plans how to reduce risks and handle possible emergencies or accidents.

Children and Adolescents

School Performance

- The youth performs in school at a level consistent with his or her ability, as indicated by reasoning abilities evident during discussion and problem-solving activities, and by standardized achievement and intelligence tests.

- The youth effectively communicates with teachers and other school personnel and desires and enjoys these exchanges.
- The youth participates in both planned school-related social activities (e.g., sports, dances, and clubs) and in spontaneous activities involving other students and peer group.
- The youth (in keeping with age level) is interested in learning about job possibilities and educational requirements and opportunities related to various career choices.
- The youth is able to attend school without concern for personal safety.

Relationship to Parents, Siblings, and Family

- The youth usually does what is expected by the parent. He or she performs household chores and other assigned duties that are appropriate to age and ability (e.g., taking care of clothing, cleaning room, supervision of younger siblings, etc.).
- The youth frequently joins in the family's recreational, social, or spiritual activities, such as family gatherings, going to church, shopping, and so on.
- The youth regularly interacts with extended family members such as grandparents, aunts, uncles, and cousins.
- The youth joins with friends and peers in activities intended to improve the neighborhood or community.

Child or Adolescent Sexuality

- The youth is comfortable with the biological, social, and psychological aspects of his or her own sexuality.
- The youth (consistent with age level) has basic knowledge of sex. He or she seeks out accurate information about sexual matters and expresses comfort with this information.
- The youth often talks with parents about feelings, thoughts, and questions related to sexual matters.
- The youth is respectful of his or her dating partner and makes decisions concerning sexual activity accordingly. Sexual activity is kept within the limits of the partner's and own sense of morality. Participation in sexual activity is not compulsive nor forced; he or she does not coerce or force others to participate.

Ordinary Problems of Childhood and Adolescence

- The youth is able to cope with feelings and emotions without letting them interfere with the activities of everyday living or seriously disrupt relationships at home and in school.
- The youth (if necessary to adjust to new parent figures) accepts the emotional support and guidance offered by the new parent figures such as stepparents, guardians, or foster parents.
- The youth acknowledges and faces up to his or her problems. He or she can recognize a problem that is blocking positive interactions and neither underestimates nor exaggerates its effect.

■ The youth plans clear and specific actions intended to avoid a recurrence of prior problem behavior.

SELECTED BIBLIOGRAPHY

Daniel Memorial Institute. *Independent Living Skills Assessment.* Jacksonville, FL: Daniel Memorial Institute, 1995.

MacNair, Ray. *Assessment of Social Functioning: A Client Instrument for Practitioners. Vol. 6, Human Service Series.* Athens: Institute of Community and Area Development, University of Georgia, 1981.

MacNair, Ray, and Elizabeth McKinney. *Assessment of Child and Adolescent Functioning: A Practitioner's Instrument for Assessing Clients.* Athens: Institute of Community and Area Development, University of Georgia, 1983.

11.14   ASSESSING A CLIENT'S MENTAL STATUS

Purpose: To determine if the client's thoughts and behaviors indicate serious mental illness and the need for a psychiatric referral.

Discussion: Not infrequently, the social worker will encounter a client who has an undiagnosed mental illness, neurological disorder, or dementia. It is important for the worker to know the fundamentals of a mental status exam so he or she will be able to recognize symptoms and refer the client for a psychiatric or neurological examination. Because some symptoms may be caused by physiological changes in the brain (e.g., tumors, neurological disease, etc.), proper referral can mean the difference between life and death (see Items 15.10 and 15.13).

A *mental status exam* consists of conducting a careful observation and asking a set of simple questions that attempt to gauge the client's orientation to time and place, short- and long-term memory, accuracy of perceptions, judgment, and appropriateness of affect. For example, these are the typical questions asked to assess memory: How old are you? In what year were you born? What did you have to eat at your last meal? Can you count backward from ten? What is the name of the building we are in?

To the extent possible, these questions should be worked into the ordinary flow of conversation. If asked one question after another, the client may be offended, and if the client cannot answer the questions, he or she will feel embarrassed. Engaging the client in a description of his or her typical day—from awakening to bedtime—provides a context for asking specific questions. Following are 11 categories of information that should be considered in assessing mental status:

1. *General appearance and attitude* considers whether the client's appearance is appropriate and consistent with his or her age, social, and economic status. The client's dress, hygiene, speech, facial expressions, and motor activity provide information about his or her self-perception and awareness of others. Marked inappropriateness in appearance may be associated with psychological disturbance, particularly if these characteristics have changed over a short period of time.

2. *Behavior* is concerned with the appropriateness of the client's conduct during the interview and with any reports of bizarre behavior by others or the client. Irrational behaviors, such as compulsions (repeated acts that the client feels compelled to do) and phobias (avoidance of places, persons, or objects because of unfounded fears), are characteristics of many disorders.

3. *Orientation to time and place* refers to whether the client is aware of who he or she is, where he or she is, and what time it is (year, month, date, and day). Disorientation is a symptom of brain dysfunction.

4. *Memory* deficits may be associated with psychiatric as well as physical disorders. Four types of memory may be assessed:

- *Immediate recall* refers to the ability to recall things within seconds of their presentation.
- *Short-term memory* is generally defined as covering events transpiring within the last 25 minutes.
- *Recent memory* refers to the client's recollection of current events and situations occurring within the few weeks preceding the interview.
- *Remote memory* refers to the recollection of events occurring months or years ago and of a significant life happening, such as marriage, first job, high school graduation, and so on.

Immediate and short-term recall are generally assessed by instructing the client to remember something (a word, number, or object) and then asking him or her to recall that item after the lapse of a few minutes. Recent memory can be tested by asking questions such as these: Where do you live? and How long have you lived there? Remote memory can be tested by asking: Where were you born? Where did you go to school? and Who was president of the United States when you got married?

5. *Sensorium* refers to an individual's ability to utilize data from his or her sense organs (hearing, vision, touch, smelling, and taste) and more generally to his or her overall attentiveness and alertness to the surroundings. If a client cannot comprehend visual symbols (and has no visual impairment), touch, or ordinary conversation (and has no hearing impairment and can be presumed to understand the language) or otherwise demonstrates an inability to respond to sensory stimuli, he or she may have an organic brain disorder.

6. *Intellectual functioning* is screened by evaluating the client's abilities to read, write, and follow simple instructions, to do simple arithmetic, to think abstractly (e.g., How are an apple and orange alike?), and the client's awareness of common knowledge consistent with his or her level of education. Poor comprehension as well as deficits in abstract thinking and intellectual performance are commonly noted as symptoms of various psychological disorders. Gauging educational attainment is important because low levels of intellectual functioning may be attributable to a lack of education. Poor intellectual functioning among educated persons, however, may be indicative of organic disorders. Intellectual deterioration is most apparent among individuals with central nervous system disorders but may also be evident in other disturbed individuals.

7. ***Mood and affect*** refer to the client's prevailing emotional state and the range of emotions displayed during the interview. Moods include such emotions as anger, irritability, elation, exhilaration, anxiety, fear, depression, sadness, apathy, and indifference. In assessing mood and affect, two questions are important:

- Is the client's emotional state a reasonable response to his or her situation? For example, it is important to determine whether a client's depression is the result of recent events (e.g., the death of a spouse).
- Does the client show emotions that correspond to the topic being discussed? Inappropriate smiling or laughter when talking about sad events or rapid changes in emotional expression, such as laughing or crying without relevance to the conversation or circumstances, may be indicative of a psychiatric disorder. Emotional lability can also have an organic origin (e.g., after a stroke).

8. ***Perceptual distortions*** may be exhibited by some psychologically impaired individuals. Two of the most significant perceptual problems are illusions and hallucinations. Illusions are misinterpretations of actual stimuli. Hallucinations are perceptual experiences in the absence of external stimuli (e.g., hearing voices).

9. ***Thought content*** refers to the logic and consistency of an individual's attitudes, ideas, and beliefs. Examples of thought content problems include delusional thinking (false beliefs that cannot be altered by logical arguments) and obsessions (fixed or repetitive ideas that the client cannot get out of his or her mind).

10. ***Insight*** can be evaluated by asking questions that determine whether the client understands and is aware that he or she has a problem or is exhibiting behavior that is of concern to family members, the social worker, or a physician, and whether the client can describe reasons why he or she might be having this problem. Ironically, the more severe the disorder, the more likely it is that the client will be unaware of that his or her behavior is unusual or symptomatic of a mental disorder.

11. ***Judgment*** refers to the individual's ability to make responsible and rational decisions in relation to obvious problems. It also refers to a client's mental capability to make decisions related to daily living and particularly his or her physical well-being and survival.

SELECTED BIBLIOGRAPHY

Kaplan, Harold, and Virginia Sadock. *Synopsis of Psychiatry,* 9th ed. Baltimore: Williams and Wilkins, 2004.

Sands, Roberta. *Clinical Social Work Practice in Behavioral Mental Health,* 2nd ed. Boston: Allyn & Bacon, 2001.

Sommers-Flannigan, John, and Rita Sommers-Flannigan. *Clinical Interviewing,* 3rd ed. New York: John Wiley and Sons, 2003.

11.15 IDENTIFYING DEVELOPMENTAL DELAYS IN YOUNG CHILDREN

Purpose: To identify possible developmental delays in a young child.

Disucssion: A social worker in contact with families is often in a strategic position to observe preschool-age children and to conduct a cursory assessment of a child's physical and mental development. The early identification of possible developmental delays and proper referrals for further evaluation and intervention are of critical importance. Once children enter school, teachers will usually identify developmental delays.

Children who are malnourished or chronically ill, many who are abused and neglected, and, of course, those who have mental retardation or sensory or neurological problems will fall behind developmental norms. However, there can be considerable variation in the development of normal children at a particular age. Moreover, for a given age, it is not unusual to find some unevenness across the various domains of development. For example, a child who is quick to walk but slow to talk can most likely be considered normal in terms of development.

Figure 11.9 lists a number of easily observed developmental markers that can be used to judge a child's developmental progress. If it appears that a child cannot perform the motor, mental, language, and social skills and tasks expected of a given age, he or she should be referred to a specialist for further screening or an in-depth evaluation. A governmental website designed especially for parents concerned about possible problems in their child's development is http://www.cdc.gov/ncbddd/autism/actearly/interactive/milestones/index.html.

Here are some early warning signs of sensory problems and developmental delays:

Indicators of Vision Problems
- Holds head in strained or awkward position when trying to look at a person or object
- Is often unable to locate and pick up small objects within reach
- Has one or both eyes crossed

Indicators of Hearing Problems
- Exhibits delays in speech and language development
- Does not turn toward source of strange sounds or voices by six months of age
- Has frequent earaches or runny ears
- Talks in a very loud or very soft voice
- Does not respond when you call from another room
- Turns the same ear toward a sound he or she wishes to hear

Indicators of Delays in Speech Development
- Does not say "Mama" and "Dada" by age 1
- Does not say the names of a few toys and people by age 2

FIGURE 11.9   Developmental Markers

At about 1 month, child will:
- Turn eyes and head toward sound
- Cease crying if picked up and talked to
- Lift head when lying on stomach
- Follow a moving light with eyes
- Stretch limbs and fan out toes and fingers
- Display pupil response when a flashlight is moved in front of eyes

At about 3 months, child will:
- Make cooing sounds
- Respond to loud sounds
- Turn head toward bright colors and lights
- Move eyes and head in same direction together
- Recognize bottle or breast
- Make fists with both hands
- Grasp rattles or hair
- Wiggle and kick with legs and arms
- Lift head and chest while on stomach
- Smile in response to others

At about 6 months, child will:
- Babble
- Recognize familiar faces
- Turn toward source of normal sound
- Follow moving object with eyes when head is held stationary
- Play with toes
- Roll from stomach to back
- Reach for objects and pick them up
- Transfer objects from one hand to other
- Help hold bottle during feeding
- Bang spoon on table repeatedly
- Look for fallen object

At about 12 months, child will:
- Have a 5- to 6-word vocabulary
- Sit without support
- Pull self to standing position
- Crawl on hands and knees
- Drink from cup
- Wave bye-bye
- Enjoy peek-a-boo and patty cake
- Hold out arms and legs while being dressed
- Put objects into container
- Stack two blocks

At about 18 months, child will:
- Use 8 to 10 words that are understood
- Feed self with fingers
- Walk without help
- Pull, push, and dump things
- Pull off shoes, socks, and mittens

- Step off low object and keep balance
- Follow simple directions ("Bring the ball")
- Like to look at pictures
- Make marks on paper with crayons

By age 2 years, child can:
- Use 2- to 3-word sentences
- Say names of favorite toys
- Recognize familiar pictures
- Carry an object while walking
- Feed self with spoon
- Play alone and independently
- Turn 2 or 3 pages at a time
- Imitate parents
- Point to own hair, eyes, ears, and nose upon request
- Build a tower of four blocks
- Show affection toward others

By age 3 years, child can:
- Use 3- to 5-word sentences and repeat common rhymes
- Walk up stairs or steps alternating feet
- Jump, run, climb
- Ride a tricycle
- Put on shoes
- Open door
- Turn one page at a time
- Play with other children for a few minutes
- Name at least one color correctly
- Use toilet with occasional accidents

By age 4 years, child can:
- Ask "what," "where," "who" questions
- Give reasonable answers to simple questions
- Give first and last names
- Show many different emotions
- Say "no" or "I won't" with intensity
- Balance on one foot for 4 to 8 seconds
- Jump from a step and maintain balance
- Dress and undress with little help
- Cut straight with scissors
- Wash hands alone
- Play simple group games

By age 5 years, child can:
- Speak clearly,
- Print a few letters
- Count 5 to 10 objects
- Skip, using feet alternately
- Catch a large ball
- Bathe and dress self
- Draw a body with at least five parts
- Copy familiar shapes (e.g., square, circle, triangle)

- Cannot repeat common rhymes or TV jingles by age 3
- Does not talk in sentences by age 4
- Cannot be understood by people outside the family by age 5

Indicators of Delays in Motor Development

- Unable to sit up without support by age 1
- Cannot walk without help by age 2
- Does not walk up and down steps by age 3
- Unable to balance on one foot for a short time by age 4
- Cannot throw a ball overhand and catch a large ball bounced to him or her by age 5

Indicators of Delays in Social and Mental Development

- Does not react to his or her own name when called by age 1
- Does not play games such as peek-a-boo, patty cake, and waving bye-bye by age 1
- Unable to identify hair, eyes, ears, nose, and mouth by pointing to them by age 2
- Does not imitate parents doing routine household chores by age 2 to 3
- Does not understand simple stories told or read by age 3
- Does not enjoy playing alone with toys, pots and pans, sand, and so on by age 3
- Does not play group games such as hide-and-seek, tag-ball, and so on with other children by age 4
- Does not give reasonable answers to such questions as "What do you do when you are sleepy?" or "What do you do when you are hungry?" by age 4
- Does not seem to understand the meanings of the words *today, tomorrow,* and *yesterday* by age 5
- Does not share and take turns by age 5

SELECTED BIBLIOGRAPHY

Berk, Laura. *Child Development*, 7th ed. Boston: Allyn & Bacon, 2006.
Chess, Stella, and Alexander Thomas. *Know Your Child*. Northvale, NJ: Jason Aronson, 1996.
Leach, Penelope. *Your Baby and Child: Birth to Age Five*, 3rd ed. New York: Alfred A. Knopf, 1997.

11.16   THE PERSON-IN-ENVIRONMENT (PIE) SYSTEM

Purpose: To describe, classify, and code problems in adult social functioning.

Discussion: The PIE system is designed for use by social workers and is built around two key social work concepts: social functioning and the Person-In-Environment construct. According to Karls and Wandrei (1994a), the PIE provides social workers with the following:

- common language . . . to describe their clients' problems in social functioning.
- a common capsulated description of social phenomena that could facilitate treatment or amelioration of the problems presented by clients.

- a basis for gathering data required to measure the need for services and to design human services programs and evaluate effectiveness.
- a mechanism for clearer communication among social work practitioners and between practitioners and administrators and researchers.
- a basis for clarifying the domain of social work in the human services field. (p. 7)

The PIE system groups client problems into four classes or *factors*. Basically, a factor is a category or a general type of problem. The terminology used for Factor I (*social functioning problems*) and Factor II (*environmental problems*) is unique to social work practice. Factor III (*mental health problems*) utilizes the clinical syndrome and personality and developmental disorders terminology found in the *DSM*. Factor IV (*physical health problems*) records diseases and health problems that have been diagnosed by a physician or reported by the client or others. It should be noted that the PIE is not intended as a substitute for the *DSM* but rather is a complementary system. (See Item 11.18 for information about the *DSM*.)

An abbreviated outline of Factor I and Factor II categories and subcategories is presented here.

PIE Factor I: Social Functioning Problems

1. Social role (see Item 11.7) in which each problem is defined (four categories and numerous subcategories):
   - Familial roles (parent, spouse, child, sibling, other family member, and significant other)
   - Other interpersonal roles (lover, friend, neighbor, member, and other)
   - Occupational roles (worker-paid, worker-home, worker-volunteer, student, and other)
   - Special life situation roles (consumer, inpatient/client, outpatient/client, probationer/parolee, prisoner, immigrant-legal, immigrant-undocumented, immigrant-refugee, and other)
2. Type of problem in social role (nine types: power, ambivalence, responsibility, dependency, loss, isolation, victimization, mixed, and other)
3. Severity of problem (rated on a 6-point scale)
4. Duration of problem (six categories)
5. Ability of client to cope with problem (six levels)

PIE Factor II: Environmental Problems

1. Social system where each problem is identified (six major systems and numerous subcategories):
   - Economic/basic needs system problems
   - Education and training system problems
   - Judicial and legal system problems
   - Health, safety, and social services problems
   - Voluntary association system problems
   - Affectional support system problems
2. Specific type of problem within each social system (71 subcategories; number varies for each of six social systems. Examples of social system problem subcategories: lack of regular food supply, absence of shelter, lack of culturally relevant education,

discrimination, lack of police services, unsafe conditions in home, regulatory barriers to social services, absence of affectional support system, lack of community acceptance of religious values, etc.)

3. Severity of problem (rated on a 6-point scale)
4. Duration of problem (six categories)

SELECTED BIBLIOGRAPHY

Karls, James. "Person-in-Environment System: Its Essence and Applications." In *Social Workers' Desk Reference,* edited by Albert Roberts and Gilbert Greene, 194–198. New York: Oxford University Press, 2002.

Karls, James, and Karin Wandrei, eds. *Person-in-Environment System.* Washington, DC: NASW Press, 1994a.

———. *PIE Manual.* Washington, DC: NASW Press, 1994b.

———. Compu PIE [computer software]. Washington, DC: NASW Press, 2000.

11.17   REFERRAL FOR PSYCHOLOGICAL TESTING

Purpose: To make appropriate use of psychological testing in the assessment of client functioning.

Discussion: Not infrequently, the social worker will refer a client to a psychologist for testing. Such testing can provide information on the client's intellectual capacity, patterns of motivation and coping behavior, self-concept, level of anxiety or depression, and general personality integration. Even so, it is important to remember that psychological tests focus on certain variables while neglecting others that may be important. In sum, a psychological test can provide valuable information on which to base a decision, but one should not rely exclusively on test results, especially if based on a single test instrument. Presented here are brief descriptions of some of the tests administered by psychologists:

Infant Development Scales

■ *The Brazelton Neonatal Behavioral Assessment Scale* tests an infant's (1) neurological intactness, (2) interactive behavior (including motoric control such as putting the thumb in the mouth and remaining calm and alert in response to stimuli such as a bell, a light, and pinprick), and (3) responsiveness to the examiner and need for stimulation.

■ *The Bayley Scales of Infant Development* test mental abilities, including memory, learning, and problem-solving behavior; motor skills; and social behaviors, such as social orientation, fearfulness, and cooperation.

■ *The Gesell Developmental Schedules* test for fine and gross motor behavior; language behavior; adaptive behavior, including eye-hand coordination, imitation, and object recovery; and personal/social behavior, including reaction to persons, initiative, independence, and play response.

■ *The Denver Developmental Screening Test* is widely used and can be administered by a person with only limited training. It is a screening tool, not a diagnostic test.

It is used to discover possible developmental delays in the four areas of personal/social, fine motor/adaptive, language, and gross motor skills that should be more carefully evaluated with other tests.

Intelligence Tests for Preschool- and School-Age Children

- *The Wechsler Scales* include separate forms for preschool- and school-age children. The preschool form is called the *Wechsler Preschool and Primary Scale of Intelligence (WPPSI-R)*, and the school-aged form is called the *Wechsler Intelligence Scale for Children (WISC-III)*. The WISC-III is the test most likely to be used to assess the cognitive functioning of school-age children. It has six verbal and six performance subtests.
- The *Stanford-Binet IV* can be used with both preschool- and school-age children. Examples of tasks include remembering where an object was hidden, building a block tower to match an existing tower, explaining the use of common objects, and identifying pictured objects by name. The Stanford-Binet may not provide an accurate assessment of bilingual or bicultural children.

Intelligence Tests for Adults

- *The Wechsler Adult Intelligence Scale (WAIS-III)* is usually considered to be the best general intelligence test for persons age 16 and older. Six subtests (information, digit span, vocabulary, arithmetic, comprehension, and similarities) make up its verbal scale, and five subtests (picture completion, picture arrangement, block design, object assemble, and digit symbol) make up the performance scale.

Special Abilities Tests

- *The Bender Visual Motor Gestalt Test* is used to assess visual perceptual skills and eye-hand coordination. The client is given nine geometric figures, one at a time, and asked to copy each.
- *The Peabody Picture Vocabulary Test* assesses familiarity with vocabulary words without requiring the child to speak. The client is shown four pictures at a time and must point to the one that corresponds to the word the examiner says. The test was originally designed to be used with persons who are nonverbal, mentally retarded, and/or have cerebral palsy.
- *The Detroit Test of Learning Aptitude* measures auditory and visual memory and concentration.

Testing for Cognitive Delay

An IQ score below 70 indicates that a client may have cognitive delay or mental retardation. However, a low IQ score by itself is not sufficient for diagnosis; the client's adaptive behavior must also be measured. *Adaptive behavior* refers to the person's ability to carry out everyday living skills, such as dressing, eating, washing, playing, functioning independently, and cooperating with others. Several instruments measure age-appropriate adaptive behavior: *The Vineland Adaptive Behavior Scale* (*VABS*), *The American Association on Mental Retardation's* (*AAMR*) *Adaptive Behavior Scales,* and *Scales of Independent Behavior.*

Personality Tests

Objective-type personality tests such as the following are pencil-and-paper tests designed to determine predominant personality traits or behaviors:

- *The Minnesota Multiphasic Personality Inventory* (*MMPI-2*) is probably the most often used objective personality test. It consists of 567 self-descriptive statements to which the client answers either true, false, or cannot say. It is used with persons 16 years of age or older.
- *The Personality Inventory for Children* (*PIC*) is one of the few objective tests for children. It has forms for both the parent and the youth.

Projective tests provide a stimulus (e.g., inkblots, a set of pictures, or incomplete sentences) and ask the client to respond to it. These tests rest on the assumption that the client's responses will reveal his or her unique view of the world, troublesome thoughts, and inner conflicts. Another type of projective test provides instructions for the client to draw a picture, again with the idea that the drawing will reveal information about the inner self. The *Rorschach Test,* the first inkblot test, is the most commonly used projective test for adults. The *Holtzman Inkblot Technique* may substitute for the Rorschach. The most common picture-story type tests are the *Thematic Apperception Test* (*TAT*), the *Michigan Picture Test,* the *Tasks of Emotional Development Test,* and the *Make-a-Picture-Story Test.*

Referring a Client for Psychological Testing

1. Before deciding on a referral, be very clear about why you are seeking a psychological evaluation of your client.

2. When making a referral to a psychologist for testing, explain how and why you and your agency are involved in providing service to this client, the case management decisions you face, and the type of information that would be helpful. List the questions you would like the psychologist to answer.

3. Provide the psychologist with information concerning the client's age, sex, education, occupation and employment history, ethnicity, and any special disabilities, such as hearing or visual problems or physical limitations. Also provide the results of any previous testing, including the dates of testing and the names of the tests used.

4. After consulting with the psychologist who will do the testing, prepare the client by giving him or her basic information on what to expect, where the testing will be done, and about how long it will take.

5. Have realistic expectations of psychological testing. In many cases, the results of testing will simply confirm the conclusions already reached by people who have observed the client for a matter of weeks or months.

6. Ask the psychologist to explain the strengths and limitations of the testing procedures used with your client, so you can decide how much faith to place in the results.

SELECTED BIBLIOGRAPHY

Aiken, Lewis, and Gary Groth-Marnat *Psychological Testing* 12th ed. Boston: Allyn & Bacon, 2006.

Neukrug, Edward. *Essentials of Testing and Assessment: A Practical Guide for Counselors, Social Workers, and Psychologists.* Belmont, CA: Brooks/Cole, 2006.

11.18   *THE DIAGNOSTIC AND STATISTICAL MANUAL OF MENTAL DISORDERS (DSM)*

Purpose: To use proper terminology and classifications when exchanging information about a client's mental disorder.

Discussion: In order to communicate accurately with other professionals about a client's mental disorder and to understand reports prepared by psychologists and psychiatrists, the social worker should be familiar with the *Diagnostic and Statistical Manual of Mental Disorders* (*DSM*), published by the American Psychiatric Association. Knowledge of the *DSM* is also important because many social workers and agencies look to third-party payments from Medicaid, Medicare, private insurance companies, and managed care companies as sources of fees for the psychotherapy they provide to clients. Prior to submitting a claim for such a fee, the client must be assigned to a specific diagnostic category from the *DSM*.

In the *DSM,* nearly 300 disorders are classified within 17 broad categories. Each disorder is described in terms of symptoms, diagnostic criteria, usual age of onset, prevalence, level of impairment, and so on. The major categories are as follow:

1. Disorders Usually First Diagnosed in Infancy, Childhood, or Adolescence
2. Delirium, Dementia, and Amnestic and Other Cognitive Disorders
3. Mental Disorders Due to a General Medical Condition
4. Substance-Related Disorders
5. Schizophrenia and Other Psychotic Disorders
6. Mood Disorders
7. Anxiety Disorders
8. Somatoform Disorders
9. Factitious Disorders
10. Dissociative Disorders
11. Sexual and Gender Identity Disorders
12. Eating Disorders
13. Sleep Disorders
14. Impulse-Control Disorders Not Elsewhere Classified
15. Adjustment Disorder
16. Personality Disorders
17. Other Conditions That May Be a Focus of Clinical Attention

A clinician using the *DSM* must evaluate the client within five separate clusters or categories of information, each of which is called an *axis:*

Axis 1: Disorders with usually obvious symptoms and often the primary focus of clinical attention (e.g., anxiety disorders, schizophrenia, substance abuse, eating disorders)

Axis 2: Long-standing problems that might be overlooked when a client has an Axis 1 disorder (e.g., mental retardation, personality disorders)

Axis 3: Medical conditions or diseases that may be relevant to the understanding, treatment, and management of a person's mental disorder (e.g., high blood pressure, pregnancy, brain injury, infection, diabetes)

Axis 4: Psychosocial and environmental problems or situations that may have a bearing on the understanding, treatment, and management of a client's mental disorder (e.g., lack of family support, lack of housing, unemployment, poverty, life cycle transitions)

Axis 5: A rating of the client's overall psychological, social, and occupational functioning using the Global Assessment of Functioning (GAF) Scale

Using these five axes forces the clinician to gather and consider a range of data and observations.

The *DSM* is a classification of mental disorders, not a classification of people. Thus, a term such as *schizophrenic* should be avoided in favor of an expression such as *an individual with schizophrenia.*

The American Psychiatric Association (2000) warns users of the *DSM* about the inherent difficulties of assessing the behavior of a person from an ethnic or cultural group different from that of the clinician: "A clinician who is unfamiliar with the nuances of an individual's cultural frame of reference may incorrectly judge as psychopathology those normal variations in behavior, belief, or experiences that are particular to the individual's culture" (p. xxxiv). Moreover, when using *DSM* nomenclature, it is well to remember these other cautions and warnings issued by the authors of the manual:

> No definition adequately specifies precise boundaries for the concept of "mental disorder." The concept of mental disorder . . . lacks a consistent operational definition that covers all situations. . . .

> In the *DSM-IV,* each of the mental disorders is conceptualized as a clinically significant behavioral or psychological syndrome or pattern that occurs in an individual and that is associated with present distress (e.g., a painful symptom) or disability (i.e., impairment in one or more important areas of functioning), or with a significantly increased risk of suffering death, pain, disability, or an important loss of freedom. . . .

> Neither deviant behavior (e.g., political, religious, or sexual) nor conflicts that are primarily between the individual and society are mental disorders unless the deviance or conflict is a symptom of a dysfunction in the individual. (pp. xxx–xxxi)

While recognizing the necessity of social workers using the *DSM* in a large number of practice settings, many in the profession question the appropriateness of this diagnostic manual for social work practice and are troubled by its impact on the profession. Many are bothered by the labeling inherent in the *DSM* system and by the manual's exclusive focus on pathology. Fortunately, the Person-In-Environment (PIE) is available as a supplement to the *DSM* (see Item 11.16).

SELECTED BIBLIOGRAPHY

American Psychiatric Association. *Diagnostic and Statistical Manual of Mental Disorders,* 4th ed., text rev. Washington, DC: APA, 2000.

Corcoran, Jacqueline, and Joseph Walsh. *Clinical Assessment and Diagnosis in Social Work Practice.* New York: Oxford University Press, 2006.

Fauman, Michael. *Study Guide to DSM-IV-TR.* Washington, DC: American Psychiatric Publishers, 2002.

Turner, Francis, ed. *Social Work Diagnosis in Contemporary Practice.* New York: Oxford, 2005.

11.19   ASSESSING A CHILD'S NEED FOR PROTECTION

Purpose: To identify a child who has been abused or neglected and to determine if the child is at risk of further harm.

Discussion: State laws require social workers to report cases of suspected abuse or neglect. (Many states also mandate the reporting of elder abuse.) The observation of several of the physical and behavioral indicators suggest the possible existence of child abuse or neglect. These indicators are summarized here:

Indicators of Physical Abuse
- Unexplained bruises or welts, especially if on both sides of face or body, or on back, buttocks, or torso
- Bruises in different stages of healing
- Multiple bruises clustered in one area, forming symmetrical patterns or reflecting the shape of an instrument (e.g., loop marks, lineal or parallel marks, punch marks, etc.)
- Bruises regularly appear after a weekend or a visit
- Bruises on shoulders or neck displaying shape of hand and fingers (e.g., grab marks)
- Unexplained burns, such as those caused by cigarettes, and especially if on palms, soles, back, or buttocks
- Hot water immersion or dunking burns (e.g., socklike, glovelike, or doughnut shaped on buttocks or genitalia)
- Burns patterned like electric stove burner, hot plate, curling iron, etc.
- Rope burns on wrists or ankles (i.e., tie marks)
- Unexplained mouth injuries such as frenulum tears or broken teeth (caused by rough feeding)
- Human, adult-size bites to child's body
- Unexplained broken bones or head injuries such as skull fractures or subdural hematoma
- Retina detachment or whiplash injuries to neck caused by violent shaking
- Internal injuries caused by punch

- Poisoning caused by ingestion of street drugs, alcohol, prescription medicines, or household chemicals
- Attempts by child to hide injuries with clothing; embarrassment or shame over injury, reluctance to talk about injury (nonabused children proudly display injuries)
- Hyper-vigilant, fearful, and guarded around adults; avoids physical contact with people including his parents (i.e., fearful of human touch).
- Overly adaptive behavior in an attempt to meet parents' needs (i.e., by taking care of and comforting parent, the child seeks to keep things calm and prevent abusive episodes)
- Becomes uneasy when another child cries or acts up (i.e., has learned to associate crying with pain of abuse)
- Serious behavioral problems at young age (e.g., runs away, self-mutilation, suicide attempts, violent, withdrawn, etc.).

Indicators of Neglect

- Begging, stealing, or hoarding food; underweight; failure to thrive; bald patches on scalp
- Poor school attendance (sometimes the neglectful parent is so lonely he or she keeps the child home for company; sometimes the child remains home to care for younger siblings)
- Untreated medical and dental problems, even though parent has resources to get medical services
- Unsocialized and primitive in eating and toilet behaviors
- Unusual fatigue and listlessness; falling asleep at unusual times
- Stays at school, in public places, or at other homes for extended periods
- Poor hygiene, filthy clothing, clothing inappropriate for weather
- Child not supervised or protected from dangerous activity

Indicators of Sexual Abuse

- Bruises, scaring, or tissue tears around vagina and anus; bruised or swollen penis (caused by rough fondling and masturbation)
- Blood on child's underwear
- Redness or rash in genital area in child not wearing diaper (caused by frequent fondling)
- Redness or abrasions between upper legs (caused by penis placed between child's legs)
- Recurrent bladder infections (i.e., bacteria from rectum introduced into vagina when there is both anal and vaginal intercourse)
- Pregnancy or a sexually transmitted disease in younger child
- Semen in vagina, rectum, or mouth (can be detected by medical exam within three days of intercourse)
- Inappropriate masturbation that has a driven or compulsive quality
- Unusual sexual play and exploration of pets or dolls
- Aggressive and forced sexual activity with other children, usually of a younger age
- Inappropriate sexual behavior toward adults

- Unusual level of knowledge about sexual activity (e.g., can describe sexual movement, smells, taste, feelings, etc.)
- Preoccupation with sexual matters or unusual fear of anything sexual
- Unusual fear of showers, bathrooms, bedrooms
- Unwilling to change clothes for gym or to expose body (caused by extreme shame of body)
- Frequent and patterned absences from school that are justified by one adult, the offender
- Unusual or bizarre sexual themes in artwork
- Wearing many layers of clothing (protection of body)
- Frequent use of dissociation as coping mechanism
- Unusually close relationship with adult that has secretive or sexual overtones
- Extreme protectiveness of child by an adult who keeps child from talking to or getting close to responsible adults

It is important to understand that while the presence of certain signs and symptoms can establish that a child has experienced abuse or neglect, it does not determine with certainty who was responsible for the maltreatment or injury.

In the United States, about 50 percent of all cases of child maltreatment are cases of neglect. Moreover, about one-half of all child maltreatment–related fatalities are caused by neglect. A high percentage of the neglect cases occur in families where the parents are abusing alcohol or addicted to drugs.

Many parents believe in and utilize corporal punishment as discipline. Thus, in assessing a situation, the social worker must be able to differentiate physical abuse from ordinary spanking or corporal punishment. That decision will, of course, be tied to the definition of physical abuse found in a state's legal code. In addition, we offer three criteria for making that distinction:

1. In corporal punishment, the child experiences some pain and discomfort. In abuse, there is injury to body tissue.

2. In using corporal punishment, the parent maintains self-control and is aware of where and how hard the child is being hit. In an abusive situation, the parent loses control over his or her emotions and strikes the child with excessive force or hits the child in places that are easily injured.

3. Nonabusive parents using corporal punishment may occasionally get carried away and hit too hard but they quickly realize what has happened and are able to make changes in how they discipline the child so this does not happen again. In situations of abuse, there are repeated episodes of excessive corporal punishment and injury because the parents are unable to gain control of their anger and make changes in how they respond to the child.

It is tragic but true that child sexual abuse is not an uncommon occurrence in our society. Most children who are sexually abused do not tell anyone because they are either afraid or feel great shame. Most cases of child sexual abuse involve fondling and masturbation but *not* penetration. Penetration might be of the child's mouth, vagina, or rectum. Even if there has been penetration of the vagina or rectum there will be no physical evidence in most cases.

It is also important to understand that the majority of sexually abused children do *not* exhibit unusual sexual behavior. However, sexually abused children are more likely than nonabused children to display adultlike sexual behavior.

The social worker must report suspected cases of child sexual abuse. However, he or she must also be alert to the fact that false or mistaken accusations do occur. Both children and adults are suggestible and may misinterpret facts, and occasionally false accusations are used as a means of hurting someone. False allegations by a child are relatively rare but the rate increases if the child's accusation is being encouraged by a parent and the rate becomes even higher in cases involving child custody fights between parents.

Once a case of abuse or neglect has been identified, the question of risk must be addressed. In other words, is the child at risk of serious harm and in need of immediate protection? Presented here are factors that should be considered in the assessment of risk.

Child-Related Factors

- Child's young age and/or presences of serious illness or physical or mental disability (i.e., vulnerable and unable to protect self, need for medication, etc.)
- Prior history of being target of abuse
- History of severe or frequent abuse or neglect
- Injuries to child at vulnerable body locations (e.g., head, face, genitals, etc.)
- Injuries that require medical attention or hospitalization
- Child's behavior and special needs (e.g., disability or illness) place great and stressful demands on caregiver
- Perpetrator has access to child
- Child's relationships with siblings or others in the household are strained or troubled (i.e., decreasing chances that others will offer protection)

Parent/Caregiver-Related Factors

- Presence of condition that limits ability of caregiver to care for or protect child (e.g., existence of a serious physical or mental illness, mental retardation, extreme immaturity, etc.)
- Presence of serious drug or alcohol dependency
- History of domestic violence (e.g., spouse abuse) or other violent criminal activity
- History of having abused or neglected other children
- Lack of basic parenting skills or knowledge
- High levels of anger, hostility, or rejection toward child
- Existence of other serious family problems that place added stress on family (e.g., marital conflict, financial, health, chaotic life-style, etc.)
- Unrealistic and unreasonable expectations of child
- Denial of problem; evasiveness or refusal to cooperate with agency personnel or other helpers
- Prior efforts to work with family have been rejected or ineffective

Environmental Factors

- Physical conditions of home presents serious danger to child (e.g., exposed electrical wiring, unprotected household chemicals, etc.)
- Family is socially or physically isolated from social supports and other forms of assistance in times of emergency

In some cases, the removal of the child from his or her own home is necessary. However, because the separation of parent and child is so traumatic to the child and so disruptive to the family, an out-of-home placement should be used only in those cases where the child is at high risk of serious harm and there is no less drastic method of protecting the child. The following principles should guide placement decisions:

- If a child must be placed into foster care, it is to be done for one reason only: to protect the child from harm. For example, it would be unethical and unprofessional to place a child in order to coerce the parent into taking some action.
- A child should be placed in the least restrictive alternative; moreover, the parent(s) and child should, to the extent possible and appropriate, participate in the placement decision and the preparation of the child for the placement.
- Efforts to assure protection for child are to be those that are the least intrusive and least disruptive for both the child and family.
- During the placement, respect and maintain the child's cultural heritage and religious beliefs (*Note:* See the special requirements and provisions of the Indian Child Welfare Act, a federal law.)

SELECTED BIBLIOGRAPHY

Brittain, Charmaine, and Deborah Esquibel Hunt. *Helping in Child Protection,* 2nd ed. New York: Oxford University Press, 2005.

Giardino, Angelo, and Eileen Giardino. *Recognition of Child Abuse for the Mandated Reporter,* 3rd ed. Elk Grove Village, IL: American Academy of Pediatrics, 2002.

Myers, John, Lucy Berliner, John Briere, C. Terry Hendrix, Theresa Reid, and Carole Jenny. *The APSAC Handbook on Child Maltreatment,* 2nd ed. Thousand Oaks, CA: Sage, 2002.

SECTION B

TECHNIQUES AND GUIDELINES FOR INDIRECT PRACTICE

Large system change is difficult and time consuming. Rarely can a single person, or even a few people, decide on changes to be made and implement the actions to bring about that change. It takes careful planning, education, negotiation, and patience to achieve meaningful changes, such as in agency policies and programs or the legislative changes that affect the larger community.

Data-Collection Activities. The first step in preparing for agency or community change is to collect sufficient information to be well informed. In an agency, for example, change requires working through, or sometimes around, the agency's or community's decision-making structure. To do this, the worker needs to learn about the feasibility of various options, the costs (in dollars and the expenditure of human resources) of changing the current situation, the positive and/or negative implications for other associated individuals or systems, and the most effective ways to bring about change.

Like direct practice data collection, indirect practice requires that the worker be skilled at interviewing people to obtain information regarding their experiences and attitudes about the situation being considered for change. However, these impressions typically are obtained from a number of people who have knowledge of or may be affected by the situation. The worker must also be able to accumulate data regarding differing perceptions and accurately summarize the information obtained.

Often, this data collection occurs in a staff meeting, in a board meeting, or from members of a committee appointed to consider the situation. On other occasions, focus groups (see Item 11.22) are created where intensive verbal interaction is stimulated in order to air various opinions on a topic. Another format for data collection involves creating a standardized questionnaire that invites written responses to a series of questions that can be tabulated and summarized to yield a description of the thoughts and opinions of the respondents. Finally, data collection may mean securing relevant reports and documents and then writing a report that organizes these data so that they might be readily analyzed.

Assessment Activities.   Once data are collected and summarized, the social worker must have some tools to help interpret the meaning of the data and to arrive at conclusions. When working at the organizational level, a social worker is typically concerned with issues such as understanding alternative ways to structure the work to be done in a human services agency (see Item 11.20) or ways to organize data that leads to an assessment of needs that clients typically experience (see Item 11.21).

At the community level, a social worker needs to be able to assess the factors that impinge on decision makers in that particular community (see Item 11.23). Also, before moving to action, the social worker must accurately assess the social policies that are in place and understand the ramifications of various changes that may be proposed. Having at least a general sense of the elements of a sound policy analysis (see Item 11.24) is important for any social worker.

11.20   ASSESSING AGENCY STRUCTURE

Purpose: To identify alternative ways to structure staff roles and responsibilities in order to achieve efficient and effective agency operation.

Discussion: The organizational structure of an agency has a significant impact on the ability of the social worker to provide effective services. In any type of organization, the structure can be expected to vary according to the complexity of the tasks being performed, the amount of authority reserved for central decision making, and the degree to which policies, rules, and procedures are formalized. For example, many successful industrial organizations are based on the bureaucratic model. That model is most viable when the work requires the performance of relatively simple tasks (e.g., putting together parts on an assembly line) that are coordinated through a carefully structured process and very specific rules of operation. The bureaucratic organizational model, however, is much less viable in human services agencies where the work is complex and must be adapted to the unique needs of clients. This work requires individualized judgments by professionals that cannot be readily subjected to centralized control and formalized rules and procedures.

In human services agencies, a variety of structures exist that range from highly bureaucratized operations to those that permit considerable worker autonomy. For example, public agencies tend to be bureaucratized, allowing the policymakers and program administrators to maintain a high degree of control over agency functioning. Private nonprofit agencies, by contrast, are usually smaller, offer fewer programs, and tend toward decentralized authority and a minimum of rules and regulations, thus allowing staff members more control over their practice activities and substantial flexibility in how they perform their jobs.

For social workers in all types of human services organizations, it is useful to recognize that various degrees of bureaucratization can exist and that adaptations can be made that create a balance between management and worker in order to facilitate the provision of high-quality services. At times, workers must advocate for structural changes when they find that the agency's structure interferes with service to clients. To inform these advocacy efforts, it is useful to examine several examples of structural formats commonly found in human services agencies.

At one end of the continuum of organizational structure is the ***bureaucratic model.*** In its pure form, a bureaucracy has an elaborate *division of labor* in which work activities are clearly defined and assigned to specialized workers; a *hierarchy* of several of layers of managers, supervisors, and front-line workers is developed; a formalized set of very specific *rules and regulations* is rigidly applied; and the work is carried out in a *spirit of impersonality* that is not adjusted to accommodate individual uniqueness. Bureaucracies are characterized by fairness and equal treatment, but they suffer from lack of flexibility and the ability to individualize. They are stable and consistent yet slow to change.

At the other end of the continuum of organizational structure is the ***adhocracy*** (i.e., the organization that forms internal structures on an issue-by-issue basis with various collectives of staff members addressing each issue). Ad hoc groups have considerable authority and operate with few agencywide rules and regulations. These organizations have a "flat" administrative structure, in which all staff positions are somewhat equal. Ad hoc agencies are weak on both structure and stability, but are able to respond to new issues and undergo change rapidly. They are particularly effective when the nature of the work is dynamic or fluid.

In reality, most human services agencies fall somewhere between a fully developed bureaucracy and a completely ad hoc structure. In smaller agencies, it is possible to have a relatively flat structure with an executive director heading the organization (e.g., representing the staff with the board and community) and the other staff member reporting directly to that executive.

As agencies become larger and more complex and when the span of control or number of contacts becomes too great for one person to manage, the work must be divided into segments. In this situation, a functional structure is likely to serve the agency well. In the ***functional model,*** a second-level administrative layer reports to the director and also leads a program unit or supervises a group of workers. A family services agency, for example, might have a counseling unit, a day treatment unit, a social action unit, and an administrative support unit—each with its own unit manager. The executive director would facilitate coordination of these units and oversee the work of the unit managers.

At times, an agency may temporarily supplement one of these structures with a ***project-team approach.*** This model provides for groups of staff to be organized around specific tasks for limited periods of time. In addition to being assigned to a specific unit or supervisor for their primary job, workers may be temporarily assigned on a full- or part-time basis to a team that cuts across units to address a specific problem. For example, staff from a family agency's clinical and day treatment units may temporarily join with a staff member from the social action unit to plan and carry out a strategy of public education and legislative advocacy to reduce the incidence of spouse abuse.

SELECTED BIBLIOGRAPHY

Brueggemann, William G. *The Practice of Macro Social Work,* 3rd ed. Belmont, CA: Brooks/ Cole, 2006.

Schmid, Hillel, ed. *Organizational and Structural Dilemmas in Nonprofit Human Service Organizations.* Binghamton, NY: Haworth, 2004.

11.21 ASSESSING HUMAN SERVICES NEEDS

Purpose: To provide data on the utilization of and/or need for specific human services offered in a community or region or to an identified population group.

Discussion: Although the perspective of the agency board and staff is a valuable source of information for determining agency goals and services, it is also important that decisions be based on a formal evaluation of the need for these services. Agencies should periodically conduct needs assessments.

Needs assessment refers to the process of identifying the incidence, prevalence, and nature of certain conditions within a community or target group. The ultimate purpose is to assess the adequacy of existing services and resources in addressing those conditions. The extent to which those conditions are not adequately addressed denotes a need for different services or resources.

Before conducting a needs assessment, two decisions must be made by those conducting the analysis and those who will use the findings (e.g., agency board, city council, United Way). First, there should be agreement about what constitutes a need.

Second, there must be a willingness to take action if an unmet need is identified. It is not a good use of time or resources to conduct a needs assessment if there is not recognition in advance that if needs are discovered some corrective action is both possible and probable.

Guidelines for Conducting a Needs Assessment

These guidelines should be kept in mind when conducting a needs assessment:

1. It is essential to have a clear understanding of the policy issues and administrative concerns that prompted the decision to conduct a needs assessment. In other words, what problems do the decision makers hope to address through the use of a needs assessment?

2. The goals and objectives of the needs assessment must be clear before it is possible to select appropriate methods of data collection and analysis. All too often, those planning a needs assessment jump ahead to the question of what questions to ask the people being interviewed before they are clear on exactly what kind of data will be useful in the planning of new services or the modification of existing services.

3. It is helpful to know how other communities or agencies have approached the task, but it is usually a mistake to borrow someone else's objectives and methodology. Those who are in a position to use the data should decide what approach would be useful and work best in their community. Such decisions should not be made by outside consultants or by persons or agencies that have a vested interest in seeing the assessment yield certain results.

4. In planning a needs assessment, it is important to anticipate possible reasons why situations of unmet need might exist. For example:
- Insufficient services are available in the community.
- Existing services are not accessible because of transportation problems, eligibility criteria, and the like.
- Persons in need are not aware that services exist.
- Existing services are not integrated to provide a continuity of service to multiproblem individuals and families.
- Existing programs do not have adequate resources to provide quality service.
- Existing services are unacceptable to residents of a particular community. For example, they may be perceived as degrading, threatening, or in conflict with existing ethnic, religious, or cultural norms and values.

5. A needs assessment should not only identify unmet service needs; in addition, it should shed light on the quantity, quality, and direction of existing services. For example:
- *Quantity.* Does the level of service meet the need? This involves some assessment of the number of persons in need of service compared with the capacity of providers to serve those persons.
- *Quality.* Are the services effective? Do they accomplish what they are intended to do? Do they work?

■ *Direction.* Are the approaches used in service delivery appropriate or possibly out of touch with the real needs of clients? Does the philosophy that gave rise to existing programs coincide with the generally accepted philosophy espoused by current experts in the field?

6. Do not attempt a needs assessment until there is evidence that the agency(s) and community possess the administrative and political readiness to use the data once it is gathered. If they are not ready, the report will gather dust on a shelf.

SELECTED BIBLIOGRAPHY

Altschuld, James W., and Belle Ruth Witkin. *From Needs Assessment to Action: Transforming Needs into Solution Strategies.* Thousand Oaks, CA: Sage, 2000.
Brun, Carl F. *A Practical Guide to Social Service Evaluation.* Chicago: Lyceum, 2005.

11.22   FOCUS GROUPS

Purpose: To acquire in-depth responses from a group of human services consumers or research subjects regarding an agency, program, service, or other topic.

Discussion: Human services agencies and qualitative researchers have followed the marketing branch of the business community in the use of focus groups as a technique for collecting valuable information. A *focus group* is a small group of people (usually 8 to 12) who have had a common experience or share common knowledge and are led through a one- to two-hour discussion of a particular topic. The goal is to explore the topic by allowing the ideas of participants to create a synergy that promotes in-depth discussion until the points of agreement or disagreement emerge and become clear. Focus groups are particularly useful in identifying why the participants think or feel as they do about the subject.

When used for administrative purposes, focus groups can supply information that may be helpful in activities such as planning new services, assessing the needs of current consumers of services, developing marketing strategies, or identifying the implications of terminating a particular program. This technique might be used with existing groups such as agency boards, advisory committees, and staff members or with groups of clients or community members. In research, focus groups are used in association with qualitative approaches, in which content analysis of transcriptions of the meetings serve as a data source for the identification of important themes and fleshing out the meaning participants attribute to them. In addition to members extending their thinking from the ideas presented by others, focus groups are a relatively inexpensive and usually a readily available source of data.

There are four essentials of a successful focus group meeting. First, the participants should be selected carefully. They should represent a broad range of the people who are familiar with the topic and should be people willing to speak their minds. The atmosphere of the meeting and the meeting place should be conducive to freewheeling discussion, and the participants should be protected from retribution for any remarks they might make. Thus, the results should be viewed cautiously and considered only one data source for making decisions.

Second, the moderator should be well prepared. It is the leader's responsibility to introduce the topic without suggesting a bias and to facilitate open discussion of the topic. The moderator must listen carefully and explore the meaning behind the participants' statements, constantly probing for greater depth and clarity. He or she must also be flexible in allowing the group to explore the topic as the flow of their discussion leads, but at the same time be able to bring the group back to the topic when tangents are no longer productive. The moderator must assure that no one member dominates the session and that everyone has an opportunity to speak on each dimension of the topic being explored.

Third, there should be a carefully developed plan for the group meeting that includes the preparation of a series of open-ended questions or statements that stimulate discussion of the topic. The persons planning the focus group meeting should develop an outline known as a *moderator guide* that introduces the subject matter in a logical order (i.e., usually from the most general areas to the most specific) and probes for what the participants perceive to be the relevant diminsions of the topic. The moderator guide can be used as a checklist during the meeting to assure that all important aspects of the topic are addressed before the meeting is concluded. Time should be reserved at the end of the meeting for participants to add topics that may have been omitted and for the moderator to summarize what he or she saw as important themes in the discussion, allowing participants to reply to that summary.

Finally, the information provided by the group members must be recorded and accurately interpreted. Often, audiotapes or videotapes of the sessions are used, along with notetaking by observers, to record the information that emerges in the meeting. Again, it is important to minimize any biases or self-interests when interpreting the information.

SELECTED BIBLIOGRAPHY

Greenbaum, Thomas L. *Moderating Focus Groups: A Practical Guide for Group Facilitation.* Thousand Oaks, CA: Sage, 2000.

Rubin, Herbert J., and Irene S. Rubin. *Qualitative Interviewing: The Art of Hearing Data,* 2nd ed. Thousand Oaks, CA: Sage, 2005.

11.23   COMMUNITY DECISION-MAKING ANALYSIS

Purpose: To assess the factors that influence the actions of elected officials and other decision makers.

Discussion: As social workers seek to influence decisions that affect the quality of human services in a community, they must develop a strategy for convincing the person or persons in authority that a particular course of action is the best choice among the possible options. Ideally, decisions should be made on the merit of the proposal; in reality, however, decision makers usually respond to external pressures and various personal considerations. The social worker must be alert to the factors and forces that may sway a decision maker.

Research on community decision making and community power structures does not yield a consistent picture of the forces that lead to these decisions. However, several generalizations can be made regarding variables that at least partially explain why some communities tend to center the decision making in a small, elite group of people while others are more pluralistic and involve a broader spectrum of the community:

1. *Size.* Large cities tend to be pluralistic. They are likely to become more diverse and competitive as they grow, resulting in a greater range of people and interest groups involved in making decisions.

2. *Population diversity.* Communities that have more varied and complex class and ethnic structures develop more special interest groups and more community organizations that compete for power and resources. Consequently, there are more challenges to any dominant elite group and a tendency to increase pluralism in decision making.

3. *Economic diversity.* More diversified communities in terms of varied sources of employment, high levels of industrialization, and the presence of absentee-owned industry (as opposed to local people owning the major industries) all tend to make communities more pluralistic in how decisions are made.

4. *Structure of local government.* Reformed governments (i.e., cities with council-manager format, nonpartisan-at-large elections) tend to be more elitist than those partisan governments with representatives elected by districts. Further, the greater the competition or balance among political groups, the more likely the community will have a pluralistic decision-making structure.

Increasingly, communities in the United States have a pluralistic type of decision-making structure, although some small rural communities maintain elite power structures. The worker in most communities, then, should be aware that the task of influencing decisions requires a careful assessment of the people who are authorized to make the decisions. For example, the critical *decision maker* regarding an issue of interest may be an agency board member, an elected official, or the manager or management team for a social program. In most cases, relatively few people are involved in making a decision, and they will tend to be focused on particular issues where they have a self-interest (e.g., realtors and bankers focused on housing and economic issues, physicians and other health care professionals focused on health care, etc.).

One task for the social worker is to assess the various factors that may affect a decision maker's choice. As identified in Figure 11.10, *personal charactistics* of the person or persons attempting to influence the decision maker, as well as the *institutional power* the influencer represents, will potentially affect the decision. Also, *personal considerations* such as the repercussions of the decision on one's finances, self-esteem, judgment about the merits of the proposed change, and so on, will affect

FIGURE 11.10   Factors Influencing Community Decision Makers

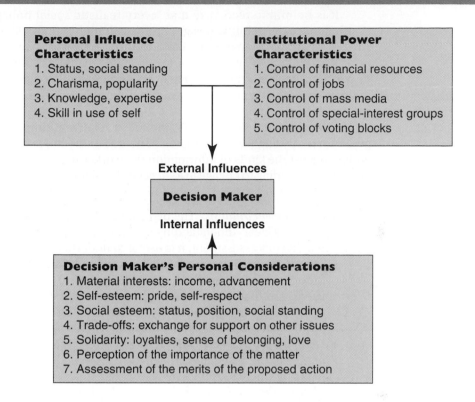

Personal Influence Characteristics
1. Status, social standing
2. Charisma, popularity
3. Knowledge, expertise
4. Skill in use of self

Institutional Power Characteristics
1. Control of financial resources
2. Control of jobs
3. Control of mass media
4. Control of special-interest groups
5. Control of voting blocks

External Influences

Decision Maker

Internal Influences

Decision Maker's Personal Considerations
1. Material interests: income, advancement
2. Self-esteem: pride, self-respect
3. Social esteem: status, position, social standing
4. Trade-offs: exchange for support on other issues
5. Solidarity: loyalties, sense of belonging, love
6. Perception of the importance of the matter
7. Assessment of the merits of the proposed action

the choice. An assessment of the sources for influencing the decision makers for both the proponents and opponents of the change, as well as the personal issues that might affect the decision, should serve as the basis for mapping a strategy for change.

SELECTED BIBLIOGRAPHY

Chaskin, Robert J. *Building Community Capacity.* New York: Aldine de Gruyter, 2001.
Pilotta, Joseph J. *Communication and Social Action Research.* Cresskill, NJ: Hampton Press, 2001.
Scott, John. *Network Analysis: A Handbook,* 2nd ed. Thousand Oaks, CA: Sage, 2000.

11.24   ANALYZING SOCIAL POLICY IMPLICATIONS

Purpose: To assess an existing or proposed social policy in order to guide community change activities.

Discussion: When a social worker engages in activity to change an existing social policy or to introduce a new one, it is important that he or she conduct a careful analysis of that policy. Otherwise, the chance of success will be minimized. The depth of that analysis will depend on the social worker's role in making the analysis and the scope of the change to be accomplished.

It is helpful to recognize that "every realistic social policy is a compromise that balances desirability, design, and feasibility" (Burch 1999, 28). In short, the worker must be prepared to compromise. However, a compromise must be informed by knowledge of the consequences of the various policies that might be adopted. At a minimum, every social worker should be prepared to analyze the major elements of a policy proposal to assure that compromise does not negate the central goal of the change.

Chambers and Wedel (2005) provide a relatively simple and straightforward guide for analyzing policy proposals. The questions in each of the following categories suggest the kinds of information the worker might seek in order to gain sufficient understanding to engage in a successful policy change process:

1. *Social problem analysis.* The first step in the analysis of a social policy or program is to have a clear understanding of what created the situation requiring such a policy. To make this assessment, it is useful to undertake the following activities:

- *Identify how the problem is defined, and establish who and how many people are affected.* For example, what definition of this problem is commonly used? Are there other definitions that might be more appropriate? How many people experience this problem as it is defined? What particular subpopulations are most likely to experience this problem?
- *Determine the causes and consequences of the problem.* What forces or factors have caused the problem? Are there multiple causes? Are there multiple consequences from a single cause?
- *Identify the ideological beliefs embedded in the description of the problem.* The definition of a problem is influenced by beliefs about what "ought to be," or the values one holds. Is there a difference of opinion about the seriousness of the problem? Do different groups hold varying views about the nature and cause of the problem?
- *Identify the gainers and losers in relation to the problem.* Who gains from the existence of the problem? What do they gain and how much? Who loses? What do they lose and how much? How serious are the negative consequences on the lives of the losers?

2. *Social policy and program analysis.* Once the problem is understood, the second step is to assess the social policy and/or program being considered as a means of addressing the problem or offering relief to the victims of the problem. The following are useful for this analysis:

- *Search out the relevant program and policy history.* Is this a new problem? Have conditions, values, or perceptions changed over time? What is different about the proposed program or policy from past efforts to deal with the problem?
- *Identify the key characteristics of the proposed policy or program.* What are the goals and objectives of the proposal? Who would be eligible to benefit

from the plan? What benefits or services would be delivered if this proposal gains approval? What administrative structure would be required and how would it work? How would the program be financed and how much money would be required?

3. *Draw conclusions.* After the preceding information has been collected, it is necessary to judge the merits of the policy or program under analysis. Ultimately, it is the weight of the evidence matched with one's beliefs about what the quality of life should be for members of the society that results in a recommendation favoring or opposing the proposal—or suggesting compromise.

Answers to the following questions might be considered in arriving at conclusions about this program or policy proposal: Does the remedy proposed adequately deal with the causes as well as the consequences of the problem? Will it yield an outcome different from ones attempted in the past? Would the costs associated with the proposed remedy justify the possible outcomes? Are there better remedies that might be proposed?

When addressing a social policy, it is particularly important to be conscientious about using accurate data. If challenged by those with competing interests, credibility can be lost by not having sufficient and accurate data to support conclusions and underpin recommendations for change.

With a solid analysis of the policy or program proposal in hand, the social worker is prepared to influence the decisions that would impact the problem under consideration. At times, the social worker will work through committees or other groups to affect these decisions; on other occasions, it is appropriate to contact a policymaker directly and express a position on the proposal.

SELECTED BIBLIOGRAPHY

Burch, Hobart A. *Social Welfare Policy Analysis and Choices.* New York: Haworth, 1999.

Chambers, Donald E., and Kenneth Wedel. *Social Policy and Social Programs: A Method for the Practical Social Policy Analyst,* 4th ed. Boston: Allyn & Bacon, 2005.

Meenaghan, Thomas M., Keith M. Kilty, and John G. McNutt. *Social Policy Analysis and Practice.* Chicago: Lyceum Books, 2004.

12 Planning and Contracting

INTRODUCTION

Once the client and social worker have completed an assessment of the situation, they move on to formulating an action plan and entering into a formal or informal contract for implementing the plan. During this phase, the people and organizations with whom the client and worker will work to achieve the goals are identified and actions to be taken for accomplishing the needed changes are agreed upon.

Planning is the bridge between assessment and intervention. It begins with (1) specifying goals the client hopes to achieve, then (2) identifying what changes need to be made to achieve those goals, (3) selecting from among alternative change strategies the interventions most likely to reach the goals, (4) determining which actions will be taken by the client and the worker, and (5) establishing timelines for completing those actions. Clients, and sometimes inexperienced workers, may want to shortcut this planning activity. However, action without a clear plan is a recipe for failure. In efforts to change complex systems such as organizations and communities, the length of the planning phase will often exceed the time required for the intervention itself.

Effective planning places a special demand on the creativity of the social worker and the willingness of the client to consider alternative courses of action. Each possible option must be evaluated in an effort to predict any helpful or harmful impacts on the client or others, to identify the resources required, and to estimate the time frame for carrying it out. The worker must also determine the most appropriate practice frameworks—perspectives, theories, and models—that might be used to guide the process (see Chapter 6). Recognizing that some methods of securing change may be effective but unethical, the *Code of Ethics* should be considered at this point, as it is an important screen or filter when planning intervention strategies (see Item 8.8). Finally, to the extent possible, the worker should base the planning decisions on hard facts and objective evidence that was collected during the data collection and assessment phase.

Once a plan has been developed, it is important for the worker and clients to develop a *contract* (i.e., an agreement between the worker and client that spells out the activities to be conducted by each, along with a timetable for action during the intervention phase). A contract can be written, oral, or even an implied agreement, although the more specific the contract, the more likely it is to prevent misunderstandings. A written contract, in particular, is useful because it provides an explicitness that helps clarify points of agreement and disagreement between the worker and client; it serves as a basis for demonstrating accountability to both the client and the agency; and it can be an effective tool in facilitating the transfer of cases to another worker, should that become necessary.

The language and format of contracts may vary, but the content is essentially the same whether working at the individual, family, group, organization, or community level. At a minimum, a contract should delineate the following:

- Problems or concerns to be addressed
- Goals and objectives of the intervention
- Activities the client will undertake
- Tasks to be performed by the worker
- Expected duration of the intervention (in weeks or months)
- Schedule of time and place for interviews or committee meetings
- Identification of other persons, agencies, or organizations expected to participate and clarification about what they will be expected to contribute to the change process

Recognizing that even the most carefully developed plan may need to be modified as the intervention evolves, the worker and client must be open to revising the contract.

SECTION A

TECHNIQUES AND GUIDELINES FOR DIRECT PRACTICE

When working with individuals, families, and groups during the planning and contracting phase, the social worker should pay particular attention to the principles of maximizing client participation and self-determination. After all, it is the clients who must live with the outcome resulting from the plans selected and the accompanying interventions. Specifically, the worker recognizes that the client should have the following rights:

- Make decisions and have input concerning the intervention goals and objectives, as well as the general approach to be used to reach those goals.
- Know what approach the worker proposes to use, the likelihood of success, and if there are any anticipated risks or adverse effects associated with the proposed intervention.

- Know how long the intervention will last and/or about how long it will take to achieve the agreed upon objectives.
- Know how much time and money (if any) will be required of the client.
- Know any consequences for terminating the intervention against the advice of the social worker or agency.
- Know what rules of confidentiality apply and who else (e.g., court, probation officer, school officials, parent, etc.) will have access to information about the client's participation and the outcome of the intervention.
- Know how the success of the intervention will be evaluated.
- Know about appeals or grievance procedures that can be used to challenge a decision made by the social worker or agency.

Planning Activities.   Some of the most critical decisions a social worker must make occur as part of planning. These can have lifelong consequences for a client—for example, whether to plan the separation of an abused child from his or her parents, whether to recommend probation or incarceration for a youth, and so on. Therefore, it is important to proceed in a thoughtful and methodical manner and to avoid making serious errors.

One possible mistake is to move too quickly toward selecting an intervention without having devoted sufficient time and effort to clarifying and assessing the client's presenting problem or concern and exploring various options on how it could be addressed. That error can result in a misdirected plan and an ineffective intervention. A related error is to make decisions on the basis of untested assumptions without first probing for information that might contradict the client's or the worker's beliefs and presumptions about the nature, cause, and solution to the client's problem. Also, mistakes may result when the worker considers only a narrow range of strategies for change due to hurried decision making, laxness, or rigid interpretation of agency policy. The creativity that is an essential part of the art of social work (see Chapter 3) is particularly important when identifying a range of possible interventions. Finally, the routine or uncritical application of a particular practice theory or model can lead to bad decisions. Conceptual frameworks tend to create mindsets about the nature and causes of psychosocial problems, and a social worker too committed to a certain way of thinking may overlook or disregard important information that does not fit his or her preferred approach or theory.

Contracting Activities.   The best plans are of little value if there is not clear agreement and understanding about how they will be implemented. The greater the specificity about who will do what, when, and how, the greater the chances of the plan being fully implemented. The temptation for the social worker who has been through the change process many times is to assume that the client, too, knows what lies ahead. The discipline of carefully developing a contract is often reassuring to clients, while also encouraging the social worker to rethink steps that may have become routine.

Of the three forms of service contracts—implied, oral, and written—implied contracts typically offer the least clarity and are probably the least beneficial for the client. Oral contracts between the client and worker add an element of clarity, but the details of oral communication can be quickly forgotten and it is difficult to document the degree to which both the client and worker have been accountable. Although more time consuming to develop, written contracts (see Item 12.6) are the most useful for both the client and worker. They can be reviewed between sessions to remind the participants of their responsibilities and serve as the basis for future evaluation and accountability reporting. As suggested by Items 12.7 and 12.9, implied or oral contracts are also important when using group processes and in work with various informal helping resources.

12.1   SELECTING TARGET PROBLEMS AND GOALS

Purpose: To select the target problems and goals that will give direction to the social work intervention.

Discussion: A *goal* is a desired end toward which an activity is directed. Thus, the goal of a social work intervention is the end or outcome sought by the client and his or her social worker. This goal should logically flow from prior data gathering and assessment that examined both the client's strengths and resources and his or her problems and needs. The goals of intervention can take many forms. For example:

- *Learn a skill or acquire needed knowledge* (e.g., learn how to interview for a job, manage time, make decisions, resolve interpersonal conflict, manage stress, take care of a child, etc.).
- *Make an important decision* (e.g., decide on a college major, whether to get a divorce, whether to relinquish custody of a child, whether to seek help for an emotional problem, etc.).
- *Gather information* needed to make a plan or make a decision.
- *Assess a problem or concern* (e.g., conduct a careful assessment of some concern in order to decide if it is a serious problem needing attention, what the nature of the problem is, etc.).
- *Make a plan* (e.g., formulate a plan on how best to address the concern or problem).
- *Change a behavior* (e.g., increase a desirable behavior, decrease or eliminate a troublesome behavior).
- *Alter attitudes* about self or about some other person(s).
- *Gather information about availability of certain types of services or programs.*
- *Become linked to or enrolled in a program or service* provided by some agency or professional.
- *Rebuild a damaged relationship* (e.g., reach out to and reestablish relationship with estranged parent or child, improve husband-wife relationship, etc.).

■ *Change the way life circumstances or a life event is perceived or interpreted* (e.g., learn to assign new meaning to events and circumstances, view things from a different angle, develop new perspectives, etc.).
■ *Achieve a more satisfactory adjustment* to an unchangeable condition or situation (e.g., a chronic illness or permanent disability or the death of a loved one).

Sometimes, the social worker and client can quickly agree on the goal. This is likely when the client's need or problem is readily apparent to both the client and worker. However, in many cases, the social worker and client will see things differently and must struggle to reach agreement on the nature of the problem and on what can and should be done about it. Often, the worker and client must also devote considerable time to the task of priority setting in order to decide which of the client's many problems and concerns should become a target for intervention. Until those decisions are made, they cannot formulate a feasible intervention plan.

The value-based principle of *client self-determination* dictates that the client has the right to select the concerns to be addressed by a social work intervention. There are also very practical reasons for expecting the client, rather than the social worker, to select the target problems and goals of the intervention. Namely, it is seldom possible to encourage or motivate a client to do something that he or she does not consider a priority. Unless the problem to be worked on is important to the client and unless the goal and method of the proposed intervention seem reasonable and make sense, the client will not invest himself or herself in the process of change. Even in work with the nonvoluntary client, it is important to give the client as much choice as possible. In such a case, the worker or agency might require or mandate working toward one goal while encouraging the client to select an additional goal that he or she considers important.

Many of the clients served by social workers have multiple and complex problems and concerns. Both research and practice wisdom suggest that, in order to be effective, the helping process must concentrate available time and energy on just one, two, or three problems at a time. If priorities and a clear focus are not established, the helping effort flounders and usually ends in frustration for both client and worker. The following steps will help the client and worker set *priorities:*

1. The client identifies and lists what he or she sees as problems or concerns (i.e., what the client wants to change).

2. The social worker offers his or her recommendations, if any, and explains why they also need to be considered. The worker makes sure that any mandated problems are included (mandated problems are ones imposed on the client by some legitimate authority such as a court, probation officer, or child protection agency).

3. The problems and concerns are reviewed and sorted into logical groupings or combinations so that interrelatedness is identified.

4. The client examines the list and selects the two or three problems or concerns of highest priority.

5. The worker selects the two or three items he or she considers to be of highest priority.

6. Together, the client and worker discuss the concerns identified in steps 4 and 5 and examine them against the following criteria:

- Which ones weigh most heavily on the client's situation (e.g., which ones cause the most worry and anxiety)?
- Which ones, if not addressed and corrected, will have the most negative and far-reaching consequences for the client?
- Which ones, if addressed and corrected, would have the most positive effects on the client (e.g., provide the client with greatest sense of relief, make it easier to solve other problems, etc.)?
- Which ones are of greatest interest to the client (e.g., which ones the client is most motivated to work on at this time)?
- Which ones can be addressed and corrected with only a moderate investment of time, energy, and other resources?
- Which ones are relatively unchangeable or would require a extraordinary investment of time, energy, or resources?

7. After considering these criteria, the three problems of highest priority are selected. As mentioned earlier, it is usually counterproductive to try to address more than about three concerns at one time. Task-centered practitioners have termed this principle *the rule of three*.

8. It is important for the social worker to remember that the client's problems and concerns will almost always affect or involve significant others (e.g., spouse, children, parents, close friends, employer, etc.). Unless these individuals, who are either part of the problem or part of the solution, are considered in the intervention planning, there is good chance that they will—knowingly or unknowingly—become an obstacle to the change process. In some cases, they may actively sabotage the client's attempt to make desired changes.

SELECTED BIBLIOGRAPHY

Epstein, Laura and Lester Brown. *Brief Treatment and a New Look at the Task-Centered Approach,* 4th ed. Boston: Allyn & Bacon, 2002.

Reid, William, and Anne Fortune. "The Task-Centered Model." In *Social Workers' Desk Reference,* edited by Albert Roberts and Gilbert Greene, 101–104. New York: Oxford University Press, 2002.

Rooney, Ronald. *Strategies for Work with Involuntary Clients.* New York: Columbia University Press, 1992.

12.2 THE PROBLEM SEARCH

Purpose: To engage the reluctant client in a process designed to identify a problem on which he or she is willing to work.

Discussion: The technique often termed a ***problem search*** is a "mini-contract" or negotiated agreement between the client and worker to devote a couple of sessions to discussing the client's situation in order to determine if the client has a problem and, if so, whether it should be addressed by some type of professional or agency intervention.

A problem search is often used by a worker either when (1) the client has been referred by an authoritative agency (court) or by his or her family but does not acknowledge the existence of a problem as defined by others or (2) the client has requested a specific agency service, but in the worker's opinion, it is desirable to help the client expand that request or redefine the presenting problem. In this later situation, the social worker is concerned that the client's definition of the problem is not accurate or realistic and/or that his or her request for a specific service will not resolve the problem. An example might be the father who requests foster care placement for his children because he and his wife are having marital problems.

Essentially, the problem search asks the client to participate in one or two additional sessions in order to explore the situation in more depth. The client is asked to withhold judgment about the need for service and the worker's usefulness until after these meetings. In using this technique, the social worker moves through these four steps:

1. *Explain why you are suggesting a further exploration of the client's situation.* Briefly identify your concerns and the advantages of an additional session or two. For example: "I realize that you see no problems that deserve my attention, but what you have said about getting fired leads me to believe that you really try to get along at work but for some reason you and your supervisors often clash on how best to do the job. Because of that, I suggest we meet two times and talk more about your job experiences. If, after the second session, we cannot figure out what might be done to improve the situation, we will stop meeting."

2. *Solicit the client's thoughts and feedback on the proposal.* For example: "What do you think about my suggestion that we meet two times to review and discuss the stress you experience on the job?" (If client responds with a no, say, for example, "Well, I can understand your reluctance and I will respect your decision, but let me give you one other reason why I think it is a good idea. . . .")

3. *Set up a plan for a future meeting.* For example: "I am glad that you agreed to meet again. As I said, we will meet two times. If it proves useful, that will be great. But, if after the second session, it doesn't seem useful, then we will not continue. How about meeting the next two Wednesdays at 4 P.M.?"

4. *Identify two or three topics to be discussed.* For example: "When we meet next week, let's start with a discussion of the jobs you have really liked and why. Second, I would like to discuss the type of supervision you expect to get on the job. Does that sound like a reasonable place to begin?"

SELECTED BIBLIOGRAPHY

Epstein, Laura, and Lester Brown. *Brief Treatment and a New Look at the Task-Centered Approach,* 4th ed. Boston: Allyn & Bacon, 2002.
Marsh, Peter, and Mark Doel. *The Task Centered Book.* New York: Routledge, 2005.

12.3   USING CHECKLISTS IN GOAL SELECTION

Purpose: To assist the client in identifying and selecting intervention goals.

Discussion: Some clients have difficulty articulating their concerns and identifying their goals for change. In such cases, some type of goal checklist may be useful. Basically, this tool is a list of possible intervention goals from which the client can select ones that are relevant to his or her situation. For example, Figure 12.1 is a goal checklist developed for use in work with parents who had abused their children. A worker familiar with the problems and concerns of a particular client group can construct a goal checklist and tailor it to a particular practice setting or type of service available. A goal checklist can also be translated into a format for evaluating client perceptions of the progress achieved during an intervention (see Item 14.3).

SELECTED BIBLIOGRAPHY

Horejsi, Charles. *Assessment and Case Planning in Child Protection and Foster Care Services.* Englewood, CO: American Humane Association, 1996.

Horejsi, Charles, Ann Bertsche, and Frank Clark. *Social Work Practice with Parents of Children in Foster Care: A Handbook.* Springfield, IL: Charles C Thomas, 1981.

12.4   THE CLIENT NEEDS LIST

Purpose: To remind the worker and client of concerns and needs that should be addressed in a service contract or case plan.

Discussion: A ***needs list*** is a tool used to guide case-management activities related to a certain category of clients. This list is most often used with clients who are highly dependent on the services provided by health care and social agencies (e.g., the frail elderly, children in foster care, people who have serious developmental disabilities or mental illness, etc.). A needs list reminds all involved of the concerns that should be addressed in a service plan. Those involved in formulating this plan—including the client—must decide how the client's needs and concerns can best be addressed by the service providers and which person, professional, or agency will be responsible for addressing a particular concern or issue. The client needs list is especially useful when the case-planning activity is being performed by a multiagency or a multidisciplinary team; namely, using the lists helps clarify assigned responsibilities, facilitate interagency coordination, and reduce misunderstanding within the team.

Figure 12.2 is an example of a needs list used in work with adults who have developmental disabilities but are capable of living in a semi-independent living arrangement. Also see Item 11.13 for ideas on specific areas of client functioning that might be included in a needs list.

FIGURE 12.1   Sample Goal Checklist

A List of Goals for Parents

Explanation: Having a clear goal in mind is one important step in dealing with problems and concerns. Once there is a goal, it is possible to develop a plan for reaching that goal. Below is a list of goals that have been mentioned by parents. Place a check (✓) by those that are similar to your goals. This checklist can help you and your social worker formulate a workable plan of action.

_____ Talk to people about my concerns, problems, and worries.

_____ Budget my money and keep track of bills.

_____ Prepare meals that are healthy.

_____ Clean and take care of my apartment or house.

_____ Find and make use of services such as day care, counseling, and legal services.

_____ Cope with daily pressures and demands on my time.

_____ Show greater affection toward my child.

_____ Make friends, mix, and feel comfortable with people.

_____ Learn skills needed to get a job.

_____ Have good visits with my child in foster care.

_____ Get along well with my spouse or partner.

_____ Learn to recognize when I am at risk of doing something I may regret.

_____ Find a better and safer living arrangement.

_____ Talk with my child in ways that make him or her feel secure.

_____ Discipline and control my child without hitting him or her.

_____ Talk to and plan with the foster parents who are taking care of my child.

_____ Talk with my social worker and make use of the help he or she can provide.

_____ Learn to calm myself down when I start to get angry or agitated.

_____ Find friends or a support group that will understand my situation and help me deal with problems.

_____ Learn what to expect from children and what is "normal" behavior for a child of a certain age.

_____ Be more assertive and direct in making my thoughts and feelings known to other people.

_____ Get along without alcohol or drugs.

_____ Learn how to deal with conflicts with my parents and relatives.

_____ Learn how to deal with emergency situations and with times when I feel overwhelmed.

_____ Learn to cope with strong emotions such as guilt, sadness, fear, and anger.

FIGURE 12.2 Sample Needs List

Needs List for Independent Living

1. Housing suitable for client's level of mobility and physical limitations (consider stairs, wheelchair accessibility, etc.)
2. Safe heating and electrical system and usable toilet facilities
3. Home furnishing (chairs, tables, TV, radio, etc.)
4. Bed, blankets, sheets, etc.
5. Clothing for all seasons of the year
6. Food, food storage, stove
7. Telephone or other means of requesting assistance
8. Items needed for food preparation (e.g., utensils, pots, pans)
9. Items needed to maintain personal hygiene (razor, soap, sanitary napkins, etc.)
10. Financial resources/money management system
11. Transportation
12. Medical and dental care
13. Medication and monitoring of dosage, if needed
14. Social contacts and recreational activities
15. Concern and interest shown by family, friends, and neighbors
16. Protection from harm or exploitation
17. Appropriate level of supervision
18. Training (job-related, community, survival skills, etc.)
19. Employment or work-related activity
20. Adaptive aids (e.g., eyeglasses, hearing aids, leg braces, etc.)
21. Therapy and other special treatments (e.g., physical therapy, speech therapy, etc.)
22. Maintenance of cultural and ethnic heritage
23. Participation in spiritual or religious activities
24. Legal advice

SELECTED BIBLIOGRAPHY

Frankel, Arthur, and Sheldon Gelman. *Case Management*, 2nd ed. Chicago: Lyceum Books, 2004.

Rothman, Jack, and Jon Simon Sager. *Case Management*, 2nd ed. Boston: Allyn & Bacon, 1998.

Summers, Nancy. *Fundamentals of Case Management Practice*, 2nd ed. Belmont, CA: Brooks/Cole, 2006.

12.5 FORMULATING INTERVENTION OBJECTIVES

Purpose: To develop objectives that are measurable and relevant to the client's concerns.

Discussion: Unless there are agreed upon objectives for an intervention, the helping process will flounder and its evaluation will be impossible. Unless the client and social worker are clear about what they are trying to achieve, they cannot determine when or whether they achieved it. Although the terms goals and objectives are often used interchangeably, they do not mean the same thing. A *goal* is usually a broad and rather global statement (e.g., "to better cope with the demands of a child who has a disability"). Not infrequently, a goal is simply a restatement of a problem in a way that suggests a solution. For example, if a family's lack of money creates stress that erupts in violence against children, a logical goal would be to increase that family's financial resources in order to reduce stress.

As compared to a goal, an *objective* is more specific and written in a manner that allows and facilitates measurement and evaluation. Consider these examples:

Statements Prepared by a Hospital Social Worker

Goal: Improve responsiveness of social work staff to new referrals.

Objective: To conduct at least 80 percent of initial patient or family member interviews within four hours of receiving a referral from a doctor or nurse.

Statements Prepared by the Administrator of a Big Brother/Big Sister Program

Goal: Obtain more Big Brothers for our children.

Objective: To recruit, train, and match 35 new Big Brothers before August 1.

Statements Prepared by a Child Welfare Worker

Goal: To promote better parent-child relationships.

Objective: To encourage and facilitate parental visitation so that by January 15 at least 70 percent of parents in my caseload visit their children in foster care at least once a month.

A properly written objective will answer a five-part question:

1. Who . . .
2. will do what . . .
3. to what extent . . .
4. under what conditions . . .
5. by when?

When an objective is complex and cannot be written in a single sentence, it will be necessary to attach to a general statement a list of conditions and criteria as a means of further clarification. *Conditions* describe the situation or context in which the desired behavior or action is to take place; *criteria* are the rules or the definitions that will be used to decide whether the desired behavior or action has occurred at an acceptable level.

Inherent in the writing of an objective is the use of verbs that describe an action to be taken, such as the following:

attend	contact	answer	write	demonstrate	list
decide	discuss	plan	select	purchase	obtain
bring	supervise	practice	arrange	utilize	apply
implement	display	recognize	join	contribute	transport

When developing an objective, it is important not to confuse an *input* with an *outcome*. This common error results in statements like "Mr. Jones is to obtain counseling," which describes an input (counseling) but says nothing about the intended outcome. In this example, counseling is presented as an end, but in reality, it is only a means to an end. What is the intended outcome of the counseling? What is the counseling to accomplish? A better statement would be "Mr. Jones will obtain counseling focused on his physical abuse of his son, Johnny, and designed to help him learn to use time out and positive reinforcement as alternatives to harsh spanking and screaming as discipline."

In writing an objective, *positive language* should be used whenever possible; the words used should describe what the client will do, not what the client will not do (e.g., "learn and follow table manners" versus "stop being so messy when eating"). Also, it is important that objectives be formulated in *behavioral language*—using words that describe observable actions in terms of their frequency, duration, and intensity.

A *timeframe* is an essential part of an objective. In interpersonal helping, for example, an objective should not take more than a few weeks to accomplish. Thus, an objective that would probably take many months to accomplish should be broken down into several smaller ones. This is important because the client needs to see evidence of progress. If the client can perceive he or she is making concrete gains (i.e., reaching an objective), even if the steps are small, he or she will feel more hopeful and more motivated to continue.

The concept of a task, as used by social workers favoring the task-centered approach, is both similar to and different from the concept of an objective, as presented here. Basically, a *task* is some specified and observable problem-solving action or step that can be evaluated in terms of whether it was achieved or completed. Preferably, a task is an action that can be accomplished in a matter of days or at most a couple of weeks. A task can be viewed as one of the many steps or short-term activities that must be completed to achieve an objective. Thus, in working toward a single goal, the client may need to achieve several objectives, and in order to achieve a given objective, he or she may need to work on and complete numerous tasks (see Figure 12.3).

Generally speaking, an objective is something that a client might achieve in a couple of months or a matter of weeks (e.g., "Learn new methods of discipline with the help of a parent training program"), whereas a task is something that can be completed in a matter of days or a couple of weeks (e.g., "Call a friend to arrange transportation to the parent training program"). Regardless of the terminology used, the point to remember is that an intervention must have a clear purpose and direction.

Objectives are intended to give direction and structure to the helping process, but they should never stifle the humanness and individualization that are essential ingredients in effective helping. A willingness to revise objectives to meet changing circumstances is critical to effective helping. In summary, a properly developed objective meets the following criteria:

1. It usually starts with the word *to*, followed by an action verb.
2. It specifies a single result or outcome to be accomplished.
3. It specifies a target date for its accomplishment.
4. It is as specific and quantitative as possible and, hence, measurable.

FIGURE 12.3   **Relationship of Goals, Objectives, and Tasks**

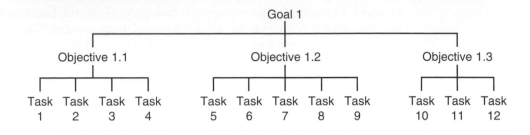

5. It is understandable by the client and others who will be contributing to or participating in the intervention.
6. It is realistic and attainable but still represents a significant challenge.
7. It is agreed to by both client and worker without pressure or coercion.
8. It is consistent with agency policies and with the social work *Code of Ethics*.

SELECTED BIBLIOGRAPHY

Gronlund, Norman. *How to Write and Use Instructional Objectives*, 6th ed. Upper Saddle River,
NJ: Merrill, 2000.
Mager, Robert. *Goal Analysis*, 3rd ed. Atlanta: Center for Effective Performance, 1997.
———. *Preparing Instructional Objectives*, 3rd ed. Atlanta: Center for Effective Performance, 1997.

12.6   WRITTEN SERVICE CONTRACTS

Purpose: To provide direction and focus during intervention.

Discussion: Arriving at an agreement on the service to be provided by the worker and used by the
client is fundamental to social work practice. In most cases and in most agencies and
programs, a verbal agreement is sufficient. However, many social workers use
written service contracts (or service agreements). This is especially true in public
agencies and in the fields of child welfare, developmental disabilities, and probation
and parole. Some providers of psychotherapy and other mental health services also
use written contracts as a means of reducing the possibility of a serious misunderstanding and a malpractice suit.

A ***written service contract*** is a document that specifies the desired outcome of
the service(s) to be provided, the key actions that will be taken to achieve this outcome,
the major roles and responsibilities of those involved in this effort, and the relevant
timelines. Typically, the document is signed by the client and service provider(s).
The core elements of a contract are depicted in Figure 12.4.

Except in those cases in which the contract is written into a court order, a service contract is not viewed as legally binding. However, it is intended to describe a clear
commitment to pursue a mutually agreed upon course of action. While the authors

FIGURE 12.4 **Sample Form for Client-Social Worker Contract**

This agreement is between ____(client's name)____ and ____(social worker's name)____, who is employed by the Mountain State Department of Family Services.

The purpose or goal of this agreement is to _____

_____

_____

In order to achieve this purpose or reach this goal, the following objectives must be met:

1. _____ (by date) _____
2. _____ (by date) _____
3. _____ (by date) _____

In order to reach these objectives, ____(client's name)____ is to perform or engage in the following tasks or activities during or before the dates shown:

1. _____ (by date) _____
2. _____ (by date) _____
3. _____ (by date) _____

In order to reach these objectives, ____(social worker's name)____ is to perform or engage in the following tasks or activities during or before the dates shown:

1. _____ (by date) _____
2. _____ (by date) _____
3. _____ (by date) _____

Progress toward the objectives will be reviewed and evaluated by means of the following procedures or methods:

_____

_____

The consequences, if any, of not reaching the objectives are the following:

_____

_____

The following steps or actions are required to renegotiate terms of this agreement:

_____

_____

Signed _____ Date _____

Signed _____ Date _____

prefer the term *service contract*, other practitioners or agencies may use the terms *service agreement, case plan, treatment plan, intervention plan*, or *individual family support plan* when referring to this type of document. Often these terms are used interchangeably.

A service contract should answer the following questions:

- What is the desired outcome of the worker's and/or agency's service to the client?
- What is to be done by the client? By when?
- What is to be done by the client's significant others (family, friends, neighbors, etc.)? By when?
- What is to be done by the worker and other agency staff? By when?
- What services are to be obtained from other agencies? By when?
- What events will trigger a reassessment of the client's situation and/or a revision of the service contract?
- What are the consequences, if any, for not adhering to the plan?

Service contracts should not be confused with *behavioral contracts* (see Item 13.6). The two have similarities but also important differences. A behavioral contract is much more specific and covers a shorter period of time—often a matter of days or a week or two. The period covered by a service contract may be several months, although it is ordinarily renegotiated and rewritten every three or six months.

Follow these guidelines for using written service contracts:

1. Understand agency policy regarding written service contracts and any legal requirements or legal interpretations relevant to their use with the clients you serve. In the fields of child protection and probation, it is common for a service contract to be incorporated into a court order. The following statement, taken from a public agency manual concerning the handling of certain cases of child abuse and neglect, is fairly typical of agency policy on using a written service contract (treatment plan) when court involvement is possible:

The tasks of identification, assessment and formulation of treatment recommendations rest primarily with the social worker working with the family. The results of these formulations are set forth in the written treatment plan to advise the parents and the court of the problems identified and the course of action recommended to remedy these problems. The treatment plan should contain the following elements:

- Identification of the problems or conditions which resulted in the abuse or neglect.
- Treatment goals for the family which address the needs identified and which, when attained, will assure the adequate level of care for the child.
- Specific treatment objectives, or tasks, which outline in detail the series of steps which must be taken by each member of the household to reach the treatment goals. These objectives should clearly define the separate roles and responsibilities of all of the parties involved in the treatment process. Objectives should clearly state the actions which are necessary, and the time period in which the objective should be accomplished. The objectives should be reasonably attainable and designed to fit the capabilities and existing circumstances of the family involved.

2. Understand the advantages and disadvantages of using written service contracts. The major advantages are that they clarify purpose, set priorities, delineate roles and responsibilities, increase ownership of the plan, provide a means of measuring progress, and reduce the potential for client-worker misunderstanding. Needless to say, contracts work best with voluntary and motivated clients. They do, however, have a special advantage when working with a reluctant or involuntary client because they facilitate clear and above-board communication, reducing the client's hostility and fear of being manipulated or set up by some hidden agenda.

An obvious disadvantage of written service contracts is that considerable time may be needed to prepare a clearly written and easily understood contract. Also, there is the danger of having the powerless client agree to a contract out of fear of somehow being punished or penalized if he or she does not agree with what the provider has suggested. Another disadvantage is the possibility of focusing on trivial outcomes in order to more easily attain success while avoiding objectives that are more important but difficult to achieve. Despite these potential problems, Epstein and Brown (2002) conclude that written contracts

> can and should be used in the bulk of ordinary practice. However, written contracts should not be viewed as a remedy for all difficulties nor as rigid machinery for pushing a case toward some hard and fast end. If a contract has been agreed upon and put into writing, it represents a degree of commitment to an arrangement worked out between the client and practitioner—a promising basis for positive movement. . . . Without mutual agreement and continuous work, the contract has little force for change. (pp. 168–169)

3. Develop the contract only after a thorough social assessment during which you and the client study and agree on the problems to be tackled. The terms of the contract should be consistent with the client's capacities, the worker's skill, and the agency's mission.

4. By definition, a contract specifies what the client will do and what the worker/agency will do. A contract must never be one sided and list only that which the worker or agency expects of the client.

5. The contract should be phrased in simple, clear language so that the client will know exactly what it means. The wording should not confuse or intimidate the client. It may be necessary to prepare the contract in the client's first language (e.g., Spanish) if he or she has a poor understanding of English. In cases where the client cannot read, the worker should consider recording the agreement on a cassette tape, in addition to preparing a written statement.

6. A contract should be developed in a way that makes success probable without, of course, sacrificing relevance. If the worker believes that the client will be unable to meet the terms of a particular contract, that alone is an indication that its objectives are too ambitious, or the timeframe is too short.

7. From the client's viewpoint the objectives identified in the contract must be realistic and worth achieving. Since the purpose of the contract is to facilitate change, it must focus on behaviors or situations that can, in fact, be changed. Do not focus on things that are beyond anyone's control.

8. When selecting and formulating objectives, logical sequences must be built into the plan. Some problems must be tackled one step at a time and in a certain order, and new behaviors may need to be learned in a particular sequence. For example, the client who wants a job must first learn how to complete a job application.

9. Do not propose to do something for the client if the client can do it himself or herself. Sometimes a busy social worker will do for the client rather than taking the time to teach or encourage the client to carry out the action. Unnecessarily doing things for a client can also occur when the worker is overly eager to be helpful or overlooks client strengths and abilities.

10. Provisions of the contract should be modified as necessary to stay in step with changing realities of the situation. This flexibility is important in maintaining the trust of the client.

SELECTED BIBLIOGRAPHY

Epstein, Laura, and Lester Brown. *Brief Treatment and a New Look at the Task-Centered Approach*, 4th ed. Boston: Allyn & Bacon, 2002.

Rothman, Juliet. *Contracting in Clinical Social Work*. Chicago: Nelson-Hall, 1998.

Wodarski, John, Lisa Rapp-Paglicci, Catherine Dulmus, and Arthur Jongsma. *The Social Work and Human Services Treatment Planner*. New York: John Wiley and Sons, 2001.

12.7   MAKING USE OF INFORMAL RESOURCES

Purpose: To assist the client in identifying and utilizing informal resources.

Discussion: When possible and appropriate, the intervention plan should utilize the ***informal resources*** available within the client's social support network, such as his or her extended family, friends, neighbors, church groups, and service clubs. These are in contrast to ***formal resources***, such as agencies, hospitals, and trained professionals. Informal resources can provide emotional support, material assistance (e.g., money, loans, food, housing), physical care (e.g., child care, supervision of frail elderly persons living in their own homes), information, and the mediation of interpersonal conflict.

Many people prefer to use informal resources over formal ones, for several reasons:

- No stigma is attached to receiving help from an informal resource.
- Informal helping is available 24 hours a day, seven days a week, at no cost.
- One does not have to be categorized, labeled, diagnosed, or otherwise meet eligibility requirements in order to secure needed help.
- Informal helping involves a reciprocal relationship—the give and take among two equals or peers—rather than the expert-client relationship that is so often a part of the professional helping process.

A self-help group is usually considered to be an informal resource, even though some are affiliated with a state or national organization and may use professionals as advisors. Another important informal resource is the ***natural helper***, an individual who has often resided in the community for a long time and is known for his or her ability to help others. An example is the "neighborhood Mom" to whom children gravitate for nurturing and advice. Other natural helpers include respected elders, religious leaders, and healers. Another informal resource—one often overlooked by professionals—is other agency clients. Clients can often be of help to each other; however, in some cases, they can also exacerbate each other's problems.

Although informal resources are the oldest and most common form of helping activity, some professionals are reluctant to encourage or assist their clients in using these resources. Possible reasons include the following:

- They assume that formal resources and other professionals are inherently more effective than nonprofessionals, regardless of the client's problem or situation.
- They have little awareness of the informal helping networks and informal resources.
- They assume that the client has already thought about using informal resources and for some reason rejected the idea.
- They doubt the capacity of informal resources to protect a client's right to confidentiality.

When considering the appropriateness of looking to informal resources as a source of help and assistance for a client, the social worker should keep the following guidelines in mind:

1. The fundamental goal of social work practice is to help clients improve their social functioning. The resources used—whether formal, informal, or a mix of both—are simply the means to that end. Both formal and informal resources are important, and both may be needed. A professional should not feel threatened by a client's use of or preference for informal resources. While invaluable in many situations, informal resources are neither a panacea nor an inexpensive alternative to professional services and the formal resources needed by a client.

2. The client's social support network should always be viewed as a potential reservoir of helping resources. The client's relationships—past and present—with relatives, friends, neighbors, churches, and service organizations should be explored in an effort to identify potential sources of help. If a source is identified, the advantages and disadvantages of attempting to use it should be discussed with the client. However, in the final analysis, it is the client who decides whether to contact others and involve them in the helping process. Some clients may need guidance on how to reach out to an informal resource and also handle the expectation of reciprocity (see Item 11.3).

3. The ethical and legal codes concerning client confidentiality need not be a barrier to the use of informal resources. Most often, the client first approaches the informal resources. Thus, the client is in control of what he or she chooses to reveal. In cases where the social worker needs to talk with an informal resource, he or she must, of course, first secure the client's permission, just as is done when the worker communicates with another professional or agency.

4. Some clients are reluctant to approach or join a support group or a self-help group because they do not want to admit that they have a problem. They may find the group more attractive if they come to view their own participation as a means of helping others. Thus, a worker trying to connect a client with such a group might emphasize that the client's life experiences and efforts to cope with a problem may offer encouragement and helpful insights to the group's members.

5. A worker should not attempt to "professionalize," train, or direct the actions of an informal helping resource. Generally, these resources are most effective when they follow their own best judgments and respond spontaneously.

SELECTED BIBLIOGRAPHY

Gitterman, Alex, and Lawrence Shulman, eds. *Mutual Aid Groups, Vulnerable Populations and the Life Cycle*, 3rd ed. New York: Columbia University Press, 2005.

Kurtz, Linda. *Self-Help and Support Groups.* Thousand Oaks, CA: Sage, 1997.

Maguire, Lambert. *Social Support Systems in Practice.* Washington, DC: NASW Press, 1991.

Norcross, John, John Santrock, Linda Campbell, Thomas Smith, Robert Sommer, and Edward Zuckerman. *Authoritative Guide to Self-Help Resources in Mental Health*, rev. ed. New York: Guilford, 2003.

12.8   FAMILY GROUP CONFERENCING

Purpose: To plan for a child's safety and care by involving the child's parents, adult family members, relatives, and other concerned individuals in a meeting that focuses on decision making and planning.

Discussion: The technique termed ***family group conferencing*** (also called *family group decision making* and *family unity meetings*) was first developed in the late 1980s by child welfare personnel in New Zealand in order to engage members of large extended families and kinship groups (which are common to indigenous peoples) in decision making and planning for a child who has been abused or neglected by a parent. Essentially, a *family group conference* (*FGC*) brings together for a face-to-face discussion the parent and other persons who are concerned about both the parent and the child and asks them to come up with a feasible plan for keeping the child safe. In many cases, making a plan for the child involves making a plan for the parent to change his or her behavior or situation. A typical FGC lasts from 2 to 3 hours, but some go on for an entire day. Young children do not attend, but in some cases, an adolescent might be invited to participate.

In addition to the parent and his or her family and relatives, those attending the FGC may include close friends of the parent, the parent's clergy person, the child's school personnel or day-care providers, attorneys, foster parents, social and mental health service providers, and others who are somehow involved with and concerned about the child and the child's parent. However, the nonfamily members who attend an FGC are there only to provide information, not to propose solutions or make decisions.

The FGC technique is based on these assumptions, values, and beliefs:

- The individuals who are most deeply concerned about and committed to the long-term well-being of the child are, most likely, his or her blood relatives and very close friends of the family.
- Family members know one another's histories as well as their strengths, limitations, and problems.
- A plan that is developed by family members and close relatives (i.e., parents, grandparents, aunts, uncles, etc.) and trusted family friends is more likely to be understood, accepted, and implemented than is a plan developed by a social worker, a social agency, or even a court.

The FGC approach is attractive to many social workers because it is inherently culturally sensitive. In addition, it is family centered and builds on family strengths. An FGC has the effect of demonstrating to the parent that many people care and want to help, which often breaks through the parent's denial and resistance and mobilizes the resources of the parent's extended family or kinship group. Those who are experienced in the use of the FGC technique often express amazement at the creativity and resourcefulness that is displayed by people attending a family group conference, as they strive to come up with feasible solutions to the problem. In fact, an FGC meeting often initiates reconciliation and begins the healing of ruptured family relationships. The family group conferencing technique is being used increasingly in other practice settings, such as juvenile probation, education, and mental health.

Here are several guidelines for using family group conferencing:

1. An FGC can be utilized only when the parent has agreed to its use. All of those invited to attend the meeting first must be "nominated" by the parent. The parent is encouraged, however, by his or her social worker to invite all family members, relatives, and friends who are genuinely concerned about the situation and who may be possible resources, even if the parent does not like them. If the parent wants his or her attorney present, the attorney can be invited, if he or she will allow a free-flowing discussion and a nonadversarial approach to problem solving. In some states, the child protection agency is required to invite the parent's attorney to a family group conference.

An FGC can be used with most families. Those most likely to benefit are the ones in which family members (and others) can focus on the needs of the *child*, rather than their own issues and agendas. FGCs are most effective with families that can take the risks needed to communicate honestly and that can work toward reaching a consensus in decision making.

When making decisions about whom to invite to the conference, the coordinator and the parent also must consider safety issues. A person who is extremely intimidating, violent, or under the influence of drugs or alcohol may need to be excluded.

2. An FGC can be used at any point in the course of a case, but it is usually tried in these situations: (a) when the agency and the parent have reached an impasse; (b) when the out-of-home placement of a child or the child's return home is under consideration by a child protection agency or court; and (c) when the parent's work toward change has become "stuck" and his or her family and friends need to decide how to help bring about the needed changes or better cope with current problems. In some states, the use of an FGC can be court ordered in an effort to arrive at a plan for a child in need of care.

3. The *facilitator* of the meeting (often termed the *family group conferencing coordinator*) should have a neutral attitude toward the parent and not have an ongoing or prior relationship with the parent or family. Thus, the parent's current social worker, caseworker, case manager, therapist, or service provider should not assume the role of facilitator.

4. For a family group conference to be successful, the coordinator or facilitator of the meeting should carefully prepare the potential participants. During this preparation phase, the FGC coordinator should meet with each potential participant (i.e., someone nominated by parent) to explain the purpose and process of the FGC, to answer any questions he or she may have, to encourage him or her to attend, and, if necessary, to arrange for transportation, child care, and so on. If a potential participant appears fearful or hesitant to express his or her thoughts at an FGC, the coordinator should work with him or her and offer encouragement to voice any concerns. Typically, a coordinator will invest 30 to 40 hours in preparing for a single FGC meeting.

5. At the beginning of an FGC session, certain ground rules must be displayed for all to see. For example:
- The coordinator will guide the process without imposing his or her views or ideas on the group.
- Maintain focus on the needs of the child—that is, What plan of action will be in the best interests of the child?
- Keep the focus on finding solutions. Talk about what can be done in the future, not on what happened in the past.
- Be respectful of each other. There can be no name calling, blaming, shaming, or threatening. No one will be allowed to intimidate another person or keep someone from saying what he or she believes is important and relevant to the purpose of the meeting.
- It is important for everyone to voice his or her ideas and suggestions. It is OK to disagree, but do so in a respectful manner.
- Only one person will speak at a time.
- After this meeting, be sure to maintain confidentiality about what was discussed.

6. A typical FGC session will unfold as follows:

- The coordinator welcomes the participants and explains the purpose of the meeting. For example: "We are here to see how we can help Margaret and her children and thereby make it possible for the family to stay together."
- The coordinator explains the ground rules for the meeting (see item 5). At the beginning of the meeting, a ritual that is meaningful to the family may be used to set the tone for the discussion. This ritual might be, for example, reciting a prayer, recalling the family's traditions, or recalling some special time in the family's history.
- All who are present introduce themselves and briefly explain their relationship to the parent/family.
- The parent is asked and helped, if necessary, to describe his or her goals for the meeting and the hoped-for or preferred outcome.
- The coordinator guides a discussion of the parent's and the family's strengths.
- The coordinator guides presentations by selected child protection personnel, service providers, and family members, which serves to clearly describe the current problem (e.g., nature of abuse), the needs of the child, and the possible legal ramifications if the problem is not resolved. The professionals in attendance answer all questions asked by the parent and his or her relatives and friends.
- The family and friends are asked to propose their ideas on how the child can be protected from further maltreatment and how the parent might be helped to make needed changes. In cases in which the child must be placed away from the parent, the group decides where the child might live. (This discussion may take place with or without the coordinator being present.)
- The decisions made are reviewed by the coordinator, and a plan for necessary follow-up is formulated.
- The meeting is adjourned and often followed by a celebration ritual and sharing of food.

7. The use of family group conferencing does not abrogate the responsibilities of the social worker, agency, or court in protecting the child. They can, if necessary, veto the plan. However, if the plan generated by the family conference will keep the child safe, it will be approved by the child welfare agency or court.

8. Following the meeting, the coordinator compiles notes on the meeting and puts the agreed-upon plan into written form and sends this report to all participants.

SELECTED BIBLIOGRAPHY

American Humane Association. *Family Group Decision Making: Technical Assistance Notebook.* Englewood, CO: American Humane Association, 1998.

Burford, Gale, and Joe Hudson, eds. *Family Group Conferencing.* New York: Aldine de Gruyter, 2000.

Connolly, Marie, and Margaret McKenzie. *Effective Participatory Practice: Family Group Conferencing in Child Protection.* New York: Aldine de Gruyter, 1999.

Pennell, Joan and Gray Anderson, eds. *Widening the Circle: The Practice and Evaluation of Family Group Conferencing.* Washington, DC: National Association of Social Workers, 2005.

12.9   THE SMALL GROUP AS A RESOURCE

Purpose: To develop groups that can be resources to clients.

Discussion: Small groups can be an invaluable resource to both individuals and families who are struggling with some problem in social functioning or simply trying to better cope with a difficult situation. Group experiences provide their members with a sense of acceptance, encouragement, and challenge. When a client, as a group member, communicates and interacts with others, he or she is presented with valuable opportunities to acquire new skills, develop greater self-awareness, and help others.

In many instances, a group experience is superior to one-on-one work with an individual. Many clients are more open to ideas, suggestions, and confrontations voiced by peers or other clients than by a professional. For example, an adolescent client is more likely to listen seriously to another adolescent than to a social worker. Moreover, group members are often willing to say things and make observations to one another that a social worker holds back out of fear of offending a client or making a mistake. For example, a social worker might be reluctant to confront a client who seems deceptive or manipulative without certain evidence, but another group member may not hesitate at all before voicing such a suspicion. Groups are viewed as essential in work with clients who are often defensive and manipulative, as is frequently the case with clients whose problems revolve around substance abuse, sexual offenses and related crimes, and domestic abuse.

Despite the many advantages of group work in the delivery of direct services, many practice settings do not make group experiences available to their clients. Workers sometimes presume that their clients do not want to be part of a group. While this may be the case, it should never be presumed. If asked, many clients will react favorably to the idea of joining a group. Another reason some workers do not attempt to develop groups for their clients is the practical difficulty of bringing several clients together at a convenient time and place. Still another barrier is the erroneous belief that for a group to be helpful, the members must all have similar problems, concerns, and backgrounds. While it is true that the development and utilization of a group experience can pose some challenges, the authors urge social workers to expand the use of groups because the advantages and potential benefits for clients far outweigh the difficulties involved.

For the most part, the groups utilized in direct practice are *formed groups*, meaning that they are purposefully created by social workers. This is in contrast to so-called *natural groups*, such as those that develop spontaneously among friends, peers, and neighbors. However, there are occasions when a social worker will work with naturally occurring groups in neighborhoods, schools, and institutional settings. The use of groups in direct social work practice may have as a purpose education, recreation, socialization, therapy or behavior change, or mutual support and self-help. A basic assumption of group work is that what one learns within a small group can be applied to his or her life outside the group.

A group that meets for several sessions will typically move through various *stages of group development:* (1) preaffiliation, (2) power and control, (3) intimacy,

(4) differentiation, and (5) separation. It is during the *preaffiliation stage* that potential members size each other up, consider what they might have in common, and decide whether they want to affiliate with the others and become a part of the group. Unless individuals feel comfortable in the group and see it as somehow beneficial, they are likely to avoid meaningful involvement, even if they remain physically present. During this first stage, members tend to look to and depend on the designated leader for direction and structure.

During the *power and control stage*, members test each other and come to a decision of where they fit in the group. They may challenge each other for position and leadership. Also, members tend to challenge the designated leader. At this time, a number of informal rules develop to govern what is and is not acceptable behavior within the group.

As the members get to know each other, they gradually let down their defenses and the group enters the *intimacy stage*. Members recognize and value what they have in common. Next, the group moves to the stage of *differentiation*, wherein differences of opinion and behavior are exhibited but respected and valued. Members begin to understand that each has a life and important roles outside the group and may behave quite differently in other settings. As the life of the group approaches its ending, it enters the *separation stage* and each member must struggle with the loss of meaningful relationships.

For those who want to make a group experience available to their clients, these guidelines are suggested:

1. Before attempting to plan or design a group, be clear as to its purpose and why the group experience will be of benefit to your clients. Answers to most questions about how best to structure and guide a group will relate directly back to the group's purpose or desired outcome. As a general rule, the more narrow or specialized the group's purpose, the better it serves the members. If all the members have similar concerns and similar reasons for being in the group, they are more likely to become engaged and more willing to share personal thoughts and experiences.

2. Decide which clients are to be offered the group experience. Some social group workers hold definite beliefs about the mix of personalities they want in the group (e.g., having outgoing and verbal members to offset members who are quiet and shy). Also, some group workers may want to eliminate from consideration those who are reputed to be resistant or uncooperative. However, in many practice settings, the worker does not have the luxury of using detailed selection criteria and must simply select for possible membership those who have a need for a group experience, have some ability to tolerate differences of opinion, and have at least a basic capacity to enter into relationships. Once in the group, a voluntary member should feel free to drop out if he or she feels uncomfortable or if the group is not meeting his or her needs.

When screening or selecting potential members, the group worker must balance the needs of the individual with the needs and safety of other members. People exhibiting bizarre or truly dangerous behavior should be eliminated from consideration for membership unless the meetings occur within an institutional setting that provides close supervision. In addition, individuals who are at high risk of suicide or who are actively using or selling illegal drugs may not be appropriate for inclusion.

3. It is often not possible to predict accurately how an individual will behave and function as a group member. As a general rule, however, people will behave in a formed group about as they do in other situations. For example, if an individual has difficulty expressing feelings with family members, he or she will usually carry this same pattern into the group. Likewise, the person who controls and dominates others at work can be expected to try to dominate and control the group.

4. Decide what is an appropriate group size. Size depends on such factors as the age of the clients, concerns to be addressed by the group, and your experience as a leader or facilitator. You will want the group to be small enough so all members have a sense of belonging and a chance to participate but large enough to yield a variety of opinions and minimize pressure on those who are fearful of interaction. You will also need to consider the developmental abilities of the members. For preadolescents, a group of only three or four is often workable. For adolescents, a group of six to eight is about right. For adults, a group of eight to ten is a comfortable size. You must also anticipate the inevitable problem of nonattendance and dropouts. The group must be large enough to continue functioning when some members miss a meeting and after a member or two decides to drop out.

5. Decide on the frequency of meetings and the length of each session. For most adults, a meeting lasting 1 1/2 to 2 hours is about right. Because of limited attention span, shorter but more frequent meetings are usually best for children and adolescents. The practice setting will also dictate the frequency of meetings. In an institutional setting, daily meetings are often possible and desirable. When members are drawn from the larger community, it may not be feasible to meet more often than weekly or monthly.

6. Decide when and where the group will meet. A meeting space should be quiet, private, comfortable, and large enough for people to move around and to accommodate a circle of chairs. The decision of when to meet must consider each member's work and family responsibilities, matters of personal convenience, and, of course, the availability of a meeting room.

7. Decide on the approximate number of times the group will meet. This is, of course, tied to purpose. An information sharing or training group might meet only once or twice, whereas a support or therapy group might meet weekly for several months or longer. Consider setting a limit (e.g., three, five, or ten meetings) with the understanding that at the end of that period, you and the group will decide whether the meetings should continue. This can help keep members involved because they will know there is a planned time to terminate, and it can prevent a group from continuing to meet even when there is no longer a clear purpose for doing so.

8. Decide whether the group will be open or closed to additional members. This is sometimes a decision for the group to make. If it is to be decided by the group, the decision needs to be made during the first or second meeting. Incorporating new members into an already functioning group has the advantage of maintaining group size if some members drop out. Also, new members may bring fresh perspectives. However, the frequent introduction of new members is a barrier to the development of group cohesion and it may limit the intensity of interaction.

9. Decide if the group is for voluntary clients, involuntary clients, or both. Obviously, there are advantages to limiting membership to persons who want to attend. Although involuntary members can be forced by court order to attend, they cannot be forced to interact in a meaningful and productive manner. Nevertheless, the successful utilization of group methods in correctional, chemical dependency, and child abuse treatment programs demonstrates that groups made up of involuntary clients are feasible and can be effective. However, the leader of such groups must be strong and skilled in confronting resistant and manipulative members.

The addition of involuntary members to a basically voluntary group will usually work if the group has been functioning quite well for a time and the involuntary member is willing to cooperate to at least a minimal degree. On the other hand, it is not likely to work if the group is newly formed or has not been functioning well and/or if the involuntary member is highly resistant and disruptive. Before adding a new involuntary member, it is best to wait until the group has reached the intimacy stage. The addition of new members, especially resistant ones, should be avoided during the power and control stage.

10. When extending an invitation to join a group, be prepared to explain how the group will be of benefit, what will happen during the meetings, and the atmosphere you hope to create (e.g., informal, fun, learning, sharing, etc.). Also, offer information that might raise interest and reduce fears about participating.

11. As the group moves through the usual stages of development, assess the functioning of each group member and consider the use of various techniques to deal with identified problems (see Items 8.4, 11.10, and 13.27). The answers to the following questions will help the worker in this assessment:

- Is the member in agreement with the group's purpose and format?
- Is the member personally involved—sharing feelings, opinions, and experiences?
- Does the member attend on a regular basis and participate in discussion or activities?
- Does the member enjoy being with other members?
- Does the member engage in a mix of confrontation and support of others?
- How might the group's activities be modified to address the problems or concerns identified?

12. Be prepared to establish rules (possibly written) to govern the behavior of group members. Possible rules include the following:

- Members are expected to attend all meetings.
- Members are expected to maintain confidentiality.
- Members cannot smoke or do drugs during the meeting.
- Members are not allowed to remain at the meeting if they are under the influence of alcohol or drugs.

- Minor-aged members must have parents' written consent to participate.
- Members are to avoid romantic involvement with other members.
- Members who bring weapons, threaten violence, or engage in sexual harassment will be excluded.

13. Select activities (programs) for each meeting (e.g., introductions, ice breakers, refreshments, structured discussion, role-play, guest speaker, etc.). These activities should be consistent with the group's overall purpose and encourage the type of activity relevant to the group's stage of development (see Item 13.23).

14. Anticipate how you can handle the numerous practical problems associated with a meeting, such as the room is too hot or cold or too large or small; the leader must miss a meeting; members arrive late; members bring uninvited friends; deciding if there will be refreshments and, if so, who will pay; conflict between smokers and nonsmokers; who will remind members of the next meeting; and so on.

SELECTED BIBLIOGRAPHY

Corey, Gerald, Marianne Schneider, and Patrick Callanan. *Group Techniques*, 3rd ed. Belmont, CA: Brooks/Cole, 2004.
Garvin, Charles, Maeda Galinsky, and Lorraine Gutierrez. *Handbook of Social Work with Groups*. New York: Guilford, 2004.
Haslett, Diane. *Group Work Activities in Generalist Practice*. Belmont, CA: Brooke/Cole 2005.
Jacobs, Ed, Robert Masson, and Riley Harvill. *Group Counseling Strategies and Skills*, 2nd ed. Belmont, CA: Brooks/Cole, 2006.

SECTION B

TECHNIQUES AND GUIDELINES FOR INDIRECT PRACTICE

It is especially important for social workers engaged in indirect service activities to give careful attention to the planning and contracting phase of the change process. As systems become more complex, it is increasingly difficult and time consuming to promote meaningful change in a system's ways of operating. When working with organizations and communities, one should also be aware that a change in one system will reverberate not only through that system but through related systems, as well. Therefore, change efforts must be carefully planned and the responsibilities of each actor in the process should be clearly identified.

Planning Activities.   Organization and community planning are forms of social work practice typically performed by social workers with specialized education and training. This book does not intend to address these more complex processes; rather, it provides some guidelines (see Items 12.10 through 12.14) that are useful for the front-line social worker (i.e., the direct practice worker whose job sometimes involves indirect practice activities).

Much of the front-line worker's planning activity related to organizations and communities involves the ability to assess various alternatives for remedying a problem, selecting the best alternative for achieving a positive outcome, and plotting the schedule of tasks and activities to make the change process as efficient and effective as possible. These planning activities should be based on knowledge of how organizations can be changed from within, how ongoing agency planning should occur, the process of planning special projects, and understanding the requirements for developing a primary prevention program.

Contracting Activities.   Once plans for organizational and community change have been developed, there must be explicit agreements among the participating parties about the responsibilities and timetable for carrying out the associated activities. In a community change effort, for example, once an assessment is made and a plan developed, individual or committee assignments for implementing the plan must be agreed upon. Typically, someone must prepare a position statement, someone must organize the people concerned with the issue to take action, someone must contact the media, someone must lobby the decision makers, and so on. These actions must be orchestrated to be sure that they are done in a timely manner, as subsequent actions may depend on those tasks having already been completed.

12.10   ESTABLISHING AND CHANGING ORGANIZATIONS

Purpose: To establish or modify agency goals, policies, and programs.

Discussion: Social agencies stake their claim to specific areas of service provision. They must clearly state their mission, the goals they intend to achieve, the services they will provide, and the policies and procedures they will follow. Only then can the public be accurately informed about the nature of the agency, can clients know what services to expect, can unplanned duplication and overlap of services among agencies be minimized, and can staff members plan and coordinate their work.

An effective social agency is dynamic; it must constantly adapt to community and societal changes, to new knowledge about the nature of personal and social problems, to changes in public attitudes, and to ever-changing fiscal and political realities. Thus, a social worker can expect to participate, to some degree and at some level, in efforts to modify agency goals, structure, and operations.

Public agencies are particularly reactive to any change in the state and federal laws relevant to their areas of service and to budget modifications. In response to such changes, the agency's own policies and procedures may need to undergo significant change during a short period of time.

Private agencies, too, must be capable of responding to a variety of forces. When a private agency is created, the bylaws spell out its mission and decision-making structure. Although the original bylaws may capture the intent of the founders, such agencies must change over time to keep pace with changing community needs and new concepts of service. Leadership for needed change by a private agency often falls first to the executive director and the staff, with the board and/or a broader membership group subsequently amending the bylaws or revising its policies to reflect the needed changes.

Although change is inevitable, an agency, like all social systems, will resist change; in fact, it may take considerable effort to make needed change. The following guidelines suggest what to consider when planning and initiating organizational change:

1. Begin by describing as precisely as possible the change that is needed and why. Then secure and study all documents that may pertain to the desired change. These may include, for example, federal and state laws and regulations, administrative and personnel manuals, union contracts, accreditation standards, agreements and contracts involving other agencies, and so on. The information drawn from these sources will determine, to some degree, what changes are possible, how the change process must proceed, and who else must support or approve the change.

2. Assess the organization's readiness for change. Review its prior experience in accepting change. People are likely to resist change if prior change efforts have been misguided, ineffective, or frustrating. On the other hand, they will tend to accept change if they trust those promoting or leading the change effort, when they believe the proposed change is needed and feasible, and when the proposal has addressed their questions, concerns, and fears about changing.

3. Determine if the desire for change is shared across the various levels, departments, and units of the organization. Pay special attention to the views of those who will be affected most directly by the proposed change. A common and serious error in planning change is to overlook or disregard the opinions of line workers and clerical staff—those who may know most about how the proposed change will affect day-to-day agency operations and agency clients.

4. Assess the degree to which the change is compatible with the agency's mission, traditions, and current goals. Determine the degree to which the change is desired and likely to be supported by top management and the board of directors.

5. Identify and assess the relative strength of the organizational subsystems and individuals who are likely to favor the change and those who will oppose it. Determine who stands to gain and who stands to be hurt by the proposed change. A strategy most likely to overcome resistance is one that either (a) increases the power of those within the agency that favor the change or (b) introduces innovative programs or brings new resources into the organization that will minimize the impact of the change on those who are resistant.

6. The agency, or a unit of the agency, will most likely adopt a proposed change if it can be shown that the change will result in an increase in scope, authority, autonomy, or funds and other resources. A change that decreases power and resources will be resisted. People will favor a change that makes their work easier or more successful; they will resist a change that makes their work more complex or demands more of their time.

7. The members of an organization will strongly resist a change that they perceive as a threat to their jobs, advancement, or opportunities within the organization. Also, they will be resistant to change whenever they suspect others are withholding information about the true intentions of the change.

8. An organization will be more open to a proposed change if it can be demonstrated that other similar organizations have successfully made this change.

9. A change is most likely to be accepted by the organization after its advantages have been demonstrated in a trial run or implemented within only a part of the organization. Thus, it is desirable that the first phase of a more far-reaching change effort begin by focusing on a specific program or activity of limited scope.

10. Whenever possible, changes should be integrated into current structures and procedures so as to minimize the disruption of existing relationships and patterns.

SELECTED BIBLIOGRAPHY

Kaplan, Howard B. *Organizational Innovation: Studies of Program Change in Community Agencies*. New York: Plenum, 2003.

Tropman, John E., John L. Erlich, and Jack Rothman, eds. *Tactics and Techniques of Community Intervention*. Itasca, IL: F. E. Peacock, 2001.

Weinbach, Robert W. *The Social Worker as Manager*, 4th ed. Boston: Allyn & Bacon, 2003.

12.11   THE PROCESS OF AGENCY PLANNING

Purpose: To formulate plans to guide an agency's operations and to maximize its performance.

Discussion: In order to operate in an effective and efficient manner and to grow and develop as an organization, a social agency must formulate both short-range and long-range plans that will guide its ongoing activity and decision making. All too often, agencies neglect long-term planning and then find that they must make hasty decisions and rapid changes in agency operations in response to a situation or crisis they did not anticipate and for which they were unprepared.

Ideally, an agency's planning process is proactive and forward looking. The plan should include a description of how it will utilize its resources (i.e., staff time, money, knowledge, skills, etc.), how it can capitalize on its strengths and opportunities, how it will correct its weaknesses, and how it can respond to certain unwanted but possible future events such as increased demand for service, loss of staff, or a reduction in funding.

A fruitful planning process is complex and time consuming. It can be especially difficult because all planning decisions rest on a set of predictions as to what will happen in future months and years. Unfortunately, it is a complex task to predict accurately the ever-changing political, economic, and public opinion forces that may affect an agency operation. Given these uncertainties, even the best of plans must be constantly reviewed and revised.

Despite all the challenges inherent in planning, an agency must devote time and energy to this activity. Broadly speaking, there are three types of planning processes: (1) problem-solving planning, (2) operational planning, and (3) strategic planning. They differ primarily in terms of the time period covered.

Problem-solving planning has a lifespan of 60 to 90 days. It focuses on some specific problem that is having an adverse effect on the agency's usual activity. The process involves (1) identifying and examining the problem, (2) selecting a set of corrective actions or measures, (3) planning the implementation of these measures, and (4) monitoring the effectiveness of the corrective action. If the agency is successful in its operational and strategic planning, the need for problem-solving planning will be minimized.

Operational planning refers to short-range planning covering a period of 6 to 12 months or perhaps one budget cycle. This planning process formulates objectives, details performance standards, and prepares an action plan to reach the stated objectives.

Strategic planning may cover a period of 3 to 10 years. Basically, the strategic planning process strives to develop a plan for achieving the agency's mission or long-term goals. This type of planning calls for the identification and analysis of broad social and economic trends, for speculation on what challenges and opportunities the agency will face in the next few years, and for forward-looking decisions about how best to use agency resources. Strategic planning is based on the belief that it is important to have a plan that considers all conditions and factors that may impact the agency, regardless of how uncertain the future must be. Because it is so speculative and based on so many uncertain variables, a strategic plan must be continually reviewed and revised.

Following these guidelines will enhance the planning process:

1. Make certain that adequate and accurate data are readily available to those engaged in the planning process. Such data should describe these factors:

- The agency's mission and goals
- Current and projected budgets and a history of the agency's fiscal condition
- Programs and services provided and the number of clients/consumers participating in each program or service area
- Characteristics of the persons served by the agency (e.g., age, income, ethnicity, religion, etc.)
- Agency staff (e.g., education, training, interests, skills, etc.)
- The agency's relationship with other agencies in the community
- Requests and concerns voiced by staff/clients/consumers and other agencies and community groups
- Trends and projections (i.e., demand for services, capacity to raise funds, demographic changes in the community)
- Special problems faced by the agency

2. Keep the planning process as simple as possible so that all those who should participate can do so despite the day-to-day pressures of their other responsibilities. Do not demand more of their time than is absolutely necessary. Keep the number of meetings and the paperwork required to a minimum.

3. Make sure that all who might be affected by a decision or proposed change are invited to participate in the discussion and encouraged to voice their thoughts and concerns. Avoid *top-down planning* (i.e., decision making and planning by only the upper-level administrative personnel).

4. Gather and organize ideas and promote creativity by performing a SWOPA analysis of the agency. The acronym *SWOPA* stands for Strengths, Weaknesses, Opportunities, Problems, and Action.

- *Strengths.* Identify the services, programs, and activities currently provided at a level of quality that meets or exceeds professional standards.
- *Weaknesses.* Identify the services, programs, and activities that fall below acceptable levels of quality or needed levels of quantity.
- *Opportunities.* Identify the service or program activities that are promising for future development or expansion because of growing demand, available funding, staff interest, and so on.
- *Problems.* Identify the areas of agency performance that are especially troublesome.
- *Actions.* Identify activities or changes that would build on agency strengths, exploit opportunities, address areas of weakness, or better manage the problems faced by the agency.

5. Perform a *competition analysis.* This requirement asks those participating in the planning process to examine the activities of other agencies, organizations, or professional groups to determine how they compete with the agency's current programs and services. For example, are other organizations developing services that would attract your agency's clients or staff or are other agencies making requests for the funds now utilized by your agency?

6. Perform a *stakeholder's analysis.* Stakeholders are those individuals, groups, or organizations that have an interest in the agency. Their beliefs, values, and possible reactions to changes in the agency must be given serious consideration. Examples of internal stakeholders are clients/consumers, agency staff, unions representing staff, members of the board of directors, and so on. Examples of external stakeholders include professional associations, politicians, other agencies, businesses and corporations, local newspapers, citizen groups, taxpayers, contributors, former clients, and the like.

7. Perform a *threat analysis.* A threat is some possible future circumstance or action by others that could harm the agency. Examples might include a lawsuit against the agency, an employee strike, loss of funding, loss of key staff, rapid change in community demographics, significant changes in the laws or regulations that affect the agency, damaging news stories, and so forth.

8. Make sure that the many facets of the planning process are coordinated and well integrated. For example, decisions concerning budget, staffing patterns, performance standards, and programs and services to be offered are all interrelated. In particular, financial planning must be incorporated into all other areas of planning. If the many components of the process are not properly coordinated and integrated, much time will be wasted, confusion will occur, and the planning process will flounder.

SELECTED BIBLIOGRAPHY

Chen, Huey I. *Practical Program Evaluation: Assessing and Improving Planning, Implementation, and Effectiveness.* Thousand Oaks, CA: Sage, 2005.

Pawlak, Edward J., and Robert D. Vinter. *Design and Planning Programs for Nonprofit and Government Organizations.* San Francisco: John Wiley and Sons, 2004.

Rogers, Gala, Donna S. Findlay, and John R. Galloway, eds. *Strategic Planning in the Social Services.* Toronto, Canada: University of Toronto Press, 2001.

12.12   SELECTING CHANGE ISSUES FOR ADVOCACY

Purpose: To assist in choosing issues that can bring about change and improve a harmful social condition.

Discussion: Social workers regularly encounter individuals, families, neighborhoods, and various vulnerable population groups who experience social problems that are caused by discrimination or societally imposed factors based on race or ethnicity, gender, age, sexual orientation, and disabling conditions. These people face social problems that diminish the quality of their lives and even make their lives more difficult. At times, a social problem may become so pervasive that it affects many people and it becomes necessary to take action and bring about change.

The social worker can help people recognize and express their concerns about a problem or situation and begin to define the issue. The social worker also can serve an additional important function by mobilizing people to form coalitions to attempt to resolve these issues.

Si Kahn (1991, 84–87), a well-known folk musician and social worker who has been successful in grass-roots organizing, provides a helpful list of items to consider when selecting an issue to address:

- A good issue is winnable (i.e., it is reasonable to believe the desired change can occur).
- A good issue builds the organization or strengthens the group of concerned people.
- A good issue unites people.
- A good issue affects a lot of people.
- A good issue is strongly felt.
- A good issue is simple enough to be stated in one sentence.

Another important part of planning to address an issue is assessing the readiness of the community to change. These questions might prove helpful in examining the capacity of a community to engage in a change effort:

- Are efforts, programs, or policies already in place that attempt to address this issue?
- To what extent do community members know about these efforts and their effectiveness?

- How much do members of the community know about the extent of the problem and the consequences for the persons affected, as well as its impact on the community at large?
- Do elected officials and other influential members of the community support addressing this issue? If not, why?
- Is the prevailing attitude in the community toward this issue one of resignation or one of willingness to assume responsibility for addressing the matter?
- To what extent are people likely to commit time and other resources to bring about change in this situation?

As suggested by these questions, those people who select and define the issue to be addressed must grapple with the fundamental question of whether a particular change effort is feasible, realistic, and likely to succeed. The issue selected must be one that will motivate people and attract their involvement in the change process.

Once an issue has been selected and it has been determined that the community is ready to address it, the next critical step is to build a membership base. Typically, the effort to seek change is initiated by a few highly committed people, but unless the membership can build to a more substantial number, there is little hope for success. Politically, economically, and socially powerful people can best be influenced by an advocacy group when the group's power comes, for example, from having members who might boycott a company or product, form a voting block, or conduct a public demonstration. In other words, the advocacy group must make the general public aware of the unwillingness of those in power to change. Of course, using these confrontational approaches may not be necessary if less polarizing tactics are successful, such as negotiating, collecting and analyzing data for a position paper, conducting a public education campaign, or using other techniques described in the following chapter of this book. However, knowing that an organization has the capacity to mobilize a large group of people for action will help to get the attention of powerful people and encourage them to consider solutions (perhaps requiring compromise from both sides) before a more conflictual situation develops. (For additional information on social change and advocacy, see Items 11.24, 13.33, and 13.40.)

SELECTED BIBLIOGRAPHY

Chaskin, Robert J., Prudence Brown, Sudhir Venkatesh, and Avis Vidal. *Building Community Capacity*. Hawthorne, NY: Aldine de Gruyter, 2001.

Kahn, Si. *Organizing: A Guide for Grassroots Leaders*, rev. ed. Washington, DC: NASW Press, 1991.

Plested, Barbara A., Ruth W. Edwards, and Pamela Jumper-Thurman. *Community Readiness: The Key to Successful Change*. Fort Collins, CO: Colorado State University, Tri-Ethnic Center for Prevention Research, 2003.

12.13   PROJECT PLANNING AND EVALUATION

Purpose: To plan, coordinate, and schedule project activities.

Discussion: The introduction of a new service or special project into the day-to-day operation of a social agency can be disruptive unless it is carefully planned and integrated into the life of the organization. Efficient planning of new activities involves selecting the most effective strategy for accomplishing objectives, scheduling activities to maximize efficiency, and carefully planning the manner in which tasks are completed so as not to disrupt other parts of the agency.

Strategy Selection

Achieving the goals and objectives of a new project calls for the selection of the best possible course of action or strategy from among available alternatives. Craig (1978) identifies five criteria that should be considered in this selection:

1. *Appropriateness.* Is this strategy consistent with the agency's overall mission and goals? Is it consistent with the agency's experience and usual methods and standards of operation? Does the use of this strategy raise any legal or ethical concerns?
2. *Effectiveness.* Given the nature of the problem or issue being addressed by the project, is this strategy likely to be successful in reducing or eliminating it?
3. *Efficiency.* Given the agency's current resources (e.g., funding, available staff time, expertise), is this strategy a more efficient use of those resources?
4. *Adequacy.* Are the actions called for by this strategy ones that will have a real and lasting impact on the problem or issues to be addressed by the project?
5. *Side effects.* What positive and negative side effects could result from using this strategy?

By charting each alternative according to these five criteria, it is possible to compare the advantages and disadvantages of each. Figure 12.5 is an example of a chart that might be developed to compare strategies for increasing the number of minorities and women on the staff of a human services agency.

Scheduling

A variety of techniques have been developed to help schedule specific project activities. One frequently used scheduling tool called a ***Gantt chart*** provides a visual means of depicting the relationship between the activities required for a project and the timeframe for completing each. The activities are listed down the left column, and the periods of work on each activity, charted by month or week, are shown across the top of the page (see Figure 12.6). A Gantt chart is useful because it helps to identify the sequencing required for the entire project and helps to keep track of the completion dates for specific activities.

The Program Evaluation and Review Technique *(PERT chart)* is another useful scheduling tool. This chart is especially helpful for sorting out the proper sequencing of events and estimating the amount of time required to complete each activity or event. When developing a PERT chart, an *activity* is defined as requiring staff time to

FIGURE 12.5	Example of an Alternative Comparison Chart

Objective: To analyze different strategies for creating a process for recruiting and promoting minorities and women that has the support of employee unions and minority advocacy groups

Strategy	Appropriate Yes/No/Maybe	Adequacy Hi/Med/Low	Effectiveness Hi/Med/Low	Efficiency Hi/Med/Low	Side Effect Good/Bad
A. Develop task force of employees and advocates to write a minority recruitment and mentoring plan.	Maybe	Hi	Hi	Med (probable benefits high, so is cost)	*Good*—precedent for better decision-making process. *Bad*—time consuming citizen involvement.
B. Ask for suggestions first, then circulate plan, ask for comments.	Yes	Med	Med	Hi (probable benefits high, cost not so high)	*Good*—precedent for more input in decision making. *Bad*—hostility if we don't adopt their comments.
C. Write plan, then circulate for comments.	Yes	Low	Low	Med (probable benefits low, but so is cost)	*Good*—avoid direct confrontation. *Bad*—plan may not have real support.
D. Copy plan from another city where it was implemented without conflict.	Maybe	Low	Low	Low (low cost, but low benefit too)	*Good*—maybe no one would know we'd done a plan. *Bad*—plan might not fit this community

Source: Craig 1978, p. 52. A Learning Concepts Publication, distributed by University Associates, San Diego. Used with permission of University Associates.

complete. Thus, by adding up the days or hours devoted to the various activities, it is possible to estimate the cost in staff time to carry out the project. An *event* is an action taken by someone other than staff on a target date that affects the timeline of the project. By first identifying the dates on which various events are likely to be completed and then charting the activities that must occur to prepare for each event, it is possible to start with the intended completion date for the project and work backward to build the PERT chart. Figure 12.7 illustrates a section of a PERT chart developed for a client survey regarding the effectiveness of an agency's services.

FIGURE 12.6   Sample Gantt Chart

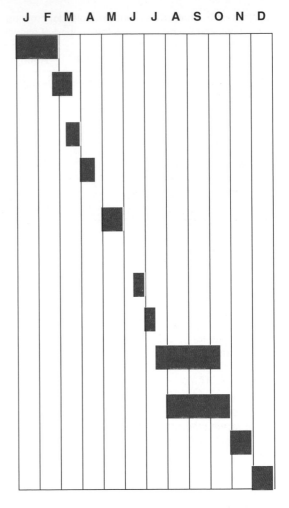

Activity	J F M A M J J A S O N D
1. Collect literature on parent-effectiveness training.	
2. Secure permission to initiate parent-effectiveness training group from supervisor.	
3. Interpret parent-effectiveness training in staff meeting.	
4. Request all workers in unit to nominate families for parent-effectiveness training.	
5. Send letters to nominated families, inviting them to parti-cipate and asking for preference on which night to meet.	
6. Set meeting times, reserve room, and notify families of first meeting.	
7. Make day-care plans for children of the participants.	
8. Prepare presentations and materials for parent-effectiveness training sessions.	
9. Hold 12 weekly meetings with participants.	
10. Assess the value of the sessions to the participants.	
11. Report results to supervisor and other staff members.	

Task Planning

The final step in completing a special project is to identify and carry out the activities required to implement the strategy that has been selected. This step involves identifying the tasks to be completed and the rationale for engaging in this activity, noting when it must be completed and who should be involved, and specifying the time or other resources required for completing the task. Figure 12.8 is an example of a chart that might be developed for this purpose when establishing a task force.

It is noteworthy that if seeking funding to support a project (see Item 13.39), evidence of the careful planning represented by Figures 12.5 through 12.8 can be effective in indicating to funding sources that you have thought out how your plan would be carried out.

FIGURE 12.7   Sample PERT Chart for Client Survey Proposal

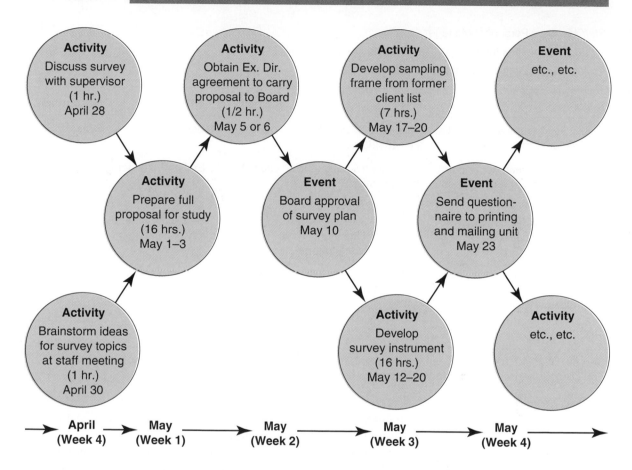

SELECTED BIBLIOGRAPHY

Callahan, Kevin R., and Lynne M. Brooks. *Essentials of Strategic Project Management.* Hoboken, NY: John Wiley and Sons, 2004.

Horine, Greg. *Absolute Beginner's Guide to Project Management.* Indianapolis, IN: Que, 2005.

12.14   PLANNING A PRIMARY PREVENTION PROGRAM

Purpose: To develop a human services program or change strategy intended to prevent problems in social functioning.

Discussion: Most social programs are created as a reaction to an existing problem and are designed to offer treatment or assistance to the people who experience this problem. Equally important are programs designed to prevent the problem from developing

FIGURE 12.8	Example of a Task Planning Sheet

Staff Member: Personnel Manager
Strategy: Form task force to develop Affirmative Action Plan
Activity: Get agreement of members to serve on task force

Tasks	Why?	When?	Who?	Resources?
1. List key groups and potential task force members.	Make sure all possibilities are considered.	Jan.3	Self	3 hrs.
2. Go over list with department director and agree on whom to approach.	Get director's perspective and approval.	Jan. 4	Self and director	2 hrs.
3. Review overall strategy with department director.	Make sure we're on same wavelength, confirm commitment to strategy.	Jan. 4	Self, director, and key clerical staff	same meeting as #2
4. Arrange meetings with some potential members for preliminary discussion.	Person-to-person, informal approach most likely to succeed.	Jan 15–22	Self and potential members	6 hrs.
5. Etc.				

Source: Craig 1978, p. 80. A Learning Concepts Publication, distributed by University Associates, San Diego. Used with permission of University Associates.

in the first place. Prevention efforts are desirable and logical, but the actual design of an effective prevention program is complex and difficult.

Although many view prevention as essentially different from intervention, it is useful to treat prevention as a type of intervention. ***Primary prevention*** consists of a set of actions intended to intervene and modify those conditions or situations that will, if not changed, lead to a significant problem. Thus, those engaged in planning a prevention effort must be able to identify the specific factors, conditions, and situations that cause or give rise to a problem and then identify a set of actions and activities that will reduce or eliminate their impact.

Increasingly, primary prevention programs are built around ideas of risk and resiliency. In relation to children and youth, for example, considerable research identifies a high correlation between certain negative family, neighborhood, and community influences and the development of social problems such as delinquency, drug and alcohol abuse, school dropout, emotional disturbance, gang activity, and teen pregnancy. Among the corrosive influences that give rise to these problems are poverty, discrimination, lack of opportunity, family breakdown and dysfunction, feelings of low self-worth, easy access to drugs and alcohol, and poor schools. For reasons not well understood, some young people are more "resistant" to these influences than others. They have within their personalities, environment, and life experiences certain protective factors that shield them from the full force of negative influences. They are said to possess *resiliency* in that even when exposed to stress, trauma, and adversity, they do not develop serious problems. A variety of protective factors appear to contribute to resiliency in children and youth. Benard (1991), for example, believes that three protective factors are of critical importance:

- The child has a caring and supportive relationship with at least one adult (this may or may not be a parent).
- Some meaningful person(s) in the child's life communicates consistently high expectations of the child.
- The child has ample opportunity to participate in and contribute meaningfully to others in his or her social environment.

Resiliency-related research suggests that both children and adults are more adaptive and flexible than we often assume, and that the process of human development and adjustment includes many self-righting mechanisms that can compensate for trauma and life stressors. Some of these protective factors are found in the person's personality and behavior patterns (e.g., self-confidence, self-esteem, problem-solving skills, etc.), warm and supportive relationships within his or her family, the presence of caring people in the school or work environment, and/or supportive factors in one's ethnic, neighborhood, or community interactions. This is not meant to suggest that stages of human development do not exist or that what happens at one point in a person's development has no impact on what follows. Rather, it suggests that the developmental stages and the impact of significant events are more elastic than often assumed and it is possible for people to overcome serious problems that arise in their lives.

As part of their commitment to facilitating change in both the person and the environment, social workers must be skilled at designing and implementing primary prevention programs. Following these general guidelines will help those planning to engage in primary prevention:

1. Enter the initial planning stage with caution and thoughtfulness; a poorly designed program is likely to fail. Early in the planning process, consult with those people who have experience in designing prevention programs and review the literature that reports efforts to address these target problems.

2. Clearly define and describe the problem or condition you are attempting to prevent. Without an operational definition of your target problem, you cannot design an effective program of prevention.

3. Identify the indicators of the problem you are addressing and its current level of seriousness so that you can later measure the impact of your prevention effort. Without a way of measuring success, your program is not likely to attract funding and support for more than a brief demonstration period. Make sure that these indicators are understandable, measurable, and important to those who are paying for this prevention program. Consult the literature and people skilled at program evaluation (see Item 14.9) early in the planning process.

4. Recognize that any plan you may select to prevent a problem rests on the knowledge, beliefs, and assumptions made about when, why, and how this problem develops, as well as judgments about which individuals or groups are most likely to experience this problem. Thus, a critical step in planning is to formulate and articulate one's beliefs about the nature and causes of the problem to be prevented. This is a challenge because the social and behavioral sciences are seldom able to identify clear cause and effect relationships. Social problems are complex and a whole host of interrelated factors contribute to their development.

5. Once the factors that cause the problem have been identified, it is necessary to decide which contributing factors, if any, can be influenced and changed. Identify the specific risk and protective factors related to the problem you want to prevent. A *risk factor* is a condition, situation, or set of circumstances that increases the likelihood that a person will develop the problem you seek to prevent. A *protective factor* is a condition or circumstance that reduces the chance that the problem will develop. The prevention program should be designed to weaken or reduce risk factors and, at the same time, strengthen or expand protective factors. As a general rule, a prevention program is most likely to be effective and efficient if it targets those at greatest risk of developing the problem.

6. Finally, determine how the necessary changes can best be accomplished. In many cases, important contributing causes (e.g., large-scale economic and societal forces) are beyond the reach of community-based programs. A social worker may choose instead to engage in advocacy for change at the state or national levels. In other cases, the action plan would require intervention at the local level or at both the local and national levels.

SELECTED BIBLIOGRAPHY

Gullotta, Thomas P., and Martin Bloom, eds. *Encyclopedia of Primary Prevention and Health Practice*. New York: Plenum, 2003.
Simeonsson, Rune, ed. *Risk, Resilience and Prevention*. Baltimore: Paul Brooks, 1994.

13 Intervention and Monitoring

INTRODUCTION

Intervention and monitoring is the most visible phase in the change process. Sometimes called the *action phase*, it is the time the client, the social worker, and others take the steps and complete the tasks that will implement the plan they believe will bring about the desired outcome. During this phase, all prior efforts to examine the presenting concern and to formulate a workable plan are transformed into action.

Each phase of the change process builds on and is dependent on the prior phases. Thus, whether the intervention actually achieves the desired outcome will depend upon the accuracy, completeness, and validity of the conclusions reached and the decisions made during the prior phases, such as problem definition, data collection, assessment, and planning.

Perhaps because intervention requires concrete actions and typically takes up most of the time and energy expended during a change process, many helpful intervention techniques have been developed. Often, the greatest challenge for the social worker serving individuals, families, groups, organizations, and communities is to select the most appropriate approach and techniques to facilitate change.

As the interventive activities unfold, another task of the social worker is to *monitor,* or keep track of what is happening and continuously evaluate the progress of the intervention. Depending on how well it is succeeding, the social worker must decide if the intervention should be continued, modified, or possibly aborted and a new plan and contract negotiated. Monitoring differs from evaluation in that monitoring occurs while the intervention is happening, whereas evaluation takes place at the end of the change process—looking back to assess what happened.

One often overlooked element of monitoring is continuing to examine the situation for a period of time before completely terminating the professional relationship and the change process. Whenever change occurs, various systems are disrupted, and progress will possibly deteriorate over time. The social worker should therefore attempt to determine if the change is more than a temporary accommodation to the interventive activities and to ensure that the desired change has become firmly established as part of the ongoing functioning for the client and/or the relevant environment.

363

SECTION A

TECHNIQUES AND GUIDELINES FOR DIRECT PRACTICE

When working with individuals, families, and small groups, the social worker's responsibility is to adapt the intervention approach to the uniqueness of the people involved and to support the clients as they take the necessary actions to bring about the planned change. The worker, too, must constantly monitor the client's response to the process and regularly assess progress toward the agreed upon objectives.

Intervention Activities.   As the social worker engages a client in a helping relationship and introduces the client to the process of change, the social worker must select an appropriate practice framework to guide this process (See Chapter 6). In addition, the worker must choose a number of specific techniques and guidelines that are likely to facilitate and support change. In Section A of this chapter an array of direct-service techniques and guidelines are presented. These are but a selection or a sampling. Social work literature, supervisors, colleagues, and workshops are sources of still others. None, however, is likely to be effective unless it is used by a caring and competent social worker.

Monitoring Activities.   Monitoring involves keeping watch over the change process. To do this, the social worker must regularly interact in person or through other communication forms with the clients. The worker must be sensitive to how the change activities are affecting the client, but also to how other people or related social systems are being affected. If progress toward the agreed upon objectives is lacking, the worker then should suggest needed modifications in the intervention plan and possibly even cycle back to the beginning phases of the process to reexamine and clarify the issues being addressed and to look for other solutions.

Whenever possible, the social worker should share the results of this monitoring with the clients. When clients are aware of the changes that are occuring, whether positive or negative, they are more likely to involve themselves more deeply in the change porcess and come up with useful modifications to the intervention plan. Most often, these results are fed back to the client in an informal manner as part of regular counseling or therapy sessions. Increasingly, however, social workers are collecting empirical data about client change and feeding that information back to clients to assist them in understanding the affects of the services being provided. Some of the commonly used tools for organizing data regarding changes that result from direct practice interventions can be found in Chapter 14.

As explained in Chapter 7 and elsewhere in this book, the process of making change happen is often difficult, frustrating, and slow. When clients do not find a quick solution to their problems or when they slip back into an old and troubling pattern or habit, they may become discouraged and tempted to give up. Change can be scary because it usually requires that clients do things differently, make difficult decisions, learn new skills, view their situation from a different angle, or place themselves in an unfamiliar social environment. When clients are hesitant or fearful about moving ahead, it can be helpful to remind them that "when nothing changes, nothing changes." In other words, achieving a desired change requires a genuine effort to try something new. Without that effort, nothing can possibly change.

13.1   PLANNING AN INTERVIEW

Purpose: To formulate a tentative plan for an interview or contact with a client.

Discussion: One of the most common errors made by new workers is to go into a session without a clear purpose. Just as there should be an overall intervention plan, there should be a plan for each contact with the client. However, this plan must be tentative and flexible in order to respond to client concerns that could not be anticipated. The following questions can help the worker formulate such a plan:

1. What are the overall goals and objectives of the intervention with this client? How will my next session or contact relate to these goals and objectives?

2. What needs to be accomplished during the interview or meeting? What decisions need to be reached during the session?

3. Should the next contact be a face-to-face or a telephone interview? One-on-one, family, or group session? Who needs to be present?

4. Will other professionals and/or concerned individuals participate in the session (e.g., a family conference in a medical setting)? What objectives do these other participants have, and how might differences in expectations be resolved?

5. How much time do I have to devote to the interview or meeting? How much time can the client devote to the session?

6. Where and when will the interview take place? What arrangements are necessary prior to the interview (e.g., scheduling interviewing room, transportation, care for client's children)?

7. What techniques might be used during the session to complete important tasks and work toward intervention goals and objectives?

8. What factors related to the client's current emotional state (e.g., anger, fear, confusion, depression, etc.) need to be considered in preparing for the session?

9. What factors related to the client's current physical functioning (e.g., mobility, pain, discomfort, hearing problems, effects of medication, etc.) need to be considered in preparing for the interview or meeting?

10. What factors related to the client's values or religious beliefs and social and family network need to be considered in preparing for the session?

11. What documentation of this contact is necessary for the agency record?

SELECTED BIBLIOGRAPHY

Kadushin, Alfred, and Goldie Kodushin. *The Social Work Interview*, 4th ed. New York: Columbia University Press, 1997.

Murphy, Bianca, and Carolyn Dillon. *Interviewing in Action*, 3rd ed. Belmont, CA: Wadsworth, 2007.

13.2   INFORMATION AND ADVICE

Purpose: To enhance the client's problem-solving capacity by providing needed information and guidance.

Discussion: *Information giving* refers to providing a client with information he or she needs to make a decision or carry out a task. As used here, the term *advice giving* refers to worker statements that recommend what a client should do. In information giving, the client feels free to use the information as he or she sees fit; in advice giving, the client clearly senses the social worker's preference.

One of the common errors made by inexperienced social workers is to give advice when the client has not asked for it. This is an understandable error because often the worker has known other clients with similar problems or has had personal experience with the concern faced by the client, and naturally, the worker wants the client to benefit from those experiences. However, there are many pitfalls in advice giving, and the worker needs to be very cautious in using this technique. Follow these guidelines for advice giving:

1. Before giving advice to a client, reflect on how you feel when someone gives you advice. In most instances, we feel uncomfortable when on the receiving end of someone's advice, regardless of their good intentions. Also, remember that most of us do not always follow advice, even when we have requested it. When we do follow advice, it is usually advice provided by a person we know very well and trust completely.

2. Whether the giving of advice is appropriate depends largely on the purpose of the worker-client interaction. If it is a counseling-therapy relationship, giving advice is seldom appropriate. If the purpose relates to referral, obtaining a needed service, or advocacy, advice giving may be important and necessary.

3. Consider the issue of legal liability if you advise a client and he or she later experiences an adverse personal or financial consequence as a result of your recommendation. For example, beware of advising a client who asks questions such as "Do you think I should get a divorce? Do you think I should quit my job and look for another? Do you think it would be OK if I cut down on my medicine?"

4. Be alert to the dangers of giving advice to a manipulative client, who may then hold you responsible if things do not turn out well (e.g., "I did what you said and it didn't work, so it's your fault"). Also be alert to the danger of encouraging dependency in a client who can and should take responsibility for decision making.

5. Do not offer advice until you have determined that the client genuinely wants your opinions and suggestions. Test the client's receptivity to advice by asking questions such as "Have you asked others for suggestions?" and "May I tell you what other people usually do in that situation?"

6. When you do give advice, present it in a way that says, "This is what I would do," or "This is what others have done." But leave the responsibility for deciding what to do to the client. Explain the reasoning behind the guidance you offer. Never give advice on a topic outside your area of training and expertise.

When providing information to a client, keep these guidelines for information giving in mind:

1. Carefully consider the client's state of mind. For example, if the client is anxious or overwhelmed, he or she may not comprehend or remember the information or instructions you provide. Adapt what you say to the client's educational background, intelligence, command of the language, and the like. If it is likely that the client will not understand or will be confused by your message, seek his or her permission to also convey this information to family members or trusted friends so they might help the client understand and make use of the information.

2. Provide information or directions in a logical, step-by-step fashion. Give the client time to think about what you are saying, and invite him or her to ask questions to clarify any uncertainty. After giving information to a client, it is desirable to end your message with something like "Now I want to make sure that I was clear in what I have been telling you. Would you please repeat back to me what you heard me say?" Do not simply ask "Do you understand?" All too often, people will answer by saying that they understand even when they do not. It is important always to check that your message was understood.

3. Complicated, multistep instructions (e.g., how to get to another agency) may need to be written down. Also write out names, addresses, and phone numbers needed by the client.

4. Use pronouns (e.g., *it, this, that, those, them*) with caution. For example, the statement "Fill out the form and take it to the person at the desk over there" could be very confusing to someone who does not know what the "form," "it," "person," or "over there" mean specifically. It is best to use the exact word rather than a pronoun, or provide sufficient description so there can be no mistake about what or to whom you are referring.

SELECTED BIBLIOGRAPHY

Murphy, Bianca, and Carolyn Dillon. *Interviewing in Action*, 3rd ed. Belmont, CA: Brooks/Cole, 2007.

Shebib, Bob. *Choices: Counseling Skills for Social Workers and Other Professionals*. Boston: Allyn & Bacon, 2003.

Shulman, Lawrence. *The Skills of Helping Individuals, Families, Groups, and Communities*, 5th ed. Belmont, CA: Brooks/Cole, 2006.

13.3   ENCOURAGEMENT, REASSURANCE, AND UNIVERSALIZATION

Purpose: To enhance the client's problem-solving capacity by providing supportive and encouraging statements.

Discussion: The interrelated techniques of encouragement, reassurance, and universalization are used to help a client move ahead and get past the barriers of self-doubt and uncertainty. These techniques are especially important when working with clients who lack self-confidence or are fearful about taking necessary steps in the process of change. The word *encouragement* literally means to give courage or help another overcome fear. Thus, providing encouragement often takes the form of worker statements that express confidence in the client's ability to overcome an obstacle. The social worker's words of encouragement must be genuine and individualized to the client's situation. For example:

> "I know that the reoccurrence of your cancer is devastating news and that you do not want to tell this to your children. However, they are waiting to hear what you have learned from the doctor. This is one of those times when it is very difficult to be a mother. Telling them the truth is a way of showing your love for them. This is a time when you must be very strong for your children. It will be hard but it needs to be done."

Statements of *reassurance* are appropriately used when the client is doubtful or unsure of his or her decisions and actions when they are, in fact, reasonable and realistic. Such worker statements must be based in reality or else the client will conclude that the worker does not fully comprehend the situation. Trite comments such as "I am sure everything will be OK," or "You can do anything you set your mind to" will be of little help. At best the client will accept such a statement as a gesture of politeness: at worst, he or she will feel patronized and insulted. By always tying words of reassurance to the facts of the client's situation, the worker will avoid sounding phony or naïve. For example:

> "Even though you are now feeling scared and unprepared, I am confident that you will be able to handle this new job assignment. I say that because over the past two months you have successfully taken on three new and difficult job-related responsibilities. That shows you have the ability."

Universalization is a form of reassurance that consists of statements explaining to the client that his or her thoughts, feelings, or behavior are similar to those of other people—for example, "I have known many people who had to place their parent in a nursing home and they described the same feelings you are expressing." This technique is intended to counteract the client's perception that how he or she is feeling or behaving is strange or unusual.

In every session with a client some time should be devoted to talking about client experiences that are positive and that make the client feel good about himself or herself. This is important because so often counseling or therapy sessions focus mostly on problems and on what is going wrong in the client's life. To counterbalance this attention to the negative, a social worker should create opportunities for clients to recognize and verbalize their successes and strengths.

SELECTED BIBLIOGRAPHY

Kottler, Jeffery. *Nuts and Bolts of Helping.* Boston: Allyn & Bacon, 2000.

Woods, Mary, and Florence Hollis. *Casework: A Psychosocial Therapy*, 5th ed. New York: McGraw-Hill, 2000.

13.4 REINFORCEMENT AND RELATED BEHAVIORAL TECHNIQUES

Purpose: To modify the frequency, intensity, or duration of a specific behavior.

Discussion: Behavioral techniques are some of the most powerful available to the social worker when the intervention objective is to help the client learn a new behavior or modify an existing one. The social worker employs behavioral techniques when trying either to strengthen (increase) or weaken (decrease) a particular target behavior. The term *target behavior* refers to an operationally defined and measurable behavior that is the focus of the intervention.

Reinforcement is any event or activity that increases the likelihood that a target behavior will occur more frequently. Thus, a reinforcer is anything that strengthens a target behavior. There are two forms of reinforcement: positive and negative. *Positive reinforcement* involves adding, presenting, or giving something to the client (such as attention, objects of value, or privileges) that has the effect of increasing the target behavior. A positive reinforcer is usually something that is desirable or pleasurable (e.g., praise, money, candy), but for some individuals, a painful event could actually be a reinforcer (e.g., self-mutilation, head banging). Thus, only by observing the effects of what is assumed to be a reinforcer can the worker know for sure what is and is not a reinforcer for a given individual. In order to observe the effects, it is necessary to establish a *baseline measurement* that describes the frequency, intensity, or duration of the target behavior prior to intervention.

There are two kinds of positive reinforcers: primary and secondary. *Primary reinforcers* are inherently rewarding and almost universally reinforcing. Examples include food, water, sex, and so on. *Secondary reinforcers* are learned, usually as a result of having been associated with primary reinforcers. Examples include money, tokens, and new clothes. Social reinforcers—such as praise, attention, and hugs—are usually considered to be secondary reinforcers, but there is some evidence that they are universally reinforcing. As a general rule, what a person chooses to do when he or she does not have to do something else is an indicator of what is reinforcing for that person (e.g., how a person spends extra time and money).

Both positive and negative reinforcement increase the frequency, intensity, or duration of a target behavior. ***Negative reinforcement*** involves subtracting or removing some condition that is aversive or unpleasant to the client, which has the effect of increasing or strengthening the target behavior. Negative reinforcement is often confused with punishment, but they are not the same. Punishment weakens the target behavior, whereas negative reinforcement strengthens the behavior.

As a technique of behavior change, ***punishment*** involves the presentation of an unwanted or unpleasant stimulus (event) that has the effect of suppressing a target behavior or reducing its strength. For ethical and legal reasons, the social worker must usually avoid the use of punishment. Most agencies and treatment programs prohibit the use of punishment for one or more of the following reasons:

1. Often, the results of punishment are short term. When the threat of punishment is not present, the target behavior often recurs.
2. The use of punishment provides a poor behavioral model for the client.
3. Punishment can become excessive when administered by a person who is angry or frustrated.
4. Punishment may also suppress desirable behavior and make the client afraid to respond in normal ways.
5. The use of physical punishment may make the worker vulnerable to a civil lawsuit or criminal charges (e.g., assault).

A behavior that is not reinforced tends to decrease in frequency, duration, or intensity. The term *extinction* describes the planned withdrawal of whatever reinforces a target behavior so as to eliminate or weaken that behavior.

There are two basic ***reinforcement schedules:*** continuous and intermittent. *Continuous reinforcement* provides a reinforcer each time the desired target behavior occurs. In *intermittent reinforcement*, the target behavior is not always rewarded. Continuous reinforcement is often used in the first stages of a program designed to teach a new behavior because it allows faster learning than intermittent reinforcement. However, a behavior that has been continuously reinforced is comparatively easy to extinguish. To make the newly learned behavior resistant to extinction, continuous reinforcement should be replaced by intermittent reinforcement. A behavior that is maintained by *random reinforcement* (e.g., slot machine, bingo, fishing, etc.) or learned during a time of high emotion or personal crisis is highly resistant to change and difficult to extinguish.

When one behavior is described as being incompatible with another, it means that a person cannot perform both behaviors concurrently. For example, a child cannot play basketball and watch TV at the same time. A highly useful technique in planned behavior change is to recognize such an incompatibility and ignore an unwanted target behavior while at the same time reinforcing an incompatible desired behavior. This is called ***differential reinforcement***.

The techniques of chaining, prompting, fading, and shaping are useful when the objective is to help a client learn a new behavior. These are frequently used in training programs for people who are mentally retarded, in speech therapy, and in certain aspects of physical rehabilitation. *Chaining* refers to a procedure that breaks down a complex behavior (e.g., dressing) into many separate steps or components and teaches only one of these steps at a time. As new components are learned, they are "chained," or linked, to the ones already learned. The number of steps needed to teach a particular behavior will depend on the complexity of the behavior and the capacity of the client. There are two types of chaining: forward and backward.

In *forward chaining*, the first step in a chain is taught first. For example, in teaching a client to put on his trousers, the client would first be taught how to pick up and hold his pants. All subsequent steps are taught in order of their natural sequence. This sequence is determined by observing several people perform the behavior and noting the most common sequence of steps.

In *backward chaining*, the last step in the chain is taught first. Thus, all of the steps in the sequence would be done for the client except the one being taught. For example, in dressing training, the first step to be taught would be "pulls pants up to the waist." One advantage of backward chaining is that the last step in the chain is always the one that is reinforced. Thus, the client is always reinforced at the very end of the behavior chain (e.g., when he has finished putting on his pants). For some self-help skills, such as hand and face washing, backward chaining is not feasible.

The term *prompting* describes any form of assistance given by the worker to help the client perform the target behavior. A prompt may be a verbal cue or instruction, a gesture or other nonverbal cue, or physically moving or guiding the client through the behavior. Prompting should be used only when necessary.

Fading is the process of gradually withdrawing prompts and decreasing the frequency of reinforcement as the client begins to learn the desired behavior. In the first steps of a training program, the worker will use continuous reinforcement and frequent prompting to help establish the new behavior. Later, when the client regularly performs the target behavior, the worker will gradually "fade out" or decrease the frequency of reinforcement and prompting.

Shaping is a technique of building a new behavior by reinforcing close approximations of the desired response. For example, a speech therapist teaching a child to say "cookie" may reward the child when he says "gowk." Perhaps later, the child is reinforced for saying "gook-koo" and still later, "gookie." Finally, after many weeks of reinforcing the child for closer and closer approximations of the desired sound, the child is able to say "cookie."

Much of what one learns—especially social or interactional behavior—is learned by observing others and subsequently imitating their behavior. This learning process is termed *modeling*. Needless to say, both functional and dysfunctional behaviors are learned this way. A social worker can enhance the learning of functional behavior by keeping several principles in mind:

- Individual A is most likely to imitate the behavior of individual B (the model) if he or she views B as having some valued status (e.g., power, prestige, attractiveness, etc.) and if he or she observes B being rewarded for the behavior.

■ In addition, individual A must in some way identify with B and feel similar. If A views B as being completely different, individual A may conclude there is no chance he or she could actually perform the behavior and/or that there was little or no chance that it would be rewarded.

■ Individual A is most likely to learn B's behavior if he or she has an opportunity to perform or practice the behavior soon after observing it and is then rewarded for the behavior.

Under ordinary conditions, licensed foster parents and child care staff working in hospitals, treatment centers, and group homes are prohibited from using any form of physical punishment. The procedure termed ***time out*** is an alternative to physical discipline. Its purpose is to reduce or eliminate a problem behavior by temporarily removing the client from an environment that is reinforcing the unwanted behavior. Consider this set of instructions given to a foster parent who is learning methods of nonviolent child care for use with a 7-year-old, male, foster child:

1. Find an area in your home that can be used for time out. If he kicks, throws things, or has tantrums, be sure to choose an area that has no breakable or dangerous objects. You might use his bedroom or other quiet area that is well lighted and ventilated.

2. Identify the undesirable or unacceptable behaviors that will result in time out (i.e., clearly define the target behavior). For example, you may decide to use time out whenever he hits other children.

3. Each time a target behavior occurs, use the time-out procedure immediately. Walk up to the child, explain what rule was broken, and tell him what must now happen—for example, "Johnny, whenever you hit your sister, you must go to time out." Accompany the child to the time-out area; do not look at or talk to him on the way. If he resists, carry him there as quickly as possible.

4. Leave him in the time-out area for a preselected period of time. As a rule of thumb, use the formula of one minute per year of the child's age. At the end of the time period or when he is quiet and behaving well, go to the door and ask if he is ready to come out and behave correctly. For example, if Johnny threw toys, ask him, "Are you ready to come out and put your toys away?" If he hit his sister, ask, "Are you ready to come out and be friendly to your sister?"

5. If he answers this question yes, have him come out and correct the earlier behavior. Reinforce the correct behavior with praise. For example, say, "I like the way you are picking up your toys."

6. If he does not answer yes or screams, cries, throws a tantrum, or displays other undesirable behavior, walk away from the door and wait until he is again quiet and behaving appropriately. Then go back and repeat the question.

7. At first, you may have to question him several times before he is ready to come out and correct the bad behavior. Do not be discouraged—just continue to follow these rules.

8. Try to arrange a special activity, privilege, or treat at the end of each day that he did not have to be taken to the time-out area, and tell him that the reward is for his good behavior.

SELECTED BIBLIOGRAPHY

Hersen, Michel, ed. *Encyclopedia of Behavior Modification and Cognitive Behavior Therapy* (three volumes). Thousand Oaks, CA: Sage Publications, 2005.

Martin, Gary, and Joseph Pear. *Behavior Modification*, 8th ed. Englewood Cliffs, NJ: Prentice Hall, 2005.

Sundel, Martin, and Sandra Sundel. *Behavior Change in the Human Services*, 5th ed. Thousand Oaks, CA: Sage, 2005.

Thyer, Bruce, and John Wodarski. *Handbook of Empirical Social Work Practice*. New York: Wiley, 1998.

13.5 BEHAVIORAL REHEARSAL

Purpose: To assist the client in learning a new behavior to better cope with a particular situation.

Discussion: *Behavioral rehearsal* is a technique designed to teach a client how to handle a specific interpersonal exchange or a situation for which he or she feels unprepared. Essentially, it is a form of role-playing that makes use of modeling and coaching. Like other forms of role-play, behavioral rehearsal provides the client with an opportunity to try out new behaviors in a protected or safe environment. For example, the technique can be used to prepare a client for a job interview (e.g., the social worker takes the role of the employer and conducts a simulated job interview). As the client practices the behavior, the worker provides feedback and offers suggestions and alternative ways of behaving. The worker may demonstrate or model the desired behavior, so it can be imitated by the client. Whether used during a one-to-one interview or during a group session, the steps are basically the same:

1. The client identifies the problem situation and then describes or demonstrates how he or she would usually behave in that situation.
2. The worker (and/or group members) makes suggestions on how the situation might be handled more effectively.
3. The client is given an opportunity to provide additional information about the problem or concern and to ask the worker (or group members) to further explain the suggestions.
4. A role-play is used to demonstrate the behavioral changes suggested to the client. The worker (or group members) will usually take the role of the client. However, the client may enact the behavior if he or she feels ready and understands the changes being suggested.
5. After the role-play, the worker (or members) first identifies the positive aspects of the performance, then makes additional suggestions for improvement. If necessary, the role-play is repeated to further illustrate the preferred way of behaving.
6. When the client understands how he or she ought to behave, he or she practices the behavior until satisfied with the performance.
7. Homework outside the session can be used to further the client's learning of the new behavior.

A possible limitation of behavioral rehearsal is that the client may perform well in the presence of the worker but may not be able to generalize this behavior to the real world. Sometimes the real situation poses problems that cannot be anticipated during a practice session.

SELECTED BIBLIOGRAPHY

Rose, Sheldon. *Group Therapy: A Behavioral Approach*. Englewood Cliffs, NJ: Prentice Hall, 1977.
Spiegler, Michael, and David Guevremont. *Contemporary Behavior Therapy*, 4th ed. Belmont, CA: Wadsworth, 2003.

13.6   BEHAVIORAL CONTRACTING

Purpose: To modify a behavior through the mutual exchange of reinforcers.

Discussion: A ***behavioral contract*** is an agreement designed to bring about a change in a person's behavior. It usually involves an exchange of rewards or positive reinforcements between two or more persons. DeRisi and Butz (1975, 1–2) explain that behavior contracting "is a technique used to structure behavioral counseling by making each of the necessary elements of the process so clear and explicit that they may be written into an agreement for behavior change that is understandable and acceptable to everyone involved."

There are two forms of behavioral contracting. In a ***contingency contract***, one person (often a professional) arranges for a positive consequence to follow performance of a given behavior by another person (such as a client). For example, a group home manager may agree to take a resident to a movie if the resident cleans his or her room five days in a row. By contrast, a ***reciprocal behavior contract*** is an agreement between the members of a dyad (e.g., husband-wife), in which each agrees to reward the other for the performance of a desired behavior. For example, the husband agrees to take his wife to a movie of her choice if she will take the car to the repair shop, and she agrees to cook his favorite meal if he will clean the house.

Thus, we see that a behavioral contract might be negotiated between the social worker and the client, or the worker may help two or more clients (e.g., a husband and wife, parent and child) negotiate their own behavioral contract. Any behavior can become the focus or target of a contract so long as the behavior can be described clearly. Target behaviors should be described in positive terms; the contract should describe what a person *will* do rather than what he or she *will not* do. Also, the contract should be developed in a way that makes success likely, for success sustains motivation.

When helping to formulate a reciprocal behavioral contract to be used by a couple or family, the following guidelines are important:

1. Assist all parties to select a change (or target behavior) that will provide some immediate reward or relief from their problems. Make sure that each person stands to receive some desired payoff for participating and completing the tasks.
2. Select tasks that everyone agrees are worthwhile and possible, given the current circumstances.

3. Select tasks that can be easily observed so there will be no disagreement as to whether a task was completed.
4. Select tasks that allow for approximation. It should be possible to observe even a partial success and a person's genuine effort to complete the task.
5. Set up a simple plan for recording task completion and the exchange of rewards.
6. Before the participants leave the negotiation session, ask each one to describe and explain the contract and the tasks he or she has agreed to carry out. Make sure there is no misunderstanding.

Variations of the contingency behavioral contracting, often called ***point systems*** or ***token economies***, are frequently used in special educational settings and residential treatment facilities. Under such systems, a client earns points or tokens for performing desired behaviors (e.g., completing homework, saying thank you, cleaning one's room) and can then use the tokens to "purchase" desired objects or privileges.

When using a contingency contract, the reinforcement (rewards) for compliance, along with any adverse consequences for noncompliance, should be clearly described and understood by all. Whenever noncompliance can have serious consequences for a client, the contract should be in writing. In other situations, a verbal agreement may suffice.

SELECTED BIBLIOGRAPHY

DeRisi, William, and George Butz. *Writing Behavioral Contracts.* Champaign, IL: Research Press, 1975.

Gambrill, Eileen. *Social Work Practice,* 2nd ed. New York: Oxford University Press, 2006.

Stuart, Richard. *Helping Couples Change: A Social Learning Approach to Marital Therapy.* New York: Guilford, 1980.

13.7   ROLE REVERSAL

Purpose: To assist the client in understanding the viewpoint and feelings of a significant other.

Discussion: When people begin to understand one another's viewpoints, their relationship begins to change. When applying the technique known as ***role reversal***, the social worker asks a client to take on the perspective or vantage point of another person in an effort to better understand that person. This technique allows the individual to observe and hear his or her own attitudes and messages, as interpreted and dramatized by another. It is especially useful during marriage and family counseling when, for example, a husband and wife or a parent and child are in conflict and one or both have little awareness of how the other is thinking and feeling. The best time to use role reversal is when the communication between the two individuals has reached an impasse or when one or both is "stuck" in a particular assumption or notion about why the other is behaving in a certain way.

The worker might initiate the role reversal by saying something like "Joe and Susan, would you two be willing to try something? I would like you to reverse roles to see how it feels being the other person." The two people are then asked to switch chairs; if the clients do not change chairs, they often become confused as to which role they are playing. The worker should explain, "In this chair, you are yourself. In that chair, you are Joe."

Once they are in the role or mindset of the other, the social worker might get the discussion going by focusing attention on a particular line of repetitious or contentious dialogue—for example, "Joe, I want you to start playing Susan's part in this conflict and begin with the line 'Joe, you don't care about me.' And Susan, in the role of Joe, I want you to respond by saying how those words make you feel." As the discussion unfolds, the worker uses various interviewing techniques to encourage the expression of thoughts and feeling. Given the nature of this technique, the clients should be instructed to approach their effort at role reversal with a spirit of lightheartedness and humor so they can, hopefully, laugh at themselves and the situation.

After a few minutes of role reversal, the worker asks each person to return to his or her own chair. The content of what was said during the reversal is then discussed in a way that helps each to better understand how the other is thinking and feeling about the issue causing the conflict. The role reversal technique may be adapted for use as homework, asking the couple or family members to take time to experiment with role reversal prior to the next session.

SELECTED BIBLIOGRAPHY

Brock, Gregory, and Charles Barnard. *Procedures in Marriage and Family Therapy*, 3rd ed. Boston: Allyn & Bacon, 1999.

Sprafkin, Robert, N. Jane Gershaw, and Arnold Goldstein. *Social Skills for Mental Health*. Boston: Allyn & Bacon, 1993.

13.8   MANAGING SELF-TALK

Purpose: To assist the client to manage emotional reactions by modifying distorted interpretations of reality.

Discussion: Social work places much emphasis on viewing the client within an environmental context. The profession is particularly concerned about how the realities of life affect one's social functioning. However, in many situations, the client is more influenced by his or her interpretations and assumptions than by reality itself.

The term *self-talk* refers to the messages that we give ourselves. What we "say" to ourselves reflects our unique interpretation of what we have experienced. Our self-talk evokes emotional reactions, which, in turn, give rise to behaviors. If a person habitually thinks about his or her experiences in distorting and irrational ways, he or she generates much inner turmoil and also creates problems in interpersonal relationships. Here are some common types of distortions:

- *All or nothing.* We evaluate experiences in terms of the extremes of black and white, all right or all wrong; there is no gray area or middle ground (e.g., we conclude that a single mistake proves we are a complete failure).

- *Jumping to conclusions.* We draw a conclusion on the basis of little or no evidence (e.g., we conclude that something is undesirable or unworkable even before we have gathered information).
- *Selective attention.* We pay attention only to those facts that support our preconceived ideas; we dismiss facts that point to a different conclusion.
- *Catastrophizing.* We anticipate the worst possible outcome; we always expect something bad to happen.
- *Magnification of failure.* We exaggerate the meaning or importance of a setback or mistake (e.g., we may have ten successes and one failure, but we only think about the failure).
- *Minimization of success.* We disregard or downplay a positive experience or success (e.g., we attribute our success to dumb luck).
- *Negative beliefs about self, others, and the world.* We hold tightly to the belief that everything and everybody, including ourselves, is bad, hopeless, and getting worse.
- *Personalization.* We assume every problem or negative happening is caused by our inadequacy. We take responsibility for things over which we have little or no control.
- *External locus of control.* We believe we have no control over our lives; whatever happens to us is caused by factors beyond our influence.

Many individuals hold irrational beliefs and unfounded assumptions that cause them much distress and unhappiness, such as the following:

"I will be alone and rejected by everyone unless I am able to meet all of their expectations."

"Worthwhile people give 110 percent effort to everything they do."

"I cannot be happy until I lose 100 pounds."

By helping a client learn to think more critically, the worker can help him or her control troublesome emotions and behave more effectively. This is, of course, more difficult than it sounds. Patterns of thinking are habits; they are not easily changed and are themselves a barrier to change.

The social worker can use a five-step approach to help a client modify distortions in self-talk. Ask the client to do the following:

1. Identify what you are feeling and thinking right now.
2. Get in touch with your self-talk. Pay attention to extremes in thinking, as suggested by the use of words such as *never, always, everybody, completely,* and so on.
3. Examine the objective reality of your situation. Once the facts have been identified, relax, take a deep breath, and repeat them out loud three times.
4. Notice that, when you hold to the facts and avoid using inaccurate words, you begin to feel differently and things do not seem as bad as before.
5. Keeping the facts of your situation clearly in mind, consider what you can do about it.

This five-step method is illustrated here in a dialogue between a social worker and a college student who has just learned that he failed a math exam:

Client: I cannot believe I am so stupid. I had a B average in math and got an F on the last test. I might as well leave school and get a job as a dishwasher. I am a complete failure. I don't deserve to be in school.

Worker: Wait a minute! You have said before you wanted to learn how to stop putting yourself down. Let's try something. Start by telling me again what you are feeling and thinking right now.

Client: Well, I just can't pass math tests. I'm stupid. I am embarrassed and I hate myself. I am never going to get through college. My parents are going to kill me for this. This is the worst possible thing that could have happened. My future is down the drain. Everything is just awful.

Worker: Let's take a look at that kind of self-talk. Try to recognize what you are saying to yourself; notice your extreme language. Let's take a look at the way things are in reality. Is it true you cannot pass math tests?

Client: Well, not really. I passed all of them before this one and I still have a B average in college.

Worker: Are your parents really going to kill you?

Client: Well, no, but they will be disappointed.

Worker: Is failing a test really the worst possible thing that could happen to you?

Client: Well, no, but it seems awful right now.

Worker: Does failing this test really mean you have no future?

Client: Well, I still have a future. I know what you are saying, and I agree that I am overreacting. But I don't know how to put a lid on those thoughts and feelings.

Worker: Do this for me. Repeat the truth—the reality—of your situation, which is as follows: I flunked one math test. My parents will be unhappy. I have a B average in college. I can remain in college. My life is not over.

Client: (repeats above)

Worker: Now take a couple of deep breaths and relax. Now say that again, three times.

Client: (client follows instruction)

Worker: How do you feel when you change your self-talk?

Client: Well, I guess it isn't as bad as I thought. I feel less upset than before.

Worker: Our emotions react to what we tell ourselves about our experiences. If your self-talk is distorted, your emotions are going to be more extreme and more negative than they need to be. You can use this technique yourself when your feelings start to get out of control. Certainly, your situation is not as bad as it seemed when you were telling yourself those awful things. But you still have to make some plans on how to prepare for your next math test. Now let's talk about that.

Once a client is able to describe his or her pattern of maladaptive self-talk, the cognitive restructuring techniques of self-instruction, visualization, and journaling may prove helpful. ***Self-instruction*** (also termed *positive self-talk, covert speech,* and *countering*) refers to a set of statements that are repeated by the client on a regular basis, perhaps three times a day, and especially in times of distress. Often, they are said aloud in front of a mirror. These messages are incompatible with the client's habitual negative self-talk and are intended to counteract the dysfunctional pattern and to foster self-acceptance and self-confidence. The use of this technique rests on the observation that when an individual actively argues against his or her own irrational thoughts, those thoughts are weakened.

This technique should not be confused with positive thinking that is blindly optimistic and may gloss over important realities and allow self-deception. Rather, self-instruction requires that the messages be truthful and realistic, given the client's abilities and situation. Also, the messages should be as specific as possible and tied directly to the client's concerns. Self-instruction works but it works slowly. Consistent practice for a year or more may be needed to effect a significant and lasting change. Consider the client who avoids taking a better job because her dysfunctional self-talk tells her "If I make a mistake on the job, people will think I am stupid and will criticize me." This woman might be taught to repeat the following message: "Each time I make a mistake on the job, I have an opportunity to learn something very important. If someone criticizes me, he or she is either right or wrong. If the person is right, I have learned something. If he or she is wrong, I can ignore it."

In using the technique of ***visualization***, the client is taught to prepare himself or herself to deal with a worry-causing event by repeatedly imagining this event and mentally rehearsing the steps necessary to handle it successfully. It is important that the images are ones of action and activity; the more vivid and detailed, the better. For many individuals, visualization reduces their fear of the event and builds confidence in their ability to do what they know they must do. For example, a client might prepare for a frightening job interview by visualizing being asked hard questions and giving clear and appropriate answers. Such a visualization would need to be practiced dozens of times before the interview.

The technique of ***journaling*** asks the client to keep a daily log of significant thoughts and feelings. It is especially useful for clients who like to write. It helps them recognize recurring themes and patterns in the meaning assigned to their experiences. As a way of structuring this homework, the client might be instructed to respond in writing to specific questions, such as the following: What have I learned about myself today? What feelings and moods did I experience? What thoughts gave rise to these feelings? What were the two most significant events of the day? What thoughts and feelings did I have in relation to these events? What personal strengths did I observe in myself today? What troublesome thoughts do I need to work on and what is my plan for doing so? How will my plan build on my personal strengths?

SELECTED BIBLIOGRAPHY

Berlin, Sharon. *Clinical Social Work Practice.* New York: Oxford University Press, 2001.

Corcoran, Jacqueline. *Cognitive Behavioral Methods: A Workbook for Social Workers.* Boston: Allyn & Bacon, 2006.

McMullin, Rian. *New Handbook of Cognitive Therapy Techniques.* New York: W. W. Norton, 2000.

13.9   BUILDING SELF-ESTEEM

Purpose: To assist the client in coming to a more positive evaluation of self.

Discussion: The term *self-esteem* refers to one's belief about one's own worth. Individuals who do not value or respect themselves struggle with a multitude of self-imposed limitations. Often, they lack self-confidence, engage in self-defeating and destructive behaviors, and are vulnerable to exploitation and abuse by others. Because the effects of low self-esteem are so far reaching, social workers have wished for a magic wand that could quickly transform a client's negative self-evaluation into a more positive one. Unfortunately, no such magic exists. Movement toward self-esteem is a slow journey. By following these guidelines the social worker can help the client along that journey:

1. Help clients with low self-esteem understand that feelings of personal worth (i.e., our level of self-esteem) arise from one's self-evaluation. Our self-esteem is rooted in how we think about ourselves and how we compare ourselves to others. These self-evaluations are highly subjective, not always accurate, and not necessarily consistent with the judgments and evaluations of those who know us. Consequently, Person A, who is violent, narcissistic, and dishonest, may have high self-esteem, whereas person B, who others view as a genuinely good and wonderful human being, may have low self-esteem.

2. A change in one's self-esteem must grow from within. Self-esteem cannot be taught, but it can be learned. Certain types of experiences can provide learning opportunities that draw the client into a reconsideration of his or her beliefs about self. In many ways, efforts to help others improve their self-esteem involve placing the client into situations or environments that create some cognitive dissonance and compel the client to reconcile a seemly positive outcome or experience with their own negative opinions of self. For example, if an individual participates in a support group, personal growth group, or faith community they usually have an experience of being accepted, valued, and respected by others. They must then reexamine their assumptions and, hopefully, conclude that they are indeed valuable and worthwhile. Other opportunities for clients to recognize their strengths and abilities and revaluate their beliefs about themselves might involve taking a job, changing jobs, returning to school, becoming a volunteer, and forming new friendships. Needless to say, persons with low self-esteem are usually fearful about entering into new experiences. They will need encouragement and emotional support.

3. People with low self-esteem often have a habit of comparing themselves with the "best in the field" (e.g., with the best musician, the best student, the most attractive person, etc.). Given that mode of thinking they will always suffer by comparison, and this reinforces their beliefs that they are not as good or as worthwhile as other people. Help clients recognize this self-defeating pattern of thinking. Help them to see that another person may indeed be outstanding in a certain area but will not be outstanding in all areas. All people have strengths and limitations. Self-awareness and self-acceptance are the building blocks of self-esteem.

4. As a way of helping the clients to examine their beliefs and assumptions about themselves, encourage them to imagine specific conditions or circumstances that—if they existed—would elevate their feelings of self-worth. Then engage them in an examination of the values implicit in those conditions and whether these values are indeed suitable criteria for measuring the worth of a person. For example, many people assume that they would have higher self-esteem if they were more attractive, a better athlete, or had more money, power, and social status. A critical look at those desires reveals that they are the shallow values of a society obsessed with physical appearance, possessions, and self-aggrandizement. There are numerous examples of people who seemingly "have it all" but still lack feelings of happiness, contentment, self-worth, and a sense of purpose in life. Other values—such as generosity, compassion, and friendliness—are more authentic, noble, and lasting measures of personal value. Help clients to understand that their own personal worth is not dependent on what other people may think is important and that they can choose how to think about themselves and life.

5. Self-esteem grows from experiences of success and achievement. Thus, encourage clients to establish realistic and achievable objectives for themselves. Assist them in working toward those objectives and call to their attention their successes (see Item 12.5).

6. Encourage and assist clients to develop a sense of purpose and meaning and a healthy spirituality. Self-worth grows from knowing that you are living your life in accord with your own ideals, values, and moral standards. For this reason, when clients are facing difficult decisions they should be encouraged to do what they know in their heart is the right thing to do so they can maintain a sense of personal integrity (see Item 15.18).

7. For some clients, low self-esteem is tied to one or more significant separation and loss experiences (e.g., separation from bio-family, loss of one's childhood through sexual abuse, loss of respect from valued others, etc.). Help these clients recognize and grieve for what they have lost (see Item 15.17).

SELECTED BIBLIOGRAPHY

Kernis, Michael. *Self-Esteem: A Sourcebook on Current Perspectives*. New York: Psychology Press, 2006.
McKay, Matthew. *Self-Esteem Companion*. Oakland, CA: New Harbinger, 2005.
Mruk, Christopher. *Self-Esteem: Research, Theory, and Practice*, 3rd ed. New York: Springer, 2006.

13.10   CONFRONTATION AND CHALLENGE

Purpose: To increase the client's self-awareness, especially in regard to self-imposed barriers to change.

Discussion: The technique of **confrontation** (also called a *challenge*) refers to gentle and respectful efforts to help the client recognize that he or she is using distortions, deceptions, denials, or manipulations that are self-defeating and getting in the way of desirable change. It challenges and invites the client take a careful look at a thought or behavior that is harmful to self or others and to take action to change it.

The particular focus of a challenge or confrontation will depend on the worker's judgment as to what changes are essential for a client and what stands in the way of those changes. Most often the challenge will focus on the client's avoidance or self-deception, such as failure to acknowledge or "own" an obvious problem; rationalizations, evasions, and game playing; unwillingness to recognize the consequences of one's behavior; discrepancies between what the client says and does; unwillingness to take steps to correct a problem or deal with an issue; or failure to live up to stated values and moral principles.

Here is an example of a challenge or confrontation:

> *Client:*   I should be more involved with Jason, my son. His mother, my former wife, says that Jason feels like I don't care about him. I feel bad about that, but I don't have the time. I have a new wife, and my job is very demanding.
>
> *Social Worker:*   What do you mean by the word *involved?*
>
> *Client:*   Oh, you know, I should spend time with Jason—take him to a ballgame, that sort of stuff.
>
> *Social Worker:*   I recall you saying this same thing several times over the past few weeks. You say that you should be more involved with Jason, but it is obvious that you are not doing what you think you should be doing. You say one thing but do another. I am aware that you want to make your new marriage work and that you are a very good and responsible employee. But I cannot help but feel that deep down, you have decided to give up your role of father and turn over complete responsibility for raising Jason to his mother. What is your honest reaction to what I am saying?

For a challenge to be effective, it must be used at a time when the client seems most ready to hear and consider the message. There is always some risk in using this technique. If used with a client who is depressed, the client may feel criticized and withdraw from the relationship. Clients who are highly defensive will usually reject the message by rationalizing, verbally attacking the worker, or minimizing the matter. Several guidelines need to be considered in the use of this technique:

1. Do not challenge when you are feeling angry. Unless you have a genuine concern for the client, its use may be little more than an expression of frustration or a desire to punish a difficult client.

2. Do not challenge or confront a client if you cannot or do not intend to become more deeply involved. Once offered, it is the responsibility of the worker to help the client deal nondefensively with the message, to understand it, and to consider what it means for future choices. Unless you have the time to help the client make use of the message, do not use this technique.

3. A challenge that is offered by someone whom the client does not like or respect will have no beneficial impact whatsoever. A challenge will be effective only if the client feels respected by the social worker and if the client has similar feelings toward the worker.

4. Couple the challenging message with positive observations about the client. In other words, present the message within a context of recognizing and supporting the client's strengths.

5. Make sure your message is descriptive and nonjudgmental. Be prepared to give a detailed description of the client's self-destructive or negative behavior, and provide concrete examples of how this behavior creates problems. Judgmental statements tend to trigger anger, whereas descriptive statements provide information that can be used in problem-solving efforts.

6. Always present the observations or data on which your message is based. For example, if the confrontation focuses on self-defeating behavior, present detailed descriptions of that behavior before trying to explain how the behavior is counter-productive for the client. Make sure the client understands the distinction between your observations and the inferences you have drawn from those observations. An *observation* can be stated directly: "I saw you . . ." or "Last Friday you specifically told me that . . ." or "I have had seven separate reports that describe your fights." An *inference* should be stated tentatively: "Because of what I have been told, I have concluded that . . ." or "Unless you can offer another explanation, I have to assume that . . . " Strive to use I-statements throughout the challenge (see Item 8.2).

SELECTED BIBLIOGRAPHY

Cormier, Sherry, and Paula Nurius. *Inteviewing and Change Strategies for Helpers*, 5th ed. Belmont, CA: Brooks/Cole, 2003.

Egan, Gerard. *The Skilled Helper*, 8th ed. Belmont, CA: Brooks/Cole, 2007.

Hepworth, Dean, Ronald Rooney, Glenda Dewberry Rooney, Kim Strom-Gottfried, and Jo Ann Larsen. *Direct Social Work Practice*, 7th ed. Belmont, CA: Brooks/Cole, 2006.

13.11   REFRAMING

Purpose: To assist the client in viewing a behavior or experience from a different perspective and in a more positive light.

Discussion: The technique known as **reframing,** sometimes called *relabeling* or *redefining*, is used to help a client modify the meaning he or she assigns to a particular event, behavior, or life experience.

It is especially useful in work with clients having interpersonal conflicts. It encourages them to reexamine their definitions of the problem and their beliefs about why others are behaving as they do. When a person perceives things in a new way, he or she usually begins to feel differently and behave differently. Reframing recognizes the wisdom of the first-century philosopher Epictetus, who said, "It is not the things themselves which trouble us, but the opinions we have about these things.

The following example illustrates a social worker's use of reframing:

Foster Parent: I get so upset with Anna (foster child). So often, she blows up and gets angry with me. But I haven't done anything to make her angry!

Social Worker: That must be frustrating—to know you do not deserve to be the target of her anger. As you know, Anna is an angry child because of the severe abuse she experienced before you ever met her. But, in one way of looking at it, Anna is paying you a big compliment. When she gets angry in your presence, she is demonstrating that she feels safe with you and trusts that you will not retaliate and hurt her. If she didn't feel safe, she would be afraid to express her anger in your presence.

Another example of reframing is illustrated in the following statement made to a 35-year-old client who has experienced a lifetime of physical and emotional pain related to a disabling car accident and having been physically and sexually abused as a child:

Social Worker: I have been thinking about your life and all that you have experienced. Despite all you have been through, here you are at age 35 still alive and still struggling to do the best you can. In the school of life, you have received a very expensive and a very good education—much better than what a Harvard or a Yale could provide. You have learned things about people and about life that most people never learn, no matter how long they go to school, no matter how much money they spend on college tuition. Your tuition has been paid in the form of personal pain and suffering but in return you have acquired great wisdom.

An alternative to the social worker providing the client with a new perspective is to encourage the client to brainstorm several different interpretations. For example, the worker might begin by explaining that there is a difference between the facts that describe a particular life experience and the story an individual tells himself or herself about that experience. The client will usually agree that five people will most likely tell five slightly different stories about the same experience. Using that agreement as a foundation, the worker can now encourage the client to come up with additional stories (interpretations) about the particular behavior or life experience being discussed. After thinking up several alternative perceptions, the client will usually soften his or her position and acknowledge that there may indeed be a different way to interpret his or her situation.

Still another approach to reframing is to redefine a client's problem or irresponsible action as a basically positive behavior or motive taken to an extreme. In other words, a problem is viewed as a strength spinning out of control. For example, consider the young mother who has injured her 3-year-old child as a result of using excessive spanking as discipline. The discussion of her behavior might be approached by first recognizing that the mother wants to teach the child proper behavior but in this situation her motive to be a good mother jumped the track or went spinning out of control. When the worker can redefine a client's problem as a strength or a good motive that has gone wild, the client feels less defensive and more hopeful. Somehow it seems easier to tone down or control a strength than to get rid of a problem behavior. The words a helper uses do make a difference.

SELECTED BIBLIOGRAPHY

Berg, Insoo Kim. *Family Based Services.* New York: W. W. Norton, 1994.

Ronen, Tammie, and Arthur Freeman. eds. *Cognitive Behavior Therapy in Clinical Social Work Practice.* New York: Springer, 2006.

Schuyler, Dean. *Cognitive Therapy.* New York: W. W. Norton, 2003.

13.12 HELPING CLIENTS MAKE DIFFICULT DECISIONS

Purpose: To assist the client in considering alternatives and making a decision.

Discussion: Because many of the problems that clients face involve having to make difficult decisions and choosing different courses of action, helping them make decisions is an important social work skill. Decision making can be especially difficult for clients who face multiple problems and feel overwhelmed. All too often, these individuals either avoid or delay making hard decisions or they make them impulsively, without adequately considering the advantages and disadvantages of each option. To facilitate decision making by clients, the social worker can use some relatively simple ideas and tools.

An important first step in examining any troublesome situation is to make a clear distinction between the problem to be solved and the options available for dealing with that problem. To do so, the social worker must help the client ***distinguish the means from the end***. Consider, for example, the client who asks for assistance in figuring out how to get money to buy a car because he needs to get to and from a new job. In this case, the client has confused means and ends. The client's problem is a lack of transportation, not the lack of a car. A car is only one means of transportation; others might include public transportation, paying a private car owner for a ride, walking, or taking a taxi.

Creating a simple list may help the client keep the ends and means separate. The following list was developed during an interview with a young single mother who had requested foster care placement for her child because she could not care for the child while holding a job:

End	*Means*
Child care while mother works to secure money to support self and child	Licensed day-care center
	Paid babysitter
	Informal babysitting exchange with friend
	Babysitting (relative)
	Change jobs or hours of work
	Welfare assistance

As can be seen, once the client's presenting problem was redefined as a need for child care, rather than a need for placement, several new options emerged.

A ***decision-making matrix*** can help a client think through the pros and cons of each option and arrive at a decision. The matrix has three columns: (1) Alternative, (2) Cost, and (3) Benefit. In the Alternative column, the client lists the options being considered. Then, across from each alternative, in the other columns, the client describes both the drawbacks (costs) and the advantages (benefits) associated with each option. Finally, after all the pros and cons have been outlined, the client compares each option and makes a decision. Figure 13.1 is an example of a matrix completed by a social worker and a battered wife during an interview focusing on the decision of whether she should return to her husband or end her marriage.

A social worker who is familiar with the key issues and common thoughts and feelings surrounding a particular type of decision can facilitate the client's decision making by constructing a ***decision-making worksheet***. This worksheet will focus the client's attention on the important questions, factors, and possible consequences that should be considered in arriving at a decision.

Figure 13.2 contains excerpts from a decision-making worksheet designed for use with pregnant teenagers who are considering whether to relinquish their babies for adoption. As can be seen from this sample, a worksheet is simply

FIGURE 13.1	Sample Decision-Making Matrix

Alternative	Cost	Benefit
1. Return to John	a. Abuse would probably continue b. Children are fearful c. Would have to face same hard decisions in future d. I could get seriously hurt or killed e. Medical expenses	a. Preserve family b. Hard decision is delayed until later c. Would have place to live and money d. John says he cares for me
2. Leave John and end the marriage	a. Fear of the unknown (I need to be with somebody) b. Trauma of divorce for me and kids c. Would have less money to live on d. Legal costs e. Custody battle over children	a. Abuse, pain, and fear would end b. Decision would have been made and I could try to put my life together c. Children would be less nervous and upset d. I could find out if I can function on my own e. Opportunity for fresh start

FIGURE 13.2 **Sample Decision-Making Worksheet**

Planning for My Baby

I. Questions about my relationship with my baby's father.
   A. Can I count on him for financial support?
   B. Can I count on him for emotional support?
   C. Has my relationship with him changed since I got pregnant?
   (and so on)

II. Questions about my relationship with my parents.
   A. What do my parents want me to do?
   B. Can I go against their wishes?
   C. If my mother helps take care of my baby, is it possible the baby will become "her baby"?
   (and so on)

III. Questions about my life after having the baby.
   A. If I keep the baby, how will this affect future dating, marriage, and children?
   B. If I give my baby up for adoption, how will this affect my future dating, marriage, and children?
   (and so on)

IV. A daydream exercise.
   A. If I could pick the ideal time for having a baby, when would it be? Where would I be? What would the baby's father be like?
   B. How does the above ideal situation compare with my real situation?
   (and so on)

V. Picturing myself.
   A. Draw a picture of yourself one year ago. Around your picture, indicate in words or pictures the things that were important to you then. What were your activities, how did you use your time? What were your goals and aspirations one year ago?
   B. Think about yourself now. Change the above picture of yourself one year ago to fit things today. Cross out those activities in which you are no longer involved. Have your goals and aspirations changed?
   C. Draw a picture of yourself one year from now. Again, around your picture, write in those things that you will be involved in one year from now. How will you spend your time? In one year, what will be your goals and aspirations?
   (and so on)

Source: Lutheran Social Services, mimeographed item (no date), pp. 1–2, 4–5. Used with permission.

a format for raising questions and helping the client analyze his or her situation. Obviously, skilled interviewing could accomplish the same thing, but the worksheet can provide added structure and can be used as homework between sessions.

SELECTED BIBLIOGRAPHY

Lutheran Social Services. "Decision-Making Plans for the Baby." Missoula, MT: Lutheran Social Services, no date.

McClam, Tricia, and Marianne Woodside. *Problem Solving in the Helping Professions*. Belmont, CA: Brooks/Cole, 1994.

13.13   THE "TALKING STICK"

Purpose: To structure discussion within a group session or family interview.

Discussion: For centuries, many American Indian tribes have used a symbolic, decorated stick called the "talking stick" to govern small-group discussion and encourage listening behaviors. Instead of a stick, some tribes use an eagle feather or other sacred object. During a discussion, the talking stick or special object is passed around the group, from person to person. Whoever holds it has permission to speak; all others are to give that person their undivided attention. This ensures that everyone will have a chance to speak and be heard by the others. Reverence for the object serves to limit verbose group members and to encourage those who are timid or otherwise uninclined to speak.

This method of structuring discussion can be used with a small group or a family. It may be especially useful if members tend to talk all at once or do not listen to each other. In place of the talking stick or feather, a family might use some other object that illicits reverence and respect (e.g., a family picture, a Bible, etc.).

SELECTED BIBLIOGRAPHY

Locust, Carol. "The Talking Stick." Tucson, AZ: Native American Research and Training Center, no date.

13.14   HOMEWORK ASSIGNMENTS

Purpose: To assist the client in learning a new behavior by assigning specific tasks and activities to be worked on between counseling sessions.

Discussion: The term ***homework*** refers to various types of activities that the client is asked by the social worker to perform between sessions. Homework is often used when the objectives of the intervention involve teaching the client new skills that need to be practiced within the client's natural environment. For example, given a client whose problems revolve on low self-esteem, shyness, and an inability to interact comfortably with others, a homework assignment might be for the client to strike up at least two conversations a day while riding to and from work on the bus.

The homework assignment must be given with clear and precise instructions. Often, these need to be written instructions. Both the client and worker should have copies. The instructions that accompany homework might include, for example, one or more of the following types of statements:

- *Do statements* that begin with action words such as *talk, read, write, observe, count, obtain*, and *give*.
- *Quantity statements* such as "Observe three people who are doing . . . " and "Spend 30 minutes talking to . . . "
- *Recording statements* such as "Write down the number of times that you . . . " and "Mark on your chart . . . "
- *Bring statements* such as "Bring your list of . . . to our next session."
- *Contingency statements* such as "If you . . . , then reward yourself by . . . " and "Each time you . . . , you are to donate \$2 to an organization that you dislike."

Obviously, the homework assignment must seem possible and make sense to the client. The use of this technique presumes that the client is willing to accept direction from the worker.

SELECTED BIBLIOGRAPHY

Hecker, Lorna, and Sharon Deacon. *The Therapist Notebook II: Homework Handouts, and Activities for Use in Psychotherapy.* New York: Haworth, 2007.

Rosenthal, Howard. *Favorite Counseling and Therapy Homework Assignments.* Philadelphia: Brunner-Routledge, 2001.

Schultheis, Gary. *Brief Therapy Homework Planner.* New York: Wiley, 1998.

13.15 ENVELOPE BUDGETING

Purpose: To assist the client in money management.

Discussion: Many of the clients served by social workers are poor and find it difficult to stretch their very limited incomes to cover the bare essentials. Moreover, most of their money transactions are conducted using cash. ***Envelope budgeting*** can be taught to clients who need a simple method for keeping track of their money.

The first step in setting up this budgeting system is for the client to identify the key categories of expenditure: rent, food, clothing, transportation, household supplies, and so on. The next step is to determine how many dollars need to be spent on each category during a spending cycle, such as a one-month or a two-week period. An envelope is then prepared and labeled for each category. In the "food envelope," for example, the client places the money allotted for food. All of the envelopes are kept together in a box.

As money is removed from an envelope and spent, the client has a tangible measure of cash outflow and can view the balance that remains. The client is encouraged to resist the temptation to shift money from one category to another, but this may sometimes be necessary. When the client obtains additional income, cash is again placed in the envelopes for the new spending cycle.

This technique can be used with clients who have limited computational skills. If the client can only count, he or she can usually use envelope budgeting. Subtraction and addition skills are helpful but not essential. This technique helps people plan and monitor expenditures but it is not a permanent solution for those who are overwhelmed by debt or have expenditures that far exceed their income. In such cases, more complex approaches—such as consumer credit counseling, debt consolidation, or even bankruptcy—may be necessary (see Item 13.16).

SELECTED BIBLIOGRAPHY

American Association of Retired Persons. *A Primer on Personal Money Management for Midlife and Older Women.* Washington, DC: AARP, 1991.

Drenth, Tere. *The Everything Budgeting Book.* Avon, MA: Adams Media, 2003.

National Endowment of Financial Education. *Family Money Basics.* Denver: American Humane Association, 2002.

13.16   MANAGING PERSONAL DEBT

Purpose: To assist the client in handling large bills and debt.

Discussion: An individual or family with too many bills and too little money will experience much stress. A shortage of money can be made up by borrowing or buying on credit, but this only makes the problem worse in the long run. Paying some bills while neglecting others may be necessary, but doing so will ultimately result in a damaged credit rating and possible legal ramifications.

There is no easy way to climb out of debt, but several things can be done to gain control of the situation. The following suggestions may be relevant in working with a client who is trying to deal with financial problems:

1. Recognize that financial problems are often more complex than simply not having enough money. The problem is often rooted in a set of personal values, attitudes, and shopping behaviors that lead to overspending. The power of advertising, peer-group influences, and feelings of low self-esteem push many people into buying more than they need and can afford. When excessive spending is driven by emotional needs and a lack of self-discipline, participating in the self-help group Debtors Anonymous may prove helpful. The ease with which credit cards can be obtained is a cause of money problems for many individuals. No one should enter into a credit card contract without first reading the fine print and understanding completely the amount of interest and late charges that will be assessed. Paying a high rate of credit card interest often sets in motion a spiral of ever-growing debt. In order to get out of debt, some significant changes in behavior are required.

2. When a client's bills always exceed his or her income, he or she must find a way to decrease spending, increase income, or both. The client should begin immediately to cut spending. And since accumulating additional debt will make the problem even worse, the client should stop purchasing items on credit, close out revolving credit accounts at stores, and avoid the temptation to buy more than is really needed. If the overuse of credit cards has caused financial problems, the client should destroy the cards. If the use of credit cards is necessary, the client should strive to pay each credit card bill before incurring interest payments or late fees.

3. Help the client conduct a careful analysis of what is owed. To do so, make four columns on a piece of paper. In column 1, list all of the items that are billed on a regular basis (e.g., loan and credit card bills, utilities, rent, car payment, dental and medical, insurance, and the like). In column 2, list the expected payment due for each item in column 1. In column 3, list the amount that can actually be paid each month toward each item. In column 4, total the amount owed for all items. Next, have the client mark all of the items for which interest is charged; these should become high-priority targets for payment. If the client must skip a payment or reduce the amount paid toward a bill, it should be on an item that does not involve interest charges or overdue charges. Also prioritize the interest-related bills according to the amount still owed. The client should concentrate on paying off those on which the least amount is owed, which will eliminate all credit charges associated with that bill and free up money for other bills. Completely paying off a bill also helps the client feel he or she is making progress on debt reduction. Moreover, this record of progress can be used to argue for payment extensions because it demonstrates the client's ability to pay bills.

4. If a client cannot pay a bill or must miss a monthly payment, he or she should immediately contact the creditor or business to which the money is owed and explain the problem. If he or she can demonstrate a genuine desire to pay, the creditor or business may be willing to make an adjustment to the bill. In some situations, a creditor may be willing to rewrite a payment plan or the loan in order to lower the monthly payment or spread the payments over a longer period.

If a business concludes that an individual is ignoring a bill, the company may turn the matter over to a collection agency or seek legal action such as the garnishment of wages. A collection agency does not really want to repossess property or do anything that will decrease the individual's ability to pay in the future. What it wants is payment. If the individual avoids the bill collectors and shows no effort to make or arrange payments, the collection agency will do whatever is legal to recover the money owed or repossess the items not yet paid for.

5. Consider referring the client for *credit counseling*. A consumer credit-counseling program can help a client construct a workable budget, develop self-discipline, and possibly avoid bankruptcy. However, do not confuse credit-counseling services that are available for little or no cost from nonprofit agencies with those offered by for-profit businesses that do debt adjustment for a high fee. Some for-profit credit-counseling services promise more than they deliver. Before referring a client to any program, be sure to find out who sponsors the program, what fees are involved, and the program's reputation for honesty and effectiveness.

6. To reduce debt, the client should consider selling off unneeded possessions and then use the money from such sales to pay off debt. He or she might consider selling a car—unless it is needed for work-related transportation—if it is being bought on an installment plan. A car loan creates a cycle of debt because by the time it is finally paid off, the car must often be replaced. The client might use a less expensive form of transportation in lieu of having a car.

7. When other less drastic methods fail to reduce or contain the client's debt, loan consolidation must be considered. With a ***consolidation loan,*** one takes out a new loan that is sufficient to pay off all other loans and overdue accounts. The single payment on this new loan is designed to be smaller than the combined total for the prior monthly payments, and it is easier to keep track of the payments on just one loan. However, a consolidation loan typically stretches one's payments over a longer period of time. The client must still pay the whole amount before becoming debt free, and that requires paying interest throughout the life of the consolidation loan. Another disadvantage of consolidation is that the monthly payment seems small in comparison to previous bills and it is easy to forget how much is actually owed, making it tempting to take on new credit obligations.

8. When all reasonable efforts fail to pay off the debt owed, a client may find it necessary to seek the legal protections offered by a court declaration of ***bankruptcy***. For individuals and married couples, the Federal Bankruptcy Act provides two types of bankruptcy: *Chapter 7 (called a straight bankruptcy or a liquidation proceeding)* and *Chapter 13 (called a wage-earner plan)*. A means test, used to assess the petitioner's ability to pay his or her debts, determines which of these two bankruptcy options can be used. As a general rule, if the individual earns more than the median income for his or her state, that individual must file for a Chapter 13 proceeding, rather than Chapter 7. A Chapter 13 bankruptcy requires payment of some or all debt over a designated period of time. Those seeking bankruptcy protection must avail themselves of credit-counseling services (see paragraph 5 above).

In the case of a Chapter 7 bankruptcy proceeding, a bankruptcy judge notifies the people to whom the individual owes money (i.e., the creditors) of their right to file claims for their losses and to question the individual filing for bankruptcy on the witness stand. The creditors are given the opportunity to object to the individual not having to pay what is owed. If there are no objections, the bankruptcy judge grants *a discharge in bankruptcy*, which relieves the individual from legal liability for all debts at the time of this bankruptcy. All the person's possessions, except those exempted by law, are then turned over to a trustee to be sold, and the proceeds from this sale are distributed to the creditors who filed claims. The remaining dept is then legally erased. Certain debts such as child support, alimony, taxes, fines, and/or debts obtained under false pretenses cannot be discharged.

A Chapter 13 bankruptcy proceeding allows the individual to keep his or her possessions while he or she pays the debts under an installment plan monitored by a court-appointed trustee. The installment plan provides for the repaying of debts over a designated period, usually three to five years. If the judge approves this plan, creditors must stop all collection efforts and stop charging interest and late charges on most types of depts. Each payday, a fixed amount of the client's wages or other income is turned over to the trustee, who then pays the creditors.

Bankruptcy has a number of negative consequences. For example, it is a matter of public record and, consequently, it can never be hidden from those who take the time to find this information. Also, a bankruptcy remains on one's credit report for many years and affects the person's credit rating and ability to secure loans and other forms of credit. If a client reaches a point of needing to consider bankruptcy, he or she should consult with an attorney and carefully weight the pros and cons of this legal procedure.

SELECTED BIBLIOGRAPHY

Gallen, Ron. *The Money Trap*. New York: Harper Collins, 2002.
Leonard, Robin. *Credit Repair*, 8th ed. Berkeley, CA: Nolo, 2007.
Sutton, Garrett. *The ABC's of Getting Out of Debt*. New York: Warner Business Books, 2004.

13.17   THE FEELINGS LIST

Purpose: To assist a client in the identification and expression of feelings.

Discussion: Many of the clients seen by social workers grew up in dysfunctional families (e.g., alcoholic, abusive, etc.) where they learned to suppress their feelings. Often, they were punished for expressing emotion or for asking the "wrong" questions. Many were exposed to a childrearing pattern that invalidated or discounted the feelings that they did express (e.g., when a mother tells her angry child, "You're not really angry; you're just tired"). As these individuals grow older, they carry with them a tendency to suppress, misinterpret, or mistrust their own emotions and feelings. Many are unsure of their true feelings; many cannot distinguish one from another and can speak of feelings in only broad terms such as *sad, upset,* or *OK.*

Simplistic as it sounds, a written list of feeling words can help a client identify and express feelings. As the client struggles to identify and sort out personal feelings, he or she is encouraged to review the list as an aid in finding the words needed to describe feelings. Even a short list of 25 to 50 words can serve as a starting place and help the client distinguish one feeling from another—for example:

controlled	embarrassed	attached	abandoned
excited	courageous	worthless	serene
concerned	tender	secure	curious
manipulated	tough	lost	ashamed
hateful	sarcastic	protected	guilty
desperate	competitive	isolated	vulnerable
joyful	confident	relieved	apathetic
disloyal	fearful	detached	warm

The client should be helped to understand that feelings and emotions are a normal human experience. Although some are pleasant and some unpleasant, they are neither good nor bad. How one chooses to behave in response to feelings may be appropriate or inappropriate, but the feelings themselves simply exist and are neither right nor wrong in a moral sense.

A feelings list can prove useful in work with individuals, families, and groups. If you believe the use of a feelings list would help your clients, the authors suggest that you prepare one consisting of words that will be meaningful to individuals served by your agency. A client's age, life experience, culture, and educational level need to be considered when compiling a list. (Also see Item 8.5 for additional information on emotion.)

SELECTED BIBLIOGRAPHY

Black, Claudia. *It Will Never Happen to Me,* 2nd ed. Center City, MN: Hazelden, 2002.

Mayer, Adele. *Incest: A Treatment Manual for Therapy with Victims, Spouses and Offenders.* Homes Beach, FL: Learning Publications, 1983.

Porter, Eugene. *Treating the Young Male Victim of Sexual Assault.* Syracuse, NY: Safer Society Press, 1986.

13.18   CLIENT ADVOCACY

Purpose: To secure services that the client needs and is entitled to but is unable to obtain on his or her own.

Discussion: When the social worker assumes the role of ***client advocate,*** he or she speaks, argues, bargains, and negotiates on behalf of a client. This form of advocacy is also termed *case advocacy*, in contrast to what is known as *class advocacy* (see Item 13.33). An advocacy stance may be necessary when a client has been unable to obtain services to which he or she is entitled; has been subjected to discrimination or unfairness by a professional, agency, or business; and is unable to respond effectively to these situations without help. Because advocacy is a form of confrontation and one cannot be sure how those to be confronted will respond, some risks are involved in choosing this tactic. The worker should remember these guidelines:

1. Make sure your client wants you to become his or her advocate. Do not engage in advocacy unless you have an explicit agreement with your client and he or she understands both the potential benefits and risks. To the extent possible, involve your client in all decisions concerning the actions you will take.

2. Realize that your advocacy can damage your relationship or your agency's relationship with another agency or professional and that this damaged relationship may create problems in the future when you need their cooperation to serve other clients. Do not use advocacy until you have tried approaches that are less likely to polarize the parties involved.

3. Your decision to assume the role of client advocate should arise out of a genuine desire to be of service to your client and never from a wish to punish or embarrass another agency or organization.

4. Before you decide to use this confrontational tactic, be sure you understand the facts of the matter. Do not base your decisions on hearsay or on a one-sided description of what happened and why. Realize that clients sometimes misunderstand or misinterpret the explanations given to them by professionals and agency representatives. Get the facts before you decide how to proceed.

5. Once you decide that the tactic of advocacy is required, arrange a meeting with the appropriate agency or program representative. Face-to-face meetings are almost always more effective than phone calls and letters. However, a letter outlining your client's situation and your concern may be needed prior to the face-to-face meeting. Respect an agency's chain of command (e.g., do not ask to speak with a supervisor until you have spoken to the line worker who was in contact with your client; do not ask to speak with the administrator until you have spoken with the line worker's supervisor).

6. Before you speak with the agency representative, write down exactly what you intend to say and the questions you will ask. Begin your conversation with a courteous request for an explanation of why your client was denied service or treated in a certain way. Communicate your concerns in a factual and nonabrasive manner, but speak in a tone that conveys that you feel strongly about the matter. Keep a written record of who you talk to, their position and responses, and the time, date, and place of the communication. Secure and retain copies of all letters sent and received, completed forms, and other documents relevant to the issue.

7. If the agency wanted to provide the service requested by your client but could not because of a technicality or an unreasonable procedural or policy requirement, ask for information on how the decision can be appealed and who else you and your client should speak to. Ask if administrators, board members, or a legislative committee should be informed of the difficulty faced by your client or perhaps consulted on how this matter can be resolved.

8. If the agency treated your client in an unfair or inappropriate manner, seek the resolution or outcome desired by your client. Explain to the agency that if the matter cannot be resolved or corrected at this organizational level, you will take your concern to those higher in the chain of command and if necessary make a formal complaint or file an appeal.

9. If further action is required, you will need to secure information on how to file a complaint or initiate an appeal. In some cases, you will need legal advice before proceeding. As preparation for an appeal or formal complaint, you will need detailed documentation of what happened and what was attempted, step by step, to resolve the matter. You will need names, dates, and the content of all communications and copies of all letters sent and received.

SELECTED BIBLIOGRAPHY

Ezell, Mark. *Advocacy in the Human Services*. Belmont, CA: Brooks/Cole 2001.

Hoefer, Richard. *Advocacy Practice for Social Justice*. Chicago: Lyceum, 2006.

Katz, Marsha. *Don't Look For Logic: An Advocate's Manual for Negotiating the SSI and SSDI Programs*. Missoula, MT: University of Montana Rural Institute on Disabilities, 2005.

Schneider, Robert, and Lori Lester. *Social Work Advocacy*. Belmont, CA: Brooks/Cole 2001.

13.19   CLIENT EMPOWERMENT

Purpose: To assist a client in developing a sense of power and control in his or his life.

Discussion: Many of the clients seen by social workers in direct-service agencies have been "beaten down" by oppression, poverty, abuse, and other harmful life experiences. They want better lives for themselves and their families, but they feel powerless to make the necessary changes. Some have a pervasive sense of failure and feel rejected by other people.

In order to counter or modify clients' negative feelings and self-limiting perceptions, social workers and social agencies need to emphasize empowerment in their work with these individuals. The word *empowerment* literally means to invest another with power or to authorize or permit another to exercise a certain power. As used in social work, the term ***empowerment*** refers to a way of working with clients that emphasizes helping them to acquire the personal, interpersonal, and political power they need to take control of their lives and also to bring about changes in the policies, organizations, and public attitudes that are adversely impacting their lives.

Clients who see themselves as powerless will begin to reevaluate this presumption about themselves and their situations when they experience success, power, and control. It is through experiencing success as a result of their own efforts that clients most clearly recognize that change is possible and that they do, in fact, have the capacity to shape their lives. Thus, the empowerment approach seeks to engage clients in activities that prepare them to experience success.

Clients experience a sense of power in their lives when, for example, they voice their concerns to decision makers and discover that they can shape public opinion and influence the organizations and systems in their environment. People cannot bring about change until their ideas for doing so are taken seriously by others (e.g., social workers, agency administrators, government officials, politicians). Before people invest themselves in the difficult process of change, they must be given responsibility for defining the problems they face and for selecting solutions that are relevant to their concerns. In addition, they must have access to the resources they deem important to implementing those solutions. Basically, the empowerment strategy asks social workers and agencies to take the principle of client self-determination very seriously, to work in partnership with their clients, and to find ways of sharing power and responsibility with their clients. To apply this approach, the social worker should adhere to these guidelines:

1. Fundamental to empowering others is the firm conviction that all individuals and all communities are capable of improving their situation. By working together, people can bring about social and political change. This approach views the individual as an important resource to others and a potential participant in social and political action. Through the process of cooperating and sharing, teaching and learning, clients come to understand the social, economic, political, and historical context that underlies their situations; they grow in self-confidence, learn leadership skills, and take action—both individually and as part of a group—to improve their lives.

2. View your client as an expert on his or her life and situation. Thus, the client's definition of the problem and his or her thoughts on what should be done about it are pivotal to the change process. View your helping role as primarily that of a teacher-trainer or consultant. Take steps that will help your client view the client-worker relationship as a partnership in problem solving.

3. Help your client build self-confidence and self-respect. Encourage him or her to take the risks necessary to learn new skills and to break out of self-defeating and self-limiting beliefs and behaviors. The small group is an ideal environment in which the client can learn and practice skills in communicating, problem solving, leadership, critical thinking, persuasion, assertiveness, negotiation, and mutual support. In addition, small-group experiences can help the client overcome feelings of being alone and different from others and realize that people have many of the same struggles in life (see Item 12.9).

4. Help your client experience personal power by allowing and encouraging him or her to make decisions, individually and as part of a group, and then to follow through on those decisions. Be prepared to respect the client's decisions and allow him or her to experience the consequences of those choices, both positive and negative. One does not learn to make decisions unless given the opportunity to do so. In empowerment-oriented practice, you must integrate the principle of client self-determination into all aspects of your involvement with clients.

5. Help your clients understand the factors that contribute to their feelings of powerlessness. This is best done within the context of small-group discussion. When some clients seriously begin to examine how they have been mistreated or held back in life, they become engulfed by resentment. Some get stuck at this point and become prisoners of their own anger. Help these clients express and understand their feelings but then move beyond the bitterness to take positive action.

Also make frequent use of reframing (see Item 13.11) to help the client view his or her prior experiences of mistreatment and injustice from a different angle. For example, help him or her view the past as a painful but invaluable source of wisdom about what is really important in life and how and why people behave as they do. Help the client see that if one chooses to be taught rather than hurt, then he or she will uncover many opportunities to grow as a person. Help the client recognize that even distress can be beneficial if it pushes one to carefully reexamine his or her situation and take action to change those things that are causing pain or discomfort.

6. Encourage your clients to seek out learning opportunities (e.g., presentations, visits to agencies, etc.) that will help them understand the people, organizations, and systems they would like to influence. Assist clients in making arrangements to attend or perhaps host such events. As a general rule, when clients meet face to face with program administrators, politicians, and community leaders, they come away with renewed hope that change is possible and that they have some power to shape the outcome.

7. The term *power* refers to an individual's or a group's capacity to influence the behavior of others, such as the decisions of a politician, government official, program director, or agency board of directors. Assist clients in making an inventory of the types of power they possess, such as knowledge derived from life experience, motivation, time, energy, knowledge of the community, understanding of particular problems, sense of humor, willingness to take risks, right to vote, solidarity with others, membership in an influential organization, and the like.

8. Once your clients realize and understand that they are not helpless and do possess some power, help them use this power in a planned, disciplined manner to bring about desired change. However, keep in mind that there are some pitfalls at this stage. When persons who have been oppressed finally realize that they have some power, they may not use it in an appropriate manner. Sometimes built-up anger and a sense of injustice lead people to make impulsive decisions and to become aggressive or combative; consequently, they alienate potential supporters or attract added opposition to their goals. While encouraging clients to use their power, also help them understand that making change can be frustratingly slow and that numerous realities may limit how quickly others respond to their ideas and requests. For example, an agency may not be able to make immediate or far-reaching changes in its policies or programs because of budget limitations, existing laws, and the needs of others that they serve.

9. Empowerment, as an overall strategy and guiding philosophy, is applicable in work with all clients and in all settings. However, what a social worker can actually do to empower others will vary, depending upon the practice setting and the types of clients served. For example, the empowerment approach is highly applicable in work with women who have been abused and with persons with physical disabilities. It is less applicable with clients who are inmates of a correctional facility or who are mentally confused residents in a nursing home. In selecting this strategy, you are assuming that the client (individual or group) already has or can learn the prerequisite competencies needed to effect changes in his or her environment and also that his or her current difficulties are caused primarily by social or political barriers and a lack of resources. If these are not valid assumptions for a given client (individual or group), you will not likely find this approach, by itself, effective or sufficient.

SELECTED BIBLIOGRAPHY

Lee, Judith. *The Empowerment Approach to Social Work Practice*, 2nd ed. New York: Columbia University Press, 2001.

Linhorst, Donald. *Empowering People with Severe Mental Illness*. New York: Oxford 2005.

Wise, Judith. *Empowerment Practice with Families in Distress*. New York: Columbia University Press, 2005.

13.20 RESOLVING CONFLICT THROUGH COUNSELING AND MEDIATION

Purpose: To assist people in resolving conflicts using peaceful means of dispute resolution.

Discussion: Social workers are frequently involved in helping clients resolve conflicts. For example, conflicts might arise between spouses or partners, perhaps over divorce and child custody, between a parent and child; between landlords and tenants, and even between social workers and clients regarding issues at a human services agency. These interpersonal conflicts may be rooted in opposing beliefs and values, in disagreements related to inaccurate or incomplete information, or in misunderstandings. Improved communication and mutual understanding fostered by the social worker can resolve some issues as part of a counseling process, but resolving a fundamental disagreement requires a more structured means of intervention known as *mediation*.

For some social workers, conflict resolution has become a practice specialty. Organizations such as the American Arbitration Association (AAA), the Association for Conflict Resolution (ACR), and the Institute for Advanced Dispute Resolution offer training programs and issue certificates to social workers and other professionals who have the knowledge and skill needed to address conflictual situations. In addition, the AAA and ARC, along with the American Bar Association, have created a "model of conduct" for mediators (2005) that like the *NASW Code of Ethics* offers guidelines for persons engaged in conflict resolution interventions.

Counseling Strategies

Compared to many social work interventions that involve advocating on behalf of a client, successful conflict resolution typically involves taking a neutral position while helping the affected parties examine their situation, clarify the factors that contributed to the conflict, and consider alternative solutions.

During counseling that focuses on resolving a conflict, the social worker should first help the parties determine if the conflict is possibly caused either by a *misunderstanding* (i.e., simply not having or comprehending the facts of the situation) or a *disagreement*, in which the facts are well-understood but there is fundamental disagreement about the outcome of the situation. Basic social work counseling and facilitation skills that help people explore issues, engage in effective communication, and identify common interests should help to resolve many conflicts. Some guidelines to keep in mind when counseling clients and others in relation to a conflict include:

- As part of planning and scheduling a meeting to address the conflict, urge the parties to consider these questions: Do I really want to resolve this conflict, or do I have another motive relative to this matter? Is what I have stated regarding this matter true, or have I exaggerated or given only partial truth? What relevant information can I add to the discussion during the session? What can I offer as a constructive step toward resolving this matter?
- When beginning the session, appeal to the parties to demonstrate mutual respect while discussing the issue, to reflect willingness to listen to one another, and to make an honest effort to understand their different perceptions of the situation.
- Invite the parties to designate you as the person in the discussion who will enforce basic rules of fairness so that each can speak his or her mind without interruption.
- Use basic helping skills (e.g., clarifying, paraphrasing, reframing, and summarizing) to assist and encourage each party to clearly express and explain his or her viewpoint. It may be useful, at times, to ask each party to repeat what he or

she heard the other party say in order to help each clarify points and develop some level of empathy for the other person's perspectives and feelings.

■ Once there appears to be sufficient understanding of the issues, use brainstorming to identify several potential solutions to the conflict (see Item 13.32). During this process, look for opportunities to remind the parties of their common interests and what they have already agreed upon (e.g., values, compromises, concern for a third party who is potentially affected by the outcome) and to build possible solutions that do not violate those areas of agreement.

Mediation

A more structured alternative to counseling in reference to a conflict is *facilitative mediation*, a method where a neutral third party, who has no authority or decision-making power in the situation, works with both sides to help them agree to terms for settling the dispute. As opposed to *arbitration*, where the participants are bound by the decisions of the third party, mediation engages the disputing persons as active participants in addressing the issue and arriving at a mutually agreed upon solution, which leads to a win-win situation. ***Mediation***, then, is essentially a dialogue between parties who are in conflict over such things as values, power, status, or access to resources, in which a social worker or other third party facilitates a balanced and even-handed search for a solution.

Moore (2003, pp. 64–65) has developed a typology that distinguishes five forms of conflict often addressed by mediation:

■ *Relationship conflicts* are caused by such things as strong emotions, poor communication, misperceptions, and negative behaviors or actions. In addressing this type of conflict, interventions should include helping participants to control emotions, to promote expression of emotions that will clarify feelings, and to encourage positive problem-solving approaches.

■ *Data conflicts* are created by lack of information or misinformation, competing views on what is relevant information, or different interpretations of data. Addressing these conflicts requires determining which data are important, how data might be collected and analyzed, and resolving issues about interpretation of the data.

■ *Interest conflicts* are caused by competition over substantive interests or resources. Thus helping parties resolve these conflicts requires minimizing entrenched positions, looking for objective criteria for developing possible solutions, and developing trade-offs to arrive at a mutually agreeable solution.

■ *Structural conflicts* are created by destructive patterns of behavior, imbalance of power or resources, and time or geographical constraints that hinder cooperation. Perhaps the most difficult conflicts to mediate, structural conflict interventions often require the parties to modify destructive behavior patterns, establish a mutually agreeable decision-making process, and/or modify the influence of external pressures on the parties.

■ *Value conflicts* often develop when the parties come from very different family or cultural backgrounds, have basically different goals, or operate from different religious perspectives or ideologies. To assist persons in minimizing value conflicts, the mediator might help them search for agreement on a broader or more important goal, agree to disagree on some issues in order to move on, or seek a way to define the problem in some way other than a value conflict.

Because the mediator does not operate from a position of power or authority, his or her primary strengths must be the ability to quickly build a trusting relationship with both parties and to effectively use basic social work helping skills (see Chapter 8). Especially important is the ability of the social worker to guide the change process (see Chapter 7) in order to assure that the parties are indeed equal and active participants.

SELECTED BIBLIOGRAPHY

American Arbitration Association, American Bar Association, and Association of Conflict Resolution. "Model Standards of Conduct for Mediators." http://www.adr.org/si.asp?id=2095, 2005.

Barsky, Allan. *Conflict Resolution for the Helping Professions,* 2nd ed. Belmont, CA: Brooks/Cole, 2007.

Mayer, Bernard S. *The Dynamics of Conflict Resolution: A Practitioner's Guide,* 2nd ed. San Francisco: Jossey-Bass, 2007.

Moore, Christopher W. *The Mediation Process: Practical Strategies for Resolving Conflict,* 3rd ed. rev. San Francisco: Jossey-Bass, 2003.

Stoesen, Lyn. "Mediation a Natural for Social Workers." *NASW News* 51 (September 2006): 4.

13.21   ANIMAL-ASSISTED INTERVENTIONS

Purpose: To use companion animals in assisting clients to express feelings, build self-confidence, and enhance their quality of life.

Discussion: Recognition that interactions with animals can have a significant influence on the well-being of humans has long been present, yet the use of animals as an intervention is relatively recent. The term ***animal-assisted intervention*** is defined as "any therapeutic intervention that intentionally includes or incorporates animals as part of the therapeutic process or milieu" (Kruger et al, 2004). Although research into best practices regarding the use of animals in social work practice is sparse, the use of animals has been effective in the following ways:

- As companions for persons who live alone or are otherwise isolated
- As guide dogs for persons with handicapping conditions
- As a source of comfort and mental stimulation (i.e., animal-assisted activities [AAA]) for persons who are hospitalized or residing in care facilities
- As part of a human-animal team (animal-assisted therapy [AAT]) working with clients where the animal serves as an intermediary point of contact to address problems in physical, emotional, social, or cognitive functioning

For centuries, people have observed that *companion animals* (e.g., dogs, cats, rabbits, farm animals, and even dolphins) enhance the lives of children and older people. Recent research confirms a positive association between pet ownership and an individual's health and improved social relationships (Wilson and Turner, 1998). Consequently, it is not uncommon for social workers and other professionals to recommend pet ownership or an association with animals for persons with limited opportunities for communication and social interaction. It is thought that the attachment to and bonding with another living creature and the acceptance and stimulation by the animal affects one's level of happiness and sense of well-being. According to research reported by the Delta Society, the following are some benefits experienced by people who own pets:

- Children who have dogs tend to be more self-reliant, sociable, and less selfish than children without pets.
- Elderly people with dogs are better able than non-pet-owning elderly people to cope with daily activities.
- Owning a dog gives isolated people a routine, a sense of purpose, and a sense of fulfillment that helps prevent depression and loneliness.
- Stroking and petting a dog can be relaxing, which is measured by a slower heart rate and a drop in blood pressure.
- The presence of a dog can ease the effects of Alzheimer's disease.

Known as *service animals,* the use of dogs to assist persons experiencing a handicapping condition has also been a long-standing intervention in health and human services. Seeing-eye dogs provide a form of vision for persons who are blind, hearing dogs assist deaf people by responding to sounds, and guide dogs aid persons with other physical and mental disabilities to successfully navigate in a society where the person's condition limits safe mobility. Dogs have even been trained to anticipate a stroke or heart attack in humans. For many people, these highly trained animals are their ticket to being full participants in society.

The term *Animals-Assisted Activities* (AAA) refers to forms of contact with human-animal teams involving such sources of comfort as petting or speaking to the animal where the interactions are largely controlled by the client. This form of intervention has been especially effective in hospice settings and long-term care facilities. The acceptance and nonjudgmental response offered by an animal invites a person to respond even when his or her ability to speak and relate has been compromised by an illness or disability. The opportunity to pet, scratch, or snuggle with the animal can be a great source of comfort to someone who is lonely. Originally known as "pet therapy," this human-animal interaction has been embraced by human services agencies as being both safe and inexpensive, given the minimal amount of staff time and other resources needed to provide the service. The term '*therapy*' was dropped for AAA because most members of the human-animal teams were not professionally prepared therapists and thus the term overstated the level of care being provided.

Animal-Assisted Therapy (AAT), however, does involve professionals working with animals (usually dogs or horses) to provide a therapeutic service intended to affect a condition experienced by the client. The standards for the practice of AAT specified by the Delta Society (1996) indicate that AAT is delivered and/or directed by a health or human service provider who includes an animal as part of practice when working within the scope of his/her profession to promote improvement in human physical, social, emotional, and/or cognitive functioning. Studies of AAT document such changes in clients as increased attention skills, increased self-esteem, reduced anxiety, and improved social behaviors. In Alzheimer's patients, AAT contributes to increased vocabulary, improved speech, increased long-and short-term memory, and improved understanding of concepts such as size and color.

Animal-assisted intervention involves much more than simply linking clients with animals. For this to be a safe and productive experience for the client, the animal, and associated humans, careful planning is essential.

Screening and Training of the Animals

Only certain pets are suitable for animal-assisted intervention. The animal must be physically healthy (a thorough examination by a veterinarian is essential), must demonstrate that he or she likes people, and must possess a high degree of self-control. To serve as an AAA or AAT animal, for example, a dog must demonstrate the ability to accept a friendly stranger, sit politely, walk on a loose leash, walk through a crowd that includes wheelchairs, sit on command and stay in place, react well to another dog, and react appropriately to distraction—like loud noises (Delta Society, 2006). The animals must also have the maturity to handle a human-animal bond situation. Dogs, for example, should be at least two years old before beginning to serve in this capacity. In addition, dogs intended for AAT intervention are trained at an advanced level, require advanced behavioral screening, and must learn additional commands.

Care and Training of Human Participants

Except for companion animals, the human part of the human-animal team must also be trained to provide these forms of intervention. Organizations are springing up around the United States that prepare human-animal teams for AAA and AAT interventions. Human-Animal Bond in Colorado (HABIC), for example, prepares teams for work in long-term care and rehabilitation programs, schools, hospitals, hospice agencies, child advocacy centers, residential treatment facilities, mental health centers, and youth corrections (Granger and Granger, 2006). The training of HABIC teams typically involves an orientation session, a pre-evaluation of the animal, and, at the beginning level, several training sessions. At the advanced level for AAT, requirements include an additional six weeks of training, plus observation/supervision of the team at the facility where the service will be provided. Periodic special training sessions are also provided the HABIC team members.

SELECTED BIBLIOGRAPHY

Delta Society, http://deltasociety.org. Retrieved 9/29/06.

Fine, Anthony H. *Handbook on Animal-Assisted Therapy: Theoretical Foundations and Guidelines for Practice*, 2nd ed. Atlanta: Elsevier, 2006.

Granger, Georgia, and Ben Granger. "From the Desk of the Co-Directors." In *Human-Animal Bond in Colorado*. Fort Collins: Colorado State University School of Social Work, 2006.

Kruger, Katherine A., Symme Trachtenberg, and James. A. Serpell. "Can Animals Help Humans Heal? Animal-Assisted Interventions in Adolescent Mental Health." Philadelphia:

University of Pennsylvania School of Veterinary Medicine, Center for the Interaction of Animals and Humans. Retrieved 2005 from http://www2.vet.upenn.edu/research/centers/cias/publications.html.

Wilson, Cindy C., and Dennis C. Turner, eds. *Companion Animals in Human Health*. Thousand Oaks, CA: Sage Publications, 1998.

13.22 INDIRECT DISCUSSION OF SELF IN SMALL GROUPS

Purpose: To make it easier for group participants to discuss personal concerns.

Discussion: This technique is designed to stimulate and structure small-group discussion of the participants' concerns while at the same time protecting individual privacy. This technique can draw a reluctant client into the discussion. Essentially, the technique calls for each participant to respond to a set of questions by writing answers on 3" × 5" cards. The unsigned cards are collected, shuffled, and then randomly passed out to the group members. The members then discuss and analyze the responses, problems, or concerns found on the cards.

To begin the process, each participant is given three 3" × 5" cards; each card is labeled A, B, or C. The participant will use each card to write a response to a specific question: question A, question B, question C. Before they write, tell them exactly how the cards will be collected, shuffled, and then redistributed randomly for discussion. Warn participants against writing a response in a way that might reveal their identity. Encourage the group to be honest in answering the questions, since the identity of the person writing the card will be protected.

The social worker using the technique preselects the questions. The following is a sample set of stem sentences used in a session with physically abusing parents:

On Card A: (complete the statement) "Before a hitting episode, I feel . . . "

On Card B: (complete the statement) "The thing I feel most after a hitting episode is . . . "

On Card C: (complete the statement) "One thing I could do to decrease the hitting episodes is . . . "

The technique is also useful in training sessions. The next sample is a set of stem sentences used in a training session for foster parents concerned with improving their work with the biological parents of children in foster care:

On Card A: (complete the statement) "In my work with biological parents, I find it most difficult to . . . "

On Card B: (complete the statement) "I know I shouldn't have this negative feeling toward biological parents, but I feel . . . "

On Card C: (complete the statement) "The thing that would help me to improve my work with biological parents is . . . "

After all of the participants have finished writing their responses, collect the cards in sequence: first, all of the A cards, then the Bs, and then the C cards. Shuffle each stack separately. Then pass out all of the A cards randomly, then the Bs, then the Cs. This procedure ensures that each participant receives a response to each of the three questions or stem sentences.

The next step is to have groups of three or four members, if part of a large group, study and discuss the cards they have been given. They might be asked to summarize what the cards seem to be saying. For example, the foster parents might be asked to study the cards and answer the following:

1. Identify the difficulties experienced in work with biological parents.
2. Identify the possible causes of these difficulties.
3. Identify methods of improving relationships with biological parents.

After a small group has studied its cards, participants are encouraged to trade their cards with other small groups in order to obtain even more data. Typically, the participants discover that they share common worries, problems, and feelings. This can be reassuring. Use of the technique helps counteract feelings of isolation and the belief that "no one else feels like I do."

The technique works best in groups larger than about 15, but it can be adapted for use in smaller groups and even with families. When used with a small group, the social worker should also submit a set of cards. Sometimes, the worker can move things along by writing responses that are sure to provoke discussion.

SELECTED BIBLIOGRAPHY

Haslett, Diane. *Group Work Activities in Generalist Practice*. Belmont, CA: Wadsworth, 2005.

Reid, Kenneth. *Social Work Practice with Groups: A Clinical Perspective*, 2nd ed. Belmont, CA: Brooks/Cole, 1997.

Zastrow, Charles. *Social Work with Groups*, 6th ed. Belmont, CA: Brooks/Cole, 2006.

13.23 PROGRAMMING IN GROUP WORK

Purpose: To encourage individual and group development by selecting and arranging group activities that promote specific types of interaction.

Discussion: The technique of ***programming*** originated within the group work tradition of social work. It refers to the planful selection and use of recreation, nonverbal media, and other activities to create opportunities for clients to learn new behaviors or experience positive interpersonal relationships and to move the group process in certain directions. Participation in a group activity can effect how members feel about themselves and each other and can affect the structure and norms that develop within the group.

A broad range of activities can be used in programming: camping, puppet shows, drama, care of animals, art, dance, music, crafts, basketball, parties, work tasks, and the like. Games can be useful in group work with all ages but they are especially important with children. Games are fun and engaging—they often allow for creativity and fantasy, they teach the importance of rules and boundaries, and they challenge the player to test himself or herself against others. Complex games may teach a variety of important skills such as self-control, problem solving, communication and cooperation, leadership, and handling feelings related to authority.

An individual's behavior during an activity can provide important assessment and diagnostic information. For example, a child's interaction with peers during a game may garner insights into the child's behavior that could not be obtained from a battery of psychological tests.

The type of programming used will depend on the social worker's assessment of individual members, the functioning of the group as a whole, the group's purpose, and the group's size. Guidelines include the following:

1. The selection of a particular activity is always tied to the question: What behaviors, attitudes, and skills do I want to encourage and teach? Activities should elicit and reinforce the behaviors that will benefit group members and help the group achieve its purpose.

2. The appropriateness of an activity will depend on the group's stage of development. For example, in the get-acquainted stage, you would select an activity that encourages communication and friendly interaction but you would avoid one that requires competition or that requires a member to assume a leadership role (see Item 12.9).

3. When selecting an activity, consider such factors as the members' ages, intellectual abilities, physical capacities, motor skills, endurance, attention span, need for control and protections, social skills, and so forth. Also, carefully consider the prerequisite skills or knowledge required by the activity. For example, does the activity require writing, reading, oral communication, cooperation, competition, initiative, memory, quick judgment, self-control, or the ability to follow detailed instructions? An activity should offer some challenge to the members but not generate excessive frustration.

4. A group activity should be attractive, interesting, and possible. For example, young adults are often attracted to activities such as car maintenance, woodworking, and cooking because such activities are age appropriate and combine the learning of useful skills with social interaction. Those who are physically fit might enjoy hiking, volleyball, or swimming. Older people might prefer more sedentary activities such as bingo, cards, and sewing; they might enjoy dancing but only if the music is familiar.

5. Carefully consider what the activity will require of the social worker. For example, does the activity require the worker to function as a teacher, leader, advisor, planner, enforcer of rules, umpire, timekeeper, transporter, supplier of food, or what?

6. Consider how the rules of the activity will affect the members. For example, does a game involve the selection or ranking of participants, the choosing of sides, or the elimination of a "loser" from further competition? Can the members cope with the limits imposed and whatever frustration the rules may create?

7. Consider how the activity fits with scheduling constraints and the physical environment. How much time is required? How much space? Is it safe? Is it noisy?

SELECTED BIBLIOGRAPHY

Barlow, Constance, Judith Blythe, and Margaret Edmonds. *A Handbook of Interactive Exercises for Groups.* Boston: Allyn & Bacon, 1999.

Carrell, Susan. *Group Exercises for Adolescents: A Manual for Therapists.* Thousand Oaks, CA: Sage Publications, 2000.

Cheung, Monit. *Therapeutic Games and Guided Imagery.* Chicago: Lyceum, 2006.

Ephross, Paul, and Thomas Vassil. *Groups That Work*, 2nd ed. New York: Columbia University Press, 2005.

SECTION B

TECHNIQUES AND GUIDELINES FOR INDIRECT PRACTICE

Due to the complexity and multiple layers of decision making in organizations and communities, facilitating change in these large systems is usually a time-consuming and labor-intensive process. The social worker engaged in these activities should recognize that these complex social organizations were built by people and can be changed by people, but the process of changing them is often difficult. Typically, large system change efforts must be sustained over a long period of time, although occasionally intensive work on a project during a somewhat limited time period is as effective. Successful outcomes depend on such factors as timing (Is the organization or community ready to consider alternative ways of operating?), knowledge of alternative programs (Are there viable solutions to the issues being addressed?), and involvement of key people in the organization or community.

Intervention Activities.   Like all social work practice, much of the activity by social workers to change human services organizations and communities is based on relationships. As compared to direct-service practice where the central relationship is with clients, these relationships are with administrators, board members, the media, elected officials, and others who may be in a position to make or influence decisions. Many of the actions of the social worker to interpret problems or promote changes in the functioning of the agencies or the community occur through informal conversations with decision makers. We sometimes neglect to consider these actions as intervention, yet they serve to promote change.

Some actions by social workers in organizations and communities are best described as maintenance or incremental change activities. Much of that work is geared toward facilitating teamwork, resolving disputes within an agency, generating ideas for new or innovative services, raising funds for programs, or developing grant applications. These forms of intervention are central to improving the services to clients or the future clients of human services agencies.

The more dramatic change activities are those that attempt to solve immediate and stressful problems. Those interventions include activities such as pressing for changes in agency programs, organizing staff to address issues, chairing a committee or leading a problem-solving group, designing new programs, helping the media interpret social problems to the public, advocating for vulnerable groups, and lobbying key decision makers.

Monitoring Activities.   Similar to the direct services, the monitoring of indirect-service activities uses techniques that can be used either to inform actions while the change effort is in process (i.e., formative evaluation) or to sum up the results of an action after it is completed (i.e., summative evaluation). The tools for monitoring and evaluating practice are combined in Chapter 14.

13.24   WORKING WITH A GOVERNING OR ADVISORY BOARD

Purpose: To understand the responsibilities of governing and advisory boards in the operation of human services organizations.

Discussion: With the exception of for-profit human services agencies, social agencies operate at the will of the people. Governing or advisory boards made up of community representatives play a critical role in establishing and/or shaping the policies and programs that these agencies provide and also serve as the interface between the community and staff. The board's actions and decisions, therefore, affect the resources (e.g., funds, volunteers) that are available to support the services provided by the agency. Thus, it is essential that the social worker understand the authority and responsibilities of the agency's board. Furthermore, if the policies and programs currently in place fail to adequately meet the needs of clients, the social worker must understand how the agency's board functions in order to effectively advocate for change.

In private and nonprofit social agencies, the ***governing board*** is the body that is sanctioned to manage the organization. Legally, the board is responsible for the total management of the organization and the members are personally liable for its financial viability. However, board members cannot and should not be present on a day-to-day basis to manage the operation of the agency. That is the job of the executive director or chief administrator. When a governing board shares its authority with the executive director, who then engages other staff members to provide the services, the lines of authority must be clearly drawn so there is no confusion that interferes with the provision of client services.

Raymond (2000) suggests that the board should have these responsibilities:

1. Determining the long-term impact to be caused by the organization's existence;
2. Specifying the boundaries around the executive director's and the board's behavior;
3. Monitoring the performance of the executive director against the board's clear expectations;

4. Assuring that the organization has the resources to cause the impact decided by the board; and
5. Developing and maintaining relationships with key organizational stakeholders. (p. 2)

The governing board of an agency, then, is responsible for *policymaking* to establish the goals, operating policies, and programs; *planning* to link the agency with the needs of the community; *fund-raising* to assure the resources needed to operate the organization are available; *staffing* to carry out the programs under the guidance of the executive director; providing *facilities* in which to deliver the programs; *communicating* with the public regarding the agency's successes; and conducting *evaluations* to assure accountability for the trust placed in them to govern the organization.

Particularly in a private agency, the composition of the board is important. It should be representative of the community but also bring expertise or resources that are needed. Some agencies, but not all, select members with the expectation that they will be major fund-raisers or donors (i.e., the principle of the 3Gs applies: get money, give money, or get off the board).

In a public agency, by contrast, the ***advisory board*** (also called an *advisory council* or *advisory committee*) has no legal authority or responsibility for the operation of the organization. It is established either because the public officials responsible for the operation of the organization desire citizen input and/or because public law requires an advisory body as a channel for citizen participation. As the name implies, it offers advice but cannot require compliance with that advice. Why, then, would an agency have an advisory board? Advisory boards exist for these purposes:

1. To help identify the needs of the community and recommend new or revised programs
2. To evaluate agency programs and propose new procedures for conducting the agency's business
3. To assist in fund-raising (see Item 13.38) and public education regarding the agency's work

Typically, the members of both governing and advisory boards volunteer their time and talents to the agency. The motivations of board members may vary from a desire to help others, to a desire to use their special knowledge to benefit the community, to seeking personal recognition and social status. It is important to understand these motivations and use this resource in a manner that both serves the agency and satisfies the board member's need.

SELECTED BIBLIOGRAPHY

Perlmutter, Felice Davidson, and Wendy P. Crook. *Changing Hats while Managing Change: Social Work Practice to Administration*, 2nd ed. Washington, DC: NASW Press, 2004.

Tropman, John, and Elmer J. Tropman. *Nonprofit Boards: What to Do and How to Do It.* Washington, DC: Child Welfare League of America, 1999.

13.25   CONDUCTING EFFECTIVE STAFF MEETINGS

Purpose: To plan and conduct efficient staff meetings that promote intraagency communication.

Discussion: An important factor in the successful operation of a social agency is the quality of staff communication, making the staff meeting a critically important tool in agency management. Properly used, the staff meeting enhances communication and can prevent organizational problems caused by staff who act on inaccurate or incomplete information. Improperly used, staff meetings can be both costly for the agency and frustrating for the staff. A one-hour meeting involving a staff of eight, for example, is the equivalent of a day's salary for one person. The cost of the meeting should be justified by its benefits for achieving the agency's purpose, as compared to the staff providing service to clients during that time.

It is important to distinguish between a staff meeting and other types of meetings, such as case staffings and consultations and the meetings used for case assignments or by special committees and project teams. The distinction between staff meetings and team meetings can be made in terms of *purpose* (e.g., exchange of information regarding the agency versus practice techniques related to specific cases); *content* (e.g., discussion of policies, procedures, organizational maintenance, and professional practice issues versus a specific issue of practice activity regarding a case situation); *formality* (e.g., a formal decision-making structure), *membership* (e.g., inclusive of practitioners and support staff); and *size* (e.g., typically larger than a team meeting).

Staff meeting time should not be spent on routine or easily understood information that can be disseminated by other means, such as memos and email. Staff meeting time is best spent only on matters that require verbal clarification, feedback from staff, or a staff decision. Also, staff meetings should be held at the same time each week or month, have a set starting and ending time, and last not more than one hour. Attendance should be mandatory, and the leader should prepare and circulate an agenda in advance of the meeting and take responsibility to keep the discussion moving. However, staff meetings are not solely a management responsibility. All staff should be expected to contribute agenda items, be prepared for discussion of those items, and assume responsibility for following through on items that require their attention. If an issue requires extensive discussion, a separate meeting should be scheduled. In many settings, the preparation of minutes is useful to disseminate information and properly record staff decisions in order to keep upper levels of administration informed of the activities of this unit.

Barretta-Herman's (1990, 145) analysis of staff meetings in human services organizations identifies three elements of successful meetings:

1. They should fulfill their objectives by jointly involving management and practitioners.
2. They should provide a forum for active discussion, creative problem solving, and participation of staff members.
3. The structure of the meeting should ensure that decisions made are followed through with action.

SELECTED BIBLIOGRAPHY

Barretta-Herman, Angeline. "The Effective Social Service Staff Meeting." In *Business Communi-cation: New Zealand Perspectives*, edited by Frank Slegio, 136–147. Auckland, New Zealand: Software Technology, 1990.

Brody, Ralph. *Effectively Managing Human Service Organizations*, 3rd ed. Thousand Oaks, CA: Sage, 2005.

Tropman, John E. *Making Meetings Work: Achieving High Quality Group Decisions*. Thousand Oaks, CA: Sage, 2003.

13.26   BUILDING TEAMWORK AND COOPERATION

Purpose: To encourage and develop interagency and interprofessional cooperation.

Discussion: Given the complexity of human services, often requiring the involvement of both multiagency and multidisciplinary workplaces, there is a need for social workers to have good teamwork skills. Providing services through teams and cooperative efforts not only draws together the resources of multiple agencies but also provides opportunities for the knowledge and skills of several disciplines to be brought into a service plan. Thus, if the client is to be served, the social worker must be prepared to work as a team member and to generate teamwork and cooperation from others.

Following these guidelines can encourage cooperation and teamwork:

1. In general, individuals and organizations cooperate with each other when it is of benefit to do so. Those benefits may be personal, professional, organizational, political, or financial. Cooperation is fostered by emphasizing what the parties have in common and how they and the client will benefit from working together.

2. Genuine teamwork and interagency cooperation does not occur by accident; they must be encouraged and nurtured. Statements of thanks, recognition, praise, and taking a personal interest in other team members help to reinforce cooperative behavior. Where appropriate, invite other members of the team to social gatherings as a way of building relationships and promoting goodwill. Do not engage in activities that might diminish respect for other professionals or agencies.

3. Teamwork and cooperation is built on a common purpose. That purpose is to serve the client and to accomplish what no one professional or single agency can achieve alone. Whenever necessary, help the team members or agency representatives revisit the question What are we trying to achieve for our clients?

4. Encourage the selection of a leader or chairperson who is nondefensive, supportive of others, and respected by the group. Strive to be proactive and willing to plan and prepare carefully for team meetings and assume a leadership role when appropriate.

5. Concern for client confidentiality is a reason commonly given for not working closely with other agencies and professionals. Sometimes this issue is more imagined than real. Clients can be asked to sign a release of information, thus removing this barrier. If professionals or agencies want to work together but are hesitant to do so because of confidentiality, they should ask their agency's legal counsel to recommend a workable procedure.

6. Be alert to the fact that many interagency conflicts center on questions of which agency has primary fiscal responsibility for providing a particular service. In other words, many disagreements boil down to the question of whose budget is to be used to pay the cost of services.

7. Understand your role and responsibility and those of the people with whom you are working. Make sure everyone knows what they can and cannot expect of each other. Several forms of documents might be used to define interagency expectations such as contracts, letters of agreement, protocol statements, and purchase of service agreements.

8. Remember that even under the best circumstances, teamwork can be challenging. This is especially true when the team is attempting to make difficult, value-laden decisions. Members should be willing to address directly and openly the conflicts or hidden agendas that disrupt team efforts. Conflict that arises from thoughtful differences of opinion is healthy. However, conflict that stems from bias or thoughtless loyalty to actions of the past is disruptive. Attempts to suppress or avoid conflicts or significant differences of opinion by denial, capitulation, or domination often make the problem even worse. When it is necessary to express a difference of opinion, use I-statements and other communication skills that convey your message in a clear, straightforward, and nonthreatening manner. Try to resolve interprofessional and interagency conflicts by focusing on shared values and goals and by using negotiating skills.

9. Realize that some of those with whom you must work may not be committed to teamwork. When this is evident, be firm but diplomatic in expressing the need for cooperation and for putting the good of the client before other considerations.

SELECTED BIBLIOGRAPHY

Garner, Howard. *Helping Others through Teamwork: A Handbook for Professionals*, 2nd ed. Washington, DC: Child Welfare League of America, 2001.
Gold, Natalie, ed. *Teamwork: Multi-Disciplinary Perspectives*. New York: Macmillan, 2005.

13.27   LEADING SMALL-GROUP MEETINGS

Purpose: To schedule and conduct efficient and productive committee and group meetings.

Discussion: Group decision making has become increasingly popular in the human services. Therefore, social workers spend considerable time participating in groups, agency staff meetings, interagency team meetings, and various agency and community committees. While group consideration of issues potentially leads to better decisions, group meetings, without proper planning and direction, can waste much valuable time and reduce the opportunity for making change. As the leader of a small group, the social worker is responsible for making the meeting as productive and efficient as possible. The following principles and guidelines should be followed by the worker when he or she is in a leadership position:

1. *Prepare for the meeting by engaging in the following activities:*
   - Clearly identify the purpose of the meeting.
   - Decide who should participate.
   - Identify objectives for the meeting and anticipate what the participants will and should expect. You may want to involve them in the planning.
   - Decide the best time and place for the meeting, and determine how participants will be notified of the purpose, agenda, starting time, and location of the meeting.
   - Decide how much time will be required for the meeting and construct a realistic agenda. Plan to address high-priority items first.
   - Decide what physical arrangements are necessary (e.g., room reservations, seating arrangements, audiovisual equipment, refreshments, etc.).
   - Decide if a written report will be needed and, if so, who will prepare it and how it will be distributed.
   - Decide if a follow-up meeting will be needed.

2. *Get the discussion off to a good start.*
   - Make sure that all members are introduced to each other. Use name tags if members do not already know each other.
   - Explain the purpose of the discussion and its relevance to the participants.
   - Distribute materials needed for the discussion (e.g., fact sheets, outlines, case examples).
   - Create an atmosphere that helps the participants feel valued, appreciated, and responsible for contributing to the discussion.

3. *Give all members an opportunity to participate.*
   - Explain in your opening remarks that the role of the group leader primarily will be that of coordinator to ensure that all members have an opportunity to be heard.
   - Address your comments and questions to the group as a whole, unless specific information is needed from a particular person.
   - Scan the group every minute or two. Look for indications that a member wants to speak. If this is seen and the member has been quiet, bring that person into the discussion by asking if he or she would like to add something to the discussion.
   - If the group contains members who dominate the discussion, try to control them for the benefit of the group. A number of techniques can be

used; begin with a more subtle approach and become directive only if necessary. Here are some possible ways to deal with such members:

   a. Seat the talkative members where they are more easily overlooked by other members.

   b. When a question is asked of the group, meet the eyes of those members who have spoken infrequently and avoid eye contact with the dominant talkers.

   c. When a frequent talker has made a point, cut in with something like: How do the rest of you feel about that idea?

   d. Propose a rule that each person can make but one statement per topic.

   e. In private, ask the excessive talkers to help in getting the quiet members to speak more often.

   f. Point out the problem and ask others to contribute more—for instance: "We have heard a lot from John and Mary, but what do the rest of you think about . . . ?"

- If asked by a member to express a personal opinion about a controversial issue, try to bounce the question back to the group, unless members already have expressed their opinions. Say, "Well, let's see how others feel about this first." If you must express a personal opinion, do so in a manner that will not inhibit others from speaking on the topic.
- Avoid making a comment after each member has spoken. Doing so tends to create a "wheel" pattern of communication, with the leader becoming the hub of the wheel and thus the center of attention.
- React to what members say with acceptance and without judgment, showing only that a point is understood or that it needs clarification. If evaluation seems necessary, invite it from others with a question such as "Does that fit with your perception on the matter?"
- Use nonverbal communication to promote discussion. Nods and gestures can be used to encourage participation, especially from the quiet members.

4. *Promote cooperation and harmony in a small group.*

- Be alert to the possibility of counterproductive hidden agendas, and, if necessary, call them to the attention of the group. The group usually can solve a problem of conflicting purposes if it is brought into the open for discussion.
- Emphasize the importance of the mutual sharing of ideas and experiences and the need for clear communication.
- Use the word *we* often to stress the group's unity of purpose.
- Keep conflicts focused on facts and issues. Stop any personal attacks.
- Do not let the discussion become so serious that the members do not have some fun. Humor can reduce tension. Effective discussion is characterized by shifting between the serious and the playful.

5. *Use questioning techniques to maintain attention on a topic and encourage analytical thinking.*

- Use open-ended questions, such as "What do you see as the merits of . . .?"
- Questions should be understandable to all. Vague or obtuse questions frustrate the members.

- Questions should be asked in a natural and conversational tone of voice.
- Questions should usually be addressed to the group as a whole, rather than to a particular individual. This motivates everyone to think and respond.
- Questions occasionally should be asked of persons who are not giving their attention to the discussion. This usually stimulates the individual and the whole group to redirect its attention to the topic.
- Questions should be asked in a manner that indicates the leader's confidence in the person's ability to respond.
- Questions should be selected to maintain the focus on the topic under discussion. Avoid questions that would cause the group to leave its task and go off on a tangent.
- Ask for more detail and specification. Dig for the rationale and assumptions behind an opinion or a belief. Help those offering opinions to furnish evidence for the positions they take.
- See that the evidence offered for a position is tested and not accepted at face value.
- Assign one or two members of the group to challenge ideas and play devil's advocate so that differences are aired openly.

6. *Keep the discussion orderly, efficient, and productive.*
   - Keep the participants focused on the meeting's goals and purpose. For example, occasionally ask, "Are we still on target for reaching our objectives?"
   - Be alert to extended departures from the topic. If the group is drifting away from the topic, call this to everyone's attention. Ask if the digression means that there is disagreement on the goal or if it is an indication that the group is ready to move on to another topic.
   - If there is much repetition in the discussion, ask if the group has exhausted the subject at hand. If so, help them get started on a new topic.
   - Be the group's timekeeper. Keep the group informed of the time limits so high-priority topics will get the attention they deserve.
   - Bring the discussion to a conclusion, which might include any of the following:
     a. A summary of progress made by the group
     b. Comments about planning and preparation for another meeting
     c. Assignments for follow-up and implementation
     d. Commendations when appropriate
     e. A request for an evaluation of the meeting in order to improve future meetings

SELECTED BIBLIOGRAPHY

Brilhart, John K., Gloria J. Galanes, and Katherine Adams. *Effective Group Discussion: Theory and Practice*, 11th ed. Boston: McGraw-Hill, 2004.

Ephross, Paul H., and and Thomas V. Vassil, *Groups that Work: Structure and Process*. New York: Columbia University Press, 2005.

Kaner, Sam. *Facilitator's Guide to Participatory Decision Making*, 2nd ed. Hoboken, NJ: John Wiley, 2007.

Tropman, John E. *Making Meetings Work: Achieving High-Quality Group Decisions*, 2nd ed. Thousand Oaks, CA: Sage, 2003.

13.28   THE RISK TECHNIQUE

Purpose: To facilitate committee or group members in expressing their fears or concerns about an issue or proposed action.

Discussion: At times, committees (and especially staff committees) need to address fears and concerns related to some perceived risk or threat. For example, when new policies are adopted by a board, when new legislation is passed that affects a social program and/or the resources available, or when administrators establish a change in routine, it becomes important to identify and clarify the facts and issues in the situation and set aside rumors and fantasized outcomes. In these situations, the *RISK technique* can be useful.

To use this technique, the leader must take a nondefensive posture and communicate an interest in having the group members express all fears, issues, concerns, complaints, and anticipated problems. By maintaining this approach, the leader encourages members of the group to express their views and to listen and understand one another's fears.

For example, assume that a change is proposed in an agency that would double the number of days that social workers are on 24-hour call. To address concerns about this proposal, the supervisor might elect to use the RISK technique by taking the following steps:

1. The leader schedules a meeting with all agency workers and presents a detailed description of the proposed change in the on-call section of the agency's personnel policy.

2. The leader explains that he or she will utilize the RISK technique to help workers identify all of their concerns about this proposed change.

3. The leader begins by asking workers to voice any and all fears, concerns, and worries they have in relation to the proposed change. These "risks" are written on newsprint for all to see, with the wording of the statement acceptable to the person raising the concern. Discussion of the items is not permitted at this time. (Note that up to this point, the RISK technique is similar to brainstorming, Item 13.32.)

4. The leader continues to encourage workers to voice additional concerns about the proposed change. It is important to allow adequate time for this session because the concerns that are most disturbing and threatening often will not surface until late in the session.

5. The initial session ends and the leader schedules a second meeting to occur in the next three to seven days. Meanwhile, all workers receive a written listing of the risk items identified during the meeting.

6. At the second meeting, the leader encourages workers to voice any additional risks they may have thought of since the initial meeting or to change the wording of any risk statements. The group is then asked to discuss and react to each risk item and decide if it is, indeed, a serious and substantive concern or issue. The risks considered to be minor or of little concern are dropped from the list. Those remaining are further discussed and clarified. At this point, the second meeting is ended with the understanding that the identified risks are viewed as those of the group as a whole, and not the person who first identified any risk.

7. The leader places the group's identified risks (i.e., the final list from the second meeting) on an agenda for a meeting between the workers and administrators.

SELECTED BIBLIOGRAPHY

Brilhart, John K., Gloria J. Galanes, and Katherine Adams. *Effective Group Discussion: Theory and Practice*, 11th ed. Boston: McGraw-Hill, 2004.

13.29   THE NOMINAL GROUP TECHNIQUE (NGT)

Purpose: To help consensus-oriented groups arrive at decisions.

Discussion: Committees that depend on a consensus approach sometimes get stuck in reaching a decision. One technique that helps bring issues into the open and moves the group toward consensus is the ***Nominal Group Technique (NGT).*** It is particularly suited for groups of six to nine people; if used with a larger group, the committee should be divided into smaller groups. Depending on the scope and complexity of the matter being addressed, it might take from little as an hour and a half to a much longer period to complete the process.

There are four main elements in the NGT process:

1. The participants generate ideas in writing.
2. Round-robin feedback is given from group members with each idea recorded in a terse phrase on a flipchart.
3. Group discussion of each recorded idea is held for clarification and evaluation.
4. Individual voting establishes priorities among ideas with a group decision being mathematically derived through rank ordering or rating.

The following guidelines are suggested to help structure a NGT session:

1. The chair acts as facilitator and does not vote.
2. The issue is stated on a flipchart.
3. The pros and cons are freely discussed for 10 minutes.
4. Each person is asked to spend 5 to 15 minutes working silently, writing down ideas or solutions on a piece of paper. The chair polls each committee member for one idea or solution.
5. Each idea or solution is listed on the chart and numbered. The chair then polls each member for a second idea or solution and repeats this process until the lists have been exhausted.
6. An additional 10 more minutes are allowed for clarification of the ideas or solutions presented—not for defense of the position.

7. All members vote on a secret ballot, ranking their top five choices 1, 2, 3, 4, 5. By adding the scores for each idea or solution, the lower scores will reflect the most favored positions.
8. Discuss the several items at the top of the list. Encourage critical thinking, invite disagreement, and seek careful analysis of the items.
9. If a clear consensus is not reached, revote and then discuss the items again. This can be repeated until a synthesis of ideas is developed or there is clear support for one idea.

The NGT process encourages active involvement by all participants as they consider and write down their ideas. Too often, in a group process, a few members carry the discussion and others do not actively and creatively think about the issues from their own perspectives. The interactive presentation of the issues allows all committee members an opportunity to express themselves and respond to the ideas from both the verbal and less-verbal members.

SELECTED BIBLIOGRAPHY

Brilhart, John K., Gloria J. Galanes, and Katherine Adams. *Effective Group Discussion: Theory and Practice*, 11th ed. Boston: McGraw-Hill, 2004.
Toseland, Ronald W., and Robert F. Rivas. *An Introduction to Group Work Practice*, 5th ed. Boston: Allyn & Bacon, 2005.

13.30   CHAIRING A FORMAL COMMITTEE

Purpose: To effectively serve as chair of a committee and lead it to successful action.

Discussion: The committee is a particular type of small group for which the social worker might assume a leadership function. As chairperson of a committee, the social worker should make use of the guidelines for working with small groups (see Item 13.27). In addition, chairing a committee requires the use of a formal task-oriented approach to groups.

Essential knowledge for both the chairperson and committee members is familiarity with parliamentary procedures. For more than a century, *Robert's Rules of Order* (Robert 2000) has been the accepted procedures to be followed in formal committee proceedings. Table 13.1 provides a summary of these rules.

Above all else, a committee chair must believe in the worth and wisdom of group decision making. The decisions made by a small group, as compared to those made by a single individual, are more likely to be based on accurate and complete information and on a wider range of considerations; thus, the decisions are more likely to be the best ones possible. That is not to say that committees do not make bad decisions. They do. But a group is less likely to make a bad decision or a serious error in judgment than is an individual acting alone.

Tropman, Johnson, and Tropman (1992) remind us that the committee chair must be alert to the danger of *groupthink*, a situation of false agreement or false consensus that arises when a powerful committee member takes a strong stand on an issue and other members simply acquiesce rather than argue an opposing point of view. Soon after the meeting, the other members will usually complain and agree among themselves that the decision reached was a bad one. Needless to say, this conflict could have been avoided if the chair had made sure all points of view were expressed and debated and no one member or faction dominated the meeting.

People are usually willing to serve on a committee if they believe their time will be used efficiently and the committee's work will result in a real and positive change. On the other hand, many people have reasons for disliking and avoiding committee work:

- There is a lack of clear purpose (e.g., members are not sure why they are meeting or what they are to accomplish).
- There is a lack of leadership and direction by the chairperson (e.g., the chair does not keep the group moving and focused; real issues are not addressed or difficult decisions are avoided).
- The chair and/or members do not take the assignment seriously (i.e., lack of motivation or interest in the work of the committee).
- The committee's work is disregarded by top management (e.g., a committee is asked to study an issue and make a recommendation but the recommendation is ignored; sometimes the committee discovers that there was never an intention to follow the committee's recommendation).
- Committee discussion is controlled or dominated by one individual or a clique.
- There is a lack of preparation for the meetings (e.g., no agenda, needed information is not made available, etc.).
- There is a lack of follow through (e.g., members or the chair promises to do something but fails to do so).
- The chair or members have a hidden agenda (e.g., some members have an ax to grind or will accept only one outcome, regardless of majority opinion).

One means of helping a committee avoid pitfalls that can lead to unproductive meetings is to engage the members in setting goals and operating procedures for the committee. Whether it is new or a committee that has continued over an extended period of time, it is useful for the chairperson or other members to periodically review and renegotiate the objectives and methods of operation so that all members can fully participate in the work. Dyer (1995) identifies several steps that should be followed in building a productive committee:

1. *Give the work realistic priority.* It is important to give members a chance to discuss why they are serving on the committee, clarify the relative importance of this work in the context of their total responsibilities, and indicate the amount of time they are able to commit to this activity. Sharing these matters helps to establish the

TABLE 13.1   Summary of Parliamentary Procedure

Guidelines/Description	Type of Action	Purpose of Action	Interrupts Debate?	Requires Second?	Debatable?	Amendable?	Vote Required?
	PRIVILEGED MOTIONS						
■ #1–12 in order of priority	1. Fix time to adjourn	Establish plan to discontinue meeting	No	Yes	No	No	Majority
■ #1–4 supersede all other actions	2. Recess	Temporary break in meeting	No	Yes	Yes	Yes	Majority
	3. Question of privilege	Challenge rights of assembly or a member to take an action	Yes	No	No	No	None
	4. Point of order	Clarify or challenge process	Yes	No	No	No	None
	SUBSIDIARY MOTIONS						
■ #5–12 facilitate action on other motions	5. Table the motion	Delay action to a specified meeting	No	Yes	No	No	Majority
	6. Previous question	Close debate and vote immediately	No	Yes	No	No	2/3
	7. Limit debate	Set limits on future debate	No	Yes	Yes	Yes	2/3
	8. Postpone definitely	Temporarily delay action to a specified time	No	Yes	Yes	Yes	Majority
■ Each may be made while motion below is on the floor	9. Refer to committee	Delay until committee can review matter and report back	No	Yes	Yes	Yes	Majority
	10. Amend the amendment	One amendment to primary amendment is permitted at a time	No	Yes	Yes	Yes	Majority
	11. Primary amendment	Propose change in main motion	No	Yes	Yes	Yes	Majority
	12. Postpone indefinitely	Remove motion from consideration	No	Yes	Yes	No	Majority

Process Starts Here		Interrupt debate?	Require second?	Debatable?	Amendable?	Approval
MAIN MOTION OR RESOLUTION						
Routes to opening main motion — New motion	Introduce action for first time	No	Yes	Yes	Yes	Majority
Reconsider prior action	Reconsider previous vote	Yes	Yes	Yes	No	Majority
Resume consideration	Take up motion previously tabled	No	Yes	Yes	No	Majority
INCIDENTAL MOTIONS						
No order of precedence — Move to appeal	Challenge ruling of the chair	Yes	Yes	Yes	No	Majority
Arise from process of debate and may occur at any time — Move to suspend rules	Override existing procedures	No	Yes	No	No	2/3
Request point of order	Correct parliamentary process error	Yes	No	No	No	None
Yield only to privileged motions — Withdraw motion	Remove motion from consideration	Yes	No	No	No	None
Division of question	Act on parts of motion or amendment	No	No	No	No	None
Division of assembly	After voice vote, request vote count	Yes	No	No	No	None
Request for information	Seek clarification	Yes	No	No	No	None

Note: Parliamentary procedure requires study and practice before it becomes useful. An action can only occur after a motion or resolution is introduced, as indicated in the left column by "Process Starts Here." One of the three routes to opening the main motion must be selected, and then the chair can track across the columns from left to right to determine the process to follow. Does it interrupt debate? (Yes/No) Does it require a second? (Yes/No) Is it debatable? (Yes/No) Can it be amended? (Yes/No) Is a vote required, and if so, what proportion of the voters must support it if it is to be approved? For any subsequent motion, the same process applies. Note that moving vertically up the page, the "Privileged" and "Subsidiary" motions are listed in order of priority from the top (#1) to the bottom of the first page (#12). The "Incidental" motions (listed below the main motion) may be made at any time during debate, but they do not override the privileged motions.

pace at which the committee can operate and allows the chair to identify persons who have the time and interest to carry major responsibilities.

2. *Share expectations.* Each person should be asked to identify his or her greatest concerns about working on this committee, how he or she sees it functioning, and what actions are necessary to ensure positive outcomes.

3. *Clarify goals.* The committee members should collectively discuss and write down a statement that represents the group's *core mission*. Subgoals can then be developed to reflect the intermediate or short-range objectives necessary to accomplish this mission. During subsequent committee work, each decision and action should be examined for its contribution to the mission or subgoals that have been established.

4. *Formulate operating guidelines.* The committee members should then establish procedures for their operation. Answers to the following questions will provide guidance for the chair and allow members to know how to proceed:
- How will we make decisions?
- What will be our basic method of working as a group?
- How do we make sure everyone gets a chance to discuss issues or raise concerns?
- How will we resolve differences?
- How will we ensure that we complete our work and meet deadlines?
- How will we change methods that are not producing results?

In addition, it should be recognized that the formality with which a committee operates often depends on its size, the existing relationships among the members, and the speed with which it needs to make decisions. The purpose of some committees is best served by an open dialogue that explores topics in depth before action is taken. For others, the work is more task oriented. Subcommittees consider the issues and prepare reports of their deliberations on which the full committee will act.

SELECTED BIBLIOGRAPHY

Dyer, William G. *Team Building: Issues and Alternatives,* 3rd ed. Reading, MA: Addison-Wesley, 1995.

Robert, Henry M., III, William J. Evans, Daniel H. Honemann, and Thomas J. Balch. *Robert's Rules of Order Newly Revised, in Brief.* Cambridge, MA: DaCapro Press, 2004.

13.31   PROBLEM SOLVING BY A LARGE GROUP

Purpose: To help a large group of people arrive at a decision.

Discussion: At times, it is necessary for a social worker to initiate problem-solving activity within a large group. The technique described here is intended to elicit ideas from all members and provide an opportunity for participation, even when as many as 30 or more people are involved.

The technique begins with the group leader explaining the purpose of the meeting—for example: "We need to come up with a method of collecting information from the agencies in town on trends in the number of homeless people applying for help." These steps should then be followed:

1. *Each individual is asked to think privately about the problem and possible solutions.* Members are asked to make written notes on their thoughts.

2. *Dyads are formed.* Each person in the dyad is instructed to interview his or her partner and to try to understand that person's perspective on the problem and proposed solutions. The dyads work for 10 minutes.

3. *Quartets are formed.* For 15 minutes, each group of four people discusses the problem and possible solutions. Each quartet records the key points of its deliberation on a large piece of paper, which is hung on the wall for all to see.

4. *Each individual studies the papers for 10 minutes.*

5. *The whole group reassembles and shares their analysis of the problem and proposed solutions.* This final step sets the stage for the prioritizing of proposed solutions to be explored in more depth.

SELECTED BIBLIOGRAPHY

Brody, Ralph. *Effectively Managing Human Service Organizations,* 3rd ed. Thousand Oaks, CA: Sage, 2005.

Tropman, John E. *Making Meetings Work: Achieving High-Quality Group Decisions,* 2nd ed. Thousand Oaks, CA: Sage, 2003.

13.32   BRAINSTORMING

Purpose: To help a participant identify several possible solutions to a problem.

Discussion: Problem solving includes the important step of identifying all possible alternatives or solutions. Too often, some potential solutions are overlooked because they do not fit preconceived notions or expectations. Being rigid and following old habits of thought can limit creativity during the problem-solving process. The technique of **brainstorming** is designed to overcome this limitation. It can be applied to any problem for which there may be a range of solutions. The objective of brainstorming is to free persons temporarily from self-criticism and from the criticism of others in order to generate imaginative solutions to a specific problem. However, it should not be used until the problem has been clearly defined. Brainstorming is most often used in work with groups or committees, but many workers adapt its principles for use in one-on-one counseling sessions.

A brainstorming session begins with the identification and listing of a wide variety of possible solutions. Many may be unrealistic, but it is only after all alternatives have been identified that the participants are permitted to evaluate the proposed solutions in search of those that are feasible. A social worker setting up a brainstorming session should give several instructions:

1. Encourage participants to develop a large number of solutions. The goal is to generate a quantity of solutions—quality will be determined later.
2. Encourage participants to be freewheeling in their thinking. Even wild ideas should be welcomed and accepted without judgment.
3. Recommend that participants combine and elaborate on the solutions that are offered.
4. Do not allow participants to criticize or evaluate one another's proposed solutions.

During the brainstorming session, a recorder writes down all the ideas as fast as they come up. Do this on a blackboard or flipchart so the visual record stimulates additional ideas. The leader of the session should quickly stop any criticism of ideas, whether verbal or implied by tone of voice or nonverbal gesture. Also, the group leader needs to keep the participants focused on the problem under consideration.

Once all of the proposed solutions or ideas have been heard and recorded, the session moves to a second stage: the critical examination of each idea. De Bono (1992) suggests a useful technique for ensuring that six types of questioning and thinking are applied during the evaluation stage. Each of these six categories of thinking is called a "hat," and each hat has a color. Thus, for example, when the group is asked by the group leader to "put on your red hats," the group is being asked to evaluate the proposed solutions in terms of hunches, intuition, and gut feelings. If asked to put on the "black hat," the group is to view the solutions in a highly critical and skeptical manner.

The six thinking hats are as follow:

1. *White hat* (focus on objectivity and data): What information do we have? How reliable is this information? What additional information do we need?
2. *Red hat* (focus on hunches and intuition): What are our gut feelings about this proposed solution? Does it "feel" right? Let's trust our instincts!
3. *Black hat* (focus on caution and risk): What are the legal, policy, political, and funding problems we will encounter? This cannot be done and will not work because . . .
4. *Yellow hat* (focus on optimism): It needs to be done, so let's try! Who cares if it has never been done before? Let's try something different! It will work if we really want it to work!
5. *Green hat* (focus on creativity and other combinations of ideas): Are there still other ways of thinking about this? Can we combine the best parts of several different proposals?
6. *Blue hat* (focus on the big picture and holistic thinking): How does this idea fit with other things we know about this issue? Are we missing something important? Let's summarize the conclusions we have reached and the decisions we have made so far. Is our way of discussing and approaching this issue working for us? Are we making progress toward a decision or solution?

Be sure to provide sufficient time for a brainstorming session. Considering that many ideas might be generated in a single session and that time will be needed to evaluate each proposed solution, a brainstorming session could easily take more than an hour.

SELECTED BIBLIOGRAPHY

De Bono, Edward. *Serious Creativity*. New York: HarperCollins, 1992.

Paulus, Paul B., and Bernard A. Nijsted, eds. *Group Creativity: Innovation through Collaboration*. New York: Oxford University Press, 2003.

13.33   CLASS ADVOCACY

Purpose: To advance the cause of a group in order to establish a right or entitlement to a resource or opportunity.

Discussion: The term ***class advocacy*** refers to actions on behalf of a whole group or class of people. This is in contrast to *client advocacy* (see Item 13.18), in which the advocacy is on behalf of a specific individual. Because class advocacy seeks change in law and public policy at either the local, state, or national level, it is essentially a political process aimed at influencing the decisions of elected officials and high-level administrators. It entails building coalitions with other groups and organizations that share concerns about a social issue. The social worker typically participates as a representative of an organization, rather than as an independent practitioner.

Since the goal is to bring about a change, opposition should be expected. Not everyone is comfortable with this type of advocacy. Further, each organization must examine the pros and cons of taking on an advocacy role and decide whether having its representatives perform this role fits with the purpose of the organization.

For those who choose to become engaged in class advocacy, following these guidelines may increase the chance of success:

1. Realize that advocacy intends to help bring about needed changes in laws, policies, and programs. Bringing about change is difficult—but not impossible.

2. Remember that you cannot do it alone. Individual social workers will need to join with others. A group has more power than an individual, and several organizations working together have more power than a single organization working alone. Working with other organizations will mean that your own organization will have to share some resources, make some compromises, and perhaps do some things differently. In the long run, however, you will accomplish more as part of a coalition than by working alone.

3. Many improvements are needed in our human services systems. Since you cannot do everything that needs to be done, you must decide which concern has the highest priority. If you or your organization take on several causes at one time, you may be spread too thin. It is better to make real gains in just one area than to make minimal gains or fail completely in several.

4. It is also important to choose a cause where success is possible. Be realistic! Do not waste your time and energy on a lost cause. A successful experience generates hope and a feeling that other successes are possible. If participants can see even small successes, they will be more willing to invest themselves in future advocacy efforts.

5. Successful advocacy is built on a foundation of careful analysis and planning. It is important to define what you see as a problem and carefully study the problem—before you make a decision on what to do about it. Do not launch an effort to change something until you know exactly what has to be changed, why it has to be changed, and what will be involved in bringing about the change.

6. Before you take action, carefully assess what achieving your goal will require in the way of time, energy, money, and other resources. Do you have the resources? If not, it is best to scale down your goals or wait until later when you are better organized and more capable of reaching your goal.

7. Try to understand those who oppose you. There is always resistance to change, and analysis of the situation should include understanding why there is resistance. The advocate needs to be able to put himself or herself in the opponent's shoes (i.e., have empathy). People always have reasons for opposing change. You may not agree with their reasons, but you must understand them if you are to figure out a way to successfully overcome that resistance.

8. Successful advocacy requires self-discipline. One of the most serious errors one can make in advocacy is to act impulsively. If that happens, the other organizations in the coalition may pull back or be reluctant to cooperate because they fear that your recklessness will cause damage to their organization or to the coalition. Also, if you act impulsively, those who oppose you can more easily discredit you.

9. Advocacy involves the use of power. You may not have as much power as you want, but do not overlook the power you do have. Essentially, **power** is the ability to make others behave the way you want them to behave. Think of power as a resource that can be used or "spent" for a particular purpose. There are different kinds of power. It is important to study your own organization and its membership in order to discover the type of power that you possess.

Among the types of power social workers have is the power that comes from knowledge and expertise. For example, if you are advocating on behalf of children, you have detailed information about children and troubled families, and you know how the system works or does not work for the benefit of children and families. Information, if carefully assembled and presented, can have a powerful impact on legislators, agency administrators, and the public.

Perhaps some members of your organization are highly respected in the community. They are held in high esteem by the public because of their past achievements. They have credibility that gives them a type of power. Individuals who are respected can have a significant influence on legislators and administrators. You need to encourage and help those respected individuals to advocate actively in behalf of the issue.

Do not forget that personal commitment, time, and energy are also types of power. Much can be accomplished just by sticking with a task and seeing it through to the end. Organizational solidarity is also a type of power. If legislators and decision makers can see that members are solidly behind their organization, they will pay attention to what the organization's leaders have to say.

Within your organization are members who are natural leaders. Some may be charismatic and articulate. They can excite people and get them to work together on a cause. Charisma is a rare quality, but it is definitely a type of power. Identify those individuals in your organization and let them speak for your cause.

10. There are times when class advocacy must take the form of a lawsuit. Many changes and reforms would never have happened without lawsuits and court decisions. For example, many of the reforms in the areas of mental health and mental retardation have grown out of legal actions. An organization committed to advocacy will, at times, need to encourage and support lawsuits that have potential for bringing about a needed change.

11. Most people in the United States depend on television and newspapers for information. If one wants the public to understand and support a cause, it is important to learn to work with the media (see Item 13.37). If there is someone associated with the organization who knows how to work in advertising and the use of media, make use of that person's talent. If not, approach an advertising agency or perhaps a school of journalism and ask if someone would be willing to help you get your message on TV or in the newspapers.

SELECTED BIBLIOGRAPHY

Ezell, Mark. *Advocacy in the Human Services*. Belmont, CA: Brooks/Cole, 2001.
Haynes, Karen, and James Mickelson. *Affecting Change: Social Workers in the Political Arena*, 6th ed. Boston: Allyn & Bacon, 2006.

13.34 TEACHING AND TRAINING

Purpose: To guide and assist others in the acquisition of information, knowledge, or skills.

Discussion: Social workers do a lot of teaching. They frequently teach skills related to parenting, interpersonal communication, stress management, job seeking, independent living, and so on. Their teaching may be directed to clients, volunteers, colleagues, or concerned citizens. It may occur within the context of a one-to-one relationship, a workshop, or a formal classroom situation. Several guidelines can help the social worker increase his or her effectiveness as a teacher:

1. The adage "It hasn't been taught until it has been learned" underscores the difference between teaching and learning. Teaching activities are planned and controlled by the teacher, but learning is not. Learning occurs within the learner and is tied to such factors as motivation, ability, and readiness. The teacher's job is to find a way of engaging and motivating the learner to examine and consider the materials to be taught.

2. That which we teach and learn falls into three broad categories: knowledge, beliefs and values, and skills. Of these three, *knowledge* is the easiest to teach because there is an agreed upon language to explain facts, concepts, and theories. This is not so when we focus on values and attitudes. In fact, *values* and *attitudes* cannot be taught directly, but they can be "caught" or learned from a teacher. If the teacher models or exhibits the desired beliefs, values, and attitudes, the learners may modify their own in order to imitate those of the teacher. *Skills*, too, are best learned through modeling and demonstration. They then can be performed and practiced in a real or simulated situation in order to master the behaviors or actions related to the skill.

3. It is said that the truly educated person is one who has learned how to learn. How we learn varies with such factors as our sensory preferences (hearing, seeing, kinesthetic, etc.), our need for or resistance to structure and direction, our desire for either competition or cooperation, our tendency to move from the specific (parts) to the general (whole) or vice versa, our tendency to either break apart or build concepts, our need to read and write in order to learn, our preferences for either solitary or group learning, and so forth. An important first step in teaching, then, is to plan for differences in how people learn. An effective teacher must be prepared to use several different methods when teaching a single topic.

4. When teaching, identify and teach essential terminology and concepts. Language is the foundation of learning because we use language to communicate ideas and experiences. The acquisition of specialized vocabulary is a fundamental step in the acquisition of new learning. For example, before someone can learn to do the work of the social worker, he or she must first master the terminology and basic concepts related to the profession's values, roles, principles, and practice theories. The teacher, however, should carefully pace the introduction of new concepts in order to avoid overloading the learner with too much new material at one time.

5. Help people learn by helping them practice skills and techniques.

6. When planning a class or training session, begin with an analysis of learner characteristics (e.g., developmental stage, formal education, prior experience, etc.) and the identification of the knowledge, values, and skills they are expecting (and expected) to learn. Then select or design the methods that are most likely to engage the learners and push and pull them toward the learning objectives.

7. Review and consider using existing curricula and teaching materials, but realize that such materials nearly always need to be modified and adapted. Materials and methods that worked well with one group of learners may not work for others.

8. To the extent possible, use teaching techniques that actively engage both the learner's mind and body (e.g., role-plays, simulation exercises, debates, and discussions). Reduce to a minimum the time spent in formal presentations. Lectures are among the least effective methods. In order to teach, we must attend to the learner's thinking, feelings, and behavior.

9. When teaching a skill, utilize the model known as "watch one, do one, teach one." First, have the learners observe someone performing the skill activity, then have them do it, and, finally, have them teach it to someone else. Another model is to understand the skill, use the skill, find new uses for the skill, and, finally, teach the skill to someone.

10. Place emphasis on helping the learner immediately use the information, knowledge, or skill being taught. In the human services the primary reason for learning is to do something with whatever has been learned. Thus, encourage the learner to ask Why am I interested in this topic? What can I do with it? How can I apply it? How will it help me answer some other question or solve a problem?

11. Critically evaluate your teaching. We can assess our effectiveness as teachers on these four levels:

- *Level 1.* We may simply ask the learners if they liked it. This is the most commonly used method of evaluating teaching. The problem is that one can enjoy a class or a workshop, but learn little or nothing. Moreover, learning is not always an enjoyable experience.
- *Level 2.* We can determine if the learners actually learned something new. Did they leave the session with knowledge or skills that they did not have when they began? To assess training at this second level, some type of presession and postsession testing is necessary.
- *Level 3.* Assuming that new learning occurred, we can then ask if the new knowledge and skills were used after the session. To assess training at this level, we need a follow-up system for monitoring the learner's behavior subsequent to the training session.
- *Level 4.* Finally, we can determine whether the learners' application of the new knowledge and skills had a positive impact on their lives or work. Unless what is learned has a real and a positive impact, the session was of little value no matter how enjoyable or how much was learned.

SELECTED BIBLIOGRAPHY

Basarab-Horwath, Janet A., and Tony Morrison. *Effective Staff Training in Social Care: From Theory to Practice.* New York: Routledge, 1999.

Dolgoff, Ralph. *An Introduction to Supervisory Practice in Human Services.* Boston: Allyn & Bacon, 2005.

13.35 PREPARING A BUDGET

Purpose: To prepare an estimate of income and expenditures for a human services agency or a special project.

Discussion: A budget is an important planning tool that lists an agency's anticipated income and its intended use during a designated period, usually one or two years. Typically, a budget will be revised several times during the period it is in use. A *preliminary budget* is often used to estimate expenses and serve as the basis for securing funding. That budget will be revised once various commitments have been made by the funding sources. An *operating budget*, when approved by a legislative body (in the case of a public agency) or by a board of directors (in the case of a private agency), becomes the authorization for the agency's executive director to spend the amounts listed for each budget category. However, in the course of the budget period, there may be a shortfall in one or more income categories, unanticipated costs in expenditure categories, or emergent reasons to shift funds from one category to another. Given the relative fluidity of demand for services, agencies must have the capacity to make changes in programming or staffing during budget periods.

As part of the process of building a budget, many questions should be asked and answered:

- What agency goals and objectives are to be emphasized during the budget period?
- How do changes in program emphasis affect the agency's income and expenses?
- What types and how many employees are needed to carry out the agency's current programs? What salaries and benefits are needed to attract and retain them? What liability insurance is needed to protect the employees and the agency? What training will be required for staff and volunteers—and what is the cost of that training?
- How might changes in program activities affect budget items such as numbers of staff with various competencies, training expenses, travel, supplies and equipment, consultation, and so on?
- What central office space and outreach locations are needed? What is required to keep the space clean, well maintained, and safe? What will be the cost of rent, utilities, insurance, security, and so forth?
- What is required to develop and maintain community support for the agency such as printing and publications, postage, public relations materials, membership development activities, audits, and the like?
- What total income will be needed to carry out the anticipated programs during the budget period? What are the sources of this income (e.g., agency fund-raising efforts, United Way, government appropriations, fees for service, grants, contracts, bequests, etc.) and how reliable is each as a base of support?
- If the budget must be cut at some later time, what reductions could be made that will do the least damage to the agency's capacity to carry out its mission?

In a stable organization, the budget should be built on past experience with allowance for anticipated changes in income or expenditures or to accommodate new programming. Without the infusion of new resources, the personnel aspects of the budget become the most critical to consider if any substantial change is anticipated, since most human services agencies are highly labor intensive. In addition, the constant tug between *efficiency* (cost per unit of service) and *effectiveness* (ability to achieve service objectives) should be addressed as part of the budgeting process.

Three types of budgeting are commonly found in human services agencies: (1) line-item budgeting, (2) incremental budgeting, and (3) program or functional budgeting. Each yields different information about the cost of doing business.

Line-Item Budgeting

This type of budget is the most commonly used in social agencies. It requires that the various income and spending categories be identified and that the amount of money anticipated in each category be stated (see Figure 13.3). The accounting system of

FIGURE 13.3 Sample Line-Item Budget

Categories	Last Actual Year	Year-to-Date	Current Budget	Proposed Budget
Income				
Beginning Balance	6,375	10,648	–0–	3,000
Contracts for Service	17,358	7,156	18,000	18,000
Contributions	5,392	938	5,000	5,000
Grants	5,000	2,500	5,000	–0–
Gifts and Bequests	14,321	7,106	10,000	10,000
Investment Income	4,987	2,386	5,000	5,000
Membership Dues	2,510	1,050	2,500	2,500
Program Service Fees	98,746	44,657	100,000	112,000
Sales	–0–	–0–	3,000	–0–
United Way Allocation	20,000	10,000	20,000	29,000
Total Income	174,689	86,443	168,500	184,500
Expense				
Salaries	112,518	50,447	115,894	129,650
Employee Benefits	9,756	7,557	10,146	10,265
Payroll Taxes	2,171	1,180	2,360	2,385
Consultation and Audit Fees	10,000	4,120	10,000	11,000
Professional Development	2,500	1,195	2,500	2,500
Total Personnel	136,945	64,499	140,900	155,800
Supplies and Equipment	8,938	6,053	9,000	9,500
Telephone	3,063	1,600	3,200	3,200
Printing and Photocopying	984	407	600	600
Occupancy	12,000	6,300	12,600	13,200
Travel	570	287	600	600
Membership Dues	1,000	1,000	1,000	1,000
Miscellaneous	541	295	600	600
Total Operating Expenses	27,096	15,942	27,600	28,700
Total Expenses	164,341	80,411	168,500	184,500
Ending Balance	10,648	6,020	–0–	–0–

the agency is usually organized around these categories, making it possible to obtain a historical picture of the income and expenditures that will serve as the basis for projecting the future. Since a preliminary budget is a planning device, it must be prepared in advance of the year it will be in effect. In other words, next year's budget must be based on incomplete information about how well this year's budget estimated income and expenses. Thus, a preliminary line-item budget will reflect educated guesses about how each budget line will play out during the remainder of the current year and how it will change during the subsequent year.

The line-item budget must then be backed up by an audit report verifying the last year's actual income and expenditures and listing the amounts of any other assets, endowment, or building fund reserves that are excluded from the operating budget.

Incremental Budgeting

Based on estimates of increases or decreases in revenue, a series of budget projections might be built on the basis of the current line-item budget. That is, using a "what if?" approach, the expense items of a budget might be developed to reflect the impact of 5 and 10 percent income reductions, no change in revenue, or 5 and 10 percent revenue increases. An incremental budget is particularly helpful in reflecting the impact of inflation and identifying the service implications of increases and decreases in revenue. Such a budget is useful in assessing the cost of adjusting an organization's current program to provide new services. The availability of computer spreadsheet programs (see Item 9.4) has simplified the process of developing incremental budgets and thus examining the impact of various alternatives.

Program or Functional Budgeting

A final type of budget used by social agencies is the program or functional budget. Again, this is based on a line-item budget and adds the feature of attributing portions of the total cost in each income and expense category to the various components or functions of agency operation. This approach makes it possible to estimate income and expenditures related to any function of the agency, thus providing a picture of the cost-effectiveness of that function. Attributing the income or expenses to particular program areas calls for careful estimates (e.g., the amount of staff time devoted to fundraising) and an accurate identification of how income is generated (e.g., fees received for a particular service).

Preparing a program budget involves using the income and expense items from the "Proposed Budget" column (see Figure 13.3) of the line-item budget and projecting a distribution of those items according to both the operational support services (e.g., management, fund-raising, etc.) and each of the various service programs (e.g., adoption, foster care, family counseling, etc.) of the agency.

SELECTED BIBLIOGRAPHY

Edwards, Richard L. and John A. Yankey, eds. *Effectively Managing Nonprofit Organizations*. Washington, DC: NASW Press, 2006.

Kettner, Peter M. *Achieving Excellence in the Management of Human Service Organizations*. Boston: Allyn & Bacon, 2002.

13.36 THE 5 Ps OF MARKETING HUMAN SERVICES

Purpose: To interest the public in participating in or supporting the work of a human services organization.

Discussion: Increasingly, human services agencies draw on the marketing technology of modern business to attract needed resources. Most social workers are not accustomed to thinking about their agency's services as a product to be advertised, displayed, and sold. Doing so, however, helps workers better understand what actions are necessary to attract funding, the clients who need their services, competent board members and volunteers, and paraprofessional staff members such as foster parents.

Five concepts—the 5 Ps—should be considered when developing a human services marketing strategy.

Product

Successful salespeople are enthusiastic about their product and they can explain its advantages, as compared to the other products, which might attract the potential customer's interest. Thus, social agency personnel must truly believe in the worth of their product (service). They must be able to explain its worth and advantages in simple language and, if possible, back up their beliefs with data drawn from independent evaluations.

Potential Buyer (or Consumer)

In order to understand what attracts supporters and clients to a service program, it may be necessary to conduct some type of market survey. What are the characteristics of those who use this service? What are its most attractive features? Who has used the service in the past? If other programs have stronger community support, why are they more attractive than yours? The answers to such questions help an agency better understand its potential supporters and consumers and help target marketing efforts toward those groups most likely to respond.

For purposes of marketing, it is important to remember that there is no such thing as a general public. There are, however, subgroups of people who share common interests and values. It is useful to determine which subgroups are most likely to be interested in a particular program. An agency should not waste time and resources trying to attract those unlikely to ever develop interest in supporting or using its services.

For human services agencies, there are several important subgroups or stakeholders that a marketing strategy might address, depending on what aspect of the agency or program is being promoted:

- *Agency family.* This includes the board, members of various committees, and the staff.
- *Volunteers.* People who have volunteered their time to assist an agency in providing services have a special commitment to that agency and are especially interested in its activities.

■ *Clients, former clients, and their families.* Those who have benefited from the agency's efforts can become valuable advocates for an agency. One negative evaluation from this group can offset the public relations benefits from several satisfied clients.

■ *Supporters.* Many agencies have a group of members or other interested supporters who provide various forms of assistance such as financial contributions, assistance with fund-raising efforts, and speakers' bureau participants.

■ *Community influencers.* Each community has a few people who help shape public opinion (e.g., the media, people who speak out on issues, etc.) or make important decisions that affect human services (e.g., elected officials, directors of other agencies, United Way board members, etc.). They must be informed about the services of your agency.

■ *Special-interest groups.* Associated groups that have a particular interest in your agency's work might include such professional bodies or organizations as NASW, the AMA, the local bar association, related human services agencies, or influential groups such as the League of Women Voters, NAACP, and so on.

Place

Once the attention of the target audience has been attracted, the agency needs a place or location where the services can be provided and an identity for the program established. In the human services field, this place of business is typically a social agency, school, hospital, or clinic. Whether the targets of the marketing approach decide to contribute or use an agency's services will depend, in part, on their first impressions of the agency's building and offices, its personnel, and its program. First impressions are exceedingly powerful. Consumers will appreciate an appropriate atmosphere when entering the agency and expect respect, courtesy, and fairness in their treatment from clerical and professional staff.

Price

In the marketplace, price is measured in terms of dollars (i.e., how much a customer has to pay to get the wanted product). In the human services, price is more appropriately viewed as what an agency supporter or consumer must give up in order to support or utilize the services. If contributors or volunteers give their money and time, they are not able to give those dollars or hours to some other worthy cause. Thus, they want to know that their gifts are appreciated and will make a real difference in someone's life. Or perhaps they want to make sure their association with the agency will yield some personal benefit, such as interesting training, job-related experience, or a feeling of being useful.

Promotion

Working with the media (see Item 13.37) is an effective way to reach a large number of people with a message about an agency. Stories in newspapers and on TV can make people aware of a particular agency and its needs, but they are not usually effective in bringing people to the decision that they will support it with their time or money. The same can be said for presentations and public appearances at service clubs, schools, public meetings, and so on; they help, but it takes something more to get a real commitment. When it comes to making that final decision of whether to support an agency, face-to-face interaction with agency personnel is of critical importance.

As in business, a satisfied customer is the best advertisement an agency can have; on the other hand, a dissatisfied customer can do a lot of damage to an agency's image and reputation. As a general rule, presentations by satisfied customers (e.g., long-time financial supporters, enthusiastic volunteers, clients pleased with agency services, etc.) are more persuasive than presentations by agency staff.

SELECTED BIBLIOGRAPHY

Andreasen, Alan R., and Philip Kotler. *Strategic Marketing for Nonprofit Organizations*, 6th ed. Upper Saddle River, NJ: Prentice Hall, 2003.

Sargeant, Adrian. *Marketing Management for Nonprofit Organizations,* 2nd ed. New York: Oxford University Press, 2005.

Wymer, Walter, Jr., Patricia Knowles, and Roger Gomes. *Nonprofit Marketing: Marketing Management for Charitable and Nongovernmental Organizations.* Thousand Oaks, CA: Sage, 2006.

13.37 DEALING WITH THE MEDIA

Purpose: To inform the public and generate support for the services offered by an agency.

Discussion: The public has a right to know about the social programs and agencies supported by taxes or voluntary contributions. All too often, the public hears only negative information about these services and the people who use them. Social workers have a responsibility to help the public fully understand the impact of human services on the quality of life for all persons. Social workers can make a valuable contribution to their agencies, clients, and community by developing the skills to work with the media in providing this information.

General Advice

Social workers should keep in mind these points when working with the media:

- *Be proactive.* Rather than hoping the media will come to you for information or a story, reach out to them. Work at creating opportunities to describe your agency and program in a positive way. Remember that human-interest stories are especially attractive to reporters.
- *Have the authority to speak for the agency.* Make sure you are authorized to represent the agency and, if more than one person from the agency is authorized to deal with the media, make sure the efforts are coordinated. Also, be clear if at any time you are speaking for yourself rather than for the agency and avoid professional jargon.
- *Establish personal relationships with the media.* If the reporters and photographers know and trust you and are aware that you are willing to help them, it can mean the difference between your agency or program just getting covered and getting good coverage.

- *Be available.* Make it easy for the media to contact you by providing all reporters who cover your agency with your home and office telephone numbers and the name and numbers of someone else to call if you are not available.
- *Observe deadlines.* Know the deadlines of news shows and do not expect reporters to attend to your interests when they have deadlines to meet. If necessary, be willing to reschedule so they can give your story full attention.
- *Be fair.* When you release a story, make sure that all media organizations get your news release or a phone call as close to the same time as you can manage.
- *Be understanding.* If your story does not run, there may be good reasons. It could have been thrown out at the last minute for something of more urgent news value. It is all right to ask if there was something wrong with the story—something that could be corrected in future stories.
- *Make corrections when necessary.* Handle errors in stories carefully. Unless a serious error has been made, no comment is usually necessary. When a comment is in order, go to the reporter who made the error and handle the correction in private. Explain the error and indicate any damage that may have been caused. Control your emotions and focus only on the facts.
- *Say thanks.* Express your appreciation every time you submit material, whether it is used or not. At least once a year, thank your media professional's boss for the interest and investment in your program.

The Press Kit

A useful tool for establishing and maintaining relationships with either the print or electronic media is to prepare a press kit for distribution to editors and reporters. A press kit is simply a folder that contains information that interprets the agency and suggests stories for the media. The folder should be colorful or in some way attract the attention of the reporter. A cover letter should be included that draws attention to the contents of the press kit.

Meltsner (no date, 4) suggests the following materials as the minimum for inclusion in a press kit:

- *Agency information.* This may be a brochure, annual report, or a brief description of the agency's goals, programs, and clientele.
- *Business card.* This card should contain the agency contact person's name, address, and telephone number. This should be displayed prominently, perhaps by stapling it to the pocket of the folder.
- *Campaign or public relations effort information.* If you have a particular goal for this public relations effort, such as raising funds for a specific program or recruiting volunteers to work with troubled children, explain this with a brochure about the project or a short information sheet.
- *At least one backgrounder.* A backgrounder is a sheet that familiarizes the reader with concepts, terms, and data that might be useful in preparing a story about the agency—for example, What is mental health? What kind of problems are addressed in family counseling? What is the legal definition of child abuse?

What is a developmental disability?

- *A fact sheet or news release.* Depending on what you want the media to cover, you may include a fact sheet that contains basic information (who, what, where, when, why, and how) that allows the reporter to create his or her own story. A news release is a one- to three-page story that can be printed as is or reduced or expanded into the reporter's own story.
- *A public service announcement.* Prepare a draft of a 30-second radio spot describing your project.
- *At least one reprint.* To suggest ideas for a story, include previously published articles about the agency or the project.

The Newspaper Release

When preparing a newspaper release, you will improve the chances of it being used if the format is familiar to the reporter and the information requires a minimum of editing. For example, a newspaper may want a news release typed double or triple spaced and with wide margins so it can be easily edited or transmitted electronically. Contact each newspaper for specific instructions regarding their preferences.

Write in a clear, simple, and logical style. Use short sentences and paragraphs. Remember that reporters are interested in the who, what, where, when, and why of a story. Begin with the most important information and place the less critical information and supplemental details at the end. Keep in mind that editors often shorten a story by cutting from the end. Remember, too, that editors like direct quotations and that by providing one or two glossy print photographs it is possible to add human interest to the story.

Be sure to clearly identify your agency's name, address, and phone number and provide the name of the person to be contacted for further information. The newspaper will need to know if the item is for "immediate release" or if it should be held for release on a specific date.

Radio and Television News

Information presented on a television or radio news broadcast can reach a large segment of the public. The human-interest flavor of stories originating from social agencies is especially amenable to the images of television. The social worker attempting to utilize these forms of media should know how to prepare materials for broadcast and be well prepared if being interviewed for radio or television.

If you expect to be interviewed or be a guest on a talk show, be clear about what you want to say and then rehearse. Have in mind some case examples, but be sure to disguise them in a way that will protect confidentiality. Radio and television news stories are almost always concise, making it necessary to limit your message to 30 to 60 seconds. Also, avoid using words or giving examples that would be offensive or misunderstood by the public.

SELECTED BIBLIOGRAPHY

Bonk, Kathy, Henry Griggs, and Emily Tynes. *Strategic Communications for Nonprofits.* San Francisco: Jossey-Bass, 1999.

Meltsner, Susan. "Public Relations Tools for Human Service Providers: The Press Kit." No publisher, no date.

13.38   FUND-RAISING FOR A HUMAN SERVICES AGENCY

Purpose: To secure funds from the community to support a special project or the ongoing work of a social agency.

Discussion: If a private, not-for-profit human services agency is to survive and develop its programs, it must have a secure and diversified funding base. In the final analysis, that depends on the willingness of people to contribute their money to the agency rather than to another cause.

A key to agency survival is what some prefer to call *friend-raising*. This refers to the identification and nurturance of contributors who genuinely believe in the value of the agency and can be counted on to make a significant contribution, year after year.

Many local health and human services agencies are affiliated with large federated campaigns such as the United Way or the American Cancer Society. A small, independent agency must compete with these experienced and sophisticated fund-raising agencies for the interest, goodwill, and money of potential contributors.

For some agencies, a major fund-raising campaign is an occasional event in which funds to start a new program or build a facility are solicited. Inexperienced persons are seldom prepared for the demands and complexity of such a campaign. It takes time, energy, and know-how to successfully raise funds. It is estimated that it will take a minimum of three months to plan and raise funds from individuals and local businesses (e.g., through canvassing and direct mail); three to six months to raise funds from local foundations, service clubs, and unions; and at least six to eight months to raise funds from a national foundation, United Way, or financial institution. Also, that investment of time and energy usually means that other responsibilities in the agency must be set aside in order to free time for fund-raising. Thus, it is important to assess the need and the chances of success before embarking on a fund-raising effort.

Guidelines for Fund-Raising

Following these principles can assist social workers in fund-raising:

- Realize that even under the best of circumstances, raising money for human services agencies is a difficult and time-consuming activity.
- Fund-raising for the ongoing work of a social agency should employ methods that can be repeated each year.
- Prerequisite to success in fund-raising is a sound marketing program that keeps the public well informed about the agency and its services.
- It is critical to plan ahead. Allow plenty of time (i.e., several months), remembering that the most difficult time to raise funds is when you urgently need them.
- Look for money at the local level first. Local people are the ones most likely to have a vested interest in seeing the program succeed.
- Fund-raising is a very personal activity. In reality, people usually give money to other people, not to an organization or cause. Build networks and get to know

key people in the organizations you plan to solicit and have those individuals help you gain access to and establish credibility with others in that organization.

- It costs money to raise money. Make sure that the cost of fund-raising is built into the agency's budget.
- Get volunteers and the agency board of directors involved. They will have credibility in the community and their involvement increases their ownership of the program.
- It is important to research the priorities of potential funding sources and match their priorities with yours.
- Fund-raising involves asking people for their money. If you do not ask, you will not get it. (Some suggestions on how to ask are given later.)
- Get expert advice if you are unsure of how to proceed in a fund-raising campaign. You can damage future efforts if you attempt to carry out a poorly developed plan.

Elements of a Fund-Raising Campaign

Hundreds of decisions and actions make up a successful fund-raising campaign. Here are some of the major steps to follow:

1. *Formulate a goal.* After a careful examination of agency needs, establish a realistic goal as to how much money is to be raised and set a realistic time frame for reaching that goal.

2. *Consult those with expertise.* Draw together those who have worked on previous campaigns and determine what has and has not worked. Consider hiring a professional fund-raiser if your own prior efforts have not been successful, if you are unsure how to proceed, or if you need to raise more than $100,000.

3. *Develop a plan.* Draw on the agency's former experience and use an approach that has worked in the past. Be cautious about attempting an approach with which you have no experience. When constructing your budget, factor in the amount of staff time needed and the cost of postage, supplies, public information materials, and travel.

4. *Select a chairperson.* This person should be a respected and trusted individual with good name recognition in the community. Most important, the chairperson must be someone who has the energy and time required and is committed to achieving the campaign goal. Recruit the chairperson during the planning stage so he or she can shape the overall strategy. This individual must be capable of recruiting many other volunteers.

5. *Build an organizational structure.* A successful campaign requires an organizational structure that ensures rapid communication, coordination, and careful monitoring of campaign activities and volunteers. Because many of the contributions will come from those working on the campaign, the effort should embrace and involve a great many individuals, community groups, and organizations. Many campaigns use some type of pyramid structure made up of several team captains, each responsible for overseeing the work of several campaign workers. A campaign might also have several divisions or special units that seek contributions from certain segments of the community (e.g., labor unions and small businesses).

6. *Recruit and train the campaign workers.* Workers must be asked to help—people seldom volunteer for fund-raising. The campaign chair, board members, and friends of the agency must actively recruit as volunteers persons who have the contacts and influence necessary to secure contributions. Some of the individuals willing to help may not be comfortable asking for money. They can help with other important tasks, however, such as preparing informational packets, office work, and bookkeeping.

7. *Prepare informational material.* Simply written brochures should explain the agency's program, what money is needed, and how it will be spent. This information may also need to be presented in the form of newspaper, television, and radio ads. Agency staff who best know the various programs the agency offers should play a key role in identifying appropriate content.

8. *Maintain proper records.* The campaign must maintain a complete and accurate record of contributions and expenses. Any hint of dishonesty, fraud, or incomplete bookkeeping will seriously damage the agency's ability to raise funds in the future.

9. *Provide recognition.* All those who contributed and all those who worked on the campaign should receive recognition and thanks. This creates a sense of pride and goodwill and increases the chances that these people and groups will assist in future campaigns.

10. *Evaluate the campaign.* After the campaign is complete, the agency board, campaign chairperson, and other key leaders should carefully evaluate what worked, what did not work, and how future campaigns could be improved.

Asking for Money

Many of us are hesitant to ask others for money, but that is what fund-raising is all about. Following these suggestions may help reduce this problem:

- Those who ask others for money must have already given their fair share. Those doing the asking must be able to say, "I have given $500; I am asking that you give at least $250."
- It is critically important that the right person ask another for money and that the request be made in the right way, for the right reason, and at the right time. This is a further reminder that people do not give money to agencies or even causes; people give primarily because a specific person (e.g., someone they know and trust) has asked them to give.
- Small amounts of money can be raised by mail, e-mail, and telephone campaigns. Big money is raised through face-to-face contact with the donor.
- Ask for a specific amount of money and be sure to ask for enough (e.g., "We need $1,000 to send five children to camp").

- Assess the person's capability of giving before you ask. In other words, do some background research and determine what an individual or company is capable of giving. Ask for that amount.
- Be persistent. Keep asking until you get what you want or receive a firm "no."
- If an individual cannot make a cash donation, ask if an in-kind donation might be possible (e.g., time, used equipment, expertise, etc.).

SELECTED BIBLIOGRAPHY

Alexander, G. Douglas, and Kristina J. Carlson. *Essential Principles for Fund-Raising Success.* San Francisco: Jossey Bass, 2005.

Dove, Kent E. *Conducting a Successful Development Services Program: A Comprehensive Guide and Resources.* San Francisco: Jossey-Bass, 2002.

13.39   DEVELOPING GRANT APPLICATIONS

Purpose: To secure funding from a governmental agency or private foundation.

Discussion: The resources available to a social agency are usually fully committed for operating existing programs. Any incremental increases in funds that might be obtained each year are often consumed by normal salary increases and inflation. The opportunity to demonstrate or test program innovations or conduct research on some aspect of the agency's program frequently cannot be done without the infusion of grant funds. A social worker who is knowledgeable about locating sources of grant funds and skilled at preparing applications for such funds is a valuable asset to his or her agency.

Before a social worker (or team of workers) can begin the grant-writing process, three prerequisites must be met. First, the idea or program innovation to be demonstrated or studied must be clearly thought out. Second, in addition to the persons developing the program or project, the agency's administrators and governing body must be committed to the idea. Finally, an assessment of the competence and capacity of both the individuals and the agency to carry out the activity must indicate that this work can be successfully completed. The worker should be prepared to invest considerable up-front time and effort into preparing a grant application, which frequently must be done in addition to ongoing work assignments. Yet, it is often the only way to improve services.

Sources of Grant Funding

A variety of funding sources might be considered. Sometimes, a local or national business will underwrite a project that is of interest to them. A computer company, for example, might donate equipment to demonstrate the potential effectiveness of a computerized interagency referral network. Other times, a group of persons interested in a project might undertake a fund-raising effort to help support this activity. However, the primary sources for a project are grants from government agencies or private foundations.

Government Grants.   The largest amount of money is available through agencies of the federal government, although states may also allocate such funds. Most government grants relate to areas that the sponsoring agency has defined in relation to its purpose and priorities. The public is notified of available funding through a *Request for Proposals (RFP)* or *Request for Applications (RFA)*. Grant applications are reviewed by a panel of experts and awarded on a competitive basis. Some discretionary funds may also be available to allow for innovative program ideas that are not currently among the granting agency's established priorities. It is helpful to discuss your ideas with persons in the regional and national offices of the government agencies who administer the funds in your area of interest (e.g., aging, child welfare, AIDS, etc.) before investing much time and energy in developing a proposal. These staff members can help you assess the fit between your proposal and the agency's interest and provide such facts as the typical size of grants and the odds of success.

Two published sources of information are particularly useful regarding grant possibilities from the federal government. The *Catalog of Federal Domestic Assistance* is an essential sourcebook published each year with a supplement that updates after six months. It contains a comprehensive listing and description of federal programs. Programs are cross-referenced by function (e.g., housing, health, etc.), by subject (e.g., drug abuse, economic development, etc.), and by the federal agency in which the program is administered. The description of each program includes information such as uses and restrictions on the funds, eligibility requirements, and the application and award process. A second source is the *Federal Register*. It is published every government working day and contains notices, rules and regulations, guidelines, and proposed rules and regulations for every federal grant-giving agency. Both the *Catalog of Federal Domestic Assistance* and the *Federal Register* are usually available through libraries and on the Internet (see Item 9.4).

Private Foundations.   Another potential source of support for innovative program ideas is the private foundation. Small agencies and service demonstration projects are more likely to obtain support from these private sources than from government agencies. Most foundations develop specialized areas of interest, and some make resources available only for programs located in a specific geographic region. Perhaps the most helpful source is *The Foundation Directory*. Part 1 of that directory includes those foundations that give away more than $200,000 per year, and Part 2 contains those that give smaller amounts. The Foundation Center periodically publishes a series of specialized directories of grant sources that are focused on areas such as children, youth, and families; aging; the economically disadvantaged; health; and women and girls. Another directory, *The Directory of Corporate and Foundation Givers*, provides background information about potential funding sources in the private sector. Once again, many local libraries and universities will have copies of these publications.

Computer Searches.   Several databases are also available to aid in searching for funding sources—both governmental agencies and foundations. Searches by topic (key words), geographic region, funding agency, and program area make it possible to narrow a vast amount of information to a small number of organizations or RFPs that are appropriate for the project.

Guidelines for Developing a Proposal

The planning and preparation of a proposal is a labor-intensive process. Make sure you have the necessary time and motivation. A hastily written proposal, or the so-called all-purpose proposal, has little chance of success. Several guidelines are of critical importance:

1. *Do your homework.* Make a thorough study of the potential funding source (foundation or government agency) before deciding to submit a proposal. Pay special attention to the published funding priorities, history of prior awards, eligibility, geographical limitation, type and size of grants available, funding cycle, process for selection, and so on. Secure the name, address, and phone number for the proper contact person.

2. *Make informal inquiries.* Save time for yourself and for the funding agency by informally inquiring about its possible interest in your ideas. However, assume that the recipient of your inquiry is busy, impatient, skeptical, not especially interested in your problems, and faced with many more requests than he or she can even read thoroughly, let alone fund. Be very businesslike in your approach. Be prepared to describe your proposal clearly and concisely in one or two pages or in five minutes on the phone. If you think you will be making an application, obtain an application packet and all relevant instructions.

3. *Write the proposal.* Study the instructions in the RFP or RFA and follow them to the letter. Be prepared to answer each and every question. You should anticipate answering at least the following questions:

- What do you want to do, how much will it cost, and how much time will it take?
- How does the proposed project relate to the funding agency's area of interest and priorities?
- Are there other projects like the one you are proposing? How is yours similar or different?
- How do you plan to carry out the project? Does the proposed staff have the necessary training and experience? Why should you conduct this project, rather than someone else?
- Who stands to benefit from the proposed project? What impact will it have on your agency, clients, discipline, community, state, or nation? How will you measure, evaluate, and report the impact? Will the project be able to continue after the grant support has ended?

The written proposal must be very clear and well organized, with justification for the various expenditures described in detail. Often, the proposal cannot exceed a certain number of pages and has a firm closing date. Sometimes, the closing date is a designated postmark, but usually, the proposal must be in the hands of the granting agency by that date. If a team is writing a proposal, designate one person who will have final authority to edit the materials into a coherent document.

4. *Be a good salesperson for your project.* Your written proposal and/or oral presentation should reflect knowledge, enthusiasm, and commitment. Focus your proposal on its alignment with the funder's goals and how you can contribute to clients or improve the provision of human services if you are funded. Coming across as helpless and needy (e.g., "We really, really need the money") will pretty much assure that you will not be funded. However, if those selecting proposals to be funded become convinced that the people associated with the program are especially capable and responsible, they may work especially hard on finding a way to fund the proposal. Obtaining substantive letters of support from related agencies and key people in your community can help sell your proposal. Ask these people to address specific areas of the proposal (e.g., the need, the agency's history of sound management, the staff's ability to carry out the project, community support for the program, etc.).

5. *Be accountable.* If you receive the grant requested, be prepared to carry out the project according to your written plan and within the proposed budget. The acceptance of a grant carries with it the responsibility for managing the money properly, submitting regular progress reports, reporting project results, and giving appropriate credit to the funding source. Good stewardship of the grant funds is very important.

Proposal Contents.   Stress the quality of what you can do with grant support, as opposed to stressing why you have not done it before. Remember that your proposal is in competition for scarce grant resources and that it likely will be evaluated against the criteria set out in the RFP. Thus, you should carefully follow the outline required by the funding source; explicitly address each of the criteria, and answer every question asked in the RFP. In general, the following components will be expected:

1. *Cover page.* Include the project title, principal investigators, name of agency, dates for project activity, total budget request, and signatures of authorized agency personnel approving the application.

2. *Abstract.* Prepare a short statement of the objectives and procedures to be used, methods of evaluation, and plan for disseminating results.

3. *Statement of problem and objectives.* Indicate the rationale for this project and prepare a clear statement of the objectives in measurable terms.

4. *Methodology, procedures, and activities.* Describe the design and approach of the project, who will be served, and the administrative structure for the project. Lay out a clear plan of action with phases and dates for activity detailed. The use of Gantt and PERT charts (see Item 12.13) can help make processes and timelines clear to reviewers.

5. *Evaluation methods.* Describe how the results or outcomes of the activity will be assessed. Your application will be strengthened if the evaluators are not directly associated with your agency or personally invested in the outcome of your demonstration or research project.

6. *Dissemination of results.* Indicate how the results of the project will be disseminated so that others can benefit from the knowledge gained from this activity.

7. *Personnel and facilities.* Describe the staff required to carry out the project, include short resumés of key personnel who will be assigned to this activity, and indicate how new staff will be selected. Also, describe any special equipment required, and indicate how the agency will make space available to accommodate project activities.

8. *Budget.* Provide a detailed budget of the anticipated costs of the project. Indicate what will be required from the funding source and what will be contributed by the agency or other sources. Many funding sources require that matching funds from local sources be identified as a requirement for funding. In some instances, a cash match is required, but in others, in-kind contributions (e.g., staff time or office space) are acceptable. A budget will usually include personnel costs (including fringe benefits), outside consultants or evaluators for the project, consumable materials (supplies, printing, postage, etc.), equipment, travel, and indirect costs. The latter relates to the real costs to an agency (space, heat, light, etc.) consumed by the project staff. Some federal agencies limit the indirect cost to as little as 8 to 15 percent of the project expenses. Also, be prepared to describe what will happen to the project after the grant funding has ended.

SELECTED BIBLIOGRAPHY

Browning, Beverly A. *Winning Strategies for Developing Grant Proposals*, 2nd ed. Washington, DC: Thompson Publishing, 2005.

Catalog of Federal Domestic Assistance. Available online: http://12.46.245.173/cfda/cfda.html.

Directory of Corporate and Foundation Givers, The. Washington, DC: Taft Group, most recent edition.

Federal Register. Available online: www.gpoaccess.gov/fr/index.html.

Greever, Jane C. *The Foundation Center's Guide to Proposal Writing*, 5th ed. New York: The Foundation Center, 2006.

13.40 INFLUENCING LEGISLATORS AND OTHER DECISION MAKERS

Purpose: To influence the actions of legislators and other community decision makers regarding human services issues.

Discussion: Decisions that are made at the local, state, and national levels by elected representatives and other public officials have substantial impact on the human services. Because social workers are in a unique position to observe how public social policy helps or hinders the most vulnerable members of society, their perspective needs to be communicated to public officials. When social workers do not engage in the politics related to shaping social welfare policy and the allocation of funds for social programs, client needs and concerns are often overlooked. When social workers are not politically involved, the insights and experiences of the social work profession are not made available to the policy development process.

When planning an effort to influence a decision maker, the worker should keep several guidelines in mind. First, a social worker is more likely to influence a decision when he or she has an established relationship with the decision maker. Of course, when a social worker is new to a community or organization it will take time to build such relationships and, as new decision makers appear on the scene, it will also take time to cultivate a relationship with them. The worker should make a point to initiate such relationships before attempting to influence a particular decision if at all possible. Second, the decision maker is more likely to be influenced by the worker if the worker and his or her information can be trusted. The social worker should make a careful analysis of the issue and the people making the decision (see Items 11.23 and 11.24), never distort the facts or give information that cannot be substantiated, and be thoroughly prepared to discuss the matter. Finally, the worker should be selective about the issues presented to decision makers. One's credibility with decision makers can be diminished if too many issues are addressed or if the worker is not sufficiently prepared to speak to the matter knowledgeably.

When a social worker decides to attempt to influence a decision, it should be done in an assertive and planful way. In formulating an approach, the worker should remember that decision makers are most likely to be persuaded by persons they perceive as having these qualities:

- Intelligence, self-confidence, and competence
- Life experiences, values, and a personal style like their own
- Power and the ability to deal out rewards or punishments
- Individuals with whom they can expect future interaction and from whom they seek social acceptance

Because social workers do not usually have the power or status necessary to directly persuade decision makers, they must often work through others who are in a better position to exercise influence. At other times, however, the worker should directly communicate with the decision maker through personal contact, in writing, or both.

Visiting with a Policymaker

Many legislators and other key decision makers spend their time in a somewhat restricted environment; they speak primarily with staff members, lobbyists, and colleagues. Hence, they often welcome the opportunity to hear the positions of people who have firsthand knowledge of issues they must decide. This communication might occur by attending a legislator's open forum or town meeting or by talking individually with the decision maker. Sometimes, when a decision maker is difficult to schedule, effective communication on a subject can occur with an aide or advisor to the decision maker.

The following guidelines can help to make visits with decision makers (or their advisors) effective:

- *Use time efficiently.* The decision maker's time is valuable. If you are to get that person's full attention and have a favorable climate for communicating your information, you must be efficient. When planning an individual meeting, schedule an appointment in advance and ask that a specific amount of time be reserved for the meeting. Be on time, even though you may have to wait for the legislator to complete other responsibilities before meeting with you. Also, get to the point quickly. Have your presentation planned so that you can pack a lot of information into a short time period.

- *Be positive.* Begin on a friendly note. Find a reason to praise the decision maker for some action taken in relation to prior contacts (if appropriate) and thank him or her for being willing to take time to hear your position on this matter.
- *Express your conviction.* Let the legislator know that, as a social worker, you are in a unique position to recognize the implications of this decision. Leave no doubt in the legislator's mind that you believe in what you are proposing. Back up your view with facts and examples. If the information is at all detailed, prepare a handout that can be left with the decision maker and others who may be present.
- *Be specific.* Be very sure that the person knows what you want him or her to do. For example, do you simply want him or her to understand the situation better? Do you want him or her to propose an amendment to a piece of legislation? Do you want him or her to vote in a particular way?
- *Follow up in writing.* Send or leave a statement that reflects your position and provides the facts that you presented. The purpose of this document is to supply material that will be placed in the legislator's file on the topic and to remind him or her of your position when it is time to take action. Be sure that your name, street address, email address, and telephone number are on the materials so you can be contacted to clarify points or provide information on related matters.

Writing a Policymaker

Although face-to-face contact is probably the most effective way to influence a legislator or other decision maker, many times that is not possible because of constraints of time, distance, resources, or the availability of the decision maker. Letters, fax messages, email, and telephone calls, when properly timed, can also be effective in influencing decisions. The addresses and telephone numbers of public officials will usually be listed periodically in newspapers or available at the local library. Locating other officials may require more research.

Observe these guidelines when writing to a decision maker:

- *Be accurate.* Be sure that you use the correct spelling of the person's name, the proper title, and the accurate address. Be sure that the decision maker has correct information about you in case he or she wants to respond to your communication.
- *Be brief and to the point.* Limit your communication to one page. Focus only on one issue or piece of legislation in each communication. If you are interested in several matters, send separate correspondence so each can be filed with materials about those matters.
- *Clearly identify the issue or bill that concerns you.* Provide identifying details (e.g., the bill's number, name, and dates) so there can be no misunderstanding of what you are writing about.
- *Write simply and clearly.* Remember that those who will read your material are very busy and may receive many pieces of correspondence each day. Make it easy for them to understand the points you wish to make.
- *Begin in a positive manner.* Address the legislator in a respectful manner and use titles appropriate to the office. If possible, praise or compliment the

legislator for some previous action or statement and relate the preferred action on this matter to other positions he or she has supported.

- *Provide facts and figures that support your position.* Explain the impact of the decision and how many people will be affected. Short case examples are often effective in helping the reader understand how the issue affects individuals.
- *Clearly identify the action you desire.* Make sure the reader knows what you want to happen (e.g., vote for HR 254, oppose the filibuster of SB 1543, etc.).
- *Pay attention to timing.* Be sure to time communicating your opinion to just precede the debate on the topic. Typically, a legislator will make up his or her mind early in the hearing process and long before time for a final vote.
- *Follow up the action.* After the decision or vote is completed, write again, thanking the legislator for considering your viewpoint if he or she took the action you requested. If not, express regret about that action. Such follow-up reminds the person that you are truly concerned about the issue and will continue to observe his or her actions on this matter.

SELECTED BIBLIOGRAPHY

Richan, Willard C. *Lobbying for Social Change*, 3rd ed. New York: Haworth Press, 2006.

Schneider, Robert L., and Lori Lester. *Social Work Advocacy: A New Framework for Action.* Belmont, CA: Brooks/Cole, 2001.

Evaluation and Termination

INTRODUCTION

Every helping relationship must end. Counseling must be concluded and groups or committees must eventually be disbanded. The change process ends with the termination of service and a final evaluation of the intervention. ***Termination*** is that important final phase in planned change when the worker guides concluding activities of the process in a manner that is sensitive to issues surrounding the ending of a relationship.

If a meaningful relationship has been formed between client and worker (a key to successful helping), it is not surprising that this ending phase is often experienced with mixed emotions. One common reaction is that the client and worker are pleased that the work together has been concluded. Consequently, the client will no longer need to invest time, resources, and emotional energy in the change process and the worker can move on to new responsibilities. A competing emotion is the sense of loss. Clients sometimes feel anger, rejection, sadness, and anxiousness when the relationship ends. Thus, the worker must provide an opportunity for the client to express his or her feelings and concerns and the worker must lay the groundwork for a resumption of service in the future, should that be needed.

Occasionally, service will unexpectedly end at a time other than that originally planned or expected by the worker and client. For example, an abrupt termination may occur in these circumstances:

- The client, for personal or financial reasons, decides to stop participating.
- The worker accepts employment elsewhere.
- The helping process is blocked by a problem in the worker-client relationship necessitating transfer to another worker.
- The client requires specialized services that are best provided by another social worker, professional, or agency.

If the termination is prompted by the worker or agency, the worker should clearly explain what is happening and why. If the client simply stops participating, the worker should attempt to make a final contact to bring their relationship to an amicable closure.

Also, a final ***evaluation*** should occur at the conclusion of the change process. At this time, the degree of client change is measured and the social worker assesses the success of the intervention. The growing impact of managed care on the practice of social work today (see Item 16.8), coupled with an already important obligation for accountability to clients, agencies, and the community, makes it imperative that social workers are skilled at evaluating their practice. As compared to the ongoing monitoring that occurs throughout the helping process, the final evaluation occurs during or after termination. In essence, the worker assesses the degree to which the intervention was effective in improving the client's functioning or situation.

Two forms of evaluation are of primary concern to the social worker. **Direct practice evaluation** is the assessment of a worker's interventions and their impact on a specific client (e.g., an individual, family, or small group). This evaluation can serve two purposes. It can be *formative evaluation*, which is used to inform and guide the ongoing practice decisions and, as such, is a tool for monitoring the intervention and changing the planned intervention when necessary. Direct practice evaluation can also be used as a *summative evaluation*, in which one assesses the final outcome and identifies the factors that contributed to the relative success or failure of the intervention.

The second form, **program evaluation**, attempts to evaluate the effectiveness and efficiency of a program serving a large number of clients or perhaps even a whole community. Program evaluation, too, can be both formative and summative. It is formative if it is used for assessing a program and changing aspects of its functioning to better serve the agency's clients or community. It is summative when, for example, it is used to report the results of a demonstration program to a board of directors or a funding source.

Evaluation planning begins at the point the intervention is selected and the goals expected to be achieved are selected. Unless the desired outcomes are specified in the early phases of the change process, the worker will not be able to measure its effect. Additionally, the worker must select the criteria by which to measure the variables (e.g., client behaviors, community knowledge) that are expected to change during the intervention. In research terms, the client's, agency's, or community's functioning is considered the *dependent variable* and the intervention used is the *independent variable*. In the evaluation of a family counseling program, for example, improvement of client functioning (dependent variable) may be viewed as an indicator of the success of services (independent variable).

The position reflected here is that social work practice is all about change—helping clients change, helping their environments change, and helping agencies or communities change in order to prevent social problems from occurring in the first place. The philosophy behind the evaluation of social work practice, then, is that change that occurs during a practice intervention can be measured for the following reasons:

- If a social problem or negative social condition does not exist, then there is no need for intervention.
- If a problem or negative situation exists for a client, then it exists in some quantity and thus the amount of that factor can be identified and measured.
- If the factor can be measured, then the degree of change that occurs over time can be documented.

In short, the outcomes of all social work practice can be evaluated. The difficulty is to determine how, or to find ways to measure the dependent variables and to establish the amount of change that occurred.

When deciding what procedures to use to measure change in client functioning, the social worker should consider the following questions:

- *Validity.* Does the procedure measure what it is assumed or believed to measure?
- *Reliability.* Does the procedure yield similar results when the measurement is repeated under similar circumstances?
- *Ease of application.* Is the procedure sufficiently brief, easy to use, and understandable to the nonspecialist?
- *Sensitivity.* Is the measurement procedure able to detect relatively small levels of change and degrees of difference?
- *Nonreactivity.* Can the procedure detect differences without modifying or influencing the phenomena being measured?

When selecting standardized measurement tools, the social worker should review the manuals that accompany the instrument for descriptions of how they are to be used. The worker should also examine the social work and psychology literature for information on their strengths, limitations, and psychometric properties. If this information is not available, the social worker should make only tentative and cautious judgments based on this measurement.

The measurement techniques included in this chapter can be used for both monitoring practice (formative evaluation) and making a comprehensive or final assessment of the intervention activity (summative evaluation). Thus, these techniques could be placed in either Chapter 13 or Chapter 14 of this book. Due to the large number of intervention techniques reported in Chapter 13, measurement techniques are located in this chapter to give them more visibility.

SECTION A

TECHNIQUES AND GUIDELINES FOR DIRECT PRACTICE

The social worker is ethically obliged to be accountable for the quality of services provided. The *NASW Code of Ethics* recognizes that "social workers should monitor and evaluate [their] . . . practice interventions" (Section 5.02.a). Clearly, it is important to engage clients in the final review of the change process, encouraging them to judge the success and usefulness of the experience from their vantage point, and to express their thoughts on the worker's performance. From this information, the worker can more accurately assess his or her practice strengths and limitations and, where appropriate, seek consultation or training to enhance the quality of future practice.

There is a growing emphasis on the need for data-based or empirical evaluations of social work practice, as characterized by the call for social workers to become *scientific practitioners.* This development is not without controversy. Four primary themes are reflected in this debate:

1. It is argued that social work intervention is primarily an act of human caring and that the whole person cannot be broken down into discrete components and measured in any meaningful way. Proponents of direct practice evaluation, however, argue that while social work includes the artistic expression of the social worker and concern for all aspects of a person's life, people come to social workers for help with specific problems and conditions. Unless the social worker and client isolate those issues for attention, practice will lack the focus required to be successful. If social work practice were only an act of caring, professional knowledge and skill would not be required.

2. Opponents of the empirical evaluation of practice contend that it is too time consuming and that to select or design measurement scales, collect and analyze data, and then interpret the results takes valuable time away from therapeutic interactions with clients. Those on the other side of the debate contend that the data needed for evaluation purposes are usually gathered for assessment and monitoring purposes anyway. The difference is that the data are organized for systematic analysis; once the workers develop skill in this form of evaluation, it takes relatively little additional time. In fact, when this process actively engages the client, it can help increase his or her involvement and motivation and thus focus and enhance practice.

3. Persons who object to empirical practice evaluation suggest that only a relatively few social workers and agency administrators have the skills needed to use this type of evaluation effectively. And until it is used throughout social work practice and such data collection becomes the norm, clients will object. Proponents, however, contend that the profession cannot wait until more social workers are trained to use these evaluation techniques, given the demands from managed care companies and the public in general for evidence that social workers' practice makes a difference. Further, it is the social workers, not the clients, who tend to resist collecting these data. Most clients are accustomed to physicians measuring and recording changes in their body temperature, blood pressure, and weight—or even asking for a patient's judgment on a 1 to 10 scale regarding less quantifiable factors, such as how much pain is being experienced. For the clients of social workers, there is little difference among being asked to record the number of anger outbursts experienced in a week, to rate their degree of anxiety, or to complete a questionnaire that measures the level of marital conflict.

4. Some social scientists contend that it is not possible to arrive at clear cause-and-effect conclusions from the methodologies available for this type of evaluation. These scientists suggest that there is too little control over extraneous variables, that the designs must be adapted to unique client situations (thus minimizing one's ability to generalize the results to other cases), that the range of designs is too limited to accommodate the breadth of social work practice, and that the conclusions a practitioner reaches are suspect because the practitioner-researcher cannot remain sufficiently objective. Proponents contend that this form of evaluation is not intended to yield the same kind of information as traditional research, and they agree that the results should not be generalized to other clients. Rather, these methods are primarily intended to help assess one social worker's work with one client (or group of clients). Also, proponents call for caution in concluding that the measures alone provide sufficient evidence to prove that an intervention by itself *caused* a change in a client's attitudes, behaviors, or actions. Additional information would be needed to arrive at a cause-and-effect conclusion. Even so, those supporting empirical evaluation conclude that it is valuable for what it can measure—for example, to substantiate that the client or situation did change, that the change occurred following introduction of a specific intervention, or that the client's condition improved and that the improvement was sustained over time.

These four basic criticisms of the empirical evaluation of social work practice should signal the worker to be cautious not to overestimate the power of the data to predict outcomes. These data should supplement, rather than replace, other indicators of practice success. The worker can feel most confident about measurements of client change when empirical data are consistent with his or her own practice observations, the client's perceptions, and the views of collateral resources, such as parents or other professionals. If at least three assessments are comparable (i.e., *triangulation*), the social worker can feel relatively confident about the results.

The social worker engaged in direct practice evaluation will find these guidelines useful:

1. *The informed consent of the client is more important than the data.* The client should be fully informed about how these data will be collected and used and should give his or her consent for participation in the evaluation process (see *NASW Code of Ethics*, 1999, Section 5.02.e). Clients may fear that the data collected could potentially be used against them, for example, by a court, school, or family member and should have the right to refuse to supply this information. In addition to the obvious ethical matter of collecting and maintaining such information without client permission, it is also unlikely that much useful data will be obtained if the client is not an active participant in the process.

2. *Practice requirements should take precedence over data collection.* It is sometimes tempting to manipulate service delivery to assure good data collection. But compromising client services for the purpose of evaluation (e.g., delaying intervention to obtain baseline scores, continuing services beyond the client's needs to obtain additional data) is not in the best interest of the client and thus should be avoided.

3. *The questions to be answered through the practice evaluation should be viewed as fluid.* The traditional research process begins with identifying the research question, selecting the methods for data collection, determining the sampling process for the population to provide data, and so on. There is little flexibility once the process is begun. By contrast, direct practice evaluation begins with developing a service plan for a client (individual, family, group) and only after that is the research question (or questions) generated, the measurement tools selected, and the evaluation design adopted. The questions one might attempt to answer could relate to any of these topics:

- *The client.* A fundamental purpose of monitoring and evaluating practice is to determine if the client was helped. For example: Did change occur in the intended direction? Did the family or group show positive change, and, if so, did each member also experience positive change? Did the client accomplish the agreed upon tasks? To what extent did the client achieve his or her goals? Was the change accomplished during the intervention sustained after termination?
- *The intervention.* To help inform future practice, we often want to study the effectiveness of the interventions we use. We might ask questions such as these: Was the change a client experienced associated with the intervention? Was one intervention more effective than another? Was an intervention more effective when used alone or in combination with other interventions?
- *The worker.* We also may want to use practice evaluation as a means of answering questions about ourselves and the success of our service provision—for instance, To what extent do my clients achieve their goals for this service activity? Do I provide some services more successfully than others?

Also, unlike traditional research, the questions one attempts to answer may change as practice unfolds. For example, a service plan may begin with the premise that a particular intervention approach will be the best means of serving a client and the worker may formulate a question regarding the success of this intervention with this client. Tracking the client's progress may lead the worker to conclude that this approach is not working adequately and that a different intervention approach should be selected. Thus, a new question could be asked and answered regarding the comparative success of each approach in this practice situation.

4. *The evaluation design should be viewed as changeable.* Once the questions have been framed, the worker can select the most appropriate ways to measure change in the dependent variables (i.e., the client's actions, emotions, behaviors) and establish the process by which measurements will be taken, organized, and analyzed. If the anticipated service plan for the client changes, it may be necessary to revise the evaluation process, as well.

A critical feature of any evaluation is to accurately measure the factors the intervention is intended to change. One form of measurement is to count and record such factual information as school attendance, acts of violent behavior, number of family arguments, and so on. A second form of measurement is to develop a tool specifically tailored to the issues experienced by the particular client (see Item 14.1), or an *individualized scale*. Finally, in some cases, scales may already exist that will accurately measure the client on the factors being considered (see Item 14.2). These *standardized scales* might be utilized both to assess and periodically measure changes in the client's condition.

With measurement data in hand, the social worker can then organize the information in a manner that will allow him or her to answer the practice evaluation questions and reach conclusions about his or her degree of success. Items 14.3 through 14.6 provide examples of tools one can use to conduct these tasks.

Termination Activities. Although termination is recognized as a key element in planned change, it has been given surprisingly little attention in the social work literature. With the increased limits placed by managed care on the number of sessions a social worker can have with a client, this ending point increasingly is arbitrary and often premature. However, termination should be discussed during intake and at appropriate times throughout the helping process, and concluded in a manner that leaves the client with positive feelings and improved capacity to sustain gains made during the period of service. Item 14.7 provides some guidelines for the worker closing a case and terminating a professional relationship.

Social workers should remember, too, that the *NASW Code of Ethics* (1999, Section 1.16) states that termination should be planned with the needs of the client as the primary consideration. If termination is necessary before the change process is completed, there should be an appropriate referral to other helping sources.

SELECTED BIBLIOGRAPHY

Corcoran, Jacqueline, and Joseph Walch. *Clinical Assessment and Diagnosis in Social Work Practice.* New York: Oxford University Press, 2006.

Cournoyer, Barry R. *The Evidence-Based Social Work Skills Book.* Boston: Allyn & Bacon, 2004.

National Association of Social Workers. *NASW Code of Ethics.* Washington, DC: NASW, 1999.

Nugent, William R., Jackie D. Sieppert, and Walter W. Hudson. *Practice Evaluation for the Twenty-First Century.* Belmont, CA: Brooks/Cole, 2001.

14.1 MEASURING CHANGE WITH INDIVIDUALIZED RATING SCALES

Purpose: To prepare a scale that is unique to an individual client or client group to measure the client's condition.

Discussion: Social workers often need to measure various factors that are related to client conditions or situations that are the focus of practice. Accurate assessment of the duration, intensity, frequency, severity, and so on, of a client's condition is prerequisite to determining if an emergency exists, if the client or someone else is at risk, or if a referral should be made. The assessment is also informative in selecting an intervention technique.

Another reason for developing ways to measure factors affecting the client is to be able to track the amount and direction of change that occurs as the helping process unfolds. This allows the worker to correct the course of service if the selected interventions do not accomplish the desired goals.

Finally, measurements taken at the beginning and end of a service period can help a social worker examine his or her practice effectiveness (e.g., Did my client's condition improve? How much? In what practice issues and with what practice approaches am I most effective? Least effective? etc.). The answers to those questions can lead to a professional development plan to strengthen one's competence or, if applied to a number of workers, to accumulate data that can help an agency design its staff development plan.

In short, accurate measurement can benefit clients, workers, and agencies alike. How does a social worker accurately measure a client condition or situation? In truth, measurements of human behaviors, attitudes, feelings, and interactions are rarely completely accurate. Yet, with careful selection of appropriate indicators and a rigorous process of data collection, usually a good approximation of the factor being measured can be achieved.

One approach to measuring factors related to the client's actions and feelings is to construct an ***individualized rating scale*** that is developed or adapted to fit the client's unique situation. A homemade scale is particularly useful if the client can be involved in the process of developing the scale. Often, clients become more clear about their situations and what it might take to bring about change in a situation by working to create a scale in which abstract feelings or concerns are translated into concrete statements that describe degrees of change. Thus, the development of the measurement tool becomes a part of the practice activity. Further, when scales reflect the client's own descriptions of the variables, the face validity of the scale is high and repeated measurements can be relatively accurate indicators of the client's experience. Finally, some factors that social workers help clients address defy standardized descriptors (see Item 14.2) that can be universally interpreted for the purpose of measurement. For example, how does one standardize a person's feeling of grief, or a spouse's level of listening, or someone's motivation to change? With individualized scales, it is possible to "start where the client is" and construct measures of change from the perspective of that client.

Follow these steps when constructing an individualized rating scale:

1. *Help the client recognize the value in measuring behaviors, attitudes, and feelings.* Unless the client is invested in measuring his or her condition, the results are unlikely to be very helpful. Measurement of one's condition, however, should be a familiar experience for most clients. Just as other professionals routinely utilize indices of a patient's physical health, social workers require indices of a client's social health to perform most effectively in providing assistance. Many clients want such indicators and find the results confirming of their own observations.

2. *Carefully identify what is to be measured.* Many times, the problem or concern being addressed cannot directly be measured. If measured indirectly, it is critical that the items selected for measurement are valid or logical indicators of the problem being addressed. Just as an elevated temperature might be an indicator of infection, the number of arguments a couple has might be an indicator of marital discord. It is also important that each scale is designed to measure only one dimension of client functioning. If more than one dimension is involved, scales that measure each dimension should be created. Further, if there are multiple indicators for a single dimension, the use of several indicators can help to confirm or raise caution about the results from any one indicator.

3. *Develop a scale in which the client's status on a continuum from negative to positive functioning can be designated.* When developing a scale, one task is to determine how many points on a continuum—that is, from most to least or best to worst—will be identified. There can be as few as 2 points (e.g., yes or no, more or less), whereas other scales typically range anywhere between 3 and 10 points. A general guideline is to have only as many points as the client can clearly distinguish—usually 3 to 7 points. Whether to have an odd or even number of points depends somewhat on the item being scaled. For some items, it is appropriate to have a midpoint, but often that creates a situation in which the respondent simply takes a noncommittal middleground that provides little useful information. An even-numbered scale, by contrast, forces the respondent to at least lean one direction or the other.

Once the number of points on the scale is determined, anchoring statements can be developed that describe each point. One method is to describe the most negative point on the scale (e.g., "I lost my temper at least once each day") and then define the most positive anchor point (e.g., "I did not lose my temper at all during the week"). With the two ends of the continuum identified, some or all of the points between them can be defined. Care should be taken that the client can identify differences in the increments between points. Another method for developing anchor points is to begin describing the client's functioning at the current time and making that description the midpoint. A description of what it would be like if things should get worse (a worst-case scenario) would become the negative end of the continuum and progressive levels to the midpoint on the negative side identified. Then the process is repeated on the positive side of the continuum.

When the anchor points use the client's own words (e.g., "I feel encouraged," "I am furious," "My thoughts are fuzzy," "I flew off the handle," etc.), the scale is referred to as a *self-anchored scale* and the face validity of the scale is enhanced. At other times, it is helpful to use anchor points that have been utilized in other scales and are generally known to reflect differing scale values. When numerical categories are placed on a scale, be sure there are no gaps or overlaps in the numbers. It must be possible to place every potential number on the scale and impossible for any score to fall into more than one category. Some frequently used response categories include the following:

- *Frequency*
  rarely > seldom > occasionally > frequently > almost always
  none > 1 or 2 times > 3–5 times > 6–7 times > more than 7 times
  never > rarely > sometimes > often > very often > always
- *Duration*
  0–20% of the time > 21–40% > 41–60% > 61–80% > 81–100% of the time
  never > some of the time > most of the time > almost always
- *Intensity*
  strongly disagree > disagree > agree > strongly agree
  totally disagree > disagree slightly > neutral > agree slightly > totally agree
  not at all > slightly > moderately > very much > extremely
- *Change*
  strong decrease > some decrease > no change > some increase > strong increase

One last decision is whether to present the scales horizontally or vertically. Most people are accustomed to horizontal scales, as they are convenient to produce on a computer and are regularly used in survey instruments. Usually, the negative end of the continuum is placed on the left side of a page and the progressive steps (i.e., identified by the anchor points) flow from left to right. For some clients, however, a vertical scale communicates the more or less dimension more clearly. Children, for example, sometimes find a scale that looks like a thermometer or a height chart more understandable.

4. *Determine how the data will be collected.* Determining a process for completing the scales is the next step. Who should do the rating? The client? The worker? A teacher? A relative? When should the rating be made? The rating scale might be completed just before each counseling session, first thing each morning, Sunday evenings, and so forth. Where should the rating be done? At home? In the agency's waiting room? In the worker's office with the worker participating? There are any number of suitable places where the client can give thoughtful responses. Perhaps the most important general guideline is to attempt to achieve consistency regarding the conditions under which the ratings are made.

5. *Present the data in a form that allows them to be easily interpreted.* Just charting before and after scores, possibly in different colors, on the scale itself is often sufficient visual evidence of change. However, if a series of measurements are taken to reflect change over time or to compare changes in two or more variables, it is useful to create simple line graphs to track the progression. Such organization of the data can provide a useful basis for discussion of change or lack of change with clients.

SELECTED BIBLIOGRAPHY

Bloom, Martin, Joel Fischer, and John Orme. *Evaluating Practice: Guidelines for the Accountable Professional*, 4th ed. Boston: Allyn & Bacon, 2003.
Nurius, Paula S., and Walter W. Hudson. *Human Services: Practice, Evaluation, and Computers.* Pacific Grove, CA: Brooks/Cole, 1993.

14.2 MEASURING CHANGE WITH STANDARDIZED RATING SCALES

Purpose: To use predeveloped and tested scales to measure various dimensions of client functioning.

Discussion: In many instances, the social worker can measure a client's social functioning by using one of the many standardized measuring instruments. ***Standardized rating scales*** are indices of behaviors, attitudes, feelings, and so on, that represent a set of questions to measure a clearly defined construct. These scales have been subjected to sufficient psychometric testing to confirm the instrument's reliability when used with various populations. As opposed to individualized rating scales that are designed for a specific individual client or client group (see Item 14.1), standardized indexes can be used to measure the experiences of many different clients.

Using standardized scales has three main benefits. First, because they have already been developed and tested, standardized scales are ready for immediate use and can be applied in a practice situation even before the client and worker have established the rapport necessary for an ongoing professional relationship. Thus, they can be used for diagnostic purposes in case situations where it is necessary to assess the severity or intensity of a client's situation.

Second, periodic application of standardized assessment scales when working with a client can identify changes as they occur during the intervention to inform practice decisions regarding the desirability of continuing or changing the intervention plan. These scales can be used to help a social worker sum up the results of the intervention with one client (i.e., comparing the client's score on the scale before the intervention begins and at the conclusion of service). In addition to the social worker's general ethical obligation to be accountable to clients and agencies for the quality of services provided, empirical analyses of practice outcomes as reflected by standardized measurement tools are increasingly requested by managed care companies.

Although standardized scales vary in length, most contain between 15 and 30 one-sentence statements that a client is asked to rate on a 3- to 7-point scale. Therefore, these scales can be completed in a short period of time. One set of scales, known as the *WALMYR Assessment Scales*, illustrates a typical format used to measure constructs applicable to social work practice. For example, one of the WALMYR scales, the *Index of Self-Esteem (ISE)*, is designed to measure the extent of a client's problems with self-esteem. Here are 5 of the 25 items on that scale:

    1. I feel that people would not like me if they knew me really well.
    4. When I am with others I feel they are glad I am with them.
    8. I feel that I need more self-confidence.
    16. I feel very self-conscious when I am with strangers.
    20. I feel I get pushed around more than others.

The client then rates each item on a 7-point scale with (1) none of the time, (2) very rarely, (3) a little of the time, (4) some of the time, (5) a good part of the time, (6) most of the time, and (7) all of the time. To prevent respondents from falling into a pattern of responses in which each item is not carefully considered, some of the items are presented as a positive statement and others as negative. In these cases, the responses must be "reverse scored." To illustrate, an answer of "most of the time" on Item 1 (above) would be a negative statement about the client's self-esteem, while on Item 4 a response of "most of the time" would reflect a positive attitude. Clear instructions are provided with the scales to guide the worker in reverse scoring.

A well-established research methodology underpins the development of standardized instruments known as *psychometrics*. During the process of development, the scales are examined to assure that they not only represent the meaning of the construct being measured (validity) but that the scale would also yield approximately the same result each time it is administered (reliability). In the development phase, the scales are administered to a large number of respondents and the responses are statistically analyzed; then the results are compared to other indicators of that condition. The scale is then revised and adjusted until it meets the criteria for a valid measure.

The descriptions provided with the scales help inform the social worker when making a selection. For example, data should always be available on the instrument's validity and reliability. Although there are no strict guidelines, generally when judging a scale's *validity* in the human services area, a correlation coefficient of +.60 or greater when compared to other indicators is acceptable. For *reliability*, an Alpha score of +.80 or greater is sufficient. Some scale descriptions will also specify the age and reading levels for which the measure is acceptable. Finally, the worker must decide if it is feasible to use the instrument in the particular practice situation. For example, the worker should determine if the measure has been normed with the cultural or age group that includes the client, is of appropriate length to use in the practice situation, is sensitive to the issues on which the practice is focused, and does not take an inordinate amount of money to secure or time to score.

Another feature of some scales is that cutting scores can be established. *Cutting scores* indicate the point on a scale where a client's score reflects a very serious problem or, at the other end of the continuum, does not represent a problem that would require professional intervention. Many of the WALMYR scales, for example, measure the severity of problems with scores ranging from 0 (low severity or intensity) to 100 (extremely high level). A cutting score of 70 on these scales has been standardized to indicate the level of severity at which the client begins to be at high risk to self or others. Similarly, a score below 30 is an indication that intervention is probably not required.

Finally, to interpret the scores from a standardized scale, it must be recognized that the scale contains a certain amount of error in representing the factor it measures. Just as various political polls in an election year present their data with a plus or minus error factor, so do the standardized scales used by social workers. Known as the *standard error of measurement (SEM)*, this SEM represents the amount of change in either direction that can be considered significant. Typically, the SEM for a scale is around +/- five points, but the specific factor should be available in the psychometric reports on any scale.

Reports on standardized scales are scattered throughout the social work and psychology literature and are often difficult to locate. Three excellent resources for finding useful scales are described in Figure 14.1.

SELECTED BIBLIOGRAPHY

Bloom, Martin, Joel Fischer, and John G. Orme. *Evaluating Practice: Guidelines for the Accountable Professional*, 4th ed. Boston: Allyn & Bacon, 2003.

Jordan, Cathleen, and Cynthia Franklin. *Clinical Assessment for Social Workers*, 2nd ed. Chicago: Lyceum Books, 2003.

FIGURE 14.1	Basic Sources of Standardized Scales for Social Workers

➤ Corcoran, Kevin, and Joel Fischer. *Measures for Clinical Practice: A Sourcebook*, 4th ed. New York: Oxford University Press, 2009.

This two-volume handbook of measures appropriate for social work practice describes more than 300 different standardized instruments. Volume 1 contains scales for use with children, couples, and families; Volume 2 is focused on scales for measuring adults. A partial list of topic areas for which multiple scales are reported includes the following:

Anger and hostility	Marital/couple relationships
Anxiety and fear	Parent/child relationships
Assertiveness	Phobias
Children's behaviors/problems	Satisfaction with life
Depression and grief	Self-concept and esteem
Family functioning	Social support
Health issues	Substance abuse
Interpersonal behavior	Treatment satisfaction

For each scale, a short description is provided, its psychometric properties presented, and sources for obtaining permission to use the scale (with or without a fee) included.

➤ Hudson, Walter W. *WALMYR Assessment Scales Scoring Manual*. Available online: www.walmyr.com. WALMYR Publishing Co., P.O. Box 12217, Tallahassee, FL 32317–2217. E-mail: walmyr@walmyr.com.

This is a collection of nearly 30 paper-and-pencil short self-report scales. The scales include "personal adjustment measures" that assess levels of depression, stress, anxiety, substance abuse, and so on; "problems with spouse or partner" such as marital discord, physical or nonphysical abuse; "family relationship problems," including a child's attitude toward mother or father, sibling relations, and family relations; and measures of "organizational outcomes" such as a person's job-related distress or a client's satisfaction with the services provided. The psychometric properties and a description of the construct being measured by each scale are also included with the set of scales.

➤ Rush, A. John, et al., eds. *Handbook of Psychiatric Measures*. Washington, DC: American Psychiatric Association, 2000.

This sourcebook contains 230 carefully selected measures of various psychiatric conditions, including the following:

Diagnostic interviews for adults	General psychiatric symptoms
Mental health status and functioning	Quality of life
Patient perceptions of care	Practitioner and system evaluation
Stress and life events	Family and relational issues
Suicide risk measures	Measures related to the *DSM-IV-R* categories

For each measure, the authors identify the goal of the measurement tool; describe what it measures; identify practical issues of test administration, availability, and cost of instruments; report the psychometric properties (including reliability and validity); discuss its clinical utility; and refer the reader to more in-depth sources. An accompanying CD-ROM contains the complete text and reprints of 108 of the measures.

14.3   THE SERVICE PLAN OUTCOME CHECKLIST (SPOC)

Purpose: To record the client's perception of progress on a menu of outcome goals and/or to accumulate the outcome scores for multiple clients in order to assess success in achieving desired outcomes.

Discussion: The *Service Plan Outcome Checklist (SPOC)* is a recording and monitoring tool for collecting summative data on client progress in achieving identified outcomes. Unlike most other monitoring tools, the SPOC can be developed and used with multiple clients (e.g., a group or a worker's caseload), as well as with an individual client.

A SPOC is relatively easy to construct and is an extension of client problem or goal checklists used as assessment tools (see Item 11.12). The central feature of the SPOC is a menu of outcome goals the agency or worker typically helps the clients address. The SPOC is also useful for identifying the content that group members hope to address during group sessions, information that can help in planning the group experience, as well as in assessing what was actually achieved during the group sessions. Although the format of the SPOC is standardized, the list of outcomes included in the menu will be unique for each type of service offered. Such a list can be derived from an analysis of client records, a review of the agency's mission and policies, and interviews with experienced workers. The menu of outcomes in Figure 14.2 was created for clients in a pain management group.

The first step in using the SPOC is to ask the client or clients during the initiation of service to review the list of desired outcomes (left-hand column of Figure 14.2) and to place a check (✓) by each goal he or she wants to achieve. This selection might be done independently by the client or with the assistance of the worker. Workers often find that discussion of these items yields helpful information and provides a way to focus an initial interview or adapt plans for a group's content or activities. To assist in prioritizing services, the two or three most important service outcomes for the client should also be identified.

If used with a client over an extended period, the client's perception of achievement might be obtained at interim points in the change process to assess the progress of the intervention effort. At a minimum, all items on the menu of possible outcomes should be rated at the point of termination (shaded section of Figure 14.2). A by-product of this final evaluation is that clients find it helpful to revisit their initial selection of outcome goals, as well as the other outcomes addressed, and reflect on what was actually achieved. When applied to an individual client, examination of the client's view of the level of outcome achievement is an indicator of the success of the intervention relative to the various items the client believed were important.

When the SPOC is applied to a group of clients, it yields information that can help the worker identify both the importance of and level of achievement for the various menu categories. The menu in Figure 14.2 was developed in relation to the items the worker anticipated addressing when using a cognitive-behavioral approach in a

FIGURE 14.2   Service Plan Outcome Checklist (SPOC): Northside Health Clinic Pain Management Group

Kate Miranda
_____
Client/Family

Maureen Carney
_____
Worker

7/6/2008
_____
Service Initiation Date

Instructions: Complete Steps 1–2 within two weeks of the initiation of service.

Step 1   In the far left column, select and (✓) all outcomes for intervention. If a desired outcome does not appear on the menu below, add items in the space provided at the end of the questionnaire.

Step 2   Review the items checked in Step 1 and circle the two or three that you consider the most important or of highest priority.

When services are terminated and/or at an interim point in service activity, complete Step 3 (i.e., the shaded area).

Step 3   Rate each checked item from "no progress" to "fully achieved" by circling the number from 1 to 5 that best represents your judgment about progress made to date.

Place a (✓) by each desired outcome for this service. Then circle the two or three most important outcomes.	Circle Your Assessment at Time of Discharge				
	No Progress	About Half Achieved		Fully Achieved	
1. Understand the connection between stress and pain.	1	②	3	4	5
✓ 2. Learn coping skills to use during a pain episode.	1	2	3	4	⑤
✓ 3. Improve outlook for my pain.	1	②	3	4	5
4. Change my beliefs about pain.	1	2	③	4	5
5. Help me communicate more directly with others about my pain.	1	2	3	④	5
6. Learn to manage my emotions better.	1	2	③	4	5
✓ 7. Learn how my pain impacts relationships.	1	2	3	4	⑤
✓ 8. Be less dependent on medication for pain relief.	1	2	3	④	5
9. Learn better self-expression about my pain.	1	2	3	④	5
10. Develop coping skills for stress management.	1	2	③	4	5
11. Reduce fear associated with pain.	1	2	③	4	5

Place a (✓) by each desired outcome for this service. Then circle the two or three most important outcomes.	Circle Your Assessment at Time of Discharge				
	No Progress		About Half Achieved		Fully Achieved
✓ 12. Improve self-confidence	1	2	③	4	5
✓ 13. Increase my level of physical activity and socialization.	1	2	3	4	⑤
_____ 14. Learn more about the connection between my thoughts and behaviors.	1	2	3	④	5
_____ 15. Additional outcome I would like to address: _Referral to different clinic_	①	2	3	4	5
_____ 16. Additional outcome I would like to address: _____	1	2	3	4	5

Source: Adapted and modified from evaluation conducted by Maureen Carney, Colorado State University.

chronic pain group offered by a family health center.* Before the group sessions began, the worker constructed the items in the menu (left column) by scanning literature on chronic pain and listing items that typically concern patients, interviewing staff members who regularly work with persons experiencing chronic pain, and discussing a draft menu with potential group members. The group members were subsequently given a copy of the SPOC and asked to place a checkmark by every item they would like to address while in the group and then to circle the two or three items that would be their highest priority. In addition, a final item was an open-ended question allowing group members the opportunity to identify topics to address that may have been omitted from the menu. At the last group session, the worker returned the SPOCs to the group members and asked them to rate their achievement for each items on a five-point scale.

To determine the importance of each item to the group members, the social worker then summarized the group members' responses as reflected in Columns 2 through 4 in Figure 14.3. The steps followed were as follows:

- In Column 2, the worker recorded the number of group members who had selected that item and computed a percentage of the total (i.e., 3 of the 15 clients, or 20.0 percent, selected item 1, "Understand the connections between stress and pain" as an issue they wanted to address).
- In Column 3, the worker followed the same procedure and arrived at the number and percentage for each item selected as one of the two or three priority issues to address by the group members.

*Prior editions of this book contained outcome menus from a child and family services agency (4th edition), a community mental health center (5th edition), a hospice agency (6th edition), and a medical trauma center (7th edition).

FIGURE 14.3	Northside Health Clinic Pain Management Group: Service Plan Outcome Checklist Summary

	Column 1	Column 2		Column 3		Column 4	Column 5
Item #	Issue Selected	# and % Selected		# and % Priority		Importance Index	Mean Achievement
2	Learn to cope with pain episodes	12	80.0%	9	60.0%	140.0	4.50
8	Be less dependent on pain medications	12	80.0	8	53.3	133.3	4.00
12	Improve self-confidence	11	73.3	5	33.3	106.7	3.00
13	Increase physical activity and socialization	12	80.0	4	26.7	106.7	4.53
3	Improve outlook on my pain	10	66.7	5	33.3	100.0	1.75
5	Communicate more directly about my pain	6	40.0	3	20.0	60.0	3.55
7	Learn how my pain impacts relationships	5	33.3	2	13.3	46.6	4.33
6	Learn to manage my emotions better	4	26.7	2	13.3	40.0	2.75
9	Better self-expression about my pain	4	26.7	1	6.7	33.4	3.82
10	Develop coping skills for stress management	4	26.7	1	6.7	33.4	4.22
11	Reduce fear associated with pain	4	26.7	1	6.7	33.4	3.67
14	Connection between thoughts and behaviors	5	33.3	0	0.0	33.3	2.22
1	Connection between stress and pain	3	20.0	0	0.0	20.0	3.22
15	Other: Referral to different clinic	2	13.3	0	0.0	13.3	1.69
4	Change my beliefs about pain	1	6.7	0	0.0	6.7	2.31
16	Other: None Identified						
						Group Mean	3.30
	Overall Achievement	N = 15 clients				**Possible Range** = 1.00 to 5.00	

Source: Adapted and modified from evaluation conducted by Maureen Carney, Colorado State University.

- Given that both the expression of interest and the priority given an item are valid indicators about how important an item is for each member, an *importance index* (Column 4) was compiled by adding the two percentages from Columns 2 and 3. Note that this is an index number, not a percentage.
- At the point of termination, each group member rated his or her achievement on the five-point scale in the shaded section of the SPOC form (see Figure 14.2). The social worker then recorded each client's rating, computed a mean achievement score for each item, and entered that in Column 5.
- Finally, the worker used a spreadsheet program to sort the items, using Column 4 (in descending order) as the first sort. Doing so produced a list of the items in order of the Importance Index score, with the most important items at the top of the chart. The mean or average score for the group members was 3.30.

Having completed these calculations, the worker could then interpret the group members' perceptions of success by visually comparing Columns 4 and 5. For example, in Figure 14.3, Item 2 had a 140.0 importance index and a high achievement score, suggesting the group was very successful in achieving this outcome. However, Item 3 had a high importance index (100.0), but only a 1.75 achievement mean. According to these data, the group was not successful in helping members improve their outlook on pain. This would suggest that the worker should seek additional knowledge or training about how to help group members in this area. Also, the "other" item mentioned by two members would suggest that it should be added to the menu the next time this SPOC is used.

Two additional uses of the SPOC might be used to strengthen social work practice. First, a social worker might administer the SPOC to all or a sample of his or her clients and compute the scores as in the group example above in order to identify areas where clients could benefit from the worker gaining additional knowledge and skill. Second, a supervisor on a unit of an agency might give an SPOC with a menu of unit services to a sample of clients to judge overall unit performance and to identify workers who are particularly strong in addressing specific outcomes so that the most competent workers could be assigned to clients with these specific needs.

SELECTED BIBLIOGRAPHY

Horejsi, Charles. *Assessment and Case Planning in Child Protection and Foster Care Services.* Englewood, CO: American Humane Association, 1996.

14.4   TASK ACHIEVEMENT SCALING (TAS)

Purpose: To determine the degree to which the client has completed agreed upon intervention tasks.

Discussion: *Task Achievement Scaling (TAS)* is a tool that measures success in completing specified tasks. This evaluation procedure was developed for use in task-centered practice wherein work toward the client's goals and objectives is broken down into

FIGURE 14.4	Task Achievement Scale (TAS)

Overall Goal: Better Interpersonal Relationships
Client: Devin W.   *Worker: Tamera Ford*
Date: 10/7/2008   *Week #3*

	Task 1: **Meet More People** **at School**	Task 2: **Prepare to Start** **Dating**	Task 3: **Increase Social Skills**
No Progress (0)	Do nothing for now	Don't waste time on this as it won't happen (✓)	Don't even think about it
Minimally Achieved (1)	Create list of interesting clubs on campus	Create compatibility choice list	Identify specific social skills to work on
Partially Achieved (2)	Choose which club to join (✓)	Describe what a fun, budget-conscious date would be like	Be able to describe the process of using one's social skills
Substantially Achieved (3)	Attend a club meeting, introduce self, socialize, and get involved	Research different venues for meeting women (internet, campus, etc.)	Expose self to opportunities to practice new social skills (✓)
Completely Achieved (4)	Invite someone to do something outside of group	Be willing and prepared to make sacrifices with time and money	Integrate new social skills into daily interactions
Change Score	2	0	3
Possible Change	4	4	4
% of Possible Change Achieved	50%	0%	75%
Total Percent of Change for all Three Tasks: 41.7%			

Source: Adapted and modified from evaluation conducted by Tamera Ford, Colorado State University.

many small and separate tasks and then worked on sequentially. A ***task*** is an action or decision by the client or worker that is necessary in order to reach a desired outcome. A task is usually something that can be accomplished in a matter of days or, at most, in a few weeks. Usually, not more than three or four tasks are worked on at a time. Each session with the client begins with a review of the progress on tasks selected for attention during the previous session and ends with identifying tasks to be undertaken before the next session. Because the TAS reports the percent of attempted tasks that were actually achieved, some tasks may be completed or judged to be no longer needed and dropped, some may be continued, and others added at each session.

TAS is especially applicable as a means of evaluation when the service is relatively brief and when activities are concrete. For purposes of illustration, consider the client in a university counseling center who is feeling isolated due to his poor ability to establish positive interpersonal relationships. The goal seemed unattainable to the client until the worker, drawing on the task-centered practice approach, helped the client break this down into three specific tasks he could perform: (1) meet more people at school; (2) prepare to start dating; and (3) increase social skills. The worker and client then identified four incremental steps the client might take to move toward each goal and assigned a numerical value to each step. By combining the percentage of change score for each task, an overall task achievement score could be readily computed each week when the client and worker met, and discussion of how to make better progress the next week could ensue.

Figure 14.4 represents one week's task achievement scale completed by the client and worker in this university counseling center. The client "partially achieved" the tasks set out for the week by creating a list of campus clubs that interested him and choosing a club to join. He made "no progress" in preparation to start dating, but "substantially achieved" the task for increasing social skills when he put himself in a position to practice some new social skills he was developing. His percent of achievement compared to what might have been achieved for each task appears near the bottom of the figure, and his overall percent of achievement (a total change score of 5 compared to a possible change score of 12) was scored as 41.7 percent.

A useful means of tracking a client's level of task achievement is to cast the weekly scores into a time-series chart as described in Item 14.6, where various single subject designs are introduced. Such graphing of the percent of task achievement from week to week can be useful in reinforcing positive task achievement, or a downward trend can signal a decline in client interest or motivation. Using the time-series format also makes it possible to graphically compare the percent of task completion with some other variable to answer a practice question such as "To what extent is the level of task achievement associated with the client's level of self-esteem?"

SELECTED BIBLIOGRAPHY

Epstein, Laura, and Lester Brown. *Brief Treatment and a New Look at the Task-Centered Approach*, 4th ed. Boston: Allyn & Bacon, 2002.

14.5 GOAL ATTAINMENT SCALING (GAS)

Purpose: To measure the degree to which a client has reached individualized goals.

Discussion: *Goal Attainment Scaling (GAS)* is a procedure that provides an estimate of the degree of movement toward goals that accrues from an intervention with an individual or family. The application of GAS begins during the contracting and goal-setting phase of the change process. The basic format for a GAS is the same for all clients, although adjustments must be made to accommodate the number of goals selected. It consists of several five-point scales (usually two to four or five) that are individualized for the specific client to represent a set of possible outcomes—both positive and negative— related to the agreed upon goals. These may be individualized scales (see Item 14.1) or may reflect differing scores on a standardized assessment instrument (see Item 14.2). Here are the steps in constructing a GAS:

1. *Identify two to five goals, and develop a five-point scale for each.* To establish a GAS, the worker and client begin by describing in a few words the client's condition or situation before the intervention was started in relation to each identified goal. Ideally, this description should be viewed as indicating the second-lowest point on a five-point scale; a score of 2 is assigned. The lowest point (assigned a score of 1) on the scale is then described, indicating what a step backward would represent. Next, the best outcome that could reasonably be expected should be described; a value of 5 is assigned. Then, two levels of improvement between the current situation and the best possible scenario can be described and assigned scores of 3 and 4. In sum, the scores should reflect the conditions described below. (However, the worker and client should create more explicit descriptions of the variable at each of the five levels.) The scores represent these conditions:

1 = Most unfavorable outcome thought likely
2 = No change or less than expected success
3 = Some favorable change or expected level of success
4 = Substantial change or more than expected success
5 = Most favorable outcome thought likely

The GAS in Figure 14.5 was created by a school social worker who was helping a 13-year-old girl diagnosed with a Significant Identifiable Emotional Disability (SIED) to improve her behaviors in order to be accepted for transition to mainstream classes in her school. The social worker and client identified three goals to address during the intervention period: (1) increase self-esteem; (2) reduce anger outbursts with peers; and (3) decrease frequency of discipline referrals to the principal's office. Using a strengths-based approach to individual counseling (see Chapter 6) and placing the girl in an anger management group, the worker and student developed scales to measure her success (or lack of success) in attaining each goal. Five levels of change, ranging from "Most unfavorable" to "Most favorable," were identified for each goal. In this example the worker used all three forms of measurement including a standardized scale (Index of Self-Esteem), an individualized scale (based on the student's estimate of the percentage of time she used anger coping skills), and frequency data (based on the number of discipline referrals each month).

2. *Assign a weight to each goal area to indicate its importance in relation to the other goals.* Since most people are accustomed to working in sets of 100, clients

FIGURE 14.5	Goal Attainment Scale for Anne Christopher, 9/27/2008 and 12/15/2008

Client: Anne Christoper
Worker: Erin Burke

(✓) = Beginning Level (✗) = Terminating Level	Goal 1: **Increase Self-Esteem**	Goal 2: **Reduce Anger Outbursts with Peers**	Goal 3: **Decrease Frequency of Discipline Referrals**
Attainment Level	Weight: 40	Weight: 35	Weight: 25
(1) Most unfavorable outcome thought likely	Index of Self-Esteem Scale score = 70 or above	Does not make effort to control anger outbursts	4 or more discipline referrals per month ✓
(2) Less than expected success	Index of Self-Esteem Scale score = 57-69 ✓	Learns new skills for coping with anger ✓	3 discipline referrals per month
(3) Expected success	Index of Self-Esteem Scale score = 44-56	Uses anger coping skills less than 50% of the time when angry ✗	2 discipline referrals per month
(4) More than expected success	Index of Self-Esteem Scale score = 31-43 ✗	Uses anger coping skills 50% to 75% of the time when angry	1 discipline referral per month
(5) Best anticipated success	Index of Self-Esteem Scale score = 30 or lower	Uses anger coping skills more than 75% of the time when angry	0 discipline referrals per month ✗
Summary	Goal 1: Self-Esteem	Goal 2: Anger Outbursts	Goal 3: Discipline Referrals
Weight	40	35	25
Change Score	2	1	4
Weighted Change Score	80	35	100
Possible Weighted Change	120	105	100
Percentage Attainment	66.7%	33.3%	100.0%
Total Weighted Change (215) / Total Possible Weighted Change (325) = 66.2%			

Source: Adapted and modified from evaluation conducted by Erin Burke, Colorado State University.

usually understand dividing 100 points among the several goals to reflect the degree to which each is important. In Figure 14.5, the social worker and client decided that increasing self-esteem would partially contribute to reducing anger outbursts and would thus cut down on discipline referrals. Therefore they gave Goal #1 the highest weight of 40. They then gave Goal #2 a weight of 35, and Goal #3 a 25 weighting. By assigning a weight to each goal, not only could the progress on each goal be identified, but an indicator of overall goal achievement (due to the fact that the goals were interrelated) also could be computed.

3. *Place a checkmark (✓) in the cell that best describes the client's condition for each goal at the point that intervention begins.* Usually this checkmark will appear in the "2" cell, the "Less than expected success" level, since at the start of the intervention the client is likely to be having difficulty in the area to be addressed. Sometimes, however, the checkmark will appear in a different attainment level, as for Goal #3 in Figure 14.5. The checkmarks, then, become the baseline or "before" measurement for the GAS.

4. *When the service or intervention is terminated, place an (X) in the cell that best describes the client's condition for each goal at that time.* This mark (✗) represents the "after" measurement, and the difference in measurement from the initial checkmark (✓) reflects the change that occurred during the time of service. In some long-term cases, however, it may be useful to locate an interim attainment level for each goal as a means of monitoring the change process.

5. *Determine the weighted change score for each goal.* Computing the change score involves subtracting the beginning score (✓) from the ending score (✗) and multiplying by the weight assigned to that goal. In Goal #1 of Figure 14.5, for example, the client's level of self-esteem increased from the "2" attainment level to the "4" attainment level—a change of two levels. The change score is then multiplied by 40 (the established weight for Goal #1), and a weighted change score of 80 was recorded.

6. *Compute the percentage of possible change for each scale.* Determine the highest score a client might generate for each scale by identifying the change that would have occurred if the client had fully reached the goal (i.e., the "5" level) and record that score. Then divide the actual weighted change score by this possible change score. For Goal #1 in Figure 14.5, this would involve dividing 80 by 120, yielding a percentage change score of 66.7 for that goal.

7. *Compute an overall goal attainment score.* Perhaps the most valuable information derived from a GAS is the combined score from the several scales, which gives a comprehensive indication of the client's level of goal attainment. To derive that score, the possible weighted change scores for all the goals are summed and then divided into the sum of the actual weighted change scores. In Figure 14.5, the percentage of overall change is reflected at the bottom of the chart (i.e., total weighted change [215] divided by possible weighted change [325], which yields a percentage change of 66.2 percent). In sum, using the strengths-based perspective and involving this student in an anger management group resulted in a generally favorable outcome, although the reduction of anger outbursts with peers might continue to require attention.

If goal attainment scaling is used widely in an agency, data can be gleaned from GAS charts that will be useful in program evaluation. For example, data might be accumulated regarding the following:

- The types of goals chosen as targets for intervention, their frequency, and the percent of goal achievement on each
- The amount of progress made on particular goals by the clients served by a specific worker
- The relative success in goal achievement with particular groups of clients (e.g., age, ethnicity, gender, etc.)

SELECTED BIBLIOGRAPHY

Bloom, Martin, Joel Fischer, and John G. Orme. *Evaluating Practice: Guidelines for the Accountable Professional*, 4th ed. Boston: Allyn & Bacon, 2003.

Kiresuk, Thomas J., Aaron Smith, and Joseph E. Cardillo. *Goal Attainment Scaling: Applications, Theory, and Measurement*. Hillsdale, NY: Erlbaum, 1994.

14.6   SINGLE-SUBJECT DESIGNS (SSDs)

Purpose: To evaluate changes in client actions, feelings, or attitudes over a specified period of time.

Discussion: The most well-known methods for direct practice evaluation are single-subject research designs—also known as single-system, single-case, $N = 1$, and time-series designs. As compared to more traditional forms of research that accumulate data from multiple respondents either before and after or with experimental and control groups, *single-subject designs (SSDs)* involve accumulating repeated measurements from a single subject (e.g., individual, couple, family, or group) over time. An SSD might also be used to examine a single intervention with multiple applications (e.g., multiple clients, multiple targets of change, or in multiple settings).

Two fundamental assumptions underpin SSD. First, it is assumed that if left unattended, the client's condition or problem will stay about the same or worsen. Second, it is assumed that barring evidence to the contrary, one can cautiously conclude that if change occurs after the introduction of an intervention, the intervention is a dominant force in that change. Thus, by clearly specifying the client's behavior, attitude, or functioning *before* the intervention begins (i.e., a baseline measurement), any change that occurs during the period of intervention can be attributed to the intervention. Although it is not possible to conclude that the intervention *caused* an identified change, it can be said that there is (or is not) an *association* between the change and the intervention.

There is no uniform format for single-subject designs. In fact, one of the strengths of this methodology is its flexibility. Because the SSD monitors what occurs in practice, the design must be adaptable to changing practice situations. Unlike traditional social science research, therefore, it is appropriate to modify the design during the change process if a decision is made, for example, to alter the intervention plan or to take advantage of a temporary secession of service such as a vacation period to obtain another baseline. The following steps reflect a process for conducting a single-subject evaluation:

1. *Select a case situation in which it will be possible to take several measurements over time.* Because data that reveal trends in a client's actions or feelings provide the basis of this design, repeated measurements must be taken. These measurements might occur before the intervention is begun, during the intervention, and even after the intervention is completed. The frequency of measurement will depend on the case situation and could be daily, weekly, or monthly. The characteristic way of organizing SSD data is on a graph that depicts the independent variable (e.g., attitude, behavior, etc.) on the left axis (*y*-axis) and a timeline in days or weeks along the bottom (*x*-axis). Figure 14.6 depicts the typical format for graphing the basic components of a single-subject design.

2. *Select the target behaviors/attitudes/beliefs, and determine how each is to be measured.* During the assessment and planning phases of the change process, the factors, conditions, or patterns targeted for change will have been identified and, in order to monitor change, a valid and relevant numerical measure must be selected. This may be a frequency count (how often something happens) or a score on a standardized or individualized scale (see Items 14.1 and 14.2). The worker and client should establish a plan for taking the measurements under similar conditions (e.g., same location, just prior to counseling sessions)

| FIGURE 14.6 | Components of Single-Subject Design (SSD) Graphing |

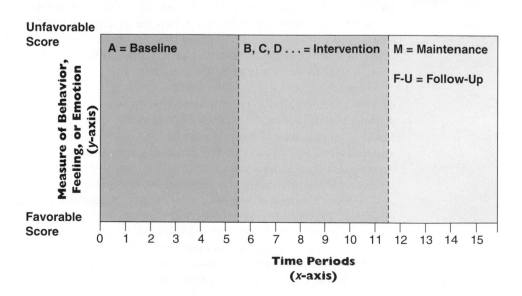

so that as far as possible, each time a measurement is made, the context when collecting data will be consistent.

3. *Select a single-subject design, and designate the phases of the process on the chart.* The different phases (e.g., baseline, intervention, and follow-up) of the process are identified across the top of the graph with dashed vertical lines separating each phase. *A* is used to represent a *baseline period*. The letters *B, C, D,* and so forth, identify distinctly different interventions. If multiple interventions are used simultaneously, a slash is placed between the letters representing those interventions (e.g., *B/C*). If there is a modification in the frequency or intensity of an intervention (e.g., shorter sessions or increased medication), those modifications can be noted with a superscript designation (e.g., B^1 B^2). *M* designates a period in which a minimum level of service is maintained before a case is closed (the maintenance phase) and *F-U* denotes a follow-up measurement after service has been terminated. Either include a descriptor (e.g., *B* = family therapy, *C* = individual supportive counseling) or provide a key for each phase of the process somewhere on the chart.

The variations in SSD depend on the practice situation, the worker's creativity, and the questions the worker intends to answer. The most elementary SSD is the *B* design or a case study in which there are no baseline or follow-up data and the worker simply tracks what happens in regard to the independent variable(s) while the intervention is occurring. This approach allows the worker to record what is happening during the intervention phase in order to adjust the practice approach, if necessary, or to inform future practice decisions.

The most commonly used form of SSD allows the worker and client to examine any changes in a relevant client characteristic between a baseline period and the intervention phase (e.g., an *AB* design). This type of study might also allow the worker to examine any client change associated with changing to a different intervention (an *ABC* design) or adding a second intervention, such as group therapy, to the task-centered individual counseling already in process (an *ABB/C* design) to assess the relative effectiveness of each approach or combination of approaches. In sum, these designs can be used to provide data to guide practice decisions (i.e., if an intervention isn't working, it can be replaced with another) or to adapt to changing practice activities to track the relative success at each phase of the process.

Figure 14.7 reflects a single-subject practice evaluation conducted in a hospice setting. The client, Gail Winder, was a 52-year-old woman who lost her mother a few months before visiting the hospice agency to request help in dealing with her grief. Ms. Winder had been her mother's primary caregiver during the last year of her life and had given up her job to serve in this capacity. During this time her relationship with her sisters had deteriorated to the point that they were barely speaking to each other and were squabbling over the mother's few remaining possessions.

Having a history of depression, Ms. Winder recognized that the symptoms were returning. The social worker identified that Ms. Winder was experiencing extreme guilt as she reevaluated herself as a not very adequate caregiver for her mother. In addition, she was sad over the strained relationships with her sisters, as well as angry with her husband, whom she thought did not give her assistance in caring for her mother during the last stages of her life. Warden (1982) identifies sadness, anger, and

FIGURE 14.7   **Generalized Contentment [Depression] Scores (GCS) for Gail Winder**

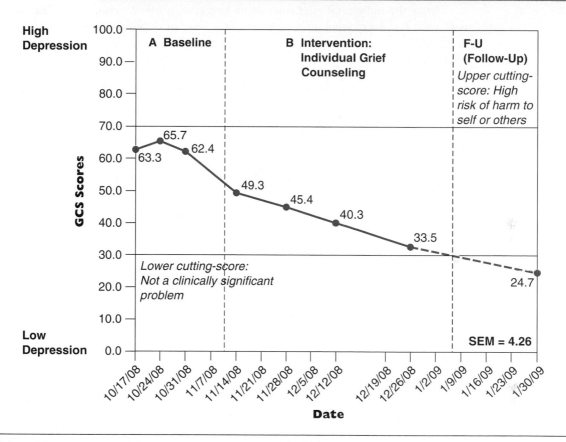

guilt as common symptoms of grief, and Zisook and Shuchter (2001) report that when bereavement is complicated by a major depressive episode, individual grief counseling can be an effective intervention to reduce depression and promote well-being.

When assessing this case situation, the social worker had Ms. Winder complete the Generalized Contentment Scale (GCS) (Hudson, 1997) to help determine the extent of the depression she was feeling. As indicated in Figure 14.7, she scored 63.3, a relatively high level of depression. Because he was not going to be able to schedule her into his workload for several weeks, he gave Ms. Winder two extra copies of the GSC to complete and mail to him so he could judge if the depression was substantially deepening, thus requiring a more immediate intervention. Those two scores changed slightly but were well within the Standard Error of Measurement (SEM = 4.26) for that instrument (see Item 14.2). These three scores were plotted on the single subject design (SSD) chart as the baseline scores (A), suggesting that a stable pattern of relatively high depression was present.

Once the individual grief counseling began with Ms. Winder, the social worker meet with her every week and measured her level of depression every other week. During this intervention phase, the B phase on the SSD chart, the CGS scores declined, reflecting a decrease in the client's level of depression. In fact, the scores neared the lower cutting score of 30, indicating that the depression had decreased to the point that it was unlikely that Ms. Winder was experiencing a clinically significant problem. Further, the change far exceeded the SEM of 4.26, indicating that the positive change was more than just error in the instrument (the GCS) and that Ms. Winder's decrease in depression was substantial. To keep tabs on Ms. Winder's depression, the social worker sent her another copy of the GCS a month later (the Follow-Up Phase), and her score of 24.7 indicated that she had maintained a level of depression that did not suggest the need for additional counseling at that time.

In the case of Ms. Winder, only one variable (depression) was measured. If the social worker and client had wanted to determine if Ms. Winder's level of stress was declining along with her level of depression, a second measure (e.g., the Index of Clinical Stress [ICS]) might also have been administered (perhaps on the alternate weeks to the GCS so as not to overload Ms. Winder). By plotting both sets of scores on the SSD chart, the change in ICS scores could be compared to change in the GCS scores and the interrelatedness of the two emotions (i.e., stress and depression) examined.

Single-system designs also can be used in more elaborate ways to test the impact of an intervention. As indicated earlier, by establishing the baseline (A) level for a client characteristic and then starting an intervention (B) to establish the amount of change in that condition, one can reach the reasonable conclusion that initiating the intervention was associated with the change. One could be even more confident in that conclusion if the intervention was withheld and the measurements continued for a time (perhaps while the worker or client was on vacation), providing another baseline (A) period and then resuming the intervention (B). If improvement in the client's condition was found in conjunction with the intervention during both B phases in this ABAB design, there would be strong evidence that the intervention was a key factor in that change. Another variation might be to assess change associated with an intervention in a group. A group average score from measurements taken at each session might be useful, but the chance that a group approach might be helpful for most members yet damaging to others would have to be considered. The scores for all members could be charted, as well as the mean score for the group, to compare both individual and group scores. In sum, once the rudiments of SSD are mastered, the opportunities for developing a wide variety of designs to inform one's practice are limited only by the worker's creativity.

4. *Collect and record baseline, intervention, maintenance, and/or follow-up data on each factor.* When scores are obtained on each variable, the score should be plotted on the client's graph. Because the chart reflects the sequence of related scores through time, a *line chart* is the preferred format. The known data points should be connected with solid lines. If there are missing data at an interval when data regularly would have been collected, the two known points should be connected by a dashed line, which depicts an assumption that the missing data would have fallen along the line between the two known points.

Ideally, baseline measures should be repeatedly taken until a stable score on the variable is established. However, the realities of social work practice rarely permit many measurements. A minimum of three baseline measurements (before the intervention is begun) should be collected if at all possible. These measurements might be made during the assessment and planning phases of the change process (*current baseline* data) or might possibly be based on information already on record (*retrospective baseline* data), such as attendance records or previous scores on assessment instruments. It is also important to note on the *y*-axis if a high score represents a positive or negative outcome on each factor.

5. *Interpret the data and compare empirical evidence with other practice observations.* When data points have been entered on a graph, it is then possible to examine the data and make judgments about the success of the intervention. Several cautions should be considered when interpreting SSD data. First, if there is a sequence of interventions being evaluated, such as in an ABCD design, there could be a *carryover* effect in which the change made in one phase affects the next. Withdrawing all interventions (i.e., returning to a second baseline) can help to reveal if there has been a cumulative influence from the series of interventions. The *order of presentation* of various intervention strategies can also affect the impact of a specific intervention. This problem can be addressed in subsequent practice situations by changing the order of introducing the various intervention strategies. If one strategy appears most effective regardless of order, a worker can feel more confident about using that strategy in similar practice situations. Finally, SSDs often suffer from *incomplete and inaccurate data*. The realities of practice are that clients miss sessions, data collection instruments are not completed, clients sometimes provide incorrect information, and so on. These problems should not mitigate against conducting direct practice evaluation, but rather they argue for cautious interpretation of the results and reinforce the importance of triangulation.

Visual examination of the direction of change will often produce a clear picture of the client's situation. However, when data are erratic, it may be difficult to detect trends. When this happens, it is helpful to compute a *mean* or *median* score (see Item 16.11) to identify the most typical responses. For each phase of the process, then, horizontal lines represent the central tendency. When a small number of measurements are taken, an extreme score may distort a mean. In these cases, a *trimmed mean* can more accurately reflect central tendency. It is computed by dropping both the highest and lowest 10 percent of responses and then computing the mean score. Other more sophisticated analyses of data can be conducted, in which *trend lines* or *celeration lines* project the future direction of client performance on the factor being measured. Moreover, if there are sufficient data, it is possible to determine if a change is *statistically significant*. Rubin and Babbie (2001), for example, describe procedures for determining if the intervention phase scores are more than two standard deviations from the baseline scores (i.e., statistically significant at the 0.05 level). Also, statistical tables have been developed that identify levels of significance based on the proportion and frequency of observations. However, one should be cautious about using elaborate statistical manipulation, as it can imply more rigorous data collection than the SSD methodology permits. The effort devoted to determining statistical significance might be better spent on examining the *practical significance* of the information (i.e., the importance of the change).

SELECTED BIBLIOGRAPHY

Bloom, Martin, Joel Fischer, and John G. Orme. *Evaluating Practice: Guidelines for the Accountable Professional*, 4th ed. Boston: Allyn & Bacon, 2003.

Hudson, Walter W. *WALMYR Assessment Scales Scoring Manual*. Tallahassee, FL: WALMYR Publishing, 1997.

Rubin, Allen, and Earl Babbie. *Essential Research Methods for Social Work*. Belmont, CA: Brooks/Cole, 2007.

Worden, J. William. *Grief Counseling and Grief Therapy*. New York: Springer, 1982.

Zisook, Sidney, and Stephen R. Schuchter, Treatment of the Depressions of Bereavement. *American Behavioral Scientist* 44, no. 5: 782–797.

14.7 — TERMINATION OF SERVICE

Purpose: To terminate the professional relationship between social worker and client in a timely and responsible manner.

Discussion: Closing a case, or terminating services to a client, should be viewed as a planned component of the helping process. When deciding if termination is appropriate, the following factors should be considered:

- Have the intervention objectives been achieved?
- Has an agreed upon time limit to service provision been achieved?
- Is the problem or situation that brought the client to the agency sufficiently resolved so the client can now function at an acceptable level and not be at risk of being harmed by self or others?
- Has the worker and/or agency made a reasonable investment of time, energy, and skill without sufficient results?
- Has the client and/or worker reached a point where one or both do not anticipate benefit from future contacts?
- Has the client become inappropriately dependent on the worker or agency?
- Would the client benefit by changing to another agency or professional?

In some situations, a transfer of the client to another worker within the agency is necessary. This, too, is a type of termination. An intraagency transfer is necessary when any of the following occurs:

- The worker will no longer be available to serve the client (e.g., worker moving to another job, etc.).
- The client will be better served by another agency staff member.
- A conflict between the worker and client cannot be resolved and is interfering with service provision or client progress.

- For some reason, the worker cannot develop necessary empathy and warmth.
- There is a serious and insurmountable gap in mutual understanding and communication caused by difference in values, religious beliefs, language, or cultural background.

Ideally, termination is a mutual decision by worker and client that occurs when the service objectives have been reached. Many situations are far from ideal, however. All too often, the client decides to end the relationship before reaching the objectives, and sometimes circumstances dictate that the worker decide unilaterally to terminate. Examples of the latter include the following:

- The client is considered to be a physical danger to the worker or continually harasses the worker.
- The client files a lawsuit or an official complaint against the worker.
- The client violates, without good cause, a financial agreement regarding the payment of fees for service.

In the case of an intraagency transfer and in the case of a termination by the worker, the client should be notified in writing, and, if possible, during a face-to-face meeting. The reasons and circumstances surrounding the transfer or termination should be clearly documented in the case record.

The social worker has an obligation to make a termination or transfer as positive an experience as possible. Several guidelines can aid in this process:

1. The worker should do everything possible to keep termination from being abrupt or unexpected. Termination should be discussed during the planning and contracting phase of the helping process and the client should be reminded from the beginning that intervention is goal oriented and time limited. The client will be gradually prepared for termination if the intervention includes, as it should, an ongoing monitoring of progress.

2. In a case where an adult client wants to terminate but the social worker thinks he or she should continue, the worker should explain to the client the possible consequences of terminating. If the client still wishes to terminate, his or her decision should be respected. Usually, a child or adolescent client does not have the authority to decide the termination of services; in cases involving a minor, the minor's parent or guardian must make the decision.

3. Special attention should be given to any termination prompted by an administrative decision to cut back on services provided, restrict case transfers within the agency, or modify a client contract due to either a change in the worker's status with the agency, or the end of financial reimbursement from a third-party payer (e.g., an insurance company, Medicaid, etc.). When necessary, the worker is obliged to advocate on behalf of the client. Additional care must be observed if services were being provided under court order to be sure that all terms of the order have been met. When making decisions about termination, the worker should be guided by Section 1.16 of the *NASW Code of Ethics* (1999).

4. The social worker must anticipate how the termination might affect other people in the client's family and social network. In situations where a termination may place the client or others at risk of harm, it may be appropriate to notify others of the termination. This notification must, of course, be done in ways consistent with the law and ethics concerning confidentiality.

5. In some cases, termination can be difficult because of a social worker's own psychological needs. A worker may want to be needed and appreciated so strongly that he or she maintains regular contact with a client even when there is no professional reason for doing so. This should be avoided.

6. As termination approaches, it is desirable to gradually decrease the frequency of contact. If the client is quite dependent on the worker, this weaning process should be accompanied by efforts to connect the client with natural helpers and informal resources within his or her neighborhood or social network.

7. The feelings of loss and anger that often accompany the ending of any important relationship should be broached by the worker, even if not mentioned by the client. The scheduling of a follow-up interview or telephone contact several weeks after official termination may be reassuring to the client who fears separation. Also, the client should be informed that he or she can return to the agency if the need arises.

8. The ending of a meaningful professional relationship should utilize some type of ritual to mark this transition. Fortune (1995) notes that such markers include culturally appropriate good-byes such as hugging and shaking hands and, in the case of terminations within a support group or treatment group, they might involve the exchange of small gifts, potluck meals, and celebrations at which the participants recall highlights in the group's experience. Such ending rituals are especially important in work with children.

SELECTED BIBLIOGRAPHY

Fortune, Anne. "Termination in Direct Practice." In *Encyclopedia of Social Work*, 19th ed., vol. 3, edited by Richard L. Edwards, 2398–2404. Washington, DC: NASW Press, 1995.
Hull, Grafton H., and Jannah Mather. *Understanding Generalist Practice with Families*. Belmont, CA: Brooks/Cole, 2006.
National Association of Social Workers. *NASW Code of Ethics*. Washington, DC: NASW, 1999.
Walsh, Joseph. *Endings in Clinical Practice*. Chicago: Lyceum, 2007.

SECTION B

TECHNIQUES AND GUIDELINES FOR INDIRECT PRACTICE

When engaged in indirect practice activities, social workers must also pay attention to issues that arise in the termination and evaluation phase of practice. When the work has resulted in meaningful experiences and relationships for the participants, bringing them to a close must be done carefully and thoroughly. Many of the guidelines for termination and evaluation identified in the introduction to Section A of this chapter also apply to indirect practice. However, a few modifications should be made.

Termination Activities.   Organization and community change do not come easily. Although the effort to prevent problems can lead to dramatic savings in both human and financial costs, efforts to make agencies run more smoothly or to help communities address problems are not usually included in a social worker's job description. In order to engage in large system change, social workers typically invest or contribute their personal time or squeeze indirect service work into an already packed schedule. The conclusion of a successful organization or community change effort is therefore a time for celebration, or if unsuccessful, a time for critique and recognition of the significance of making the effort. Usually, such change effort is undertaken by a team of staff members or a special committee from the community. Pizza in a conference room, dinner out together, a gathering at someone's home, or some other symbolic recognition can be important concluding activities that terminate the process.

Evaluation Activities.   A number of techniques are available for evaluating indirect practice. Some are used in conjunction with the evaluation of an agency's workers, and other techniques offer guidelines for a comprehensive program evaluation.

14.8   WORKER PERFORMANCE EVALUATION

Purpose: To understand the purpose and procedures of performance evaluations in order to make such assessments productive for both workers and agencies.

Discussion: *Worker performance appraisal* involves systematically assessing how well agency staff members are performing their jobs. Performance evaluations are designed to measure the extent to which the worker is achieving the requirements of his or her position through regular evaluation. The regular appraisal of its employees is a fundamental part of the agency's obligation to be accountable to its clients, its community, and those who provide financial support.

When a performance evaluation is conducted for the purpose of facilitating worker development, the evaluation tools used will likely engage the person being evaluated in the process. Known as *empowerment evaluation* (Fetterman 2001), some performance reviews involve considerable self-assessment and reflection by the worker. Guided by a trained evaluation coach, the worker is assisted in candidly evaluating his or her strengths and limitations in an environment in which merit pay, job promotion, and the like are not at stake. The steps of this process require the worker to take stock of himself or herself, set performance goals, develop strategies to reach those goals, and document progress over time.

Matheson, Van Dyk, and Millar (1995, 1) suggest that if properly conducted, the following positive outcomes can accrue from worker performance evaluations:

- Increase the person's motivation to perform effectively.
- Increase the self-esteem of the person being evaluated.
- Allow new insights for the person(s) doing the appraisal.
- Promote more clarification and better definition of the job of the person being evaluated.
- Facilitate valuable communication among the individuals taking part.
- Promote a better understanding among participants, of themselves, and of the kind of staff development activities that are of value.
- Clarify organizational goals and facilitate their acceptance.
- Allow the organization to engage in human resource planning and to develop training programs.

Certainly, the outcome of a performance evaluation may have either positive or negative consequences for the worker. To minimize the negative factors, an evaluation should be factual and objective to the degree possible. However, even a well-designed procedure requires judgment by the supervisor. Consequently, there will be times when the supervisor and the supervisee disagree on the conclusions.

In general, an evaluation can be considered relevant when the following criteria are met:

- It focuses on areas of performance or competency that are related to the supervisee's job and the agency's mission and goals.
- The evaluation criteria and standards, as well as the agency's preferred practices and outcomes, are clearly stated in writing and are made known to the supervisee at the beginning of the time period to be evaluated.
- The supervisee's work is compared to written performance standards and criteria that are realistic for the work assigned.
- The supervisee has been given ongoing feedback regarding his or her performance prior to the formal evaluation.
- The supervisor can cite and describe examples of performance that form the basis of the ratings.
- The evaluation process identifies and records differences in level of performance among supervisees.
- The evaluation takes into consideration the nature and complexity of the assignments given the supervisee.

Horejsi and Garthwait (2002) warn supervisors of the pitfalls that exist whenever one person attempts to evaluate or rate another's performance:

- The *halo effect*. A supervisee is rated the same in all standards based on the observed performance in a few areas.

- The *attraction of the average*. Every supervisee is evaluated about the same or about average, regardless of real differences in their performances.
- The *leniency bias*. All supervisees are evaluated as outstanding or are assigned inflated ratings so as to avoid arguments or conflict or to avoid hurting their feelings.
- The *strictness bias*. All supervisees are evaluated and rated on the low side because the supervisor has unrealistically high expectations or holds the belief that low ratings will motivate them toward even higher levels of performance.

These three elements are critical to conducting a useful and valid performance evaluation:

1. *People*. The evaluator must be competent. That person must know what constitutes good practice and be able to develop a trusting relationship with the worker. That trust must center on the desire to help the worker develop his or her potential as a social worker. The evaluator must be able to identify both worker competencies and deficiencies in performance and be able to articulate them in a way that builds on worker strengths in order to correct deficiencies. The evaluator must understand that new workers can be expected to have unevenness in their performances.

2. *Criteria*. The criteria on which the evaluation will be based must be made clear *before* the worker enters the time period to be covered by the evaluation. The lack of clear criteria can cause confusion and hard feelings. A typical direct-service worker's performance appraisal would focus on areas such as these:

- Capacity to establish and maintain appropriate relationships with clients (e.g., attitudes, values, and ethics as manifested in behavior toward clients; self-awareness and self-discipline; ability to manage especially difficult relationships)
- Knowledge and skills in the helping process (e.g., engagement of clients, data collection and assessment, planning and intervention, interviewing and communication skills, documentation of work and recordkeeping)
- Knowledge of and adherence to agency policies, procedures, and objectives
- Use of supervision and learning opportunities
- Management of workload and job stress
- Intraagency relations (e.g., communication and teamwork with other staff members)
- Interagency relations (e.g., creation and maintenance of working relationships with other agencies, programs, and resources)
- Productivity (e.g., numbers of clients served, new programs started, fees generated)

3. *Process*. The examination of performance must focus on worker behavior, not on explanations or rationalizations for the behavior. The written aspect of the evaluation may take the form of a narrative statement, rating scales, or a combination. Once prepared, these written materials should be reviewed, discussed, revised, if necessary, and signed by both the worker and supervisor, with notation regarding any disagreements, and then placed in the worker's permanent record. The documentation of disagreements could help the worker defend against arbitrary personnel actions. From discussion of the evaluation materials, the worker and supervisor can establish goals, adjust assignments, and plan activities that will strengthen the worker's performance prior to the next evaluation.

SELECTED BIBLIOGRAPHY

Fetterman, David M. *Foundations of Empowerment Evaluation.* Thousand Oaks, CA: Sage, 2001.

Horejsi, Charles, and Cynthia Garthwait. *The Social Work Practicum,* 2nd ed. Boston: Allyn & Bacon, 2002.

Matheson, Wayne, Cornelius Van Dyk, and Kenneth Millar. *Performance Evaluation in the Human Services.* New York: Haworth, 1995.

Weinback, Robert W. *The Social Workers as Manager: A Practical Guide to Success,* 5th ed. Boston: Allyn & Bacon, 2007.

14.9   PROGRAM EVALUATION

Purpose: To determine how well a social program is meeting its objectives.

Discussion: Because each program is a planned sequence of activities designed to achieve desired individual and social change, its success in achieving that change is partially determined by its ability to respond to changing human needs. Thus, every social program should be evaluated on a regular basis. **Program evaluation,** then, is the systematic examination of a program to determine the degree to which and the means by which it is achieving its goals and objectives. Unless programs are regularly evaluated, they can rapidly become out of touch with client needs and lose the support of the community. Furthermore, sound program evaluation and the correction of deficiencies that are identified is essential if the program is to be supported by funding agencies or if services are to reimbursed by managed care companies.

The following guidelines should be followed when considering a program evaluation:

1. *Identify the users of the evaluation data and report* (e.g., administrators, practitioners, program planners, legislators, fund-raisers, etc.). What do they really want and need from this evaluation? What type of information can they understand and use? Is it reasonable to believe that evaluation results will affect the continuation, modification, or termination of the program? Do not begin a program evaluation effort unless the results can make a real difference in terms of the program's operation and the services provided.

2. *Decide if an evaluation is feasible.* Do you have the necessary time, money, and skill available? Do you have access to experts in program evaluation? Are the data

you need actually available? Are all key staff members committed to the idea of evaluation? Is the program stable enough to undergo scrutiny? Has the program been in operation long enough to make an evaluation worthwhile?

3. *State the goals and objectives of the program.* Are there clear statements of the program goals and objectives? You cannot evaluate a program until you know precisely what it is trying to accomplish.

4. *Describe the program's interventions that are to be evaluated.* Intervention activities must be logically connected to program goals and objectives and must focus on factors or forces over which it has control. Clearly describe the units of intervention or the services. For example, to describe when an intervention activity is happening, you might ask: When does it begin and end? Does the worker decide when an intervention has occurred or does the client or someone else? Can you distinguish an intervention from other client-staff interactions? Can you decide when a service has been used? (For example, if a client attended only two of five scheduled sessions of a parenting class, has he or she received parent training?)

5. *Select measurable indicators of change.* Once you are clear as to the specific attitudes, behaviors, or conditions your program is trying to change, and you are clear as to the interventions used to bring about those changes, you need to select indicators of change that can be detected and measured. Make sure these indicators are ones that can be reasonably attributed to your program's intervention. Also, decide if it is reasonable to believe that the desired effects of the intervention will occur within the time frame you are using. If you cannot wait to measure long-term benefits, you must choose indicators that reflect more immediate changes.

6. *Select appropriate and feasible data collection and measurement tools and/or instruments.* Developing a valid and reliable instrument is a complex, time-consuming, and expensive process, so try to use available instruments. Examine evaluations done on similar programs and use instruments that others have found useful.

7. *Plan how you will collect, tabulate, and analyze the data.* Do not collect more data than you can manage and use. Make sure the data you want are actually available. For example, if you plan to gather data from case files, are you sure all of them contain the information you need? If your data are stored in the computer system, can you get them out? Can the information you seek be obtained without a release from the client? If your evaluation design involves contacting former service consumers, will you be able to locate them?

8. *Interpret the results of your evaluation.* The final product of your effort is to report the results. Caution should be used in making this interpretation. Factors other than the nature of the intervention may account for a program's success or failure. For example, low staff morale may produce poor outcomes despite a well-conceived program.

A useful model for guiding program evaluation is known as the ***logic model.*** The essence of this model is to create a structure appropriate for the evaluation to be conducted and to ensure a rigorous and logical assessment of each aspect of a program.

According to the logic model, the following items should be considered in conducting a program evaluation:

1. *Priorities established for the program.* The fundamental criteria for evaluating a program are first expressed in the "broad strokes" of the agency's mission, vision statement, expressions about whom to serve and how to serve them, mandates from the public, and so on. Thus, the first step in program evaluation is to review these priorities as expressed when the program was created and then to update them to reflect any changes in emphasis that have occurred.

2. *Inputs into the program.* Inputs are the resources the agency invests in the program—for instance, staff, volunteers, money, equipment, information technology, and other factors necessary to carry out the day-to-day program activities. How much of each is needed? How much is being used? What does each cost?

3. *Outputs from the program.* Outputs are the characteristics of a program's activities—for example, the manner in which the various programs are delivered, the successful engagement of the people/clients who are served, and the more tangible products that are produced. An evaluation must carefully identify the desired outputs in order to develop appropriate measures of a program's format and method of functioning. Some human services programs can be evaluated in terms of the individual/family/group sessions conducted, others in terms of the training provided to volunteers, and yet others in the amount of consultation given or the number of research studies conducted. Outputs, too, might be reflected in the number of clients served, participants in community education meetings, or decisions made by the agency's governing board.

4. *Outcomes, impacts, and results.* These factors might take the form of learning—for instance, people gaining awareness or knowledge of a social issue, developing attitudes or skills for addressing personal problems, or clarifying values. They might also be measured in terms of results achieved, such as actions taken, behaviors learned, decisions made, and so on. Finally, the outcomes might be assessed for their long-range implications, such as impact on social or economic conditions, civic pride, or protection of the environment.

In sum, the logic model provides a tool for carefully specifying the factors that should be considered when engaging in program evaluation. Particularly good illustrations of this model can be found online at many cooperative extension programs throughout the United States (e.g., www.uwex.edu/ces/pdande).

SELECTED BIBLIOGRAPHY

Chen, Huey-tsyh. *Practical Program Evaluation: Assessing and Improving Planning, Implementation, and Effectiveness.* San Francisco: Jossey-Bass, 2005.
Fretchling, Joy A. *Logic Modeling Methods in Program Evaluation.* San Francisco: Jossey-Bass, 2007.
Weinbach, Robert W. *Evaluating Social Work Services and Programs.* Boston: Allyn & Bacon, 2005.

14.10   THE CLIENT SATISFACTION QUESTIONNAIRE (CSQ)

Purpose: To determine clients' satisfaction with the services received.

Discussion: The *Client Satisfaction Questionnaire (CSQ)* is a method for soliciting client opinions about the services provided by a human services agency. It asks clients to rate important aspects of the helping process, such as the atmosphere of the agency, the success of the intervention, the competence of the staff, and so on. Typically, a questionnaire is administered at the point of termination or shortly thereafter, although some agencies administer a CSQ after three to five interviews and periodically thereafter if the client receives services for a longer period.

Figure 14.8 is an example of a typical CSQ. Although CSQs vary in length, they should be easy for a client to complete; therefore, they should not request too much detailed information. If more information is desired, administration of the CSQ might be coupled with an in-depth interview (by phone or in a face-to-face setting) on specific variables related to the client's satisfaction or dissatisfaction.

A limitation of the CSQ format is that it records only the client's perceptions of what happened as a result of the intervention. Certainly, reality may differ from that perception or the perception may change over time. Also, there is a tendency for satisfied clients to return a greater portion of the questionnaires (particularly if a mailed questionnaire is the process selected) than those who are dissatisfied—skewing the data toward positive responses.

The process for implementing a CSQ is as follows:

1. *Decide what population of clients to sample.* The sample could be representative of agency clientele in general, of clients who have received a particular type of service, or of clients who make up a particular demographic group (e.g., clients over age 60). A basic knowledge of sampling methods is required in order to draw a representative sample. Criteria for CSQ distribution should be determined by the evaluator and relate to the purpose of the evaluation, statistical requirements, and administrative convenience.

2. *Design the questionnaire.* Keep it as simple and brief as possible and avoid professional jargon. The agency may want to gather certain client and demographic information in order to determine if satisfaction with or complaints about services are related to factors such as the client's ethnicity, age, socioeconomic status, and the like. However, asking for such information tends to weaken assurances of anonymity.

3. *Administer the questionnaire.* This step can often be carried out by clerical staff, volunteers, or social service aides; however, those administering the questionnaire must be trained in its use in order to increase reliability. The assurance of confidentiality to respondents is very important. A mailed CSQ can provide the client with anonymity but does presume that the client can read. If the target population consists of former clients, the questionnaire can be either mailed or administered by phone. If it includes clients who are still in regular contact with the agency, the questionnaire can usually be administered by a receptionist. The greatest amount of

FIGURE 14.8   Sample Client Satisfaction Questionnaire

Evaluating Your Experience at ABC Agency

Thank you for taking a few minutes to evaluate the services you have received at our agency. Your answers to this brief questionnaire will help us improve our services. Feel free to offer additional comments in the space provided or on the back of this page.

Instructions: For each question below, check (✓) your answer.

A. How do you feel about the way you were treated by the receptionist?
—— (1) dissatisfied
—— (3) no feelings either way
—— (5) satisfied
Comments:

B. How do you feel about the length of time you had to wait before our agency provided you with service?
—— (1) unhappy or dissatisfied
—— (3) no feelings either way
—— (5) pleased or satisfied
Comments:

C. Did you accomplish what you expected to achieve when you came to this agency?
—— (5) yes, completely
—— (4) mostly accomplished
—— (3) some accomplishment
—— (2) no real progress
—— (1) worse off than before
Comments:

D. Did you feel your situation/problem(s) changed when you became involved with this agency?
—— (1) things became much worse
—— (2) things somewhat worse
—— (3) no change
—— (4) things somewhat better
—— (5) things became much better
Comments:

E. Which of the following statements comes closest to your feelings about the impact of this agency's services on your situation or problem?
—— (1) made things much worse
—— (2) made things somewhat worse
—— (3) no change
—— (4) made things somewhat better
—— (5) made things much better
Comments:

F. How competent do you feel the social worker was to deal with your situation or problem?
—— (5) very competent
—— (4) moderately competent
—— (2) somewhat incompetent
—— (1) very incompetent
Comments:

G. If a friend needed services from an agency like ours, would you recommend our agency?
—— (1) never
—— (2) probably not
—— (4) probably yes
—— (5) definitely yes
Comments:

H. Overall, how do you feel about your experience with our agency?
—— (1) very dissatisfied
—— (2) dissatisfied
—— (4) satisfied
—— (5) very satisfied
Comments:

It is helpful to know something about the person completing this questionnaire.

		Client's age:	
—— Male	—— Client		
—— Female	—— Parent of agency client	—— under 21	—— 51–65
	—— Spouse of agency client	—— 21–50	—— over 65

work in administering the questionnaire will probably be in following up on those clients who fail to return the questionnaire; these clients will have to be called or sent a letter to obtain a reasonable return rate. If the responses are to be anonymous, there will be problems in follow-up; therefore, a guarantee of confidentiality without the added assurance of anonymity may be preferable. Statistical techniques can determine whether there are significant differences between those who return the questionnaire immediately and those who require urging.

4. *Tabulate and analyze the questionnaire data.* Manual tabulation may be possible for short questionnaires. Computer processing is desirable for long questionnaires and when a large number must be tabulated.

SELECTED BIBLIOGRAPHY

Royse, David, Bruce A. Thyer, Deborah K. Padgett, and T. K. Logan. *Program Evaluation: An Introduction,* 4th ed. Belmont, CA: Brooks/Cole, 2006.
Sue, Valerie, and Lois A. Ritter. *Conducting Online Surveys.* Thousand Oaks, CA: Sage, 2007.

14.11   AGENCY EVALUATION

Purpose: To identify data that should be collected to assess the ongoing performance of a social agency.

Discussion: Social agencies are expected to demonstrate that they are efficient and effective in the provision of services. Agency boards, legislative bodies, and other funding sources regularly demand that agencies review their functioning and report the results of that evaluation. Individual workers, too, are often interested in performance indicators that might stimulate organizational changes necessary to improve the quality of services provided. Thus, it is useful for social workers to be familiar with some of the indicators typically used in agency performance reviews.

Evaluation must be preceded by a clear statement of goals. Often, the first task in agency evaluation is for the governing board or other policymakers to explicate the current goals and objectives for the organization. It is only with this information that appropriate performance indicators can be selected and methods of data collection identified.

An agency's evaluation should address the degree to which its programs respond to community need, the quality of services offered, the satisfaction of clients, efficiency in use of resources, and so on. Here are some of the areas that should be considered in specifying an agency's goals:

- *Responsiveness.* Does the agency and its programs respond to public and community needs and identified concerns?
- *Relevance.* Do sponsors, constituents, and consumers find the programs appropriate to the needs they seek to address and do they consider them supportive of community values?
- *Availability.* Are the amount and type of services provided sufficient to meet the needs of the community?

- *Accessibility.* Is the location, cost, and times services are offered appropriate for the clientele of the agency? Are there other potential constituent groups who do not receive services due to accessibility issues?
- *Quality.* Do the services meet expected standards of quality as judged by client satisfaction and expert opinion?
- *Awareness.* Is the general population, as well as other human services providers, sufficiently aware of the services offered to assure that persons who need the services know how to obtain them?
- *Productivity.* Does the program efficiently use its resources to accomplish the agency's goals?

With clarity about the questions to be answered when collecting data, it is then possible to select a set of *performance indicators* that will help to measure the agency's level of success and, when appropriate, lead to changes for improving its functioning. Selecting appropriate indicators and finding accurate data regarding them is a complex task. The following sampling of indicators illustrates a few essential areas to include in measures of agency success:

- *Personnel-related factors.* Rate of turnover, absenteeism, staff vacancies, number of hours contributed by volunteers, frequency of in-service training, and so forth
- *The intake process.* Data on the number and sources of referrals, number of telephone contacts, number of people on the waiting list, average length of time between first contact and initiation of service, and so on
- *Service-related factors.* Number of new cases opened each month, average length of service per case, number of clients served, number and type of cases referred elsewhere, number of former clients returning for service, average cost per client, client satisfaction with services, and so on
- *Staff productivity.* Size and type of caseload per worker, number of counseling sessions provided each day, number of hours spent per case, amount of inter- and intraagency contacts per month, number of miles of work-related travel each week, and the like
- *Cost of providing services.* Average cost of staff time per case, number of clients paying a fee for service, average travel cost per case, average time spent in case recording, estimated value of volunteer hours per week, and so on

These data, once collected, must be carefully analyzed. Data collected over time will allow for the examination of trends within the agency and adjustments to improve the efficiency and effectiveness of the agency. Also, the data can be compared to data from similar agencies, making it possible to gain a relative picture of the agency's functioning.

SELECTED BIBLIOGRAPHY

Harrison, Michael I. *Diagnosing Organizations: Methods, Models, and Processes*, 3rd ed. Thousand Oaks, CA: Sage, 2005.
Posavac, Emil J., and Raymond G. Carey. *Program Evaluation: Methods and Case Studies*. Upper Saddle River, NJ: R. G. Carey and Associates, 2007.

PART 5

Specialized Techniques and Guidelines for Social Work Practice

Most of the techniques and guidelines described in prior sections of this book could be used by almost any social worker, in almost any social work position, in almost any human services agency. In addition to the generic tools of the social worker's trade, specialized knowledge and skills are required for some social work practice activities. Part V concludes the book with two chapters on these specialized aspects of social work.

Some client groups require special sensitivity by the social worker. For example, unique insight and understanding is required to help a client deal with the devastating impact of poverty, to serve a client who has been battered by a spouse, or to carefully assist a client who is at risk of committing suicide. Clients from different age groups call for special sensitivity, too. Working with a child or adolescent requires knowledge of developmental factors and communication skills that are unique to young people, and at the other end of the age spectrum, older people also have unique needs that a social worker should recognize. These and other client conditions (e.g., cognitive delay, brain injury, physical disability, chemical dependence, serious mental illness, eating disorders) are often encountered in social work practice. Chapter 15 identifies guidelines for working with clients experiencing these circumstances and conditions.

Another set of specialized guidelines can help the social worker obtain employment and have a satisfying and productive experience as a social worker. Chapter 16 presents guidelines that will assist the worker in dealing with the demands of a social work job. Items about managing stress, preventing worker burnout, working within and coping with life in a bureaucracy, and giving and using supervision can improve a worker's effectiveness and efficiency. In addition, there are guidelines for performing the challenging tasks of testifying in court and dealing with managed care. And given the times in which we live, items on dealing with sexual misconduct and avoiding malpractice suits have been included, as well. Finally, to support the social worker in carrying out his or her professional obligations, this chapter provides guidelines for consuming and contributing to social work knowledge, improving the social work image, and becoming a leader in the human services.

491

15 Guidelines for Working with Vulnerable Client Groups

INTRODUCTION

Social workers practice within a wide variety of settings, and consequently, they encounter a wide variety of clients with a wide variety of concerns, problems, and requests. Although it is not uncommon to find that many of the clients served by a particular agency or program have the same presenting problem, each client is an individual and will react to his or her situation and to the social worker in a unique way. Thus, social workers must always adapt their approaches and techniques to the special needs, characteristics, and circumstances of the clients they serve.

For this chapter, items were selected to illustrate how a social worker might adapt his or her approach to the client by providing information on several different client groups and offering guidelines for addressing the special needs, characteristics, and challenges presented by each group. By comparing the approaches recommended for these diverse client groups, the reader will come to a deeper appreciation of why direct-service practitioners, as well as those who design and administer programs, must always consider the uniqueness of the clients they serve. In addition, the reader will understand more clearly why an approach that works well for one group may not be appropriate for another.

15.1 THE CLIENT WHO IS POOR

Purpose: To adapt direct-service approaches to the concerns of persons living in poverty.

Discussion: As a profession, social work has always focused attention on poverty and the difficulties faced by persons who do not have enough resources to obtain the basics of life, such as food, shelter, and medical and dental care. Poverty has devastating effects on individuals, families, and communities. It is a contributing factor to many other problems, such as the breakup of families, violence, crime, substance abuse, suicide, and a multitude of health problems. Poverty is especially injurious to children because they are most vulnerable to the effects of poor nutrition, disease, family insecurity, and social instability.

The causes of poverty are always complex and will vary somewhat, depending on whether one is examining poverty in a first-world, modern country or in a third-world, developing country. Among the economic forces that give rise to poverty in a developed country such as the United States are recession, downturns in regional economies, widespread job layoffs, shifts in the types of skills needed to secure a job, and rapid increases in the costs of essential goods and services (e.g., housing, electricity, health care). Racism and job discrimination can also restrict the economic opportunities available to whole segments of a population. And in some instances, poverty results from the social dislocation and economic disruption caused by war or political turmoil. Natural disasters, such as floods and earthquakes, can have similar social and economic effects.

Even in good economic times, some individuals and groups are at risk of being poor, including those with inadequate education and few job skills and those who have significant intellectual limitations, a serious mental illness, an addiction, or a debilitating health problem. Moreover, individuals and families who are economically independent can quickly slide into poverty after a tragedy such as a house fire, a serious injury or illness, or the death of the family's breadwinner. People who are elderly and live on a fixed income are also at risk of slipping into poverty whenever there are significant increases in the cost of living.

In the United States, many of those who are poor are the so-called ***working poor***. Typically, they are holding down two or three part-time jobs but not earning an adequate income or receiving important benefits such as health insurance. Many of those living in poverty are mothers and their children. Families headed by young mothers are at risk of being poor because many of these women lack needed job skills. Mothers who are raising their children after a divorce are often at risk, as well, because many fathers do not or cannot pay adequate child support. As a group, women with limited education face special challenges; many of the jobs available to them (e.g., waitress, maid) pay low wages, and often the time of work for these jobs is at night or on weekends, when child care is especially expensive and transportation is harder to arrange.

Poverty is fundamentally an issue of social and economic justice. No matter what the cause—whether primarily individual factors or large-scale economic forces—no person should have to live in poverty. No one should have to go without minimum levels of food, safe housing, medical care, and protection from preventable disease and injury. Social workers, regardless of their practice settings and job titles, have the responsibility to collaborate with others to develop social and economic policies that will reduce the incidence of poverty and directly assist those who are poor.

Social workers who directly serve individuals and families who are poor will find this additional information and guidance useful:

1. When designing or selecting an approach to working with clients who are poor, recognize that once an individual becomes poor, he or she encounters a multitude of forces and barriers that keep him or her poor. For example, in order to get a job, an individual must have appropriate clothing, transportation, recent job experiences, a telephone, and a permanent address—things that many poor people do not have. A mother who wants to work may discover that the cost of child care will consume much of the pay she will receive from a minimum-wage job. Working one's way out of poverty requires not only the motivation and the capacity but also the opportunity to do so. It is a slow process that requires planning and methodically executing a multitude of small steps. Changing one's life circumstances is difficult for anyone, but doing so when one is poor is especially difficult given the demoralizing and exhausting effects of poverty.

2. If you frequently encounter clients living in poverty, you must have a working knowledge of the government programs and private agencies in their communities that may be of assistance. Because the causes of an individual's or a family's poverty are usually multifaceted, the most effective programs are those designed to address an array of personal and family problems and issues. All such programs must be able to address the financial emergencies that are so common among people living in poverty. In addition to providing services for job training, job finding, job retention, and the like, programs must also address common barriers to employment, such as the lack of child care and transportation. Providing access to education and technical training is one of the most cost-effective approaches to addressing the problem of poverty among people who are healthy and of working age.

While programs that provide education, job training, and financial subsidies are needed by and helpful to many who are economically poor, these programs are usually not, by themselves, sufficient for those individuals who are also suffering the psychological effects of domestic violence, child abuse and neglect, death of a loved one, and other traumatic life events. Thus, counseling and therapy are essential components of successful programs.

Economic self-sufficiency is a desirable goal and a realistic one for many poor persons. However, for some individuals of working age, this goal is not realistic because their capacity for work has been severely limited by serious and chronic conditions such as mental illness, mental retardation, brain injury, and substance abuse.

3. Be alert to the fact that existing welfare policies, program rules, and eligibility criteria can be barriers or obstacles to people who are in need of assistance and services. *Client advocacy* by the worker is often needed to help an individual secure needed services. *Class advocacy* is also necessary, but the process of changing welfare policies and bureaucratic structures is definitely slow and difficult (see Items 13.18 and 13.33).

4. Understand that a client's views about being poor are important because his or her response to current circumstances, sense of hope about the future, and level of distress about being poor are shaped by prior life experiences and by the people with whom he or she frequently interacts. Among people who are poor, you will find a variety of beliefs, attitudes, and feelings about being poor. For example, an individual who has always been poor will view living in poverty somewhat differently than an individual who had an adequate income for many years before becoming poor. Moreover, a person who lives in a community made up of mostly poor people will view poverty differently than the person who lives in a community where few are poor. Some people who are poor, as officially measured by government standards or other objective criteria, may not define themselves as poor.

Unless you understand the client and his or her situation, you will be unable to make informed decisions concerning what options are possible and what might be the best course of action for him or her. To better understand the client's situation, keep the following questions in mind:

■ What is the client's specific concern, problem, or request? Is it related to a lack of money or to some nonmonetary concern?

■ What are the client's goals, and what needs to happen in order for him or her to achieve these goals?

■ What strengths has the client developed in order to survive and cope with his or her very difficult circumstances?

■ What personal and family characteristics, situational factors, and economic forces are contributing to the poverty experienced by this individual?

■ Was there a time when the client was self-sufficient and making an adequate living? If yes, what happened to change the situation?

■ Did the client grow up in a family living in poverty or in a family with adequate economic resources? Has he or she always expected to be poor, or is being poor an unexpected development in life?

■ Did the client grow up in a community where many others were poor? If yes, what meaning did he or she assign to being poor, and was that similar to or different from most others in the community?

■ Does the individual have family and close relatives who are poor, or is he or she economically different from family and relatives?

■ Has the client been abandoned or rejected by family and relatives who are better off economically? If yes, did a problem such as mental illness, substance abuse, or criminal activity contribute to this ostracism?

■ Who are the client's sources of social support and everyday assistance? Are these persons also poor?

■ What strengths or resiliency factors has the client relied upon to survive and cope with the challenges and stressfulness of living in poverty?

5. Strive to understand the emotional and mental state of the person who is poor. Living in poverty is extraordinarily stressful because so many aspects of a poor person's life are uncertain, unpredictable, and beyond his or her control. This gives rise to anxiety, fear, and frustration. Consequently, some people who are poor are quick to anger and resentful toward anyone who somehow makes their life even more difficult. Still others feel hopeless and respond to their circumstances and to service providers with passivity and emotional dependency.

Because the dominant American culture values work, money, material possessions, independence, and outward appearance, persons who are poor are prone to developing feelings of inferiority and shame. They often feel rejected and treated as social outcasts. They may feel guilty about being poor, especially if they are the parents of young children and see that their children are being harmed by their life circumstances. Some cope with these painful feelings by withdrawing from ordinary social relationships. Some express their embarrassment and resentment by criticizing and tearing down the work and efforts of other people, including those working in programs that attempt to address the problems faced by the poor.

Some of the people who live on the streets or in shelters for the homeless are especially challenging clients. Their economic situation is often interrelated with problems of substance abuse, personality disorders, mental illness, brain injury, inadequate nutrition, and other disabling health problems. Some of these individuals are so immersed in a lifestyle of day-to-day survival that they approach every relationship in a calculating and manipulative manner in order to meet their daily basic needs. Some become belligerent and aggressive.

Those who are poor must be approached in ways that recognize their uniqueness along with their worth and dignity. It is also important to recognize that a client's sense of frustration and hopelessness, unpredictable lifestyle, and preoccupation with immediate needs can become barriers to his or her effective use of professionals and human service programs that expect cooperation, adherence to schedules, and follow through on plans.

6. Those who struggle with the effects of poverty need to tell their stories and come to understand that their circumstances are similar to those of many others. Doing so helps them feel less isolated and more connected to other people. People who are poor need to build or rebuild their self-respect and self-esteem and learn to take control of their lives. This is most likely to occur when they join with others to bring about positive change in their life situations and communities and to advocate for needed legislation, public policies, and programs. As these individuals participate in social and political action, many will learn the leadership and organizational skills and gain the self-confidence that are important to achieving economic self-sufficiency (see Items 11.4, 11.5, 13.9, and 13.19).

7. Identify and arrange opportunities for clients to share their knowledge and skills for dealing with poverty. For example, many who are poor have learned how to be frugal and thrifty in shopping and otherwise stretching their limited resources. Many have located and learned to use various programs and community resources that are overlooked by others. Many are very creative in cooperating with others and working out arrangements that permit several individuals or families to share what they have and to help each other cope. Still others have arrived at profound insights into the human condition and developed a truly inspiring spirituality. These are all important strengths that need to be recognized and, if the client is willing, shared with others who struggle with many of the same issues.

8. Strive to reduce the social distance and power differential between yourself and the client. Do this by looking for opportunities to talk with clients about the very ordinary aspects of life, such as family and friends, interests and hobbies, special times in their lives, and today's experiences. Meet with clients at times that are most convenient for them, possibly in their homes or at their worksites. When it is appropriate to the practice setting, share meals with clients. Also invite them to share their music, art, and other creative skills.

9. Offer people opportunities to shape the programs they utilize and to learn leadership skills by serving on agency boards and advisory committees. People often have a need to express appreciation for help they have received and perhaps even to reciprocate. If you believe this is important to a particular client, arrange opportunities for him or her to make some contribution to the appropriate program or agency. For example, a client might be eager to do some cleaning at a shelter for homeless persons or otherwise assist other clients. Unfortunately, issues of facility insurance and legal liability may be barriers to arranging reciprocity.

10. Appreciate the fact that the person living in poverty often leads a life of desperation. Frustration can push this person into making impulsive decisions. For example, a mother may buy her child a pair of expensive shoes or splurge on a restaurant meal. Fear and worry over a lack of money can also draw a person into activities that are illegal and that violate their conscience. For example, in an effort to secure money, someone may sell drugs, steal, or engage in prostitution. You will feel frustrated when these choices make matters even more difficult for clients. And while you cannot condone illegal behavior, you must understand why clients make these choices and avoid becoming judgmental or moralistic. Doing so would create a barrier to additional work with the client.

11. Many professionals (e.g., social workers, physicians, nurses, psychologists) admit to feeling somewhat uncomfortable when working directly with persons who live in truly desperate economic circumstances. This discomfort stems, in part, from the obvious fact that the client has so little and that, by comparison, the professional has so much—more than he or she really needs. In addition, the professional realizes that he or she does, in fact, have the ability (i.e., the money) to alleviate this client's immediate financial distress, at least for a few hours or a few days. It is this awareness that tugs on the professional's conscience and sense of fundamental justice. In working with clients who have other types of problems, the professional knows that he or she does not have the ability to bring about such an immediate change. In work with the economically poor, the professional must struggle with the question If I have the ability, do I have the responsibility?

SELECTED BIBLIOGRAPHY

Albert, Raymond, and Louise Skolnik. *Social Welfare Programs: Narratives from Hard Times.* Belmont, CA: Brooks/Cole, 2006.

Levitan, Sar, Garth Mangum, and Stephen Mangum. *Programs in Aid of the Poor*, 8th ed. Baltimore: Johns Hopkins University, 2003.

Shlomo, Sharlin, and Michal Shamai. *Therapeutic Intervention with Poor, Unorganized Families.* New York: Haworth, 1999.

15.2   THE CLIENT WHO IS A CHILD

Purpose: To adapt basic social work techniques and approaches to the special needs of children under age 12.

Discussion: Children are not miniature adults. Thus, the techniques and approaches that are effective with adult clients may not work with children. Social workers whose clients are children must add some new skills to their repertoire, such as the use of play.

The sections that follow provide guidelines for a range of tasks that are involved in working with a child.

Planning the Interview

1. Anticipate how the child's level of development will affect his or her capacity to understand situations and to use language. How and what children think and feel are closely tied to their developmental stages. Realize, however, that there is much variation among the children in a particular age group.

2. Be clear about why you are meeting with the child and what you hope to accomplish. Plan several alternative methods to accomplish your goal. Anticipate what might go wrong (e.g., child will not talk, child cries, child will not leave parent, etc.) and consider how you might handle such situations.

3. Play is a child's natural means of communication and interacting with others. Thus, consider using some form of play to put the child at ease and facilitate communication. Prior to the interview, assemble play materials that may be needed. For young children, provide art materials (e.g., finger paints, clay, building blocks) as well as objects that can be used to portray family members and situations (e.g., dolls, hand puppets, doll house, toy animals). For older children, consider simple card or board games, toy telephones, puzzles, and electronic games.

4. Conduct the interview in a room that is familiar and comfortable to the child. If that is not possible, consider an open space such as a park or playground where you can be some distance from other people. Be cognizant that little or no confidentiality can be provided to a child. Parents and other professionals will often have access to the information revealed by a child.

Introducing Yourself and Getting Started

5. Place yourself at the child's level physically; sit or squat so you do not tower over the child. Introduce yourself by explaining who you are and how you want to be addressed. Also, give a simple description of your role (e.g., "My name is Ron Hoffman. Please call me Ron. My job is to help children who have problems at home."). Be prepared to offer a simple and truthful explanation as to why you want to speak with the child.

If the child is at least 6 or 7 years of age, ask what he or she has been told about the purpose of the interview. This may reveal what the child is expecting. You might ask if someone (e.g., a parent) has told the child what to say or do during the interview. It may be necessary to assure the child that he or she is not in trouble and that the interview is not a punishment.

6. You might begin the interaction with some friendly conversation by showing an interest in items the child is wearing or carrying or ask about the child's school or favorite games or TV shows. If the child is frightened, attempt to normalize the situation by saying something such as "When I was your age, I was afraid to talk to new people." If the child appears reluctant to talk for fear of retaliation by others, you may need to describe what you can do to keep him or her safe. But do not make promises you cannot keep.

If the child refuses to talk or interact, try engaging him or her in a parallel activity and then gradually initiate conversation about the activity. For example, if the child does not talk but begins to play with a doll, pick up another doll and engage in similar play. This will often lead to some interaction and opportunity for verbal exchanges.

Young children who are frightened and withdrawn will sometimes relax and let down their guard in response to a bit of clowning around; however this clowning must be done in a way so the child knows that you are trying to be silly. For example, if you put on a clown nose, the child will understand your intentions. Another technique is to do something unexpected (e.g., "Brian, while we are talking, we may get thirsty. Should we get some juice now or should we wait until later?").

Gathering Information from Children

7. Because young children have limited verbal ability, much of the information you gather will come from observing the child's nonverbal behavior during play and social interactions. However, in order to draw valid inferences about a child's personality or behavioral patterns, you must observe the child in several different situations. Do not base conclusions on a single observation.

8. Children "act out" their concerns in play and project their thoughts and feelings into the stories they make up and into their drawings and art. Thus, consider using such activities to set up make-believe situations that are relevant to the topics you wish to explore. For example, present the child with a set of dolls and ask the child to make up a story about the dolls. Or, you might ask the child to draw a picture of a family or of some children at school and then tell a story about the people in the picture. You may need to initiate the storytelling about the dolls or pictures, but once the child is attentive, you can ask the child to continue the story.

However, you must be cautious about interpreting your observations. Indeed, young children incorporate their thoughts, feelings, and recent experiences into their play, stories, and drawings but they will also incorporate themes drawn from TV programs, books, and incidents described by their friends. Thus, it may be difficult to pinpoint the source of the themes that appear in play activities. Also, it is important to remember that themes of violence are quite common in the play of normal children. Thus, violence-related talk and play, especially by boys, is not by itself an indicator that a child has personally experienced violence.

9. Children between the ages of about 3 and 6 are usually eager to please adults. They are also suggestible, especially if asked leading questions. Children of this age may modify their story or what they have to say in order to make it fit with what they believe the adult wants to hear. If the child concludes that you disapprove of what he or she is saying, the child may stop talking.

Young children are rather easily distracted and will move quickly from one topic to another. Consequently, they may express what they think or feel about a particular concern only once. Asking a child to stay focused on a topic is seldom successful. If pressured to remain focused on a painful or sensitive topic, the child may become noncommittal or silent.

10. Most children older than about 6 years are able to use sufficient words to communicate their ideas and answer questions, if the questions are simple and age appropriate. However, they may need assistance to fully describe a situation or event. For example, you may need to ask: What happened next? Then what did you do? Where were you when this happened? Who was with you? As a general rule, avoid asking "why" questions because children find it difficult to accurately describe the reasons behind their behavior.

11. By age 9 or 10, most children can think conceptually and will pay attention to the meaning of words used by others. They can often detect phony or insincere messages and will become suspicious when they observe incongruence between a person's words and actions.

12. Special techniques like story completions, doll play, and drawings may still be necessary and useful when interviewing children between 7 and 9, but many children who are older than this will usually give thoughtful responses to questions that are clear and age appropriate. Many children find it easier to talk about personal matters if they can do so while engaged in some nondemanding activity such as a simple card game or a board game like checkers that does not require much concentration. The use of hand puppets in puppet-to-puppet talking can facilitate communication. And talking back and forth on a toy telephone works well with many children. Sentence completions (i.e., projective questioning) may prove useful with older children (e.g., "When at home, I am afraid of . . . ").

13. To make a discussion or exploration more specific, the game of Hot or Cold may prove useful. For example, if the child is having difficulty articulating a concern, you might say something like the following:

> "Jimmy, I am going to make some guesses about what is bothering you. If my guesses are getting closer to what is troubling you, tell me that I am getting warm. If my guesses are wrong, tell me that I am getting cold."

How Children Think

14. Children between the ages of about 3 to 6 are subjective, concrete, and egocentric in their thinking. For example, they believe an event or activity that makes them happy will have the same effect on all people. Their thinking is characterized by an all-or-nothing pattern. That is, things are either good or bad; the child is unable to understand mixed feelings or ambivalence. The child may describe a person as mean and then just minutes later describe the same person as nice or fun. Such thinking in extremes and absolutes leads them to categorize both themselves and others as, for example, either good or bad, smart or dumb, and so on. Children of this age describe themselves and others in terms of external characteristics (e.g., age, hair color, grade in school, etc.); they do not mention personality traits except in global terms such as "She is happy" or "He is a bad person."

15. Beginning at about age 6, the child's thinking becomes more objective and logical. Gradually, the child acquires the ability to imagine himself or herself in the place of another and to understand that people differ in how they think and feel.

However, even a 7-year-old may still believe that he or she is the total cause for how others, especially parents, feel and behave. It is not until about age 9 or 10 that children truly understand that they do not cause all of the behaviors and emotions they observe in others.

16. By about age 10, the child no longer thinks in absolutes and views himself or herself as an individual who is separate from others and a mixture of characteristics and abilities (e.g., someone who is skilled at some things but not others or good sometimes and bad other times). At this age, he or she realizes it is possible to have conflicting thoughts and to feel opposing emotions simultaneously (e.g., to be angry at someone you love). Also, the child now has the ability to reflect on his or her own thoughts and actions and can figure out how others will probably react in a particular situation or react to certain information. Thus, the child can now manipulate words and information in order to influence how others will behave.

Assessing the Truthfulness of Children's Statements

17. If you investigate reports of abuse and neglect or conduct child custody evaluations, you will often make judgments about whether a child is telling the truth. As a general rule, the younger the child, the less able and the less likely he or she is to fabricate a falsehood. However, it is important to remember that children, like adults, can and do misunderstand and misinterpret their experiences and will at times lie.

18. Children from about 4 to 6 years old can and will tell a simple lie in order to avoid punishment (e.g., "I didn't break the cup"), but they do not have the cognitive abilities necessary to fabricate a complex story having several interrelated elements, actions, or actors. In trying to describe something that happened, they can often recall central actors or central events but not the connecting details, such as what happened before and after and how one action lead to another. They have what some call a *script memory*, which means they can remember events (e.g., a birthday party) and rituals (e.g., going to bed, mealtime, etc.) but not accurately remember events that are not part of their usual routines. Children this age frequently exaggerate events or boast when describing their abilities and experiences; however, when asked, "Is that pretend or real?" or "Is that an 'I wish' story or is it true?" they generally can articulate the difference between what was true and what was an exaggeration.

19. Children between the ages of about 7 and 11 usually value honesty and fairness. They may, however, lie in order to avoid punishment or to get what they want. At this stage, they possess the cognitive abilities necessary to deliberately mislead others by selectively withholding information and using other forms of deception. They often embellish the truth in order to tell an exciting story. Children in the age range of about 9 to 11 are usually eager to please adults and inclined to say what they believe adults want to hear. They have good memories of central actors and events and good free recall (i.e., able to recall and describe without the aid of detailed questioning by an interviewer).

20. The social worker should not assume that a young child can accurately describe when an event happened. Young children do not use clocks or calendars to measure time. In fact, preschool children do not grasp the concept of time; young grade school–age children typically use events such as nap time, lunch time, Christmas, start of school, and other events as markers of time. Such markers, rather than clock times and dates, should be used to establish timeframes.

21. Sometimes, a parent or another adult will pressure a child to lie to a social worker in order to avoid the disclosure of some problem or criminal activity or perhaps as a way of hurting another person, such as an ex-spouse. If an adult has coached a child on what to tell a social worker, the child will often speak in adultlike language, use few gestures and facial expressions, and not display genuine and appropriate emotions. Moreover, the child will be either inconsistent regarding the major elements of the story or, on the other hand, extremely consistent but unable to describe supporting or connecting details.

22. Assessing the truth of a child's statement is a special challenge in the case of alleged child sexual abuse. As a general rule, sexually abused children are reluctant to report the abuse and do not want to talk about it. When children do self-report sexual abuse, they seldom lie about such matters. Deliberate false reports (i.e., actual lying by the child) are rare among children below age 12 and infrequent among teenagers. Nonetheless, the child's lying about, misunderstanding, or misinterpreting the situation, along with the child's having named and accused the wrong person, are all possibilities that must be kept in mind. The likelihood of deception and making a deliberate false report becomes greater when the child is the focus of a custody or visitation dispute and is instructed by one parent to accuse the other parent of some wrongdoing.

Indicators of a possible deception by a child and/or by his or her parent include the following:

- Disclosing of and talking about the incident seems too easy for the child (i.e., is not afraid or reluctant to tell others what happened).
- The child does not show expected or authentic emotion when describing what happened (e.g., does not cry or display distress, embarrassment, fear, anger, etc.).
- The child uses adultlike words to describe sexual activity (as if coached or rehearsed by an adult).
- The child describes the sexual activity using only visual images and not information drawn from the other senses (i.e., smell, taste, touch, sound).
- The child does not seem to be afraid of the alleged offender; for example, the child does not seem hesitant to meet with or confront the alleged offender when the possibility of doing so is mentioned.
- The child is not hesitant to talk about the sexual abuse in the presence of a nonoffending parent. (Most children try to shield the parent from the details and thus the pain of what happened.)
- The child talks about having been sexually abused but does not display any of the other behavioral signs and symptoms associated with child sexual abuse. (See Item 11.19, Assessing a Child's Need for Protection.)
- When a parent is encouraging the child to report the sexual abuse, the parent does not display the emotions that are normal in such a situation. For example, the parent does not seem genuinely shocked, sad, depressed,

anxious, worried, alarmed, and/or fearful. The parent may also express anger at the alleged offender and seek revenge yet not display genuine alarm or distress over what has supposedly happened to the child.

Additional Suggestions

23. Realize that during an interview, you get only a sample of the child's behavior. The child may behave differently in other situations and with other people. The farther removed the child is from his or her usual social and family context, the more cautious you must be in drawing conclusions about the child's behavior. For example, the child who appears anxious or withdrawn during an office interview may simply be fearful of an unfamiliar environment. In-home interviews are important to an accurate assessment of a child's functioning.

24. Allow the child to set the pace of the interview. Permit him or her to move around and explore the room. Children—especially young children—have a short attention span. Excessive squirming and a lack of attention probably indicates that the child is tired and the interview should end.

25. The vocabulary you use in an interview should be appropriate to the age of the child. For example, with a 12-year-old, you can use words and expressions very similar to those used with an adult, but with a 5-year-old, your speech must be simple and concrete.

26. Because young children are responsive to nonverbal communication, you will likely find it helpful to make frequent use of facial expressions, touch, changes in voice tone, and gestures. However, do not hug or caress a child, for this makes many children feel uncomfortable. In addition, this could be misinterpreted as inappropriate sexual contact. Touch can be especially confusing and even threatening to a child who has been physically or sexually abused.

27. Answer a child's question honestly and directly (e.g., "I believe you will be in foster care until the school term ends"). Do not use euphemisms; do not beat around the bush. Avoid giving elaborate explanations. When giving important information to a child, try to present it in phases and small doses.

28. When behavior-control rules are necessary during an interview, explain the rules, along with any consequences for breaking them (e.g., "You are not permitted to hit me; if you do hit me, I will put away the toys.").

29. During an interview, give the child as much choice and control as possible. But be sure to offer choices among alternatives that you can accept. This point is illustrated in the following statements:

> *Misleading:* "Well, Ellen, what would you like to do? We can do whatever you like."

> *Correct:* "Ellen, today you can use the finger paints or the crayons. Which one do you want to use?"

30. Outings, treats, or gifts should be used judiciously. Although they are an extension of normal adult-child interaction and may be helpful in building a relationship, they are easily misinterpreted. Also, be careful that your gift of even a small toy is not viewed as competition with the child's parents.

31. Children are protective of their parents. A child will usually defend his or her parents, even abusive parents. Be objective and concrete in talking about the parent-child relationship and the parents' behavior (e.g., "Your dad does have a problem with alcohol. He gets drunk about once a week. He cannot stop drinking. That is why your parents are getting a divorce."). Do not criticize the parents.

32. A series of interviews should usually have structure and a routine, depending on each child's needs. For example, some children like interviews that have definite beginning and ending rituals. Others, however, may want relief from structure and need freedom to do more of what they feel like doing.

Children in Out-of-Home Placements

33. Many of the children known professionally to social workers are in out-of-home placements (i.e., foster family care, group homes, institutional care, etc.). Many of these children have been exposed to severe abuse or neglect. Regardless of the reason for the placement, a separation from parents and family is usually a disruptive and emotionally traumatic experience for children. Children often blame themselves for the family problems that led up to the placement and view their separation from family as a punishment for some real or imagined wrongdoing. Once apart from family, many worry intensely about the well-being of their parents and siblings still at home. Some will be uncertain or confused about why they are in placement. Assume that the child has many questions about his or her past, current situation, and future. Make it as easy as possible for the child to ask questions, and be as factual and honest as possible in answering.

34. Do everything possible to maintain frequent contacts and visits between the child in placement and his or her parents, siblings, and other close relatives. If a child has little or no contact with family, he or she will usually create an elaborate fantasy that explains the situation. In the long run, frequent visitation is helpful to the child, even if the visits are at times upsetting. If, for example, the child's mother is addicted to drugs and acting irresponsibly, it is important for the child to see this and know that the parent is in no shape to provide care. It is better for the child to struggle with and adjust to an unpleasant reality than to live within a pleasant fantasy.

35. Relationship losses, especially a series of losses, have long-lasting, negative effects on a child. Thus, it is critically important to minimize the number of separations experienced by a child. If a child must be separated from someone to which he or she is emotionally attached, the move should be as gradual as possible, thus giving the child an opportunity to prepare and time to adjust. A ritual such as a going-away party helps the child make this transition by symbolically ending one relationship and beginning another. Without such a ritual, the child might feel as if he or she was given away or rejected; a transition ritual gives the child permission to let go of one relationship and begin a new one. After the physical separation, it is important that the child be able to return to his or her former home for occasional visits.

36. Because foster children experience so much change and because their lives are so unpredictable, you must be prepared to become a predictable figure in their lives. The foster child is especially sensitive to any hint of rejection. Contacts should occur on a regular basis. If you must miss an appointment, explain the reason directly to the child. If you may not be able to keep a promise, do not make it!

37. Children often feel shame and embarrassment about being in foster care, and consequently they fabricate a story to explain their situation. When the fabrication is discovered, the child acquires a reputation for being a spinner of tall tales or a liar. Thus, it is important to help these children develop an understandable and acceptable explanation of why they are in an out-of-home placement so they can more comfortably describe their living situation to teachers, friends, and others.

38. When speaking with foster parents, adoptive parents, or group care staff, be truthful about the child's behavior, situation, and history. Efforts to conceal the child's life experience in an attempt to protect the child or because you fear others will not understand or accept the child almost always backfire.

SELECTED BIBLIOGRAPHY

Poole, Debra, and Michael Lamb. *Investigative Interviews of Children.* Washington, DC: American Psychological Association, 1998.

Rose, Steven R., and Marian Fatout. *Social Work Practice with Children and Adolescents.* Boston: Allyn & Bacon, 2003.

Sommers-Flanagan, John, and Rita Sommers-Flanagan. *Tough Kids, Cool Counseling,* 2nd ed. Alexandria, VA: American Counseling Association, 2006.

Timberlake, Elizabeth, and Marika Cutler. *Developmental Play Therapy in Clinical Social Work.* Boston: Allyn & Bacon, 2001.

Wilson, Claire, and Martine Powell, eds. *A Guide to Interviewing Children.* New York: Brunner-Routledge, 2001.

15.3   THE CLIENT WHO IS AN ADOLESCENT

Purpose: To adapt basic social work techniques and approaches to the needs of adolescents.

Discussion: The developmental period known as *adolescence*—between about ages 12 and 18—is a time of rapid physical and psychological change and awakening sexual desire. It is often a time of conflict and tension between adolescents and their parents, frequently regarding issues of authority and control. Parents typically worry that their adolescent children will become involved with drugs, have irresponsible sexual experiences, or be injured by recklessness. A small percentage of parents become so frustrated with their adolescent children that they kick them out of the home.

The problems most likely to bring adolescents to the attention of a social worker include family conflict, alcohol and drug use, running away, behavior problems in school, violence, delinquency, pregnancy, threat of suicide, and the need for foster care or residential treatment. The following background information and guidelines are useful when working with adolescents:

1. Adolescents are typically idealistic, painfully self-conscious, struggling with authority issues, fiercely attached to peers, preoccupied with their appearance and sexuality, seeking popularity and conformity within their peer group, and desperately trying to develop an identity apart from their family. Adolescents need and want positive adult role models and mentors who can prepare them for adulthood. Ironically, they often resist the influence and teachings of their parents but will accept guidance from adults outside their own family.

2. Many of the adolescents encountered in social work practice are involuntary clients who have been brought to or sent to a social worker or a social agency by parents, school officials, a juvenile court judge, or a probation officer. This is an uncomfortable and awkward situation for the adolescent because of the authority struggles common to this developmental period. The adolescent may respond to you with silence as a means of resisting adult intrusion, or he or she may challenge you and any other adult authority by being noncooperative and rude and by using abusive language. In such a situation, your patience and self-control can be severely tested. Also, be aware that your own unresolved parent-child and authority issues may surface in the professional relationship.

Despite the challenges they present, adolescents are resilient and have a great capacity to grow and change. Because these clients are often lively, inquisitive, and questioning, your work with adolescents can be stimulating, fun, and truly rewarding. Effective social work intervention during this developmental period can prevent serious problems and have lifelong, positive effects.

3. Adolescents need an environment that is predictable and provides structure and limits. In many practice settings, such as group homes and treatment centers, social workers have the responsibility for creating this environment and deciding what rules are necessary. Adolescents will typically test the rules and limits put in place by adults. Thus, before you create a new rule, make sure it is really necessary, can be enforced, and is worth fighting over. Then, once you have decided that a particular rule is necessary, inform the adolescent of the rule and the consequences for violating it. When enforcing rules and imposing consequences with adolescents, it is critically important to be fair and consistent.

4. Because the peer group is so important during adolescence, group approaches (e.g., group discussion, psychodrama, and group counseling) can be useful. Most adolescents are more accepting of a group-related intervention than a one-to-one interview. Adolescents in need of out-of-home placement usually do better in a group home setting than in foster family care. Behavioral contracting works fairly well with adolescents (see Item 13.6).

5. Because of adolescents' high energy level, interactions with them should be planned around movement and physical activity. If possible, avoid office interviews; rather, try talking with adolescent clients while walking, shooting baskets, working out in a gym, or riding in a car. Movement seems to make it easier for adolescents to talk and express feelings.

6. Adolescents are sensitive to any hint of artificiality in others, even though they themselves may pretend to be someone they are not. Thus, it is important to be genuine. Do not try to talk and act like their peers. It is nearly impossible to keep up with the latest adolescent fads, music, and slang. Imitating adolescent talk is likely to make you appear phoney.

7. Most adolescents are focused on the here and now. They tend to be somewhat impulsive in their decision making and may not anticipate the consequences of particular actions. This, of course, can lead to bad choices that are harmful to themselves and others. Gently encourage adolescent clients to examine their options and possible decisions in light of their hopes, dreams, and goals. When their thinking is clearly unrealistic or dangerous, it is usually best to tell them so along with the reasoning behind your conclusion.

8. Adolescents have an intense need to be heard. They want others to pay attention and take them seriously. Yet, they usually find it difficult to talk openly with adults. Listen carefully and be nonjudgmental. Be alert to the underlying meaning in what they are saying. Encourage them to share their perspectives and experiences. Ask about their hopes, dreams, values, significant life experiences, times when they learned something important, and what others do not understand about a teenager's life, problems, and challenges.

9. Strive to promote mutual understanding and improved communication between the adolescent and his or her parents. By helping parents recall and talk about their own behaviors, thoughts, and feelings during their adolescent years, you can often increase their understanding and acceptance of their teenager. Keep the parents informed and involved when working with their adolescent child. At the same time, provide the adolescent with as much confidentiality as is legally permissible.

10. Because of high rates of divorce, estrangement and conflict between the divorced parents, and high rates of single motherhood, many children do not have a meaningful relationship with their biological fathers. In the United States, for example, about 40 percent of boys are "fatherless" in the sense that they are being raised apart from their biological fathers and have little or no contact with their fathers. The absence of an interested and caring father in the lives of children has effects that are especially noticeable among boys. The absence of a father is correlated with a boy's poor school performance, school dropout rate, delinquency, drug use, violence, and gang membership. One of the most reliable predictors of whether a boy will succeed or fail in high school is whether he has in his life a responsible and positive adult male model and mentor. Both girls and boys need healthy adult role models. Ideally, the parent will be this positive model but when that is not the case, modeling by other adults (e.g., concerned relatives, family friends, big brothers, big sisters, etc.) is critically important.

11. During their adolescence, some individuals are drawn into gang activity. Youth join gangs for a variety of reasons, but it is often because the gang meets their needs for peer recognition, a sense of identity and belonging, self-esteem and pride, and excitement and camaraderie. For many, the tribal culture of the gang serves as a substitute family. In some instances, youth join a gang because it offers some safety and protection from other gangs in their neighborhood.

Youth gangs or street gangs have existed in major U.S. cities since the late nineteenth century. In the past, their illegal activity was mostly theft. In recent years, many youth gangs have adults as leaders, have grown more violent, and are often involved in serious criminal activity such as drug dealing and murder. Economic gain from drug dealing has become a driving force behind the expansion of gang activity. Consequently, it is increasingly difficult to distinguish between some youth gangs and organized crime.

SELECTED BIBLIOGRAPHY

Geldard, Kathryn, and David Geldard. *Counseling Adolescents*, 2nd ed. Thousand Oaks, CA: Sage, 2005.

Gullotta, Thomas, and Gerald Adams, eds. *Handbook of Adolescent Behavioral Problems*. New York: Springer, 2005.

Malekoff, Andrew. *Group Work with Adolescents*. New York: Guilford, 2004.

Taffel, Ron. *Breaking Through to Teens*. New York: Guilford, 2005.

15.4   THE CLIENT WHO IS A PARENT OR GRANDPARENT

Purpose: To understand and respond to the special challenges faced by persons raising children and adolescents.

Discussion: Many social work clients are parents, and many of the organizations that employ social workers are ones that provide services focusing on the role of parent and the parent-child relationship. A significant number of grandparents also provide full-time care for their grandchildren when the child's parents are incapacitated, called for military duty, or otherwise absent or unavailable. Below are some factors that social workers should keep in mind as they work directly with parents or grandparents or work on behalf of them when administering or designing programs that impact children and families.

1. A social worker must be always cognizant of a parent's fundamental legal rights and responsibilities. According to the American Bar Association (2004, 62), "Parents have a right to direct the care, control, and upbringing of their [minor-aged] children. . . . This gives them the power to make various decisions on behalf of the child including where to live, what school to attend, what religion to follow, and what medical treatment to obtain. Only in life threatening or extreme situations will the court step in to override the parents decisions."

Parents have a right to control, discipline, and punish their child but they may not injure the child, for that would constitute abuse. They have the right to control and manage their child's earnings and property and to receive proper legal notice of any action instituted on behalf of or against the child. Parents have the right to consent to (i.e., decide) marriage and military service by their minor-aged child and the right to consent to medical procedures and surgery needed by the child. It must be noted, however, that specific statutes may allow a "mature minor" to obtain certain forms of health care (e.g., mental health counseling, birth control, treatment for venereal disease, abortion) even without parental permission.

Parents also have certain legal responsibilities. These include the responsibility to provide the child with maintenance (e.g., food, shelter, clothing), to provide the child with basic health care, to supervise and protect the child from harm, and to provide the child with a basic education. A failure to meet these responsibilities may constitute child neglect (see Item 11.19).

2. Some of the grandparents who are raising their grandchildren, are ambivalent about assuming this responsibility. On one hand, they want to provide this care out of their love for the children but, on the other hand, caring for grandchildren may strain their finances and disrupt a hoped-for retirement. Some find this responsibility burdensome because it often comes at a time when they are experiencing more health problems and lack the energy needed to look after a young child or teen. It is important for agencies to develop programs that will address the concerns of these grandparents.

3. When we become parents we tend to raise our children the way we were raised. If we were lucky to have experienced a loving and caring relationship with our parents, this tendency is indeed helpful. On the other hand, if our parents were troubled, dysfunctional, or violent it may give rise to parenting behaviors that are ineffective and damaging.

An individual may enter parenthood resolving never to repeat the mistakes of his or her parents but later discover (or worse, be unaware) that he or she is visiting those same dysfunctional patterns on the next generation. Many parents have been jolted when they have heard themselves saying things to their children that they hated hearing from their own parents. The parent who grew up in a troubled home is often more sure of what he or she does not want to do than what he or she should do. When stressed and frustrated, these parents often dip into their childhood experiences and say and do what their own parents said and did. Needless to say, not all parents repeat the mistakes or the dysfunctions of their own parents, but breaking this cycle takes self-awareness, conscious efforts, and often parent training and counseling.

4. When parents do not have easy access to persons who are experienced in the ways of parenting, they can easily feel alone, unsure, and overwhelmed. Stress and social isolation are contributing factors to the problems of child abuse and neglect. A parent who has little or no contact with other parents and children may form unrealistic expectations of his or her own child. Social workers should look for opportunities to promote friendships and build social support networks among parents so the parents gain new perspectives on how to be a parent.

Parents cannot give what they do not have. For example, if a mother does not feel physically safe, it will be difficult for her to help her child feel safe. If a father does not possess a sense of personal worth, it will be difficult for him to help his child develop healthy self-esteem.

In order to be effective, a parent must have the emotional and psychological maturity and capacity to make sacrifices and manage emotions of anger and frustration. Parents who are fearful, frustrated, or preoccupied will have difficulty being attentive and responsive to their children and are likely to act impulsively and make bad parenting decisions. Those with serious personal problems (e.g., addiction, mental illness, domestic violence) and those who grew up in families that experienced such problems will, almost always, face some special challenges in the parenting role. The young and immature parent and the parent with cognitive delays will also find the demands of parenting especially difficult. In order to help a parent become more effective in the parent role, the parent's personal concerns and problems must first be addressed.

5. A social worker must guard against the possibility of favoring the child to the detriment of the parent. Since a child is more vulnerable than an adult, it is natural to be especially attentive to the needs of the child and possibly value the child over the parent, especially when the parent has been irresponsible or damaging to the child. This very human inclination can, however, give rise to an unfair and biased treatment of the parent.

6. Social workers need to be sensitive to differences in parenting styles and child-rearing practices that are often rooted in the parent's own childhood experiences, family of origin, ethnicity, religion, and socioeconomic class. Fabes and Martin (2000, 280–283) describe four such styles. *Authoritarian parents* are parent-centered and demanding. They require their child to follow their orders without question and discourage verbal give and take or negotiation when conflicts arise. They believe that allowing the child to "win" is an indication of parental weakness. They are often reluctant to show affection or to praise, and often use physical punishment as the primary means of enforcing discipline. *Permissive parents*, by contrast, are child-centered. They make few demands on their child, avoid conflicts whenever possible, and generally tailor their lives to the tempo, wants, and desires of their child. *Uninvolved parents* are primarily concerned with their own needs, wants, and convenience. They make few demands of their children and invest only minimal time and effort in the parent–child relationship. In their interactions with their child, these parents are often critical, rejecting, or unresponsive. *Authoritative parents* are child-centered but they also place realistic demands on the child. While they set high standards for responsible behavior, they are willing to discuss the reasons for their rules with their child and at times negotiate reasonable compromises. They display both warmth and consistent discipline, finding no contradictions in the two.

Experts in the field of child development believe that the authoritative style is the one most likely to form children who are confident, responsible, and socially competent. However, it is important to understand that these various parenting styles tend to be engrained attitudinal and behavioral patterns and not easily modified, even when the parent wants a change. When a child's two parents or other caretakers have different styles and beliefs about how children should be reared, the child may receive confusing and contradictory messages on rules and expectations.

7. Most parents struggle in their efforts to create and enforce rules. To be effective in the area of discipline, the parent must, first of all, have a truly caring, trusting, and loving relationship with his or her child. Within the context of that positive relationship, the parent must be able to distinguish between behavior that arises from the child's immaturity, inexperience, or developmental stage and behavior that is truly defiant and a deliberate violation of known and reasonable rules. Boundaries and protections should be the response to immature behavior. To truly defiant behavior, the parent needs to respond firmly with nonviolent but real and realistic consequences.

8. Most parents can benefit from parent training, parent support groups, and counseling focusing on the parent–child relationship. The most effective programs zero in on concerns that are of high priority to the parent. They strive to reach out to parents during especially difficult times, such as soon after the arrival of a first child or when the child enters the teen years. Successful programs recognize the unique challenges faced by certain groups of parents. For example, a foster parent, an adoptive parent, and the parent of a disabled child will usually have a unique set of concerns and questions about being a parent. Being a single parent is inherently stressful simply because all of the responsibilities fall upon one person. Because of societal attitudes and prejudices, parents in same-sex relationships and those in interracial marriages sometimes face special challenges, too.

Successful programs build on the parents' strengths. They operate on the assumptions that most parents do the best they know how but often have difficulties in the parent role because the parent lacks important knowledge and skills or is overwhelmed by other personal, family, or economic problems. Rather than focusing solely on the parent role, the successful programs also give attention to the situational and contextual factors that are adversely impacting on the parent. Successful parent training programs collaborate with other agencies and connect parents to other needed resources (e.g., health care, financial assistance, housing, counseling, job training).

As a general rule, fathers are less involved than mothers in the care of children and less likely to avail themselves of opportunities to learn parenting skills. Thus, the professionals and agencies that offer these services must actively reach out to fathers and design programs that will connect with the ways men think and feel. Whenever possible, parenting classes for men should be taught by a man.

Most parent training programs presume that the parent can read and write and can, therefore, make use of written materials, workbook assignments, and the like. Unfortunately, there are many parents who are not literate. Special efforts should be made to identify those parents so alternative modes of teaching can be utilized.

Ironically, the parents most likely to utilize parent training and other parenting resources are parents who are already doing an adequate job. The parents who are most in need of these services seldom seek them out. In order to attract those parents, programs must be welcoming and have a vigorous outreach component.

9. Most agencies deliver parent training within the context of a small group because that environment provides the participants with opportunities to learn from
each other and receive assurance that they are not alone in having worries, self-
doubts, and questions about being a parent. A typical parent education group meets
once a week for about eight weeks. A session should last about one and one-half
hours. The optimal size is between 8 and 16 parents. The group can be larger if the
teaching format is mostly didactic; smaller if it utilizes techniques of role-play and
discussion. It is usually preferable to have both members of the parenting couple
participate. Parents are expected to attend all sessions. Members should not be
added after the group is formed and underway. Ideally, groups for parents should be
led by two trainers, a male and a female. It is best to have separate groups for the parents of teens since their concerns are significantly different from the parents of
young children.

When feasible, each potential participant should be interviewed before being
admitted to the group in order to determine if what the group has to offer is needed
by and appropriate for the parent. The parents who have been referred to the group
by a child protection agency or mandated to attend by court order should be carefully assessed because such parents are often angry and resistant and sometimes
disruptive to the group process. However, a skilled facilitator can usually successfully
integrate them into the group (see Item 12.9).

For parents who will not attend a group because of fear or other reasons, the
use of home visitation and a parent-to-parent approach is a helpful alternative. In a
home visitation program, a parent trainer or a "resource mom" meets the parent in
the parent's own home and their discussion focuses on this parent's child and
unique circumstances. This highly individualized approach to parent training is tu-
torial in nature.

10. Social workers often find themselves in practice situations that require an assessment of the parent's capacity to provide his or her child with appropriate and acceptable care. For example, a social worker might be asked to prepare a report to the court
concerning whether a mother who had neglected her child is able to resume care of her
child now in foster care. When conducting such evaluations the social worker must
remember that there is no one, always right, way of raising a child and that every parent
makes some mistakes. It is also important to recognize that the parent–child relationship is always two-sided; the child's behavior affects the parent and the parent's behavior affects the child. A parent may do an adequate job with a child at a certain stage
of development but encounter difficulty when the child moves into another stage.
Similarly, a parent may be effective with a normal child but ineffective and overwhelmed by a child who has special needs or highly unusual behavioral problems.
Moreover, since every child is a unique personality, different children will respond
differently to various parent behaviors. An approach to discipline and guidance that
works well with one child may not work with another. Most parents find their parental
abilities severely tested when their child enters adolescence, a time when the teen is
inclined to resist the parent's rules and values and is being strongly influenced by peer
pressure. Children do not need perfect parents but they do need and deserve parents
who can provide at least a minimally acceptable level of care.

Some special challenges and conflicts can arise if the parent and child are "mismatched" or very different in terms of their temperaments, intellectual abilities, or interests. For example, a gregarious and outgoing parent may feel inept and frustrated if his or her child is by temperament shy and introverted. A father who loves sports may secretly resent a son who shows no interest in athletics.

In order to assess a parent's capacity and performance in the parent role, it is essential to observe the parent interacting with his or her child in several different situations and social contexts. It is also important to gather information on parent-related values, attitudes, and knowledge, as well as about how these individuals have come to terms with their own parents and childhood experiences. Within the context of a nonthreatening interview, a social worker can often initiate a discussion about parenting by asking a number of simple questions, such as: Tell me about your child, Mary? In what ways is Mary like other kids her age? In what way is she different from other children? Does Mary have a personality that is similar to yours or different from yours? In what ways are Mary's experiences as a child similar to or different from what you experienced as a child? What have you liked most about being a parent? What do you find to be most difficult about being a parent? Is being a parent fun for you? Has being a parent gotten more or less demanding as your child has grown older? How would you rate the parenting abilities of your own parents? Many people say they want to be a better parent than their own parent; have you ever had that thought? If you could start over, is there anything you would do differently in your approach to being a parent? Have you ever made a big mistake in how you dealt with your child? What is it like for Mary to have you as a parent? (See Item 11.7 and Item 11.9.)

SELECTED BIBLIOGRAPHY

American Bar Association. *Family Legal Guide*, 3rd ed. New York: Random House, 2004.

Bigner, Jerry. *Parent-Child Relations: An Introduction to Parenting*, 7th ed. Columbus, OH: Pearson/Merrill, 2006.

Bornstein, Marc, ed. *Handbook of Parenting*, 2nd ed. (in five volumes). Mahwah, NJ: Lawrence Erlbaum, 2003.

Campbell, Deborah, and Glen Palm. *Group Parent Education*. Thousand Oaks, CA: Sage, 2003.

Fabes, Richard, and Carol Martin. *Exploring Child Development*. Boston: Allyn & Bacon, 2000.

Istar, Arlene. *The Complete Lesbian and Gay Parenting Guide*. New York: Berkeley Books, 2004.

15.5   THE CLIENT WHO IS AN OLDER PERSON

Purpose: To adapt social work techniques and approaches to the special needs of older people.

Discussion: In most developed countries a growing percentage of the population is in the older age range. For example, in the United States by the year 2030, about 20 percent of the population will be over 65 years of age. Given this trend, social workers and human services programs must give increased attention to the needs and concerns of older people, especially those who are in their seventies, eighties, and nineties. The following background information and guidelines will assist the social worker serving these clients:

1. As people grow older, they experience many losses (e.g., deaths of loved ones, loss of health, restricted mobility, etc.) and usually feel less independent and more vulnerable. They begin to worry about their ability to take care of themselves and about becoming a burden to their children or other family members. In response, many elderly persons hold on tightly to whatever freedom and independence they still possess. Some staunchly resist any service or professional they perceive as somehow limiting their freedom. When working with elderly clients, allow them to retain control, make choices, and maintain independence to the greatest extent possible.

2. Most older persons will prefer a friendly and outgoing social worker, but some will react negatively to a professional who seems too casual and informal or appears to take the relationship for granted. When addressing the client, use the title Mr., Mrs., or Miss until you have received permission to use his or her first name. Be alert to the fact that some older persons may be bothered or offended by what they judge to be unusual, inappropriate, or immodest clothing, hairstyles, or jewelry worn by a professional.

3. For both physical and psychological reasons, it is usually more comfortable for the older client to be interviewed at home rather than in an office setting. A good way to break the ice and start a conversation is to show an interest in the family pictures, furnishings, homemade items, or decorations in the client's home or room. Then begin building the professional relationship by focusing first on the client's most obvious concerns and concrete needs such as social activity and friendships, transportation, medical care, living arrangement, home maintenance, and the like. Only after a positive professional relationship has been formed is the client likely to feel comfortable discussing more personal concerns such as family conflicts, fears, feelings of isolation, grief, money problems, and so on.

4. Many older clients are concerned about the cost of services and their ability to pay. Some will simply reject service rather than reveal their inability to pay. Many older people find "taking charity" and using public programs to be especially difficult and humiliating.

5. Most older people have some degree of vision and hearing loss. Thus, it is important to speak clearly and repeat yourself as often as necessary. Your nonverbal communication is important as a means of compensating for the client's auditory deficit. Also, the pace of an interview will usually be slower with an older person, and the client's lack of energy may limit the length of the interview.

6. During their later years, people become increasingly aware of their unique relationships with their children and grandchildren. It may be of great importance for them to stay in contact with offspring or to reactivate relationships that have deteriorated. Some may want to reach out to estranged family members and patch up differences or make amends for harm they caused. Do everything possible to facilitate intergenerational family communication.

7. As people grow older, they often think more about the meaning and purpose of life and the achievements and disappointments of their own lives. For many, spirituality takes on added importance. Look for opportunities that allow them to share their thoughts and what they have learned about life.

8. Allow and encourage the older client to reminisce. Thinking and talking about the past is a normal activity—it is not a sign of deteriorating mental abilities. Listen carefully to the reminiscence; it will reveal much about the client's values, feelings, and current concerns. A few open-ended questions will often encourage an older client to speak about meaningful life experiences. For example: What was the world like when you grew up? What was the most significant event of your childhood? How did you meet your spouse? What was the happiest time of your life? What do you consider to be your greatest accomplishment? What do you consider your greatest disappointment or regret in life? What are you most thankful for? What do you most want the younger generations to know about life?

9. Given the impact of racism, discrimination, and prejudice on people, be especially sensitive when interacting with older people who are members of racial or ethnic minorities. As a general rule, they will be more suspicious and distrustful of agencies and more sensitive to anything that might appear demeaning and disrespectful. The values common to a particular ethnic group may make life more or less difficult for the aging person. For example, in certain ethnic groups (e.g., Chinese American, Native American), older people occupy a position of respect and influence within families. On the other hand, the importance of hard work as a value within some ethnic groups (e.g., Slavic American) may make the nonworking elderly person feel particularly unworthy and unimportant.

10. Be alert to indicators of elder abuse and neglect (especially self-neglect), such as bruises, cuts, burns, or untreated injuries that are explained in a vague or defensive manner; improper clothing for the weather; wandering outside at odd hours or into dangerous areas; mail, newspapers, or other deliveries that are not picked up; unusual activity or no signs of movement from their home; unpleasant odors associated with hygiene or housekeeping; the person does not recognize you or does not know where he or she is or the day or time; the person has means to meet basic needs but is facing an eviction, utility shutoff, or has many unpaid bills; or the person is dependent on a stressed, chemically dependent or mentally ill caregiver and basic needs are not being met.

SELECTED BIBLIOGRAPHY

Berkman, Barbara, ed. *Handbook of Social Work in Health and Aging.* New York: Oxford University, 2006.

Lymbery, Mark. *Social Work with Older People.* Thousand Oaks, CA: Sage, 2006.

Naleppa, Matthias, and William Reid. *Gerontological Social Work.* New York: Columbia University Press, 2003.

Solie, David. *How to Say It: Closing the Communication Gap With Our Elders.* New York: Prentice Hall, 2004.

| **15.6** | **THE CLIENT WHO IS IN CRISIS** |

Purpose: To assist the client in coping with a personal crisis.

Discussion: The social worker will encounter many clients who are in a state of crisis. Although the word crisis is widely used, it has a specific meaning within the field of mental health. Essentially, a *crisis* consists of a perception and the reaction to that perception. When an individual is in crisis, he or she perceives a particular situation to be an intolerable and overwhelming difficulty and one with which he or she is unable to cope. The individual reacts with anxiety, panic, despair, and disorganization. A crisis is a sudden but temporary breakdown in a person's capacity to cope with and manage one's life. Among the events that can precipitate a crisis are the death of a loved one, loss of a job, divorce, birth of a child with a severe disability, serious illness or accident, house fire, rape or mugging, or other traumatic event.

A personal crisis is a time of both danger and opportunity. It is dangerous because if the crisis is not resolved constructively, it can set in motion a downward spiral that leads to a level of functioning lower than that which existed prior to the crisis. On the other hand, a crisis can be an opportunity to learn new coping skills and actually elevate one's usual level of functioning. A crisis is *time limited*; within a matter of about 4 to 6 weeks, the person will come to some level of adjustment and steady state. And as suggested, that adjustment may be either positive or negative, depending in part on how others respond to the person during the crisis.

It is important to distinguish between a genuine personal crisis (i.e., a short period of distress and readjustment) and a lifestyle characterized by one emergency after another, year after year, but in which nothing is done to face or change the circumstances that give rise to these emergencies. For individuals immersed in this crisis-ridden mode, life is like a roller-coaster ride, and the emergencies they experience are energizing and addicting, rather than deeply distressful.

The concept of crisis overlaps, to a degree, with two mental disorders: Acute Stress Disorder and Posttraumatic Stress Disorder (PTSD). The essential feature of an *Acute Distress Disorder* is the appearance of certain symptoms within 1 month after exposure to an extremely traumatic event. Symptoms include anxiety, "numbing" (or an absence of emotional responsiveness), reduced awareness of one's surroundings, a feeling that life is unreal, a feeling of being detached from one's body, an inability to concentrate, and an inability to remember the important details of the traumatic event. If this condition goes untreated and/or if the person experiences additional traumatic events, the second condition, PTSD, may develop.

Posttraumatic Stress Disorder is characterized by the occurrence of the above-mentioned symptoms plus flashbacks, recurring frightening dreams about the event, and extreme distress reactions when reminded of the event. PTSD may arise 3 or more months after exposure to an intensely emotional and/or life-threatening experience, such as rape, war-related combat, kidnapping, torture, an automobile accident, and witnessing the traumatic death of another person.

If an individual is not making progress in working his or her way through the crisis period and if symptoms of an Acute Stress Disorder or PTSD become evident, he or she should be referred for appropriate psychiatric treatment.

The following guidelines will be useful when dealing with a person in crisis:

1. Listen actively and offer emotional support. A person in crisis is in a heightened state of either anxiety or depression and also feels a sense of failure because he or she is unable to cope. The client is probably preoccupied with the precipitating event and will have difficulty focusing attention on anything else. Before the client can consider alternatives, make decisions, or plan ways for resolving problems, he or she will need much emotional support from the worker and significant others. This support may range from simply acknowledging the existence of the upsetting experience to offering strong reassurance (e.g., "You did the right thing in leaving that violent situation and coming to our shelter").

2. Involve others in the helping process. People in crisis are often most receptive to assistance provided by those whom they already know and trust (e.g., family, friends, employer, minister, neighbors, etc.). Encourage the client to reach out to others, or, with his or her permission, contact these significant others and enlist their help on behalf of the client.

3. Allow the client to express emotion, whether crying or expressing feelings of fear or anger, while you continue to provide emotional support and acceptance. The client's strong emotions and intense feelings will diminish with time.

4. Communicate hope. A hopeful attitude is an essential element in responding to a person in crisis. If you communicate a belief in the client's ability to cope, he or she will be less fearful and will gradually regain self-confidence.

5. People in crisis are preoccupied with their pain and problems. They have tunnel vision and can think of little else. Consequently, they are not able to step back and objectively analyze their situation. Ask questions and actively examine the details of their situation as a way of helping them think more clearly.

6. Use partialization. The person in crisis feels as if he or she is facing a giant and completely unmanageable problem. By breaking the problem down into several smaller ones, to be addressed one at a time, the client will feel more hopeful about regaining control.

7. Provide factual information. Often, a crisis arises because the person has misconceptions about his or her situation or because intense feelings have distorted his or her perception of reality (e.g., "I just know that I'm going to lose my job" or "This goes to prove that no company is going to hire someone in a wheelchair like me"). Provide factual information related to the person's concern (e.g., "No, I don't think it is because you are in a wheelchair that you weren't hired; there are laws against discrimination of that kind"). When appropriate, give honest feedback needed to correct misunderstandings (e.g., "Mr. Jones told me that you weren't hired because you were belligerent and sarcastic during the interview").

8. A person in crisis has difficulty making decisions and anticipating the consequences of his or her actions. Thus, you may need to provide highly specific directions as to what the person needs to do or what will probably happen if he or she takes a certain course of action. It is especially important to help the client anticipate the consequences of destructive behaviors (e.g., "If you lose control and again injure your child, she will be placed in a foster home") (see Item 13.12).

9. Reinforce adaptive behavior. Help the individual identify what worked in the past; encourage the client to take similar actions to address his or her current problem. An important part of crisis intervention is to encourage clients to take action so they begin to regain a faith and trust in their own capabilities.

10. Consider using a behavioral contract (see Item 13.6) as a means of providing the client with structure and direction. This helps the client mobilize inner resources, and it also sends the message that you have confidence in his or her ability to take the steps needed to get through the crisis.

SELECTED BIBLIOGRAPHY

James, Richard, and Burl Gilliland. *Crisis Intervention Strategies*, 5th ed. Belmont, CA: Brooks/Cole, 2005.
Kanel, Kristi. *A Guide to Crisis Intervention*, 3rd ed. Belmont, CA: Brooks/Cole, 2007.
Roberts, Albert. *Crisis Intervention Handbook*, 3rd ed. New York: Oxford University, 2005.

15.7   THE CLIENT WHO IS A BATTERED WOMAN

Purpose: To understand domestic abuse and respond appropriately to a battered woman.

Discussion: As used here, the term *battered woman* refers to an adult female who has been physically, sexually, and/or emotionally abused by a spouse or intimate partner. Unfortunately, this type of abuse is common and results in many serious injuries and deaths. In the United States, a woman is more likely to be assaulted, injured, raped, or killed by a her male partner than by a stranger or any other type of assailant. The vast majority of the abusers are men and the abuse occurs most often within a heterosexual relationship. However, it may also occur within gay and lesbian relationships. (For ease of discussion, the authors will refer to the offender or abuser as the male and to the victim as the female.)

The abuse can take several forms, but all are intended to control the woman— for example:

- *Physical injury or threats of injury* (e.g., pushing, choking, punching, beating, hitting with objects, forcing sex, threatening to hurt her or the children)
- *Emotional abuse* (e.g., humiliating her, making her the object of demeaning jokes, blaming her, undermining her confidence, saying she is crazy, insisting that she deserves to be punished, denying her opportunity to make decisions)

- *Isolation* (e.g., controlling what she does, who she talks to, and where she goes, closely monitoring her activities)
- *Economic manipulation* (e.g., controlling her access to money, giving her an allowance, preventing her from getting or keeping a job, threatening to take all possessions and leave her with nothing)
- *Intimidation* (e.g., displaying weapons, abusing pets, destroying her property, threatening to commit suicide if she does not do what he wants)
- *Using the children* (e.g., threatening to take the children, threatening to report the woman for child abuse)

Typically, there is a cycle of abuse with three major phases: (1) tension building, (2) the explosion, and (3) the "honeymoon." In some cases, the cycle may be quite short, such as a matter of days; in other cases, it may take several months to cycle through these phases:

- *Phase 1—Tension building.* Tensions between the two people begin to rise. Some outbursts may occur but these are minimized and rationalized away by both parties. The woman typically tries to protect herself and maintain some control over the situation by being compliant and not showing anger.
- *Phase 2—Explosion.* The abuser finally explodes. Anger is expressed in extreme verbal abuse, physical violence, and/or rape.
- *Phase 3—Repairing the damage (Honeymoon).* The abuser expresses sorrow for what he has done. He fears that she will leave, and to keep her from leaving, he becomes very attentive, loving, and thoughtful. Since this loving behavior does not fit with his prior behavior, she becomes confused and may doubt her own perceptions and sanity. She probably wants to believe that the episode of abuse was atypical and out of character. She may conclude that she is the one responsible for the abuse and think: "If only I would have done things right, he would not have gotten angry." This period of good behavior by the abuser eventually runs its course and the cycle begins again.

Those who believe they must hurt others in order to solve a problem are, in fact, the problem. Men who abuse women have several of the following characteristics:

- Extreme and irrational jealousy and possessiveness toward the woman, often coupled with an unjustifiable belief that she is interested in other men
- Desire to control the woman and isolate her from friends and family by saying such things as "All we need is each other—no one else"
- Quick to anger and have an explosive temper
- Moods and behavior may fluctuate from being kind and gentle to being violent and oppressive
- Refuses to take responsibility for his own behavior; blames others, especially the woman, for whatever goes wrong in his life
- Often a history of having been abused as a child or a witness to frequent family violence

- Often a history of legal violations related to violence
- Denies or rationalizes his outbursts and abusive behavior
- Usually feels remorse after a violent episode, promises that it will never happen again, and, for a time, becomes a very devoted and loving partner; however, this does not last and eventually he repeats the abusing and violent behavior

There are a number of reasons battered women are reluctant to leave an abusive relationship or return to it after only a brief separation:

- Fear of retribution and even more serious violence
- Lack of money and no suitable place to live
- Fear of losing her children, home, possessions, and economic security
- Feelings of self-doubt, low self-esteem, shame, or a distrust of other people
- Fear of not being believed or of being blamed for causing the abuse
- Religious beliefs and morals that emphasize maintaining a marriage
- Desire to preserve the family for benefit of the children
- Wanting to believe that the abuse will stop or a tendency to deny or minimize the seriousness of the abuse
- A tendency to equate love with dependency

An abusive situation should be considered especially dangerous if there is a pattern of frequent and/or severe violence, the abuser and/or the abused woman use drugs or alcohol, the woman or her children have been threatened with death, the abuser has access to deadly weapons, either the abuser or victim has a psychiatric impairment, the abuser has a history of criminal activity, the abuse has taken the form of forced sexual acts, the abuser has threatened suicide, the abuser has tortured or killed animals as a display of his willingness to take extreme action, and the woman has made suicide threats or attempts.

Social workers and programs offering services to battered women must strive toward the following goals:

- Ensure that the woman and her children are safe and protected.
- Help the woman understand the nature and cycle of abuse and that she has options that can keep her and her children safe.
- Help her make decisions, formulate plans, and obtain the services she will need in order to ensure safety in the future.
- Help her and her children heal from the psychological effects of abuse and reestablish a sense of personal boundaries.

Those working directly with abused women should keep the following guidelines in mind:

1. Give immediate attention to helping the woman with her basic needs such as the need for safety, food, shelter, transportation, assistance in caring for the children, legal counsel, and so on. Do not immediately assume that the battered woman is in a heterosexual relationship; refer to the abuser as "partner" until you learn the gender of the offender.

2. Because a woman caught up in a abusive relationship is prone to self-doubt and self-blame, establish a warm, caring, and nonjudgmental relationship; listen attentively and respectfully to her story, her fears and confusion, and her reasons for wanting to maintain the relationship. She may want to remain in the relationship because she and/or her children love him and believe that he will change.

3. Focus on the woman's strengths, such as the decisions and behaviors that have kept her alive or that protected her children; help her to identify and name her survival skills as a way of counteracting her feelings of self-doubt and helplessness.

4. If she decides to remain with the abuser, assist the woman in developing an escape plan (safety plan) that she can immediately implement if she is again threatened. The plan should include her packing and then hiding from the abuser a bag that contains money, clothing, personal items, and copies of legal documents that she (and her children) would need to live apart from the abuser.

5. Anticipate that the woman's emotions and moods will fluctuate widely and that she will experience great ambivalence about ending the relationship; discourage her from speaking with the abuser when she is feeling especially insecure and confused. At such times she is vulnerable to his influence and is likely to return to him without really considering the danger.

6. If the woman's children have witnessed the abuse of their mother, anticipate that they, too, are feeling frightened and confused and are in need of counseling.

7. Do not assume that the woman has some underlying emotional need or problem that causes her to remain in an abusive relationship. However, as a response to ongoing abuse, the woman may indeed develop problems such as alcohol or drug abuse, depression, anxiety and posttraumatic stress disorder.

8. Understand that the woman may have to leave and return to the abuser several times before she is finally convinced that the abuse will not end unless the abuser is motivated to make use of a program of therapy and training. Couples counseling (i.e., both partners attend at the same time) is not an appropriate mode of intervention because the abused woman will be afraid to speak honestly in the presence of the abuser and the abuser will typically deny or minimize the abuse.

9. After leaving an abusive relationship, it may take from two to four years before the battered woman recovers emotionally and becomes significantly less fearful, anxious, and depressed. The same can be said for the children who have experienced the terror of seeing their mother beaten and threatened.

SELECTED BIBLIOGRAPHY

Barnett, Ola, Cindy Miller-Perrin, and Robin Perrin. *Family Violence Across the Lifespan*, 2nd ed. Thousand Oaks, CA: Sage, 2005.
Roberts, Albert, ed. *Battered Women and Their Families*, 3rd ed. New York: Springer, 2007.
Walker, Lenore. *The Battered Woman Syndrome*, 3rd ed. New York: Springer, 2006.

15.8	**THE CLIENT WHO IS AT RISK OF SUICIDE**

Purpose: To assess risk of suicide and take preventive action.

Discussion: Given the high rate of suicide among teenagers, young adults, and the elderly, the social worker will encounter clients who are at risk of taking their own lives. The warning signs of *suicide* include depression, preoccupation with death and pain, giving away prized possessions, unexplained changes in behavioral patterns, sudden increase in the use of drugs and alcohol, and impulsive or reckless behavior. Clinical data indicate that most suicide victims have consulted a physician within six months of their suicide.

Although not all people who end their lives are clinically depressed, studies reveal that depression is often present. The symptoms of *depression* include pervasive sadness, feelings of hopelessness, lack of interest in activities once enjoyed, inability to concentrate, thoughts of suicide, unexplained aches and pains, fatigue and restlessness, changes in appetite and sleep habits, withdrawal from others, early waking from sleep or erratic sleep patterns, irritability, and unexplained crying. Whereas depression in adults usually results in a retardation of activity, depression in children and youth is often expressed in agitation.

Legally and ethically, the social worker must make every reasonable effort to prevent a client's suicide. This includes providing counseling, staying with the person during times of high risk, and, if necessary, calling the police. State laws dictate when police can detain a suicidal person and when involuntary hospitalization is permitted. However, it must be noted that it may not be possible to prevent the suicide of a person who is firmly committed to taking his or her own life. If the person wants to die, he or she will eventually find the opportunity and the means. Professional intervention, close monitoring, and hospitalization may delay a suicide but such efforts cannot always prevent it.

For the person thinking about suicide, the following factors or situations suggest a high risk of suicide:

- Has a history of prior suicide attempts
- Has a plan for the suicide and access to the chosen method (e.g., has a gun or a supply of sleeping pills)
- Is in a very troublesome or painful situation that is growing worse
- No longer has access to a person who has been an important source of support, encouragement, and meaning in life
- Has noticeably and rather quickly changed from being distressed and in turmoil to being at ease and content (an indicator that he or she has finally made the decision to commit suicide)

The following guidelines will help the social worker in assessing a client's suicide potential and responding to the client who is at risk of suicide:

1. Take every message about suicide seriously. It is very significant that the person is talking about harm to self rather than expressing his or her frustration in other ways. It is a myth that people who talk about suicide will not kill themselves. Unfortunately, the message may be veiled and, in some cases, it is not until after the death that its meaning becomes clear. In 10 to 20 percent of suicides, there are no noticeable warnings prior to the death.

2. If you believe that a client is at risk of suicide, consult with other professionals on how best to proceed. Do not allow yourself to be "hooked" by the suicidal client into a promise of complete confidentiality. Ordinary rules of confidentiality must be broken in order to prevent a death.

3. Listen for subtle and indirect statements of suicidal intent, such as "I won't be around much longer," "There is nothing worth living for anymore," and "I just can't stand the pain any longer." Be especially concerned about such statements if the person has recently experienced the loss of an important relationship, a loss of status among peers, an episode of family violence, or is in the throes of adjusting to chronic pain, a life-threatening illness, or a serious physical limitation.

4. Keep in mind that the person thinking about suicide is experiencing intense feelings of ambivalence—the desire to live and, at the same time, the desire to escape pain, even if by death. The person does not really want to die but wants desperately to escape his or her pain. Thus, assume that the person talking about suicide is ambivalent and hoping for your assistance. Reach out and support that part of the person holding to life.

5. Do not be afraid to ask if he or she is thinking about suicide. Speaking openly will not increase the likelihood of suicide. Direct questioning tells the suicidal person that you are concerned and not afraid to talk straight. Examples of questions include the following: Are you thinking of killing yourself? Can you tell me why suicide seems like the answer? Who else knows you are thinking about suicide? What has happened recently that caused you to think more and more about suicide? Why do you believe your situation will not improve or change? How might your situation be different six months from now? Have you ever sought professional help? Have you attempted suicide in the past? If you thought about suicide in the past, what caused you to change your mind?

6. Determine whether the person has worked out a specific suicide plan. Ask questions such as Do you have a plan for killing yourself? How do you plan to get the gun you intend to use? Where do you plan to kill yourself? and What time of day or night do you plan to kill yourself? The more detailed and specific the person's plan, the higher the risk of suicide. Many suicidal people have thought about their suicide plan, but most have not thought about an alternative or a "plan B." Thus, if you can interfere with a key element of their plan, you can often thwart their suicide.

7. Determine whether the person has chosen a specific method (shooting, hanging, pills, etc.) and if he or she has access to the method. The person who has selected a method and has access to it is at high risk.

8. Determine the lethality of the method. Highly lethal methods include shooting, jumping, hanging, drowning, carbon monoxide poisoning, car crash, or taking high doses of barbiturates, sleeping pills, or aspirin. Less lethal methods include wrist cutting, gas stove, or tranquilizers and nonprescription drugs (excluding aspirin and Tylenol). The more lethal the method, the higher the risk and the greater the chance that a suicide attempt will result in death.

9. Most suicidal people have "tunnel vision"—they can think only about their pain and helplessness. It is important to help them identify and consider alternative methods for dealing with the situation. How has the individual managed stressful situations in the past? Will any of these methods work in the present situation?

10. Determine whether the suicidal person has anyone to rely on during a time of crisis. Many who commit suicide feel ignored or cut off from the people around them. The risk of suicide increases when a person is widowed, divorced, or separated. It is important to help significant others come to the support of the suicidal person.

11. Help the person see that suicide is a permanent solution to a temporary problem. Identify other possible solutions to dealing with the pain the individual is experiencing but do not lie or offer false hope. Ask the client to immediately enter counseling as an alternative to suicide. If necessary, ask him or her to agree not to commit suicide for a specific period (e.g., two weeks) or to promise not to commit suicide before talking to you one more time. If a referral for counseling is made, you or someone else should accompany the client to the initial interview. Follow-up is necessary to ensure that the client is making use of the service.

12. In extreme situations and when nothing else seems to be working, attempt to engage the person in a discussion of what will happen after he or she is found dead. Sometimes this will jar the person into thinking more clearly about the consequences of a suicide—for example, What kind of a funeral service do you want? Who should be notified of your death? Should the people to be notified of your death be approached or talked to in a certain way? Can we make a list of all the people who should be contacted and invited to your funeral? Who do you want to have your favorite possessions? What do you want your obituary to say?

13. When dealing with persons who are actively suicidal, it is important to remember that they may have no hesitation about also killing you or someone else in the process of taking their own life. For example, a suicidal person with a gun may shoot you if you attempt to take away the gun.

SELECTED BIBLIOGRAPHY

Jacobs, Douglas, ed. *Suicide Assessment and Intervention*. San Francisco: Jossey-Bass, 1998.
Quinett, Paul. *Suicide: The Forever Decision*. New York: Crossroad, 2004.
Schneidman, Edwin. *Comprehending Suicide*: Washington, DC: American Psychological Association, 2001.

15.9   THE CLIENT WITH COGNITIVE DELAY

Purpose: To adapt usual social work methods to the special needs of an adult with cognitive delay (mental retardation).

Discussion: The two key features of ***mental retardation*** are significantly subaverage general intelligence and significant limitations in adaptive behaviors such as communication, self-care, and academic skills. There are many forms of mental retardation and dozens of causes, such as inborn errors in metabolism, chromosomal aberrations, ingestion of toxic chemicals, malnutrition, viral infections, and head trauma.

Roughly 3 percent of the population has mental retardation. Of those, about 80 percent have delays in the mild to moderate range and 20 percent in the ranges termed severe and profound. Signs of cognitive delay are usually apparent early in childhood. Early diagnosis and medical and educational intervention are of critical importance to minimize the effects of the condition (see Items 11.15 and 11.17).

Because of the stigma attached to the word *retardation*, the term *cognitive delay* is increasingly used by educators and parents as a substitute, especially when speaking about children. However, mental retardation is a diagnostic category in the *Diagnostic and Statistical Manual of Mental Disorders* (see Item 11.18) and a term frequently used by physicians and health care professionals.

The term *developmental disability* is a legal and programmatic category of mental disability. Although definitions may vary slightly from state to state, a ***developmental disability*** is often defined as a severe disability caused by physical or mental impairment that limits a person's development, appears before the age 18 (or 22), is likely to be lifelong, and affects the person's functioning in self-care, learning, self-direction, language, independent living, mobility, and/or economic self-sufficiency. The developmental disabilities are mental retardation, cerebral palsy, autism, severe dyslexia, and epilepsy. Of these, mental retardation is the one most frequently diagnosed. Thus, all persons with mental retardation have a developmental disability, but not all persons with a developmental disability have mental retardation.

Most adults with mild to moderate levels of mental retardation can hold jobs (albeit low-paying ones), and some may marry and have children. Because they are usually trusting, naïve, and gullible, they are easily tricked and vulnerable to exploitation and abuse. Because they often experience frustration and social rejection, they are at risk of developing emotional problems and unusual and inappropriate behaviors.

The following guidelines will aid the social worker serving an adult client with cognitive delay:

1. Individualize the client. Focus mostly on the client's abilities. Discard any stereotypes you may have concerning people with this condition. They have the same physical, emotional, social, sexual, and spiritual needs as everyone else.

2. Adapt your approach to the client's abilities (e.g., his or her intellectual level, language skills, etc.). To the extent possible, clients should participate in making decisions that affect their own lives. This may be limited in the case of one who has a very severe disability, but other clients may be excellent sources of information about their own preferences, abilities, and limitations.

3. People with cognitive delay have limited verbal skills and difficulty with abstract thinking. Thus, be prepared to utilize alternatives to verbal communication and the ordinary helping skills. Behavioral techniques, special teaching methodologies, non-verbal group work, modeling, and the creative arts are examples. (This is not to say that verbal techniques cannot be effective with some clients.)

4. Because the client's attention span may be short, the length of interviews will need to be adjusted accordingly; and because the client's memory may be limited, each contact and communication should be planned as a discrete event rather than as a continuation of previous conversations. When you give explanations, you may need to repeat them and use several concrete examples and illustrations. Your language must be clear, straightforward, and simple but never patronizing.

5. Because the client's life situation is heavily influenced by the people in his or her immediate environment (e.g., family members, group home manager, neighbors, employers, etc.), the social worker must be prepared to formulate interventions designed to change these people's level of understanding and the expectations they place on the client. The practice roles of client advocate, case manager, and broker, are especially important in work with this client group (see Item 12.4).

6. In your interactions with your client, do nothing that might reinforce inappropriate behaviors. For example, hugging is not a conventional greeting among adults who do not know each other very well. Thus, initiate a handshake rather than allow yourself to be hugged by the client.

7. Address adults with cognitive delay as you would any other adult. For example, always use *Mr.* or *Miss*, unless you know each other so well that you are on a first-name basis. Avoid demeaning language, such as referring to an adult as a "kid."

8. Certain behavioral patterns and medical disorders are associated with some forms of mental retardation. This area of knowledge is of critical importance in assessment and case planning and in working as part of a team with other disciplines, such as psychology, physical therapy, occupational therapy, medicine, speech therapy, special education, and vocational rehabilitation.

9. In order to maximize learning and socialization by persons with mental retardation and also to reduce the chances that they will be stigmatized and possibly learn inappropriate mannerisms and behaviors, the principles of normalization and social integration should guide the design and delivery of social services and the formulation of client habilitation plans. *Integration* exists when persons who have a disability participate, to the greatest extent possible, in the ordinary and usual activities of family, community, and society. *Normalization* is a philosophy of service planning and delivery that emphasizes the utilization of helping approaches and services that are culturally normative. The phrase *culturally normative* refers to that which is typical, ordinary, or conventional within the community.

An example may illustrate the normalization principle. Where does the ordinary or typical man get his haircuts? The answer is at a barbershop. Thus, a man with mental retardation should also obtain his haircut at a local barbershop. It would be a violation of the normalization principle for a case manager to arrange for a barber to visit a group home in order to give haircuts to all the residents.

The term *normalization* should not be misunderstood as "being normal" but rather as efforts to decrease separation and deviance (i.e., socially created differences). Moreover, normalization does not dictate that a person with a disability should be placed in situations that would generate unusual frustration or impossible completion just because those situations are typical for the "average person." However, it does call for the removal of overprotection and recognizes that learning and living involves a degree of risk taking and possible failure.

10. It is in relation to clients with severe disabilities that a social worker is likely to encounter the legal procedures known as guardianship and conservatorship. In a ***guardianship*** arrangement, a court finds a person to be legally incompetent because of young age or mental or physical incapacity and therefore invests another person (the guardian) with the power to manage the incapacitated person's money and property and to make certain other decisions such as those related to health care. In a ***conservatorship***, the court appoints another (the conservator) for the more limited purpose of managing the legally incompetent person's estate. Neither of these two procedures should be confused with ***power of attorney***, which does not involve a court finding of legal incompetence but simply involves the use of a notarized document in which one legally competent person voluntarily gives to another the legal power to take certain actions such as selling a property, depositing or withdrawing funds from a bank, or paying bills.

SELECTED BIBLIOGRAPHY

Graziano, Anthony. *Developmental Disabilities.* Boston: Allyn & Bacon, 2002.

Luckasson, Ruth. *Mental Retardation.* 10th ed. Washington, DC: American Association on Mental Retardation, 2002.

Parette, Howard, George Peterson-Karlan, and Ravic Ringlaben, eds. *Research-based Practices in Developmental Disabilities.* Austin, TX: Pro-Ed, 2007.

15.10 THE CLIENT WITH BRAIN INJURY

Purpose: To consider the aftereffects of brain injury in assessment and case planning.

Discussion: Recent advances in emergency medical treatment have made it possible to save the lives of many people who have a stroke or a traumatic head injury. Consequently, a growing number of individuals in society have survived a life-threatening event but struggle with the aftereffects of brain injury.

The actual effects of an injury depend primarily on what parts of the brain are damaged and the extent of damage. For example, the effects of stroke (*cerebral vascular accident,* or *CVA*) can be quite circumscribed because a blocked blood vessel will cause damage to a very specific area of the brain. For this reason, once the location of stroke-caused damage is known, the aftereffects can be predicted with some accuracy. By contrast, the aftereffects of a traumatic brain injury, such as one acquired in an auto accident or a beating to the head, can be defuse and unpredictable because the tearing and shearing of tissue occurs in several areas of the brain.

Individuals with significant brain injury, especially if caused by trauma, will often develop a pattern of rigid thinking. Because they have difficulty detecting subtle differences among ideas and nuances in meaning and are frustrated by complexity and ambiguity, they tend to hold tightly to their understandings and interpretations. They are inclined to view an issue or position as either entirely right or entirely wrong. They have difficulty accepting a middle ground and considering both the advantages and disadvantages of a proposal. This black-or-white type of thinking makes it difficult for them to make workable decisions and may cause others to perceive them as rigid, abrasive, opinionated, and narrow minded.

Stroke

Typically, the most visible sign of a stroke is a paralysis on one side of the body. Damage to the left side of the brain results in right-sided paralysis and problems with speech and language (termed *aphasia*). In addition, the person tends to be slow, hesitant, and disorganized when faced with an unfamiliar situation.

CVA damage to the right brain results in left side paralysis and causes difficulties in perception. The person tends to be impulsive, have poor judgment, and overlook his or her limitations. This individual can often describe and explain tasks that need to be done but is not able to do them. He or she has trouble both expressing emotions and perceiving the emotional signals of others.

Many of those who have had a stroke have what is termed *one-sided neglect*, meaning that they may have lost sections of their visual field or have lost sensory signals to parts of their bodies. For example, a man with a paralyzed arm may be unaware that his arm is dangling near a hot stove. Another illustrative example is the woman who looks at her own leg and then becomes upset because she concludes someone is laying in bed beside her. Persons with such perceptual problems can easily become confused while traveling or moving about.

Other problems commonly associated with a stroke include (1) the person becomes careless and neglectful of personal grooming and appearance; (2) loss of memory retention span (i.e., a decrease in the number of things that can be retained and attended to at one time); (3) decreased capacity for short-term memory, which makes new learning difficult; (4) difficulty in generalization (i.e., applying what was learned in one situation to another); (5) emotional lability (i.e., laughing or crying for no apparent reason); (6) sensory deprivation (i.e., loss in the ability to taste, hear, see, perceive touch, etc.); and (7) fatigue.

Traumatic Brain Injury

Trauma to the brain may result in paralysis or other physical symptoms such as seizures and a decrease in strength and coordination; however, it is common for the person to appear physically normal but experience a number of cognitive, behavioral, and emotional problems. Difficulties in memory, judgment, attention, perception, and impulse control can result in major problems in social interaction and job performance.

For the social work practitioner who may encounter a client who has had a stroke or a traumatic brain injury, several guidelines are important:

1. Be alert to the possibility of brain injury effects whenever presenting problems involve personality changes, impulsiveness, poor memory, and poor judgment. Inquire as to a history of a concussion, coma, stroke, skull fracture, or other injuries to the head caused by, for example, car accidents, sports injuries, or violence. If there is reason to suspect the existence of a brain injury, consult with a rehabilitation specialist, neurologist, or neuropsychologist concerning the symptoms and determine if a referral for an in-depth evaluation is indicated. A medical doctor who specializes in physical rehabilitation and in treating the aftereffects of stroke and head injury is called a *physiatrist*. This medical specialty is known as *physiatry* (not to be confused with *psychiatry*).

2. Rehabilitation programs can be successful in teaching patients how to compensate for some of the deficits caused by brain injury. They are most beneficial when started as soon as possible after the brain damage has occurred.

3. The family of a person who has had a stroke or acquired a head injury will need information, guidance, and support in learning to cope with the many changes they face in relating to a loved one who may seem like a different person. Also, the family should be encouraged to review relevant legal documents, contracts, wills, financial agreements, and the like and to develop legal protection against impulsive decisions and poor judgments made by a family member who experiences the effects of a head injury.

4. Individuals with brain injury may fabricate an explanation or make up a story in order to cope with or hide their problems of poor memory and learning difficulties. They may hold tightly to false beliefs because the beliefs help them make sense out of the unorganized bits of information they possess and the confusion they experience. The family may be distressed and angry when the person with brain injury insists that an obviously false belief is true. Organizations such as the National Head Injury Foundation and the American Stroke Association provide information as well as support to the survivors of head injury and stroke and their families.

5. State departments of vocational rehabilitation may have special employment programs for persons with serious cognitive deficits caused by head injury. Such services may include job coaching and extended or supported employment programs. Cognitive deficits that preclude competitive employment may qualify a person for Social Security Disability Income benefits (see Item 15.11).

SELECTED BIBLIOGRAPHY

Berg, Richard, Michael Franzen, and Danny Wedding. *Screening for Brain Impairment*, 2nd ed. New York: Springer, 1994.

Dell, Arthur, and Paul Power. *Brain Injury and the Family*, 2nd ed. Houston, TX: HDI Publishers, 2000.

Miller, Laurence. *Psychotherapy of the Brain-Injured Patient*. New York: W. W. Norton, 1993.

Senelick, Richard, Peter Rossi, and Karla Dougherty. *Living with Stroke: A Guide for Families*. Chicago: Contemporary Books, 2000.

15.11   THE CLIENT WITH A SERIOUS PHYSICAL DISABILITY

Purpose: To adapt social work techniques and approaches to the client with a serious physical disability.

Discussion: Nearly 20 percent of the people in the United States experience some sort of physical or mental impairment that limits their functioning. For about 8 percent, that impairment affects their ability to secure employment, thus further limiting their ability to fully participate in society. For social workers in many settings, but especially those employed in hospitals and rehabilitaion centers, understanding the impact of a disabling condition is critical to effective practice.

A grasp of certain terminology is important to any discussion of disability. The term **impairment** refers to a long-term or permanent bodily, sensory, or cognitive limitation caused by a disease or injury or by advanced age. If the impairment significantly hampers a person's capacity to perform his or her major social roles and other normal and usual activities (e.g., self-care, moving about, and communicating with others), it is termed a **disability.**

To a considerable extent, the degree to which an impairment becomes a disability depends on the physical and social barriers the person encounters in his or her environment or situation. An example of a *physical barrier* for a person using a wheelchair is a set of stairs. An example of a *social barrier* for the same person is the prejudice or discrimination that keeps him or her from securing a job for which he or she is qualified and for which the ability to walk is not required. Thus, a *disability* is the outcome of an interaction or interplay between the person's impairment and existing physical, social, and attitudinal barriers. The terms **handicap** and **handicapping condition** often are used to describe an impairment or a disability that imposes a very serious limitation on a person's capacity to function physically, socially, or economically in a normal or usual environment.

From this discussion, we can see that eliminating physical and social barriers and using adaptive technology and equipment can go a long way in keeping an impairment from actually becoming a significant disability or handicapping condition. In recent decades, federal laws such as the 1973 Rehabilitation Act, the 1975 Education for All Handicapped Children Act, and the 1990 **Americans with Disabilities Act (ADA)** have greatly benefited persons with disabling conditions. The ADA, which has been described as the "emancipation proclamation for the disabled," provides a national mandate and the legal mechanisms to remove barriers for and eliminate discrimination against persons with disabilities, especially in the areas of employment, access to public services and public transportation, access to goods and services offered by businesses, and access to telecommunications. The ADA is a solid basis for social work advocacy with and in behalf of persons with disabilities.

It is important for the social worker to be familiar with the various programs and services a client with a physical disability might need. The two most significant federal programs are worker's compensation, which provides financial assistance to a person recovering from a work-related injury, and programs under the Social Security Act, including Supplemental Security Income (SSI) and Social Security Disability Insurance (SSDI). In addition, a number of local programs that focus on specific disabling conditions (e.g., cerebral palsy, arthritis, multiple sclerosis, spinal cord injury, blindness) can be found in most communities.

The social worker should remember these useful guidelines when working with persons who are physically disabled:

- Work first with the person and then the disability.
- Use a strengths perspective and look for abilities to offset disabilities.
- Maximize client self-determination.
- Seek to normalize as much of the client's life as possible.
- Empower the client by asking how you might help, rather than assuming he or she needs assistance.
- Be prepared for advocacy.
- Engage the client's family and friends in providing services.
- Above all, treat the client with dignity.

SELECTED BIBLIOGRAPHY

May, Gary, and Martha Raske. *Ending Disability Discrimination: Strategies for Social Workers.* Boston: Allyn & Bacon, 2005.

Oliver, Michael, and Bob Sapey. *Social Work with Disabled People*, 3rd ed. New York: Palgrave Macmillan, 2006.

Rothman, Juliet. *Social Work Practice across Disability.* Boston: Allyn & Bacon, 2003.

15.12   THE CLIENT WHO IS CHEMICALLY DEPENDENT

Purpose: To engage the person who is chemically dependent in ways that will increase the chances that he or she will seek treatment and deal effectively with the addiction.

Discussion: Many of the individuals and families receiving services from social agencies are affected directly or indirectly by alcohol and/or drug dependency. The abuse of chemicals is a contributing factor in many other problems, such as marital discord, parent-child conflict, spouse abuse, child abuse and neglect, suicide, homicide, financial problems, crime, and auto accidents. Substance abuse also contributes to the spread of AIDS due to intravenous injections and indiscriminate sexual behavior related to the disinhibiting effects of drugs and alcohol. The use of alcohol and drugs by a pregnant woman can damage the fetus and result in various birth defects and neurological and developmental problems.

Individuals who are alcohol dependent and/or drug dependent are usually difficult and challenging clients because of the pathological denial, rationalization, and self-delusion that are part of the addiction process. These individuals typically reject offers of professional help and will see an addictions counselor only after being court ordered or coerced into treatment by family or friends. The social worker's response to these clients must be based on an understanding of how alcohol and drugs affect the mind and body and on the realization that it is seldom possible for an individual to break an addiction without great and persistent effort and specialized treatment.

Some professionals find it useful to distinguish between dependency and abuse. *Chemical abuse* or *substance abuse* refers to occasional use that has negative consequences for the individual, but perhaps in only one area of functioning (e.g., occasional missed work, an arrest for drunk driving). By contrast, *chemical dependency* refers to a pattern of frequent and possibly compulsive use that is often accompanied by the existence of tolerance and symptoms of withdrawal and has a negative impact on several areas of functioning (e.g., family, job, health, finances, etc.).

Many of the abused chemicals alter the body's neurochemistry and physiology resulting in the development of *tolerance* (i.e., an ever increasing amount of the chemical is required to bring on the desired mood-altering effect) and symptoms of *withdrawal* (i.e., the individual becomes anxious, panicky, or physically ill when unable to take in the chemical). An individual may engage in reckless and extreme behaviors (e.g., stealing, violence, deceit) in order to escape distressing withdrawal symptoms.

Patterns of dependency and addiction are rooted in a learning process. Each time a mood-altering substance provides the user with a desired effect (e.g., relaxation, self-confidence, euphoria) usage is thereby rewarded or reinforced, thus increasing the likelihood that the substance will be used again and again. Individuals who suffer from a mood disorder (e.g., depression, bipolar disorder, anxiety) are particularly vulnerable to developing a dependency. Individuals with low self-esteem, feelings of powerlessness, loneliness, and other types of emotional pain are also drawn to the mood changing and numbing effects of certain chemicals.

An individual with an alcohol or drug problem (e.g. chemical dependency) will typically exhibit several of the following behaviors and patterns:

- Continues to use the chemical or substance even though its use is causing personal, family, health, and work-related problems
- Displays an increased tolerance to the chemical
- Experiences symptoms of withdrawal and often uses the chemical to relieve or avoid the onset of those symptoms
- Uses more of the chemical, uses it more often, and uses it over longer periods than intended or planned and as a result is often late for or misses work-related appointments and family events
- Abandons previously important activities and relationships in favor of drinking and/or drug use
- Voices a desire to cut back on use but is unsuccessful in efforts to control use
- Neglects appearance, grooming, and hygiene

- Experiences a decrease in physical and intellectual capacities, such as physical stamina and ability to concentrate and think logically
- Participates in reckless and/or illegal activities in order to obtain the chemical

It is important to note that the information presented here is of a basic and general nature. The reader should consult the DSM for more precise criteria used in diagnosis and identifying the existence of tolerance and withdrawal. (See Item 11.18).

Generally speaking, the chemicals or substances most sought after are those with a rapid onset of effects. Onset of effect is related to chemical properties, dose, method of intake, and the users personality characteristics. The psychosocial setting of its use also influences a person's response to a chemical.

There are local and regional differences in the popularity of various substances and preferred methods of intake. There are continual changes in the street lingo applied to illegal substances and new chemical combinations appear frequently. Presented below are brief descriptions of the legal and illegal chemicals and substances that are most often abused and that give rise to dependency problems.

Nicotine

The nicotine found in tobacco is highly addictive. Because this stimulant is so widely used and is a contributing cause in cancer and heart and lung disease, nicotine may cause more illness and death than all of the illegal street drugs combined. Tobacco is usually smoked but is also chewed or placed next to the gums in the form of "snuff."

The cessation of smoking brings on a physical withdrawal syndrome and a craving that is particularly uncomfortable and drawn out. These effects can be alleviated almost immediately, however, by a return to the use of nicotine. This makes quitting exceedingly difficult.

Alcohol

If one considers the number of individuals and families affected, the number of injuries and deaths caused by drunken driving, and the number of health problems either caused or exacerbated by drinking, the abuse of alcohol (a legal drug) is the number one drug problem in the United States. Because alcohol depresses the central nervous system (CNS), it can be very dangerous when used with other drugs or medications that also depress the CNS.

The American Medical Association, the National Council on Alcoholism, and the American Society of Addiction Medicine all view alcohol dependence as a chronic disease that is often progressive and fatal. Genetic, psychosocial, and cultural factors influence the development and manifestations of this disease. The individual who will eventually develop a dependency can often consume a great deal of alcohol without showing the effects; this phenomenon may be genetic in origin.

There is no cure for this disease; at best, it can be controlled through complete abstinence from alcohol. Treatment experts generally agree that once addicted, the individual can never again become only a casual user of alcohol (i.e., a social drinker). If the alcohol-dependent person tries to drink in moderation, he or she will soon resume a pattern of uncontrolled problem drinking. There is some research to support a so-called harm reduction model of treatment, but the vast majority of experts continue to endorse abstinence as the only sure way to maintain control over alcohol addiction.

In its early stage, alcohol dependence is difficult to recognize because the symptoms are subtle. Moreover, the dependent person's drinking pattern may be almost indistinguishable from that of a person who drinks too much only occasionally. However, one may observe that the dependent person drinks a greater amount and more often than others and that drinking plays a part in most of his or her activities. Yet during this early stage, the consumption of alcohol may not significantly interfere with job or family functioning.

In the middle stage, the alcohol-dependent person becomes physically addicted. When his or her blood-alcohol level is lowered, he or she will experience withdrawal symptoms, including anxiety, agitation, tremors, and sweating as well as fluctuations in blood pressure and blood-sugar levels. Increasingly, the individual will have trouble remembering what occurred while drinking, a phenomenon called a *blackout*. He or she will drink more, more often, and for longer periods than intended, and as a result, he or she will be late for or miss work-related appointments and family events. Family and job functioning also will be adversely affected at this point, and family and friends will commonly ask the individual to cut back. The individual may quit drinking for a few weeks at a time but will eventually start again. Experiencing these short periods of abstinence will convince the dependent person that it is possible to quit whenever he or she really wants to and that drinking is not a problem. Concerned family members may reach out for professional help, but typically, the alcohol-dependent person will deny there is a problem.

In the late stage, the seriousness of the problem is apparent to everyone but the alcoholic, for paradoxically, the more serious the addiction becomes, the less he or she will be aware of what is happening. By this point in the addiction process, the individual may have lost his or her family and job and may have alcohol-related health problems. However, the denial and self-delusion will continue, and only experiencing a major personal or health crisis will temporarily shake him or her into reality.

The progression of alcohol dependency may be somewhat different for different individuals. For example, an adolescent who engages in heavy drinking may develop a dependency after only 6 or 18 months of drinking. Other individuals may drink for 15 or 20 years before the onset of dependency.

Amphetamines

There are several forms of amphetamines. All are CNS stimulants. Some (e.g., Dexedrine and Benzedrine) are prescription medications prescribed in the treatment of narcolepsy, brain dysfunction, and obesity. When laws were put in place to control the abuse and illegal distribution of these medications, related forms (i.e., the methamphetamines) were produced illegally and are now widely abused because of their strength, low cost, and the ease with which they can be manufactured in simple laboratories. Among the chemicals used in making methamphetamine are cold remedies that contain Ephedrine, acetone, ether, sulfuric acid, rubbing alcohol, brake cleaner, rock salt, farm fertilizer, iodine, red phosphorus from matches or road flares, and lithium.

Many of these chemicals are extremely toxic and flammable. Dangerous "meth labs" have been found in basements, bathrooms, kitchens, garages, and hotel rooms. People have died or have become ill from exposure to these labs.

Among the forms of methamphetamine are methamphetamine sulfate (i.e., "crank"), methamphetamine hydrochloride (i.e., "crystal meth"), and dextromethamphetamine (i.e., "ice"). These highly addictive chemicals produce feelings of self-confidence and an intense and long-lasting euphoria. Depending on their form, they may be snorted, swallowed, smoked, or injected.

The abuse of these stimulants is indicated by hyperactivity, nervousness and anxiety, dilated pupils, irritability, and going for long periods without sleep or food. Some users experience a dry mouth, sweating, headache, blurred vision, dizziness, and sleeplessness. High doses can cause dangerously rapid or irregular heartbeat, tremors, loss of coordination, and physical collapse. Long-time and heavy use can lead to malnutrition, skin disorders, ulcers, weight loss, kidney damage, dental decay, depression, and speech and thought disturbances. A methamphetamine injection causes a sudden increase in blood pressure that can precipitate a stroke or heart failure.

Heavy use can result in a psychosis involving hallucinations (seeing, hearing, and feeling things that do not exist), delusions (having irrational thoughts or beliefs), and paranoia (feeling as though people are out to harm him or her). In such a state, the person may exhibit bizarre and sometimes violent behavior. Methamphetamine use is a major factor in some cases of child abuse, domestic abuse, and other forms of violence. Withdrawal from this drug (often referred to as "crashing") is uncomfortable and often characterized by fatigue, nightmares, insomnia, depression, and a wildly fluctuating appetite.

Cocaine

Cocaine, like the amphetamines, is a CNS stimulant. Derived from the coca plant native to the high mountain regions of South America, cocaine is smuggled into a country as a fine, white, crystalline powder (cocaine hydrochloride). This powder is then diluted, or "cut," to increase its bulk and stretch the supply for sale.

The most common method of administration is intranasal, or "snorting" the diluted powder. When snorted, the euphoric effects begin within a few minutes, peak within 15 to 20 minutes, and disappear within about 45 minutes. During this brief period, the user often feels confident, energetic, talkative, and omnipotent.

Chemical procedures can be used to separate or free the pure cocaine from the other usual additives in powdered cocaine. This results in "freebase" that can be smoked—a more direct and rapid way to transmit the chemical to the brain. Smokeable "crack" or "rock cocaine" is particularly potent and highly addictive.

The smoking of "crack" produces a short but very intense "high." Whereas the users of powdered cocaine may develop their addiction over many months or even years, "crack" smokers can become addicted in a matter of days.

Since freebase cocaine is water soluble, it can also be injected. This is the most dangerous method of administration. Because it produces an immediate and intense euphoria, intravenous use is highly addictive.

Regular users of cocaine often report feelings of restlessness, irritability, anxiety, and sleeplessness. Cocaine causes physical and mental damage similar to that caused by the amphetamines. High doses over a long period may precipitate a "cocaine psychosis" with hallucinations of touch, sight, taste, or smell. Because cocaine stimulates the body and its nervous system, it is not uncommon to experience a physical "crash" and a mental depression following a period of use. These depressions and mood swings can be debilitating and last from a few hours to several weeks. The uncomfortable psychological and physiological effects of withdrawal are a constant source of anxiety for cocaine abusers.

Marijuana

Marijuana is the common name for a tobacco-like dried leafy substance made from the plant *cannabis sativa*. The main psychoactive ingredient in marijuana is THC (delta-9-tetrahydrocannabinol). The amount of THC in the marijuana determines how strong its effects will be on the user. Hashish, or hash, is made by taking the resin from the leaves and flowers of the plant and pressing it into cakes; it contains more THC than crude marijuana. Marijuana and hash are usually smoked but sometimes taken orally.

Research and the clinical experience of drug treatment programs identify several adverse effects. Some individuals become psychologically addicted, and heavy users may develop *amotivational syndrome*, such that they generally lose interest in life's major activities and feel increasingly passive and sluggish. Marijuana addicts do not experience the physiological withdrawal syndrome that commonly follows use of so-called hard drugs, but it is not uncommon for these individuals to report a psychological withdrawal that includes intense feelings of craving.

An individual "high" on marijuana or hashish will feel euphoric and may speak rapidly and loudly and have dilated pupils. Some individuals experience sensory distortions. The drug can impair short-term memory, alter sense of time, and reduce the ability to do things that require concentration and quick reactions such as in driving a car. A possible response to marijuana use is an acute panic reaction.

Because many people view marijuana as relatively harmless, it is the most politically controversial of all illegal substances. Some groups advocate for the legalized use of marijuana as a regulated medicine because it holds promise as a treatment for glaucoma and for the side effects of chemotherapy.

PCP

PCP (phencyclidine) was developed as an anesthetic but later taken off the market for human use because it sometimes caused hallucinations. It continues to have use in veterinary medicine. PCP is easily manufactured and is available in a number of forms (i.e., white crystal-like powder, tablet, or capsule). It can be swallowed, smoked, sniffed, or injected. PCP powder, sometimes referred to as "angel dust" or "dust," is sprinkled on marijuana and smoked.

The sought-after effect is euphoria. For some users, small amounts act as a stimulant. For many, PCP changes how they perceive their own bodies and things around them; movements and time are slowed. The effects of PCP are unpredictable, and for this reason many "experimenters" abandon its use. Others, unfortunately, become dependent. Negative effects include increased heart rate and blood pressure, flushing, sweating, dizziness, and numbness. When large doses are taken, effects include drowsiness, convulsions, coma, and sometimes death. PCP can produce violent or bizarre behavior. Regular use affects memory, perception, concentration, and judgment. Users may show signs of paranoia, fearfulness, and anxiety. When under the drug's influence, some become aggressive; others withdraw and have difficulty communicating. A PCP-induced psychosis may last for days or weeks.

Hallucinogens

Hallucinogens, or psychedelics, are drugs that affect a person's perceptions, sensations, thinking, self-awareness, and emotions. This category includes such drugs as LSD, mescaline, and psilocybin. *LSD* is manufactured from lysergic acid, which is found in a fungus that grows on grains. LSD is sold on the street in tablets, capsules, or occasionally in liquid form. It is usually taken by mouth. *Mescaline* comes from the peyote cactus and, although it is not as strong as LSD, its effects are similar. Mescaline is usually smoked or swallowed in the form of capsules or tablets. *Psilocybin* comes from certain mushrooms. It is sold in tablet or capsule form or the mushrooms themselves may be eaten.

The effects of psychedelics are unpredictable and depend on dosage as well as the user's personality, mood, expectations, and the surroundings. The person's sense of time and self change. Several different emotions may be felt at once or swing rapidly from one to another. Sensations become mixed and seem to "cross over," giving the user the feeling of hearing colors and seeing sounds. For some, these strange sensations are frightening and cause a "bad trip" that may last a few minutes or several hours and involve confusion, suspiciousness, anxiety, feelings of helplessness, and loss of control. Physical effects include dilated pupils, higher body temperature, increased heart rate and blood pressure, and often sweating, irregular breathing, and tremors. Some users sit in a stupor, whereas others become agitated.

In recent years, a manufactured hallucinogenic known as *MDMA*, or "Ecstasy," has become popular in the United States and Europe. It is usually taken by capsule or tablet. Its use brings on mild distortions of perceptions, has a calming effect, and, for many, creates a feeling of empathy with others. It does not cause the visual illusions often associated with the psychedelics. Physical dependency is not a major problem, but psychological dependence does develop in many users. Growing evidence indicates that frequent and heavy use of MDMA causes damage to the brain.

The use of hallucinogens can unmask underlying mental or emotional problems. Also, some users experience *flashbacks*, which are intense and intrusive memories and emotions that can occur days and even weeks after having taken the drug. Heavy users sometimes develop impaired memory, loss of attention span, confusion, and difficulty with abstract thinking.

Sedative Hypnotics

Sedative hypnotics are prescription drugs often referred to as sleeping pills, sedatives, and tranquilizers (antianxiety medications). Two major categories are the barbiturates and the benzodiazepines, which include Xanex, Valium, Librium, Ambien, and Ativan.

These manufactured pharmaceutical drugs are usually obtained with a prescription from a physician, but prescriptions are commonly altered or forged by addicts. These pills are sometimes stolen and sold on the street, as well. Because they depress the central nervous system, they have a calming effect and promote sleep. An individual who has taken a higher than prescribed dosage may give the appearance of being drunk (e.g., staggering, slurred speech, sleepiness, etc.) but not smell of alcohol. When taken with alcohol (also a depressant), these drugs can cause unconsciousness and death.

The sedative-hypnotic drugs can cause both physical and psychological dependence. When regular users suddenly stop, they may develop withdrawal symptoms, ranging from restlessness, insomnia, and anxiety to convulsions and death. Barbiturate overdose is a factor in many drug-related deaths; these include suicides and accidental poisonings.

Inhalants

Inhalants are chemicals that produce semitoxic vapors. The vapors are concentrated and then inhaled in a practice sometimes called *huffing*. The inhalants are grouped into four classes: (1) volatile solvents (e.g., certain glues, gasoline, paint thinner, nail polish remover, lighter fluid); (2) aerosols (e.g., spray paints); (3) anesthetics (e.g., ether, chloroform, nitrous oxide); and (4) amyl and butyl nitrates. Nearly all of the abused inhalants act to depress the body's functions. At low doses, users may feel slightly stimulated and some, like butyl nitrite, produce a "rush" or "high" lasting for a few seconds or a couple of minutes. Young people are likely to abuse inhalants, in part because these chemicals are readily available and inexpensive.

Possible negative effects include nausea, sneezing, coughing, nosebleeds, fatigue, bad breath, lack of coordination, and a loss of appetite. Solvents and aerosols decrease the heart and breathing rates and affect judgment. Deep breathing of the vapors may result in a loss of self-control, violent behavior, and unconsciousness. Inhalants can cause death from suffocation by displacing oxygen in the lungs and by depressing the central nervous system to a point that breathing stops. Moderate to long-term use can damage the brain, liver, kidneys, blood, and bone marrow.

Opiates

Opiates (narcotics) are a group of drugs used medically to relieve pain, but they also have a high potential for abuse. Some opiates (opium, morphine, heroin, and codeine) come from the Asian poppy. Others, such as meperidine (Demerol), are manufactured. Heroin accounts for most of the opiate abuse in the United States.

Opiates are ingested, snorted, smoked, or injected intravenously. After causing an initial rush, they tend to relax the user. Indicators of opiate abuse include needle scars on the arms and the backs of hands, drowsiness, frequent scratching, red and watering eyes, sniffles, and a loss of appetite overall but an attraction to sugar and candies. In contrast to the effects of most other abused drugs that dilate the eye's pupils, the opiates constrict the pupils. When an opiate-dependent person stops taking the drug, withdrawal symptoms begin within 4 to 6 hours; symptoms include anxiety, diarrhea, abdominal cramps, chills, sweating, nausea, and runny nose and eyes. The intensity of these symptoms depends on how much was taken, how often, and for how long. Withdrawal symptoms for most opiates are stronger approximately 24 to 72 hours after they begin but subside within 7 to 10 days.

Most of the physical dangers of opiate abuse are caused by overdose, the use of unsterile needles, contamination of the drug by other chemicals, or combining the drug with other substances. Over time, opiate users may develop infections of the heart, skin abscesses, and congested lungs.

Pain Medication

Addiction to prescription pain medication is perhaps the fastest-growing addiction problem in the United States. These addictive compounds include Darvon, Darocette, Percodan, Percocette, Demerol, Vicodin, Hydrocodone, and Oxycodone. Many individuals get caught up in dependency and illegal use after first taking one of these drugs as a prescribed and legitimate medical treatment. Once dependent, the individual goes through withdrawal symptoms that are similar to those associated with withdrawal from an opiate. Being addicted to pain medication may give rise to reckless and criminal behavior, as the individual desperately attempts to secure the drug. Prescription forgeries and pharmacy and hospital robberies are both associated with the abuse of these addictive pain medications.

Guidelines for Dealing with a Chemically Dependent Client

Throughout their relationships and interventions with a chemically dependent client and his or her family, social workers should carefully consider the following guidelines:

1. Because the abuse of and dependence on alcohol and other drugs is so pervasive in society, the social worker should be alert to the possible existence of such a problem even when neither the client nor the client's family has mentioned it. In all individual and family assessments, some questions should be asked about the current use of alcohol and drugs. However, it must be recognized that chemically dependent persons are seldom willing or able to accurately describe the frequency or quantity of their use. Typically, they are adamant in denying any connection between their personal problems and their use of alcohol or drugs.

2. Never underestimate the psychological power of alcohol and drugs. In order to appreciate its effects on people, it is helpful to view a dependency or addiction as a pathological relationship with a mood-altering substance. The dynamics of this relationship resemble those of a neurotic love affair, but in this case, the love object is a chemical. A chemical dependency or addiction can turn a kind and honest person into a self-centered individual who may lie, cheat, and even injure loved ones in order to obtain and use a chemical.

3. When, in the course of your professional activity and/or when within your agency setting, you encounter an intoxicated individual you must be alert to the potentially life-threatening danger of delirium tremors or a drug overdose and to matters of personal safety. A consideration of legal and ethical duties would suggest that a professional person must make a reasonable effort to prevent a foreseeable injury, death, or tragic occurrence. For example, if you know that this intoxicated person intends to drive a car, you have a duty to attempt to prevent that from happening and if necessary, to notify law enforcement in order to prevent an auto accident.

4. If your client is intoxicated when he or she arrives for a scheduled interview or meeting, explain in a polite but firm manner that you need accurate information and his or her full attention to do your work so you must reschedule the session for a time when he or she is sober. The client may argue and become angry but remain calm and hold firm to your decision.

5. Do not allow yourself to become part of an enabling system. For example, do not lend the client money and do not write letters or make phone calls that provide excuses or "cover" for the client and protect him or her from the real-life consequences of chemical abuse.

6. Learn the basic principles and techniques of *motivational interviewing*, an approach being used increasingly with substance-abusing clients. It has the effect of decreasing these clients' resistance and increasing their motivation to change (i.e., to enter treatment and continue efforts toward recovery). This approach rests on the observation that clients tend to be more committed to a plan (e.g., treatment, sobriety) when they perceive it to be one of their own choosing and one that will addresses their personal concerns. Also, clients tend to become even more resistant when a professional insists that they have a "problem" and that they must accept the label of being an "alcoholic" or "drug addict." The underlying strategy of motivational interviewing is to engage the client in a discussion of his or her current situation in a way that will create a dissonance or a perceived discrepancy between his or her drinking or drug use and what he or she considers to be important (e.g., self-esteem, health, success on the job, being a good parent, etc.). This approach strives to help clients verbalize what they really want and then conclude for themselves that their drinking or drug use is a barrier to reaching their own important goals.

7. Learn about the behavioral pattern of *codependency* that develops as a result of living for many years with someone who is chemically dependent. Typically, the codependent assumes responsibility for the behavior of others (e.g., the alcoholic) while neglecting his or her own needs. They are often hostile because of how they have been treated by someone they love, controlling because their situation is so out of control, manipulative because manipulation seems to be the only way to get things done, and indirect and vague in their communication because they live in a family system that cannot tolerate honesty.

8. Because a person who is chemically dependent is seldom able to stop using without the help of a treatment program, a referral for treatment likely will be necessary. However, before attempting a referral, it is best to consult with a treatment specialist on how to approach the client on this matter and how you might handle his or her probable resistance to the idea of securing treatment.

The available options for securing treatment will need to be examined and structured within the client's health insurance program (e.g., HMO, managed care) or applicable tax-supported programs. In some cases, inpatient medical care will be needed to manage physiological withdrawal (detoxification). After undergoing medically supervised detoxification, if needed, the individual will enter a treatment program that will take one of several forms (e.g., inpatient, outpatient, day treatment). Ongoing weekly or twice-weekly outpatient counseling sessions (both individual and group) may continue for six months to one year or longer.

Most recovering addicts will likely be involved in a *12-step program* (e.g., Alcoholics Anonymous, Cocaine Anonymous, Narcotics Anonymous), which provides encouragement and teaches methods of day-to-day coping. These self-help programs emphasize the development of spirituality and help the individual develop a life-style free of alcohol and drugs.

9. The assistance and support of the client's family and friends will probably be needed in making a referral to a treatment program. Thus, it may be necessary to reach out to these individuals and engage them in the assessment, planning, and helping process. However, be alert to the possibility that they too may have a substance abuse problem and/or may be contributing to your client's problem through denial, enabling, or codependency behaviors.

10. Learn about 12-step recovery programs by attending open meetings. Members are usually eager to consult with professionals who want to learn about the effects of addiction, the nature of the recovery process, and effective ways of dealing with the challenges presented by clients who are chemically dependent.

11. Encourage family members to make use of Al-Anon and Alateen groups, along with other resources such as COA (Children of Alcoholics), ACOA or ACA (Adult Children of Alcoholics), and programs that address the problem of codependency.

12. Once the individual stops using chemicals, special attention must be given to planning for relapse prevention. This involves helping the individual develop a plan for coping with those times and situations when he or she will be at highest risk of resuming the use of alcohol and drugs. Also, it is important to remember that once an individual has been addicted to one type of chemical, he or she will be vulnerable to become addicted to another type. Help the recovering addict be vigilant with regard to use of both prescription and over-the-counter medications. Recovering addicts should inform their physicians of their prior problems with the abuse of chemicals.

SELECTED BIBLIOGRAPHY

Doweiko, Harold. *Concepts of Chemical Dependency*, 6th ed. Belmont, CA: Brooks/Cole, 2006.

McNeece, C. Aaron, and Diana DiNitto. *Chemical Dependency*, 3rd ed. Boston: Allyn & Bacon, 2005.

Miller, William, and Stephen Rollnick. *Motivational Interviewing*, 2nd ed. New York: Guilford, 2002.

Smith, Jane, and Robert Meyers. *Motivating Substance Abusers to Enter Treatment*. New York: Guilford, 2004.

Straussner, Shulamith, ed. *Clinical Work with Substance Abusing Clients*, 2nd ed. New York: Guilford, 2004.

Thombs, Dennis. *Introduction to Addictive Behaviors*, 2nd ed. New York: Guilford, 2006.

15.13   THE CLIENT WITH SERIOUS MENTAL ILLNESS

Purpose: To adapt social work techniques and approaches to the special needs of a client with serious mental illness.

Discussion: There are three major categories of serious mental illness: schizophrenia, bipolar disorder, and major depression. All three are diseases of the brain caused primarily by biochemical and structural changes in the brain tissue. Each may be episodic and vary in intensity and the degree to which it impairs a person's functioning. Some of those who experience these illnesses may lose touch with reality (i.e., become psychotic), whereas others may have trouble with memory, judgment, or feelings of low self-worth.

Schizophrenia is a baffling and debilitating illness. About 1 percent of the population is afflicted with this disturbance of the thinking processes. The usual age of onset is between 15 and 25 years old, when the frontal lobes of the brain are rapidly maturing. Many experts believe that a stressful environment, infections, and other physiological conditions may trigger the onset of this illness in those predisposed by heredity.

An individual with schizophrenia will exhibit several of these symptoms:

- *Delusions* (e.g., has false beliefs that have no factual basis)
- *Hallucinations* (hearing voices is the most common hallucination; visual hallucination [seeing nonexistent things] is relatively rare but is more likely if the individual is also abusing illegal drugs or psychiatric medications; olfactory and tactile hallucinations are less common but possible)
- *Disordered thinking* (e.g., making loose or illogical connections between thoughts; shifting rapidly from one topic to another; reaching conclusions that are unrelated to facts or logic; making up words or using sounds or rhythms that have no meaning to others)
- *Blunted or inappropriate affect* (e.g., narrow range of emotional reactions; the emotions or feelings do not fit the situation; speaks in monotone)
- *Extreme withdrawal* (e.g., withdrawal from ordinary life experiences and social interaction; deterioration in work or school performance; apathy in regard to appearance and self-care)

About one-fourth of those who have a schizophrenic episode get well and never have another episode. Some have occasional relapses. Between 20 to 30 percent develop symptoms that are persistent throughout life.

The other two types of serious mental illness—major depression and bipolar disorder—are known as *mood disorders* or *affective disorders*. Individuals with a **major depression** experience persistent feelings of sadness and melancholy. They often become tearful, irritable, or hostile for no apparent reason. Other symptoms common to depression include the following:

- Poor appetite and weight loss or increased appetite and weight gain
- Change in sleep pattern (sleeping too little or too much)

- Excessive fatigue; loss of energy
- Change in activity level (either increased or decreased)
- Loss of interest in being with others
- Loss of interest or pleasure in usual activities
- Decreased sexual drive
- Diminished ability to think, concentrate, or make decisions
- Anxiety and rumination over problems
- Feelings of worthlessness or excessive guilt that may reach delusional proportions
- Recurrent thoughts of death or self-harm; wishing to be dead or contemplating or attempting suicide

About 1 percent of the population suffer from ***bipolar disorder***, which is characterized by swings between periods of depression and mania (a hyperactive state). Mania is often characterized by these qualities:

- An exaggerated or irritable mood
- Decreased need for sleep
- Inflated self-confidence and grandiose ideas
- Increased energy and activity
- Overoptimism, poor judgment, quick and impulsive decision making
- Unusually high levels of involvement in work, pleasurable activities, and sexuality
- Rapid and pressured speech and racing thoughts
- Distractibility

Most often, the depressive phase follows the manic phase. Sometimes, the two phases are separated by periods of near normal functioning. These episodes may come and go and last from several days to several months. Without treatment, there is usually an increase in the severity of the symptoms and the frequency of the episodes.

Some individuals experience the bipolar disorder with only the depressive or manic symptoms rather than both. These are termed *bipolar disorder, depressive type* and *bipolar disorder, manic type*. Often, a person's mental health history will predict how the bipolar disorder will manifest itself in the future. For example, a person who historically experiences depression in the autumn may continue to experience more severe symptoms during these months of the year. There is evidence that this disorder has a basis in heredity.

When working with a client with serious mental illness, the social worker should follow these guidelines:

1. These illnesses, especially the mood disorders, can usually be treated effectively with proper medications. Thus, an individual with a serious mental illness should be under the care of a physician, preferably a psychiatrist, who can prescribe medications and monitor their effects. A combination of medication and other forms of mental health care, such as psychotherapy and supportive services, is the preferred treatment for most persons with a serious mental illness. (See Item 15.14 on psychotropic medication.)

2. Because depression gives rise to intense emotional pain and feelings of hopelessness, the risk of suicide must always be considered. (See Item 15.8 on suicide risk.) Of those with schizophrenia, about one in four attempts suicide and about one in ten dies of suicide. Thoughts of suicide or self-mutilation by someone suffering from schizophrenia place him or her at extremely high risk.

3. Delusions are a common symptom in schizophrenia. By definition, a ***delusion*** is a set of ideas and beliefs that remain fixed, even in the face of clear evidence to the contrary. Be very cautious about how you respond to a person's delusions. Remember that a delusion serves a purpose; it helps the individual cope with or make sense out of some mental or perceptual confusion. The person believes in the delusions because they seem true and provide an explanation. Listen carefully to the delusion and try to understand the assumptions on which it is built, but do not judge, criticize, or argue or use logic in an effort to eliminate this symptom. Do not challenge or confront the delusional thoughts, for that will probably destroy the relationship you have with the individual and cause him or her to feel angry and misunderstood. Also, confronting a delusion increases the risk that you will become part of the delusional system of thought and perhaps defined as an enemy or part of a plot or conspiracy.

4. A very small percentage of persons who become psychotic will experience *command hallucinations,* which are voices that tell these people to hurt themselves or others (e.g., a voice telling them to jump off a bridge or kill the mayor). These command hallucinations, although rare, are very dangerous. If this symptom cannot be controlled by medication, the individual should be hospitalized.

5. The individual with persistent and serious mental illness is usually in need of services that will assist him or her with the everyday tasks of living. Such services include case management, counseling, case advocacy, budgeting, and assistance in securing income, a job, housing, transportation, medical care, and the like. The *clubhouse model*—which provides peer support, acceptance, meaningful work and activity, and other services—is especially helpful and important to persons with a persistent mental illness.

6. A family member's mental illness has a profound impact on others in the family. The social worker should address the concerns of the family by doing the following:

- Help family members grieve the loss of their loved one who, because of mental illness, may now seem like a stranger.
- Provide practical information about mental illness. Ask about their possible fear of physical assault and worry over irresponsible financial decisions by the family member who is mentally ill.
- Encourage family members to join a self-help or support group such as the National Alliance for the Mentally Ill.
- Remain accessible to the families, especially during family crises that can be precipitated by relapses.
- Help the parents and siblings recognize their rights to a life apart from the anguish and worry they feel toward the family member who is mentally ill.

- Assist family members to secure services such as case management and respite care to relieve them of the daily responsibility of care giving and provide opportunities for rest and renewal.
- Inform family members of legal issues and rights related to securing and refusing treatment.

7. It should be noted that the treatment and management of a mental illness can be further complicated by the presence of another serious problem such as substance abuse, a personality disorder, or a developmental disability. The term ***dual diagnosis*** is applied to such a situation. A *personality disorder* is a deeply ingrained, inflexible, lifelong, and maladaptive pattern of emotional responses and behaviors that are often harmful or distressful to others. However, individuals with a personality disorder seldom see anything unusual about their own behavior and typically blame others for whatever difficulties they encounter in life. Because they do not feel inner pain or anxiety, they do not usually seek treatment voluntarily. There are several types of personality disorders. They are not brain disorders and appear to develop in response to family and social influences.

SELECTED BIBLIOGRAPHY

Austrian, Sonia. *Mental Disorders, Medications, and Clinical Social Work,* 2nd ed. New York: Columbia University Press, 2000.

Gray, Susan, and Marilyn Zide. *Psychopathology: A Competency-Based Treatment Model for Social Workers.* Belmont, CA: Brooks/Cole, 2006.

Hicks, James. *50 Signs of Mental Illness.* New Haven: Yale University Press, 2005.

Mueser, Kim, and Susan Gingerich. *The Complete Family Guide to Schizophrenia.* New York: Guilford, 2006.

15.14 THE CLIENT ON PSYCHOTROPIC MEDICATION

Purpose: To provide appropriate guidance to the client taking psychotropic medication.

Discussion: The social worker will encounter many clients who take or are in need of medication to control psychiatric symptoms. These medications fall into discrete groups, each of which alleviates a particular set of symptoms. The major groups are antipsychotic, antidepressant, antianxiety, antimanic, psychomotor stimulants, and sedative-hypnotics. Each medication has a chemical name, a generic or general name, and a registered trade or brand name. Each has a specific target symptom, contraindications, and potential side effects. The selection of a medication is based on the patient's medical history, physical exam, laboratory tests, use of other medications, use and abuse of alcohol or street drugs, and, of course, the disorder being treated.

Different types and groups of medications have different side effects. Among the side effects associated with certain psychotropic medications are dry mouth; weight gain; drowsiness; oversensitivity to the sun; menstrual cycle disturbance; spasms of eye, face, neck, and back muscles; blurred vision; shuffling gait; and tremors. Children and the elderly are particularly prone to experience side effects. A psychotropic medication may exacerbate nonpsychiatric medical problems such as hypertension, liver disease, epilepsy, and glaucoma. Despite these side effects, it must be remembered that symptom control is of critical importance to persons suffering from a major mental illness. There is a benefit-risk balance with all medications. In general, a physician will reduce side effects by prescribing the lowest dosage that produces the desired effects, discontinuing a problematic medication and trying another, avoiding the simultaneous use of two medications that have a similar effect, and, whenever possible, treating only one symptom at a time.

When an individual is hospitalized and/or experiencing disabling symptoms, he or she may be started on a quick-acting medication or given a fairly large dose. Most will not need to take the same dosage after leaving the hospital or after the symptoms subside, and a physician may reduce the dosage or switch to a medication that is slower acting but has other advantages. A physician will usually reduce the dosage to the minimum effective level. Such a reduction is best done gradually—a process that may take weeks or months. Even when on a maintenance dose, some people find that their symptoms worsen from time to time. This may be due to stress, biochemical changes, or other factors.

Some patients are frightened when a doctor suggests that they take less medication because they fear a return of symptoms. On the other hand, some are reluctant take medication because they fear side effects or because it is perceived as a loss of control or a blow to their self-esteem.

When working with a client who is taking psychotropic medications, keep several guidelines in mind:

1. The decision to prescribe a medication is a complex medical judgment to be made only by a competent physician, preferably a psychiatrist. A social worker must never give medication instructions outside the physician's directions.

2. Encourage your client to maintain regular contact with a medical professional so the effects of the drug can be monitored and dosage can be properly regulated. If you observe what appears to be unusual or unexpected side effects, but your client is unwilling to see a physician, get the name and dosage of the medication and consult with a physician about what might be an appropriate course of action.

3. Make sure your client and his or her family and friends understand the dangers of modifying the prescribed daily dosage and of exchanging medications with others. Also, alert your client to the dangers of using alcohol or street drugs while taking any medication. If your client takes more than one medication, an adverse drug interaction could occur. This happens when the two drugs mixed together have an effect very different from when each is taken alone. Side effects can also occur when the client mixes a psychotropic medication with nonprescription drugs such as a cold medicine. Some foods (e.g., aged cheese) may cause adverse reactions when eaten by a person on certain medications.

4. As in the case of other forms of medical treatment, an adult has a right to refuse psychotropic medications. Exceptions are when a court has declared that the individual is legally incompetent to make that decision and/or when his or her behavior constitutes an imminent threat to self or others. Because the decision to reject a needed medication can have tragic results when symptoms recur, you should do everything possible to inform the patient and his or her family of the possible consequences. In the final analysis, however, the decision of a legally competent adult must be respected.

SELECTED BIBLIOGRAPHY

Bentley, Kia. *The Social Worker and Psychotropic Medication*, 3rd ed. Belmont, CA: Brooks/ Cole, 2006.

Dziegielewski, Sophia, and Nathan Stinson. *Psychopharmacology and Mental Health Practice*, 2nd ed. New York: Springer, 2006.

Ingersoll, R. Elliot, and Carl Rak. *Psychopharmacology for Helping Professionals*. Belmont, CA: Brooks/Cole, 2006.

15.15 THE CLIENT WHO IS GAY, LESBIAN, BISEXUAL, OR TRANSGENDER

Purpose: To address concerns and issues that may arise in the provision of services to persons who are gay, lesbian, bisexual, or transgender.

Discussion: We humans are classified and labeled by our parents and society as either male or female on the basis of physical anatomy and genitalia. However, our sexuality, sexual orientation, and sexual identity are not always so simple and clear-cut. In reality, human sexuality involves a range of orientations and identities. In all practice settings, social workers will encounter clients who are lesbian, gay, bisexual, or transgender (LGBT).

The term *sexual orientation* refers to a person's enduring romantic and sexual attractions. A majority of people are heterosexual; males are attracted to females and females are attracted to males. Possibly 6 to 10 percent of the U.S. population are *homosexual*, a term that describes individuals whose romantic thoughts and feelings of sexual attraction are for persons of the same sex. A person who is *bisexual* is sexually attracted to both males and females. It should be noted that it is difficult to determine with precision the number of people who are homosexual or bisexual because the numbers rely on self-report, and some may not want to reveal their sexual orientation.

The developmental processes that give rise to heterosexuality are not well understood; the same can be said about homosexuality and bisexuality. Researchers are not able to explain why some individuals are sexually attracted to the opposite sex, some to their own sex, and some to both sexes. However, there is growing evidence that one's sexual orientation is rooted in biological processes and, for most individuals, firmly established by adolescence. Thus, it is inaccurate to speak of either homosexuality or heterosexuality as a sexual "preference" or a "choice."

The poorly understood phenomenon of *transgender* is usually described as a matter of gender identity, rather than sexual orientation. Gender is something more subtle and complex than sexual attraction and sexual orientation. It has to do with one's sense of being a male or a female and with the feelings, attitudes, and perceptions related to femininity and masculinity. One's gender is likely formed by a complex interplay of one's genes, physiology, brain function, hormones, and culture. At a fundamental level, persons who are transgender do not feel comfortable or at ease with their physical or "assigned sex." For example, a transgender male may feel that he really "belongs" in or would be more "real" if he had a female body. Transgender individuals may feel awkward or uncomfortable wearing the clothing typically worn by their physical sex, may prefer to take part in activities traditionally associated with the other sex and, in rare instances, may seek out sex reassignment surgery in order to have a body more like the other sex. Transgender people may be heterosexual, homosexual, or bisexual.

In U.S. society and in many others around the world, people who are LGBT are often maligned. The term *homophobia* refers to an irrational fear and hatred of homosexuality and differences in expressions of gender. It can lead to discrimination in employment, housing, health care, social services, and other areas. Sometimes that fear and prejudice foments violence directed against persons who are known to be or suspected of being LGBT.

A fear of rejection, discrimination, and violence, as well as a desire to protect their families from embarrassment and worry, causes some who are LGBT to hide or deny their sexual orientation or gender identity. Needless to say, the inability to acknowledge and be at peace with something so basic as one's sexuality can be a source of emotional turmoil.

The following guidelines will be useful in working with clients who are LGBT:

1. Carefully examine your own attitudes, belief system, and moral standards for signs of possible bias, prejudice, and discrimination toward people who are LGBT. Consider, for example:

- Your beliefs on whether variations in sexual orientation and gender identity are pathological conditions or a normal variation of human sexuality
- Your level of comfort in hearing descriptions of affection and sexual activity within a same sex relationship
- Your beliefs and attitudes regarding the parenting of children by persons who are gay, lesbian, bisexual, or transgender

2. Avoid accepting or using language that implies a stereotypical view of the people identified with this group. For example, phrases such as "the gay lifestyle" or the "lesbian attitude" contradict the social work principle of individualizing the client (see Chapter 5).

3. Do not be afraid to acknowledge your lack of understanding and to face up to your own prejudices. Also, realize that an ignorance of variations in sexual orientation and gender identifications may exist among those in the helping professions, among clients who are straight, and even among some who are LGBT. Work hard to learn about the concerns of persons who are gay, lesbian, bisexual, and transgender. Get to know leaders and professionals within the LGBT community and seek their consultation when unsure about how best to work with clients who are LGBT.

Representatives of the LGBT community should be consulted regarding the design and delivery of health and social services. Such consultations will help make these services more accessible and acceptable to persons who are LGBT. And, of course, the professional staff working in these programs must be alert to how their practices and approaches fit with or accommodate differences of sexual orientation and sexual identity.

4. Realize that it is fairly common for persons who are homosexual, bisexual, or transgender to go through many years of confusion and emotional turmoil before finally recognizing and accepting their true sexual orientation or gender identity. They may deny, suppress, or hide their sexual attractions. They may become sexually active with the opposite sex and even enter into a marriage in order to reassure themselves and family that they are a "normal heterosexual." Such confusion is especially difficult for the adolescent and may lead some to consider suicide.

5. Because many who are LGBT have been hurt by prejudice and discrimination, they may be cautious when seeking services and entering into a helping relationship. Many speak openly about their sexual orientation or gender identity; others do not. When LGBT individuals seek health care, social services, or counseling, their sexual orientation or sexual identity, per se, will seldom be the presenting problem. Thus, as a general rule, it is not necessary for social workers or other helping professionals to ask about or discuss a client's sexuality unless it is clearly related to the client's concern, request, or reason why the professional is speaking with the client. In those practice settings (e.g., public health, counseling) where the professional needs to know about the client's sexuality and sexual activity, a social worker might directly approach the topic by saying something like: "In order for us to provide an individualized and appropriate service, I ask all my clients about their sexual orientation. Would you be comfortable discussing this?"

In all practice settings, a social worker should strive to create a nonthreatening atmosphere that makes it as easy as possible for a client to speak about deeply personal matters. Clients who are LGBT may hide their sexuality until they are sure the social worker is free of demonstrable prejudices. A social worker who is LGBT and who is quite sure his or her client is also may elect to self-disclose in order to lessen the client's fear. Or, a social worker might use some personal stories to reveal that he or she understands the insidious effect of stereotypes and prejudice and thereby demonstrate to the client a capacity for acceptance and understanding.

6. Do not make "coming out" a goal of your work with a client, unless that is what the client has decided to do after a careful examination of the pros and cons. On the surface, coming out may appear personally freeing and politically courageous, but a person choosing this course of action may pay a high price. Do not underestimate the possible negative ramifications of coming out, which may include alienation from one's family or even the loss of housing or a job.

7. When working with a gay or lesbian couple who are in a long-term relationship, expect that their relationship problems will be similar to those of heterosexual couples. For example, their disagreements and conflicts will probably center on matters such as money management, balancing home and work responsibilities, child care, an unsatisfactory sexual relationship, unfaithfulness, domestic abuse, and substance abuse. However, their relationship is more uncertain because it lacks the status and protection that comes with a legal marriage. Consequently, matters such as securing health insurance for one's partner, arranging survivors benefits, inheritance, child custody, hospital visitation rights, and adoption are complex and unpredictable. Help these couples find the resources they need to work out special health care and legal arrangements, such as creating a last will and testament, doing financial planning, naming a beneficiary for life insurance, and preparing a living will and durable power of attorney for health care. Laws providing for same-sex marriages and civil unions, if enacted by state legislatures and if upheld by the courts, will resolve and simplify many of these legal concerns.

8. As a group, gay men have been hard hit by *Acquired Immune Deficiency Syndrome (AIDS)*, a deadly disease caused by a virus known as *Human Immunodeficiency Virus*, or *HIV*. Many gay men have suffered the loss of friends or lovers to the disease, and others live in fear of contracting the disease. Many women and children have also been infected by the virus. The symptoms of AIDS typically do not develop until several years after being infected. HIV is spread primarily by (1) having vaginal, anal, or oral sex with someone who is infected and (2) by sharing needles for injecting drugs with someone who is infected. The use of condoms, other safe sex techniques, and HIV testing can reduce the spread of this disease. The virus can be passed from an infected mother to her baby during pregnancy or childbirth and in rare instances through breastfeeding.

SELECTED BIBLIOGRAPHY

Appleby, George, and Jeane Anastas. "Social Work Practice with Lesbian, Gay, and Bisexual People." In Armando Morales, Bradford Sheafor, and Malcolm Scott. *Social Work: A Profession of Many Faces*, 11th ed. Boston: Allyn & Bacon, 2007, pp. 329–361.

Hunter, Ski, and Jane Hickerson. *Affirmative Practice: Understanding and Working with Lesbian, Gay, Bisexual, and Transgender Persons.* Washington, DC: NASW, 2001.

Morrow, Deana, and Lori Messinger, eds. *Sexual Orientation and Gender Expression in Social Work Practice.* New York: Columbia University, 2006.

Perez, Ruperto, Kurt DeBord, and Kathleen Bieschke, eds. *Handbook of Counseling and Psychotherapy with Lesbian, Gay, and Bisexual Clients.* Washington, DC: American Psychological Association, 2000.

15.16   THE CLIENT WITH AN EATING DISORDER

Purpose: To understand the unique needs of clients with eating disorders (e.g., anorexia, bulimia, and obesity) and identify appropriate intervention techniques.

Discussion: Increasingly, social workers are serving clients with eating disorders. *Eating disorder* is an umbrella term that describes any of several problems linked to a person's relationship to food. The three most prevalent and serious forms of eating disorders are anorexia nervosa, bulimia nervosa, and obesity. At one extreme is the person who self-starves; at the other extreme is the person who eats to excess and becomes obese.

There are many other examples of actual or potentially harmful behaviors related to food and nutrition. For example, it is not uncommon for male athletes to intentionally overeat to gain weight (e.g., offensive linesmen in football) or lose weight (e.g., wrestlers seeking to reach certain weight divisions). Nor is it uncommon for older people to experience food-related problems when, for example, "cooking for one" seems like too much trouble or when one is expected to adapt to the institutional food in a nursing home. Fad diets and misguided fasting that fail to produce a balanced nutritious diet can disturb body chemistry and give rise to health problems.

Anorexia Nervosa

Anorexia nervosa is a condition characterized by intentionally maintaining one's body weight substantially below that expected of a healthy individual (i.e., 15 to 25 percent below recommended weight for a person of that age, height, and gender). This disorder is most commonly found in middle- and upper-class female adolescents, with symptoms typically beginning between ages 12 and 18. The causes of anorexia are not known, but it is often associated with high stress, pressure from one's cultural group, presence of an eating disorder among other members of the person's family, as well as the person's biological predisposition.

Some psychological indicators of anorexia are a distorted perception of one's own body size, weight, and shape; an intense fear of gaining weight; and high self-expectations or perfectionism. Some physical symptoms are excessively low weight, the absence of or irregularity in the menstrual cycle, dry skin, loss of hair, refusal to eat normal amounts of food, and anxiety about eating, with episodes of spontaneous or induced vomiting.

The recommended interventions are first to assist the person to take steps to restore physical health and regain a normal weight and then to implement the necessary interventions to prevent the recurrence of this condition. When a person is literally starving, his or her physical condition must be addressed before the social and psychological factors. Treatment may involve a period of hospitalization and the use of medications. Various drugs may be used in treatment, but the results to date of studies of drug therapy show mixed results.

When intervening with the anorexic (and also the bulimic) person, it is important to be very direct about the person's behaviors and the consequences of those behaviors, as well as to gain the person's trust as a foundation for helping him or her reestablish a sense of self-worth. Specific psychosocial interventions may include individual and family therapy, ongoing supportive treatment of the individual, cognitive therapy, behavior modification techniques, and participation in self-help groups. Recovery from anorexia nervosa requires actions on many fronts, including a team of professionals, family, and other significant people in the client's lives. Eating a sufficient amount of nutritious food is difficult for the anorexic to accomplish without considerable reinforcement from others. It is thought that about one-half of the diagnosed and treated anorexics recover within two to five years. Yet, about

18 percent never recover and, for them, the possibility of death from suicide or conditions resulting from the person's depleted physical condition is quite high.

Bulimia Nervosa

Bulimia nervosa is characterized by a morbid fear of becoming fat. With this disorder, a person usually stays within 10 percent of normal body weight but experiences lack of control over eating behaviors. As opposed to the person with anorexia who avoids food when under stress, the bulimic deals with stress by turning toward food. Periodically (i.e., three times or more a month), the person with this disorder experiences a severe craving for food and he or she binges, followed by induced vomiting, use of laxatives, severe dieting, excessive exercise, or fasting as a means of preventing weight gain. The bulimic cycle can be understood as the fear of becoming overweight leading to self-starvation, with a periodic eating frenzy followed by guilt and efforts to void the weight produced by the food, thus reinforcing the fear of becoming fat—and the cycle continues.

The causes of bulimia are not known, but symptoms usually begin in adolescence or early adulthood. The typical bulimic is thought to be a successful White woman in her mid to late twenties. Because of this stereotype, bulimia is considered a "woman's disease" and men tend to deny or hide the fact that they experience this disorder. Estimates of the number of young women experiencing bulimia are as high as 15 to 20 percent; however, young men, too, experience bulimia at the substantial rate of about 5 to 10 percent. The binge-and-purge cycle can have disastrous effects, causing fatigue, seizures, and muscle cramps as well as having long-term effects on the person's esophagus, teeth, and bone density.

It is often difficult to determine if a client might be experiencing bulimia because there are no obvious physical symptoms such as the loss of weight or emaciation found in persons with anorexia. However, some clues are periodic consumption of large amounts of food, usually eaten alone or secretly; preoccupation with food or one's weight; excessive exercise or fasting; trips to the bathroom following meals; diminished sexual interest (sometimes); and depression or self-loathing due to inability to control bingeing.

As compared to persons who are anorexic, bulimics are more likely to seek and accept treatment, but their strong need for perfection leads to frustration when there are no immediate cures. Some interventions focus on helping them become more accepting of failure to achieve perfection in their lives, improving nutrition, and the use of antidepressant medication to deal with links to depression if suspected. When social workers are involved in cases of bulimia, cognitive-behavioral therapy is most often used to assist in interrupting the pattern of eating restricted foods and bingeing, while also addressing the client's distorted view of foods and his or her body. The client is helped to reveal the problem with family and other significant people in his or her life and to seek their help in maintaining a balanced diet. Finally, group approaches have been successful in helping bulimics self-disclose to reduce guilt, learn to self-monitor their eating behaviors, gain nutrition information, discuss alternatives to the binge-and-purge cycle (e.g., relaxation techniques), and address cultural pressures they experience regarding body weight.

Overeating and Obesity

A great many people struggle to control their weight. Many are aware that they eat too much but are drawn into a pattern of overeating by the pleasure of eating, by their social surroundings, and by advertising. Weight gain occurs when an individual takes in more energy (as measured in calories) than he or she expends in physical activity. About 3,500 excess or unburned calories result in a gain of one pound of body fat.

Weight gain over a long period leads to the condition known as **obesity**. The term *moderate obesity* applies to a person who is 20 to 100 percent above recommended weight for his or her age, gender, and height, whereas a person experiencing *morbid obesity* would exceed the 100 percent level. Obesity is an epidemic in the United States and a growing problem in other developed countries. Those who are excessively overweight are more likely to experience high blood pressure, heart disease, stroke, joint problems, complications of pregnancy, and an early death than the general population.

It appears that a variety of biological, psychological, and social factors are all associated with excessive weight gain and obesity. Psychological factors include overeating as a compensation for boredom, unhappiness, depression, and painful life events. Many of those who gain excessive weight engage in binge eating. Research suggests a connection between the problem of being overweight and one's genetic makeup. Also, the eating patterns common to one's family and culture have an effect on both one's weight and the social acceptance of being overweight. People with low incomes are susceptible to excessive weight gain and obesity because they are likely to purchase inexpensive processed foods that are often high in calories and fat content.

Achieving weight loss requires a significant decrease in daily calorie intake and an increase in physical activity. While many individuals can achieve a weight loss by adhering to a prescribed diet, once they end their diet most will regain the weight in a few years. Maintaining a weight loss is a long-term, ongoing process. Changes in eating patterns are absolutely essential to weight loss and to preventing weight gain.

The goals of a social worker's interventions should include helping clients who are excessively overweight or obese to learn to self-monitor their food intake, create a social environment (e.g., family and friends) that has a positive influence on eating patterns, facilitate involvement in appropriate exercise programs, provide individual and group therapeutic services when warranted, and help the client connect to social groups wherein feelings of isolation and embarrassment can be diminished. Social workers are sometimes in a position to assist with nutrition education and to offer guidance on identifying foods that can achieve a balanced diet at a reasonable cost. Most clients will benefit from learning to apply behavior self-modification techniques designed to change eating habits and reward their commitment to a weight loss plan. Individual counseling or therapy is usually the best approach for those clients who are exceedingly self-conscious and embarrassed by their appearance. Group counseling and support groups are helpful to adults willing to speak about their problems. Group approaches can be especially useful in work with overweight children. It should be noted that, thus far, purely medical or drug interventions have not proven successful in most cases of obesity. The surgeries designed to reduce food intake carry a number of risks and are usually recommended only for persons who are under age 50, morbidly obese, and suffering from an extremely serious health problem caused by the obesity.

SELECTED BIBLIOGRAPHY

Cassell, Danak, and David H. Gleaves. *Encyclopedia of Eating Disorders*, 3rd ed. New York: Facts on File, 2006.

Cooper, Zafra, Christopher Fairburn, and Deborah Hawker. *Cognitive-Behavioral Treatment of Obesity: A Clinician's Guide*. New York: Guilford Press, 2003.

Lask, Bryan, and Rachel Bryant-Waugh, eds. *Eating Disorders in Childhood and Adolescence*. New York: Taylor and Francis, 2007.

Leach, Kathy. *The Overweight Patient: A Psychological Approach to Understanding and Working with Obesity*. Philadelphia: Jessica Kingsley Publishers, 2006.

15.17   THE CLIENT EXPERIENCING GRIEF OR LOSS

Purpose: To understand the needs of clients who are experiencing grief or suffering from the loss of a loved one and to identify appropriate intervention techniques.

Discussion: The experience of grief is as old as humanity. Virtually every social worker will, at some time, deal with a client who is experiencing the pain and turmoil of grief and loss experiences. *Grief* is defined as the intense emotional suffering brought on by the loss of or separation from someone or something that is deeply loved. A sudden and unexpected death is one of the most common precipitators of intense grief. A grief reaction to the death of a loved one, and the mourning of this loss, typically moves through four phases:

1. *Numbness*. The person is shocked, dazed, confused, and overwhelmed. Physical symptoms might include nausea, tightness in the chest and throat, shortness of breath, disturbed sleep, loss of appetite, headaches, and so on. This phase lasts from several days to several weeks.

2. *Yearning*. The person may seek somehow to recover the loved one who has been lost. He or she may become preoccupied and withdrawn and may seem to wander about as if in search of the deceased person; he or she may even report seeing and being with the deceased individual. Intense crying and feelings of anger, guilt, anxiety, and frustration are common.

3. *Despair and disorganization*. As the reality of the loss settles in, the person experiences feelings of helplessness, despair, depression, and extreme fatigue.

4. *Recovery and reorganization*. Over a period of many months, the person gradually resumes his or her usual routines at home and at work. He or she feels less depressed, sleeps better, and has more energy. Various events and recollections may bring on periods of crying and sadness, but these, too, become less frequent and less intense.

Other types of loss may also precipitate grief reactions: for example, experiencing the separation or divorce of one's parents, placing one's child in foster care, delivering a stillborn child, having a planned or spontaneous abortion, voluntarily relinquishing one's parental rights, experiencing a decline in one's physical or mental functioning, retiring or losing a job, receiving a terminal diagnosis, losing a pet, and facing the loss or destruction of one's personal possessions in a robbery, house fire, or natural disaster. Sometimes, one loss triggers others. For example, a divorce may change a family's financial circumstances so that a child not only loses his or her two-parent family but may also have to move to another neighborhood and change schools. These *secondary losses* can be very significant sources of grief. Whatever the cause, the social worker should be alert to the manifestations of grief and know of possible interventions. Experiencing one serious loss after another can have a devastating effect on a person's functioning.

The term ***acute grief*** is often used to describe the reaction that occurs at the time of the loss, such as a parent's immediate reaction to his or her child being killed in an auto accident. Acute grief typically occurs in response to a sudden and unexpected loss. A pattern of grieving known as ***anticipatory grief*** is set in motion by the realization that a serious loss will occur in the near future; the diagnosis of a terminal illness may prompt this sort of grief. The term ***anniversary reaction*** is used to describe a recurrence of grief precipitated by remembering a previous loss, such as the sadness that occurs each year during the month when one's child or spouse died.

In order to grieve successfully, people must work through certain tasks:

- Accepting the reality that the loved person or object is indeed dead, gone, or lost
- Experiencing and resolving the emotions and conflicting thoughts associated with the loss
- Readjusting to life without the loved person or object
- Reinvesting emotional energy in other relationships and the usual activities of life
- Retaining or honoring the memory of the lost person or object

These tasks are overlapping and the individual will revisit each one many times before achieving a satisfactory adjustment.

Expressions of grief are affected by one's relationship to the lost person or object, age or developmental stage, cultural background, gender, the suddenness or type of death or loss, the person's coping patterns, and so on. In Western culture, for example, women grieve more openly than men, and religious beliefs and cultural rituals vary widely in regard to accepting death and bringing closure for the survivors.

The intense grief period typically diminishes in six months to a year, but the process of grieving often takes up to three to five years (or even longer). Over time, most people are able to resolve the loss and reduce the intensive pain experienced without the assistance of professional helpers (i.e., through the support of family and friends). In fact, personal growth often occurs as a person successfully deals with grief, and the outcome can be viewed as positive. For example, people sometimes gain increased independence and self-confidence, find new areas of interest and talent, develop new and rewarding relationships, and so on.

Time is the greatest healer. Most people eventually recover to the point where they can again function effectively, even though the pain of the loss may remain with them for the rest of their lives. Sometimes, however, the normal healing process stalls and the person develops dysfunctional patterns of thought and behavior. In these situations, the social worker must use a more clinical approach.

Basic *supportive counseling* is perhaps the most useful form of social work intervention. People should be encouraged to grieve, to identify the scope of the loss they have experienced, to talk about the events of the loss, and to gain information about the process of grieving. When clients are focused on accepting the reality of the loss, it is helpful to encourage talking about the experience (usually repeatedly) and to take concrete actions related to the loss such as planning the funeral, taking care of financial matters, and so on. As acceptance of the loss begins, a worker might then help the person recall positive experiences from before the loss occurred. This might be done through talking about photographs, visiting places of special significance, or encouraging the client to use art, stories, poems, or other forms of expression. In addition, it is important to assist people in moving forward with their lives through solving problems that may have arisen from the loss (e.g., insurance claims, managing day-to-day issues, etc.), developing new roles and relationships, and engaging in new activities.

When the normal grief reaction does not begin to be resolved over time, depending on the specific circumstances, *individual, couple,* or *family therapy* might prove useful. One specific approach used when dealing with grief is termed *regrief therapy*. It is utilized when the person has not been able to complete the tasks in the grief process. Using this approach, the social worker invites the client to bring to a session items that are symbolic of the lost person or object and the client is helped to revisit the relationship and find emotional release. Another specialized technique is *guided mourning*, a cognitive-behavioral approach in which the client is encouraged to recall the details of the painful loss experience and to find appropriate ways to say good-bye through ritual and journaling about one's emotional reactions.

Support groups are useful in assisting people to deal with grief. These groups can offer advice about day-to-day tasks such as handling finances or taking on new household tasks, giving emotional support by providing a safe place where the grieving person can talk about the loss, and sharing experiences as a way of helping others see that their emotions are normal and to anticipate grief symptoms that may emerge.

SELECTED BIBLIOGRAPHY

Cassell, Dana K., Robert C, Salinas, and Peter A. S. Winn. *The Encyclopedia of Death and Dying.* New York: Facts on File, 2005.

Hooyman, Nancy, and Betty Kramer. *Living Through Loss.* New York: Columbia University Press, 2006.

Walsh-Burke, Katherine. *Grief and Loss.* Boston: Allyn & Bacon, 2006.

Worden, J. William. *Dying, Death, and Bereavement,* 2nd ed. New York: Springer, 2006.

15.18   THE CLIENT WITH CONCERNS RELATED TO SPIRITUALITY AND RELIGION

Purpose: To respond appropriately to clients who have problems, concerns, or needs intertwined with spirituality and/or religion.

Discussion: Various national surveys report that about 90 percent of adults in the United States believe in a personal god, and a majority of adults say that religion plays an important role in their everyday lives and in the formation of their spirituality. Many others who are not drawn to a religion and many who do not believe in a god also strive to develop their spirituality. Thus, if a social worker serves a cross-section of the population, religion and/or spirituality will be important to most of his or her clients. Yet, many social workers feel poorly prepared to discuss these matters with clients.

Social workers, psychologists, and other professional helpers are often taught to steer discussions with clients away from matters of religion. Even folk wisdom warns us to avoid discussing religion (and politics) with our friends because such discussions so often turn into arguments and create hard feelings. So, when it comes to the question of how a social worker should respond to clients who have problems, needs, or requests related to their religion, spirituality, and faith, the practitioner faces a dilemma. On the one hand, it is clear that religion and/or spirituality are important to most clients and, for many, a source of strength and a potential resource to the helping process. Moreover, information about a client's religious and spiritual beliefs and practices may be a key to understanding his or her motives, decisions, and behavior. On the other hand, a worker's attempt to explore these aspects of the client's life carries the risk of alienating or offending the client.

For many people, their religion and/or spirituality is a source of their sense of identity, worth, and hope and provides meaning and direction in their lives. For others, religion or spirituality is a cause of inner turmoil, family conflicts, shame, and guilt. How people define right and wrong (i.e., moral standards) is often rooted in their religion and spiritual orientation. Our feelings of self-respect and self-esteem are related, in part, to whether we are adhering to our moral code.

As suggested by the definitions of spirituality and religion offered in Chapter 2, both the cultivation of a spirituality and the practice of a religion draw one into the realm of the sacred and to an awareness of a creative life-giving force or divine presence in our lives. Spirituality is inherently difficult to define and describe because it is deeply personal and unique to each individual. Even if two people practice the same religion, their spirituality will be different.

The word *spirituality* has its origin in images of an invisible but powerful wind and the "breath of God." For many, spirituality refers to a sense of wholeness and integration and a connection between the inner-self and a higher power or ineffable presence, which many name *God*. It involves an awareness of or a mindfulness of the mystery, beauty, and awesomeness inherent in human life and the universe. Spirituality has been variously described as a holy longing or yearning for meaning; as one's most cherished and enduring values; as the essence of a person's character; as the way one lives his or her life; as how a person channels his or her deep, inner unrest and desires; and as one's lived experience with the mystery of life. The idea of mystery is a common theme in people's attempts to describe their spirituality. In this context, *mystery* refers to a dimension or level of experience and awareness that the person knows to be real but is beyond description and understanding.

At a very fundamental level, spirituality is about decision making, deciding how to live one's life and choosing between what is good and what is even better. A spiritual perspective helps people distinguish the important from the unimportant, the ends from the means, and the lasting from the fleeting. Spirituality is a certain vision of reality and a life style based on that vision.

Spirituality is the root of all religion. Broadly speaking, a **religion** is any set of beliefs and traditions that attempts to answer the overarching questions of life, such as Who am I? What is the meaning and purpose of my life? How should I live my life? Why does evil exist? What happens after death? How am I to pray (i.e., relate to my god)? Many who seek the spiritual life embrace a religion because it guides and nourishes their spiritual growth. Others seek spiritual growth apart from a religion, either because they are not attracted to the concept of a religion or because their experiences with belonging to a religion have been negative.

Given the complexity of this topic and that it is a potentially sticky issue within agencies and in the delivery of services to clients, we offer here a few additional perspectives and guidelines for the beginning-level practitioner who is working with clients for whom spirituality and/or religion is important and related to their concerns and requests.

1. Carefully and honestly examine your own experiences with and attitudes toward religion and spirituality. Be alert to any prejudices or presumptions that may limit your ability to serve clients who have beliefs or experiences different from your own. This means that you will need to be open to and accepting of persons with strong religious beliefs and those with none at all. Addressing issues and concerns related to a client's religion and spirituality requires of the social worker a high degree of self-understanding and self-discipline (see Item 16.2).

2. Approach matters related to a client's religion much as you would approach matters related to a client's culture (see Item 8.9). A person's religion is, in fact, like a culture in that it is a "lens" through which he or she views and interprets life's experiences. A client's religion or spirituality can influence what the client defines to be a problem, its cause, and its solution. The social worker must be nonjudgmental. This can be a challenge if the client's beliefs seem unusual or unreasonable. It should be remembered that a religion, like a culture, seems quite reasonable to the person who is immersed in that religion.

3. In all cases, the social worker must demonstrate an accepting attitude and readiness to discuss spiritual and religious matters if the client wishes to do so. If the client does not perceive that acceptance and openness, he or she may withhold important information out of fear of being misunderstood, judged, or ridiculed for holding certain beliefs. Also, the worker must avoid redefining a client's spiritual or religious concern as being only a psychological issue.

4. During the data-gathering and assessment phase, the social worker should do at least a cursory exploration of the client's spiritual and/or religious beliefs, values, and activities in order to identify possible client strengths and resources and to assess whether the client's presenting problem or concern is intertwined with his or her spirituality and/or religion. Simple and straightforward inquiries will usually suffice—for example, What do I need to know about your values and beliefs to better understand what is really important to you? Is religion and spirituality a part of your life? Are you a member of a church or a faith community? How do you find encouragement during difficult times? What sense do you make out of the hardship you have experienced? The nature of the client's responses to such exploratory questions will dictate if a more in-depth assessment is necessary and appropriate.

In every situation, the questions asked of a client and the information gathered about a client must be relevant and pertinent to his or her presenting concern and the reason the social worker and the client are meeting. In certain situations, however, it may be necessary to probe more deeply. A worker in direct practice (e.g., counseling, case management) might ask specific questions about the client's spirituality and/or religious beliefs and background when the client is experiencing certain troublesome thoughts and feelings, such as guilt, grief, despair, and meaninglessness or when the client is struggling with a moral dilemma. Client statements such as the following illustrate these situations: "I feel like a failure as a parent because none of my children go to church or have any interest in developing their spirituality." "I have hurt so many people; I need to make amends for the harm I have caused." "My life is empty and meaningless." "I wish I had some type of faith, but I don't know how to develop one." "The people in my 12-step program talk about their Higher Power, but I'm not sure I even have one." "So often, I pray that my illness will be cured, but my medical condition is getting worse." "As I approach my death, I wonder if there is an afterlife. Do you think there is?" "My daughter is under the influence of evil spirits." "I want to forgive my father for what he did, but I am consumed by bitterness and festering with anger."

The social worker in indirect practice (e.g., community organization, agency administration, program management) must understand the religious beliefs and practices common to a neighborhood and a community. Doing so is necessary for developing programs and policies that are sensitive, respectful, and relevant to the people who are to benefit from the social worker's actions.

5. When working with a client who desires a more fulfilling spiritual life but feels a lack of progress toward that goal, it may be helpful to explain the difference between a spiritual *search* and a spiritual *journey*. A person on a search is always looking for something more satisfying and exploring new possibilities; this often gives rise to a sense of restlessness. By contrast, a person on a journey has made a choice about where he or she wants to go and is heading in that direction; consequently, he or she can achieve a sense of inner freedom. Real spiritual growth can begin only after one chooses a path and is walking along it. In every person's spiritual search, there comes a time when, despite doubt, he or she must take a leap of faith and say, in effect, "I choose to live my life this way." The fear of choosing the wrong path will delay the development of a meaningful spirituality. Regardless of the path taken, the person will need to set aside a regular time for quiet reflection, prayer, or meditation. All of the great spiritual traditions and world religions agree on that point.

Spiritual growth is mostly a process of letting go of one's desire to have control, prestige, possessions, and power and instead embracing truly important and enduring values. The fear of letting go is, of course, the greatest barrier to the formation of an authentic and lasting spiritually.

Spiritual growth is not a solitary activity. Rather, it is communal and relational in the sense that people's deepest questions can only be answered through engaging in dialogue with others. It requires the support and guidance of others, especially persons who are more experienced in living a spiritual life, for they can help the beginner avoid problems of discouragement, self-absorption, self-deception, and spiritual arrogance. Religious institutions are centers of spiritually and exist to cultivate spiritual living. While composed of and led by persons who are flawed and very human, religious organizations are the primary means of passing on spiritual wisdom and are an invaluable spiritual resource to many.

One's spirituality is reflected in his or her everyday choices, decisions, and interactions with others. Thus, a person's spirituality and his or her behavior are interconnected. The person who seeks spiritual growth must be true to his or her conscience and beliefs about what is right and wrong. To behave in ways that violate one's own moral code precludes achieving a sense of integration and wholeness.

6. Understand the dilemmas faced by deeply religious and/or spiritually oriented individuals as they try to live, work, and raise a family within a social environment that does not support and often undermines their cherished beliefs and values. The dominant values of U.S. society are materialism, consumerism, competition, and individualism. Holding these values often leads people to create a self-centered lifestyle and to place great emphasis on the acquisition of things, power, status, and the attention of others. By contrast, authentic religion and spirituality emphasize a very different set of values and virtues, such as honesty, truthfulness, justice, humility, modesty, compassion, reconciliation, forgiveness, and service to others.

Much like those who belong to an ethnic or cultural minority group, many people who are religious and spiritual must struggle to live in "two worlds" and negotiate, socially and economically, within an environment they perceive as foreign, often unsympathetic, and sometimes hostile to their values and way of life. Parents, especially, will take action to protect their children from societal influences they perceive as destructive to their children's psychological and spiritual well-being. When people feel that their religious and spiritual beliefs and practices are threatened, they may strike out at the perceived threat. Another response is to withdraw from the mainstream societal activities they view as threatening to their values. Some, including social workers, may mistake this response for unhealthy social isolation.

7. Direct social work practice can become especially complex when the client's presenting problem involves a clash between his or her conscience, or personal moral code, and the existing legal code. Consider, for example, that for one client a certain action (e.g., abortion, blood transfusion, war) could be judged as legal but immoral whereas another client, might judge an illegal action to be morally correct (e.g., refusing to pay taxes that support a war, use of abusive punishment in child-rearing). Helping a client think through and resolve such dilemmas may call for consultation with an attorney and with those religious or spiritual leaders who have an in-depth understanding of the client's moral reasoning. It is important to recognize that some individuals misunderstand the moral principles of the religion that they purport to follow.

8. A social worker faces a challenging situation when his or her client's religious and/or spiritual beliefs and practices are unhealthy and harmful to the client or to others. In such cases, the social worker can at least try to help the client examine the effects and observable consequences of these beliefs and practices. However, the worker must realize that people hold tightly to their core ideas and values and are not easily swayed by what others view as reasonable and logical arguments.

A healthy religion or spirituality recognizes that humans are complex creatures and have many interrelated dimensions (i.e., physical, spiritual, psychological, emotional, intellectual, sexual, social). Thus, in a healthy religion and spirituality, there is an appreciation of all these dimensions, not just the spiritual. In other words, there is an emphasis on the wholeness of being. In fact, the word *holy*, as in the term *holy person*, refers to a person who has integrated these many dimensions of life and achieved a holistic balance, integration, and sense of wholeness. By contrast, an unhealthy spirituality or religion causes imbalance, division, and fragmentation internally, or within the person (e.g., a spiritual practice that harms one's body or mental health), and also externally, as for example, when one's religious beliefs fracture families and friendships or sow the seeds of violence or oppression.

9. It is important for social workers and human services programs to build working relationships with a variety of local clergy, leaders of faith communities, and trained spiritual directors so that these individuals can be consulted on how best to approach issues related to clients' religion or spirituality. When a client's concern or need is primarily within the realm of religion, faith, and spiritually and therefore outside the domain of professional social work, the social worker should refer the client to the appropriate religious or spiritual counselor or clergy person. (See Chapter 1 for a discussion of social work's domain or area of expertise.)

10. When a client is an active member of a faith community (e.g., a church, synagogue, mosque), that faith community may be a potential helping resource. Depending on the client's concern or need, the possible use of this resource might be explored. However, it is important to understand that some individuals will describe themselves as belonging to a certain religion or faith community when, in fact, they have only a tenuous or occasional connection to it. Thus, a client's self-identification with a particular religion or faith does not necessarily signify that he or she will have access to the informal social support network or other resources usually associated with active membership (see Item 12.7).

11. The social worker must avoid assuming that he or she knows about a client's specific religious beliefs and practices when all the worker knows is that the client identifies with a particular religion. Within the major religions, there are various subgroups or branches that differ in a variety of ways. For example, there are many denominations within Christianity, and each often comprises further divisions along a conservative-progressive continuum. Not infrequently, the various traditions overlap with certain nationalities and ethnic and cultural groups.

Each of the world religions has a body of writings that are viewed as extraordinary and sacred. These writings (e.g., scriptures) shape the religion's belief system and are read for inspiration and moral guidance. Within the major religions (e.g., Hinduism, Buddhism, Judaism, Christianity, Islam), different subgroups interpret their scriptures from different vantage points. For example, some utilize a literal approach, whereas others utilize a contextual, historical, and/or critical approach. Those who read the scriptures in a literal manner assume that the words mean exactly what they say. Those who apply the contextual method to reading the scriptures assign meanings to the words only after considering, for instance, the historical and cultural time in which the document was written, the writer's purpose, the intended audience, and the writer's use of symbolic language, metaphor, and other literary devices.

12. A social worker must be prepared to respond to the questions a client may ask about the worker's own religion or spiritual beliefs and practices; at the same time, the worker must recognize the need to maintain an appropriate professional boundary. A client may have several motives for asking about the worker's religion and spirituality. As a general rule, most people feel at ease with those who share their beliefs and values and have had similar life experiences. Thus, a client may want to know if the worker is capable of understanding his or her spiritual and religious beliefs and practices and perhaps whether the worker is going to be judgmental. Some clients may ask about the worker's religion simply because they are curious about how the worker approaches the "big questions" of life. Still other clients may be trying to manipulate the worker into taking their side in some interpersonal or family conflict.

How a social worker responds to such questions will depend on his or her assessment of why the client is asking them and how providing various answers will affect the professional relationship and their ongoing work together. (See Item 8.4 for guidance on how a social worker might respond to personal questions posed by a client.)

SELECTED BIBLIOGRAPHY

Becvar, Dorthy, ed. *The Family, Spirituality, and Social Work.* Binghamton, New York: Haworth, 1998.

Canda, Edward, and Lee Furman. *Spiritual Diversity in Social Work Practice.* New York: Free Press, 1999.

Derezotes, David. *Spiritually-Oriented Social Work Practice.* Boston: Allyn & Bacon, 2006.

Richards, P. Scott, and Allen Bergin, eds. *Handbook of Psychotherapy and Religious Diversity.* Washington, DC: American Psychological Association, 2000.

Van Hook, Mary, Beryl Hugen, and Marian Aguilar. *Spirituality within Religious Traditions in Social Work.* Belmont, CA: Brooks/Cole, 2002.

15.19   THE CLIENT WHO IS AN IMMIGRANT OR REFUGEE

Purpose: To consider the special issues that may arise when working with clients who are in the United States with immigrant or refugee status.

Discussion: Because a significant number of the people in need of health and human services have the designation of being an immigrant or refugee, a social worker must acquire at least a basic knowledge of the problems they face and how their special status might affect access and eligibility for human services.

The United States has been described as a country of immigrants and refugees. Nearly all U.S. citizens have a family genealogy that leads back to another nation and culture. Many of the students reading this textbook have parents, grandparents, or great-grandparents who were born in another country. Throughout its history, the United States has been a sought-after destination for persons migrating from countries that have fewer freedoms and opportunities. The United States has been a safe haven for those who sought escape from political and religious oppression and from other forms of injustice. This theme is captured by an inscription on the Statue of Liberty:

> Give me your tired, your poor,
> Your huddled masses yearning to breathe free,
> The wretched refuse of your teeming shore.
> Send these, the homeless, tempest-tossed, to me:
> I lift my lamp beside the golden door.

Those welcoming words and the country's rich immigrant history belie the challenges actually experienced by many who enter the United States as immigrants or refugees. Whether from Europe, Africa, Asia, or parts of the Western Hemisphere, these individuals commonly experience personal, social, and economic problems because of the inherent difficulty of adapting to a new culture; many lack language facility and/or job skills relevant to the American economy. Many live in or near poverty. In addition, some encounter hostility because segments of society perceive newcomers as a threat and disruption to the status quo, an added competition for jobs and housing, and an additional tax burden. Social workers often feel caught between a grudging public that wants to deny services to the new arrivals and the immigrants and refugees themselves who often face extraordinary problems and clearly need the help of educational, health, and social programs.

The Immigrant/Refugee Population

Based on data from the March 2004 "Current Population Survey" by the U.S. Census Bureau, the Pew Hispanic Center estimates that the foreign-born population in the United States had reached a total of 35.7 million persons by 2004. Included in this population were 11.3 million naturalized citizens who had formerly been legal permanent residents, 10.4 million currently legal permanent residents, and 10.3 million unauthorized migrants—some entering clandestinely or with fraudulent documents and others overstaying their visas. In addition, there were 2.5 million refugees, and 1.2 million temporary legal residents—including students and temporary workers. Among the unauthorized migrants were 5.9 million from Mexico, 2.5 million from other Latin American countries, 1.0 million from Asia, 600,000 each from Europe and Canada, and 400,000 from Africa and other countries.

The term *immigrant* refers to any person who voluntarily leaves one country in order to permanently settle in another country. However, as part of an effort to limit the allocation of resources to immigrants, various laws and regulations contain additional distinctions and difinitions. Some immigrants, for example, have been declared *legal permanent residents* as a means of recognizing those who have legally entered the country through the existing structure. Congress has established quotas for the maximum number of immigrants from each country, facilitating the entry of those who have certain job skills or close ties to family members already living in the United States. Legal permanent residents can, after a period of time and a demonstration that they possess knowledge of U.S. law and culture, become naturalized citizens. The average family income of legal permanent residents is comparable to native families and the 18–24-year-old youth are slightly more likely than resident youth to attend college (Pew 2005). This part of the immigrant population, then, is unlikely to make more of a demand on human services than other U.S. residents.

Some persons receive permission to temporarily enter the United States to attend school or perform certain needed jobs. When the visas of these *temporary legal residents* (also known as nonimmigrants) expire, they must return to their homelands. Generally speaking, this segment of the immigrant population has only limited income and few benefits. Social workers may meet persons from this group in hospitals and clinics, mental health centers, schools, and in child welfare agencies (Garrett and Herman 2006).

People who have entered the country illegally, i.e., without meeting the immigration requirements, fare rather badly in the United States. These *unauthorized immigrants* tend to be young, have limited education, live in crowded housing, and yet have high employment rates in farming, cleaning, construction, and food preparation jobs. These families have low income ($27,400 per year), 39.9 percent of the children live in poverty, and 53 percent have no health coverage (Pew 2005). Although taxes are withheld from their paychecks and they pay sales taxes, these unauthorized immigrants must live under the radar of government scrutiny, are not eligible for Temporary Assistance for Needy Families (TANF) and most other government programs, have few legal rights, and risk deportation at any time. For social workers, this population is difficult to serve. Many of the usual health and welfare resources are not accessible due to the client's legal status. Moreover, unauthorized immigrants often are reluctant to ask for services due to the risk of deportation if their status is discovered.

The Personal Responsibility and Work Opportunity and Reconciliation Act of 1996, referred to as PRWORA and commonly known as welfare reform, ". . . institutionalized the concept of immigrant exceptionalism" (Zimmerman and Tumlin, 1999, p. 5), thereby denying most public benefits to nondocumented immigrants. Specifically, that federal law bars most immigrants from receiving food stamps and Supplemental Security Income (SSI) and also blocks use of "federal means-tested benefits" for five years from their date of arrival in the United States, including TANF, Medicaid, and the Child Health Insurance Program (CHIP).

In addition, PRWORA gives states the option to deny immigrants who arrived in the United States prior to August 22, 1996, from receiving TANF, Medicaid, and services under the Social Security Block Grant. It also allows individual states the right to bar immigrants who arrived in the United States after August 22, 1996, from TANF and Medicaid, following the mandatory five-year ban. This federal legislation, in effect, denies unauthorized immigrants access to all federal public benefits, and grants to the states the legal right to discriminate through restrictive eligibility criteria for federal, state, and locally funded social services. For example, access is denied by requiring verification of immigrants' legal status prior to the provision of social services.

Refugees enter the United States under a different set of circumstances. They have been victims of oppressive conditions in their home countries and have fled persecution, usually without time to gain legal immigration status or to plan for the disposition and transfer of their property and financial resources. Often families are not able to escape together and may temporarily relocate in one or more countries before finally arriving at their final destination. Refugee status provides a temporary legal means of entering the United States and can be a first step toward becoming a legal immigrant. Social work practice with refugee populations requires that practitioners explore client problems from two interrelated dimensions: (1) issues originating from the individual's perceptions and interpretations that are a result of culture, values, or "ethnic reality" influences, and 2) the after-effects of the individual's migration journey and reception by the host country.

Because of federal legislation such as the Refugee Act of 1980, most refugees are eligible for public health and human services programs including cash and medical assistance, social services, and preventive health services. A social worker should be alert to the possibility that other organizations and social agencies working with an individual who is a refugee may not understand his or her cultural background and special immigration status and might have policies and procedures that unwittingly deny their services to refugees (see Item 8.9). In such a situation, interagency negotiation or perhaps case advocacy or class advocacy may be necessary (see Items 13.18 and 13.33). When working with refugees, social workers need to be especially sensitive to the interplay of such factors as the client's ethnicity, religion, nationality, legal and immigration status, age, gender, family context and characteristics, education, economic situation, and acceptance in the community (Puig 2001).

Guidelines for Assisting Immigrants and\Refugees

Depending on the social worker's job responsibility and agency context, a worker may have a role in assisting individuals and families in planning a migration or escaping as a refugee to a different country; the social worker might also assist those who have entered the country in successfully resetting and adapting to life in the United States.

Migration.   When clients are preparing to migrate, social workers should help them to focus on several concerns. For example, clients should be helped to address the probable economic and social impact on the family members who leave, as well as on those staying behind. Will there be a loss of income? Can they cope with the emotional pain of a separation and loneliness? Can they successfully adjust to a strange culture and new environment? Can they negotiate a language barrier? Is it safe to make this journey? How can they stay in communication with family and friends? Might this migration require detainment in a refugee camp? Does the migration require waiting for an official decision by the foreign government? If so, how long will the wait be, and what financial and other resources will be needed during the wait for an official decision? What if the person is refused entry?

Resettlement.   Social workers should help clients adjust to the new environment and learn how to secure employment, housing, health care, social relationships, and so on. In addition, social workers should help clients examine such issues as their *acculturation* (i.e., changes in beliefs toward those of the host society), *assimilation* (i.e., the degree of adoption of the values, norms, and behaviors that dominate the society), and *adaptation* (i.e., the ability to adjust one's way of life to fit into the new country). More specifically, workers should help clients consider and address possible discrepancies between their expectations and reality, the degree of stress encountered throughout the migration experience, and the effects on friends and loved ones left behind. Some other factors that social workers should help clients consider as possible impediments to or supports for successful adjustment to the new culture include the following:

- Language and the individual's degree of bilingualism
- Differences in expected housing or living arrangements between the cultures
- Variations in work patterns and expectations by employers
- The degree of commonality between values and social norms of the old and new cultures and societies
- The availability of cultural mediators or teachers for new arrivals
- Corrective feedback (positive and negative) needed to assist adaptation
- Tension between adapting to a new environment while holding on to important elements of the original culture
- The degree of similarity or dissimilarity in physical appearance with the dominant population groups in the culture

Guiding the Path to Naturalization.   Both legal permanent residents and refugees may require the assistance of the social worker in attaining naturalization. Typically the social worker helps by informing the person(s) of the naturalization process and helping to make connections to resources that help to accomplish the various steps of the process. The requirements for *naturalization* (the process of awarding U.S. citizenship to a person after birth) include the following. The individual must:

1. Be at least 18 years of age
2. Have resided continuously in the United States for at least 5 years (three years for the spouse of a U.S. citizen)

3. Have demonstrated good moral character as determined by the absence of conviction of any criminal offenses

4. Demonstrate the ability to read, write, and speak English well enough to understand commonly used English words and phrases, and

5. Demonstrate the ability to pass a citizenship exam in U.S. government and history

SELECTED BIBLIOGRAPHY

Balgopal, Pallassana, ed. *Social Work Practice with Immigrants and Refugees* New York: Columbia University Press, 2000.

Garrett, Kendra J., and W. Randolph Herman. "Foreign-Born Students in Baccalaureate Social Work Programs: Meeting the Challenges." *The Journal of Baccalaureate Social Work* 12 (Fall 2006): 24–38.

Pew Hispanic Center. "Unauthorized Migrants: Numbers and Characteristics." www.pewhispanic. org/files/reports/46.pdf. June 14, 2005.

Puig, Maria. "Organizations and Community Intervention Skills with Hispanic Americans." In Rowena Fong and Sharlene Furuto, eds. *Culturally Competent Practice: Skills, Interventions, and Evaluations*, pp. 269–284. Boston, MA: Allyn & Bacon, 2001.

Zimmerman, Wendy, and Tumlin, Karen C. *Patchwork Policies: State Assistance for Immigrants under Welfare Reform.* Washington, DC: Urban Institute, 1999.

15.20 THE CLIENT OR COMMUNITY EXPERIENCING AN EMERGENCY OR DISASTER

Purpose: To understand and respond to clients caught up in the aftermath of a disaster or catastrophic event.

Discussion: A variety of natural disasters and catastrophic events have the power to disrupt whole communities and inflict death, injury, trauma, and financial hardship on large numbers of people. Examples include earthquakes, floods, hurricanes, tornadoes, forest fires, airline crashes, terrorist attacks, school shootings, accidental spills of toxic chemicals or dangerous radiation, and war-related invasions and bombings.

The defining characteristics of a ***disaster*** are that it affects many people at the same time and that its immense scale requires a highly organized and disciplined emergency response by a range of governmental officials and organizations. The roles and activities of social workers at the site of a disaster must fit within the purposes and methods of an organized rescue and emergency response—one characterized by a military type of decision making and coordinating structure. The leaders of emergency response organizations will have certain objectives and priorities that will determine what social work services are most needed and when, where, and to whom they will be provided. In an emergency or disaster situation, the highest priorities are the following:

1. To rescue or evacuate people in danger, to treat people who are injured, and to prevent an outbreak of contagious diseases through inoculations, proper care of the dead, and reestablishment of basic sanitation facilities

2. To address the immediate physical needs of the survivors by providing emergency shelter, water, food, blankets, and the like
3. To maintain public order to prevent accidents, social chaos, and looting (This will require the use of police or military units.)

Once these priorities have been addressed, the emergency or disaster response organization will attempt to address the psychological needs of the survivors by dispatching mental health and pastoral personnel. They will assist individuals who are undergoing a mental health crisis and/or grieving the loss of loved ones and/or property.

Individual and Family Responses

How an individual responds to and adjusts to a disaster is related, in part, to the nature of the disaster and whether he or she had time to prepare for what was to occur. For example, a person who has lost his or her house to a flood or a forest fire usually had a day or two of warnings in advance of the disaster. Given that, he or she had likely considered the possibility that the water or fire could destroy the house and had discussed these fears and worries with family and friends. By contrast, to experience the effects of, say, a terrorist bomb that exploded without warning in a crowded shopping mall is quite a different type of human experience. The element of surprise that exists in the case of an earthquake, bombing, or plane crash gives rise to intense feelings of fear, horror, shock, and confusion.

People's response to a disaster often unfolds in three stages: impact, recoil, and posttrauma. During the first stage, *acute impact*, people are just grasping the reality of what has happened or is happening. During this phase, which usually lasts for an hour or two, people respond in a variety of ways, particularly when some are still in danger of injury. While a few manage to remain surprisingly calm, make rational decisions, and care for themselves and others, most people are in a state of emotional shock and disorientation and experience the physical signs of fear and anxiety, such as sweating, trembling, and having an upset stomach. These individuals are, however, able to communicate and follow the instructions given by emergency personnel. A third group—usually a small percentage—are hysterical or paralyzed by their fear. These individuals are unable to make rational choices and may run about, speak wildly, or behave in ways that are dangerous to themselves and others.

Certain individuals require special attention during the acute impact phase, even when they have escaped the disaster without physical injury. These include, for example, young children, the elderly, those who were physically or mentally disabled prior to the disaster, those who cope with life in unhealthy or self-destructive ways, and those without access to family or a social support network.

It is during the second phase, the *recoil phase*, when the survivors become fully aware of what they have been through. During this phase, which typically begins some hours after the disaster has hit, many people are in a state of emotional exhaustion; many break down and weep. Most feel a strong need to talk about their experience. Mental health counseling and crisis intervention work should begin when people are in this phase (see Item 15.6). In addition, attention must be given to meeting the immediate needs of the victims, such as food and water and shelter and sleeping arrangements. Victims also will need help securing the items needed for grooming and personal care, arranging access to communication networks (so they can contact worried relatives and friends), and replacing lost eyeglasses, prescription medications, and so on.

The third phase of adjustment to a disaster or catastrophic event is termed the *posttrauma phase.* This phase may last for months, years, or the rest of a person's life, depending in part on the adequacy of the crisis intervention services available to and used by the individuals impacted by the disaster. Often, the survivors of a disaster or a catastrophic event experience the following:

- Overwhelming feelings of grief and horror over what they experienced
- Preoccupation with death brought on by remembering the sights and sounds of people dying, persons with severe injuries, and corpses
- Preoccupation with what they have lost, such as a loved one, a house, important papers, and other meaningful possessions
- Worry over whether they ever will be able to reestablish a normal life and manage financially in the future
- Feeling that they survived at the expense of those who died (i.e., survivor guilt)
- Feelings of helplessness and a loss of trust, self-confidence, and sense of control

The major adjustments that individuals and families must make after experiencing a disaster are basically those of dealing with and grieving for their losses, rebuilding their lives, and reestablishing ordinary and predictable patterns of living. The stages or phases commonly observed among people going through these adjustments are the following:

- Accepting the reality of their loss (e.g., my child has really died; my house is gone forever)
- Acknowledging the pain of their loss (e.g., expressing rather than suppressing intense feelings)
- Adjusting to their changed personal, family, social, and economic circumstances
- Reinventing and reestablishing their sense of identity and purpose and the normal rhythms of life in the absence of whom and what has been lost

Community Responses

Webster (1995) observes that communities that have experienced a disaster typically move through four rather predicable phases: heroism, honeymoon, disillusionment, and reconstruction. The *heroism phase* occurs immediately after experiencing the disaster or during the time of the emergency, when the people of the community bond together, provide mutual support, and display cooperative behavior. Former divisions of social and economic class and race/ethnicity are set aside. During this phase, people often experience a positive sense of community and belonging. They take pride in how they have been helpful and in how well they are working together.

During a second phase, the *honeymoon*, the former or predisaster conflicts and tensions within the community are temporarily forgotten or diminish in importance. The community feels hopeful and confident that it can and will recover and perhaps be stronger than ever before.

The honeymoon phase gradually gives way to a sense of disappointment, known as the *disillusionment phase*, when the people of the community realize the enormity and complexity of rebuilding. Typically, the emergency relief programs available to the community are time limited and provide less than what people expect. These limitations and the associated eligibility rules and regulations often elicit anger and a sense of unfairness. It is during this phase that former community conflicts reappear and that people fragment into competing groups. Rumors and misinformation are special problems during this phase, which means that community meetings and disseminating accurate information are critically important.

Eventually, the community moves beyond its disillusionment and enters the long, difficult phase of *reconstruction*. Some communities are successful in rebuilding after a disaster, whereas others never recover. Among the variables that affect the capacity for and level of recovery are the nature of the disaster, the level of the destruction, the strength of the community's economic base, the abilities of the existing leadership, the cohesion of the predisaster community, and the availability of needed resources.

Guidelines for a Disaster Response

The following guidelines will help social workers to respond to the human needs and problems created by a disaster or catastrophic event:

1. Representatives of large social agencies and of social work organizations, such as the National Association of Social Workers (NASW), should be involved in statewide and local disaster-planning activities. In order to provide the appropriate services at the time of a disaster, social workers and agencies must already have a working knowledge of how emergency and disaster relief organizations function and of what is likely to happen when these organizations actually respond to a disaster or catastrophic event. In addition, each social and mental health agency should formulate its own plan as to how it will respond to a disaster in the community. An agency's plan must, of course, address the questions of how it will work with the emergency response organization and with disaster relief organizations such as the American Red Cross. Social workers who expect to work at the site of a disaster must understand that they can do so only after securing the proper authorization from those directing and coordinating the emergency response.

2. In the first hours and perhaps days following a disaster, the collection of accurate information is of critical importance to the conduct of rescue operations and other emergency responses. It is important to identify who is still missing and who has been killed or injured. Also, it is important to document where each survivor is located (e.g., whether the person was taken to a shelter, transferred to a specific hospital, etc.). Obtaining accurate and complete information will reduce the level of confusion, facilitate communication between the survivors and their worried relatives and friends, and allow for the reunification of families.

3. Information and referral services are of great importance in the months that follow a disaster. Thus, social workers who are in contact with survivors should possess a basic knowledge of state and federal disaster assistance programs that may provide direct money grants, low-cost loans, temporary housing, and other resources to victims of a disaster. Informational meetings related to these programs and eligibility criteria should be made available in the community. In order to cope as best they can, survivors need access to accurate information about the actions or anticipated actions of government agencies and emergency relief organizations. When such information is lacking, rumors develop, sometimes causing unnecessary worry, fear, and even violence.

4. Because children are especially vulnerable to turmoil and social disruption, they should not be separated from their families at times of crisis. If at all possible, families should be evacuated as units and housed together in emergency shelters.

5. If a hundred people die in a disaster, thousands of survivors must cope with the loss of a loved one in addition to the loss of property and possessions, the possible loss of jobs, and a fundamental disruption to their usual way of life. Many of the people who live through a disaster will experience adjustment problems and psychological symptoms many months and even years after the event. Many will develop Posttraumatic Stress Disorder (PTSD) (which was described in Item 15.6). Increased levels of financial problems, depression and anxiety, suicide and homicide, domestic violence, problem drinking and drug use, psychosomatic illness, poor job performance, and the like can be anticipated, as well. Thus, mental health and social services agencies should formulate plans to address an increased need for their services and engage in case finding and active outreach to those who may need them.

6. Be alert to the possibility of a professional or emergency worker developing what is known as *vicarious trauma*. After repeated exposures to clients who have been traumatized and are in great distress, social workers and other helpers may develop symptoms of trauma themselves, such as intrusive thoughts and images, sleeplessness, bystander guilt, and feelings of vulnerability, helplessness, self-doubt, and rage. Workers who feel especially overwhelmed by a disaster, those who have had a prior experience of severe emotional trauma, and those who are inexperienced in disaster-related work are especially vulnerable to developing these symptoms. Ongoing self-care, including the opportunity to talk about one's experiences and feelings and to receive reassurance and support from peers and other professionals, is of critical importance in helping social workers cope with the stress of disaster-related work.

SELECTED BIBLIOGRAPHY

Halpern, James, and Mary Tramontin. *Disaster Mental Health*. Belmont, CA: Brooks/Cole, 2007.

Ritchie, Elspeth, Patricia Watson, and Matthew Friedman, eds. *Interventions Following Mass Violence and Disasters*. New York: Guilford, 2006.

Rosenfeld, Lawrence, Joanne Caye, Ofra Ayalon, and Mooli Lahad. *When Their World Falls Apart: Helping Families and Children Manage the Effects of Disasters*. Washington, DC: NASW, 2004.

Webster, Stephen. "Disasters and Disaster Aid." In *Encyclopedia of Social Work*, 19th ed., pp. 761–771, edited by Richard L. Edwards. Washington, DC: NASW, 1995.

16 Techniques for Sustaining Social Work Practice

INTRODUCTION

Social work is a difficult and demanding profession but also a rewarding one. However, the rewards are mostly intrinsic. By selecting social work as a career, one is virtually assured of never attaining wealth or prestige. Social work is about caring, sharing, and social responsibility; these are not the values rewarded by our economic system. Gordon Allport, a respected social psychologist, once observed that the low status given to social work in the United States may be due to the emphasis social workers place on compassion and cooperation within a society that places high value on competition and individualism.

From its beginnings, the social work profession has demonstrated special concern for those who are powerless, stigmatized, and devalued—the people who others tend to avoid or ignore. Because social workers see so many people in need and the inadequacy of available professional, agency, and societal resources, they frequently experience the anguish of knowing that no matter how hard they work, many people will not receive the services and attention they need and deserve. This is a frustration with which social workers must learn to live.

Because many clients are economically poor, few are in a position to pay directly for services. For this reason, most social workers are employed by governmental or nonprofit agencies. This means that most workers find themselves in resource-poor organizations—ones with few perks and with limited opportunities for continuing education and in-service training.

This chapter provides social workers with guidance for developing their skills, coping with frustrations, and dealing with some ordinary but complex tasks. It offers background information on finding a social work job, dealing with job-related stress, making use of and contributing to professional literature, making presentations, and serving in leadership roles. In addition, the chapter provides guidance on testifying in court, avoiding malpractice suits, addressing sexual misconduct, dealing with managed care, and developing mentoring relationships.

16.1   GETTING A SOCIAL WORK JOB

Purpose: To secure employment as a social worker in a human services organization.

Discussion: Once a social worker has completed his or her professional education, the next task is to secure employment in the capacity of a social worker. That usually takes time and effort, as agencies are necessarily careful in their selection of staff to serve their clientele. (To examine this process from the viewpoint of the agency, see Item 10.12.) It is important, therefore, for the social worker who is seeking a job to present himself or herself in a manner that ensures the best chance of being hired.

The first step in finding employment is to discover the job openings. In most communities, several sources of information might be examined. Agencies will typically advertise their positions; thus, job seekers should read the classified advertisements in the local newspaper on a regular basis. The personnel departments of city, county, or state agencies will post job openings on agency bulletin boards and those should be checked periodically. Finally, informal networks among professionals are an excellent source of information. Attending local NASW meetings is a good way to tap into the professional network in most communities.

Once an open position is located, an application must be prepared. It typically has two parts: a cover letter and a professional resumé. The ***cover letter*** should focus on the particular job being applied for and stress the applicant's qualifications for that position. It should be approximately one page in length and must be carefully written with no spelling, punctuation, or grammatical errors. The letter should indicate that it and the resumé represent an application for the position, describe why the applicant is interested in that job, and discuss qualifications for the position. The cover letter is not the place to discuss salary expectations or reasons for leaving past jobs. Indicate that a list of references will be provided on request (unless the job announcement asks that references be supplied as part of the application). Be sure to obtain advance permission from the people named as references. The letter should be upbeat and positive about the position for which one is applying.

The ***professional resumé*** is more generic than a cover letter and might be used when applying for several positions. It is an organized summary of one's professional qualifications. Its purpose is to present the applicant's background in a manner that will convince the employer to invite him or her for an interview. There is no prescribed format or style for a resumé. Rather, use a creative approach to attract the attention of members of a screening committee who may be selecting a few finalists from a large number of applications; however, avoid being cute or clever. Often, photocopy shops provide layout consultation, have high-quality printers available, and can recommend distinctive paper, making it relatively inexpensive to prepare an attractive resumé. In addition, many colleges or universities have offices that provide workshops and consultation to students in preparing job applications.

At a minimum, a resumé should include the following information; other items may be added at one's discretion:

- *Personal data.* Include your name, street address, email address, and phone number. If you have a number where you can be reached during working hours, be sure to include it to facilitate scheduling an interview.
- *Education.* Give the name of your degree(s), your major, the colleges or universities you attended, and graduation dates. List all schools you have attended (listing in reverse order) and possibly add grade-point average, honors, special projects, or any special skills or training that might be relevant to a social work job (e.g., computer, foreign language, etc.).
- *Experience.* List employment in reverse order (i.e., beginning with your current or most recent job), giving the job title, name of organization, dates of employment, and job duties. It is also helpful to list any volunteer experience that might have contributed to your social work competencies.
- *Activities and interests.* Identify your professional interests as well as those that extend beyond social work. Note membership in professional organizations, your participation in various clubs or organizations and any offices held, and any hobbies or special interests.
- *References.* A statement such as "References Available On Request" is usually best to place on a resumé. If a job announcement calls for references, they should be listed in the cover letter. This flexibility allows for selecting the most appropriate references for each position. In general, the persons selected as references should be able to comment on your skills and might include a faculty member, a field instructor, and/or job supervisors or persons who supervised volunteer experiences. In many instances, an agency will contact the references by telephone rather than by letter, so give telephone numbers.
- *Other information.* It may be desirable to add other information such as publications, travel experiences, and unique experiences that may enhance your competence as a social worker.

If the application is successful, the applicant will be invited to an ***interview***. Typically, the interview process will involve appearing before a panel of interviewers, although there will usually be some one-to-one discussions, as well. Many review panels will present the applicant with hypothetical situations or case vignettes and ask how he or she would handle the situation. The interviewing procedures used by government agencies are usually highly structured and many require a written exam in addition to oral interviews.

Preparation is essential. First, research the agency thoroughly. Know the services it offers, its target clientele, and something about its structure and goals. This information might be obtained by stopping by the agency in advance to pick up informational materials, by visiting the agency's website, or by discussing the agency with clients and/or other social workers in the community. Second, dress professionally and be as relaxed as possible during the interview process. Third, be prepared for questions about your personal and professional interests, as well as your preparation for the specific job duties.

Here are some examples of questions that are commonly asked in an interview:

- What are your qualifications for this job?
- What are your strengths?
- What are your weaknesses?
- Why do you want this job?
- What are your career goals?
- Why should we hire you?
- As a social worker employed by this agency, how would you handle the following situation? (*For example:* A client tells you he plans to take his own life. How would you respond?)

Also be prepared with questions you would like to ask about the agency and the job. An interview is a two-way street—both the applicant and the agency are deciding if there is a good match between one's skills and interests and the requirements of the job.

If offered the position, be sure to know what will be expected of you on the job, and negotiate the salary or other benefits with the employer. Before accepting a new position, (1) you should obtain a letter of appointment that states the starting salary, duties, and other pertinent information; and (2) you should review the agency's personnel manual to be sure you understand the working conditions and benefits.

SELECTED BIBLIOGRAPHY

Doelling, Carol. *Career Development: A Handbook for Job Hunting and Career Planning*, 2nd ed. Washington, DC: NASW, 2005.

George, Laura, *Excuse Me, Your Job is Waiting: Attract the Work You Want.* Charlottesville, VA: Hampton Road Publications, 2007.

Ginsberg, Leon. *Thinking About a Social Work Career*, 2nd ed. Boston: Allyn & Bacon, 2005.

16.2   DEVELOPING SELF-AWARENESS

Purpose: To examine one's attitudes, personal habits, and interactional patterns in order to identify those that may obstruct work with clients.

Discussion: The social worker uses himself or herself as a tool or an instrument in the helping process. Just as a surgeon must be attentive to the condition of medical instruments, the social worker must constantly examine the self to identify barriers to his or her effectiveness. Professional social workers have always emphasized the need to develop their self-awareness and self-knowledge. The term *self-awareness* refers to an accurate perception of one's own beliefs, attitudes, and behavioral habits and their usual effects on one's own decision making and behavior in social work practice. Efforts to develop self-awareness should focus on identifying both strengths and limitations. Many of the strengths that are of importance in social work practice are discussed in other parts of this book. Chapter 3, for example, describes the qualities of courage, compassion, hopefulness, empathy, genuineness, warmth, creativity, imagination, flexibility, energy, good judgment, knowledge, and so on (also see Chapters 2 and 8). In this section, the focus is mostly on factors that can interfere with effective practice. This is not to suggest that strengths are of less importance but rather to counter the human tendency to deny and ignore personal limitations. The worker can increase his or her self-awareness through activities such as the following:

- Keep a daily journal or log. This helps one sort out and think about experiences and get in touch with feelings.
- Ask for constructive criticism. Seek feedback and evaluations from trusted and experienced colleagues familiar with your performance, responsibilities, and agency setting.
- Obtain and then study audio or video recordings of your interviews, group sessions, and other work-related meetings. (*Note:* Secure permission of others before making such a recording; clients should sign a written authorization.)
- Use role-play. Practice and evaluate your performance in simulated sessions that focus on or act out situations that are especially difficult.

Many individuals are drawn to the helping professions because they believe the problems they have faced in life give them a special understanding or sensitivity to the problems of others. Indeed, life's problems can be a powerful teacher and provide a degree of empathy that others do not have. However, this will be the case only after one has honestly examined those experiences and successfully worked through the residual feelings and emotional "baggage" associated with them.

When a social worker becomes aware of some factor that interferes with client service, he or she must be willing to correct the problem or, if change is not possible, to seek a practice setting where the factor will not have a negative impact on clients. The following list outlines some of the factors that can interfere with the formation of a professional helping relationship and client service:

1. *Personal issues.* To a considerable degree, our core beliefs and attitudes toward people and toward life have been shaped by childhood and family experiences. Most people carry a certain amount of emotional baggage into their adult lives, including unresolved parent-child conflicts, prejudice, aftereffects of traumatic events, and so on. Sometimes this baggage is carried to the workplace, where it has a negative impact on clients and work performances—for example:

- Preoccupation with personal problems, resulting in an inability to give one's full attention to the client
- Inability to control one's reactions or exercise self-discipline when in an emotionally charged situation or when under the ordinary pressure associated with social work practice

- Inability to demonstrate warmth, empathy, and genuine caring for clients served by the agency
- Inability to work cooperatively with persons in positions of authority (e.g., judges, physicians, administrators, supervisors, etc.)
- Difficulty separating personal experience (e.g., having been a victim of child abuse, growing up with alcoholic parents, etc.) from the concerns and problems presented by clients
- Defensiveness that prevents a critical examination of one's job performance
- Avoiding certain clients or difficult tasks
- Personalization of client anger and frustrations (i.e., inability to maintain an appropriate level of objectivity)
- Imposing one's values, political beliefs, religious beliefs, or lifestyle on clients
- Inability to respect the religious beliefs and cultural values of a client
- Alcohol or drug abuse
- Misuse or abuse of one's authority over clients
- Extreme level of shyness or nonassertiveness resulting in an inability to express one's opinions and engage in the give-and-take of client work, peer supervision, and team decision making

2. *Appearance, clothing, and grooming.* To a large extent, people form impressions of others—especially the powerful first impression—on the basis of physical appearance. Thus the social worker must pay attention to his or her clothing and grooming because it matters to clients and will affect how they respond to the worker and their utilization of agency services. Of course, what is offensive to one client may be acceptable to another, and what is appropriate dress in one agency setting may be inappropriate in another. The staff in a particular setting must make decisions on what is acceptable. Many agencies and most hospitals establish dress codes as a way of providing guidance to staff. When examining your appearance and its possible impact on clients, remember these guidelines:

- Some choices of clothing, hairstyle, makeup, perfume, or jewelry may offend or distract clients served by the agency.
- Deficiencies in grooming and personal hygiene may offend clients.
- Uncovered infections, skin irritations, and similar conditions may distract the client or cause him or her worry and anxiety.

3. *Behaviors that devalue or degrade others.* Social work values dictate that every client should be treated with respect. The social worker must avoid behaviors that are disrespectful, including the following:

- Using words, phrases, or gestures that are in bad taste or known to offend clients and staff (e.g., cursing, sexual overtones, etc.)
- Telling sexist or ethnic jokes
- Telling disrespectful and disparaging stories about clients
- Discriminating or showing prejudice against particular client groups
- Making sarcastic, insulting, cruel, or disrespectful comments about clients

4. *Distracting personal habits.* Most people have some undesirable mannerisms and habits that their friends and families have learned to accept. However, the social worker must be willing to modify habits that annoy clients, such as these:

- Fidgeting, pencil tapping, knuckle cracking, nail biting
- Scratching, pulling, or twisting hair
- Chewing gum or tobacco and smoking
- Scowling, frowning, or other facial gestures that seem to express scorn
- Excessive nervous laughter, frequent clearing of throat, or other distracting mannerisms

5. *Difficulties in cognitive functioning.* A social worker must absorb information quickly and apply complex principles. A capacity for abstract thinking is essential. The following examples illustrate insufficient cognitive functioning:

- Cognitive deficits that interfere with attention, memory, and judgment
- Inability to explain the assumptions and inferences behind one's judgments, conclusions, and decisions
- Difficulty processing new information, drawing logical inferences, and solving problems
- Lack of reading speed and comprehension needed to understand records and reports, agency policy, and professional books and journals

6. *Difficulties in verbal communication.* The social worker's verbal communication must be understandable to clients and other professional persons. Problems such as these could hamper work with clients:

- Mumbling, speaking inaudibly, loud or penetrating voice tones, halting or hesitant speech, rapid speech
- Frequent use of slang not understood by or offensive to clients
- Errors of grammar or awkward sentence construction that confuse clients
- Inability to adjust vocabulary to client's age or educational level
- Uncorrected vision or hearing problems

7. *Problems in written communication.* Because so much of the social worker's service to a client involves the exchange of information with other professionals, the worker must be able to communicate in writing. If letters, reports, emails, and agency records are carelessly written and difficult to understand, those attempting to read them will conclude either that the worker does not care enough to communicate clearly or is incompetent. The worker's effectiveness is seriously damaged if the client or other professional persons form such negative impressions. Serious writing problems that merit correction include the following:

- Inability to prepare letters, reports, and records that are understandable to clients, agency staff, and other professionals
- Not recognizing and correcting errors of spelling, grammar, and syntax
- Difficulty selecting words that adequately express thought
- Inability to write at a speed sufficient to manage required paperwork

8. *Poor work habits.* Poor work habits may have a direct or indirect impact on the clients served by an agency. Here are some commonly observed problems:

- Being late for client appointments, team meetings, case conferences, and other scheduled events
- Missing deadlines for the completion of written reports that are important to clients or other agencies and professionals serving the client
- Incomplete or sloppy recordkeeping
- Lack of preparation for meetings with clients and other professionals
- Not following through on assignments or tasks
- Distracting other staff members or keeping them from their work
- Unwillingness to seek and utilize direction from the supervisor
- Blaming clients or others for one's own ineffectiveness; inability or unwillingness to acknowledge mistakes or limitations of knowledge and skill
- Unwillingness to follow established agency policies and procedures
- Behaviors occurring outside work hours that draw negative attention to the social worker and thereby lessen client and public respect for the social agency and/or the worker

In order to grow in self-awareness, we need to examine our beliefs, assumptions, and behavioral patterns. We must remember, however, that our most significant advancements in self-awareness do not come from self-scrutiny but rather are "gifts" from others, such as comments made by our clients, the constructive criticism offered by a supervisor, and suggestions from our professional peers and from others who care about us and our performance as social workers.

SELECTED BIBLIOGRAPHY

Corey, Marianne, and Gerald Corey. *Becoming a Helper*, 5th ed. Belmont, CA: Brooks/Cole, 2007.
Rothman, Juliet. *The Self-Awareness Workbook for Social Workers.* Boston: Allyn & Bacon, 1998.

16.3   AVOIDING COMPASSION FATIGUE AND STRESS MANAGEMENT

Purpose: To cope effectively with the stress common to social work practice.

Discussion: Job-related stress can have three sources. First, there is the stress that is simply a part of a particular job. Everyone placed in a high-stress job will feel stressed—it comes with the territory. Second, there is stress caused by a lack of skills necessary to do the job. For example, a particular job may not be stressful for most people but will be for the individual who is poorly prepared. Third, some individuals create their own stress because they have unrealistically high expectations or take on an excessive number of responsibilities.

Every social worker responds to the demands of the profession and his or her job in a unique manner; some thrive while others grow weary. There are two especially maladaptive reactions to job stress: burnout and compassion fatigue. The term ***compassion fatigue*** (also known as secondary trauma and vicarious trauma) describes a set of reactions that may develop when a professional is helping persons who have just experienced some extremely traumatic and horrifying event, such as a destructive earthquake, a train wreck, or a terrorist bombing. The symptoms that arise in the helper include recurring images of the suffering and injured people, guilt over not being able to help certain victims, self-doubt, a dread of returning to work, anxiety, anger, difficulty sleeping, depression, and hypervigliance. The onset of those symptoms is relatively rapid and clearly connected with a particular event or experience. Efforts to treat or address this condition involve the opportunity to discuss in detail the distressing or frightening events with others who experienced it, education about the phenomena of compassion fatigue, support and reassurance, and individual counseling (see Item 15.20).

The term ***burnout*** refers to a state of physical, mental, and emotional exhaustion caused by an inability to adequately cope with the demands and stress of a job. A professional who is experiencing burnout often feels emotionally disconnected and numb, has lost interest in his or her job, dislikes going to work, is irritable and cynical, and treats clients in a routine and insensitive manner. Burnout develops gradually, often over a period of years. An affected professional may feel that something is not right about his or her job performance and attitude toward clients but usually does not recognize or acknowledge the problem. Counseling and perhaps a job change may be necessary to reverse burnout. Burnout is not inevitable; it can be prevented if the professional is committed to self-care and to developing a strategy for stress management. The following guidelines suggest ways to handle job-related stress:

1. The key to preventing negative stress reactions is to find your proper niche in the world of work. There must be a good fit or match between you as a person and the demands of your job. As a social worker, you must feel positive about your chosen profession and feel that you are effective in what you do. A century before stress reactions were studied in the laboratory, an unknown author wisely stated, "In order that people may be happy in their work, these three things are needed: they must be fit for it, they must not do too much of it, and they must have a sense of success in it."

2. Examine the fit between your work and your values. Are you spending your time and energy on activities you consider important? For example, if you value family and friends, are you making choices that enable you to be with them? On the other hand, if you find that life on the job is more exciting than your personal or family life, that, too, must be faced with honesty. As a general rule, people find time for what they really want to do and for that which they truly value. Part of stress management is to become clear about what you value.

3. Make an honest attempt to recognize stress in your life. Listen to those who care about you for clues that you are under more stress than you realized (e.g., "You're so crabby when you get home," "You're not as much fun as you used to be," "You never go anywhere anymore," and "You look so tired"). Possible signs of dangerous levels of stress include frequent colds and sore throats, skin eruptions among nonadolescents, persistent soreness in muscles and joints, frequent low-level headaches, inability to relax or sleep, fatigue, sluggishness that lingers from day to day, frequent stomach upset, weight loss, diarrhea or constipation, nervousness, depression, irritability, unexplained drop in job performance, and a loss of interest in what had been interesting hobbies and exciting activities.

4. Regular exercise, proper nutrition, and adequate sleep help to reduce stress and build natural defenses against the harmful effects of stress. Take several simple and brief physical exercise breaks during the work day (e.g., take a walk at lunch time, do some isometric exercises, or climb a few flights of stairs). Reduce or eliminate the use of alcohol, nicotine, caffeine, and other drugs. Obtain regular medical checkups. If you are having personal or family problems, seek help from trusted friends or professionals.

5. A major source of stress is the feeling that your work and responsibilities are out of control or beyond your control. In such a situation, you must start making some changes or the problem will get worse. Learn to manage your time. Time management is, in effect, stress management. When we use our time wisely we accomplish more and are more effective, and that contributes to a feeling of satisfaction and achievement (see Item 9.6). Consult with experienced workers who seem to effectively manage their workload and enjoy what they do. What are they doing that you might try? Like a long distance runner, set a pace in your work activity that you can maintain without wearing down. Arrange work activity so you will accomplish at least one really important thing each day, for this can produce a surprising amount of job satisfaction. It is usually more satisfying to have done a few things well rather than to have done many things poorly.

6. Recognize that perfection is not required in most work-related tasks. Avoid placing unrealistically high expectations on yourself and on others. Avoid dwelling on the negatives and on what is lacking in your work. Take time to recognize and enjoy the positives in both your personal and professional lives. Help yourself recover from setbacks and disappointments by recalling prior accomplishments.

7. Build a support group of friends or colleagues with whom you are able to share your frustrations. Find enjoyable ways to spend time together—eat out, see a movie, take a walk, or travel together. Also develop hobbies and outside interests that lead you into activities that are different from what you do at work. Doing something new and different can be like a mini-vacation.

8. Apply to yourself the techniques you use with clients. For example, when faced with a stressful interpersonal task, use behavioral rehearsal to reduce anxiety and build confidence (see Item 13.5). As a technique for handling your fears, try exaggerating them out of proportion. For example, if you fear being embarrassed, visualize yourself blushing to the point of turning beet red, sweating profusely, and shaking so hard your watch vibrates off your wrist. Exaggerating your fears to the point of being ludicrous may help you laugh at yourself and put your fear into perspective.

9. Apply problem-solving and organizational change techniques to the stressors common to most work settings: poor working conditions, unreasonable deadlines, heavy workloads, interruptions, and problems with co-workers and supervisors. Serious problems require careful analysis and intervention. They will not go away without intervention. Do something about them!

10. Visitors to the United States observe that the lifestyle is characterized by a fast pace, competition, materialism, and a coolness or emotional distance in human interactions. These characteristics contribute to the stress we experience, but we are not often aware of their influence. Look for ways to simplify your life and slow its pace by reducing the number of decisions you must make each day. For example, simplify your wardrobe and your meals so you have fewer decisions to make about what to wear and what and where to eat. Give up nonessential possessions and activities that demand your attention and consume your time and money but provide little in the way of joy and relaxation. Replace the things in your life with meaningful relationships with family and friends.

SELECTED BIBLIOGRAPHY

Figley, Charles R., ed. *Treating Compassion Fatigue.* New York: Brunner/Routledge, 2002.
Maslach, Christina. *Burnout: The Cost of Caring.* Cambridge, MA: Malor Books, 2003.
Rothschild, Babette, and Marjorie L. Rand. *Help for the Helper: The Psychophysiology of Compassion Fatigue and Vicarious Trauma.* New York: W.W. Norton, 2006.

16.4   COPING WITH BUREAUCRACY

Purpose: To function effectively within a large, complex organization.

Discussion: Every day, many social workers go home from their jobs feeling frustrated. Their complaints are usually not about their contact with clients but rather about the bureaucratic aspects of the agencies and service systems in which they work. Some complain that a myriad of laws, agency rules, regulations, and policies stifle their creativity and keep them from practicing good social work. Others complain that political manipulations, self-serving superiors, and power struggles between agency departments and divisions interfere with the delivery of service to clients.

Being part of a bureaucracy is unavoidable for most social workers because most social work jobs exist within large organizations. To find satisfaction in their work, social workers must develop the attitudes and skills needed to function and get things done within a large organization. Here are several suggestions:

1. Large human services agencies are by nature bureaucratic and political. This is a reality. These organizations are *bureaucratic* in that they are structured hierarchically. That is, there is an official chain of command and a clear division of labor regarding who does what and who can make certain types of decisions. These organizations are political in the sense that those who work within them use power and influence to advance their points of view on what is good for the organization and often their own career. It is essential that you learn to function effectively within this environment because it is a context of practice. You cannot do a good job with your clients unless you are able to work effectively within the organization.

2. Study your agency. Learn about its history, mission, goals, structure, culture, funding sources, budget, and decision-making processes. Strive to understand the special challenges your agency faces and the external economic, political, and community forces that push and pull it in one direction or another. Having such knowledge is a form of power that can be used to address various organizational problems, and it will help you to place your specific work and assignments within a wider context (see Item 10.11).

3. Job satisfaction is likely only when there is a good fit or match between the employee and his or her work organization. While it is unrealistic to expect a perfect fit, your professional values, beliefs, and goals must be compatible with those of your agency. You must believe in the agency's purpose and mission and have a sense that your work contributes to achieving a desired outcome. In order to achieve job satisfaction, you must be able to view yourself as a partner with your agency and not "just an employee" or a "cog in a giant wheel."

4. Identify and carefully consider your personal values, style, and strengths, and seek a niche within the organization where you will be accepted, utilized, and rewarded and where you can obtain a sense of job satisfaction. Think seriously before accepting a promotion or a transfer that would take you away from the type of work you really enjoy. If possible, maintain ongoing contact with agency clients even as you rise to a supervisory or administrative level, for this provides you with a constant reminder of the agency's purpose and what needs to be changed to improve service to clients.

5. Acquire the skills needed and valued by your agency. Examine your agency's programs and operations and then strive to develop your knowledge or skills in an area that is especially valued by the agency (e.g., computer operations, report writing, public speaking, work with a special client group, etc.). Having a special competency not only contributes to job satisfaction but it also increases your influence within the agency.

6. Respect the chain of command. Your superiors will want to be informed about any situation that could have an impact on the unit for which they are responsible. They will need to decide when and how their own superiors are to be informed. Thus, any attempt to go around or over the head of your immediate superior is likely to have negative repercussions.

7. When confused or frustrated by a specific agency rule, procedure, or policy, seek answers to the question of why it exists or why it exists in this particular form. Many rules and policies are created in reaction to an agency problem or dilemma or in response to some external force, such as a lawsuit, shift in funding sources and requirements, change in federal programs, or pressure from community groups. Some policies and procedures remain in effect even after they have outlived their usefulness. Knowing the history behind a certain requirement will at least make it more intelligible, and if you should discover that it is no longer useful, you will have taken the first step toward changing it. Also strive to develop the fine art of reframing the agency context of practice. For example, do not view existing policies and rules as barriers and constraints to be opposed and fought against. Rather, view them as guidelines to be managed and manipulated and as opportunities to be exploited in order to achieve important goals and to serve clients.

8. Although a bureaucracy can be changed, the rate of change is slow. Many months, even years, may be needed to achieve a significant change. Do not waste time on insignificant or petty concerns. Work for changes that are realistic and feasible. And always work as part of a group; a group has more influence and more knowledge than an individual.

9. When working to change your agency, select your tactics with great care. Be attentive to the question of who has power within the organization and who stands to gain or lose from a particular change in structure, policy, or procedure. Those who challenge well-entrenched power groups risk being stripped of their power or squeezed out of the organization. Be a diplomat rather than a combat soldier. Aggressive tactics seldom work within a bureaucracy.

10. As an agency employee, you must work cooperatively with other agency employees, committees, and departments, even when you disagree with their approaches and even when you do not personally like the people with whom you must work. Employment within a large agency requires that you make accommodations and adapt to administrative and organizational requirements. If you lack this personal flexibility and are unable or unwilling to make reasonable concessions, you will quickly become dissatisfied with your job.

11. Maintain a balanced perspective and a sense of humor about your job and your place within your organization. Work hard and be a responsible employee, but do not take yourself or your agency too seriously. Realize that the bureaucracy is not intended to provide a sense of meaning in life or to meet other emotional or spiritual needs. Look elsewhere for the activities and relationships that can meet those needs.

SELECTED BIBLIOGRAPHY

Ackoff, Russel L., and Sheldon Rovin. *Beating the System Using Creativity to Outsmart Bureaucracies.* SanFrancisco: Berrett-Koehler, 2005.

Ashworth, Kenneth H. *Caught between the Dog and the Fireplug, or How to Survive Public Service.* Washington, DC: Georgetown University Press, 2001.

16.5   DEALING WITH SEXUAL MISCONDUCT

Purpose: To prevent or address issues of sexual misconduct and sexual harassment in the context of social work practice or education.

Discussion: The structure of professional relationships is inherently unequal, making clients vulnerable to exploitation. Clients enter the relationship in order to receive assistance from a competent professional and trust the worker to treat their needs and interests as primary. In turn, it is expected that the professional will be responsible to avoid any misuse of this trust and will not exploit the client in any form (i.e., financial, sexual, or in any other way of personal gain). In addition, professional responsibility requires that any social worker in a position of power avoid manipulating that situation for personal advantage. For example, a supervisor should not manipulate a supervisee, an administrator should not take advantage of workers, and a teacher or a field instructor should not exploit a student.

The *NASW Code of Ethics* (1999) provides guidance in several areas in which there is a potential conflict of interest for a social worker in practice or employment situations. In recent years, there has been growing recognition that the potential for sexual exploitation in the human services is high and professions have begun to take strong positions when sexual misconduct occurs. Section 1.09 of the *Code of Ethics* is explicit in prohibiting sexual contact with clients, the relatives of clients, and former clients, as well as providing services to persons with whom the social worker has previously had a sexual relationship. In addition, Section 2.07 of NASW's *Code of Ethics* clearly prohibits sexually exploiting colleagues in a vulnerable position in the workplace (i.e., supervisees, students, trainees, or others for whom there may be a conflict of interest).

One form of sexual misconduct is ***sexual harassment*** which the federal government defines as any unwelcome sexual advance, request for sexual favors, or other verbal or physical conduct of a sexual nature made under these conditions:

- Submission to such conduct is explicitly or implicitly made a term or condition of an individual's employment or participation in an education program or activity.
- Submission to or rejection of such conduct by an individual is used as the basis for academic or employment decisions affecting that individual.
- Such conduct has the purpose or effect of substantially interfering with an individual's academic or work performance or creating an intimidating, hostile, or offensive working or educational environment. (Equal Employment Opportunity Commission, 1980)

Note that sexual harassment may comprise either heterosexual or homosexual advances.

Two strategies are available for dealing with sexual harassment: organizational and individual. At the *organizational* level, it is important to create agency policy that clearly prohibits sexual harassment and identifies procedures for making a complaint. That policy should be published in the agency's personnel manual, and the agency director should periodically post or circulate the statement. Periodic training helps to sensitize all staff to the problem and can prevent harassment.

At the *individual* level, if you feel that you are being harassed, you should first speak directly to the harasser, directing him or her to stop the offensive behaviors. If you are not able to directly confront the harasser, an effective strategy is to send a letter that specifies the nature of the harassing incidents and when they occurred, how you were affected, and how the conduct should change in the future. If the harassment persists, it is advisable to keep a diary of events and a list of any witnesses, as well as consulting with other workers, informing your supervisor, and seeking resolution using agency procedures. (*Note:* Some employers require an official complaint within 30 or 60 days of an incident.) If the situation is not resolved within the agency, consultation with a lawyer is suggested. Options include contacting your state human rights commission or the U.S. Equal Employment Opportunity Commission—making an official complaint within 180 days of the incident. If you file a complaint, be prepared for possible negative reactions from the harasser and others in the organization.

SELECTED BIBLIOGRAPHY

Boland, Mary. *Sexual Harassment in the Workplace*. Naperville, IL: Sphinx Publishing, 2004.

Equal Employment Opportunity Commission. "Guidelines on Discrimination Because of Sex, Title VII, Section 703." *Federal Register* 45 (11 April 1980): 2505.

National Association of Social Workers. *Code of Ethics*. Washington, DC: NASW, 1999.

16.6   AVOIDING MALPRACTICE SUITS

Purpose: To minimize the possibility of being named in a lawsuit alleging professional negligence or misconduct.

Discussion: Most social workers probably underestimate their legal vulnerability. But in fact, a growing number are being sued for malpractice or professional negligence. Broadly speaking, a worker may be held liable if he or she has done something or neglected to do something that resulted in causing harm or injury to a client.

In this type of lawsuit, the person who files the lawsuit and alleges malpractice or professional negligence is termed the ***plaintiff***. The person who is being accused of malpractice or negligence is termed the ***defendant***. In order to win the lawsuit, the plaintiff must prove four points:

1. The defendant (e.g., the social worker) was obligated to provide the plaintiff with a particular standard of care or professional conduct.
2. The worker was derelict because he or she breached that obligation (or duty) by some act or omission that had a foreseeable consequence.
3. The client suffered some injury or harm (physical, financial, emotional, etc.).
4. The worker's conduct was a direct or proximate cause of the injury or harm.

Whether a breach of duty has occurred is determined by measuring the allegedly harmful act or omission against published standards of practice, agency policy, and the performance of social workers in similar settings. The client's injury must be one that would not have occurred had it not been for the social worker's negligence. Despite this traditional *proximate cause* requirement, juries are increasingly finding liability without fault (i.e., finding providers of services negligent even when they are not the proximate cause of the injury).

The professional duties that, if breached, place social workers and social agencies at greatest risk of legal liability include the following:

- Duty to avoid sexual misconduct
- Duty to warn others when a client discloses intent to harm them
- Duty to prevent a client's suicide
- Duty to properly diagnose and treat a client
- Duty to ensure continuity of service to a client under the care of a worker or agency
- Duty to maintain and protect confidentiality
- Duty to maintain accurate professional records and a proper and legal accounting of payments and reimbursements

In addition to allegations of misconduct based on the preceding duties, there can be many others:

- Providing or arranging the transportation that involves a client in a vehicular accident causing bodily injury
- Failing to report or properly investigate suspected abuse or neglect
- Inappropriately placing of a child or adult into foster care, an institution, a hospital, or jail
- Inappropriately or prematurely releasing a client from foster care, a hospital, an institution, or another protective setting
- Placing or contributing to the placement of a client into a facility or foster home in which he or she is subsequently abused or neglected (i.e., failing to properly select or supervise the placement)
- Practicing while impaired by use of drugs or alcohol or failure to report a colleague known to be impaired
- Failing to inform a client of eligibility rules or regulations, resulting in avoidable financial costs to the client
- Failing to consult with or refer a client to a specialist
- Failing to recognize an obvious medical problem and not referring the client to a physician
- Practicing medicine without a license (e.g., suggesting changes in the client's use of medications)
- Misrepresenting one's professional training and qualifications
- Using a radical or untested approach, technique, or procedure
- Providing inaccurate information or advice to a client

- Providing birth control information or abortion counseling to a minor without consent of the parent
- Acting in a prejudicial manner in the selection of an adoptive home or in the licensing of a foster home, day-care facility, or the like
- Failing to be available to a client when needed (e.g., failing to provide professional coverage during the worker's vacation)
- Inappropriately or prematurely terminating a treatment relationship
- Causing alienation between parent and child or husband and wife
- Failing to supervise a child or a person with a mental disability while he or she is participating in an agency program
- Failing to supervise the work of others, including the work of volunteers and students

Of course, there is a big difference between being named in a lawsuit and actually being found negligent by a jury. But even if the suit is eventually dropped or dismissed for a lack of evidence, the worker and/or the agency will have incurred legal expenses during their defense. Most of these lawsuits are settled out of court.

Most lawsuits name as defendants both the social worker and the employing agency because the agency is assumed to be indirectly responsible for the harm caused by an employee. A social worker employed by an agency can be found personally liable, although this is not likely if the worker was acting within his or her job description, was following agency policy, and did nothing of a criminal nature.

In some cases, a social worker is held liable for harm caused by a person under his or her supervision (e.g., another social worker, volunteer, or student). Also, a worker might be held liable if he or she somehow contributed to the harm caused by another professional. An example of this is when a worker refers a client to an incompetent professional or when a worker provides a social assessment report to a psychiatrist who then makes a poor decision based on that report.

A social worker who learns that he or she has been named in a malpractice suit should immediately contact an attorney (the worker's agency may provide legal representation) and also notify his or her supervisor, agency administrator, and insurance company. The social worker should not speak with anyone about the allegations before securing legal counsel. The worker must never alter case records or other documents related to the case. Such changes are easily detected and may constitute a crime. An attempt to alter a record will be viewed as an effort to destroy evidence and cover up a wrongdoing.

Legal experts explain that the key to avoiding a malpractice suit is adherence to reasonable, ordinary, and prudent practices. In order to defend one's self against allegations, the worker must show that his or her actions were fair, in good faith, and consistent with how other properly trained professionals would behave under similar circumstances. One of the best defenses is to be able to show that the client gave his or her informed consent to the professional's intervention. This underscores the need to document client involvement in problem identification, assessment, and case planning and the value of written service agreements (see Item 12.6).

By following a number of additional guidelines, the social worker can avoid a malpractice suit or at least minimize its damage:

1. The social worker should secure malpractice insurance. It can be purchased through the National Association of Social Workers by NASW members and from some insurance companies.

2. Adhere to the *NASW Code of Ethics* and the *NASW Standards of Professional Practice* relevant to your area of practice (see NASW website). Also adhere to your agency's policies and procedures, as well as state and federal laws and regulations affecting your agency's program and services.

3. Do not become sexually or romantically involved with a client. Sexual misconduct toward a client is one of the most common allegations giving rise to malpractice suits in social work. Sexual involvement with a client is a clear violation of the *NASW Code of Ethics*, a violation of state professional licensing statutes, and, in some states, a violation of criminal law. Avoid situations that could be misinterpreted as sexually inappropriate or give rise to false allegations of sexual misconduct. For example, male workers should be very cautious about visiting a female client in her home. A third party (potential witness) should be within earshot whenever a male worker interviews a female adult or a child.

4. Do not engage in or create dual relationships. A *dual relationship* is one in which a second set of obligations or expectations is introduced into the social worker–client relationship. Examples include dating a client, renting an apartment to or from a client, loaning money to or borrowing money from a client, hiring a client to perform some service (e.g., repair worker's car), selling some item or product to a client, and so on. Dual relationships must also be avoided in supervisor-worker and faculty-student interaction.

5. Know your level of skill and practice within those limitations. Secure the training and supervision needed to perform your job-related tasks and activities responsibly. Become aware of the types of clients or situations that touch your personal issues and lessen your ability to be objective. Obtain supervision and/or consultation when you are having unusual difficulties with a client. Consult with your peers, supervisor, and/or attorney when faced with difficult ethical or legal issues.

6. Be especially careful when dealing with clients or situations that present high legal risk. Examples include clients who may attempt suicide, clients who are violent and a threat to others, clients who have a history of filing lawsuits, clients who are very manipulative, and clients who always find fault or perceive bad intentions in the behavior of others.

7. Before delivering services to a child or adolescent, be certain that your program or agency has secured proper authorization from the parent or guardian and that it is lawful for you to provide these services to the minor in question. As a general rule, the parent has the legal right to control and consent to the medical care and other professional services provided to his or her minor-aged child. However, the laws of most states allow for exceptions to this principle. For example, minors may be allowed to consent to their own medical care in regard to specific conditions such as pregnancy, sexually transmitted disease, mental illness, and substance abuse. When in doubt, consult with your agency's attorney.

8. Base your practice on a professionally recognized theory or model. Keep your client fully informed of decisions, plans, and any risks associated with the intervention. Be careful not to give your client false hope about what you will be able to do. Convey a realistic picture of what you and your agency's services can accomplish. Maintain records that document your actions and any events or circumstances that might have had an adverse impact on the client.

9. Inform clients of any circumstances that may affect confidentiality. Confidentiality must be broken in order to report suspected abuse or neglect, to warn others of your client's intention to harm them, and to alert others of your client's intention to commit suicide.

10. Reach out to the client who has been angered by your actions and attempt to rebuild the relationship and address his or her complaint. Many malpractice suits could have been prevented if only the worker or agency had followed up on client complaints. If you work for a fee-charging agency, make sure that financial arrangements are handled in a completely businesslike manner so as to minimize the possibility of misunderstanding regarding cost and the collection of insurance payments.

11. Adhere to agency policy whenever a client presents you with a gift. As a general rule, food and inexpensive gifts valued at not more than a few dollars can be accepted, but a more expensive gift should not be accepted before consulting with your supervisor.

12. Be very cautious about giving any advice that could have a significant impact on the client's life (e.g., advising a client to get a divorce, how to invest money, etc.).

13. Do not transport a client in your private car unless this is in keeping with agency procedures and allowed under your auto insurance policy.

14. If served a subpoena to release client records, immediately consult with your supervisor and agency attorney. It is important to understand that you must respond to the subpoena, but one possible response by your attorney is to claim confidentiality and contest the request to release the records. Contesting the request will result in a court hearing on the matter and then a decision by the judge on whether your claim is valid or if you must indeed turn over the records.

15. Never agree to an interview with an attorney or other investigator before first consulting with your own attorney. (It is a common practice for attorneys to attempt to secure statements or information before you are even aware that you are the target of a lawsuit.)

16. Before accepting a job with an agency, check into the agency's record of providing legal defense for employees who are named in a lawsuit.

SELECTED BIBLIOGRAPHY

Bullis, Ronald. *Clinical Social Worker Misconduct.* Chicago: Nelson-Hall, 1995.
Guttmann, David. *Ethics in Social Work.* Binghamton, NY: Haworth Press, 2006.
Madden, Robert. *Essential Law for Social Workers.* New York: Columbia University Press, 2003.

16.7   TESTIFYING IN COURT

Purpose: To prepare for a court appearance as a witness.

Discussion: Social workers employed in protective services, probation, and parole settings make frequent appearances in court. Sooner or later, nearly every social worker—regardless of agency setting—will serve as a witness. Following guidelines such as these can help the worker perform effectively on the witness stand:

1. Prepare for the court appearance. Consult with the attorney who will call you as a witness and learn about the questions he or she will ask, as well as the questions you are likely to be asked by the attorney who will cross-examine you. Your testimony will probably fall into one of three categories:

   a. *Personal observations.* Prepare to testify with little, if any, reference to your notes. If your observations occurred over a long period of time, you can prepare a chronology or list of events to refresh your memory and keep your recollections organized. The opposing counsel and judge will probably look at your list, but it will not usually be introduced as evidence unless it differs from your oral testimony. Memorize the facts, but avoid sounding as though you are giving a recitation.

   b. *Reading reports.* Portions of your case record may be admitted into evidence. If so, you may be asked to read aloud segments of the record. Prepare by being thoroughly familiar with the content and organization of the record. Make sure you can read any handwritten parts. You should be able to explain the method for producing, transcribing, and storing a case file in your office.

   c. *Expert conclusions.* An individual who the judge has designated as an expert witness is permitted to offer opinions as to the meaning of facts and observations. All other witnesses must confine their testimony to facts and observations. Opposing attorneys often argue over whether a person should be qualified as an expert. If an attorney plans to qualify you as an expert witness, be prepared to explain the following:

   - Your professional qualifications (e.g., degree, experience, special training, publications, memberships in professional associations, etc.)
   - The knowledge base, theories, and principles you used in forming an opinion
   - Your mode of practice and how it is similar to or different from that of other social workers or professionals in your field

2. Inform the attorney representing the side for which you are testifying of any uncertainty, inconsistency, or gaps in information that will be evident in your testimony. He or she should know of these concerns before you are called to testify.

3. Tell the truth. Remember that you will be under oath. Any exaggeration or departure from facts will probably be uncovered and your credibility as a witness will suffer.

4. Appearance and demeanor are critical. You should be properly dressed and well groomed to reflect the solemnity of the courtroom. When seated in the witness chair, you should be attentive and courteous.

5. Speak clearly and avoid using slang and jargon. Much of the jargon used by social workers is incomprehensible to judges, attorneys, and juries.

6. Listen carefully to the questions you are asked. If you do not understand a question, ask that it be rephrased or explained. If you do not know the answer, say so. Never speculate or guess. Answer only the question that is asked. Answer questions in a confident manner. Phrases such as "I feel" or "I guess" weaken the impact of your testimony.

7. If an objection is made during the course of your testimony, stop speaking immediately. If the judge overrules the objection, you will be told to answer the question. If the objection is sustained, you will not be permitted to answer and a new question will be asked.

8. When being cross-examined by the opposing attorney, keep in mind that he or she is not your friend. Even a polite and friendly cross-examiner is looking for ways to trip you up and discredit your testimony. Do not volunteer information that is not asked for. Do not explain why you know something unless you are asked. And finally, remember that the attorney offering your testimony has a chance to follow up and ask additional questions after the other attorney's cross-examination. This may help clear up any problems in your testimony.

9. When being cross-examined, do not lose your temper at questions you consider impertinent or offensive. Exercise self-control. If you maintain your composure, you will be less likely to become confused and inconsistent. If the questioning is truly improper, your attorney will object. Pause before answering a provocative question to allow the objection to be made, but not so long that you appear hesitant or unsure. All questions should be handled with tact and truth. Fortunately, judges are familiar with the histrionics of some trial attorneys and are rarely impressed by them.

10. Do not get caught in the "yes-or-no" trap. If, on cross-examination, the attorney asks a question and ends it with "Answer yes or no," don't feel obliged to do so if you believe such an answer will be misleading. Instead, begin your answer with "Well, that needs explaining." The attorney may again push you to answer yes or no and the judge may require you to give a yes or no answer, but the jury will understand your position and look forward to your explanation when your attorney clarifies the situation on redirect examination.

11. Many times, cross-examiners ask compound questions. When responding to a compound question, divide it into sections and then answer each part. Do not agree with a partially untrue statement, because the attorney may cut you short and not allow you to complete your response, thus giving an erroneous impression of your actions or beliefs.

12. A witness is sometimes asked a question regarding his or her sympathy for one side or the other in the case. If asked, admit your beliefs or sympathies honestly. It is absurd to deny an obvious sympathy, and an honest admission will not discredit a witness.

SELECTED BIBLIOGRAPHY

Bernstein, Barton, and Thomas Hartsell. *The Portable Guide to Testifying in Court for Mental Health Professionals*. Hoboken, NJ: John Wiley and Sons, 2005.

Vogelsang, Janet. *The Witness Stand: A Guide for Clinical Social Workers in the Courtroom*. Binghamton, NY: Haworth, 2001.

16.8   DEALING WITH MANAGED CARE

Purpose: To adapt social work practice to the requirements and restrictions of managed care arrangements.

Discussion: The term ***managed care*** refers to a variety of policies and procedures that are designed to control the costs of the services and treatments provided to individuals and also to ensure that the quality of such services and treatments is appropriate. In practice, however, efforts to minimize costs usually overshadow efforts to ensure the quality of care.

Managed care programs first developed in the areas of medical and hospital care and mental health. However, this approach and its mechanisms now influence a variety of other human services programs. A side effect of managed care is the increased privatization of social services and health care.

Managed care exists in several forms, such as Health Maintenance Organizations (HMOs), Employee Assistance Programs (EAPs), Preferred Provider Organizations (PPOs), Prospective Payment Systems (PPSs), and various approaches to utilization review. Typically, the managed care organization is a for-profit company that works under a contract with a third-party payer, such as a private health insurance company, or a government agency, similar to those that administer Medicaid and Medicare.

The employee of the managed care company (i.e., the case manager or care manger) is responsible for monitoring the use of the insurance program benefits and, where possible, for reducing the cost of patient care and treatment. The mechanisms used to control costs are usually one or more of the following: (1) to control or influence the decision on whether an individual will receive treatment, (2) to control or influence the decision on the type (or length) of treatment to be provided, (3) to control or influence the decision on what professional or facility will provide the treatment, (4) to minimize the length of stay in an expensive treatment facility and move the patient to a less expensive facility as soon as possible, (5) to determine how much the provider is to be paid, and (6) to cease payment for certain types of treatment when the patient or client is no longer making progress.

The term ***third-party payer*** has been used to refer to the organizational entity (e.g., an insurance company, Medicare, Medicaid, CHAMPUS) that is paying for the services provided by a professional and received by a client or patient. The managed care company is now a fourth-party in this already complex arrangement.

The treatment provider and the company's case manager are often separated by hundreds of miles, and their communication will be by phone and through the exchange of patient records and progress notes by surface mail, FAX, or email. In rare situations, the case manager will speak face to face with the provider and patient, but most often the case manager will base his or her decisions on the written materials submitted by the provider.

The advent of managed care has raised many legal and ethical questions for social workers and other providers of health and human services. The provider of the treatment continues to be ethically and legally responsible for making sure that the patient receives needed and appropriate care even though many of the key treatment decisions are now in the hands of a company case manager or dictated by fiscal considerations. Many of the social worker's ethical concerns relate to such issues as confidentiality, client self-determination, and the client's right to be fully informed about various treatment options.

As agencies and social workers adapt their practices and programs to the realities of managed care, it may prove helpful to follow these guidelines:

1. Decisions related to referring an individual for treatment and accepting a referral must be concerned with how managed care requirements and restrictions may affect service delivery. In many cases, it will be necessary to help the client seek information about possible managed care implications so that the client can make an informed decision on whether and from whom to seek services (see Item 10.4).

2. Learn about the procedures used in diagnosis. For the most part, third-party payers only pay for the treatment of disease and pathological conditions and thus a diagnosis is required to establish the existence of the disease or disorder. In mental health, this requires classification according to the *Diagnostic and Statistical Manual of Mental Disorders*, or *DSM* (see Item 11.18). The third-party payer will cover certain conditions, but not others, often tempting the provider to manipulate a diagnosis in order to maximize client service. However, it is important to understand that the crime of insurance fraud is committed by a provider who knowingly assigns the wrong diagnostic label in order to secure payment from an insurance company.

3. Conceptualize your treatment plan as the best intervention possible, with full awareness of what costs are involved and how managed care will limit the type and length of services that will be reimbursed. Your written plan must utilize the language and terminology used by the managed care company. Also, the arrangement, sequencing, and scheduling of specific treatment activities or procedures may need to be synchronized with the company's billing cycle and billing procedures.

4. Because the managed care company's case manager will agree to pay for treatment only so long as need can be justified and progress can be documented, it is important to use assessment tools and outcome measures that are understandable to and acceptable to the case manager (see Chapter 14). Also, the client's record and progress notes must document treatment efforts and client progress in ways required by the case manager to approve of and justify continuing the treatment.

5. Be prepared to assume the role of client advocate and develop the skills of persuasion and negotiation in order to secure the case manager's approval of treatment you consider important to your client.

6. The emphasis on cost containment has brought an added emphasis on prevention and early intervention. This development presents social workers with an opportunity to demonstrate to managed care companies the importance of psychosocial intervention as a way of reducing costs.

SELECTED BIBLIOGRAPHY

Buppert, Carolyn. *The Primary Care Provider's Guide to Compensation and Quality: How to Get Paid and Not Get Sued*, 2nd ed. Sudsbury, MA: Jones and Bartlett, 2005.

Franklin, Cynthia. "Developing Effective Practice Competencies in Managed Behavioral Health Care." In *Social Workers' Desk Reference*, edited by Albert Roberts and Gilbert Greene, 44–50. New York: Oxford University Press, 2002.

Gibelman, Margaret. "Social Work in an Era of Managed Care." In *Social Workers' Desk Reference*, edited by Albert Roberts and Gilbert Greene, 16–23. New York: Oxford University Press, 2002.

16.9   GIVING AND RECEIVING SUPERVISION

Purpose: To enhance the provision of human services through monitoring staff performance and assisting staff members to grow and develop in knowledge and skill.

Discussion: Throughout most of its history, the social work profession has looked to the process of supervision as critical to the preparation of new practitioners as well as a means of quality control in the delivery of services. Unlike those professions in which the private practice or independent practitioner model of service delivery has been dominant, social work extends the use of supervision well beyond the worker's period of training. As a primarily agency-based profession, social work depends upon a layer of the agency's administrative structure (i.e., supervisors) to continue training new workers and provide ongoing professional guidance. In order to become competent, these emerging social workers must learn how to use the supervisory process for their own professional development.

The supervisor plays dual roles. The first, ***administrative supervision***, involves monitoring the work of supervisees to assure that it meets agency standards. Thus, supervisors are part of an agency's middle-management team and play an important role in agency policy, program, and personnel decisions. The second role is called ***supportive supervision***. In this capacity, the supervisor is concerned with workers' job satisfaction, morale, and development of job-related knowledge, values, and skills. New social workers often move rather quickly into roles supervising other staff and volunteers because the basic helping skills they acquire in social work education translate into the skills needed by supervisors.

Both supervisors and supervisees should recognize that the supervisory experience merits thoughtful development and carefully planned and regularly scheduled sessions. Supervisory sessions can take several forms. Here are the most typical ways in which supervision is given and received:

- *Individual supervision.* These one-on-one meetings between the supervisor and supervisee are the most prevalent form of interaction. Every supervisee needs and deserves regularly scheduled private time with his or her supervisor during which the worker's performance can be candidly examined with sufficient emotional safety to address practice successes and failures.
- *Group supervision.* Holding regularly scheduled meetings between a supervisor and a small group of supervisees provides a time-efficient opportunity for new workers or volunteers to process events, share information and perceptions, and help each other gain knowledge and skill in service provision and meeting agency expectations.
- *Ad hoc supervision.* These brief and unscheduled meetings are designed to respond to questions and issues as they arise during daily practice activities. These impromptu meetings are particularly useful for problem solving and capturing so-called teachable moments.
- *Formal case presentations.* At these regularly scheduled meetings, one or more supervisees present in-depth descriptions of their work on specific cases and projects. The supervisor and other participants then offer advice and guidance on how each presenter's performance could be improved.

Social workers have experience with both elements of the supervisory process. As students and new workers, they must be skilled at *using* supervision to enhance their own development, and later in their careers, they must be adept at *giving* supervision to assist others in their development.

Guidelines for Using Supervision

Remembering guidelines such as the following can help the social worker make appropriate and effective use of supervision:

1. Realize that your supervisor will expect you to do these things:
   - Be effective and get results consistent with the agency's mission, program, goals, and your job description.
   - Follow agency policies, procedures, and specific instructions.
   - Consult with your supervisor when you are unsure about how to proceed or when a course of action is raising unforseen issues or encountering unexpected problems.

- Immediately inform your supervisor when you become aware of an ethical, legal, or procedural violation that could give rise to a formal complaint or in some way harm the agency or its clients.
- Demonstrate an eagerness to learn the details of your job, to become more efficient and effective, and to accept constructive criticism and suggestions on how you could improve the quality of your work.
- Take initiative and assume responsibility for work that needs to be done.
- Work cooperatively with and be respectful of colleagues and engage in behaviors that improve staff morale.
- Maintain accurate and up-to-date records of your work with clients.

2. Expect your supervisors to do the following:
   - Provide needed on-the-job training.
   - Keep you informed of changes in agency policies or procedures.
   - Provide encouragement and support when your work is particularly difficult and frustrating.
   - Evaluate your performance on a regular basis and offer specific suggestions on how it can be improved.
   - Give you a clear warning when your performance falls below standards.

3. Establish a regularly scheduled time to meet with your supervisor. This should be at least once a week. Having adequate time to discuss work and job-related concerns is of critical importance.

4. Seek your supervisor's assistance in formulating an individualized training plan that will build on your personal and professional strengths and address limitations in your performance. Such a plan should be in writing. Identify specific tasks and objectives to be accomplished over the next 6 and 12 months, and list specific learning activities (reading, study, conferences, workshops, etc.).

5. Recognize that the recommendations of experienced and respected supervisors are usually pivotal to your effort to secure a promotion or career advancement. When making such a recommendation, a supervisor will be especially attentive to the quality and quantity of your work, your understanding of the agency and the work to be done, your ability to formulate a feasible plan and carry it out, your leadership skills and the ability to win the respect of others, your time-management skills, your capacity to learn and adapt to change, your initiative and willingness to assume responsibility, and your emotional stability and dependability.

Guidelines for Social Work Students

Horejsi and Garthwait (2002, 12–13) explain that the social work student has a special set of responsibilities to his or her practicum agency:

1. Meet with the practicum instructor (field instructor) on a regular basis (at least weekly).
2. Prepare for all meetings with the practicum instructor and inform him or her of the topics that need to be discussed during the upcoming meeting.

3. Be present at the agency on days and at times agreed upon by the student and practicum instructor. If unable to attend, notify the agency supervisor prior to or at the start of the workday.

4. Behave in a professional manner, taking responsibility as an adult learner to understand and carry out assigned duties, meet all deadlines, and seek direction when needed.

5. Carry out agency-related assignments, tasks, and responsibilities in a manner consistent with agency policy and procedures and prepare all records and reports in accord with the prescribed format.

6. Identify learning needs and, if required, prepare an agreement that identifies learning outcomes and learning activities.

7. Complete all practicum monitoring and evaluation forms and reports required by the agency and school (e.g., time sheets).

8. Discuss with the practicum instructor and/or the school's practicum coordinator any areas of significant disagreement, dissatisfaction, or confusion related to the practicum experience.

Guidelines for Providing Supervision

Assuming the role of supervising other workers or volunteers is a substantial step in a social worker's career. Not only do supervisees rely on the supervisor to guide their own development, but the clients who work directly with supervisees also trust that the services they receive will be properly monitored and that their interests will be protected. The following guidelines should assist the new supervisor in carrying out his or her responsibilities:

1. Understand that social workers who assume the role of supervisor have special ethical obligations. According to the *NASW Code of Ethics* (1999), social workers who provide supervision:

- Should have the necessary knowledge and skill to supervise . . . appropriately and should do so only within their areas of knowledge and competence.
- Are responsible for setting clear, appropriate, and culturally sensitive boundaries.
- Should not engage in any dual or multiple relationships with supervisee and in which there is a risk of exploitation of or potential harm to the supervisee.
- Should evaluate supervisee's performance in a manner that is fair and respectful. (NASW, 3.01 a–d)

2. Reward good performance. Because supervisors in human services agencies can seldom offer monetary rewards, they must be creative in utilizing other types of rewards such as recognition, offering desirable or stimulating work assignments, and special privileges.

3. Hold supervisees accountable for their performance. When it is necessary to correct or discipline a supervisee, do so immediately after the infraction is discovered and in private. Disciplinary actions must be fair, decisive, very clear, and based on facts. Such actions must communicate to the supervisee exactly what is expected in the future and the consequences if performance is not improved. Failure to do so can frustrate and demoralize other agency staff and consume an inordinate amount of a supervisor's time and energy.

4. Remember that example is the best teacher. The supervisor must constantly model the values, attitudes, and behavior he or she expects of supervisees.

5. Make work assignments that are clear and appropriate to the supervisee's level of knowledge, skill, and experience. The supervisee should be helped to learn job-related skills and obtain the training he or she needs to perform at a higher level.

6. Adjust the frequency and intensity of the supervisory process to the supervisees' level of competency and experience and to their job responsibilities.

7. If dismissal of the employee is a possibility, the supervisor must understand and strictly adhere to the relevant procedures outlined in the agency's personnel manual. Such procedures should reflect state and federal law on employee-employer relations. These procedures typically require that the employee be given written warnings of possible termination, a written description of his or her unacceptable performance, and a reasonable opportunity to improve his or her performance prior to termination. When attempting to terminate the employment of an individual, the supervisor must operate on the assumption that the individual may file a lawsuit and that the dismissal will have to be explained and justified in court. Some behaviors by the employee are so serious that they should result in an immediate move to terminate employment. These include:

- Clear and serious violations of the *NASW Code of Ethics* (e.g., sexual relations with a client, abuse of client, or sexual harassment of client or staff)
- Theft of agency money, equipment, or property
- Concealing, consuming, or selling drugs on agency premises
- Reckless or threatening actions that place clients or staff at risk of serious harm
- Deliberate withholding of information from a supervisor or agency personnel that they need to know in order to properly serve clients and maintain the integrity and reputation of the agency and its programs
- Deliberate falsification of agency records and reports
- Solicitation or acceptance of gifts or favors from clients in exchange for preferential treatment
- Clear and repeated insubordination

SELECTED BIBLIOGRAPHY

Austin, Michael J., and Karen M. Hopkins, eds. *Supervision as Collaboration in the Human Services: Building a Learning Culture.* Thousand Oaks, CA: Sage, 2004.

Horejsi, Charles, and Cynthia Garthwait. *The Social Work Practicum*, 2nd ed. Boston: Allyn & Bacon, 2002.

National Association of Social Workers. *NASW Code of Ethics.* Washington, DC: NASW, 1999.

16.10   BUILDING AND MAINTAINING MENTORING RELATIONSHIPS

Purpose: To understand the nature and advantages of mentoring relationships.

Discussion: In a ***mentoring relationship***, an experienced professional and/or seasoned agency employee guides a less experienced colleague in learning the unwritten rules of the organization and how to successfully navigate the practice setting, demonstrates how to deal with common frustrations and disappointments associated with social work practice, and teaches what one should do to grow and develop as a professional. The experienced colleague is termed the *mentor*; the less experienced one is often termed the *protégé* or *mentee*.

Elements of mentoring exist within a supervisor-supervisee relationship (see Item 16.9). However, in a true mentoring relationship, the mentor is not the protégé's administrative supervisor and does not assign work to him or her, oversee his or her daily work activities, or conduct the agency's formal evaluation of the protégé's work. A mentoring relationship is characterized by friendship and mutual trust, rather than by the structure of authority or chain of command depicted in an organizational chart.

Benefits of Mentoring to the Protégé

From the vantage point of the protégé, having a positive mentoring relationship can provide these five benefits.

1. *Support and understanding.* Beginning a new job or assuming a new set of responsibilities can be a time of insecurity, self-doubt, and confusion. During such a time, a wise and seasoned employee or professional can be of considerable help to a new or less experienced employee. A mentor's support, empathy, advice, and encouragement can boost the confidence of a protégé and calm his or her fears and anxieties.

2. *Orientation to and assimilation into the agency.* A mentor can help a protégé learn about the practice setting or agency as an environment of professional activity. The mentor can orient the protégé to the organization's culture and traditions as well as help him or her understand "office politics" and avoid political pitfalls. A new employee who is mentored tends to learn the job faster, is more easily socialized into the organization, and is more likely to succeed.

3. *Access to important "insider" information.* A mentor is a valuable source of insider information that the protégé could not easily obtain through other means. Examples include information related to the key events that have shaped the organization, informal policies and procedures that do not appear in written manuals, patterns and personality traits of other colleagues, ongoing interpersonal conflicts within the organization, and the like. The protégé must honor the expectation of confidentiality and trust inherent in the sharing of this information and be prudent and discreet in using it.

4. *Career guidance.* Mentors can help protégés plan their careers, set goals, and develop the skills they need for career and professional advancement. Mentors can also help protégés connect to professional organizations, select professional learning experiences, and participate in community groups.

5. *Role modeling.* An intangible benefit of the mentoring relationship is that the mentor becomes an important role model for the protégé. Much of the protégé's learning and development will occur as a result of observing and imitating his or her mentor.

Benefits of Mentoring for the Mentor

Mentoring is a two-way interaction, and the mentor should derive at least the following benefits from the mentoring relationship:

1. *Professional stimulation.* Social work practice is far from repetitious. Nonetheless, a certain amount of routine develops in agency practice, and it is easy for workers to fall into the pattern of approaching practice on a "business as usual" basis. The fresh perspectives and insights brought to the agency by the protégé can challenge the mentor to examine his or her practice through a different lens and thus stimulate his or her own professional growth.

2. *Updated knowledge.* The protégé can help the mentor learn about and stay abreast of new developments in the field. Likewise, the protégé can motivate the mentor to reexamine old assumptions and update any outdated knowledge and skills.

3. *Agency information.* The mentor can often obtain information from the protégé about personnel, problems, and issues in the organization that other employees might be reluctant to share with a senior staff member.

4. *Professional contribution.* Helping others make the most of their potential is the primary reason most social workers enter this profession. As the protégé grows in competence and effectiveness, the mentor will have the satisfaction of contributing to the growth and development of a colleague. What's more, the mentor may become more valued and respected by others in the organization based on the success achieved by the protégé.

Matching the Protégé and the Mentor

Within most organizations, mentors voluntarily take on the mentoring role because they care about or are interested in the professional development of particular individuals. However, in some organizations, mentoring is encouraged by policy, and the organization sets up formal mentoring assignments that match new employees with more experienced ones. It is not uncommon for an organization to create mentoring relationships in order to assist women and minority employees, who may face unique challenges in performing some organizational roles, such as supervision and administration, where role models are too often in short supply.

When there are cross-gender mentoring matches, some potential problems must be considered. For example, the assignment of a male mentor to a female protégé may reinforce stereotypical roles of male power and female dependence. Others in the organization may perceive a cross-gender mentoring relationship as a romantic involvement. Mentors, protégés, and the organization as a whole must be aware of these possible complications and make sure that mentoring facilitates, rather than impedes, professional development and advancement.

Guidelines for Mentoring Relationships

A social worker who is seeking a mentor or is making a mentor/mentee assignment should keep the following guidelines in mind:

- Pick or assign a mentor with great care. Seek a mentor who has a reputation for competence and effectiveness within the agency or practice setting. The mentor must possess the knowledge and skills the protégé hopes to learn.
- The mentor/mentee relationship must be comfortable and safe, take place in an environment of open discussion and mutual trust, and maintain an atmosphere in which the protégé can freely accept advice and constructive criticism.
- The mentor and protégé must commit sufficient time and energy to the relationship. Some mentor/mentee relationships work best with regularly scheduled meetings; others work well on an on-call basis. Expectations about how the interactions will occur should be clearly established at the start of the relationship.

Social workers who are interested in mentoring or providing guidance to a protégé should keep the following points in mind:

- Pick a protégé with great care. A protégé should be someone whom you genuinely care about and someone you want to see advance within the agency and the profession.
- Above all else, be willing and able to separate your own goals and values from those of your protégé. He or she is an individual, and you must be able to recognize and honor individual differences. Do not go into a mentoring relationship expecting to create a clone of yourself.
- Listen carefully to your protégé's questions and concerns. Do not assume that he or she has exactly the same concerns that you had at a particular stage in your professional development. The younger generation of professionals grew up in a different time, received a somewhat different type of professional education, and may have a set of personal and family concerns quite different from your own.

SELECTED BIBLIOGRAPHY

Wilson, Pamela P., Deborah Valentine, and Angela Pereira. "Perceptions of New Social Work Faculty about Mentoring Experiences." *Journal of Social Work Education,* 38 (Spring–Summer 2002): 317–333.

16.11   READING, WRITING, AND INTERPRETING PROFESSIONAL LITERATURE

Purpose: To make sound judgments about the merits of the information found in the social work literature and, when possible, to contribute to that literature.

Discussion: The professional social worker makes a career-long commitment to engage in evidince-based practice. With that foundation of knowledge, the worker then selects and adapts to the uniqueness of the specific client and practice situation. Thus, social work needs a strong body of literature as a resource for practitioners, and practitioners need the ability to sort through and draw from that literature.

Analyzing the Literature

The social worker's ability to understand and apply the literature to inform practice decisions is critical to successfully serving clients. In what is known as *evidence-based practice*, the worker is obligated to locate the most relevant literature and carefully examine that material for the facts and ideas that may be most useful in work with his or her clients. Doing so may be difficult for the many social workers who have time-consuming caseloads, leaving little time to read the rapidly expanding literature. Moreover, up-to-date libraries are inaccessible to many social workers.

Fortunately, recent developments in information technology (see Item 9.4) have reduced the time and effort required to locate needed information. An increasing amount of helpful information is available online, and article reprints can readily be obtained and downloaded from one's own computer. Once articles and reports have been identified, the social worker must decide if the information is relevant to practice with his or her clients and reliable and trustworthy. A checklist such as that shown in Figure 16.1 lists the factors that should be present in a well-designed research effort. An online abbreviated version of the research report or journal article may not contain enough information on which to base a conclusive decision, but a summary will usually be sufficient to inform a decision on whether the complete article or report should be secured.

When reviewing published research, it is important to identify the basic design of the study. Although some studies combine the two basic approaches, most can be characterized as using either a qualitative or quantitative method. **Quantitative research** typically involves collecting a large amount of data from a representative sample of respondents. Statistical analysis may then be used to summarize and reduce those data to understandable generalizations and to identify relationships

FIGURE 16.1	**Checklist for Evaluating Social Work Literature**

	Yes	No	??
1. Is the question under study clearly and accurately identified?	☐	☐	☐
2. Is the literature review thorough and does it reflect current thinking on this issue?	☐	☐	☐
3. Are the key terms, concepts, and assumptions clearly defined and key variables operationalized realistically?	☐	☐	☐
4. Is the design of the research sound?			
a. Is the study design and methodology clearly described?	☐	☐	☐
b. Is the method of sampling appropriate?	☐	☐	☐
c. Is the sample of sufficient size?	☐	☐	☐
d. Are data collection instruments valid (i.e., measuring what they said they were)?	☐	☐	☐
e. Are data collection instruments reliable (i.e., consistent from use to use)?	☐	☐	☐
5. Is the data analysis appropriate?			
a. If the data were *quantitative* in nature, are the statistical tests utilized correct for the type of sample and level of data?	☐	☐	☐
b. If the data were *qualitative* in nature, was a systematic approach to recording and analyzing them used?	☐	☐	☐
6. Are the results interpreted accurately and objectively?	☐	☐	☐
7. Are limitations to the study explained?	☐	☐	☐
8. Are the research questions answered satisfactorily?	☐	☐	☐
9. Are the conclusions stated clearly and adequately substantiated by the data?	☐	☐	☐
10. Are suggested applications to practice reasonable and realistic?	☐	☐	☐

among the data. ***Qualitative research***, by contrast, has the capacity to produce a more in-depth understanding of the thoughts, values, and experiences of a smaller number of respondents. Qualitative research is most appropriate when the basic characteristics of the phenomenon being studied are unclear or poorly defined.

A reader of qualitative research literature should be aware of these research characteristics:

1. Data collection is a highly interactive process. The qualitative researcher involves the respondents in interviews, focus groups, and other interactive processes, in which the respondent is given stimulus materials. Through the use of questions and other efforts at clarification, understanding of the phenomenon is deepened.

2. The researcher delays making an in-depth literature review until the data are collected in an effort to prevent researcher bias from affecting the data. Typically, the researcher will connect the findings to the literature only after the data have been collected.

3. Because the researcher interacts with respondents and can be biased in how he or she asks questions or interprets the information gathered, the researcher is expected to acknowledge his or her perspective on the matter under study. In doing so, he or she gives consumers of the research clues to researcher bias that may have entered the process.

4. Sample size is not a significant consideration in qualitative research. Although the respondents should be representative of the population that is interested in the topic, the goal is to secure more in-depth information from a small number of respondents rather than more general information from a large number. Often, 5 to 10 respondents is seen as a sufficient sample size in a qualitative study.

5. Methods used in qualitative research include (a) direct information from respondents through interviews and focus groups, (b) case study analysis to evolve themes and patterns from case observations, and (c) ethnographic research, in which the researcher becomes immersed in the respondent's physical, social, cultural, and work environment to gain in-depth understanding of that person's perspectives and experiences.

6. The information collected is recorded as fully as possible, which is sometimes called the *thick documentation* method. It is then necessary to code the themes and subthemes that appear in order to sort, organize, and reorganize the data and thus better understand the phenomenon being studied. Several computer software programs are available to facilitate this manipulation of data.

7. A central concept that guides the interpretation and analysis of qualitative data is *triangulation*, or applying multiple data-gathering methods, multiple observers or investigators, and/or multiple perspectives to the same data set. If those results are in agreement, there can be greater confidence in the validity of the information.

When consuming qualitative research, the social worker should be especially concerned about how researcher bias may affect the conclusions drawn. As noted earlier, because the researcher usually interacts with the respondents, it is relatively easy for him or her to slant the data and/or the interpretation of what they mean.

Quantitative research is the more customary form of knowledge development and testing in Western society. It is patterned after the scientific method used in the hard sciences. If studying the success of an intervention approach, for example, the researcher might engage in the following:

1. Review the literature and determine the current state of knowledge about that approach.
2. Formulate a hypothesis about the impact of the intervention.
3. Identify, define, and isolate the various factors and elements that must be examined in order to test the hypothesis.
4. Select a statistically valid sample from the population being studied.
5. Utilize control groups to hold constant the influence of extraneous factors.
6. Apply the intervention to the experimental group.
7. Collect and apply appropriate statistical analysis to the data.
8. Draw conclusions.

While this scientific process works well under laboratory conditions, where many variables can be controlled, it is much more difficult (and sometimes inappropriate) in working with people. For example, can one ethically encourage or even require a person to remain in an abusive family in order to be part of a control group during the study of a domestic violence intervention? It is possible, however, to examine natural experimental and control groups (e.g., clients who did and did not receive a particular intervention) and then arrive at some conclusions about the merits of the intervention.

Much of the strength of quantitative social science comes from the statistical analysis of the data. ***Statistics*** are the numerical representations of the characteristics of individual cases—in social work, the characteristics of the people the researcher has chosen to study. The group of cases selected for study may be either a *sample* (i.e., part of a population) or the *population* itself (i.e., the complete group of cases to which the researcher may want to generalize the results). The consumer of this research must have confidence that the sample is indeed representative of the population in order to consider the findings valid.

The consumer must also be confident that statistical analysis was rigorous and appropriate. *Statistical analysis* involves assembling, analyzing, summarizing, and interpreting numerical data in order to inform thinking. Three general questions should guide the social worker in considering the validity of the statistical analysis conducted in a quantitative study:

1. *What was the purpose of the statistical procedure?* Some statistics simply help to reduce data to numerical indicators. These ***descriptive statistics*** include frequency distributions, percentages, measures of central tendency (i.e., reflections of the most typical response, such as mean, median, or mode), and measures of variability (i.e., descriptions of the spread or disbursement of the data, such as the range or standard deviation of responses).

A more complex set of statistical tools, ***inferential statistics***, permit the researcher to draw conclusions from a sample regarding the differences in that sample from the population. One set of inferential statistics, *measures of difference*, project the likelihood that the differences occurred because of the intervention or other factors being studied, rather than simply by chance. For example, in the social sciences, the typical criterion for accepting a finding as significant is $p < 0.05$, meaning the probability is less than 5 in 100 that the outcome will occur by chance.

A second group of inferential statistics, known as *measures of association*, measure the correlation between two or more variables. In social research, it is seldom possible to establish a clear cause-and-effect relationship, but it is possible to identify patterns of interaction among variables. If the relationship between two variables is completely random, or a zero (0.00) correlation, the variables are considered unrelated. However, if one variable increases when the other increases (i.e., a positive correlation), the correlation coefficient will be somewhere between +0.01 and +1.00. Similarly, in a negative correlation, where one variable increases as the other decreases, the scores might vary from –0.01 to –1.00. When interpreting measures of association, a correlation coefficient (either + or –) of less than 0.30 is considered a weak relationship, one from 0.30 to 0.70 is moderate, and one above 0.70 is strong. Other statistical tests reflect the relationships among more than two variables. These *multivariant statistical procedures* include multiple regression analysis, analysis of variance (ANOVA), cluster analysis, and factor analysis.

2. *Was the statistical test appropriate for the level of measurement?* The application of many statistical tests depends on the level of the data being analyzed. At the most basic level, data are simply grouped into different mutually exclusive categories. One category is not considered to have more or less value than another. Such information is termed **nominal data**. Gender, ethnicity, and various yes or no questions (e.g., parent or nonparent) are examples of nominal-level data. **Ordinal data** represent information that can be ranked from low to high, but for which it would not be reasonable to assume that there is equal value in each category. For example, many scales used in the social work literature are three- or five-point ratings of a factor (e.g., frequently, occasionally, seldom) but there is no assumption of equal intervals between ratings—only indication of more or less, or higher or lower. For example, a rating scale may be used to indicate that Client A has higher self-esteem than Client B, but in measuring a variable like self-esteem, one is not able to say that Client A has three times more self-esteem than Client B. **Interval or ratio data**, on the other hand, assume the categories are divided into equal units and thus permit more precise measures. Interval-level data might include client age or the population of the community served by social workers. As the consumer of a research report or article, it is important to be sure that the statistical procedures selected were appropriate for the level of data collected in the study. Otherwise, the statistic may misrepresent the outcome.

3. *Was the type of sample correct for the statistical test used?* The type of sample (in combination with the level of measurement) determines which statistical procedures can be appropriately used. The most powerful (i.e., more rigorous in a mathematical sense) statistical tests are **parametric tests**, which require independent or random samples and interval- or ratio-level data for at least one variable. For a sample to meet the sampling criteria for parametric tests, the different cases being compared must have been independently assigned to groups or randomly selected and there must be reason to assume that the population from which the sample was drawn has a normal distribution. **Nonparametric statistics**, in contrast, are less powerful predictors but allow work with data that are nominal and ordinal. Also, since they compare the outcomes observed in the study with expected outcomes for those respondents, they do not assume a normal distribution. Nonparametric statistics fit almost all research situations and are frequently used in social work research.

Like the ability to communicate in a foreign language, one's facility with statistics quickly diminishes if he or she does not work with these procedures on a regular basis. Thus, making judgments regarding the correct application and interpretation of statistical data is often perplexing for the social worker who works with these procedures infrequently. To help such a worker, Figure 16.2 provides a "crib sheet" for use in examining quantitative research–based literature. It identifies each of sixteen

FIGURE 16.2 Statistical Notations Frequently Used in Social Work Literature

ANOVA	*Analysis of Variance.* This test examines the variation in the means of two or more independent or predictor variables to determine the likelihood that the results could have occurred by chance. This parametric test requires that the dependent variable is measured by interval-level data, while the predictor variable or variables may be nominal or ordinal. The ANOVA is similar to the *t*-test (see below) but can also be applied when three or more groups of data are being compared. By consulting an *F* table, the probability (e.g., $p < .05$) of a distribution occurring by chance can be estimated.
DF	*Degrees of Freedom.* *DF* indicates the number of cells in a set of data that are free to vary. This freedom to vary is an important factor in estimating the probability of an outcome occurring by chance. *DF* is computed by multiplying the number of rows minus one in a table by the number of columns minus one. Thus a 2×3 table would have 2 *DF*, whereas a 3×4 table would have 6 *DF*. *DF* is a necessary number when the researcher interprets the probability tables for the different statistical tests.
f	*Frequency.* An *f* will usually be reported in a table and simply reflects the number of responses in each category or interval.
F-ratio	*F.* Usually based on an ANOVA or a multiple regression analysis, this parametric test of significance is a measure of variability that requires interval or ratio data. It tests for difference between the standard deviations of two variables or samples. The *F*-ratio compares estimates of variance *between* the samples with variance *within* the samples. If the between-group variance is higher than the within-group variance, increasing the likelihood that the variance did not occur by chance, the *F*-ratio will be larger. The *F* value has little meaning until it is applied to a table that identifies the probability of that distribution occurring by chance.
Mdn	*Median.* This is a measure of central tendency that may be used with ordinal- or interval-level data. It is the midpoint in a distribution (i.e., the score above which and below which 50 percent of the cases lie).
Mo	*Mode.* This is a measure of central tendency that may be used with all levels of data. It reflects the category that includes the most cases in a distribution and thus can be applied to nominal data. In some distributions more than one category may have the same number of cases, resulting in a bimodal or multimodal distribution.
N	*Number.* The *N* reports the total number of cases that are being considered in the statistical procedure. The *N* may vary in different analyses of a data set due to incomplete responses or test requirements that may necessitate the exclusion of some cases.
%	*Percent.* A percentage is a reflection of the share of the cases that would fall into a category if the total were 100. It is computed by dividing the frequency (*f*) in a category by the total number of cases (*N*) and multiplying by 100.
p	*Probability.* A *p*-value reports the likelihood of a particular distribution occurring by chance if a normal distribution is assumed. Thus, the lower the likelihood of a distribution occurring by chance, the more confidence can be placed in the assumption that the variables being tested indeed affected the outcome.
r	*Pearson Product-Moment Correlation Coefficient.* The *r* is a correlation coefficient (i.e., a number that represents the association between two variables). It reflects the tendency of high or low scores for one variable to regularly be associated with

(continued)

FIGURE 16.2	Continued

high or low scores for another variable. Therefore, it is possible to predict the value of one set of scores by knowing another. The nearer the r-score is to $+1.00$ or -1.00, the greater is the likelihood that the items vary together (i.e., are associated with each other). The r is a parametric test that requires interval-level data. (*Note: The Spearman Rank Order Correlation Coefficient (r_s) is a similar nonparametric test that can be applied to ordinal or ranked data. It examines the association between pairs of variables and can be computed with a relatively small number of pairs [i.e., less than 30] in the sample.*)

Range   *Range.* The range is a measure of variability that reports the span between the lowest and highest scores of the cases in the sample. Data must be at least ordinal to compute the range.

SD   *Standard Deviation.* SD tells how much dispersion from the mean exists in the scores of the sample or population being studied. The more the scores deviate from the mean, the greater the standard deviation score. When comparing samples or groups as part of a study, the ones with the largest SD scores have the greatest variability in distribution, whereas the respondents in groups with smaller SDs are more like the mean (or average) and thus are more homogeneous. In a normal distribution, about 68 percent of all cases fall within one standard deviation from the mean (34 percent above and 34 percent below) and 95 percent fall within two standard deviations from the mean.

t-test   *Student's t.* The t-test is a parametric test of significant difference between the means of two samples (or a sample and the population from which the sample was drawn). At times it is also used to test the significance of the difference between two coefficients of correlation. If the means differ substantially (i.e., a higher score), it is likely that the difference was not a result of sampling error or chance, and it is reasonable to assume that the difference is associated with actual variations in the factors being examined. A t table provides statistical estimates of the probability that the results might be due to chance (e.g., $p < 0.05$).

$\overline{X}$ *Mean.* The arithmetic mean is a measure of central tendency that requires interval- or ratio-level data. It is the sum of the values for a variable divided by the number (N) of cases.

χ^2 *Chi Square.* χ^2 is a nonparametric test of significance that may be applied with nominal data. In essence, it compares the observed and expected frequencies for a variable to determine if the differences found could be explained by chance. Until the chi square value is translated to a probability score (e.g., $p < 0.05$), it has little meaning.

z *z-score.* The z-score is used to convert the raw scores of differing individual items (e.g., psychological assessments, performance ratings, exam scores) to a common basis so they can be compared accurately. This measure is based on the assumption of a normal curve and sets the mean for each item at 0 and each standard deviation (SD) at plus or minus 1.0. Thus, regardless of the variation in a set of mean scores, the z-score will normalize the data by reflecting the distance of a score from its mean in units of standard deviation. A minus z-score (e.g., -1.47) reflects the number of standard deviations below the mean, and a positive z-score (e.g., $+0.23$) reflects the number of standard deviations above the mean.

commonly used statistical procedures by the symbol commonly used in the literature and gives a brief description of its purpose. The use of this chart will hopefully re-engage the reader in statistical thinking.

Contributing to the Literature

Social workers are not just consumers of professional literature; they are also obligated by the *NASW Code of Ethics* to build the knowledge base and make it available to other social workers (NASW, 1999). This knowledge can be made available through conference presentations (see Item 16.12), but doing so usually reaches only a handful of individuals. And while information technology offers an increasingly useful vehicle for making knowledge available to social workers, today the primary communication route of sharing that information is through publication in professional journals. The primary NASW journal, *Social Work*, for example, reaches approximately 160,000 members and hundreds of libraries with each issue.

When preparing a journal article, it is important to remember that the reader ultimately decides if the material will be read at all and, if so, how it will be approached. Some readers will begin with the first paragraph and read each word as the author has presented the material. Some will skim and return to read carefully the parts that most interest them. Others may read the introduction and conclusion and, if their interest is not captured, move on to other materials. The author, then, must write to help the reader determine if it will be worth the time to read the material and to keep the interest of those who decide to read the article carefully. The following guidelines will be useful when preparing written materials:

1. *Have a clear and important message.* Although some articles are built on original ideas and data, most update and expand existing information, synthesize or combine available knowledge in a unique way, or simply express something already known in a form that makes it more understandable. The author must help the reader understand how this message relates to what is already known and why reading this article could enhance the social worker's practice. Since articles are limited in length, the scope of the article cannot be too broad nor the content too complex. A good test of scope is to see if the key ideas can be stated in a single paragraph. If it is not possible to be this succinct, the topic is probably too broad and may need to be broken into subparts and presented in more than one article.

2. *Select an appropriate journal.* A large number of journals address matters of interest to social workers. Some publish articles on a wide range of topics, but most specialize. The NASW (1997) *Author's Guide* contains information about publishing requirements for over 130 different journals. Each has its own focus and will attract a specific readership.

Before beginning to write, examine several issues of the journal most appropriate for the content and make an assessment of the probable readership, type of articles accepted for publication, and typical format of the articles (e.g., research based, theoretical, case applications). Each journal will periodically include a statement of its publishing requirements and provide information on preferred topics, length, style, and procedures for submitting articles. Social work journals typically use the *APA style* (American Psychological Association 2001) and usually have a maximum length of 15 to 20 double-spaced pages.

3. *Picture the audience.* It is helpful to write to an individual rather than an unknown audience. Select someone who would be likely to read the article, and write to that person. Use language that communicates your ideas clearly to him or her, and use concepts familiar to that person.

4. *Prepare an abstract.* Most journals require a 75- to 100-word abstract to accompany the article. Although it is often easier to write an abstract after the article is completed, preparing a first draft before writing the article can help focus attention on the most important points. The abstract should be clear, concise, and factual, as it may ultimately appear in *Social Work Abstracts* or on other databases.

5. *Develop an outline.* The readers' ability to comprehend the information in the article will be influenced by how well it is organized. Think through the logical connections between elements to be included. Preparing an outline will help you ensure that smooth and understandable transitions are provided to link the various parts of the article in a coherent fashion.

6. *Write the introduction.* The opening two or three paragraphs should tell what the article is about, explain why it is important, and suggest which social workers might be especially interested in this material. A good introduction maintains the reader's attention and stimulates continued reading. Tying the subject to a current issue or including a short case example related to the topic may help the reader recognize the benefit in reading the entire article.

For many writers, getting started is the most difficult part of writing. Do not let frustration over the introduction block the process. Some writers find it helpful to write a rough introduction with the intent of completely rewriting it later.

7. *Set the context or background.* It is important to let the reader know where this material fits in social work (e.g., practice theory, practice techniques, social welfare policy issues, etc.). The reader also needs to know the theoretical context in which this material is placed. A literature review or even clarification of its relationship to a particular concept or school of thought helps provide this background information. However, this contextual material cannot be extensive and must be focused clearly on the topic of the article.

8. *Prepare the body of the article.* Concisely report the facts and observations that are the heart of the article. It is helpful to supplement narrative material with alternative means of presenting the information (e.g., charts, figures, tables, and lists). If case examples are used, be sure that they are presented in a way that helps the reader generalize from that example to other situations.

Make frequent use of headings and subheadings so the reader can easily follow the flow of ideas and information. Articles are most readable when they contain short paragraphs with clearly focused content.

Write simply and clearly and avoid social work jargon. Omit gender-specific language and any terms that might reflect bias or stereotyping based on race, ethnicity, gender, age, handicapping conditions, or sexual orientation.

9. *Prepare a summary and/or conclusion.* End the article with a short statement that pulls together the key points and presents conclusions that can be drawn from this material. If relevant, point out additional research that is needed to further develop the subject.

10. *Collect and format references.* Using the format appropriate for the selected journal, list the references that support the ideas and information presented. Endnotes or some type of reference list are most often used.

11. *Choose a good title.* The title will be the first clue the reader will have about the article, so be sure it clearly identifies the subject. A creative or provocative title can attract reader interest.

12. *Rewrite, rewrite, rewrite.* Expect to revise and rewrite a number of times before concluding that the article is completed. Polishing the structure, content, and language time and time again is an essential part of good written communication. It sometimes helps to read the manuscript aloud, thinking about how it might sound to someone else and checking for any errors that might have been overlooked.

13. *Let it cool.* Avoid sending an article to a journal as soon as it comes out of your printer. A few days or a week away from the material provides a fresh perspective and may yield alternative ideas for presenting the material or strengthening the way ideas are expressed. It may be helpful to use this time to get colleagues to review the work and offer comments. Remember, however, that it is your article, and you must own the final result. Do not feel obligated to incorporate all suggested changes. Also, do not allow this cooling period to become an excuse for procrastination. You may never be completely satisfied with your writing, but you must stop refining it at some point.

14. *Mail the manuscript.* Send the required number of copies to the selected journal. Typically, the publisher will acknowledge receipt of the manuscript and send it on to two or three reviewers. The review process may take several months. Remember, too, that it is considered unethical to submit an article to more than one journal at a time.

15. *Dealing with acceptance or rejection.* Reviewers will usually offer comments on the strengths and limitations of the article and how it does or does not fit the focus of that journal. Reviewers will typically conclude with a recommendation to (a) reject, (b) accept if revised in specific ways, or (c) accept the article for publication. Some journals will, on request, provide the reviewers' comments if the article is rejected. If that occurs, seriously consider those comments and either revise and resubmit the article, send it to another journal, or drop the plan to publish it.

If the article is accepted, you will work with the professional editors who will offer suggestions for strengthening the presentation. You will have the opportunity to be sure that their editing does not distort or misrepresent the content. Depending on the backlog, it may take as much as a year for the article to appear in print.

When it is printed, most journals will send the author several copies of the issue in which the article appears or provide reprints of the article for a small fee.

When an article is accepted, the author will be required to assign the legal rights to this material to the publisher. It will then be necessary for the publisher to approve any subsequent reprinting or extensive quoting of the article in other books or articles, including your own.

SELECTED BIBLIOGRAPHY

American Psychological Association. *Publication Manual of the American Psychological Association*, 5th ed. Washington, DC: APA, 2001.

Glicken, Morley. *A Guide to Writing for Human Service professionals.* Lanham, MD: Rowman and Littlefield, 2007.

National Association of Social Workers. *Author's Guide to Social Work Journals*, 4th ed. Washington, DC: NASW Press, 1997.

Neuman, W. Lawrence, and Larry Kreuger. *Social Work Research Methods: Qualitative and Quantitative Approaches.* Boston: Allyn & Bacon, 2006.

Szuchman, Lenore T., and Barbara Thomlison. *Writing with Style: APA Style for Social Work.* Belmont, CA: Brooks/Cole, 2004.

16.12   PRESENTING TO A PROFESSIONAL AUDIENCE

Purpose: To organize and plan a speech or other oral presentation to communicate professional information.

Discussion: Because social workers are expected to make presentations to decision makers and professional colleagues, it is important that they develop the skills of public speaking. Making a good presentation can be an effective way of improving services to clients. For example, a single speech to a group of community or political leaders can have far-reaching effects if that speech moves the group to modify a policy or create a needed program. Similarly, throughout their careers, social workers will be expected to make presentations at profeesional workshops or conferences in which they exchange information and describe new insights or developments in order to improve the quality of services provided to clients.

Speeches can vary considerably in structure. At one extreme is an "off-the-cuff" presentation; at the other extreme is reading from a prepared paper. Neither is usually effective. The former is likely to be difficult to follow and the latter can easily lull the audience to sleep. Somewhere between the two extremes is the recipe for an effective oral presentation.

Considerable planning is required for an effective oral presentation. The presenter must keep in mind the fact that the audience must grasp the material when it is presented. As opposed to reading a book or article, members of the audience do not have the luxury of skimming the outline to understand where the author is headed, skipping over sections of material that are not of interest, or rereading to be sure material is understood. The audience's choices are limited: to try to absorb the material the presenter delivers, to daydream through the uninteresting parts, or to make an exit.

The presenter, then, must carefully plan the speech to be sure the communication is accurately received the one time it is presented.

The first step in preparing for a presentation is to know the content and be familiar with the audience. Second, one must select and adapt the content to be presented to the interests of the audience being addressed. For example, a presentation on the tasks performed by social workers would be quite different at a junior high school career day than when presenting to a state personnel board. Third, it is essential to carefully organize the flow of information. In broad terms, the speech should include three major components: a preview of the topic, the main body of the speech, and a summary pointing out the conclusions reached about the topic. Last, the presenter should consider creative ways to make the presentation interesting and understandable to the audience.

Careful preparation and a relatively relaxed presenter are the two essential conditions for successful speeches. The following guidelines can be helpful in achieving these conditions:

1. *Be clear about the purpose of the speech.* Is the intent to inform or persuade? If the purpose is to *persuade*, the presentation should be planned to (a) identify the nature and extent of the problem using facts or case examples, (b) identify the consequences of not changing the situation for the individuals affected and the society (including the members of the audience) in general, (c) suggest solutions, and (d) propose actions the audience can take to help. If the purpose is to *inform* (e.g., a professional presentation), the presenter should (a) identify the relevance of the information to be presented, (b) explain the status of the current knowledge about the subject based on a review of the literature, (c) give a summary of the manner in which the data or concepts were developed, and (d) provide an analysis of the practice implications or conclusions drawn from the information.

2. *Carefully analyze the audience—both when preparing the presentation and just before presenting.* When planning what to present and how to present it, form a clear picture of the people who will be in the audience. It is often useful to visualize a particular person who is expected to be in attendance and prepare a presentation that will interest that person. A practice run-through and critique by a colleague can help identify areas that need reworking. To reduce anxiety and provide information to help fine-tune the presentation about to be delivered, it is often helpful for the presenter to mingle with the audience before the session begins. Introducing oneself to audience members who arrive early, asking what they hope to get from the session, and simply cultivating a few familiar and responsive faces in the audience can increase the comfort level of the presenter considerably.

3. *Be enthusiastic about the topic.* If the audience can feel that the presenter is excited and interested in the material being presented, they too will look at the material in a positive light. A little of the "salesperson" in each of us should be used to capture the attention of the audience.

4. *Be responsive to the ability of the audience to absorb the content.* The time of day, length of available time for both presentation and discussion, size of audience, atmosphere of the room, and other factors all can affect audience attention. In general, it is best to be as brief as possible. After all, the mind can absorb only what the seat can endure. A good rule is to cover the content as efficiently as possible in the presentation and to reserve time for the audience to explore the material that is of most interest to them in a question-and-answer period.

5. *Use notecards to help maintain the planned organization of the presentation.* The notecards should be numbered in case they get out of order and should be prepared in large and legible print.

6. *Use visual aids that will help the audience follow the organization of your presentation and comprehend the data that are presented.* One way to help the audience remember the key points is to put together key words that spell something (acronyms). Visual aids may take the form of handing out hard-copy materials, presenting information on an overhead projector, or using videotaped materials or sophisticated PowerPoint materials. Given the availability of portable overhead projectors and the ease of preparing outlines, charts, figures, and tables on home computers, the well-prepared presenter can readily present considerable information while holding the attention of his or her audience.

7. *Examine your mannerisms while speaking.* Words and phrases such as "you know" and "uh" are annoying and distracting, as are physical mannerisms such as elaborate hand movements or excessive pacing while presenting. Practice delivering the speech before a mirror to get a sense of the time required (although the time it takes to deliver a speech is often underestimated), and then try not to depend too heavily on notes when actually presenting. An audiotape or videotape of a practice run or the honest critique of a colleague can help to minimize distracting behaviors. Also, be sure to dress appropriately for the nature of the meeting, as attire that is out of place can be distracting to the audience.

8. *Present with an aura of confidence.* If the presenter knows the material, is well organized and enthusiastic, and responds effectively to the discussion with the audience, most errors will be forgiven. It is the message, not the messenger, that is most important.

SELECTED BIBLIOGRAPHY

Atkinson, John M. *Lend Me Your Ears: All You Need to Know About Making Speeches and Presentations.* New York: Oxford University Press, 2005.
Sprague, Jo, and Douglas Stuart. *The Speaker's Handbook,* 7th ed. New York: Harcourt Brace, 2005.

16.13   IMPROVING THE SOCIAL WORK IMAGE

Purpose: To build public understanding and a more positive image of social workers.

Discussion: Social work suffers from public misunderstanding. The typical citizen has little understanding of what social workers actually do and the impressions they have are often erroneous. On TV and in the movies, the social worker is often portrayed as either a judgmental and mindless busybody or someone who breaks up families by removing children for no good reason. All too often, the only newspaper or magazine articles that mention social workers are ones describing how the acts or omissions of an agency or a social worker contributed to a client's harm or distress. Additional image problems are created when the media uses the term *social worker* in a generic manner and applies it to all human services workers.

Social workers want a better image and want to be appreciated and understood by the public. However, such changes will not result from wishful thinking; they must be made to happen. The image will change in a positive direction when it becomes evident to the public that social workers are truly experts in what they do and are able to get results that nonsocial workers are unable to match. The financial rewards and the status associated with certain other professions (e.g., medicine, engineering, accounting) came about not through exhortation but rather because their members completed long and difficult training, acquired a definite expertise, and assumed a legal responsibility for the outcome of their decisions and actions.

In order to promote a greater public understanding, social workers should adhere to certain guidelines:

1. Use the title of *social worker*. If you must also use words such as *counseling* or *psychotherapy* to clarify your role, describe yourself as, for example: "I am a social worker—I provide psychotherapy to troubled youth," "I am a social worker specializing in the planning and development of services for persons with AIDS," "I am a social worker who administers a family support program," "I am a social worker who teaches at a university," and so on.

2. Assume a personal responsibility for improving the profession's image. Three actions are essential. First, provide the highest quality service possible. Second, behave in a highly professional and completely responsible manner when dealing with clients and the public. Third, inform those observing your performance that you are a social worker.

3. When being interviewed for a news story, make sure the reporter understands that you are a social worker and that you have a degree in social work, and perhaps describe the special training that has prepared you for the work you do. Always operate on the assumption that reporters and the public at large have little or no idea that social work is a distinct profession. Otherwise, you will probably be termed a *sociologist, welfare worker, counselor,* or *agency worker.*

4. Speak of your work with respect. If you truly value what you do, others are more likely to adopt a positive attitude toward both you and your work. Avoid any action or association that would damage your credibility and trustworthiness.

5. Work with other social workers and professional associations (e.g., the NASW) to plan and implement a media and public relations campaign aimed at educating the public about social work and social workers in your community.

6. Whenever a news story uses the term *social work* or *social worker* in an erroneous manner, send the newspaper, magazine, or radio or TV station a letter that explains the error. Also send a packet of informational materials that describes the nature of the profession and social work activities.

SELECTED BIBLIOGRAPHY

Gibelman, Margaret. *What Social Workers Do*, 2nd ed. Washington, DC: NASW Press, 2005.
Payne, Malcolm, *What is Professional Social Work?* Chicago: Lyceum Books, 2007.

16.14   BECOMING A LEADER

Purpose: To develop and utilize leadership skills in order to eliminate social injustice and improve the life situations of clients.

Discussion: Social workers encounter many situations of social and economic injustice in their communities and society. Such situations cry out for attention and change. Social workers will also discover situations in their own agencies where modifications in policies, programs, and practices are clearly needed in order to make the agencies more effective. In order to change these situations, he or she must be willing to step forward and assume the role and responsibilities of leadership. Desirable change does not happen by accident. Rather, it is set in motion by people who assert themselves, articulate their beliefs, and take on the hard work of leading.

Most efforts to define *leadership* speak of it as a process of using authority and interpersonal influence to guide people through a certain course of action and toward a particular goal. An effective leader draws upon his or her own sense of mission to create a climate and foster the attitudes that move a group or organization toward a desired end. The exercise of leadership always occurs within a context of competing and conflicting forces. A good leader can shape and guide those complex forces so as to move people toward the desired goal.

Leadership should not be equated with administration. *Leadership* is the process of bringing about some significant change by inspiring people to let go of what is familiar and to embrace a new vision or mission. By contrast, the process of *administration*, or management, seeks to bring about order and consistency within an organization through the use of various administrative tools and procedures, such as planning, budgeting, and coordinating staff. Not all who occupy administrative positions are effective leaders.

Although certain traits and characteristics—such as intelligence, dependability, verbal ability, adaptability, physical height, and attractiveness—appear to be associated with leadership, no one set of traits predicts who will become a leader. Research does not support the belief that some people are "born leaders." In order to become an effective leader, one must build on his or her strengths and learn and practice the skills of leadership, just as he or she would develop any other set of skills. An aspiring leader must consciously cultivate the development of those qualities as well as the thought processes, attitudes, and interpersonal skills associated with leadership.

Drawing upon ideas presented in Horejsi and Garthwait (2002), these guidelines are offered for those who want to become effective leaders:

1. Leaders must have a clear understanding of what they want to accomplish. They must go beyond what was and what is and articulate a vision of what could be. It is the leader's vision that gives him or her the critically important sense of purpose and direction and the self-confidence not only to make difficult decisions but to act on those decisions. However, leadership is about much more than having good ideas. In fact, effective leaders are seldom the most creative and innovative thinkers. People who are attracted primarily to ideas and theory seldom make good leaders because they often move too quickly, become impatient with the slowness of change, and get frustrated with the hesitations and limitations of those they seek to lead.

2. Leaders must articulate for their followers a vision and explain it in words that others will understand. Also, this vision must be one that can be translated into achievable objectives and programs that are feasible within the organization and its cultural, political, and economic environment.

3. Effective leaders lead by example, serving as models for others. A leader cannot ask others to do what he or she is unwilling to do. Followers are inspired and motivated by the resolve, courage, hard work, and sacrifices of an effective leader. Leaders must exhibit the behaviors and attitudes they want to see in their followers.

4. Aspiring leaders cannot lead unless people choose to follow them. In order to attract and retain followers, leaders must respect and demonstrate genuine concern for the wishes, values, and abilities of those they want to lead. Leaders must be willing and able to curtail some of their own hopes in order to avoid moving too quickly or too far ahead of their followers.

5. An effective leader must maintain clear and ongoing communication with his or her followers. This communication must keep followers focused on the desired goal while also attending to the concerns, fears, and ambivalence they may have about investing their time, energy, and money in working toward this goal.

6. Leaders must be able to make difficult decisions within social, political, economic, and organizational environments that are constantly changing. Leaders must be willing to take calculated risks, cope with uncertainty, and manage situations that are inherently unpredictable. Nothing destroys the capacity to lead more quickly than indecisiveness and unwillingness to take action when doing so is clearly necessary. It is often said that "It is better for a leader to occasionally make a bad decision than to be perceived as someone who cannot make a difficult decision."

7. A social work leader must develop and maintain a positive personal and professional reputation. The capacity to lead is often tied to having a favorable reputation within one's organization or community, to possessing special knowledge of and prior experience with the issue that has drawn people together, and to having a well-developed network of personal and professional contacts. Given this, an individual who changes jobs frequently or moves from community to community may limit his or her potential for leadership.

8. Effective leaders are skilled in the art of building consensus and coalitions. They create networks among individuals and organizations and facilitate their cooperation and collaboration. They reward others for their cooperation and share credit, even with those with whom they disagree. Leaders must also be willing to compromise when doing so is a necessary step toward reaching a sought after goal.

9. Leaders must be able to identify and understand the various motivations of followers. Leaders must also anticipate possible disagreements among followers and take steps to prevent or resolve these conflicts before they distract from achieving the goal and splinter the followers into competing factions. At the same time, leaders must be willing to remove from the collective effort those individuals or groups that are creating unnecessary conflict or setting up roadblocks to achieving essential goals.

10. A leader must be willing and able to use his or her power and influence in a thoughtful and deliberate manner. The type of power and influence available to a leader will vary, depending on the type of group or organization he or she is leading. If the leader occupies a position of leadership within a formal organization (e.g., executive director, high-level administrator, or elected official), he or she will possess the power of authority and legitimacy associated with that position. He or she, for example, may also possess the power to reward or punish the actions of others and can thereby increase their level or cooperation or decrease their level of resistance to a proposed change. If the leader has the authority to grant a salary increase or to fire an employee, he or she can effect change much more quickly than in situations where he or she does not have such authority. On the other hand, reward power and coercive power are generally not available to the leader of an organization in which membership and participation are purely voluntary and the unpaid members (or followers) can easily quit the group or organization without experiencing real consequences. In these situations, a leader may possess only the influence that comes from being a person who commands respect and attracts a following because of his or her personal charisma, attractiveness to others, and knowledge or expertise.

11. Effective leaders possess a high level of self-awareness. They understand their own strengths and limitations and constantly examine their own motives and behaviors. Many leaders destroy their capacity to lead by letting their need for public recognition and self-importance influence their decisions.

12. In addition to the factors already mentioned, the following qualities and characteristics are important to effective leadership:

- The capacity to critically evaluate various ideas and proposals, including one's own decisions, plans, and actions
- The capacity to speak and write clearly so as to articulate a vision and purpose in ways people can understand
- Perseverance even in the face of disappointment and criticism

- The ability to delegate responsibility and teach or empower others to perform as well as they can
- Willingness to take personal responsibilty for one's decisions and actions
- Openness to new ideas and acceptance of persons with various abilities and diverse backgrounds
- The ability to create a sense of camaraderie and feeling of community among one's followers
- The ability to make effective use of available time and get things done

SELECTED BIBLIOGRAPHY

Horejsi, Charles, and Cynthia Garthwait. *The Social Work Practicum*, 2nd ed. Boston: Allyn & Bacon, 2002.

Noonan, Sarah J. *The Elements of Leadership: What You Should Know.* Lanham, MD: Scarecrow Press, 2003.

Ryan, James. *Inclusive Leadership.* San Francisco: Jossey-Bass, 2006.

Schneider, Robert, and Lori Lester. *Social Work Advocacy.* Belmont, CA: Wadsworth, 2001.

Author Index

Subject Index

Note: Bold numbers indicate pages on which topics are cited as key terms.